Dear Verna

Thank you for all your support.

[illegible]

Ethics and Integrity in Educational Contexts

Volume 1

Series Editor

Sarah Elaine Eaton, Werklund School of Education, University of Calgary, Calgary, AB, Canada

The aim of this series is to provide an authoritative series of books on topics relating to ethics and integrity in educational contexts. Its scope includes ethics and integrity, defined in broad and inclusive terms, in educational contexts. It focuses on higher education, but also welcomes contributions that address ethics and integrity in primary and secondary education, non-formal educational contexts, professional education, etc. We welcome books that address traditional academic integrity topics such as plagiarism, exam cheating, and collusion.

In addition, we are particularly interested in topics that extend beyond questions of student conduct, such as

- Quality assurance in education;
- Research ethics and integrity;
- Admissions fraud;
- Fake and fraudulent credentials;
- Publication ethics;
- Educational technology ethics (e.g., surveillance tech, machine learning, and artificial intelligence, as they are used in education);
- Biomedical ethics in educational contexts;
- Ethics in varsity and school sports.

This series extends beyond traditional and narrow concepts of academic integrity to broader interpretations of applied ethics in education, including corruption and ethical questions relating to instruction, assessment, and educational leadership. It also seeks to promote social justice, diversity, equity, and inclusion.

The series provides a forum to address emerging, urgent, and even provocative topics related to ethics and integrity at all levels of education, from a variety of disciplinary and geographical perspectives.

More information about this series at https://link.springer.com/bookseries/16725

Sarah Elaine Eaton · Julia Christensen Hughes
Editors

Academic Integrity in Canada

An Enduring and Essential Challenge

Editors
Sarah Elaine Eaton
University of Calgary
Calgary, AB, Canada

Julia Christensen Hughes
Yorkville University
Toronto, Ontario, Canada

ISSN 2731-779X ISSN 2731-7803 (electronic)
Ethics and Integrity in Educational Contexts
ISBN 978-3-030-83254-4 ISBN 978-3-030-83255-1 (eBook)
https://doi.org/10.1007/978-3-030-83255-1

This Springer imprint is published by the registered company Springer Nature Switzerland AG
The registered company address is: Gewerbestrasse 11, 6330 Cham, Switzerland

The original version of this book was revised (the ISSNs for print and electronic versions have been updated in the copyright page). An erratum to this book can be found at https://doi.org/10.1007/978-3-030-83255-1_32

Acknowledgements

We begin by acknowledging those who have made major contributions to the field of academic integrity, building its foundation, inspiring us and many of the contributors to this volume.

First, we express our gratitude to Donald (Don) McCabe, the founder of the Center for Academic Integrity and the global academic integrity movement. Don was incredibly generous with his time and willingness to collaborate on the pan-Canadian study with Julia. Not only did he support arm's length data collection and analysis, but he also provided keynote addresses to various Canadian institutions, helping them interpret and take action based on their individual results. He responded to numerous inquiries from the press, and attended Canadian conferences and other academic events, contributing to discussions about what Canadian educational developers, faculty and administrators might do to enhance our cultures of integrity. Sadly, Don passed away in 2016, while in the process of conducting a follow-up Canadian study, something he aspired to do as a capstone to his academic career.

We would also like to acknowledge all of the educational developers, librarians, academic integrity officers, faculty and faculty association leaders, student leaders, and administrators who continue to support this essential work, organizing academic integrity weeks and other educational programs (for faculty and students alike), challenging and changing policies, adjudicating cases, offering inspired learning experiences and authentic modes of assessment, and supporting research, including the original Canadian study. Special thanks go to those participating institutions, who in the spirit of transparency and accountability, bravely made their institution's results publicly available.

A debt of gratitude is owed to Alastair Summerlee, who in 2001 as Provost of the University of Guelph, first asked Julia to investigate academic misconduct at the university, given his concern around growing numbers of cases of student academic misconduct. In many of these cases, students accused of "inappropriate collaboration" were successfully arguing that what they were doing supported their learning and was in keeping with the university's stated commitment to student-centred learning. This helped Julia appreciate that incidents of academic misconduct can have as much to do with faculty leadership, course design and assessment practice, as they do with the students themselves. Sincere thanks also go to Alastair's successor, Provost Maureen Mancuso, who wisely advised Julia to hold off sharing the results, until they were published through a robust peer review process, in order to ensure that the Canadian study would be viewed as credible, helping catalyze urgently needed action.

Next, we acknowledge Tracey Bretag, who passed away in 2020, while this book was under development. She travelled to Canada to keynote the inaugural Canadian Symposium on Academic Integrity in 2019 at the University of Calgary, where she inspired the attendees to further develop educational integrity work in Canada through scholarship, practice and advocacy. When Sarah told Tracey that we hoped this book would serve as a companion to her acclaimed handbook, she was genuinely pleased and supportive of the work.

We are deeply grateful to the authors who contributed to this volume. When this project got underway in 2019, none of us could have possibly imagined the unprecedented pressures and challenges that we would face during the COVID-19 pandemic that changed the world in 2020. Despite unimaginable workloads and personal struggles that included challenging caregiving roles and the loss of loved ones, our authors continued on, believing in the importance of this project. For that, we stand in awe of their resilience, and will be forever grateful.

Finally, we extend our thanks to our families and those of our contributors. We use the word "family" in an inclusive sense, embracing those to whom we are related, as well as our chosen family, and others closest to us. Without you, we would never have been able to find the time and space to complete this work during the global pandemic that continues as we submitted our collective work to Springer for publication in spring, 2022. We thank you for teaching us, inspiring us and cheering us on. It is in this spirit that Julia acknowledges her mother, Patricia Margaret Lythgoe, who passed away May 12, 2021, at the age of 89 during the book's final stages.

Calgary, Canada Sarah Elaine Eaton
Guelph, Canada Julia Christensen Hughes

Editors' Note on Peer Review

In this section, we provide details of the peer review process, outlining the criteria for assessment of the chapters. One purpose of this book is to showcase Canadian scholarly and practitioner contributions to academic integrity and mark the progress that has been made since Christensen Hughes and McCabe (2006a, b) published their two seminal studies on academic misconduct in Canada. We also wanted to produce a book that would help strengthen academic integrity practice and scholarship in Canadian higher education, which have been slow to develop, but have strengthened in recent years (Eaton & Edino, 2018). In particular, we wanted to use this book as an opportunity for scholars and practitioners to engage with one another, in a sustained manner over time, such that they would read one another's work, engage in dialogue and learn from and with one another throughout the writing and revising process.

To achieve this, we used a process of open and ongoing multi-modal peer review throughout the writing process, which involved asynchronous written review from both editors and peers, as well as oral and text chat feedback provided via video conference, during a synchronous symposium, with staggered sessions. Having chapter contributors review one another's chapter is not a new process; and it is one that both of us as editors had previous experience with. Our initial plans for the project included having an in person symposium at the University of Guelph, Julia's prior home institution. COVID-19 put a damper on those plans. Instead, we reconceptualized the notion of a traditional writing workshop, moving it into an online synchronous format, drawing from the ideas of others who had successfully used video conferences to engage in collaborative writing projects (see Eady et al., 2019), as well as more traditional concepts of academic writing groups sustained over time (Lock et al., 2019).

We hosted a virtual project launch meeting at the beginning of the project via video conference (see Eaton & Christensen Hughes, 2020). The purpose of this first meeting was to give contributors an opportunity to introduce themselves to one another, to explain the provenance and purpose of the project, outline timelines for completion of the work and offer contributors an opportunity to ask questions. During the launch meeting, we, as editors, outlined our expectations that contributors would present their work during the virtual symposium for the purposes of sharing key ideas, asking for help on any aspects they wanted advice on and receiving feedback from the editors, as well as other contributors.

The virtual symposium included seven sessions staggered over a period of four months. Each session was two to three hours long, resulting in a total duration of 15 hours of collaborative real-time chapter presentations and feedback. Authors presented their work in fifteen-minute sessions, with ample time for discussion. Contributors were invited to attend any and all of the sessions, as their schedules permitted. One or both editors organized and hosted the sessions, facilitating the discussion, offering feedback and keeping time. One editor (SEE) captured feedback shared by contributors in the text chat and sent the author(s) of each chapter a written summary of their feedback that included highlights of the spoken and text chat feedback after their session. Authors then used this feedback to develop and strengthen their work.

We used a collaborative online drive (Dropbox) for authors to save and share their work. This allowed editors and contributors to have access to others' chapters for the purposes of providing additional written feedback. The editors provided feedback in multiple stages, with each chapter being reviewed at least three times at various stages of drafting and writing. This collaborative and open approach also allowed authors to read one another's work as it was in development. In turn, this led contributors to cite and reference one another's work when it was appropriate and relevant to do so.

The result of this process of engaging in open peer review, with feedback being provided in multiple ways throughout the writing process was not only rigorous, it created a community of practice and scholarship among the contributors and the editors. Many contributors did not know one another at the beginning of the project, and due to the COVID-19 pandemic, it remains unknown when we might have the opportunity to meet in person. Nevertheless, the authors of this volume are not only contributors, but also connected and engaged members of the academic integrity community in Canada. Some have developed professional relationships of their own and are planning spin-off or subsequent projects as a result of this book. As editors, nothing could please us more.

We conclude with an expression of gratitude to those who contributed to this work. Each contributor took on multiple roles including author, peer reviewer and colleague. Some contributors faced extraordinary challenges in their personal and professional lives during this book project and yet remained committed to the project. We remain forever grateful to all of you.

Sarah Elaine Eaton
Julia Christensen Hughes

References

Christensen Hughes, J. M., & McCabe, D. L. (2006a). Academic misconduct within higher education in Canada. *The Canadian Journal of Higher Education, 36*(2), 1–21. http://journals.sfu.ca/cjhe/index.php/cjhe/article/view/183537/183482

Christensen Hughes, J. M., & McCabe, D. L. (2006b). Understanding academic misconduct. *Canadian Journal of Higher Education, 36*(1), 49–63. https://journals.sfu.ca/cjhe/index.php/cjhe/article/view/183525

Eady, M., J., Green, C., Akenson, A., B., Supple, B., McCarthy, M., Cronin, J., & McKeon, J. (2019). Supporting writing collaborations through synchronous technologies. In N. Simmons & A. Singh (Eds.), *Critical collaboration communities: Academic writing partnerships, groups, and retreats* (pp. 186–199). Brill | Sense. https://doi.org/10.1163/9789004410985_014

Eaton, S. E., & Christensen Hughes, J. (2020, February 14). *Academic Integrity in Canada: Edited Book—Project Launch Meeting.* http://hdl.handle.net/1880/113116

Eaton, S. E., & Edino, R. I. (2018). Strengthening the research agenda of educational integrity in Canada: A review of the research literature and call to action. *International Journal of Educational Integrity, 14*(1). https://edintegrity.biomedcentral.com/articles/10.1007/s40979-018-0028-7

Lock, J., Kjorlien, Y., Tweedie, G., Dressler, R., Eaton, S. E., & Spring, E. (2019). Advancing the writing of academics: Stories from the writing group. In N. Simmons & A. Singh (Eds.), *Critical collaboration communities: Academic writing partnerships, groups, and retreats* (pp. 55–65). Brill | Sense. https://doi.org/10.1163/9789004410985_005

Academic Integrity in Canada: An Enduring and Essential Challenge—Introduction

Academic integrity could not be more essential to academe. It is—and must be—at the core of our purpose, practice and the products of scholarly work. The degrees we confer (and the knowledge, skills and values they are supposed to represent) and the truths we disseminate (through research with integrity), must be beyond reproach. Yet, evidence suggests incidents of academic misconduct are rising and public confidence in the academy may be in decline.

Unfortunately, and particularly in comparison with other Commonwealth countries, as well as the United States, Canada has been slow to develop a strong scholarly community studying this essential issue and making evidence-supported recommendations for change (Eaton & Edino, 2018). We decided to address this gap. *Academic Integrity in Canada: An Enduring and Essential Challenge* makes a unique and much needed contribution to the academic integrity literature by considering its history, governance, characteristics, and prevalence within one national context—Canada. In this volume we showcase scholarly and practitioner contributions from higher education institutions across the country, and mark the progress that has been made since Christensen Hughes and McCabe (2006a, b) published their two seminal contributions on academic misconduct in Canada.

Our goal was to provide accessible chapters through a commitment to open access, that offer a rich background, a critical review of Canada's history, and informed suggestions for change. We also saw this as an opportunity for emerging and seasoned Canadian scholars, along with practitioners, to engage with one another in a sustained manner over time, such that they would read one another's work, engage in dialogue and learn from and with one another throughout the writing and revising process. We did not know as we began this project that COVID-19 would both constrain and inspire our intentions.

The period in which this book was developed and written, 2020–2021 was a time of unprecedented accusations of student cheating in the national news, and in particular, contract cheating and exam-based cheating, along with disturbing accounts of racially biased and invasive approaches to e-proctoring and student surveillance (Friesen, 2020; Panico, 2020). There have also been numerous incidents of research misconduct reported in the international press (though less so in Canada), with over a hundred scholarly papers on COVID-19 retracted, potentially fueling societal unease. There have also been increasing calls to decolonize the academy, ensuring that Indigenous ways of understanding integrity in scholarship and learning are given their proper due. Contributing authors make the point throughout, that academic integrity in Canada is indeed an enduring and essential challenge, and that history, insights and lessons learned have much relevance for our government ministries, institutional policies, practices and cultures, and personal practice.

We have organized the book into five sections, grouped by thematic content. We made an intentional decision to include the voices of academics, administrators, and higher education professionals throughout the book to signal that the work of academic integrity extends to all stakeholders and aspects of education. One of our goals with this book is to elevate evidence-informed practice, as well as practice-informed research because as much as student conduct is grounded in ethical decision-making so too, are both practice and research (Rowan et al., 2018).

Part I—The Canadian Context

The introductory section of the book includes chapters that establish the context for the exploration of academic integrity in Canada. Here, Sarah Elaine Eaton and Julia Christensen Hughes provide chapters that discuss various aspects of the history and governance of education in Canada, including our legal system that has allowed contract cheating to remain unchecked. We also question the morality of the academy, underscoring its historical roots as a colonizing force, its funding, and the deplorable treatment of Indigenous peoples. Moving to the present day, we present two chapters focused on accounts of student and faculty misconduct in the news, that give a sense of the enormity and complexity of the challenge. These various contributions include: "Academic Integrity in Canada: Historical Perspectives and Current Trends" (Eaton & Christensen Hughes, 2022) "Academic Integrity across Time and Place: Higher Education's Questionable Moral Calling" (Christensen Hughes, 2022); "Student Integrity Violations in the Academy: More Than a Decade of Growing Complexity and Concern" (Christensen Hughes & Eaton, 2022b); and "Academic Misconduct in Canadian Higher Education: Beyond Student Cheating" (Christensen Hughes & Eaton, 2022a).

Four additional chapters round out Part I, including essential contributions for building an enhanced understanding of academic integrity from Indigenous perspectives, including "Re-defining academic integrity: Embracing Indigenous Truths" by Poitras Pratt & Gladue (2022) and, Lindstrom (2022), on "Accountability, Relationality and Indigenous Epistemology: Advancing an Indigenous Perspective on Academic Integrity". This is followed by Stoesz's (2022) "Understanding Provincial and Territorial Academic Integrity Policies for Elementary and Secondary Education in Canada".

Part II—Emerging and Prevalent Forms of Academic Misconduct

This section focuses on contract cheating and the commodification of knowledge. It begins with "Contract Cheating in Canada: A Comprehensive Overview" (Eaton, 2022), followed by "EdTech, and the Rise of Contract Cheating" (Gray, 2022). Then we turn to Chibry & Kurz (2022), who share further insights in "Pay-to-Pass: Knowledge as a Commodity"; and to round out this section, Crossman (2022), "Education as a Financial Transaction: Contract Employment and Contract Cheating". Here, authors repeatedly make the point that higher education is increasingly encountering predatory and corruptive external pressures that compromise the integrity of the academy.

Part III—Integrity Within Specific Learning Environments and Professional Programs

Part III highlights aspects of academic integrity within specific learning contexts, such as service learning and distance learning, and within particular academic disciplines—the visual arts, engineering, education and law. The first three chapters address academic integrity across disciplines, but within a specific context. The section opens by addressing academic integrity and experiential learning with "Academic integrity in work-integrated learning (WIL) settings" (Miron, 2022). Then, Hunter and Kier (2022) discuss "Canadian Open Digital Distance Education Universities and Academic Integrity". Following, Foxe et al. (2022) address plagiarism in non-text based disciplines, and specifically in design-based fields, in their chapter "Visual Plagiarism: Seeing the Forest and the Trees".

Subsequent chapters in this section address academic integrity in professional programs, starting with deMontigny (2022) in "Managing academic integrity in Canadian engineering schools" followed by Peters et al. (2022) who address academic integrity in teacher training programs in their chapter, "Teaching the teachers: To what extent do preservice teachers cheat on exams and plagiarise in their written work?". The section concludes with Watson Hamilton's (2022) chapter, "The Distinctive Nature of Academic Integrity in Graduate Legal Education".

Part IV—Barriers and Catalysts to Academic Integrity: Multiple Perspectives and Supports

This section gives voice to multiple stakeholders who play essential roles in supporting institutional missions of integrity. We begin by focusing on students and their understanding of academic integrity, in a contribution by Packalen &

Rowbotham (2022), "Student insight on academic integrity", which showcases the perspectives of students in a business school. This is followed by Bens's (2022) chapter, "Helping Students Resolve the Ambiguous Expectations of Academic Integrity" which shines further light on student perspectives and how to help them embrace integrity. More chapters on student success follow, including Penaluna & Ross (2022), "How to Talk about Academic Integrity, so Students Will Listen: The Inherent Challenge in Mandated Training" and two chapters focused on helping with writing, with Rossi's (2022) "Revisioning paraphrasing instruction" and Garwood's (2022) chapter on "Supporting Academic Integrity in the Writing Centre: Perspectives of Student Consultants". Next, Morrow (2022) speaks to the role librarians and library staff play in supporting academic integrity in her chapter, "Beyond the Traditional: Academic Integrity Advocacy in Canadian Librarianship".

Part V—Institutional Responses

In the final section of the book, we turn our attention to faculty members and institutional-level initiatives. Although others have previously reported on university faculty members' reluctance to report academic misconduct in Canada (e.g., Eaton et al., 2020; MacLeod, 2014; MacLeod & Eaton, 2020; Paterson et al., 2003), Hamilton & Wolsky (2022) add much needed insights from the college perspective in their chapter, "The Barriers to Faculty Reporting Incidences of Academic Misconduct at Community Colleges".

This is followed by a series of chapters on how institutions can proactively support academic integrity through multi-stakeholder initiatives and approaches. This includes a contribution from a trio of college-based authors who present, "Promotion of Academic Integrity through a Marketing Lens for Canadian Post-Secondary Institutions" (Teymouri et al., 2022), followed by McNeill (2022), who presents original research from the University of British Columbia in her chapter, "Changing "Hearts" and Minds: Pedagogical and Institutional Practices to Foster Academic Integrity". Then, Thacker & McKenzie (2022) underscore the need to connect academic integrity to quality assurance in their chapter, "Using Quality Assurance Frameworks to support an Institutional Culture of Academic Integrity at Canadian Universities."

This is followed by two chapters on how breaches of academic integrity are addressed in Canadian post-secondary institutions. Morrison & Zacahariah (2022) write about "Student Academic Misconduct Through a Canadian Legal Lens", followed by Sopcak & Hood (2022), who discuss restorative resolutions to violations of academic integrity in their chapter, "Building a Culture of Restorative Practice and Restorative Responses to Academic Misconduct".

Then, Kenny & Eaton (2022) make the case for informing institutional change through a strengthened infrastructure, grounded in the scholarship of teaching and learning (SoTL), in their chapter, "Academic integrity through a SoTL lens and 4M framework: An institutional self-study."

We conclude the book by discussing the importance of this volume, noting its limitations. We conclude with a call to action to further strengthen academic integrity in Canada (Eaton & Christensen Hughes, 2022b).

Although collectively we have focused on the Canadian context, contributors have made an intentional effort to write for a global audience. This work provides new empirical research, advances important discussions about decolonization and Indigenization, and provides updated insights into how to support multi-stakeholder approaches to upholding and enacting academic integrity not only in higher education, but also in K-12 contexts. The book demonstrates how far Canadian contributions have come since Christensen Hughes and McCabe (2006a, b) published their two seminal articles fifteen years prior to the publication of this volume. Here, we set an agenda for how to advance academic integrity work now and in the future.

Sarah Elaine Eaton
Julia Christensen Hughes

References

Bens, S. (2022). Helping students resolve the ambiguous expectations of academic integrity. In *Academic integrity in Canada: An enduring and essential challenge*: Springer.

Chibry, N., & Kurz, E. U. (2022). Pay-to-pass: Evolving online systems that undermine the integrity of student work. In S. E. Eaton & J. Christensen Hughes (Eds.), *Academic integrity in Canada: An enduring and essential challenge*, Springer.

Christensen Hughes, J. M., & McCabe, D. L. (2006a). Academic misconduct within higher education in Canada. *The Canadian Journal of Higher Education, 36*(2), 1–21. http://journals.sfu.ca/cjhe/index.php/cjhe/article/view/183537/183482

Christensen Hughes, J. M., & McCabe, D. L. (2006b). Understanding academic misconduct. *Canadian Journal of Higher Education, 36*(1), 49–63. https://journals.sfu.ca/cjhe/index.php/cjhe/article/view/183525

Christensen Hughes, J. (2022). Academic integrity across time and place: Higher education's questionable moral calling. In S. E. Eaton & J. Christensen Hughes (Eds.), *Academic integrity in Canada: An enduring and essential challenge*, Springer.

Christensen Hughes, J., & Eaton, S. E. (2022a). Academic misconduct in Canadian higher education: Beyond student cheating. In S. E. Eaton & J. Christensen Hughes (Eds.), *Academic integrity in Canada: An enduring and essential challenge*, Springer.

Christensen Hughes, J., & Eaton, S. E. (2022b). Student integrity violations in the academy: More than a decade of growing complexity and concern In S. E. Eaton & J. Christensen Hughes (Eds.), *Academic integrity in Canada: An enduring and essential challenge*, Springer.

Crossman, K. (2022). Education as a financial transaction: Contract employment and contract cheating. In S. E. Eaton & J. Christensen Hughes (Eds.), *Academic integrity in Canada: An enduring and essential challenge*, Springer.

deMontigny, D. (2022). Managing academic integrity in Canadian engineering schools. In S. E. Eaton & J. Christensen Hughes (Eds.), *Academic integrity in Canada: An enduring and essential challenge*, Springer.

Eaton, S. E. (2022). Contract cheating in Canada: A comprehensive overview. In S. E. Eaton & J. Christensen Hughes (Eds.), *Academic integrity in Canada: An enduring and essential challenge*, Springer.

Eaton, S. E., & Christensen Hughes, J. (2022a). Academic integrity in Canada: Historical perspectives and current trends. In S. E. Eaton & J. Christensen Hughes (Eds.), *Academic integrity in Canada: An enduring and essential challenge*, Springer.

Eaton, S. E., & Edino, R. I. (2018). Strengthening the research agenda of educational integrity in Canada: A review of the research literature and call to action. *International Journal for Educational Integrity, 14*(1). https://doi.org/10.1007/s40979-018-0028-7

Eaton, S. E., Fernández Conde, C., Rothschuh, S., Guglielmin, M., & Otoo, B. K. (2020). Plagiarism: A Canadian higher education case study of policy and practice gaps. *Alberta Journal of Educational Research, 66*(4), 471–488. https://journalhosting.ucalgary.ca/index.php/ajer/article/view/69204

Friesen, J. (2020, December 16). Use of surveillance software to crack down on exam cheating has unintended consequences. *Globe and Mail*. https://www.theglobeandmail.com/canada/article-use-of-surveillance-software-to-crack-down-on-exam-cheating-has/

Garwood, K. (2022). Supporting academic integrity in the writing centre: Perspectives of student consultants. In S. E. Eaton & J. Christensen Hughes (Eds.), *Academic integrity in Canada: An enduring and essential challenge*, Springer.

Gray, B. C. (2022). Ethics, ed tech, and the rise of contract cheating. In S. E. Eaton & J. Christensen Hughes (Eds.), *Academic integrity in Canada: An enduring and essential challenge*, Springer.

Hamilton, M. J., & Wolsky, K. L. (2022). The barriers to faculty reporting incidences of academic misconduct at community colleges. In S. E. Eaton & J. Christensen Hughes (Eds.), *Academic integrity in Canada: An enduring and essential challenge*, Springer.

Hunter, J., & Kier, C. A. (2022). Canadian open digital distance education universities and academic integrity. In S. E. Eaton & J. Christensen Hughes (Eds.), *Academic integrity in Canada: An enduring and essential challenge*, Springer.

Kenny, N., & Eaton, S. E. (2022). Academic integrity through a SoTL lens and 4M framework: An institutional self-study. In S. E. Eaton & J. Christensen Hughes (Eds.), *Academic integrity in Canada: An enduring and essential challenge*, Springer.

Lindstrom, G. (2022). Accountability, relationality and Indigenous epistemology: Advancing an Indigenous perspective on academic integrity. In S. E. Eaton & J. Christensen Hughes (Eds.), *Academic integrity in Canada: An enduring and essential challenge*, Springer.

MacLeod, P. D. (2014). *An exploration of faculty attitudes toward student academic dishonesty in selected Canadian universities.* (Doctor of Education). University of Calgary, Calgary, Canada. http://hdl.handle.net/11023/1370

MacLeod, P. D., & Eaton, S. E. (2020). The paradox of faculty attitudes toward student violations of academic integrity. *Journal of Academic Ethics, 18*(4), 347–362. doi:10.1007/s10805-020-09363-4

McNeill, L. (2022). Changing "hearts" and minds: Pedagogical and institutional practices to foster academic integrity. In S. E. Eaton & J. Christensen Hughes (Eds.), *Academic integrity in Canada: An enduring and essential challenge*, Springer.

Miron, J. B. (2022). Academic integrity in work-integrated learning (WIL) settings. In S. E. Eaton & J. Christensen Hughes (Eds.), *Academic integrity in Canada: An enduring and essential challenge*, Springer.

Morrison, M., & Zachariah, P. (2022). Student academic misconduct through a Canadian legal lens. In S. E. Eaton & J. Christensen Hughes (Eds.), *Academic integrity in Canada: An enduring and essential challenge*, Springer.

Morrow, L. (2022). Beyond the traditional: academic integrity in Canadian librarianship. In S. E. Eaton & J. Christensen Hughes (Eds.), *Academic integrity in Canada: An enduring and essential challenge*, Springer.

Packalen, K., & Rowbotham, K. (2022). Student insight on academic integrity. In S. E. Eaton & J. Christensen Hughes (Eds.), *Academic integrity in Canada: An enduring and essential challenge*, Springer.

Panico, G. (2020, July 2). U of O students wary of 'extreme' anti-cheating software. CBC News. Retrieved from https://www.cbc.ca/news/canada/ottawa/exam-surveillance-software-university-ottawa-1.5633134

Paterson, B., Taylor, L., & Usick, B. (2003). The construction of plagiarism in a school of nursing. *Learning in Health & Social Care, 2*(3), 147–158. https://doi.org/10.1046/j.1473-6861.2003.00047.x

Penaluna, L.-A., & Ross, R. (2022). How to talk about academic integrity so students will listen: Engaging students in ethical decision making. In S. E. Eaton & J. Christensen Hughes (Eds.), *Academic integrity in Canada: An enduring and essential challenge*, Springer.

Peters, M., Fontaine, S., & Frenette, E. (2022). Teaching the teachers: To what extent do preservice teachers cheat on exams and plagiarise in their written work? In S. E. Eaton & J. Christensen Hughes (Eds.), *Academic integrity in Canada: An enduring and essential challenge*, Springer.

Poitras Pratt, Y., & Gladue, K. (2022). Re-defining academic integrity: Embracing indigenous truths. In S. E. Eaton & J. Christensen Hughes (Eds.), *Academic integrity in Canada: An enduring and essential challenge*, Springer.

Rossi, S. L. (2022). Revisioning paraphrasing instruction. In S. E. Eaton & J. Christensen Hughes (Eds.), *Academic integrity in Canada: An enduring and essential challenge*, Springer.

Rowan, D., Richardson, S., & Long, D. D. (2018). Practice-informed research: Contemporary challenges and ethical decision-making. *Journal of Social Work Values and Ethics, 15*(2), 15–22. https://jswve.org/download/15-2/articles15-2/15-Practice-informed-research-JSWVE-15-2-2018-Fall.pdf

Sopcak, P., & Hood, K. (2022). Building a culture of restorative practice and restorative responses to academic misconduct In S. E. Eaton & J. Christensen Hughes (Eds.), *Academic integrity in Canada: An enduring and essential challenge.*

Stoesz, B. M. (2022). Understanding provincial and territorial academic integrity policies for elementary and secondary education in Canada. In S. E. Eaton & J. Christensen Hughes (Eds.), *Academic integrity in Canada: An enduring and essential challenge*, Springer.

Thacker, E. J., & McKenzie, A. (2022). Using quality assurance frameworks to support an institutional culture of academic integrity at Canadian universities. In S. E. Eaton & J. Christensen Hughes (Eds.), *Academic integrity in Canada: An enduring and essential challenge*, Springer.

Watson Hamilton, J. (2022). The distinctive nature of academic integrity in graduate legal education. In S. E. Eaton & J. Christensen Hughes (Eds.), *Academic integrity in Canada: An enduring and essential challenge*, Springer.

Contents

About the Editors

Sarah Elaine Eaton, Ph.D. is an Associate Professor in the Werklund School of Education and the inaugural Educational Leader in Residence, Academic Integrity, University of Calgary. She is also the Editor-in-Chief of the *International Journal for Educational Integrity*and the author of *Plagiarism in Higher Education: Tackling Tough Topics in Academic Integrity* (ABC Clio, 2021). Her research focuses on ethics and integrity in higher education and she has led numerous research teams and the local and national levels. Eaton advocates for pro-active and multi-stakeholder approaches to upholding and enacting integrity throughout the academy.

Julia Christensen Hughes, Ph.D. has long advocated for ensuring the highest standards of academic integrity in higher education—in teaching, research and administrative practice. Her article, Academic Misconduct within Higher Education in Canada, with the late Don McCabe (published in 2006, in the *Canadian Journal of Higher Education*), received the Sheffield Award for research excellence (2007), from the Canadian Society for Studies in Higher Education. As former and founding Dean of the Gordon S. Lang School of Business and Economics (2009–2019) at the University of Guelph, Julia was a champion of business ethics, corporate social responsibility and the need for business schools to be aligned with the UN's Sustainable Development Goals (SDG's). In her new role as President of Yorkville Education LP, with leadership responsibilities for Yorkville University and the Toronto Film School, Julia is looking forward to supporting the long-standing commitment to integrity that is core to the values of both institutions.

Part I
The Canadian Context

Chapter 1
Academic Integrity in Canada: Historical Perspectives and Current Trends

Sarah Elaine Eaton and Julia Christensen Hughes

Abstract In this chapter we discuss the development of academic integrity in Canada. We begin by offering insights into how provincial and territorial educational governance and policy structures have affected academic integrity in Canada, compared to other countries, such as the United States. In particular, we discuss why it may not make sense for Canadian schools to try to adopt the American honour code model. We explore the evolution of higher education in Canada, highlighting the earliest incidents of academic misconduct on record as well as the development of academic integrity scholarship, focusing on significant contributions and its impact over time. In particular, we draw attention to the emergence of policies, practices, associations, and networks intended to help Canada's higher educational institutions develop and strengthen cultures of integrity. Following, we discuss how the academic integrity landscape has shifted, noting recent trends such as the rise of contract cheating. We conclude with a call to action for more enhanced support for academic integrity scholarship to support advocacy, policy, and practice.

Keywords Academic integrity · Academic misconduct · Academic dishonesty · Canada · History

Introduction

The purpose of this chapter is to provide a contextual background for understanding academic integrity in Canada. We begin with an overview of Canadian educational governance structures and historical developments that have influenced academic integrity policy and practice in this country. Because some of the seminal research on academic integrity originated within the United States, and since we share a

S. E. Eaton (✉)
University of Calgary, Calgary, Alberta, Canada
e-mail: seaton@ucalgary.ca

J. Christensen Hughes (✉)
Yorkville University, Toronto, Ontario, Canada
e-mail: jchristensen@yorkvilleu.ca

S. E. Eaton and J. Christensen Hughes (eds.), *Academic Integrity in Canada*,
Ethics and Integrity in Educational Contexts 1,
https://doi.org/10.1007/978-3-030-83255-1_1

border, it is important to be aware of similarities and differences between Canadian and US contexts and explore how the two countries differ in their approaches to education and, by extension, their approaches to academic integrity. We begin with a brief overview of Canada's educational governance model and present statistics with respect to both participation rates and performance measures. Then we examine the development of education from the 1600s up to Confederation, identifying key similarities and differences with our US neighbours during this time. We also point out key moments in the evolution of academic integrity. From there we explore the period from Confederation to World War II, as this was a major period of development in Canadian education (Gilbert et al., 1985; Jones, 2014). Following that, we examine what has happened in the post-war decades and examine current trends in the twenty-first century.

In many ways, Canada shares more in common with other Commonwealth nations than it does with the United States, at least in terms of education. In this introductory chapter, we consider questions pertaining to particular characteristics of Canadian academic integrity culture, such as how Canada has built an honour culture without the formalized honour code system that exists in the US. We offer insights into how educational governance and policy structures affect academic integrity and consider possible transferability of lessons learned to other contexts. We conclude by calling for greater support for academic integrity scholarship, recognizing its importance to the future of education in Canada and beyond. In short, this chapter is about the unique aspects of academic integrity culture in Canada and its broader implications.

Educational Governance and Structures in Canada

Education in Canada is governed through a decentralized structure. There is no federal ministry or unified national system of education (Eaton, 2019b; Jones, 2014). Each of Canada's ten (10) provinces and three (3) territories is responsible for the funding and oversight of primary and secondary (often called "Kindergarten–Grade 12" or "K-12") and higher education. Canadian K-12 education is largely governed through ministries of education and legislative acts that are implemented by district school boards.

In Canada, the term *higher education* is often used inclusively to encompass various forms of post-secondary or tertiary education, including universities, colleges, community colleges, and CEGEPs (Canadian Society for the Study of Higher Education/Société canadienne pour l'étude de l'enseignement supérieur, 2020). CEGEPs (Collège d'enseignement général et professionnel or College of General and Vocation Education) are publicly-funded institutions unique to the province of Quebec that offer pre-university, technical, and short-duration programs (Féderacion des cégeps, n.d.).

Higher education institutions across the country offer programs in either of Canada's official languages, English or French. Some institutions offer programming in both languages, but most focus on a single language of instruction. As of

2020, Canada had over 160 recognized public and private universities (including theological schools) and over 180 public colleges and institutes (Council of Ministers of Education Canada [CMEC], 2020). According to the most recent available statistics, enrollment in higher education institutions exceeds 2.1 million, including Canadian domestic and international students (Statistics Canada, 2019).

In reflecting on the characteristics of education in Canada, Glen Jones (2014) has pointed out that:

> In some important respects higher education in Canada is the story of a network of institutions that break all the rules in terms of accepted norms of organizational theory and system design. There is no national 'system', no national ministry of higher education, no national higher education policy and no national quality assessment or accreditation mechanisms for institutions of higher education. (Jones, 2014, p. 1)

Quality assurance for higher education is the primary responsibility of the provinces and territories (Thacker & McKenzie, 2022), although a common body provides oversight in the provinces of New Brunswick, Nova Scotia, and Prince Edward Island (see Maritime Provinces Higher Education Commission, n.d.).

Networks and associations of various kinds also play important roles. At the national level, for example, Universities Canada (2019), founded in 1911, represents the interests of publicly-funded universities across the country. Similarly, Colleges and Institutes Canada (n.d.) "is the national, voluntary membership organization representing publicly supported colleges, institutes, cegeps and polytechnics in Canada and internationally." Although these national associations do not have a regulatory function and nor do they provide quality assurance oversight, they provide opportunities for collaboration, strategic planning, and advocacy.

Collaboration among higher education institutions also occurs at the provincial and territorial level. For example, the purpose of the Council of Ontario Universities (COU, 2019) is to provide "a forum for Ontario's universities to collaborate and advocate in support of their shared mission to the benefit and prosperity of students, communities and the province of Ontario". Similarly, Colleges Ontario (2019) advocates for the province's twenty-four colleges. Other provinces have similar bodies that collaborate at the regional level.

Participation rates in higher education in Canada are high and growing, particularly within the university sector. According to Statistics Canada (2020):

> The participation rate of Canadians aged 18 to 24 in university or college was up by 29% from the 2000/2001 to the 2018/2019 academic years. This increase was attributable to a larger share of young Canadians going to university (+56%), as the participation rate at the college level was relatively stable. (n.p.)

In comparison with other OECD countries, Canada typically ranks amongst the highest; "In 2019, 63% of 25–34 year-olds had a tertiary degree in Canada, compared to 45% on average across OECD countries" (Organisation for Economic Co-operation and Development [OECD], 2020, n.p.), with Canadian women participating at higher rates than their male counterparts (71% vs. 55%) (OECD, 2020).

Early Development of Higher Education and Academic Integrity in Canada and the United States (1600–1867)

Canadian higher education institutions were developed under the models used in either Britain or France, with religious education (e.g., Roman Catholic, Presbyterian, Baptist, and Methodist) being a major influence throughout the 1700 and 1800s (Jones, 2014). Quebec was the first province to introduce higher education programs in the mid-1600s, through a Jesuit college (Jones, 2014). The British colonial legislatures, which later developed into provincial legislatures, followed suit shortly thereafter, founding the first English-speaking colleges in the early 1700s (Jones, 2014).

In the United States, the period from 1760 to 1860 was known as the Antebellum Period (Bertram Gallant, 2008; Lucas, 2006). This was a time when pedagogy was routinized, relationships between faculty and students became adversarial and educational institutions began to implement a system of grading to rank students (Allmendinger, 1973; Bertram Gallant, 2008). There is no parallel or specific title to describe the development of higher education during the same time period in Canada; it is important to note that education at all levels was developing in quite different ways in both countries throughout the sixteenth and seventeenth centuries.

Canada and the United States may have initially shared commonalities in the structure and approach of higher education (Jones, 2014), but the American Revolution resulted in a bifurcation of approaches that eventually led to quite different educational trajectories of the two countries. The American Revolution served as a catalyst for English-language higher education in Canada. Then British loyalists migrated north, and in doing so, dedicated life in their new country to strengthening British culture, including higher education (Jones, 2014). In contrast, the Constitution in the United States provided for a more open approach to education (Fishman, 2016; Lytton, 1996). That set the stage for more entrepreneurial approaches to higher education south of the border, with for-profit colleges emerging in the United States during the period of the American Revolution, in the late 1700s (Angulo, 2016). As a result, higher education in Canada developed in ways that made it more comparable to that of its Commonwealth cousins than to the United States.

Meanwhile in Canada, the first English-speaking colleges were opening around the same time, though under the careful watch of colonial legislatures for English-speaking institutions, while the Roman Catholic Church continued to play a significant role in Quebec, in particular (Jones, 2014). Over time, tensions between politicians and religious bodies about who should oversee education began to develop. These tensions continued throughout the first half of the seventeenth century in Canada. As a result, the period from 1800 to 1850 marked the half century where the trajectory of development for Canadian and American higher education systems began to diverge in ways that would result in drastic differences over time. Particular decisions of the two countries' respective governments and court systems solidified these diverging trajectories.

Tensions over secular versus religious-based education led to King's College at York developing into the University of Toronto in 1849, establishing it firmly as Canada's first official secular university. The establishment of the University of Toronto was a significant turning point in the country's educational history in terms of the development of higher education, however, Canada was trailing behind the United States by almost 200 years. Harvard University was founded almost two centuries prior in 1636 (Harvard University, 2020).

In 1819, the US Supreme Court made a landmark decision in Dartmouth College v. Woodward, allowing for private colleges to flourish (Angulo, 2016). As a result, by the mid-nineteenth century there were already hundreds of thousands of students enrolled in for-profit colleges in the United States, with little quality assurance oversight, which led to concerns around degree and credential fraud (Angulo, 2016). By the mid-1800's, Canada's approach to higher education was already fundamentally different to that of the United States. Little is known about Canada's approach to academic integrity from 1600 to 1867, but due to differences between the development of education in Canada and the United States during this period, it should not be assumed that matters relating to assessment, student conduct, and academic integrity were identical.

Confederation to World War II (1867–1949)

Canadian education scholars have identified the period from Confederation to World War II as being a major period of development in the country's educational systems (Gilbert et al., 1985; Jones, 2014). The Dominion of Canada was created under the British North American (BNA) Act of 1867, resulting in the confederation of the existing provinces of the time, which were Ontario, Quebec, New Brunswick, and Nova Scotia. Other provinces and territories joined later. The constitution established two levels of government: federal and provincial, with different responsibilities being assigned to each level. Education was assigned as a provincial, rather than a federal, responsibility (Jones, 2014). Even though the BNA Act of 1867 assigned responsibility for education to the government oversight of the provinces, ideological and political tensions arose over the role of religious bodies, who fought to maintain control over education.

Because the BNA Act of 1867 was pivotal in establishing education at all levels as a provincial responsibility, the period following resulted in rapid developments that had long-lasting effects. There were, however, exceptions to the federal government's abstention from intervening in matters of education. Within the first few years of education being deemed a provincial responsibility, the federal government undertook two major educational initiatives that have had an impact to the present day: the establishment of the Royal Military College of Canada (RMC) at the higher education level and, concurrently, the introduction of Indian Residential Schools for children. Both of these educational initiatives were launched in the 1870s with funding and oversight from the federal government.

The Royal Military College of Canada (RMC) was founded in Kingston, Ontario, in 1874, and was one of the only educational initiatives undertaken by the federal government (Cameron, 1991; Jones, 2014; Royal Military College of Canada, 2016). Originally named the Military College of Canada, the school was championed by then Prime Minister Alexander MacKenzie (Royal Military College of Canada, 2016). The rationale for this intervention into education was that it was a matter of the federal government's constitutional responsibility for defence (Cameron, 1991; Jones, 2014). The school accepted its first students in June 1876 and two years later, Her Majesty, Queen Victoria, granted the college the right to use the prefix "Royal" in its name, an honour the school maintains today (Royal Military College of Canada, 2016). The school's first programs were focused on military tactics, engineering, and other skills connected with the profession (Royal Military College of Canada, 2016). The school was granted the right to confer degrees in 1959.

As the federal government was planning for the education of its military personnel, it was concurrently planning for the establishment of Indian Residential Schools. The Indian Act of 1876 was formally amended in 1884 to provide for the establishment of Indian Residential Schools, whose stated purpose was to assimilate Indigenous children and "civilize the Indians" (Union of Ontario Indians, 2013, p. 3). The Government of Canada oversaw and funded the residential school system, with the collaboration of the Roman Catholic, Anglican, Methodist, Presbyterian, and United Churches, among others (Union of Ontario Indians, 2013, p. 3). Although various religious groups may have rivaled one another and opposed secular educational initiatives for control of higher education, they were united in their commitment to assimilate Indigenous children into European beliefs and behaviours.

Treatment of students at Indian Residential Schools has been documented as being excessively and horrifyingly punitive (Union of Ontario Indians, 2013, p. 6), with rule compliance being demanded at all times. Failure to comply resulted in punishments including beatings with fists and leather straps, burning and scalding of hands, and solitary confinement in closets, cages, and basements (Union of Ontario Indians, 2013). The impact of Indian Residential Schools was devastating and traumatic for Indigenous peoples (Union of Ontario Indians, 2013). The last residential school only closed in 1996 (Union of Ontario Indians, 2013) (Lindstrom, 2022; Poitras Pratt & Gladue, 2022). Today, the federal government continues to fund the education of primary and secondary education of "registered Indians living on reserves and the Inuit" (CMEC, 2001, p. 6), as well as Canadian Armed Forces members and incarcerated inmates.

Not long after the turn of the twentieth century, the development of networks and associations and conferences provided an opportunity for educators and administrators to share knowledge and work collectively. Concurrently, matters relating to student conduct have been documented as being of importance. The National Conference of Canadian Universities (NCCU) was launched in 1911, the same year Universities Canada was founded, providing an opportunity for university administrators to address common problems; they met twenty times between 1911 and 1944 (University of Manitoba, n.d.). Monohan (1971) documents how the issue of student conduct became a topic of concern during a 1922 conference, when participants:

> Heard an account of Dean Fox of Western of a case of a young lady recently expelled from a University for theft who was subsequently admitted in good faith by another University where her previous exploits were unknown. He moved the following resolution, which was adopted by the delegates, 'that this conference agree to the establishment of some sort of informal yet binding agreement by which each University will inform fully all the other Universities of the circumstances surrounding the expulsion of any student for a serious offense.' 'Serious' is not defined. Nor is it clear how the resolution was implemented. (Monohan, 1971, p. 36)

Although this matter pertained to what would be termed today as "non-academic misconduct", the division between academic and non-academic misconduct has been blurred at times. Although some behaviours can be clearly classified as non-academic (e.g., sexual violence and physical assault), and others being easily named as academic misconduct (e.g., plagiarism), overlapping cases can occur, such as when one student bullies another into completing an assignment for them or allowing them to see their answers during a test. Even today, academic and non-academic misconduct remain entangled in some cases. In the early part of the twentieth century, it would seem that a "serious offence" in terms of student misconduct was left open to some interpretation.

The Post-War-Pre-Internet Era: 1950–1991

Notable large-scale developments in educational contexts, in both Canada and the United States, occurred after World War II. Although there were some parallels, the development of the two countries differed. The post WWW II period has been identified as a period of major educational development in Canada (Jones, 2014; Summerlee & Christensen Hughes, 2010), though little is known specifically about how academic misconduct in Canada was handled during the early post-World War II years.

Educational administration emerged as a field of study in both countries during this time period. In the U.S. the first educational administration program was launched in 1950, with the financial support of the Kellogg Foundation (Gilbert et al., 1985). The same foundation also provided funding to the Canadian Education Association (CEA), two years later for Canada's first large scale project in educational leadership, which continued until 1956 (Gilbert et al., 1985). Near the end of that project, graduate programs in educational administration began to develop, with the University of Alberta being the first to admit students to a doctoral program in educational administration in 1957, conferring its first degrees a year later (Robertson, 1971). Other programs were simultaneously under development at the University of British Columbia and the University of Toronto, with the Ontario Institute for Studies in Education (OISE) at the University of Toronto being launched in 1965 (Gilbert et al., 1985). The University of Manitoba followed not long after. The Council of Ministers of Education, Canada (CMEC) was established in 1968 by provincial ministers of education, becoming "the only framework providing departments of education with an opportunity to work collectively" (CMEC, 2001, p. 8).

In the United States, William (Bill) Bowers (1964, 1966) conducted the first large-scale research on academic misconduct in the early 1960s, surveying more than 600 academic deans, over 500 student body presidents, and more than 5400 students at 99 American colleges. No similar large-scale research would be undertaken at Canadian institutions until decades later; but that is not to say that Canadian scholars were not interested in academic misconduct. One of the earliest known published papers by a Canadian scholar on academic dishonesty appeared in 1971. Written by Professor R.G. Martin (1971), from the University of Alberta, "Plagiarism and originality: Some remedies" was published in the May edition of *The English Journal*, an American publication.

The reasons why Martin did not publish his article in Canada are unknown, but it may have been partly due to the fact that there were few journals available to Canadian scholars wanting to write about academic integrity at that time. One of the first Canadian education journals was launched under the title of "*Stoa*" in April 1971, the publication later evolved into the *Canadian Journal of Higher Education* (CJHE), which addresses topics of interest in higher education. Martin's article discussed plagiarism as a general problem, with an implied focus on secondary schools, therefore it would not have been a good fit for the journal. The Canadian Journal of Education (CJE) would not be launched until five years later in 1976.

The 1960s and 1970s were a time of significant change in society and, by extension, in educational contexts. During this period of social unrest, campuses became host to student protests and the rules that had been infused into educational systems from kindergarten through to university came under scrutiny (Eerkes, 2010; Gilbert et al., 1985). In Canada, this was also the period when the professionalization of education began to advance, with teacher training moving out of teachers' colleges and into universities, a transition that was all but complete by the end of the 1970s (Gilbert, 1985).

The Constitution Act, 1982 succeeded the British North America Act (1867), when Canada's constitution was patriated from the United Kingdom, giving Canada the authority to amend its own constitution and act with sovereignty as an independent country. The Constitution Act, 1982, reaffirmed education in Canada as being primarily the responsibility of the provinces and territories, with the exceptions noted earlier (CMEC, 2001). Over time, there have been various reorganizations of provincial and territorial government ministries and departments concerning education. Some provinces have a single ministry or department responsible for education at all levels, whereas others have separate government units responsible for K-12 and advanced education. The organization of these ministries and departments can change over time, and such reorganizations are entirely within the purview of the provincial governments.

The 1980s included a period of fiscal restraint at all levels of education, following the financial boom of the 1970s. Changes in the global economy in the 1980s led to drastic changes in financial investments in education in a number of countries including Canada, the US, Australia, and the UK, among others (Eaton, 2009). In Canada, this resulted in the merging of government departments to reduce the administrative costs of education (CMEC, 2001). It also led to the development of cost-recovery educational programs in the 1980s, which morphed into revenue-generating programs in the 1990s (Eaton, 2009). International student enrollments in higher education and the establishment of revenue-generating programs, including those offering English as an Additional Language, became lucrative (Eaton, 2009). As an example, the population of EAL students in the province of British Columbia increased "334% from 1986 to 1995" (Nolan, 2001, p. 3). Such increases were common across the country as international student enrollments and English as an Additional Language (EAL) programs became a major source of income for Canadian higher education institutions (Eaton, 2009).

The Creative Disruption Era: 1992–2019

The financial restraint of the 1980s led to concerns about the commodification of education as governments systematically reduced their investment in education (Eaton, 2009). Concurrently, concerns about plagiarism and academic misconduct in Canadian higher education became more prominent (Hexham, 1992). Scholars across the world, including Canadians, have noted that there has been a correlative relationship between the commodification of education and the neoliberal university with a corresponding increase in concerns about academic misconduct (Eaton, 2021; Hersey & Lancaster, 2015; Kleinman, 2016; Saltmarsh, 2005; Whiteman & Gordon, 2001). In this section, we outline how the period of 1992–2019 was significant in terms of the development of academic integrity in Canadian education. Much of what is known about research on academic integrity in Canada during this period has been documented elsewhere (see Eaton & Edino, 2018; Eaton et al., 2019), so instead, we bring forward new insights about this influential period that supplement existing work and provide deeper insights.

1992 was a watershed year for education and for academic integrity, in particular. The term "creative disruption" was coined in 1992 by Jean-Marie Dru in France (Nora, 2016). Although the phrase refers to creative and radical innovation in business (Nora, 2016), the concept is easily transferred to educational contexts (Eaton, 2021c). Although the genesis of the Internet had begun years before, the infrastructure behind the World Wide Web flourished around this time, with the first websites coming into existence during this period of rapid innovation. In 1992, the online service askERIC was launched by the Education Resources Information Center (ERIC) in the U.S. (Sutton, 2001). Although ERIC was launched in the 1960s as a bibliographic archive, the service's adoption of the Internet as a means to share knowledge led to it becoming a "pioneering e-mail-based question–answer service" (Sutton, 2001, p. 21) and ERIC became one of the first 100 websites ever launched (Sutton, 2001). In doing so, the service democratized knowledge and disseminated content in ways previously unknown in education (Eaton, 2021c).

At the time, those who had worked on the development of the technology that evolved into the Internet had never anticipated that those who used it might do for nefarious reasons (Kleinrock, 2009, 2019). As one of its developers pointed out, the strengths of Internet technology are simultaneously its weaknesses, which have included unethical use of information, plagiarism, and misappropriation of others' creations (Kleinrock, 2009). When services such as AskERIC were being launched in 1992, those who developed the Internet noted that they "did not anticipate that the dark side of the internet would emerge with such ferocity" (Kleinrock, 2019, n.p.).

However, the signs were there. One Canadian professor in particular became vocal about academic misconduct in the early 1990s, using the Internet to sound the alarm. Dr. Irving Hexham from the University of Calgary posted at length on electronic bulletin boards and informally on his web site about the need to address plagiarism in higher education (Hexham, 1992). Although his contributions were not peer reviewed, they nevertheless stand as influential and authoritative scholarly discussions of plagiarism with numerous citations (Eaton & Edino, 2018).

As Hexham was making his views known in Canada and beyond, major developments relating to academic integrity were underway in the United States. Donald (Don) McCabe and colleagues established the Center for Academic Integrity (CAI) in 1992 (Fishman, 2016). McCabe's work built on that of Bowers (1964, 1966) and by the early 1990s, McCabe had identified a need for a large-scale initiative to address academic integrity in the US. Although the CAI was not explicitly established in response to the popularization of the Internet, the timing of its launch cannot be overlooked, as it coincided with major technological developments in education globally and also became its own form of creative disruption for academic integrity, as it was the first organized initiative to address breaches of academic integrity on a large scale. Due in a large part to McCabe's vision, the centre went on to include members from other countries, eventually changing its name to the International Center for Academic Integrity (ICAI) in 2010.

In 1999, the centre released its first iteration of the Fundamental Values of Academic Integrity, identifying five fundamental values to guide student conduct: fairness, honesty, respect, responsibility, and trust (ICAI, 2018). The document was later updated to include the sixth value of courage. Now in its third edition, (ICAI, 2021), this resource has provided the basis for dialogue, policy, and process in numerous countries, including Canada.

One of McCabe's areas of interest was the efficacy of honour codes, in both traditional and modified forms. Key components of traditional honour code systems include an orientation pledge, a commitment to report on the questionable behaviour of peers, and a student-run adjudication body to address misconduct. Later in his career, McCabe acknowledged that even if an institution calls itself an honour code school, without the necessary systems and support in place, a *culture* of honour may not actually exist (McCabe, Butterfield, & Treviño, 2012). Conversely, a school can have a culture of honour even if they do not have an explicit honour code (Fishman, 2016; McCabe et al., 2012). An honour *culture*, without explicit honour *codes*, is arguably what has existed in Canada, where honour code schools have never been the norm. It is our position that it does not make sense for Canadian schools to try and emulate the American academic honour system, given historical differences between our two counties. That being said, orientation programs in which students commit to approaching their work with integrity can serve a symbolic purpose as part of a comprehensive institutional approach to academic integrity. This argument is substantiated by Christensen Hughes & McCabe (2006a) who noted that although much can be learned from the American context with regards to academic integrity, there is a low likelihood that formal honour codes would be effective in Canada. Instead, Canadian schools have adopted a more multi-stakeholder approach, focusing not only on student conduct, but also on ethical conduct pertaining to all members of the academic community.

Systematic inquiry into academic integrity began to emerge in Canada in the 1990s, among both scholars and professional staff at universities. A few studies were published in the 1990s about academic integrity in Canada, laying the foundation for a proliferation of work after the turn of the millennium (see Genereux & McLeod, 1995; Lytton, 1996; Woods, 1998). In parallel, student affairs professionals began addressing academic integrity at events such as the Canadian Conference on Student Judicial Affairs in 1998 (Eerkes, 2010; McKenzie, 2018).

The groundwork laid in the 1990s led to major developments in academic integrity in the first decade of the twenty-first century. In a four-page exposé in *University Affairs* (a periodical dedicated to university topics in Canada) Mullens (2000) summarized a number of academic misconduct cases at universities across the country, including cases of Internet-based essay mills, which we now refer to as contract cheating. Mullens's article was a pre-cursor to the seminal papers by Christensen Hughes and McCabe. (2006a, b), the second of which was awarded with the Canadian Society for Studies in Higher Education Sheffield Award for best paper in 2007 (CSSHE, n.d.). We have elaborated on this work in Chapter 3 (see Christensen Hughes & Eaton, 2022).

Christensen Hughes and McCabe's (2006b) first contribution, based on predominantly US data, concluded that "the majority of undergraduate students [surveyed] have engaged in some type of misconduct in the completion of their academic work" while also agreeing that "such behaviour is morally wrong" (p. 52). Explanations for why students might engage in such behaviours regardless of their moral view, included a number of personal or demographic factors, such as "maturity, habit, attitude, culture and first language" (p. 53). Institutional factors were also identified; those that discouraged academic misconduct increased student risk-reward perception. Christensen Hughes and McCabe (2006a) observed:

> Higher education plays an essential role in democratic society - one that requires U.S. [sic] to provide our students with a high quality education, to develop moral and engaged citizens, and to uphold the highest standards of integrity. We need a total recommitment to this role. (p. 59)

They concluded by calling for a comprehensive Canadian study, one that would help to identify "the unique characteristics of the Canadian higher education system" in order to tailor "institutional strategies appropriate for promoting academic integrity" as well as "to identify how Canadian colleges and universities are responding to academic misconduct when it does occur and what strategies have proven most successful" (Christensen Hughes and McCabe, 2006b, p. 59).

The second article responded to this call, presenting the results of a study involving 11 Canadian higher education institutions, from five provinces, conducted between January 2002 and March 2003. Undergraduate and graduate students, teaching assistants and faculty, were surveyed about their perceptions and behaviours using a modified version of the survey developed by McCabe and colleagues via the Center of Academic Integrity's Assessment Project (Christensen Hughes and McCabe, 2006a). Given the methodological limitations of the study, the authors clearly advised, "the findings of this study should not be used to make definitive claims about the state of academic misconduct within Canada, but rather as indicators of potential areas of concern and action" (Christensen Hughes and McCabe, 2006a, p. 7).

The study concluded that "large numbers of Canadian high school, undergraduate and graduate students report they have engaged in a variety of questionable behaviours in the completion of their academic work" (Christensen Hughes & McCabe, 2006a, p. 17) and that "consistent with the view of over 40% of faculty and TAs: cheating may be a serious problem in Canadian higher education" (p. 18). The study also identified substantial differences between student and faculty "beliefs about what constitutes academic misconduct". The authors suggested that the reason many students reported engaging in "unauthorized collaboration and falsification and fabrication behaviours" may be "simply because they don't believe they are wrong" (p. 18).

The authors recommended that Canadian institutions should take a number of actions, including "recommit[ting] to academic integrity" and investigating "where existing policies are failing" (Christensen Hughes & McCabe, 2006a, p. 17). More specifically they observed, "New policies and procedures (including meaningful penalties) that have the confidence of the community are clearly needed…supported by system-wide educational efforts directed at administrators, faculty, TAs and students" (p. 17). They also called for increasing the quality of the educational experience, including assessment procedures.

With respect to honour codes—and in particular the expectation that students report on others' unethical actions—results from the seminal study conducted by Christensen Hughes and McCabe (2006a) suggest that honour codes would likely be ineffective in Canada. From the high school survey (first year students reflecting on their time in high school), "only 13% thought it likely or very likely that a student would report an incident of cheating" (p. 8). The percentage was the same for undergraduate students. For graduate students the percentage was only slightly higher (18%). Once we consider the historical factors about how the Canadian and American higher education systems developed differently, the case for honour codes in Canada becomes even weaker.

The press took notice of the results of Christensen Hughes's and McCabe's study. What followed was a provocative treatment of academic misconduct in Canada (see Christensen Hughes & Eaton, 2022). As one example, *MacLean's*, a national Canadian magazine, was somewhat misleading when it proclaimed on the front cover of its February 9, 2007 issue: "Fraud U. With more than half of Canadian university students cheating, all degrees are tainted. It's a national scandal. Why aren't schools doing more about it?" (*MacLean's*, 2007a).

Not only did this issue feature a full length article (Gulli et al., 2007), but the editors focused their comments on the topic as well, chastising administrators for certifying graduates who had not fully earned their degrees (*MacLean's*, 2007a, p. 4):

> We need to be able to trust our universities…but the fact is that few of them are moving swiftly to correct their cheating problems. Offences are observed and ignored. Processes developed to deal with culprits are bypassed. Punishments, on the infrequent occasions they are imposed, tend to be light. Simple methods of examination proven to prohibit cheating are inexplicably out of use. Universities have to do better, for their own sake, and for the sake of all who rely upon their certificates… There's a lot at stake.

The public responded with letters to the editor but university administrators and higher educational institutions were largely silent, leading the editors to further proclaim in the February 19th, 2007 issue, "go ahead and cheat" (*MacLean's*, 2007b, p. 2).

The February 26th issue featured a follow up article, on Maclean's attempt to get presidents and principals of leading research-intensive universities to comment on the findings. While few agreed to participate, those that did questioned the "prevalence of misconduct among their own students" as well as the extent to which universities were to blame (Gulli, 2007, p. 41). Instead, they suggested a range of factors were in play, including reduced government funding and increasing student/faculty ratios; the influence of parents, and primary and high school experiences; the Internet; and increasing competition for jobs.

Following, a number of universities began to take action, revisiting and revising their policies and practices, holding workshops, enhancing academic integrity resources and supports, and declaring "integrity weeks" in an effort to raise awareness. Some also made the results of their own investigations public, posting student survey results on their websites.

Other notable initiatives were also underway at this time. For example, the first federally-funded research projects relating to academic integrity were funded in this decade, supported by grants from the Social Sciences and Humanities Research Council of Canada (SSHRC), such as the one led by Lynn Taylor, University of Manitoba, who was awarded three grants totaling almost $80,000 CAD over three years ($35,785 in 2002; $22,892 in 2003; and $21,116 in 2004) (SSHRC, n.d.). This funded research project led to publications and paved the way for future research (Paterson et al., 2003; Taylor et al., 2004).

Perhaps one of the most sustained outcomes of Taylor's work was the mentorship of a graduate student, Brandy Usick (2005), who later went on to lead institutional, regional and national initiatives, such as the co-founding of the country's first and only professional and scholarly journal on the topic, *Canadian Perspectives on Academic Integrity* (Usick, 2018). In addition, Usick has been acknowledged as a prominent knowledge keeper for academic integrity in Canadian higher education (Eaton, 2021a; McKenzie, 2018).The first decade of the 2000s was also pivotal for Canada in terms of how text-matching software (e.g., Turnitin®) was used in this country. In a landmark legal case, a student from McGill University, Jesse Rosenfeld, took the university to court over the use of Turnitin during the 2003–2004 academic year (Strawczynski, 2004). Rosenfeld challenged the university on its use of Turnitin®, after he refused to submit his final semester assignment to Turnitin® and received a failing grade for doing so. The details of the case have been published elsewhere (see Strawczynski, 2004), but the key takeaway is that the courts found in favour of the student. The results of this case set a legal precedent in Canada regarding the use of text-matching software in Canada, with the long-term impact being that such software is not used in Canada to the extent that it is in other countries. There has also been limited research into how text-matching software is used in Canadian universities (for one example see Zaza & McKenzie, 2018) in part because universities have firmly limited their use of these products or declined to use them all together.

The decade that followed the publication of Christensen Hughes and McCabe's articles, from 2007–2017, was when practitioners began connecting with one another in more organized and systematic ways. Educational developers from across the country participated in events during the annual conference of the Society for Teaching and Learning in Higher Education (STLHE), sharing their results and comparing strategies for addressing them. The Academic Integrity Council of Ontario (AICO) was founded in 2008 and the Canadian Consortium became an official branch of the International Center for Academic Integrity in 2014 (McKenzie, 2018). Amanda McKenzie, from the University of Waterloo, was the first representative of a Canadian university to join the board of directors of ICAI. Also during this time, small symposia were held in Alberta and British Columbia, as individuals from multiple institutions began to collaborate more intentionally (McKenzie, 2018).

These early efforts laid the foundation for more intensive multi-institutional, cross-provincial, and national-level collaborations that began to emerge in 2018, the first of which was a national-level policy analysis designed to examine how contract cheating was addressed in Canadian higher education institutional policies (see Eaton, 2019). The project was modelled after policy research conducted in Australia (see Bretag et al., 2011a, b) and the project lead for the Australia project, Tracey Bretag, mentored the lead for the Canadian project, Sarah Elaine Eaton, offering influential advice, such as dividing the project into smaller chunks (e.g., focused on different regions of the country) and engaging individuals from each region to take part so as to build capacity across the country. The project has resulted in multiple collaborative conference presentations and publications in the phases covering Western Canada and Ontario (see: Eaton, 2019a; McKenzie et al., 2020; Stoesz et al., 2019; Stoesz & Eaton, 2020). At the time of this writing the analysis of policies at Atlantic Canadian universities is underway (see Eaton et al., 2021).

Through the mentoring of this project, Bretag and Eaton developed a professional relationship that resulted in Bretag being invited to the University of Calgary as a short-term visiting scholar in 2019. The visit evolved into a full-scale national symposium, with more than 150 participants coming from across the country, as well as from Great Britain (Canadian Symposium on Academic Integrity, 2019; Eaton, 2019c; University of Calgary, 2019). The inaugural Canadian Symposium on Academic Integrity hosted by the University of Calgary was described as a landmark event in Canadian higher education by multiple individuals (R. Mackay, personal communication to S. Eaton, April 18, 2019; T. Lancaster, personal communication to S. Eaton, December 3, 2019). This first national symposium on academic integrity brought together practitioners, educators, scholars, and leaders on a scale never before achieved in Canada. The symposium served as a launching point for the establishment of provincial academic integrity networks in British Columbia, Alberta, and Manitoba. Upon reflection, although the inaugural Canadian Symposium on Academic Integrity was not intended to serve as the culminating event of this era, that is arguably what happened. The years from 1992 to 2019 were ones of great advances in technology, education, and academic integrity; this was the era when creative disruption would characterize significant changes in education, business, and society in general. The arrival of the COVID-19 virus the following year brought with it a new era for society and education across the globe.

2020 and Beyond: Current Trends and Future Directions

In 2020, the COVID-19 coronavirus pandemic changed the world. The impact on academic integrity was notable across education globally, including in Canada. Perspectives of Canadians regarding academic integrity during the pandemic were captured in a special issue of *Canadian Perspectives on Academic Integrity*, which included more than twenty contributions from authors across the country (Bens, 2020; Denham, 2020; Eaton, 2020; Gagné, 2020; Gedajlovic & Wielemaker, 2020; Gervais, 2020; Kier, 2020; McKenzie, 2020; Miron, 2020; Nearing, 2020; Rahimian, 2020; Rovere, 2020; Scurr, 2020; Seeland, 2020; Sopcak, 2020; Stoesz, 2020; Teymouri & Boisvert, 2020; Thacker, 2020; Vogt, 2020; Wheatley, 2020; Wolsky & Hamilton, 2020). The issue, which received international acclaim (see Brown, 2021), was one of the only formal endeavours anywhere in the world to capture the experiences of those working in academic integrity during the first year of the COVID-19 pandemic.

Also in 2020, Canadians took on international leadership roles, with Jennie Miron of Humber College leading the International Day of Action Against Contract Cheating (Miron, 2020) and Sarah Elaine Eaton being named as the Editor-in-Chief of the *International Journal for Educational Integrity*, after the passing of Tracey Bretag, the Australian who co-founded the journal in 2005.

With the publication of this book, we can see that much has changed since Christensen Hughes and McCabe (2006a, b) published their two seminal articles on academic misconduct in Canada, fifteen years prior. In particular, since 2018, multi-institutional research has become the norm in Canada in both official languages of English and French. For examples of research led by Francophone scholars (published in English) see Peters and Cadieux (2019), and Peters et al. (2019, 2022).

In addition, since about 2020 Indigenous scholars have been contributing more to the knowledge base of academic integrity, showing how Indigenous ways of being, knowing, learning, and teaching are fundamentally ethical, and exist in parallel to western interpretations of values associated with academic integrity (e.g., Maracle, 2020; Gladue, 2021a, b; Lindstrom, 2022; Poitras Pratt & Gladue, 2022).

The research, resources and efforts of Canadians detailed in this chapter showcase contributions from our country that simultaneously align with internationally recognized values and approaches, while highlighting contributions and perspectives that are uniquely Canadian. We, in Canada, have become global leaders in academic integrity, with researchers, administrators, and practitioners collaborating regularly and intentionally with colleagues across the country and across the world.

However, much work remains to be done. There remains a need for enhanced support for this important work. National funding agencies must value academic integrity research and support that work with increased funding for research. There are few formal educational or professional development training programs available in Canada for practitioners and future scholars of academic integrity. Universities and colleges need more programs to train academic integrity professionals, scholars, and administrators. Ministries of education and advanced education, along with provincial and territorial quality assurance agencies and national organizing bodies for higher education, have yet to make academic integrity a priority. And as yet, there is no legislation in Canada against contract cheating companies. As Kenny and Eaton (2022) point out in this volume, much of the work relating to academic integrity is invisible and unrecognized. There is an urgent need for more Canadian post-secondary institutions to establish centralized offices of academic integrity on their campuses, with positions that are funded from regular operating budgets, rather than "soft" or project-based funding.

These gaps offer a clear direction for future opportunities and priorities. In particular, advocating for provincial and national bodies to actively recognize the importance of academic integrity in our educational systems remains a priority. Similarly, if Canada is to be successful in enacting legislation against contact cheating companies, then efforts must continue to be coordinated and sustained over time (Eaton, 2021b). This is the work of academic integrity professionals, administrators, and scholars moving forward. Canadians are poised to continue making significant and substantive contributions to the field of academic integrity, but their efforts must be sustained and supported by senior educational leaders, policy makers, and funders. The integrity of the degrees we confer and the confidence Canadians have in our higher education institutions, depends on it.

References

Allmendinger, D. (1973). The Dangers of Ante-Bellum Student Life. *Journal of Social History, 7*(1), 75. https://doi.org/10.1353/jsh/7.1.75

Angulo, A. J. (2016). *Diploma mills: How for-profit colleges stiffed students, taxpayers and the American dream.* Johns Hopkins University Press.

Bens, S. (2020). A reflection on change and academic integrity during COVID-19. *Canadian Perspectives on Academic Integrity, 3*(2), 11–13. https://doi.org/10.11575/cpai.v3i2.71637

Bertram Gallant, T. (2008). *Academic integrity in the twenty-first century: A teaching and learning imperative.* Wiley.

Bowers, W. J. (1964). *Student dishonesty and its control in college.* NY: Bureau of Applied Social Research, Columbia University.

Bowers, W. J. (1966). *Student dishonesty and its control in college.* (Doctor of Philosophy). Columbia University.

Bretag, T., Mahmud, S., East, J., Green, M., & James, C. (2011). *Academic integrity standards: A preliminary analysis of the academic integrity policies at Australian Universities.* Paper presented at the Proceedings of AuQF 2011 Demonstrating Quality.

Bretag, T., Mahmud, S., Wallace, M., Walker, R., James, C., Green, M., & Partridge, L. (2011). Core elements of exemplary academic integrity policy in Australian higher education. *International Journal for Educational Integrity, 7*(2), 3–12. https://doi.org/10.21913/IJEI.v7i2.759

Brown, J. F. (2021). *Journal issue spotlight: Canadian perspectives on academic integrity during Covid-19.* https://www.academicintegrity.org/integrity/journal-issue-spotlight-canadian-perspectives-on-academic-integrity-during-covid-19/

Cameron, D. M. (1991). *More than an academic question: Universities, government, and public policy in Canada.* Institute for Research on Public Policy.

Canadian Symposium on Academic Integrity: Program and Abstracts. (2019). In S. E. Eaton, J. Lock, & M. Schroeder (Eds.). University of Calgary. http://hdl.handle.net/1880/110293

Canadian Society for the Study of Higher Education / Société canadienne pour l'étude de l'enseignement supérieur. (n.d.). CJHE Sheffield Award. https://csshe-scees.ca/awards/cjhe-sheffield-award/

Canadian Society for the Study of Higher Education/Société canadienne pour l'étude de l'enseignement supérieur. (2020). 2020–2025 Strategic Plan. https://csshescees.files.wordpress.com/2020/06/csshe_strategicplan2019_final_may2020_e.pdf

Christensen Hughes, J., & Eaton, S. E. (2022). Student integrity violations in the academy: More than a decade of growing complexity and concern. In S. E. Eaton & J. Christensen Hughes (Eds.), *Academic integrity in Canada: An enduring and essential challenge*, Springer.

Christensen Hughes, J. M., & McCabe, D. L. (2006). Academic misconduct within higher education in Canada. *The Canadian Journal of Higher Education, 36*(2), 1–21. http://journals.sfu.ca/cjhe/index.php/cjhe/article/view/183537/183482

Christensen Hughes, J. M., & McCabe, D. L. (2006). Understanding academic misconduct. *Canadian Journal of Higher Education, 36*(1), 49–63. https://journals.sfu.ca/cjhe/index.php/cjhe/article/view/183525

Colleges Ontario. (2019). About. https://www.collegesontario.org/en

Colleges & Institutes Canada. (n.d.). https://www.collegesinstitutes.ca/

Council of Ministers of Education (CMEC) Canada. (2001). The development of education in Canada. https://www.cmec.ca/Publications/Lists/Publications/Attachments/34/ice46dev-ca.en.pdf

Council of Ministers of Education Canada (CMEC). (2020). Education in Canada: An overview. https://www.cmec.ca/299/Education-in-Canada-An-Overview/index.html

Council of Ontario Universities. (2019). Mission. https://cou.ca/about/mission/

Denham, T. (2020). My work in academic integrity 2020: Not all I hoped it would be. *Canadian Perspectives on Academic Integrity, 3*(2), 14–15. https://doi.org/10.11575/cpai.v3i2.71641

Eaton, S. E. (2009). *Marketing of revenue-generating ESL programs at the University of Calgary: A qualitative study.* Doctoral thesis, University of Calgary.

Eaton, S. E. (2019a). *Contract cheating in Canada: National Policy Analysis.* https://osf.io/n9kwt/

Eaton, S. E. (2019b). Overview of higher education in Canada. In J. M. Jacob & R. Heydon (Eds.), *Bloomsbury Education and Childhood Studies.* Bloomsbury.

Eaton, S. E. (2019c). Reflections on the 2019 Canadian symposium on academic integrity. *Canadian Perspectives on Academic Integrity, 2*(2), 1–6. https://doi.org/10.11575/cpai.v2i2.69454

Eaton, S. E. (2020). Academic integrity in 2020: Year in review. *Canadian Perspectives on Academic Integrity, 3*(2). https://doi.org/10.11575/cpai.v3i2.71636

Eaton, S. E. (2021a). *Building collaborative networks to support academic integrity.* Keynote address presented at the Academic Integrity Inter-Institutional Meeting (AIIIM) 2021. Online.

Eaton, S. E. (2021b). *Plagiarism in higher education: Tackling tough topics in academic integrity*. Santa Barbara, CA: Libraries Unlimited.

Eaton, S. E. (2022). Contract cheating in Canada: A comprehensive overview. In S. E. Eaton & J. Christensen Hughes (Eds.), *Academic integrity in Canada: An enduring and essential challenge*, Springer.

Eaton, S. E., & Edino, R. I. (2018). Strengthening the research agenda of educational integrity in Canada: A review of the research literature and call to action. *International Journal of Educational Integrity, 14*(1). https://doi.org/10.1007/s40979-018-0028-7

Eaton, S. E., Crossman, K., & Edino, R. I. (2019). *Academic integrity in Canada: An Annotated Bibliography*. http://hdl.handle.net/1880/110130

Eaton, S. E., Stoesz, B. M., Godfrey Anderson, J. R., & LeBlanc-Haley, J. (2021). *Contract Cheating in Canada, National Policy Analysis–Phase Four, Atlantic Canada: Research Project Brief*. http://hdl.handle.net/1880/113110

Eerkes, D. (2010). Student judicial affairs and academic integrity. In D. G. Hardy Cox & C. C. Strange (Eds.), *Achieving student success: Effective student services in Canadian higher education* (pp. 100–111). Montreal: McGill-Queen's University Press.

Féderacion des cégeps. (n.d). https://www.cegepsquebec.ca/en/

Fishman, T. (2016). Academic integrity as an educational concept, concern, and movement in US institutions of higher learning. In T. Bretag (Ed.), *Handbook of Academic Integrity* (pp. 7–21). Springer.

Gagné, A. (2020). Reflections on academic integrity and educational development during COVID-19. *Canadian Perspectives on Academic Integrity, 3*(2), 16–17. https://doi.org/10.11575/cpai.v3i2.71642

Gedajlovic, E., & Wielemaker, M. (2020). Neither abuse, nor neglect: A duty of care perspective on academic integrity. *Canadian Perspectives on Academic Integrity, 3*(2), 63–69. https://doi.org/10.11575/cpai.v3i2.71655

Genereux, R. L., & McLeod, B. A. (1995). Circumstances surrounding cheating: A questionnaire study of college students. *Research in Higher Education, 36*(6), 687–704. http://www.jstor.org/stable/40196166

Gervais, L. (2020). Academic integrity and student support during COVID-19. *Canadian Perspectives on Academic Integrity, 3*(2). https://doi.org/10.11575/cpai.v3i2.71528

Gilbert, V. K., Sheehan, A. T., & Teeter, K. G. (1985). *In loco parentis: A teacher's guide to educational administration*. University of Toronto.

Gladue, K. (2021a). *Indigenous academic integrity*. Calgary: University of Calgary. https://taylorinstitute.ucalgary.ca/resources/indigenous-academic-integrity

Gladue, K. (2021b). *Indigenous academic integrity: Paradigms into practice*. Paper presented at the International Center for Academic Integrity (ICAI) Annual Conference (online).

Gulli, C. (2007, February 24). Cheating? Who us? *Maclean's Magazine, 120*(7), 41–41.

Gulli, C., Köhler, N., & Patriquin, M. (2007, February 12). The great university cheating scandal. *Maclean's Magazine*. 32–36. https://archive.macleans.ca/issue/20070212

Harvard University. (2020). History. https://www.harvard.edu/about-harvard/harvard-glance/history

Hersey, C., & Lancaster, T. (2015). *The online industry of paper mills, contract cheating services, and auction sites*. Paper presented at the Clute Institute International Education Conference. https://www.researchgate.net/publication/280830577_The_Online_Industry_of_Paper_Mills_Contract_Cheating_Services_and_Auction_Sites

Hexham, I. (1992). On plagiarism and integrity in scholarly activity. *Humanist: Humanities Computing, 5*(4). http://dhhumanist.org/Archives/Virginia/v05/0795.html

International Center for Academic Integrity (ICAI). (2021). *The fundamental values of academic integrity (3rd ed.)*. https://www.academicintegrity.org/fundamental-values/

International Center for Academic Integrity (ICAI). (2018). About. https://web.archive.org/web/20180318234929/.php http://www.academicintegrity.org:80/icai/about-3.php

Jones, G. A. (2014). An introduction to higher education in Canada. In K. M. Joshi & S. Paivandi (Eds.), *Higher education across nations* (Vol. 1, pp. 1–38). B.R. Publishing.

Kenny, N., & Eaton, S. E. (2022). Academic integrity through a SoTL lens and 4M framework: An institutional self-study. In S. E. Eaton & J. Christensen Hughes (Eds.), *Academic integrity in Canada: An enduring and essential challenge*, Springer.

Kier, C. A. (2020). Reflections on COVID-19 and academic integrity. *Canadian Perspectives on Academic Integrity, 3*(2), 20–22. https://doi.org/10.11575/cpai.v3i2.71643

Kleinman, D. L. (2016). From matters of integrity to cultural transformation: Higher education in the era of neoliberalism. In T. Bretag (Ed.), *Handbook of Academic Integrity* (pp. 929–941). Springer. https://doi.org/10.1007/978-981-287-098-8_29

Kleinrock, L. (2009, October 24). Leonard Kleinrock, Mr. Internet. *Los Angeles Times.* https://www.latimes.com/opinion/la-oe-morrison-use24-2009oct24-story.html

Kleinrock, L. (2019, October 29). Opinion: 50 years ago, I helped invent the internet. How did it go so wrong? *Los Angeles Times.* https://www.latimes.com/opinion/story/2019-10-29/internet-50th-anniversary-ucla-kleinrock

Lindstrom, G. (2022). Accountability, relationality and indigenous epistemology: Advancing an indigenous perspective on academic integrity. In S. E. Eaton & J. Christensen Hughes (Eds.), *Academic integrity in Canada: An enduring and essential challenge*, Springer.

Lucas, C. J. (2006). *American higher education: A history.* Palgrave MacMillan.

Lytton, H. (1996). This is how it's always been done: The treatment of academic misconduct in Canada. *The Canadian Journal of Sociology*, 21(2), 223–235. https://doi.org/10.2307/3341978 https://doi.org/10.2307/3341978

MacLean's. (2007a, February 12). https://archive.macleans.ca/issue/20070212

MacLean's. (2007b, February 19). https://archive.macleans.ca/issue/20070219

Maracle, I. B. J. (2020). Seven grandfathers in academic integrity. https://studentlife.utoronto.ca/wp-content/uploads/Seven_Grandfathers_in_Academic_Integrity.pdf

Maritime Provinces Higher Education Commission. (n.d.). About. http://www.mphec.ca/index.aspx

Martin, R. (1971). Plagiarism and originality: Some remedies. *English Journal, 60*(5), 621–628. https://doi.org/10.2307/813078

McCabe, D. L., Butterfield, K. D., & Treviño, L. K. (2012). *Cheating in college: Why students do it and what educators can do about it.* Johns Hopkins University Press.

McKenzie, A. M. (2018). Academic integrity across the Canadian landscape. *Canadian Perspectives on Academic Integrity, 1*(2), 40–45. https://doi.org/10.11575/cpai.v1i2.54599.g42964

McKenzie, A. (2020). COVID-19: A silver lining for academic integrity from a pandemic. *Canadian Perspectives on Academic Integrity, 3*(2), 23–25. https://doi.org/10.11575/cpai.v3i2.71644

McKenzie, A., Miron, J. B., Devereaux, L., Eaton, S. E., Persaud, N., Rowbotham, K., & Thacker, E. (2020, March 8). *Contract cheating language within academic integrity policies in the university sector in Ontario, Canada.* Paper presented at the International Center for Academic Integrity (ICAI) 2020 Conference.

Miron, J. B. (2020). International Day of Action (IDoA) against contract cheating 2020—Update from the chair of the IDoA planning committee. *Canadian Perspectives on Academic Integrity, 3*(2). https://doi.org/10.11575/cpai.v3i2.71473

Monohan, E. J. (1971). Some notes for an anecdotal history of Canadian universities *STOA, 1*(1). https://journals.sfu.ca/cjhe/index.php/cjhe/article/view/35/20530

Mullens, A. (2000). Cheating to win. *University Affairs, 41*(10), 22–28.

Nearing, E. (2020). Supporting the pivot online: Academic integrity initiatives at University of Waterloo. *Canadian Perspectives on Academic Integrity, 3*(2), 29–31. https://doi.org/10.11575/cpai.v3i2.71645

Nolan, R. E. (2001). The power of theory in the administration of ESL programs. *Adult Basic Education, 11*(1), 3–17.

Nora, D. (2016, January 24). Le concept de "Disruption" expliqué par son créateur. *L'Obs.* https://www.nouvelobs.com/economie/20160122.OBS3214/le-concept-de-disruption-explique-par-son-createur.html

Organisation for Economic Co-operation and Development/Organisation de Coopération et de Développement Economiques (OECD). (2020). *Education at a Glance 2020: OECD Indicators.* https://read.oecd-ilibrary.org/education/education-at-a-glance-2020_43439e03-en#page1
Paterson, B., Taylor, L., & Usick, B. (2003). The construction of plagiarism in a school of nursing. *Learning in Health & Social Care, 2*(3), 147. https://doi.org/10.1046/j.1473-6861.2003.00047.x
Peters, M., & Cadieux, A. (2019). Are Canadian professors teaching the skills and knowledge students need to prevent plagiarism? *International Journal for Educational Integrity, 15*(10). https://doi.org/10.1007/s40979-019-0047-z
Peters, M., Boies, T., & Morin, S. (2019). Teaching academic integrity in Quebec universities: Roles professors adopt. *Frontiers in Education, 4*(99), 1–13.
Peters, M., Fontaine, S., & Frenette, E. (2022). Teaching the teachers: To what extent do preservice teachers cheat on exams and plagiarise in their written work? In S. E. Eaton & J. Christensen Hughes (Eds.), *Academic integrity in Canada: An enduring and essential challenge*, Springer.
Poitras Pratt, Y., & Gladue, K. (2022). Re-defining academic integrity: Embracing indigenous truths. In S. E. Eaton & J. Christensen Hughes (Eds.), *Academic integrity in Canada: An enduring and essential challenge*, Springer.
Rahimian, M. (2020). Academic integrity and the pandemic. *Canadian Perspectives on Academic Integrity, 3*(2), 32–35. https://doi.org/10.11575/cpai.v3i2.71666
Robertson, N. L. (1971). *The doctorate education in Canada.* Phi Delta Kappa.
Rovere, D. A. (2020). Reducing plagiarism and improving writing: A lesson from Chinese painting. *Canadian Perspectives on Academic Integrity, 3*(2), 57–62. https://doi.org/10.11575/cpai.v3i2.71211
Royal Military College of Canada. (2016). About the Royal Military College of Canada. https://www.rmc-cmr.ca/en/college-commandants-office/about-royal-military-college-canada
Saltmarsh, S. (2005). 'White pages' in the academy: Plagiarism, consumption and racist rationalities. *International Journal for Educational Integrity, 1*(1). https://doi.org/10.21913/IJEI.v1i1.17
Scurr, C. (2020). Reflections on academic integrity during COVID-19. *Canadian Perspectives on Academic Integrity, 3*(2), 36–38. https://doi.org/10.11575/cpai.v3i2.71647
Seeland, J. (2020). Reflection on academic integrity during COVID-19. *Canadian Perspectives on Academic Integrity, 3*(2), 39–40. https://doi.org/10.11575/cpai.v3i2.71648
Social Sciences and Humanities Research Council. (SSHRC). (n.d.). Award recipients. https://www.sshrc-crsh.gc.ca/results-resultats/recipients-recipiendaires/index-eng.aspx
Sopcak, P. (2020). Academic integrity and the pandemic. *Canadian Perspectives on Academic Integrity, 3*(2), 41–42. https://doi.org/10.11575/cpai.v3i2.71649
Statistics Canada. (2019). *Postsecondary enrolments, by status of student in Canada, country of citizenship and sex.* https://www150.statcan.gc.ca/t1/tbl1/en/tv.action?pid=3710008601
Statistics Canada. (2020). Education indicators in Canada. Retrieved October 2, 2020, from https://www150.statcan.gc.ca/n1/daily-quotidien/200602/dq200602b-eng.htm
Stoesz, B. M. (2020). Educational challenges of 2020 and hope for 2021. *Canadian Perspectives on Academic Integrity, 3*(2), 43–44. https://doi.org/10.11575/cpai.v3i2.71635
Stoesz, B. M., & Eaton, S. E. (2020). Academic integrity policies of publicly funded universities in western Canada. *Educational Policy.* https://doi.org/10.1177/0895904820983032
Stoesz, B. M., Eaton, S. E., Miron, J. B., & Thacker, E. (2019) Academic integrity and contract cheating policy analysis of colleges in Ontario Canada. *International Journal for Educational Integrity, 15*(4), 1–18. https://doi.org/10.1007/s40979-019-0042-4
Strawczynski, J. (2004). When students won't Turnitin: An examination of the use of plagiarism prevention services in Canada. *Education & Law Journal, 14*(2), 167–190.
Summerlee, A. J. S., & Christensen Hughes, J. (2010). Pressures for change and the future of university education. *Taking stock: Research on teaching and learning in higher education* (pp. 243–260). McGill-Queen's University Press.
Sutton, S. A. (2001). Integrating 21st century access to ERIC services and resources. *Government Information Quarterly, 18*(1), 19–30. https://doi.org/10.1016/S0740-624X(00)00063-0

Taylor, K. L., Usick, B. L., & Paterson, B. L. (2004). Understanding plagiarism: The intersection of personal, pedagogical, institutional, and social contexts. *Journal on Excellence in College Teaching, 15*(3), 153–174.

Teymouri, N., & Boisvert, S. (2020). Reflections on COVID-19 and academic integrity. *Canadian Perspectives on Academic Integrity, 3*(2), 45–46. https://doi.org/10.11575/cpai.v3i2.71650

Thacker, E. J. (2020). Reflections from a novice academic integrity researcher during COVID-19. *Canadian Perspectives on Academic Integrity, 3*(2), 47–48. https://doi.org/10.11575/cpai.v3i2.71651

Thacker, E. J., & McKenzie, A. (2022). Using quality assurance frameworks to support an institutional culture of academic integrity at Canadian universities. In S. E. Eaton & J. Christensen Hughes (Eds.), *Academic integrity in Canada: An enduring and essential challenge*, Springer.

Union of Ontario Indians. (2013). *An overview of the Indian residential school system.* http://www.anishinabek.ca/wp-content/uploads/2016/07/An-Overview-of-the-IRS-System-Booklet.pdf

University of Calgary. (2019). In *Proceedings of Canadian Symposium on Academic Integrity* (website). https://go.ucalgary.ca/Academic-Integrity.html

Universities Canada. (2019). Membership and governance. https://www.univcan.ca/fr/a-propos/adhesion-et-gouvernance/

Usick, B. L. (2005). *Is plagiarism an issue in graduate education? An examination of two graduate programs.* (MEd thesis). University of Manitoba. http://search.proquest.com/docview/305088192/abstract

Usick, B. L. (2018). Editorial: Inaugural issue-Brandy Usick. *Canadian Perspectives on Academic Integrity, 1*(1). https://doi.org/10.11575/cpai.v1i1.43363

Vogt, L. (2020). My journey to becoming an academic integrity specialist. *Canadian Perspectives on Academic Integrity, 3*(2), 49–50. https://doi.org/10.11575/cpai.v3i2.71652

Wheatley, B. (2020). The COVID cloud's Ag lining. *Canadian Perspectives on Academic Integrity, 3*(1), 51–54. https://doi.org/10.11575/cpai.v3i2.71653

Whiteman, S. A., & Gordon, J. L. (2001). Cross conversations: The price of an "A": An educator's responsibility to academic honesty. *The English Journal, 91*(2), 25–30. https://doi.org/10.2307/822339

Wolsky, K. L., & Hamilton, M. J. (2020). Faculty development and academic integrity during pandemic times. *Canadian Perspectives on Academic Integrity, 3*(2), 55–56. https://doi.org/10.11575/cpai.v3i2.71654

Woods, J. T. (1998). Academic integrity policies and practices in common law Canadian universities: An examination of compliance with natural justice. (Doctor of Philosophy). Bowling Green State University.

Zaza, C., & McKenzie, A. (2018). Turnitin® Use at a Canadian university. *Canadian Journal for the Scholarship of Teaching and Learning, 9*(2). https://doi.org/10.5206/cjsotl-rcacea.2018.2.4

Sarah Elaine Eaton Ph.D., is an Associate Professor in the Werklund School of Education and the inaugural Educational Leader in Residence, Academic Integrity, University of Calgary. She is also the Editor-in-Chief of the *International Journal for Educational Integrity* and the author of *Plagiarism in Higher Education: Tackling Tough Topics in Academic Integrity* (Eaton, 2021). Her research focuses on ethics and integrity in higher education and she has led numerous research teams and the local and national levels. Eaton advocates for pro-active and multi-stakeholder approaches to upholding and enacting integrity throughout the academy.

Julia Christensen Hughes Ph.D., has long advocated for ensuring the highest standards of academic integrity in higher education—in teaching, research and administrative practice. Her article, Academic Misconduct within Higher Education in Canada, with the late Don McCabe (published in 2006, in the *Canadian Journal of Higher Education*), received the Sheffield Award for research excellence (2007), from the Canadian Society for Studies in Higher Education. As former and founding Dean of the Gordon S. Lang School of Business and Economics (2009–2019) at the University of Guelph, Julia was a champion of business ethics, corporate social responsibility and the need for business schools to be aligned with the UN's Sustainable Development Goals (SDG's). In her new role as President of Yorkville University, Julia is looking forward to supporting and enhancing the institution's long-standing commitment to integrity.

Chapter 2
Academic Integrity Across Time and Place: Higher Education's Questionable Moral Calling

Julia Christensen Hughes

Abstract In this chapter, I call on Canada's higher education institutions to embrace Veritas (truth), in every aspect of the academy. Academic integrity must transcend discussions of student misconduct and apply to all that we are—our history, our research, our curriculum, our pedagogy, our purpose. Tracing Western higher education's development from medieval times in Europe, through to the US and Canada, I make the case that the academy has paradoxically been both a dominating and liberating force since its inception. While imposing Western conceptions of morality and truth that have shifted over time, and supporting the imperialist ambitions of Church, monarchy and state, higher education has also elevated its graduates to positions of influence within society and advanced national aims. Despite credos of truth telling and missions of character development, higher education's moral calling has been—and remains—highly questionable. Given the complex challenges the world is facing today, and the need for Canadian institutions of higher learning to confront their colonial roots, it is time for us to critically examine this history and explicitly (re)position integrity at the core of Canada's higher education institutions.

Keywords Higher Education · Medieval · Church · Missionary · Colonial · Indigenous · Slavery · Residential Schools · Morality · Truth

Introduction

In this chapter I provide a critical summary of the evolution of higher education in Europe, the US and Canada. Beginning with the medieval university as the foundation of Western systems of higher learning, this account is necessarily incomplete, given the expanse of time covered as well as the fact that Canada's educational history is currently being "researched, revisited, and retold" (Craft, 2015, p. 190). My purpose is to argue that the academy has paradoxically been both a dominating and liberating force since its inception, imposing conceptions of morality and truth that have shifted

J. Christensen Hughes (✉)
Yorkville University, Toronto, Ontario, Canada
e-mail: jchristensen@yorkvilleu.ca

S. E. Eaton and J. Christensen Hughes (eds.), *Academic Integrity in Canada*, Ethics and Integrity in Educational Contexts 1,
https://doi.org/10.1007/978-3-030-83255-1_2

over time, behaving itself in unethical ways, while elevating its largely privileged graduates to positions of influence within society and advancing national aims.

Despite credos of truth telling and missions of character development, the integrity of Western higher education has been questionable since its founding. In medieval times through to the seventeenth and eighteenth centuries, it was arguably an instrument of imperial ambition and colonial domination (by Church, monarchy and state). In the 1900s, science became the new religion, and its practice pursued by some "at all costs", with callous disregard for human rights and suffering.

Preceding my discussion of the development of higher education in Canada, I include a brief account of residential schools. This history sheds light on colonial attitudes towards the role of education in the 1800s. Consistent with recent calls for action resulting from Canada's Truth and Reconciliation Commission (CTRC), it is time for Canadian academics (beyond post-colonial theorists and Indigenous scholars, who have long-laboured at this pursuit) to critically confront this history, examine higher education's ethical shortcomings, and catalyze needed change.

In the section that follows, I consider the roots of Western society's higher education institutions and identify ways in which integrity was understood, advanced and compromised.

The Medieval University

In *The Rise of Universities*, historian Charles Homer Haskins (1923), provided a fascinating account of Europe's earliest institutions of higher learning, from the early Middle Ages, when only a very basic treatment of the "seven liberal arts" was provided, "grammar, rhetoric, logic" (the trivium), and "arithmetic, astronomy, geometry, and music" (the quadrivium) (p. 4). These early days—the Dark Ages—were followed in the twelfth century by "a great revival of learning" (p. 4)—an early Renaissance—"chiefly through the Arab scholars of Spain—the works of Aristotle, Euclid, Ptolemy, and the Greek physicians, the new arithmetic, and those texts of Roman law which had lain hidden…" (p. 5). The dissemination of these early works was catalyzed by the translation of texts originally written in Ancient Greek and Arabic, into Latin.

The work of Aristotle (384–322 BC), it is said, "reopened the question of the relation between faith and reason" (McInerny & O'Callaghan, 2018). Aristotle saw "ethical virtues (justice, courage, temperance and so on) as complex rational, emotional and social skills" (Kraut, 2018). Building on "Plato's central insight that moral thinking must be integrated with our emotions and appetites", Aristotle proposed that ethical virtue was a state of being, developed during childhood and reinforced through law and threat of punishment, in order to keep destructive psychological forces and vices at bay (Kraut, 2018).

Haskins (1923) argued that this knowledge "burst the bonds of the cathedral and monastery schools" where religious instruction was provided by monks and nuns, and created instead the "learned professions" along with the academic guilds of Paris and Bologna, "our first and our best definition of a university, a society of masters and scholars" (p. 5). These early institutions were primarily for the sons of the wealthy, preparing them for key roles in society as part of the ruling elite, whether in education, medicine, law or the Church.

The Bologna Studium, created in Northern Italy around 1088, is credited as being the "oldest university in the Western world" (Bologna, n.d.). Founded through "the spontaneous and informal initiative of a few students" (Bologna, n.d.), Bologna became a "rich and powerful medieval metropolis, capable of attracting and accommodating hundreds of wealthy young people, who brought with them not only books and servants but also a substantial amount of money" (Bologna, n.d.). Studies focused largely on civil (Roman) law and also the arts, which later influenced the development of universities in Spain and Southern France (Haskins, 1923).

In Northern Europe, church-control of higher education was more common, with Cathedral Schools (such as Notre-Dame), giving rise to the University of Paris, formed in about 1200. By 1231, the University of Paris had four faculties; arts, Canon law (i.e., law laid down by the Christian Church), medicine and theology. While theology was considered "the supreme subject of medieval study" (Haskins, 1923, p. 19), few students reportedly elected to take it, as it was considered more difficult and the books more costly than other pursuits.

Haskins (1923) described the 1200s as "a bookish age, with great reverence for standard authorities, and its instruction followed closely the written word" (p. 28). This included "intensive study of the scriptures, Old and New Testament, and of the summary of Christian doctrine" (McInerny & O'Callaghan, 2018). Philosophy also had a place of significance. So revered was Aristotle's work on logic, that "it pervaded every subject..." (Haskins, 1923, p. 30), including his contributions on Ethics and Metaphysics; "the character traits that human beings need in order to live life at its best" (Kraut, 2018).

This was also the time of St. Thomas Aquinas (1225–1274), a Catholic Priest who studied at the University of Paris before becoming a Master and occupying "one of the Dominican chairs in the Faculty of Theology" (McInerny & O'Callaghan, 2018). Aquinas interpreted and extended Aristotle's contributions. As both a philosopher and theologian, Aquinas distinguished between earthly truths (common truths known to all, discovered through human reason, argumentative structure and practical and theoretical science) and spiritual ones (faith based truths, revealed by God and Sacred Scripture). Aquinas defined the four cardinal virtues (prudence, justice, courage, and temperance) as well as the three theological virtues (faith, hope and charity).

Following Aquinas' death, some of Aristotle's and Aquinas' ideas came to be viewed as heretical. In 1277, "the Bishop of Paris, Stephen Tempier, prohibited the teaching of 219 theological and philosophical theses that were being discussed and disputed in the faculty of arts under his jurisdiction" (Thijssen, 2018). With the advent of the "Tempier Condemnation", anyone "teaching or listening to the listed errors would be excommunicated, unless they turned themselves in to the bishop or the chancellor within seven days, in which case the bishop would inflict proportionate penalties" (Thijssen, 2018). This was just one of "approximately sixteen lists of censured theses that were issued at the University of Paris during the thirteenth and fourteenth centuries" (Thijssen, 2018).

In contrast to the hierarchical governing structure imposed by the Church in Northern Europe, in Italy the earliest universities involved self-organizing student and faculty guilds. Typically away from home from the first time, students were in need of accommodation, food and other supplies. As there were initially no university buildings for classes or residences, they regularly dealt with locals who charged exorbitant rates. Working together, and through threat of boycotting particular communities, the students were able to "fix the prices of lodgings and books" (Haskins, 1923, p. 9). They similarly threatened to boycott the faculty, should they not begin and end their lectures on time, cover the full curriculum, and refrain from absenteeism. Faculty were expected to leave a deposit if they planned on leaving town, to ensure their return. The guilds also levied fines on professors who failed to be interesting enough to a secure an audience of five students per lecture (p. 10).

Haskin's (1923) research into the sermons of the faculty and other documents (including letters home) provided further insight into life as a student in the thirteenth century:

> Some who care only for the name of scholar and the income which they receive while attending the university, go to class but once or twice a week, choosing by preference the [afternoon] lectures on canon law, which leave them plenty of time for sleep in the morning. Many eat cakes when they ought to be at study, or go to sleep in the classrooms, spending the rest of their time drinking in taverns (Haskins, 1923, p. 64).

While the students may have been learning about prudence, temperance and charity from the lectures they attended, accounts of this time report on their general "debauchery", including drunkenness, gambling, frequenting prostitutes and fighting in pubs and on the streets. Following several student deaths in "a town and gown altercation" (Haskins, 1923, p. 15), the Pope confirmed the authority of the Chancellor to oversee the conduct of students, privileging and exempting the wealthy students from local laws.

Also in Italy, the professors (or masters) similarly formed guilds and later colleges, which provided a "license to teach (licentia docendi)" to graduates who were deemed to have successfully completed their examinations or "disputations", a comprehensive final oral defense overseen by the chancellor (Haskins, 1923, p. 11). In contrast, in Paris, the Chancellor "alone had authority to license teaching in the diocese and thus kept his control over the granting of university degrees" (p. 14).

Accounts of these examinations provide evidence of some of the earliest instances of academic misconduct, implicating students, faculty and the chancellor alike! According to Haskins (1923), if a student were to fail, "he may be re-examined after a year, or it may be that, through the intercession of friends or by suitable gifts or services to the chancellor's relatives or other examiners, the chancellor can be induced to change his decision" (p. 46). Students were also encouraged to "write home for more money and give a great feast for his professors; if he treats them well, he need not fear the outcome" (p. 70). Mid-course oral examinations were also subject to misconduct. Haskins observed that during the master's quiz, "the shaky scholar falls back on his only hope, a place near one who promises to prompt him" (p. 74).

Professors experienced considerable pressure to conform to the "truths" of the day, whether through authoritative doctrine, to which they were expected to be faithful, or the "tyranny of colleagues" (Haskins, 1923, p. 50). According to Del Soldato (2020), "the nature of medieval universities was such that teaching was heavily controlled by authorities, and both metaphysics and theology exercised a strong influence, limiting the number of directions in which scientific theorization could advance." Yet, Haskins (1923) suggested that few faculty would have opposed such expectations; "Accepting the principle of authority as their starting point, men did not feel its limitations as we should feel them now...He is free who feels himself free" (pp. 55–56).

Within church-run institutions, the expectation of compliance was further reinforced with the advent of the inquisitions, the first of which began in 1231 (the Papal Inquisition). By Papal decree, those accused of heresy could be prosecuted and confessions extracted by torture. By the fourteenth century, even in Bologne, Church control was assured:

> As time went by, students lost their autonomy, not only in their management bodies but also in city councils, suffering greater influence from local and papal authorities. Even the teachers, who in the meantime had formed the College of Doctors, had to accept the disciplinary measures imposed from above, and were subject to them even more from the following century, when they became public employees, who were paid with income from trade tariffs. (Bologne, n.d. b)

The Spanish Inquisition (1472–1834) was particularly tortuous. This was followed by the Portuguese Inquisition (1536) and finally the Roman Inquisition (1540s), which established a permanent body—the Congregation of the Holy Office/Congregation for the Doctrine of the Faith—to oversee inquisitions throughout the world. For much of this time, Muslims, Jews and Protestant reformers were particular targets.

About one hundred years after the first inquisition, the Renaissance (1348–1648) got underway. This was an exciting time for academics, as the teachings of many more ancient philosophers and mathematicians were translated, scientific inventions produced the telescope and microscope, and in 1450 the Gutenberg printing press provided an alternative to the lecture, allowing for the broad dissemination of scholarly ideas. Wealthy patrons supported—and thereby influenced—the work of those working in the arts and sciences, particularly if they perceived national interest; "Renaissance lords and patrons often had a particular interest in scientific works and treatises, especially those devoted to subjects of military value" (Del Soldato, 2020).

Some questioned corruption within the Church and its universities, including financial and spiritual abuses by the clergy. This gave rise to the Protestant Reformation, when in 1517, Martin Luther, a professor of moral theology at the University of Wittenberg, Germany, is said to have posted to the door of All Saint's Church, a disputation—perhaps the first academic poster presentation—the *Ninety-five Theses* (n.d.), which he hoped would stir debate.

Luther challenged the practice of priests selling indulgence certificates (forgiving sins and reduced time in purgatory in exchange for money). The money was for a capital campaign—the building of St. Peter's Basilica in Rome. Luther was essentially an early academic "whistleblower", challenging the unethical way in which money was being raised. Underscoring the strength of the bonds between the university, Church and state, Luther was tried for heresy and excommunicated in 1521. Further, the Roman Emperor declared him an outlaw, "making it a crime for anyone in Germany to give Luther food or shelter, and permitting anyone to kill Luther without any legal consequence" (Ninety-five Theses, n.d.).

The civil wars of France (1562–1598) were a direct result of growing conflict between Roman Catholics and the ever-increasing number of Protestant Reformers. Ultimately, the Edict of Nantes (1598) allowed religious toleration and freedom of conscience for France's Protestants, the Huguenots (revoked in 1685). Other countries followed suit, with Roman Catholicism having to accept its shared standing. Yet, as the inquisitions continued to unfold, the Churches' scholars were called upon as expert witnesses against the accused, including at the noteworthy trial of Galileo Galilei (1564–1642). Peers judged Galileo's academic assertions to be "foolish and absurd in philosophy", "formally heretical" and "erroneous in faith" (Van Helden & Burr, n.d.).

As a result, Galileo, who today is recognized as the "hero of modern science", was ordered by the Roman Catholic Church not to "teach or defend" the Copernican theory (Machamer, 2017). Galileo had challenged "Aristotelian categories" and offered in their place "a set of mechanical concepts" which ultimately gave rise to the "scientific revolution" (Machamer, 2017). It took the Church almost 400 years to apologize for its treatment of Galileo (Resnick, n.d.).

Threatened by growing challenge, the Roman Catholic Church underwent a renewal, a *Counter Reformation*, to reestablish its authority. Improving the quality of the priesthood became a primary strategic concern as was increasing the number of worshippers. So, the Church embraced a new strategy of building seminaries (religious colleges) and sending trained missionaries around the globe. As part of this plan, they called on the Society of Jesus (Jesuits), a Catholic religious order which had been established at the University of Paris in 1534, by St. Ignatius of Loyola. According to the Jesuits of Canada (n.d.), Loyola had written, "It is according to our divine calling…to travel to various places and to live in any part of the world where there is hope of God's greater service and the help of souls." The first Jesuits arrived in what is now Canada in the early 1600 s, with the aim of converting the Indigenous peoples.

England's Early Universities: The Influence of the Church, Monarchy and Slave Trade

The earliest universities in England were similarly influenced by the Church, but also the monarchy and the country's wealthy merchants, many who made their fortune in the transatlantic slave trade. Here, once again, integrity was both selectively advanced and compromised.

Oxford, the oldest university in the English speaking world, was initially affiliated with the Roman Catholic church, but this was changed in 1535 when King Henry VIII broke from Papal authority and declared himself head of the Church of England. Instruction began at Oxford in 1096 and "developed rapidly from 1167, when Henry II banned English students from attending the University of Paris"(Oxford, n.d.).

Cambridge was created in the 1200s by faculty and students who were dissatisfied at Oxford. The University's website describes a scholar's life in Cambridge at the time:

> In 1209, scholars taking refuge from hostile townsmen in Oxford migrated to Cambridge and settled there...King Henry III took the scholars under his protection as early as 1231 and arranged for them to be sheltered from exploitation by their landlords. At the same time he tried to ensure that they had a monopoly of teaching, by an order that only those enrolled under the tuition of a recognised master were to be allowed to remain in the town. (Cambridge, n.d., a)

Cambridge's religious affiliation was central to the purpose of the institution; "Most of the scholars of the University were at first clerks or clergymen, in holy orders of some sort, and expecting careers in the Church or in the Civil Service (as diplomats, judges or officers of the royal household)" (Cambridge, n.d. b). Classes at Cambridge began in parish churches, but eventually the University acquired its own property and buildings, the first being for the Divinity School. The first endowed university teaching post, the Lady Margaret Professorship of Divinity, was funded by the mother of King Henry VII, in 1502. Another Professorship was similarly established at Oxford.

King Henry VIII had significant influence at both schools, issuing a series of injunctions in the mid-1500 s that suppressed Canon Law and scholastic philosophy, favouring instead Greek and Latin classics, mathematics and Biblical studies. These subjects were supported by "Regius" professorships (via Royal patronage) in Civil Law, Divinity, Hebrew, Greek, Physic and Medicine.

Following King Henry's reign, in 1555, under Catholic Queen Mary I, Roman Catholicism briefly reemerged. Three Anglican bishops were tried for heresy at St. Mary the Virgin, the Church of the University of Oxford, and were burnt at the stake on university grounds for failing to renounce their beliefs. Under Queen Elizabeth I, who reigned from 1558 to 1603, the Anglican Church was reestablished. By 1571, the Church of England's key doctrine was finalized in "Thirty-nine Articles" and incorporated into the Book of Common Prayer, to which all undergraduate students were expected to commit. Oxford's motto remains *Dominus Illuminatio Mea;* 'the Lord is my light'.

The Renaissance paved the way for the establishment of learned societies. Established in 1660, the Royal Society's motto is *Nullius in verba—take nobody's word for it*. The motto expresses "the determination of [Royal Society] Fellows to withstand the domination of authority and to verify all statements by an appeal to facts determined by experiment" (Royal Society, n.d.). The Society held scholarly meetings and supported the publication of important work, including *Philosophical Transactions* (beginning in 1665), "the oldest continuously-published science journal in the world", establishing "the important concepts of scientific priority and peer review" (Royal Society, n.d.).

It was also at this time that wealthy benefactors of British universities began to exert considerable influence, supporting student scholarships and capital projects. Tobias Rustat (1608–1694), an alumnus of Jesus College Cambridge, was noted by *The Economist* (2020), for his "generosity three centuries ago [which] allowed generations of orphans to go to Cambridge and be ordained as Church of England clergymen". He was also a significant investor in the Royal African Company (RAC), which by 1672 had shipped "close to 150,000 enslaved Africans, mostly to the Caribbean" (*The Economist*, 2020). In this way, the university benefited financially by the enslavement of tens of thousands of Blacks, while helping elevate British orphans out of poverty and into the ministry.

In 2019, Cambridge acknowledged this history, announcing that it would be conducting a "two-year academic study of how much it benefited from the Atlantic slave trade and whether its scholars reinforced race-based thinking during Britain's colonial era" (Reuters, 2019).

At Oxford, Christopher Codrington's (1668–1710) endowment of the library of All Souls College has similarly come under scrutiny. Codrington's wealth came from one of the largest "sugar plantations worked by slaves in Antigua and Barbados" (Race, 2020). In January 2021, Codrington's name was removed from the library (but not his statue) and a plaque was installed, commemorating the slaves who had worked on the Codrington plantations (Shaw, 2021). The official statement by the College explained:

> rather than seek to remove [the statue] the College will investigate further forms of memorialisation and contextualisation within the library, which will draw attention to the presence of enslaved people on the Codrington plantations, and will express the College's abhorrence of slavery. (Shaw, 2021)

In May 2021, despite significant public pressure, Oxford's Oriel College similarly decided not to remove the statue of Cecil Rhodes. A spokesperson stated, "We should learn from our past, rather than censoring history, and continue focusing on reducing inequality" (Race, 2021). In 1902 Rhodes became a benefactor to the College, endowing the prestigious international Rhodes Scholarship program. Rhodes is "considered one of the founders of South African racial segregation who made his fortune from exploiting African mines worked by slaves" (Reuters, 2019).

A Brief History of Higher Education in the United States

What happens in the United States can have a profound impact on life in Canada, including within the modern academy. Our early histories also have much in common. Accordingly, it can be helpful as we attempt to understand issues of integrity in the

Canadian higher education context, to consider the evolution of higher education in the US as well. In this account, I highlight higher education's roles in colonization and the subjugation of Indigenous Peoples, complicity with slavery, evolving views on philosophical thought, approaches to teaching morality and ethics, and the rising influence of positivism and the scientific method, in shaping conceptions of truth. I also share how some US universities are responding to mounting evidence of their moral shortcomings.

Julie Reuben (1996) details the evolution of higher education in the US, suggesting that the idea that higher education should have both a "moral and intellectual" purpose was once commonplace (Reuben, 1996, p. 11). Borrowing from the traditions of Oxford and Cambridge, colonists sought to replicate aspects of British life in the Americas, with some important differences.

In New England, Puritans were a major colonizing force. Opposed to the perceived "idolatry" of both Roman Catholicism and Anglican worship, the Puritans focused on preaching scripture and salvation through Jesus Christ (Knapp, 1998, p. 112). Harvard University, the first higher education institution in North America, was founded by Puritans in New England in 1636, with the primary purpose of training clergy, who in turn were to advance "Christianity to the native peoples" (Knapp, 1998, p. 112) . Named after its benefactor the Reverend John Harvard, Harvard's Motto, first adopted in 1643, was "Veritas" meaning "truth" (Ireland, 2015).

The Puritans established segregated "Praying Towns" where "any Indian religious idea or practices were viewed as pagan and had to be rooted out" (Knapp, 1998, p. 124). "White Christian hypocrisy" (p. 121) served as a barrier to the Puritans achieving their objective of conversion:

> The most embarrassing obstacle to Indian conversion was the continued evidence of the hypocrisy which the Indians witnessed in other white 'Christians.' The brutality of the European settlers was a great impediment to the successful evangelization of the native population. (Knapp, 1998, p. 121)

In 1656, the Puritans established an "Indian College at Harvard" (Knapp, 1998). Initially housing classrooms and a dormitory (but no students), the building came to include a printing press and in 1663 Harvard produced a Bible in the Algonquian language (Knapp, 1998, p. 123). In 1817, Isaac Royall, used the proceeds from the sale of "inherited land and slaves in Antigua and in Medford…to fund Harvard Law School, the first law school in the United States" (Harris, 2020, p. 289).

Between Harvard's founding and the mid-1800s, 289 institutions of higher learning were founded across the US, 240 of them private (Goldin & Katz, 1999), with many built on the backs of slave labour. One of the most notable for doing so was Yale. Founded in 1702, Yale College's first endowed professorship (created in 1745)—the Livingstonian Professorship of Divinity—was given by Philip Livingston, who owned four slave ships, trading in people, sugar and tobacco from the West Indies and Africa. Yale later named a "prominent gateway in Branford College the 'Livingston Gateway'" (Dugdale et al., 2002, p. 4). By 1830, Yale was the largest higher education institution in the US. As at Harvard, much of Yale's growth was funded from the proceeds from slavery—providing faculty chairs, scholarships and support for the

Library. Many prominent university and church leaders of the day were also slave owners, purchasing or inheriting both Indigenous peoples and Blacks (men, women and children).

The first scholarships at Yale were named after Bishop George Berkeley, who baptized his slaves, assuring colonists that doing so would not legally "bestow freedom" (Glasson, 2010). He also sought to convert Native American "savages", peaceably if possible but otherwise, by capturing and converting their children, taking young boys (up to ten years of age) to Bermuda to reeducate them, separating them from their families and customs, before returning them as missionaries. Yale honoured Berkeley's "great missionary effort" as recently as 1999 (Hopson, 2021). Berkeley donated his plantation to Yale in 1931, which Charles Handy in turn leased from Yale, creating a scholarship fund for fifty years, for top students studying Greek and Latin (Dugdale et al., 2002 p. 5).

Timothy Dwight (1752–1817), President of Yale and a Congregationalist minister and theologian, ardently defended slavery in the US. He held the Livingstonian Professorship of Divinity and as President, taught senior students metaphysics and ethics. During his tenure, "Yale produced more pro-slavery clergy than any other college in the nation" (Dugdale et al., 2002 p. 12), considerably more than Princeton or Harvard.

In 1831, donors, law faculty and alumni from Yale vigorously and successfully opposed the establishment of a so called "Negro college" in the New Haven community, voting with local townspeople to support a formal motion that "to educate the colored population is incompatible with the prosperity, if not the existence of the present institutions of learning, and will be destructive of the best interests of the city" (Dugdale et al., 2002 p. 17). Newspaper accounts further explained opposition to the proposed college, suggesting that it would have degraded the "town's public morals" (p. 18) and upset Southern patrons.

One of Yale's most infamous alumni was John Calhoun (mentored by Dwight), who joined Yale as a student in 1802, before returning to his family's plantation in the South. Elected to Congress in 1811, Calhoun became a U.S. Vice President and Senator. An ardent advocate for maintaining slavery, he argued that the notion that "all men are born free and equal" was "utterly untrue" (Dugdale et al., 2002 p. 12). In 1933, Yale bestowed top honours on Calhoun, naming a residential college after him (overturned in 2017). It was not until 1854 that the first US college for African Americans—Lincoln University—was established, in Pennsylvania. Twenty years later, the first black student graduated from Yale.

Philosophy in the Age of Reason

The time in which higher education was being established in the Americas is perhaps ironically known as the *Age of Enlightenment.* While serving as a powerful colonizing force, the academy was considering questions of emancipation. Immanual Kant (1724–1804), identified emancipation as "the process of undertaking to think for oneself, to employ and rely on one's own intellectual capacities in determining what to believe and how to act" (Bristow, 2017).

By the early 1800s, philosophical frameworks, such as Universalism and Utilitarianism also began to hold sway. Universalism was based on the idea that while people are autonomous, they have a duty to be self-aware and behave in ways that are consistent with morally sound, personal maxims that an individual would want to see embraced by everyone as universal moral laws such as "thou shalt not steal". Kant, the founder of universalism, advocated for Categorical Imperatives (CI); "an objective, rationally necessary and unconditional principle that we must always follow despite any natural desires or inclinations we may have to the contrary" (Johnson & Cureton, 2016). Embedded within the concept of universalism is responsibility and respect for others.

Utilitarianism, from Jeremy Bentham (1748–1832) and John Stuart Mill (1806–1873), in contrast, proposed that people should pursue the greatest good for the greatest number, or "the morally right action is the action that produces the most good" (Driver, 2014). From this point of view, a principle may be discarded (such as "thou shalt not steal"), for a greater good or utility (such as feeding the hungry). Furthermore, Utilitarianism recognized that such judgements are personal (perception based) and variable; what is considered the greater good, can vary by person and change over time.

Drawing on these philosophical frameworks, in 1842 and 1843, the Yale debating club considered the question, "does the greatest good of the greatest number, justify the continuance of slavery at the South?" (Dugdale et al., 2002 p. 23). Nathanial Taylor, then President of Yale and head of the Yale Divinity School argued for it; the students declined to vote. In 1848 the question was repeated. This time both the students and the President voted in the affirmative. Such questions were used to judge final "disputations", assuring that graduates held "correct" moral beliefs.

Academics of the time subscribed to the pursuit of the "unity of truth" in which knowledge was seen to have a "moral dimension" (Reuben, 1996, p. 17). Accordingly, the primary purpose of higher education was understood to concern "educating *young men* to the highest efficiency of their intellectual *faculties* [emphasis added], and the noblest culture of their moral and religious nature" (p. 22). Offering a comprehensive curriculum, higher education institutions "aimed to train each faculty evenly and in relation to the others" (p. 22). Supporting the integration of these faculties—as at Yale—was a "senior year course in moral and mental philosophy…often taught by the college president" (pp. 22–23). Instruction was normative; "professors laid out students' proper duties to themselves, their fellow humans, and God" (p. 23).

This was also a time in which the natural sciences, rationality, reason and empiricism came to be revered, mathematical laws began to replace religious edict, and doubt and skepticism replaced faith and superstition. This shift in focus occurred across decades and institutions, including within colleges affiliated with the Protestant church:

> Christianity, or more specifically Protestantism, became synonymous with nonsectarian religion because of its conformity to science and its resonance with public sensibilities…Protestantism stood for the cause of freedom and the progress of human history. (Hart, 1999, p. 29)

The concept of "civil society" took on a new understanding at this time, incorporating the tenets of economic freedom and modern ethical theory; "As the processes of industrialization, urbanization, and dissemination of education advance in this period, happiness in this life, rather than union with God in the next, becomes the highest end for more and more people" (Bristow, 2017).

University Reform: The Rise of the Scientific Method and Declining Influence of the Church

The mid to late 1800s saw sustained efforts to transform higher education in the United States. Although "university reformers continued to view piety and moral discipline as one of the aims of higher education", they also sought to "replace older, authoritarian methods with new ones" (Reuben, 1996, p. 12). Increasing demand for scientific discovery and national advancement through the industrial complex, shaped higher education in the nineteenth century. As demand for specialized scientific and professional training grew, the curriculum became increasingly "saturated" (Reuben, 1996, p. 28), with "encyclopedic" knowledge valued over "mental discipline" (p. 62). Calls for educational reform became viewed as a matter of great national importance, in order to provide professors with the time and equipment needed for sophisticated scientific discovery, to "meet the demands of a modern, industrial society" (p. 61).

Frederick Barnard, who oversaw the transformation of Columbia College from an institution with just 100 undergraduate students studying a comprehensive curriculum, to Columbia University, with full graduate programs and a research agenda, observed that "university reform was unavoidable; if colleges did not change to meet social needs, they would die" (Reuben, 1996, p. 61). Later, Nicholas Butler, who served as president of Columbia from 1901 to 1945, emphasized the importance of higher education being in service to society; "The modern university, like the traditional college, was a servant of society, dedicated to its material and moral improvement" (p. 75).

By the late 1800s, "freedom from church control" became recognized as important for the further evolution of higher education (Reuben, 1996, p. 83). John Hopkins University was established in 1876, "on a nondenominational basis" (p. 84) as was Stanford in the late 1880s, and the University of Chicago in 1890. With this pronounced change, required courses in religious instruction, including moral philosophy and Christianity, began to disappear from the curriculum. Criticized as "too theological" (p. 89), too dogmatic, and incompatible with open scientific inquiry, such courses came to be seen as irrelevant to a modern curriculum; reformers sought philosophers who could inspire rather than preach, and "steer safely between iconoclasm and dogmatism" (p. 90). University presidents bemoaned the difficulty in finding faculty members who could teach philosophical and moral thought in a way that emerging sentiments demanded, seeking "professional philosophers" without church affiliation (p. 92). No longer part of the required curriculum, elective courses in "Elementary Ethics" and the "Philosophy of Religion" appeared in the late 1880s in part to fill this gap (p. 93).

Universities founded by religious denominations (such as Harvard and Columbia) similarly moved away from daily, mandatory chapel attendance, instead valuing "free choice" and weekly multi-denominational services that emphasized "fundamental truths" across religions, as opposed to "denominational differences" (Reuben, 1996, p. 122).

By the early twentieth century, theology as an area of study had become increasingly marginalized; religion was viewed as "having no intellectual content" (Reuben, 1996, p. 113) and biblical scholars began "to tacitly accept the separation between the intellectual and spiritual" (p. 111). The Bible itself became viewed as "a work of literature and the 'truths' contained within it seen as 'poetical' rather than 'scientific' and 'factual'" (p. 112). Demand for such programs also decreased, as students increasingly regarded programs in religious studies with "indifference" (p. 113).

Morality, Science and the Rise of "Student Life" Programs

Despite the decline of required religious and ethical instruction, in the early 1900's faculty were still expected to serve as ethical role models: upright moral conduct was treated "as an unquestioned requirement for the job" (Reuben, 1996, p. 194). Speaking in 1912, the president of Stanford opined, "teachers cannot escape responsibility for the moral and intellectual ideals of those under their charge" (Reuben, 1996, p. 194). While academic freedom supported free inquiry, presidents made clear that "moral turpitude" would not be tolerated (p. 195). Normative expectations for "appropriate scholarly presentation" were also enforced (p. 199). "Faculty could find themselves guilty of moral turpitude because they spoke in an unscholarly, undignified, or provocative manner" (p. 199). Faculty were in fact fired for speaking out about politically and morally sensitive matters, and for appearing "disloyal" (to institution and founders) and being publicly disruptive (p. 200).

As one example, in 1917 Wadsworth Longfellow Dana was fired from Columbia for his "opposition to the draft during WWI" (Reuben, 1996, p. 200). Earlier, in 1900, Edward Ross was fired from Stanford, for annoying benefactor Jane Stanford, by "speaking out against Chinese immigration and the use of coolie [sic] labor" (Reuben, 1996, p. 196). Leland Stanford, Jane's husband, was the president of the Central Pacific railway and had acquired his wealth via the efforts of thousands of Chinese railroad workers. While President Jordan was sympathetic to Ross' views, he ultimately fired him for "dishonorable behaviour" to the institution. Loyalty to institutions, donors and polite discourse, were clearly valued over personal conscience and social critique.

By the 1920s, science was positioned as the "new religion", with scientific inquiry becoming associated with morality through its highly disciplined and objective approach; "The ongoing task of scientific investigation required seriousness, diligence, and zeal, which made the scientist's vocation sacred" (Hart, 1999, p. 34). Logical positivism and the work of the Vienna Circle positioned "metaphysics not simply to be false, but to be cognitively empty and meaningless" (Uebel, 2020). Scientists were increasingly viewed as virtuous truth seekers and the pursuit of knowledge was deemed "morally relevant because it could provide standards for individual behavior and social norms" (Reuben, 1996, p. 133). "Subjected to the powerful but indirect moral discipline of scientific training, students were expected to mature into strong, honest, useful men" (p. 136).

A clear hierarchy emerged on university campuses at this time, with disciplinary specialization and "pure" research being increasingly valued. Academics moved away from pursuing a unity of truth and the moral development of their students, and instead turned to ever more atomistic areas of disciplinary interest, including establishing numerous sub-disciplines. The scientific method became revered above all else, including within the social sciences. It was at this time that "philosophical" became synonymous with "unscientific" (Reuben, 1996, p. 186) and morality was increasingly viewed "as a matter of personal preference" (p. 188). Social science research, it was said, should be ethically neutral—descriptive not evaluative (p. 188), having "no political or ethical prejudices, no preferences, no convictions" (p. 191).

Students, however, were not equally enthused with the new direction; neither the narrowing focus on science nor the poor teaching quality they experienced as faculty dedicated increasing time to scientific inquiry. Faculty recognized that "their professional advancement depended on the quality of their research, not on their position as moral leaders" (Reuben, 1996, p. 209).

By the mid to late 1920s, humanities faculty were proposing a counterbalance to the rise of the sciences, arguing "that all significant human experience was subjective and value-leaden, and that objective, value-free science was not suited to understand it" (Reuben, p. 1996, 217). Literature (including history and philosophy), it was argued, held the potential to provide a "spiritual experience" (p. 220) that could enhance empathy and provide moral lessons (p. 220).

At the same time, research suggested that efforts to develop character may be futile. An influential study by Yale psychologists Hartshorne and May (1928), found that when children were presented with opportunities to lie, cheat or steal in a variety of everyday contexts, there appeared to be little consistency in their actions. This led researchers to conclude that human behavior may be more variable than previously thought, influenced by factors such as risk perception. According to Likona (1991), this brought into question the value of character-focused education.

Higher education institutions, turned away from the curriculum towards the role of faculty advisor to support character development. While this type of position was in place in the majority of US colleges by 1928, it failed to deliver on its promise, as few faculty were apparently interested or effective in the role. The University of Michigan's dean of students, for example, observed that few faculty "are interested in the personal side of student life and who can afford to give the time and thought which proper handling of the problem requires" (Reuben, 1996, p. 253). Freshman orientation programs were also introduced, which included warnings of "moral dissipation" (p. 255), but largely also proved ineffective, given the "questionable guidance offered by upper classmen" (p. 255).

Further attempts at co-curricular moral influence followed, through the establishment of "student life" programs, including closely supervised residences (with faculty serving as dons overseeing curfews and study time), sports programs, and student clubs, with the aim of fostering "esprit de corps and moral discipline" (Reuben, 1996, p. 261). According to Rueben, "by settling on group cohesiveness as the best source of moral influence, university officials came to equate morality with morale" (p. 264).

With this new focus on positive peer influence, admissions programs also increasingly focused on accepting those judged to already exhibit moral traits, in addition to scholarly achievement (Reuben, 1996, p. 262). In practice, however, including character as an admissions criteria, reportedly aided efforts to prioritize Protestant students and "discriminate against ethnic minorities, including Jews" (p. 264). America's universities were not immune to rising anti-Semitism.

By the 1930s, "the separation of morality and knowledge came to be seen as a 'natural' part of intellectual life" (Reuben, 1996, p. 268). The rise of "logical positivism" led to the privatization of morality, and values became perceived as a matter of personal opinion (Likona, 1991, p. 8). In fact, the term "value judgment" came to refer to inappropriately imposing one's personal values or ethical beliefs on another (p. 8).

In 1947, following the end of WWII, higher education was seen as an important tool for strengthening a new set of values—democratic ideals. The President's Commission on Higher Education for American Democracy (1947) promoted the importance of providing students with the "'values, attitudes, knowledge and skills' that would allow them "to live rightly and well in a free society'", providing them with "ethical values, scientific generalizations, and aesthetic conceptions" (Hart, 1999, p. 109). This in part "fueled interest in the restoration of ethical and spiritual concerns" including "vociferous calls for a common curriculum that included instruction in values and ethics" (p. 110). The humanities were seen as a natural home for such instruction, including in religious studies, which saw increases in programs and enrolments "between 1945 and 1960" (p. 111).

In 1963, however, religion's "rightful" place in American education was challenged. A US Supreme Court ruling found that "the practice of Bible reading and prayer in public schools violated the First Amendment and thus was unconstitutional" (Hart, 1999, p. 200). Yet, the court's opinion, written by Justice Tom C. Clark, acknowledged that "a good education was 'not complete' without the study of religion" (p. 201). While private colleges and universities, whether religious or nonsectarian, could continue to provide courses in religious studies, for public institutions, including state funded universities, the situation was quite different. As recipients of tax dollars, and committed to "the separation of church and state", they were expected to maintain a "degree of impartiality" (p. 203).

Over the next several decades, within the public higher education system, departments of religious studies were further minimized or closed altogether. Yet calls for teaching character development did not vanish altogether, including within elementary schools. Writing in the 1990s Thomas Likona, author of *Educating for Character: How our Schools can Teach Respect and Responsibility* observed:

> Wise societies since the time of Plato…have educated for character as well as intellect, decency as well as literacy, virtue as well as knowledge. They have tried to form citizens who will use their intelligence to benefit others as well as themselves, who will try to build a better world (Likona, 1991, p. 6).

Uncomfortable Truths

As previously suggested, the 1900s were a time when positivism and scientific inquiry flourished, laying the foundation for the US to be positioned as the "global leader in the advancement, development, and production" of science and technology, and resulting in "dramatic improvements to American lives" (The State of U.S. Science and Engineering 2020). Some of the research undertaken during this time, however, was based on unethical and inhumane practices, arguably including advances with respect to the nuclear arms and space race, and medical and psychological research. For a chilling account of select cases of research misconduct see the *Research Ethics Timeline* compiled by bioethicist David Resnik (n.d.).

As one example, in research on yellow fever, undertaken in the early 1900s, 33 participants were "exposed to mosquitoes infected with yellow fever or injected with blood from yellow fever patients.... Six participants died, including two researcher-volunteers" (Resnik, n.d.).

Another is the horrific Tuskegee Syphilis Study. Sponsored by the Department of Health, Education and Welfare this multi-year research project, beginning in 1932, "investigated the effects of untreated syphilis in 400 African American men from the Tuskegee, Alabama area." According to Resnik (n.d.), the researchers "withheld treatment for the disease from participants even when penicillin, an effective form of treatment, became widely available".

In the 1940s, the US government launched a program to develop an atomic bomb, codenamed the Manhattan Project, involving researchers at a number of US universities, including a team of theoretical physicists at Berkeley. The Manhattan Project was seen as vital to American security. Following, the U.S. Department of Energy sponsored the scientists' research on the effects of radiation on human beings. The participants, "cancer patients, pregnant women, and military personnel" were unaware they were participating (Resnik, n.d.).

The Nuremberg trials of 1947 put the spotlight on atrocities carried out by Nazi doctors and scientists, which gave rise to the Nuremberg Code; ethical rules for engagement with "human subjects". The Code's ten items were based on the notion that "certain basic principles must be observed in order to satisfy moral, ethical and legal concepts" including voluntary consent (Holocaust Memorial Museum, n.d.).

Also in the 1940s, Nazi scientists were heavily recruited into American universities and research institutes, including NASA, through a covert government program called *Operation Paper Clip* (Records of the Secretary of Defense (RG 330), n.d.). As just one example, Dr. Hubertus Strughold, now recognized by Americans as the "Father of Space Medicine" was alledgedly once a senior Nazi official, implicated in obscene experiments on Jewish prisoners at Dachau as well as disabled children at a prominent research institute in Berlin, of which he was director (Lagnado, 2012). After the war, he was appointed "Professor of Space Medicine at the U.S. Air Force School of Aerospace Medicine", and later "co-founded the Space Medicine Branch of the Aerospace Medical Association". In 1963, the association created the Hubertus Strughold Award to "recognize excellence in space medicine" (Miller, n.d.). The award was discontinued in 2013, following allegations in the Wall Street Journal (Lagnado, 2012).

In the 1950s and 60s the US government allegedly funded psychological experiments on many American campuses and within university affiliated hospitals, under the auspices of the CIA's MK Ultra program (Mather, 2020). At Harvard, experiments reportedly involved participants being "bullied, harassed, and psychologically broke [sic] down" (Mather, 2020). In others, hallucinogenic drugs, such as LSD, were given to unwitting subjects, including college students, psychiatric patients and members of the public. The CIA was reportedly interested in learning about brainwashing and torture techniques, and university researchers were core to these efforts.

More recently, unsavoury influencers of US university research have included Jeffrey Epstein (with regard to eugenics) and the Sackler family (with regard to Purdue Pharma's complicity in the opioid crisis). Writing on Epstein's influence and privilege at Harvard, Oreskes (2020), observed:

> Harvard is not alone in accepting tainted money. Universities need to develop policies to ensure that research funding is based on merit, not cronyism, and researchers who are seeking public trust must be able to show that their own ethical compasses are not deflected by the magnetism of money. (n.p)

Growing concern with research misconduct in the US has resulted in calls to improve oversight of scientific research. In 1992, the Office of Research Integrity (ORI) was established to oversee research conducted by the Public Health Service (PHS). The PHS "provides nearly $38 billion for health research and development, primarily in the biomedical and behavioral sciences" (Office of Research Integrity, n.d. a). Today, in addition to promoting research integrity and developing policy, the ORI monitors investigations, recommends findings and posts details on cases of misconduct, naming the researcher and the institution where misconduct was found (Office of Research Integrity, n.d. b).

Another important area where "uncomfortable truths" have begun to be addressed, pertains to the complicity of many US universities in slavery. As one example, following a self-congratulatory account of Yale's history opposing slavery, published for its tercentenary, PhD students Dugdale, Fueser and Celso de Castro Alves (2002), corrected the record. As previously noted, Yale benefited financially from the proceeds of slavery. Senior leaders also taught pro-slavery ideology and along with alumni, undertook efforts to prevent Black's from participating in higher education.

As a more positive example, in 2004 the University of Alabama apologized, "for the involvement of antebellum Alabama faculty members in punishing enslaved people on campus and promulgating proslavery ideologies" (Harris, 2020). This apology is reportedly the first instance of an American university doing so (Harris, 2020).

In 2017, a memorial was erected at Harvard Law School to honor "the enslaved whose labor created wealth that made possible the founding of the Harvard Law School" (Harvard and the Legacy of Slavery, n.d.). Harvard President Faust (2016) publicly acknowledged the university had benefited financially from "racial bondage" and also called out historians who had "long ignored" this truth; "This is our history and our legacy; one we must fully acknowledge and understand in order to truly move beyond the painful injustices at its core."

In summary, higher education in the US was largely founded through missionary efforts to impose Western conceptions of civilization and morality on Indigenous peoples, while people associated with this pursuit behaved themselves in unethical ways. Slavery fueled the expansion of higher education institutions in the 1700s and early 1800s, while students who overtly supported slavery—and judged to be men of good character—graduated into positions of influence within so-called "civil" society. By the mid-1800s, universities began to shift their focus, away from character development and the humanities, towards positivist scientific research (some of it highly unethical). The 1900s saw university researchers play an increasing role in scientific advances, contributing to the country's economic and military dominance. Today, American universities have begun to acknowledge their complicity in the slave trade and systems have been put in place to help hold faculty and institutions accountable for research misconduct.

The Colonization of Canada: Higher Education's Roots

I now turn to the colonization of Canada, adding a critical view to the brief history presented by Eaton and Christensen Hughes (2022), and including the horrific treatment of Indigenous peoples, particularly First Nations, as well as the Inuit and Métis. I include an overview of the creation and aftermath of residential schools, as their shameful legacy has significant implications for the mandates of Canadian higher education institutions today. I begin with present day facts—in order to provide an essential modern lens by which to view this history.

In 1988 the Canadian government formally apologized for attitudes of "racial and cultural superiority" that led to "a suppression of Aboriginal culture and values" as well as the abuse of students in the residential school system:

> The ancestors of First Nations, Inuit and Métis peoples lived on this continent long before explorers from other continents first came to North America...Diverse, vibrant Aboriginal nations had ways of life rooted in *fundamental values* [emphasis added] concerning their relationships to the Creator, the environment, and each other, in the role of Elders as the living memory of their ancestors, and in their responsibilities as custodians of the lands, waters and resources of their homelands…
>
> Tragically, some children were the victims of physical and sexual abuse...To those of you who suffered this tragedy at residential schools, we are deeply sorry. (Gathering Strength—Canada's Aboriginal Action Plan, 1998)

This was followed a decade later by the launch of the Indian Residential Schools Truth and Reconciliation Commission (TRC), which uncovered traumatic truths about the abhorrent treatment of children, from thousands of survivors. Multiple reports and 94 explicit calls for action followed along with the establishment of the National Centre for Truth and Reconciliation (NCTR) at the University of Manitoba, described as "a place of learning and dialogue where the truths of Residential School Survivors, families and communities are honoured and kept safe for future generations" (NCTR, n.d.).

Contained within the NCTR's archive is *Honouring the Truth, Reconciling the Future: Summary of the Final Report of the Truth and Reconciliation Commission of Canada* (2015). This document contains the 94 calls for action and makes clear that Canada engaged in physical, biological and cultural genocide in dealing with Indigenous children. NCTR Director of Research, Aimée Craft observed "[we] must rise to the challenge of knowing this history, and continue to acknowledge it while moving towards a new understanding of the relationships we must rebuild" (2015, p. 190).

The first missionaries to arrive in what is now Canada, were French Catholics (Jesuits, Récollets and Ursulines), who settled in New France (Quebec) in the early 1600s. In 1632, the Jesuits "were given a monopoly over missionary activity" particularly for boys (White & Peters, 2009, p. 13.) The Collège des Jésuites followed in 1635, and the Séminaire de Québec, now Université Laval, in 1660. In 1708, the Collège des Jésuites, "opened a hydrography school where they taught mathematics, astronomy and physics to prepare students for jobs as navigators and surveyors" (Galarneau, 2006). The Ursuline nuns, who arrived in 1639, focused on educating and evangelizing girls, Indigenous and French, and later, the daughters of British officers.

In 1670, the Hudson's Bay Company (HBC) was established, after being granted control of lands surrounding Hudson's Bay. Their interest was the fur trade. The children of HBC employees and local Indigenous women were educated in a variety of formal and informal ways. While the sons of HBC officials were often sent back to England, for others, local schools trained boys for employment in the HBC and girls as "future wives" (Poitras Pratt, 2021, p. 20). The children of these unions were often given French names, and "by the 1660s governing officials considered them to be French, so long as they were baptized" (p. 20).

The Métis worked in a variety of highly skilled occupations during the peak of the fur trade, including as trappers, guides, and interpreters, and later in ranching organizations, acquiring skills through "a mentoring and apprenticeship system" (Poitras Pratt, 2021, p. 21). Following the Resistance of 1885, a highly suspect "scrip system" removed their rights to lands (Muzyka, 2019). "The landless status of many Métis coupled with extreme poverty", and the inability to pay property taxes, meant that their children were excluded from attending school, with impacts lasting for three generations" (Poitras Pratt, 2021, pp. 22–23). Others were "taken" to residential school, or enrolled by their parents. Summarizing, Poitras Pratt (2021) offered, "the Métis experience of schooling in a post-Rebellion era was marked by the removal of blended traditional and formal learning traditions into one of partial inclusion into or exclusion from, formal school systems" (p. 23). For Inuit youth, while some attended residential schools in the Northwest Territories in the 1800s, it wasn't until the 1950s, that "formal European-style education…began on a national scale…with the construction of elementary and residential schools throughout major settlements in the Arctic, including Baffin Island" (McCue & Filice, 2011/2018).

For First Nations, the situation was very different. In English-speaking Upper Canada, Governor Simcoe, who had arrived in 1792, was intent on replicating British society through education. He aspired to open several grammar (public) schools, as well as establish a university. The District School Act of 1807 called for "a Public School in each and every District":

> Their founders had in mind the great English public school, whose curriculum was largely classical and whose benefits were confined to the wealthy. These schools were not in any sense popular schools…those established by the Act of 1807 levied considerable sums in fees. They were designed to educate the sons of gentlemen. They were to prepare for professional life. They were essentially for the benefit of the ruling classes. (Putman, 1912)

In contrast, common schools, legislated in 1816, had assimilation as their central aim. As published in the Kingston Gazette (September 25, 1810):

> [O]ur population is composed of persons born in different states and nations, under various governments and laws, and speaking several languages. To assimilate them, or rather their descendants, into one congenial people, by all practicable means, is an object of true policy. And the establishment of common schools is one of those means. (cited in Robson, 2019, para. 11)

Egerton Ryerson

Of Upper Canada's "founding educational fathers", one of the most influential was Egerton Ryerson (1803–1882). A Methodist minister, Ryerson helped the Church found the Upper Canada Academy (UCA) for boys and girls in Cobourg in 1836, arguing that such a school was needed to "educate the most promising youth of the recently converted Indian [sic] tribes of Canada, as Teachers to their aboriginal countrymen" (Wilson, 1986, p. 298). Renamed Victoria College, following funding from the British Crown, UCA became a university with degree granting status in 1841. Ryerson was appointed its first principal.

Once UCA became Victoria College, female students were no longer allowed to attend. Despite Plato's view that "all the pursuits of men are the pursuits of women", in Upper Canada this view did not hold sway until many decades later.

In 1844 Ryerson was appointed Chief Superintendent of Education for Upper Canada. By this time there were "more than 2,500 elementary schools in Canada West: financed by a combination of government grants, property taxation, and tuition fees" (Gidney, 1982). Ryerson endeavoured to make education accessible to all, believing:

> Carried out in a Christian context, education promoted virtue and usefulness in this world and union with God in the next. Because it made good and useful individuals it was also a key agent in supporting the good society, inasmuch as it helped to promote social harmony, self-discipline, and loyalty to properly constituted authority. (Gidney, 1982)

Common Schools were used "as a means of entrenching a certain type of values on the growing Canadian population: middle class, British, and Christian (usually Protestant)" (Robson, 2019, pp. 37–38). Francophones (outside Quebec), Catholics and Irish-famine settlers, were amongst those targeted, and also Blacks and later Asians. "White Canadians reacted negatively to the settlement of Blacks in their communities, often refusing them entry to public schools" (Robson, 2019, p. 32). Similarly, the thousands of Chinese who came to Canada in the 1800s to help build the Canadian Pacific Railway, experienced discrimination and segregation in their children's schooling.

By 1847, Ryerson had turned his attention to the education of First Nations children (as previously discussed, differing strategies applied to the Métis and the Inuit). Ryerson advocated for Industrial Schools with the objective of creating "working farmers and agriculture labourers, fortified of course by Christian principles, feelings and habits" (Ryerson, 1847, p. 74). Further, he advocated that such schools should be run by religious orders:

> The North American Indian cannot be civilized or preserved in a state of civilization (including habits of industry and sobriety) except in connection with, if not by the influence of, not only religious instruction and sentiment but of religious feelings...The animating and controlling spirit of each industrial school establishment should, therefore, in my opinion, be a religious one. (p. 73)

Ryerson (1847) recommended that the government's role be limited to funding and oversight, with inspections "from time to time" and reports written "one or twice a year" (p. 74). Specifically, he suggested that through its power to withhold funding, the government would avoid "endless difficulties and embarrassments arising from fruitless attempts to manage the schools in detail" (p. 74).

Ryerson also advised the students should be paid a small sum for their work, be taught to keep their own accounts, and be given the money upon leaving school, in order to also learn and apply skills in business. He reflected, "it would be a gratifying result to see graduates of our Indian industrial schools become overseers of some of the largest farms in Canada" (p. 77). This is clearly not what transpired.

With Confederation in 1867, legal responsibility for "status Indians" became a federal responsibility, while "education for non-status Indian, Inuit and Métis youth…became a provincial or territorial responsibility" (McCue & Filice, 2011/2018, p. 7).

Residential Schools and Their Legacy

The Residential School system that ultimately emerged in the late 1800s was heavily influenced by Nicholas Flood Davin, a journalist and politician, commissioned by the government to produce what is now known as the "Davin Report" (Davin, 1879). Following a tour of US institutions, Davin endorsed the "aggressive civilization" policy, inaugurated by US President Grant in 1869, concluding that "day-school did not work, because the influence of the wigwam was stronger than the influence of the school" (p. 1).

Davin acknowledged the negative consequences of contracting out the running of boarding schools to religious organizations; "the children at schools under contract do not, as a rule, get a sufficient quantity of food" (Davin, 1879, p. 2). Like Ryerson, Davin supported religious oversight regardless:

> The Indians have their own idea of right and wrong, of "good" Indians and "bad" Indians, and to disturb this faith, without supplying a better, would be a curious process to enlist the sanction of civilized races whose whole civilization, like all the civilizations with which we are acquainted, is based on religion. (Davin, 1879, p. 14)

Perhaps prophetically, Davin (1879), further observed, "the character of the teacher, morally and intellectually, is a matter of vital importance. If he is morally weak, whatever his intellectual qualifications may be, he is worse than no teacher at all" (p. 15). While Davin recommended that "the schools both employ and teach Métis peoples", participation was officially restricted to "Status Indians" (White & Peters, 2009, p. 17). In practice, however, when convenient to boost numbers, Métis children were allowed to attend.

In 1883, Sir John A. Macdonald accepted Davin's recommendations and officially created Canada's residential school system. At this time, four residential schools already existed in Ontario—"The Mohawk Institute (1831), Mount Elgin Industrial Institute (1851), Shingwauk Indian Residential School (1873), and Wikwemikong Indian Residential School (1840 day school, 1879 residential school)" (Indigenous Education in Canada—Chronology, n.d.).

In 1894, through an amendment to the Indian Act, attending school became compulsory for First Nations children (whether day school, industrial school or residential school). By 1900, there were 64 residential schools and "226 federally-funded day schools on reserves" (Canadian Encyclopedia, n.d.). In 1920, attendance at residential schools was further enforced:

> Deputy Superintendent General of Indian Affairs, Duncan Campbell Scott, makes attendance at residential school mandatory for every First Nations child between 7 and 16 years of age. This policy was also inconsistently applied to Métis and Inuit children. (Canadian Encyclopedia, n.d.)

This amendment to Indian Act authorized priests, nuns, ministers, police officers, and Indian agents to forcibly seize children, and arrest and imprison parents and guardians who failed to cooperate.

By the early 1900s, the horrific consequences of residential schools were increasingly apparent. Dr. Peter Bryce, who inspected the schools, recorded the shocking conditions he witnessed in his 1922 report, *The Story of a National Crime: Being a Record of the Health Conditions of the Indians of Canada from 1904 to 1921*. After visiting 35 residential schools, he reported that due to tuberculosis and deplorable conditions, "24%, of all the pupils which had been in the schools were known to be dead, while of one school on the File Hills reserve...75%, were dead at the end of the 16 years since the school opened" (Bryce, 1922, p. 4). Those who did survive had to contend with the life-long negative consequences of inhumane treatment.

Despite this report, Canada's residential school network continued to grow, and by 1930 included more than 80 institutions, "with an enrolment of over 17,000" (Canadian Encyclopedia, n.d.). It was also about this time that the government turned its attention to the education of Inuit and Métis children. By the mid-1950s residential schools were operating in the Western Arctic and Inuvik. Attendance at these schools remained mandatory until 1969, with closures beginning shortly thereafter. The last to close was the Gordon Residential School in Saskatchewan, in 1996.

The experience of Indigenous children, and those from other marginalized groups, including racial minorities and girls, effectively restricted access to higher education well into the late nineteenth and early twentieth centuries. Further, graduates of Canada's early higher education institutions, including its seminaries and the faculty they employed perpetuated this discrimination.

Higher Education in Canada: A Brief History

Governed by the Church of England, three "Kings" colleges were amongst the first universities established in Canada (Windsor, Nova Scotia, 1789; York [Toronto], Ontario, 1827; and Fredericton, New Brunswick, 1828). These colleges were residential, tutorial and intended to "bring the ideals of the older English universities to Canada" (Anisef et al., 2015).

By the time of Confederation (1867), Canada was home to 17 degree-granting institutions across the founding provinces (Ontario, Quebec, New Brunswick, and Nova Scotia). Four were nondenominational—Dalhousie, McGill and two former

Kings Colleges (New Brunswick and Toronto) while 13 remained church controlled. Enrollments were largely small, with the majority enrolling "about 100 students" (Anisef et. Al., 2015).

Mount Allison University in New Brunswick was the first to accept female students, with Gracie Annie Lockhart earning her Bachelor of Science degree in 1875 (Archambault, 2019). Augusta Stowe was the first to earn a medical degree from Victoria College in 1883. The first female graduates in Ontario were Annie Fowler and Eliza Fitzgerald from Queen's University, in 1884. An 1876 account from the Queen's Journal, reflects attitudes toward women's participation:

> We are confident that among people who appreciate the delicate grace and beauty of woman's character too much to expose it to the rude influences, the bitterness and strife of the world, few will be found to advocate her admission to universities. (cited in Queen's Encyclopedia, n.d.)

At Kings (Toronto), despite funding from the "Anglican Church's missionary society" for a "professorship of Indian languages" (Peace, 2016, p. 2), few Indigenous students attended. One exception was a "well-known Mohawk doctor, Oronhytekha, [who] graduated from the school in 1866". Western University of London, founded in 1879 as another non-denominational school, had a mandate that included "the training of both Indian and white students for the ministry of the Church of England in Canada" (Peace, 2016, p. 1).

In 1868, changes in provincial funding resulted in consolidation and a marked decrease in the number of religious institutions through "federated" colleges; "a Canadian solution to the problem of reconciling religiosity and secularism, diversity and economic pragmatism" (Anisef et al., 2015). In Ontario, for example, Victoria College, St Michael's College and Trinity College all federated with the University of Toronto, agreeing to "restrict their offerings to the sensitive and less costly liberal arts subjects" (Anisef et al., 2015). Manitoba combined three church colleges to found the University of Manitoba. The Western provinces created a single public university each (Alberta, 1906; Saskatchewan, 1907 and British Columbia, 1908).

By the early 1900s, enrollment at Canada's now largely secular universities was 6,641 students (from a population of around seven million), with the majority male (89%); "44% of students were in the Arts and Science, while 27% were in medicine, and 11% were in Engineering" (Usher, 2018a). Considerable growth followed. By the 1940's there were almost 40,000 students, 76% male (Usher, 2018b).

During this time, as in the US, the focus of Canada's universities began to change, expanding "beyond the traditional fields of theology, law and medicine" and introducing "graduate training based on the German-inspired American model of specialized course work and the completion of a research thesis" (Anisef et al., 2015). During this time, evidence of research that would be considered highly unethical today, can be found.

As one example, in 1943 Donald Ewen Cameron became director of McGill University's Department of Psychiatry at the newly-created Allan Memorial Institute. Later, Cameron served as president of both the American (1952–1953) and Canadian Psychiatric Associations (1958–1959). His highly controversial research program, which ran until 1965, was alledgedly linked to the CIA's MKUltra program (Mather, 2020). Many of Cameron's patients were young women suffering postpartum depression.

> Ewen Cameron attempted to erase memories by repeated electro-shock treatments, forcing months of drug-induced sleep, and repeatedly administering LSD to his patients...Many of these patients came to the clinic to be treated for moderate depression and instead were subjected to months of horrific exploitation. (Mather, 2020)

An investigation by CBC's 5th Estate found that some of the victims successfully received compensation from the CIA, in an out of court settlement, while others received compensation from the Canadian Government. Both settlements were without apology or any admission of liability. While McGill's Department of Psychiatry website mentions Cameron as its founder, it makes no mention of the controversy (McGill, n.d.).

In the 1940s and 1950s, Canadian researchers studied the effects of hunger and malnutrition on Indigenous children in residential schools, maintaining control groups, depriving children of their daily nutritional allowance for years, in order to "establish a baseline against which to compare the effects"(Owens, 2013). They also restricted preventative dental care in order to assess the effects of nutritional deprivation. Mosby (2013) found that little value came from these studies and led to no positive interventions at the schools at the completion. The devastating toll residential schools took on the health of Indigenous children is well-documented (Wilk et al., 2017).

Throughout the 1960s and 1970s, enrollments and the number of Canadian universities continued to increase (Anisef et al., 2015). The 1960s also saw the introduction of the CEGEP sector in Quebec (Collège d'enseignement général et professionel), and community colleges in other regions, that focused more specifically on skill development and job preparedness. Higher education by this time was viewed as important to both economic productivity and social justice; "a major means of accommodating rising social aspirations and of enhancing the social prospects of disadvantaged social, cultural and regional groups" (Anisef et al., 2015). Given longstanding institutionalized discrimination in Canada's public schools, however, the achievement of these goals was compromised.

Ethics education "re-emerged in the 1960s in the form of practical and professional ethics education" (Maxwell et al., 2016, p. 2). While medicine was at the fore, specialized ethics courses in business, engineering and teaching followed, along with ethics-focused research centres, journals and associations. The Centre for Bioethics of the Clinical Research Institute of Montreal, established in 1976, was reportedly the first in Canada (Medical Ethics, History of the Americas: III Canada, n.d.).

Reconciling the Past While Recognizing Ongoing Concerns

According to the 2016 Statistics Canada Census, while "First Nations peoples have higher attainment rates than non-Indigenous Canadians in college and the trades", the university level participation gap "has remained at around 22 percentage points" (First Nations Post-Secondary Education Fact Sheet, n.d.) (First Nations Post-Secondary Education Fact Sheet, n.d.). For First Nations aged 25–64, by 2016 just 15% living on reserve and 23% living off reserved had attained a university-level credential (certificate, diploma or degree), in comparison to 45% of those with non-Aboriginal identity (First Nations Post-Secondary Education Fact Sheet, n.d.). Higher education has been slow to address this gap, acknowledge the impact of residential schools and colonization, and embrace the recommendations of Canada's Truth and Reconciliation Commission (2015).

Of the 94 calls to action, those that apply (directly or indirectly) to higher education, include (*TRC*, 2015): closing "educational attainment gaps" (Recommendation 10.i); providing "culturally appropriate curriculum" (10.ii); providing "adequate funding to end the backlog of First Nations students seeking a post-secondary education" (11); creating "university and college degree and diploma programs in Aboriginal languages" (16); and various calls to ensure professionals—social workers, teachers and lawyers—are properly educated, including (28) "learning the history and legacy of residential schools" and requiring "skills-based training in intercultural competency, conflict resolution, human rights and antiracism".

Colleges and universities across the country are establishing Indigenous student scholarships, faculty positions, research centres and student centres, and are critically reassessing the curriculum, pedagogy and assessment norms (see for example, Lindstrom, G., 2022; Ottmann, 2016; Poitras Pratt & Gladue, 2022), although not always successfully. In one case, Jaris Swidrovich, "the only self-identified Indigenous faculty member in pharmacy in Canada" resigned from the University of Saskatchewan citing feelings of isolation after "an extended series of incidents of racism and discrimination at multiple levels" (Sorokan, 2021). Swidrovich observed, "Verbalized or written expressions of support does not equate to action and is not a measure of an institution's level of safety for Black, Indigenous, and People of Colour" (Sorokan, 2021).

Scholars are writing on Indigenization and decolonization, providing powerful critiques of Western notions of institutionalized schooling (see for example Poitras Pratt et al., 2018) and making thoughtful and detailed recommendations for advancing and transforming the academy in Canada (Cote-Meek & Moeke-Pickering, 2020; Ottmann, 2017). The mission of the National Centre for Truth and Reconciliation (NCTR, n.d.) at the University of Manitoba is to support this work.

There have also been vociferous calls for renaming buildings and toppling statues that have honoured those implicated in Canada's colonial past, including following the discovering of the remains of 215 Indigenous children on the grounds of the former Kamloops Indian Residential School in B.C. (Fortier & Bogart, 2021). UBC is considering rescinding the honourary degree it bestowed on Catholic bishop John Fergus O'Grady, a former principal at the school (Kurjata, 2021).

Long-standing calls to remove the name of Canada's first Prime Minister, Sir John A. Macdonald are beginning to have effect. As one example, Queen's University recently removed his name from their law school building (Glowacki, 2020). Egerton Ryerson's legacy has similarly been challenged. While the Ryerson University name remains for now, in 2021 Ryerson announced they were renaming their law school after the Honourable Lincoln Alexander, the first Black person to be elected to "Canada's House of Commons, to serve as a federal Cabinet Minister and to be appointed as Lieutenant Governor of Ontario" (Ryerson Today, 2021).

At the University of New Brunswick, George Duncan Ludlow's name has been removed from the law faculty building. Ludlow was the Province's first chief justice. As the son of a slave trader, he was "one of the last judges in the British Empire to uphold the legality of slavery". Ludlow was also implicated in the abuse of Indigenous children, through his role as "a longtime member of the board of directors for the Sussex Vale Indian Day School, which contracted out First Nations children as indentured servants" (Bisset, 2019).

In Quebec, the history of James McGill has drawn attention. McGill earned his fortune as a West Indian merchant and personally owned five slaves, two Indigenous children (both of whom tragically died at the age of ten), two black women and a black man (Nelson, 2020). Former McGill faculty member Charmaine Nelson has asserted that despite the "often obvious, direct, and profound connections between the histories of western universities and Transatlantic Slavery" (p. 4), "McGill has not acknowledged, critically examined, or redressed these histories and the anti-black, anti-indigenous racism upon which McGill University was founded" (p. 4).

The Black Lives Matter movement—which many Black Canadian university students and faculty have been at the heart of—has significantly increased awareness of ongoing discrimination and harassment of marginalized groups on Canadian campuses:

> prominent young Black Canadian writers and activists, emerging from a white supremacist Canadian university system, are writing and speaking openly about the ways their experiences in higher education have shaped their activism. (Moriah, 2020)

Moriah (2020) recommended two memoirs that critique systemic racism on Canadian campuses: Desmond Cole's (2020), *The Skin We're In* (on his experience at Queen's) and Eternity Martis' (2020), *They Said This Would Be Fun: Race, Campus Life, and Growing Up* (on her experience at Western).

Although representation of female faculty and administrators has significantly improved over the past fifty years, a recent study on the "power gap" suggests gender-based discrimination within Canadian higher education is worse than in other professional domains; "As institutions of higher learning, universities have an added ethical and moral obligation to be equitable in their practices—and yet our analysis shows they have among the worst track record on gender representation" (Doolittle & Wang, 2021).

With respect to research misconduct and unethical administrative practice, Christensen Hughes and Eaton (2022a), identified numerous cases of fraud and plagiarism by faculty as well as national policy changes intended to help strengthen the culture of research integrity in Canada. Recent cases of student misconduct, which appear to be growing in frequency and complexity, were also identified (Christensen Hughes and Eaton, 2022b). Taken together, these issues point to troubling and enduring aspects of Canada's colonial legacy as well as growing concern with faculty and student misconduct.

Higher Education's Clarion Cry for Change

In bringing this chapter to a close, I first want to acknowledge that I fully recognize I have just briefly identified, and then woven together, a number of highly sensitive and complex topics, each deserving considerably more in-depth treatment than has been possible here. I also recognize my own biases and limitations. As a white woman of British heritage, with a disciplinary interest in education and organizations, much of the literature I have reviewed for this chapter is outside my traditional areas of focus. I am grateful for the thoughtful input of reviewers and look forward to further critique.

The argument I have sought to make throughout this chapter, is that Western higher education, long positioned as a bastion of integrity and truth telling, has a highly questionable and arguably–disturbing–past. In its earliest days, conceptions of truth and scientific discovery were influenced by the wealthy and controlled by the Church. In North America, higher education was a powerful instrument of colonial oppression, imposing self-serving conceptions of morality and truth, while reinforcing dominant social structures, including slavery (from which it profitted). In Canada, residential schools resulted in the "physical, biological and cultural genocide" of Indigenous children (Honouring the Truth, Reconciling the Future: Summary of the Final Report of the Truth & Reconciliation Commission of Canada, 2015). With the rise of the scientific method, a "truth at all costs" mentality took hold in some quarters, with horrific consequences. More recently, the academy has been called out for inappropriately bestowing naming honours on people central to colonial legacy, misconduct in research practice, and being an inhospitable place for BIPOC and female students and faculty. Student misconduct is an additional area of concern.

At the same time, higher education has undoubtedly produced many social benefits. It has developed philosophical thought and reason, helped found the professions, advanced the arts and humanities, fueled scientific achievement, and supported the career aspirations of its graduates. For many Indigenous Peoples, higher education is viewed as "the new means of survival, and it is also the means to achieve individual and collective self-determination" (Ottmann, 2017). Today, Canada's higher education institutions are beginning to engage in processes of Indigenization and reconciliation. Acknowledging this paradox—while essential—can be exhausting, particularly for those who have suffered and who are committed to helping advance integrity, equality and justice.

Fortunately, recent global initiatives can provide guidance. As one example, the United Nations Organisation for Economic Co-operation and Development produced a report on the *Future of Education and Skills 2030* (OECD, 2019), which acknowledged that attitudes and values are "integral to individual and social well-being" (p. 6). In this report they explicitly identified "core shared values of citizenship (respect, fairness, personal and social responsibility, integrity and self-awareness)...in order to build more inclusive, fair, and sustainable economies and societies" (p. 2). One important recommended action for academic leaders is to ensure that these values are explicitly embedded as learning outcomes in university curricula, as well as in the selection criteria for administrators, faculty and staff.

These values are also reflected in the United Nations' Sustainable Development Goals and 2030 agenda. SDG #4 calls for "Ensuring Inclusive and Equitable Quality Education". Recently, the Council of Ministers of Education Canada (CMEC) produced a report on Canada's commitment to SDG #4 (CMEC, 2020) and progress on each of SDG #4's seven targets. For Target 4.7, Global Citizenship and Sustainable Development, they reported that Canada is working on developing a "shared vision of the competencies needed for the twenty-first century...referred to as global competencies" (p. 38):

> More than any other target, Target 4.7 touches on the social, humanistic, and moral purpose of education...Global citizenship education fosters respect for all to build a sense of belonging to a common humanity... (CMEC, 2020, p. 38)

As one modest example of what addressing these issues might look like, a recent advertisement for a research seminar on "Diverse Perspectives on Knowledge Mobilization" at the University of Guelph offered:

> We have long known that we need to mobilize research knowledge more creatively if we wish to tackle 'wicked' environmental problems and put research into practice. Increasingly siloed disciplines, a disconnect between arts and science, and a lack of engagement and equity in academia and society jeopardize our capacity to collaboratively respond to environmental crises in a creative, innovative, and equitable way...diversity and inclusion perspectives can advance the way we think, do, and mobilize interdisciplinary environmental research (personal email, 2021).

Canadian faculty are beginning to engage in interdisciplinary ways, and diverse voices are beginning to be heard.

In closing, it is time for Canada's higher education institutions to fully embrace the promise of higher education that was expressed—if not enacted—in North America centuries ago. *Veritas*. For if the truth cannot be found here, where can society turn, for solving its most profound problems? Academic integrity must transcend discussions of student misconduct. Shared values of citizenship, the pursuit of social justice (including for Canada's Indigenous Peoples), and contributing to the development of "inclusive, fair, and sustainable economies and societies" should be at the core of our purpose and practice. This is the challenge of our time. Meeting it is a question of integrity.

References

Anisef, P., Axelrod, P., & Lennards, J. (2015). Universities in Canada (Canadian Universities). *In The Canadian Encyclopedia.* https://www.thecanadianencyclopedia.ca/en/article/university

Archambault, G. (2019). *The History of Canadian Women in University.* https://stfmcgill.wordpress.com/2019/02/06/the-history-of-canadian-women-in-university/

Bissett, K. (2019). N.B. University pressured to remove name of province's first chief justice from school building after slavery ties. *Toronto Star.* https://www.thestar.com/news/canada/2019/10/31/nb-university-pressured-to-remove-name-of-provinces-first-chief-justice-from-school-building-after-slavery-ties.html

Bologna. (n.d.). *Nine Centuries of History.* https://www.unibo.it/en/university/who-we-are/our-history/nine-centuries-of-history/nine-centuries-of-history

Bristow, W. (2017). Enlightenment. In E. N. Zalta (Ed.), *The Stanford Encyclopedia of Philosophy.* https://plato.stanford.edu/archives/fall2017/entries/enlightenment/

Bryce, P. (1922). *The story of a national crime: Being a record of the health conditions of the Indians of Canada from 1904 to 1921.* James Hope & Sons. https://archive.org/details/storyofnationalc00brycuoft

Cambridge. (n.d. a). Early records. *University of Cambridge.* https://www.cam.ac.uk/about-the-university/history/early-records

Cambridge. (n.d. b). Moves to independence. *University of Cambridge.* https://www.cam.ac.uk/about-the-university/history/moves-to-independence

Canadian Encyclopedia. (n.d.). Timeline. *Residential Schools.* Retrieved June 1, 2021, from https://www.thecanadianencyclopedia.ca/en/timeline/residential-schools

Christensen Hughes, J. & Eaton, S. E. (2021a). Academic misconduct in higher education: Beyond student cheating. In S. E. Eaton & J. Christensen Hughes (Eds.), *Academic integrity in Canada: An enduring and essential challenge.* Springer.

Christensen Hughes, J., & Eaton, S. E. (2021b). Student integrity violations in the academy: More than a decade of growing complexity and concern. In S. E. Eaton & J. Christensen Hughes (Eds.), *Academic integrity in Canada: An enduring and essential challenge.* Springer.

CMEC. (2020, March 19). *Ensuring inclusive and equitable quality education: Sustainable development goal 4 in Canada.* Council of Ministers of Education, Canada. https://www.cmec.ca/Publications/Lists/Publications/Attachments/407/Sustainable%20Development%20Goal%204%20in%20Canada%20EN.pdf

Cole, D. (2020). *The skin we're in.* Doubleday Canada.

Cote-Meek, S., & Moeke-Pickering, T. (2020). *Decolonizing and indigenizing education in Canada.* Canadian Scholars' Press. https://www.canadianscholars.ca/books/decolonizing-and-indigenizing-education-in-canada

Craft, A. (2015). Afterword. Gabekana. In P. Fontaine & A. Craft (Eds.), *A knock on the door: The essential history of residential schools from the truth and reconciliation commission of Canada.* University of Manitoba Press. https://ehprnh2mwo3.exactdn.com/wp-content/uploads/2021/03/A_Knock_on_the_Door_Afterword.pdf

Davin, N. F. (1879). *Report on Industrial Schools for Indians and Half-Breeds.* https://collections.irshdc.ubc.ca/index.php/Detail/objects/9427

Del Soldato, E. (2020). Natural philosophy in the Renaissance. *The Stanford Encyclopedia of Philosophy.* In E. N. Zalta (Ed.). https://plato.stanford.edu/archives/fall2020/entries/natphil-ren/

Doolittle, R., Wang, C. (2021). Explore the power gap in Canadian Universities. *Globe and Mail.* https://www.theglobeandmail.com/canada/article-power-gap-data-universities/

Driver, J. (2014). The history of Utilitarianism. *The Stanford Encyclopedia of Philosophy.* In E. N. Zalta (Ed.). https://plato.stanford.edu/archives/win2014/entries/utilitarianism-history/

Dugdale, A., Fueser, J., & Celso de Castro Alves, J. (2002). *Yale, slavery and abolition.* http://www.yaleslavery.org/YSA.pdf

Eaton, S. E., & Christensen Hughes, J. (2021). Academic integrity in Canada: Historical perspectives and current trends. In S. E. Eaton & J. Christensen Hughes (Eds.), *Academic integrity in Canada: An enduring and essential challenge*: Springer.

Economist. (2020). Ties that bind: British universities are examining how they benefited from slavery. *The Economist*. https://www.economist.com/britain/2020/02/08/british-universities-are-examining-how-they-benefited-from-slavery

Faust, D. (2016). Recognizing slavery at Harvard. *The Harvard Crimson*. https://www.harvard.edu/slavery

First Nations Post-Secondary Education Fact Sheet. (n.d.). https://www.afn.ca/wp-content/uploads/2018/07/PSE_Fact_Sheet_ENG.pdf

Fontaine, P., Craft, A., & The Truth and Reconciliation Commission of Canada. (2015). *A knock on the door: The essential history of residential schools from the truth and reconciliation commission of Canada*. University of Manitoba Press.

Fortier, B., & Bogart. N. (2021, June 1). Outrage over landmarks named for residential school leaders grows as Canada grapples with colonial legacy. *CTV News*. https://www.ctvnews.ca/canada/outrage-over-landmarks-named-for-residential-school-leaders-grows-as-canada-grapples-with-colonial-legacy-1.5452497

Frawley, J., Larkin, S., Smith, J. (eds.). (2017). *Indigenous pathways, transitions and participation in higher education*. Springer. https://doi.org/10.1007/978-981-10-4062-7_7

Galarneau, C. (2006). Collège des Jésuites. *Canadian Encyclopedia*. https://www.thecanadianencyclopedia.ca/en/article/college-des-jesuites

Gathering Strength—Canada's Aboriginal Action Plan. (1988). *Government of Canada*. http://www.publications.gc.ca/site/eng/9.849517/publication.html

Gidney, R. D. (1982). Ryerson Egerton. *Dictionary of Canadian Biography*, vol. 11, pp. 1881–1890. University of Toronto/Université Laval. http://www.biographi.ca/en/bio/ryerson_egerton_11E.html

Glasson, T. (2010). Baptism doth not bestow Freedom: Missionary Anglicanism, Slavery, and the Yorke-Talbot Opinion, 1701–30. *The William and Mary Quarterly, 67*(2), 279–318. https://doi.org/10.5309/willmaryquar.67.2.279

Glowacki, L. (2020). Queen's University to remove Sir John A. Macdonald's name from law school building. *CBC News*. https://www.cbc.ca/news/canada/ottawa/sir-john-a-macdonald-law-school-queens-university-1.5768385

Goldin, C., & Katz, L. (1999). The shaping of higher education: The formative years in the United States, 1890 to 1940. *Journal of Economic Perspectives, 13*(1), 37–62. https://scholar.harvard.edu/goldin/files/the_shaping_of_higher_education_the_formative_years_in_the_united_states_1890-1940

Harris, L. (2020). Higher education's reckoning with slavery. *American Association of University Professors*. https://www.aaup.org/article/higher-education%E2%80%99s-reckoning-slavery#.YByV5Og3nIV

Hart, D. G. (1999). *The university gets religion*. Johns Hopkins University Press.

Hartshorne, M., & May, A. (1928). *Studies in the nature of character*. Macmillan.

Harvard and the Legacy of Slavery. (n.d). *About Harvard*. https://www.harvard.edu/slavery

Haskins, C. H. (1923). *The Rise of Universities*. Cornell University Press.

Honouring the truth, reconciling the future: Summary of the final report of the truth and reconciliation commission of Canada (2015). *National Centre for Truth and Reconciliation Centre*. https://ehprnh2mwo3.exactdn.com/wp-content/uploads/2021/01/Executive_Summary_English_Web.pdf

Hopson, T. (October 1, 2021). A Portrait of George Berkeley: Philosopher or Subjugator? Yale Daily News. https://yaledailynews.com/blog/2021/10/01/a-portrait-of-george-berkeley-philosopher-orsubjugator/

Indigenous Education in Canada—Chronology. (n.d.). *Indigenous Learning—Education/Residential Schools, Laurentian University*. Retrieved May 25, 2021, from https://libguides.lakeheadu.ca/c.php?g=705780&p=5021427

Ireland, D. (2015). Seal of approval. *Harvard Gazette.* https://news.harvard.edu/gazette/story/2015/05/seal-of-approval/#:~:text=Veritas%2C%20which%20is%20Latin%20for,For%20the%20glory%20of%20Christ.%E2%80%9D

Jesuits of Canada. (n.d.). *History of the Jesuits in English Canada.* https://jesuits.ca/about-us/history/

Johnson, R., & Cureton, A. (2016). Kant's moral philosophy. *The Stanford Encyclopedia of Philosophy.* In E. N. Zalta (Ed.). https://plato.stanford.edu/archives/spr2021/entries/kant-moral/

Knapp, H. (1998). The character of Puritan missions: The motivation, methodology, and effectiveness of the Puritan evangelization of the native Americans in New England. *The Journal of Presbyterian History, 76*(2). http://www.jstor.org/stable/23335366

Kraut, R. (2018). Aristotle's ethics, *The Stanford Encyclopedia of Philosophy.* https://plato.stanford.edu/entries/aristotle-ethics/

Kurjata, A. (2021, May 31). UBC reviewing honours given to Catholic bishop and former Kamloops residential school principal. *CBC News.* https://www.cbc.ca/news/canada/british-columbia/ubc-ogrady-prince-george-kamloops-residential-school-1.6047229

Lagnado, L. (2012). A scientist's Nazi-era past haunts prestigious space prize. *Wall Street Journal.* https://www.wsj.com/articles/SB10001424052970204349404578101393870218834

Likona, T. (1991). *Educating for character: How our schools can teach respect and responsibility.* Bantam Books.

Lindstrom, G. (2021). Accountability, relationality and indigenous epistemology: Advancing an indigenous perspective on academic integrity. In S. E. Eaton & J. Christensen Hughes (Eds.), *Academic integrity in Canada: An enduring and essential challenge.* Springer.

Machamer, P. (2017). Galileo Galilei. *The Stanford Encyclopedia of Philosophy.* In E. N. Zalta (Ed.). https://plato.stanford.edu/archives/sum2017/entries/galileo/

Martis, E. (2020). *They said this would be fun: Race, campus life, and growing up.* McClelland & Stewart.

Mather, R. (2020). U.S. Government mind control experiments. *Psychology Today.* https://www.psychologytoday.com/ca/blog/the-conservative-social-psychologist/202004/us-government-mind-control-experiments

Maxwell, B., Tremblay-Laprise, A., & Filion, M. (2016). A survey of ethics curriculum in Canadian initial teacher education. *McGill Journal of Education, 50*(1). https://mje.mcgill.ca/article/view/9205

McCue, H. A., & Filice, M. (2011/2018). Education of indigenous peoples in Canada. *The Canadian Encyclopedia.* Retrieved May 31, 2021, from https://www.thecanadianencyclopedia.ca/en/article/aboriginal-people-education

McGill. (n.d.). History of the department. *Department of Psychiatry.* https://www.mcgill.ca/psychiatry/about/history

McInerny, R., & O'Callaghan, J. (2018). Saint Thomas Aquinas. *The Stanford Encyclopedia of Philosophy.* In E. N. Zalta (Ed.). https://plato.stanford.edu/archives/sum2018/entries/aquinas/

Medical Ethics, History of the Americas: III. Canada. (n.d.). *Encylopedia.com.* https://www.encyclopedia.com/science/encyclopedias-almanacs-transcripts-and-maps/medical-ethics-history-americas-iii-canada

Miller, Y. (n.d.). *Operation paperclip: The truth about bringing Nazi Scientists to America.* https://www.aish.com/ci/s/Operation-Paperclip-The-Truth-about-Bringing-Nazi-Scientists-to-America.html

Moriah, K. (2020). How anti-Black racism on Canadian university campuses robs us all. *The Conversation.* https://theconversation.com/how-anti-black-racism-on-canadian-university-campuses-robs-us-all-140927

Mosby, I. (2013). Administering colonial science: Nutrition research and human biomedical experimentation in aboriginal communities and residential schools, 1942–1952. *Social History 46*, 145–172. https://muse.jhu.edu/article/512043/pdf

Muzyka, K. (2019). What's Métis scrip? North America's 'largest land swindle,' says indigenous lawyer. Unreserved. *CBC*. https://www.cbc.ca/radio/unreserved/from-scrip-to-road-allowances-canada-s-complicated-history-with-the-m%C3%A9tis-1.5100375/what-s-m%C3%A9tis-scrip-north-america-s-largest-land-swindle-says-indigenous-lawyer-1.5100507#:~:text=What%27s%20M%C3%A9tis%20scrip,Social%20Sharing

NCTR. (n.d.). About. *National Centre for Truth and Reconciliation*. https://nctr.ca/about/

Nelson, C., & Student Authors. (2020). *Slavery and McGill University: Bicentenary recommendations*. https://www.blackcanadianstudies.com/Recommendations_and_Report.pdf

Ninety-Five Theses. (n.d.). Martin Luther and his 95 theses. *The Holy Word Church of God*. https://holyword.church/miscellaneous-resources/martin-luther-and-his-95-theses/

OECD. (2019). Conceptual learning framework: Attitudes and values for 2030. *OECD Future of Education and Skills 2030*. https://www.oecd.org/education/2030-project/teaching-and-learning/learning/attitudes-and-values/Attitudes_and_Values_for_2030_concept_note.pdf

Office of Research Integrity. (n.d. a). About ORI. *U.S. Department of Health and Human Services*. https://ori.hhs.gov/about-ori

Office of Research Integrity. (n.d. b). Case summaries. *U.S. Department of Health and Human Services*. https://ori.hhs.gov/content/case_summary

Oreskes, N. (2020). Jeffrey Epstein's Harvard connections show how money can distort research. *Scientific American*. https://www.scientificamerican.com/article/jeffrey-epsteins-harvard-connections-show-how-money-can-distort-research/

Ottmann, J. (2017). Canada's indigenous peoples' access to post-secondary education: The spirit of the 'new buffalo'. In J. Frawley S. Larkin & J. Smith (Eds.), *Indigenous pathways, transitions and participation in higher education*. Springer. https://doi.org/10.1007/978-981-10-4062-7_7

Owens, B. (2013). Canada used hungry indigenous children to study malnutrition. *Nature*. https://www.nature.com/news/canada-used-hungry-indigenous-children-to-study-malnutrition-1.13425

Oxford. (n.d.). Introduction and history. *University of Oxford*. https://www.ox.ac.uk/about/organisation/history

Peace, T. (2016). Indigenous peoples: A starting place for the history of higher education in Canada. *Active History*. https://activehistory.ca/2016/01/rethinking-higher-education-colonialism-and-indigenous-peoples/

Poitras Pratt, Y. (2021). A family of learners: The métis people of Canada and their education lifeworlds. In S. M. Brigham R. McGray & K. Jubas (Eds.), *Adult education and lifelong learning in Canada*. Thompson Educational Publishing.

Poitras Pratt, Y., & Gladue, K. (2021). Re-defining academic integrity: Embracing indigenous truths. In S. E. Eaton & J. Christensen Hughes (Eds.), *Academic integrity in Canada: An enduring and essential challenge*: Springer.

Poitras Pratt, Y., Louie, D. W., Hanson, A. J., & Ottmann, J. (2018). "Indigenous education and decolonization." In G. Noblit (Ed.), *Oxford research encyclopedia of education*. Oxford University Press. http://education.oxfordre.com/view/10.1093/acrefore/9780190264093.001.0001/acrefore-9780190264093-e-240

Putman, J. H. (1912). *Egerton Ryerson and education in Upper Canada*. William Briggs. https://www.gutenberg.ca/ebooks/putman-egertonryerson/putman-egertonryerson-00-h.html

Queen's Encyclopedia. (n.d.). *Women at Queen's, Admission of* https://www.queensu.ca/encyclopedia/w/women-queens-admission#:~:text=The%20first%20two%20women%20in,not%20come%20without%20a%20struggle

Race, M. (2021). Cecil Rhodes statue will not be removed by Oxford college. *BBC News*. https://www.bbc.com/news/uk-england-oxfordshire-57175057

Race, M. (2020). Cecil Rhodes: Oxford scholarship 'needs reform'. *BBC News*. https://www.bbc.com/news/uk-england-oxfordshire-53006735#:~:text=Campaigners%20demanding%20the%20removal%20of,since%20its%20creation%20in%201902

Records of the Secretary of Defense (RG 330). (n.d.). Foreign scientist case files 1945–1958 (Entry A1–1B). *Interagency working group.* National Archives. Retrieved June 1, 2021, from https://www.archives.gov/iwg/declassified-records/rg-330-defense-secretary

Resnik, D. B. (n.d.). Research ethics timeline. *National Institute of Environmental Health Sciences.* https://www.niehs.nih.gov/research/resources/bioethics/timeline/index.cfm#:~:text=The%20vision%20of%20NIEHS%20is,since%20its%20founding%20in%201966

Reuters. (2019). *Factbox: How have British universities grappled with links to the slave trade?* https://www.reuters.com/article/uk-britain-slavery-universities-factbox-idUKKCN1S61U5

Reuben, J. (1996). *The making of the modern university.* University of Chicago Press.

Robson, K. (2019). A historical overview of education in Canada. *Sociology of Education in Canada.* https://ecampusontario.pressbooks.pub/robsonsoced/

Royal Society. (n.d.). *History of the royal society.* https://royalsociety.org/about-us/history/

Ryerson, E. (1847). Appendix A, Report of Dr. Ryerson on industrial schools. *Statistics respecting indian schools with Dr. Ryerson's report of 1847 attached*, file 172495, AMICUS 15206086, Library and archives Canada. 73–77.

Ryerson Today. (2021). *Ryerson renames law school after the honourable Lincoln Alexander.* https://www.ryerson.ca/news-events/news/2021/04/ryerson-renames-law-school-after-the-honourable-lincoln-alexander/

Shaw, A. (2021). Decision comes as scrutiny mounts over the university's colonial legacy, including at Oriel college where a commission on Cecil Rhodes monument has been delayed. *The Art Newspaper.* https://www.theartnewspaper.com/news/oxford-university-s-all-souls-college-drops-christopher-codrington-s-name-from-its-library-but-refuses-to-remove-slave-owner-s-statue

Sorokan, K. (2021, May 22). Indigenous professor leaving University of Saskatchewan over racism concerns. *CKOM.* https://www.ckom.com/2021/05/22/indigenous-professor-leaving-university-of-saskatchewan-over-racism-claims/

The State of U.S. Science and Engineering. (2020). Introduction. Science and engineering indicators. *National Science Foundation.* https://ncses.nsf.gov/pubs/nsb20201/introduction

Thijssen, H. (2018). Condemnation of 1277. *The Stanford Encyclopedia of Philosophy.* In E. N. Zalta (Ed.). https://plato.stanford.edu/archives/win2018/entries/condemnation/

Truth and Reconciliation Commission of Canada. (2015). *Canada's residential schools: The inuit and northern experience: The final report of the truth and reconciliation commission of Canada,* Vol. 2. McGill-Queen's University Press. https://doi.org/10.2307/j.ctt19rm9tmUnitedStates

Uebel, T. (2020). Vienna Circle. *The Stanford Encyclopedia of Philosophy.* In E. N. Zalta (Ed.). https://plato.stanford.edu/archives/sum2020/entries/vienna-circle/

Holocaust Memorial Museum. (n.d.). *Nuremberg Code.* https://www.ushmm.org/information/exhibitions/online-exhibitions/special-focus/doctors-trial/nuremberg-code

Usher, A. (2018a). History of Canadian PSE Part 1 (To 1900). *Higher Education Strategy Associates.* https://higheredstrategy.com/history-of-canadian-pse-part-i-to-1900/

Usher, A. (2018b). The history of post-secondary education in Canada: Part II–1900 to 1940. *Higher Education Associates.* https://www.postsecondarybc.ca/knowledgebase/the-history-of-post-secondary-education-in-canada-part-ii-1900-to-1940/

Van Helden, A., & Burr, E. (n.d.). The Inquisition. *The Galileo Project*, Rice University. http://galileo.rice.edu/chr/inquisition.html

White, J., & Peters, J. (2009). *A short history of aboriginal education in Canada, Aboriginal Policy Research Consortium International (APRCi).* 23

Wilk, P., Maltby, A., & Cooke, M. (2017). Residential schools and the effects on indigenous health and well-being in Canada—a scoping review. *Public Health Reviews, 38*, 8. https://doi.org/10.1186/s40985-017-0055-6

Wilson, D. (1986). *"No blanket to be worn in school": The education of indians in early nineteenth-century Ontario*, 293–305. https://hssh.journals.yorku.ca/index.php/hssh/article/view/40765/36944

Julia Christensen Hughes Ph.D., has long advocated for ensuring the highest standards of academic integrity in higher education. Her article, Academic Misconduct within Higher Education in Canada, with the late Don McCabe (published in 2006, in the *Canadian Journal of Higher Education*), received the Sheffield Award for research excellence (2007), from the Canadian Society for Studies in Higher Education. As former and founding Dean of the Gordon S. Lang School of Business and Economics (2009–2019) at the University of Guelph, Julia was a champion of business ethics, corporate social responsibility and the need for business schools to be aligned with the UN's Sustainable Development Goals (SDG's). In her new role as President of Yorkville University, Julia is looking forward to supporting and enhancing the institution's long-standing commitment to integrity.

Chapter 3
Student Integrity Violations in the Academy: More Than a Decade of Growing Complexity and Concern

Julia Christensen Hughes and Sarah Elaine Eaton

Abstract Academic misconduct in Canada is a growing and complex concern, worthy of increased attention and concerted action. Yet, the press appears to be more actively engaged (at least more vocal) in raising concerns about integrity violations than many in our post-secondary institutions. This chapter presents a synopsis of the seminal work by Christensen Hughes and McCabe (in the Canadian Journal of Higher Education 36: 1–21, 2006), followed by an exploration of its treatment by the press—in particular *MacLean's* magazine—following its release. We also present select stories of student misconduct as reported by the Canadian press from 2010 to 2020. From a review of these contributions, we suggest that misconduct in the academy appears to be growing in complexity, severity and by the variety of third-party stakeholders involved. Types of cheating identified in this review include: the use of wearable, wireless high-tech devices for communicating with accomplices; paying (bribing) TAs for answers and inflated grades; exam impersonation; plagiarism; and contract cheating (customized essay buying from freelance writers and essay sweatshops). Explanations provided in the press for these behaviours, include increasing numbers of international students, the proliferation of contract cheating services, and increased use of on-line assessment, resulting from the Covid-19 pandemic. The chapter concludes with a call to action, for all post-secondary institutions, to a greater commitment to academic integrity, including stepping up efforts to educate faculty and students as well as to embrace innovation in assessment design and invigilation practice. We also suggest advocacy for introducing laws that will help to deter contract cheating services.

Keywords Academic integrity · Student misconduct · Contract cheating · Media · Canadian · Assessment

J. Christensen Hughes (✉)
Yorkville University, Toronto, Canada
e-mail: jchristensen@yorkviklleu.ca

S. E. Eaton (✉)
University of Calgary, Calgary, Canada
e-mail: seaton@ucalgary.ca

S. E. Eaton and J. Christensen Hughes (eds.), *Academic Integrity in Canada*, Ethics and Integrity in Educational Contexts 1,
https://doi.org/10.1007/978-3-030-83255-1_3

Introduction

As chapters throughout this volume suggest, academic misconduct in Canada is a growing and complex concern, worthy of increased attention and concerted action. As many institutions prefer not to publicize incidents of misconduct, we are fortunate to have a press that routinely draws attention to integrity violations in Canada's colleges and universities, that can provide insight into the types of incidents that are occurring, and help inform institutional response. We begin with a brief synopsis of the first comprehensive study of student misconduct in Canada (Christensen Hughes and McCabe, 2006a, b) and highlight some of the attention this research received by the Canadian press. Next, extending the work of Eaton (2020a, b, 2021), we briefly describe select stories of student integrity violations within higher education in Canada as reported by the press over the past decade (2010–2020). In comparing reported incidents to research on the types and frequency of misconduct self-reported by students in Canadian higher education and elsewhere, the point is made that misconduct in the academy appears to be growing, in complexity, severity and by the involvement of third party, exam impersonation and contract cheating services. The chapter concludes with a call to action, for all Canadian post-secondary institutions, to make a greater commitment to academic integrity, including championing academic integrity education, assessment design and invigilation practice, as originally advised by Christensen Hughes and McCabe (2006a, b). We also suggest that it is more than time to advocate for introducing laws which will serve to dissuade contract cheating firms from offering their services in Canada.

Academic Misconduct in Our Midst: A Canadian Contribution

In Chapter 1 of this book (see Eaton & Christensen Hughes, 2022), we provided highlights of research conducted by Christensen Hughes & McCabe (2006a, b) and here we elaborate further. In 2006, the *Canadian Journal of Higher Education* published two articles on student academic misconduct, by Julia Christensen Hughes and the late Don McCabe (2006a, b), the second of which was awarded with the Canadian Society for Studies in Higher Education's Sheffield Award (2007), as "best paper" for the previous year. These papers were the result of an investigation first launched at the University of Guelph, led by Julia Christensen Hughes, following senior administrative concern about an increasing number of student academic misconduct charges and appeals. At the time, I [Julia] was Director of Teaching Support Services, a multi-faceted support department that was responsible for enhancing the quality of teaching and learning at the University, through educational development programs as well as classroom design and learning technologies innovation.

The first publication (Christensen Hughes and McCabe, 2006a) provided an overview of predominantly US-based research that demonstrated academic misconduct was a prevalent and growing concern, explored its causes, and suggested steps that could be taken to aid with its resolution. These included:

> Revisiting the goals and values of higher education, recommitting to quality in teaching and assessment practice, establishing effective policies and invigilation practices, providing educational opportunities and support for all members of the university community, and using (modified) academic honour codes. (Christensen Hughes & McCabe, 2006a, p. 49)

We also reported that, "the majority of undergraduate students [surveyed] have engaged in some type of misconduct in the completion of their academic work" despite agreeing that "such behaviour is morally wrong" (Christensen Hughes & McCabe, 2006a, p. 52). Institutional factors that were thought to contribute to the reduction of student academic misconduct were also identified, including those that increase student risk-reward perception ("risk of being caught and the severity of possible punishments"), such as:

> Smaller institutional size, existence of an honour code, student understanding and acceptance of academic misconduct policies, severity of penalties for students found responsible for cheating, peer disapproval of cheating, certainty of being reported by a peer and peer's cheating behaviours. (p. 54)

We concluded by underscoring how essential academic integrity is to higher education institutions and society, and called for a recommitment to its achievement. We suggested that "higher education plays an essential role in democratic society" and that faculty and administrators need to recommit "to provid[ing] our students with a high quality education, to develop moral and engaged citizens, and to uphold the highest standards of integrity" (Christensen Hughes & McCabe, 2006a, p. 59).

We also called for a comprehensive Canadian study, one that would help to identify "the unique characteristics of the Canadian higher education system" in order to tailor "institutional strategies appropriate for promoting academic integrity" as well as "to identify how Canadian colleges and universities are responding to academic misconduct when it does occur and what strategies have proven most successful" (Christensen Hughes & McCabe, 2006a, p. 59).

Our second article responded to this call, presenting the results of a "grassroots" study involving 11 Canadian higher education institutions, from five provinces, conducted between January 2002 and March 2003. Undergraduate and graduate students, TAs and faculty, were surveyed about their perceptions and behaviours using a modified version of the survey developed by McCabe and colleagues via the then-named "Center of Academic Integrity's Assessment Project" (Christensen Hughes & McCabe, 2006b).

Of 25 questionable behaviours, we found that the highest rate of self-reported assignment cheating was for "working on an assignment with others when the instructor asked for individual work", reported by 45 and 29% of undergraduate and graduate students respectively (p. 13). The highest rate for examination cheating was "getting questions and answers from someone who has already taken the test", reported by 38 and 16% of undergraduate and graduate students respectively (p. 13). The three lowest rates of all behaviours were: "Turning in a paper obtained in large part from a term paper "mill"/web site that did not charge", reported by 2 and 1% of undergraduate and graduate students respectively, "Damaging library or course materials", reported by 2 and 2% respectively, and "Turning in a paper obtained in large part from a term paper "mill"/web site that did charge", reported by 1 and 0% respectively (p. 13). It is important to note that given the methodological limitations of the study, the authors clearly advised, "the findings of this study should not be used to make definitive claims about the state of academic misconduct within Canada, but rather as indicators of potential areas of concern and action" (Christensen Hughes & McCabe, 2006b, p. 7).

The study concluded that "large numbers of Canadian high school, undergraduate and graduate students report they have engaged in a variety of questionable behaviours in the completion of their academic work" (Christensen Hughes & McCabe, 2006b, p. 17) and that "consistent with the view of over 40% of faculty and TAs: cheating may be a serious problem in Canadian higher education" (p. 18). The study also identified substantial differences between student and faculty "beliefs about what constitutes academic misconduct". We suggested that the reason many students reported having engaged in "unauthorized collaboration and falsification and fabrication behaviours" may be "simply because they don't believe they are wrong" (p. 18).

We (Christensen Hughes & McCabe, 2006b) recommended that Canadian institutions take a number of actions, including "recommit[ting] to academic integrity" and investigating "where existing policies are failing" (Christensen Hughes & McCabe, 2006b, p. 17). More specifically we observed, "New policies and procedures (including meaningful penalties) that have the confidence of the community are clearly needed…supported by system-wide educational efforts directed at administrators, faculty, TAs and students" (p. 17). We also explicitly called for increasing the quality of the educational experience, including assessment procedures. With respect to the potential effectiveness of honour codes, we noted that few Canadian students appear to be willing to report incidents of cheating.

Reaction from the Press

Following the release of these two publications (Christensen Hughes & McCabe, 2006a, b), there was considerable interest by the Canadian press (print, radio and TV), including interviews with the authors on CBC TV's the National, CTV's Canada AM and CBC radio's The Sunday Edition, with Michael Enright, as well as a feature article in *MacLean's* (a national Canadian magazine) which provocatively proclaimed on its front cover: "Fraud U. With more than half of Canadian university students cheating, all degrees are tainted. It's a national scandal. Why aren't schools doing more about it?" (*MacLean's*, 2007a).

This issue (February 12, 2007) featured a full-length article, in which the importance of upholding academic integrity was emphasized, including by citing research that linked academic misconduct to ethical violations in the workforce, in business, dentistry and medicine (Gulli et al., 2007, p. 33). This same article profiled Dalhousie for hosting an "Academic Integrity Week" (p. 34) and McGill for its novel invigilation practices, including "mandatory, assigned seating" and software that checks for unlikely similarities in incorrect responses on multiple choice exams (p. 34). The article concluded by questioning the integrity of Canada's higher education institutions: "Universities—home to our healers, our bridge-builders and the CEO's who generate our wealth—are failing to demonstrate that responsibility by permitting widespread cheating among students. And we will all pay" (p. 36).

The magazine's editors focused their comments on the topic as well. Under the heading "Universities simply have to do better", they chastised administrators for certifying graduates who had not fully earned their degrees:

> We need to be able to trust our universities…but the fact is that few of them are moving swiftly to correct their cheating problems. Offences are observed and ignored. Processes developed to deal with culprits are bypassed. Punishments, on the infrequent occasions they are imposed, tend to be light. Simple methods of examination proven to prohibit cheating are inexplicably out of use. Universities have to do better, for their own sake, and for the sake of all who rely upon their certificates… There's a lot at stake. (*MacLean's*, 2007b, p. 4)

In the following issue (February 19, 2007), the public responded with letters to the editor, but university administrators and higher educational institutions were largely silent, leading the editors to headline their remarks as "Go ahead and cheat" (*MacLean's*, 2007c, p. 2):

> [T]he only knot of concern we could find in the wake of our story was among the nation's minority of honest university students…We sympathize with the honest students, but maybe it's time they faced facts. Professors, provosts, principals and presidents aren't hugely concerned with widespread cheating. What used to be considered dishonorable student behavior is in the process of being redefined as normal. (*MacLean's*, 2007c, p. 2)

The next issue (February 26, 2007) featured even more letters to the editor from faculty, alumni and students alike, with Canadian's sharing their personal experiences and perceived explanations. Comments referred to (*MacLean's*, 2007d, pp. 4–5): universities "sell"ing credentials with students as "customers"; teachers who pass undeserving students, favouring "esteem" over competence; the negative influence of unethical parents, sports stars and "entertainment idols"; increased use of freelance writing agencies; the prioritization of research over teaching; cheating during exams, including hiding materials in the washroom and writing on thighs, driven by a misplaced focus on memorization versus critical thinking; and the tension between the academy's focus on learning and society's focus on job training.

Another article in this same issue discussed *MacLean's* attempt to get presidents of Canada's leading research-intensive universities to comment publicly. While few agreed to do so, those who did questioned the "prevalence of misconduct among their own students" as well as the extent to which universities were to blame (Gulli, 2007, p. 41). Instead, they suggested that a range of external influences were at play, including reduced government funding (which had resulted in increasing student/faculty ratios); inappropriate values instilled by parents and primary and high school experiences; the Internet; and increasing competition for grades and jobs.

Interestingly, by the time of this controversy, three Canadian research intensive universities—McMaster, Calgary and Queen's—had all established academic integrity offices. These were pointed to as tangible evidence of these institutions' commitment to encouraging academic honestly amongst students. Peter George, then President of McMaster University in Hamilton observed, "I would be devastated to think that some day a credential from any of our universities would be subject to some kind of doubt because of an epidemic of cheating that went unchecked" (Gulli, 2007, p. 41).

MacLean's March 5th, 2007 issue (*MacLean's*, 2007e, p. 6), included additional letters to the editor, commenting on parents inappropriately "helping" their children complete university assignments, students who lack basis mathematical and English literacy skills (suggesting lax standards in high school), and blatant cheating on exams outside of the academy, such as technical skills certification.

Finally, the April 2, 2007 issue—the university rankings issue—included a response from Claire Morris, then President of the Association of Universities and Colleges of Canada (AUCC), in which she appropriately clarified the limitations of the Christensen Hughes and McCabe (2006b) study. She also defended the commitment of Canada's universities claiming, they are "active and vigilant in combatting academic misconduct" using such strategies as "review of regulations on examinations, online tutorials for faculty and students on how to reduce cheating, the introduction of honour codes, workshops for faculty and educational sessions for students to help them better understand the issue of academic integrity" (*MacLean's*, 2007f, pp. 4–5).

This same issue featured an interview with Nobel laureate and physicist Carl Wieman, who had just joined the University of British Columbia to head the Carl Wieman Science Education Initiative. During the interview Carl was asked about his views on student cheating. His response focused on the purpose of education and the need to switch the focus from grades to learning; "when we work quite actively to convince [students]… that the purpose of them being in class is to learn certain things, that are of value, once you do that—and we have a little bit of data to support his—the cheating goes way down. Students realize they're actually cheating themselves" (*MacLean's*, 2007f, p. 13).

Following, many Canadian universities and colleges began to take concerted action, revisiting and revising their policies and practices, holding workshops and orientation events, and enhancing academic integrity resources and supports (including developing anti-plagiarism tutorials). Some of those who had participated in the original Christensen Hughes and McCabe survey, boldly went public with their results, posting them on on-line and acknowledging that they had a problem that needed addressing. In parallel, increasing attention to the quality of teaching and learning was well underway at teaching centres across the country, with enhanced attention being paid to student engagement and authentic assessment.

This was a busy time for me [Julia], as I was regularly invited to present keynote addresses and facilitate workshops on academic integrity at higher education institutions across the country. Specifically, I encouraged Canada's universities and colleges to collaboratively develop concrete plans, using what I called "5 levers for change":

1. Recommit to integrity as a core value.
2. Provide quality education.
3. Reform assessment practice.
4. Review, revise and clarify academic integrity/misconduct policies and procedures (including invigilation).
5. Provide educational/orientation activities.

Canadian Media Reports of Student Academic Misconduct, 2010–2020

In this section, we highlight cases of student misconduct (academic and co-curricular), at least one per year, reported by the mainstream Canadian media, as well as select academic sources, that occurred between 2010 and 2020. Rather than being exhaustive, we have included a curated list, adapted and extended from Eaton (2020a, b), demonstrating various types of student misconduct and associated concerns that have been publicly reported over the past decade. While we have chosen to focus on transgressions by undergraduate and graduate students here, we fully recognize that the questionable behaviour of faculty and senior administrators is an even more important issue, as faculty serve as essential role models, and administrators set the moral tone. It is also important to note that what comes to the attention of the press is arguably a small representation of the total number of incidents, given that many higher education institutions routinely endeavour to deal with, and report on, such incidents in private. We also observed that in attempting to find at least one story for each year (and in fact struggled to find one for 2012), our task became increasingly easier across time, suggesting academic misconduct may be becoming of increasing concern and/or increasingly prevalent.

This approach of reviewing media accounts to better understand academic misconduct, was previously employed by Osipian (2007), who systematically reviewed media accounts of corruption in higher education in the US, UK and Russia between 1998 and 2017. Osipian identified accounts of "bribery, fraud, cheating, plagiarism, diploma mills, breach of contract and other forms of misconduct" as well as "credentials fraud and research fraud" (p. 35). He concluded, "corruption in higher education receives good coverage in the media… [including] its significance, scale and scope, and variety of forms in which it manifests itself" (p. 34).

2010

In 2010, the Canadian Council on Learning (CCL) issued a press release, heralding their report *Liars, fraudsters and cheats: Dealing with the growth of academic dishonesty*. In it, Paul Cappon, then President and CEO of CCL advised:

> Over the past decade internet and high-tech devices have enabled a virtual explosion of classroom cheating… As this article reveals, educators, parents and students have to work together in order to properly address what has become a serious and widespread problem. (Canadian Council on Learning, 2010)

The press release and/or report were cited in several subsequent newspaper and academic articles. One focused on the increasing frequency of academic misconduct charges at the University of Toronto, providing specific examples (Brown, 2010). As one example, a student reportedly faced 67 charges before being expelled. In another, a TA was found to have charged students $1,500 CAD for providing answers during an exam. In yet another, a student falsified a doctor's note.

2011

The *Toronto Star* published *Cheating students get second chance in Newfoundland* (Allick, 2011), which reported on a new policy in Newfoundland and Labrador's largest school district. Students caught cheating were to receive a second chance rather than a zero—the opportunity to take "an alternate and appropriate assessment" with the student's mark being determined entirely from the new assessment. Teachers complained about the new policy; "cheating is wrong and there should be an academic deterrent for it".

2012

An article in the *Toronto Sun* reported that in 2012 a University of Toronto student was recommended for expulsion following an incident of exam impersonation:

> A chemistry professor realized one student, who was failing other parts of the course, performed particularly well in her midterm and final exams… Handwriting on the two exams also differed from handwriting on other assignments. The student was found guilty of having someone impersonate her at the two exams. The tribunal recommended expulsion. (Shah, 2013)

2013

A report by *CBC News* (2013a) concluded essay buying was a growing concern on Vancouver campuses; "An official with Simon Fraser University says more and more students are cheating by buying custom written essays online, instead of writing the assignments themselves", despite the high price tag, with a "10-page essay ranging from 250 to $400". The story also highlighted the problem of detection; "While both SFU and UBC use anti-plagiarism software to catch essays that lift entire passages or completely copy papers that might be online, the custom approach used by essay sellers makes it difficult for universities to detect" (2013a).

UBC's Sauder School of Business made headlines for a pro-rape chant, as part of its orientation activities, organized by its student-run Commerce Undergraduate Society (*CBC News*, 2013b). St. Mary's Student Union similarly made headlines for a chant based on an acronym for "young"—"Y is for your sister […] U is for underage, N is for no consent […] Saint Mary's boys we like them young" (*CBC News*, 2013c).

An article in the *Toronto Sun*, *Cheaters never prosper—if universities can catch them*, reported on cases adjudicated at the University of Toronto, including impersonation, buying papers, and fraudulent university records. The article also reported that the university had "expelled 45 students and recalled five students' degrees since 2006–2007" (Shah, 2013).

2014

The CBC released the results of a study of cheating at Canadian universities. A 2012 survey of 41 Canadian universities found approximately 7,000 cases of cheating had resulted in disciplinary action, ranging from 286 cases at the University of Manitoba, representing 1.0% of the student population, to 607 cases or 2.6% of students at Carleton (Moore, 2014). The point was made that there is a large discrepancy between the high percentage of students who have self-reported engaging in academic misconduct in research studies, and those who are caught and penalized.

MacLean's reported on the rising role of technology entitled, *New frontiers in high-tech cheating: With shrinking wireless devices, online classes and the emergence of wearable technology, it's easier than ever to cheat* (Counter, 2014). The story highlighted escalating use of wireless technology, making detecting exam based cheating increasingly difficult. One example shared from the University of Victoria included a student taking a medical school admission test wearing a pinhole camera, allowing him to transmit questions to tutors, who communicated answers back through a smartphone. The tutors were unwitting accomplices, thinking they were taking an employment test. The article suggested that "Apple Watch, Google Glass and 'invisible' Bluetooth earpieces" are becoming a challenge for instructors "who may not be as tech-savvy as their students", who don't want to run classrooms and exams "like a prison" and may be reluctant to "confiscate watches" (Counter, 2014, para. 9).

A female student from the University of Waterloo made the news for allegedly paying a male student from York University $900 to write her math exam (Caldwell, 2014; *CBC News*, 2014). According to officials from the university, "a 26-year-old PhD student at Toronto's York University was contacted by the first-year student through a website connecting international students to others who are willing to write exams for compensation" (*CBC News*, 2014, para. 2). Staff had been alerted to the possibility and had increased exam security including "mandatory student card scans, which would identify any fake documentation" (*CBC News*, 2014, para. 6). Both students faced criminal charges for personation and forgery (Caldwell, 2014, *CBC News*, 2014).

2015

Alex Gillis (2015), writing for *University Affairs* highlighted increasing opportunities for students to receive unpermitted help including customized papers (contract cheating) from Internet sources. Gillis (2015), noted "sites like GradeSaver.com and StudyMode.com (which claims to have nearly 16 million members) are glitzier and offer entire libraries of past essays for a fee" (para. 4). He explained, "At StudyMode.com, students upload their own papers to the site and pay $30 a month to get full access to other uploaded essays. In spite of much badly written content, StudyMode.com claims to be making $10 million a year from the use of its 1.5 million documents" (para. 6).

The *National Post* ran a story under the title, "Canada is at the leading edge of killing the dreaded annual 'final' for good" (Brean, 2015). Brean argued that high stakes exams are not effective, referencing the now infamous photo of relatives of students in India, climbing the walls of a school, to help the students cheat.

2016

The media reported on a case of exam impersonation at Concordia University, involving a 24-year old student and his tutor (Bernstien, 2016; Meagher, 2016). Allegedly, the student hired the tutor to impersonate him during a final exam. The tutor was employed by Montreal Tutoring, which describes itself as "Montreal's premier tutoring agency focusing on Concordia University & John Molson School of Business courses" (Bernstein, 2016). Both parties faced criminal charges, including conspiracy, forgery, and identity fraud. A university spokesperson commented (Meagher, 2016): "We really value academic integrity, and students are made well aware at the beginning of their courses that issues of cheating and plagiarism will not be tolerated. It's really well set out in our own codes of academic integrity."

Meagher (2016) also made it clear that impersonation is a criminal offence, citing Article 404 of the Canadian Criminal Code:

> Everyone who falsely, with intent to gain advantage for himself or some other person, personates a candidate at a competitive or qualifying examination held under the authority of law or in connection with a university, college or school or who knowingly avails himself of the results of such personation is guilty of an offence punishable on summary conviction.

2017

A number of news stories featured incidents at the University of Regina in 2017. These included a story about engineering professors being warned about teaching assistants allegedly taking bribes from students to increase grades, when entering marks for "assignments, quizzes, and exams": professors were urged to "please discourage your graduate students from taking any bribes to help undergraduate students cheat" (Leo, 2017a). A related story focused on a dean's computer allegedly being hacked, in which failing grades for four students were adjusted to passing grades (Leo, 2017b).

2018

The University of Regina continued to be the subject of several news stories in 2018. One explored how reports of academic misconduct had nearly doubled between 2013–2014 and 2016–2017 (Leo, 2018a). It is worth noting that increases in reports of academic misconduct do not necessarily mean increasing rates of misconduct, but rather, can reflect increased vigilance on the part of instructors at the institution. Two additional media reports pointed to "a significant amount" of academic misconduct in a class on law and ethics for engineering students (Leo, 2018b). The report also discussed cheating during a fourth-year law and ethics exam that led to changes in exam invigilation, including the use of cameras in exam rooms (Leo, 2018c).

City News reported on a story of contract cheating (Sutherland, 2018). Highlighted was the proliferation of flyers on lampposts and student desks at the University of Toronto, as well as campuses across the country, advertising 3rd party assignment completion services, featuring low prices and fast turnaround ("cheap and fast"). Sutherland suggested that such assignments are often completed by graduate students. Investigating one particular service, Sutherland (2018) found that a paper could be purchased from Ehomework.ca for $25 per page. Suggesting such services don't necessarily provide high quality work, the paper she received was shorter than requested and on the wrong topic.

The *Toronto Star* put the spotlight on Niagara College, after over 400 students were required to retake an in house English language proficiency test after being found to have inconsistent skills (Keung, 2018). Niagara had decided to investigate after a significant increase in the number of students deemed to be "at risk academically". The investigation found that as many as 200 students were failing due to inadequate English skills despite having passed the International English Language Testing System (IELTS) test, a standard for Canadian higher education institutions.

In another story, an Alberta judge upheld the University of Calgary's right to rescind a Master of Arts degree it had awarded to a student in 2003 due to plagiarism (*CBC News*, 2018). According to the report, the students' examination committee had raised a concern about plagiarism and had expected the issue to be addressed. Ten years later, Saint Mary's University (SMU) in Halifax who employed the individual as an instructor, requested a copy of the thesis. SMU ran the work through text-matching software and alerted the University of Calgary, who agreed that it contained substantial plagiarized elements. Subsequently, the University of Calgary attempted to rescind the degree. After a number of unsuccessful appeal attempts, the matter went to court, where the court upheld the University of Calgary's decision, ruling; "the university was entitled to rescind the degree once it found that the thesis included substantial plagiarism, because the power to award degrees necessarily implies the power of rescission" (*CBC News*, 2018).

2019

An entire class of students in a second-year nursing course at Brandon University faced disciplinary action after a final exam for the 2019 fall semester was deemed "compromised" (Slark, 2020). The students were offered the opportunity to re-take their final exam, with the caveat that the maximum they could earn would be 70%.

Burnaby RCMP investigated allegations of someone being paid to impersonate a student during a final exam at Simon Fraser University (Bains, 2019). The test writer was arrested.

Sutherland (2019) wrote a follow-up investigative piece on the existence of academic sweatshops that serve the contract cheating market. In *EXCLUSIVE investigation: Kenyan man says he wrote essays for Canadian students*, Sutherland reported that a Kenyan man (Joseph) contacted her, claiming he had written the paper she had reported on in 2018 (for which she had paid $165). Joseph said he had been hired as a freelance writer, after responding to a Craigslist advertisement. For Sutherland's paper, he had been paid $18 and promised assistance in immigrating to Canada. Joseph further claimed that he had "written hundreds of assignments for at least 50 students over the last year…for students from schools including University of Toronto, York, University of Ottawa and Simon Fraser" (Sutherland, 2019). Underscoring the growing concern surrounding contract cheating, Sutherland (2019) observed:

> A simple online search for terms like 'essay writing' or 'contract cheating' will bring up hundreds of results for services that offer to write university papers. Many promise original term or research papers by professional writers, delivered within a quick turnaround time. The websites may be able to skirt any legal complications by claiming to provide only notes or

> structure for essay writing. However, some states in the U.S. and countries like New Zealand have set up laws against providing any form of assistance to cheat, with penalties in place if caught. (Sutherland, 2019)

The article went on to highlight a specific problem with Canadian law:

> In Canada however, the practice is legal, with the onus falling on the student to do the right thing and only submit papers they have personally researched and written. Education lawyer John Schuman says legally, there's not much that can be done to prevent students from plagiarizing or purchasing fully written essays outright. "There isn't much by way of the law in Canada that addresses this type of academic dishonesty. That's entirely within the universities and their own codes of conduct and their own disciplinary procedures," he says. (Sutherland, 2019)

In another story twenty-two (22) construction electricians had their journeyperson certificates suspended or cancelled as a result of an investigation into exam cheating at Saskatchewan Polytechnic in Moosejaw (*CBC News*, 2019). An investigation found that apprentices had accessed unauthorized materials over several years. An instructor was subsequently fired for providing answers to exam questions and a staff member resigned (*CBC News*, 2019). Following, Saskatchewan Polytechnic conducted an internal audit on exam procedures (*CBC News*, 2019).

Rivers (2019), reported that while "[i]nternational students are boosting the bottom lines of Ontario's community colleges…they also are forcing schools to pay closer attention to cheating" (para. 1). An increase in incidents of academic misconduct at St. Clair College, for example, was attributed to increasing enrolments of international students, along with different cultural understandings of what constitutes plagiarism as well as pressure to succeed. Following, the college established an academic integrity coordinator position, to help address "a spike in cases of academic misconduct including plagiarism and using prohibited materials on exams" (para. 2) as well as offer mandatory workshops. The article also suggested, however, that rather than international students actually engaging in higher rates of cheating, it may be that plagiarism is easier to detect in second-language writers.

Writing in the *Financial Post*, Francis (2019), offered, "If you think cheating at universities is just an American problem, you're wrong". This article addressed the admissions scandal in the US, that resulted in fines and jail time for wealthy elites, having paid people to write their children's admission exams or help falsify sports experience. According to the article, "British Columbia businessman and philanthropist David Sidoo [was] alleged to have paid US$200,000 to have an American fly to Vancouver to take SAT tests for his sons". She also referenced the work of Sutherland (2018), concluding:

> the reality is that the incentive to cheat, to obtain a student visa or a prestigious degree, is too great to rely simply on the honour system. The vast majority of students work hard to achieve graduation, but Canada's institutions of higher learning, and lawmakers, must smarten up and close all loopholes. (Sutherland, 2018)

2020

In an opinion piece in *The Hill Times*, lawyers Juneau and Drapeau (2020) called out Canada's Royal Military College (RMC) for its "rape culture" reporting that "68% students witnessed or experienced unwanted sexualized behaviours and more than one in seven female cadets were sexually assaulted last year (15%)". Suggesting that RMC does not live up to its "core values of honour, courage, integrity, and to display the most scrupulous regard for the truth", they also reported that "[b]etween September 2014 and December 2016 there were 87 reported incidents of plagiarism and cheating, mostly committed by third- and fourth-year cadets" (Juneau & Drapeau, 2020).

Also during 2020, many articles focused on issues of misconduct associated with students completing exams remotely, as universities and colleges grappled with how to respond during the Covid19 pandemic. One article, "Ethicist raises concerns about program's ability to lock students' computers and monitor webcams" (Grabish, 2020), focused on the University of Manitoba's official choice of *Respondus* for monitoring and recording students during exams, on the basis of an algorithm (sound, eye movements, faces). Ethicist Neil McArthur raised issues with the technology:

> To have software that not only locks a student's computer but monitors their eye movements and their physical movements I think is a clear violation of privacy…The consent is complicated because what they're consenting to is in a sense coerced in that they need to compete for this in order to get to pass the course and write the exam. (Grabish, 2020)

Instead, he suggested using take-home exams within a 24 hour window, in which students are welcome to access and apply course material. In this same article, Red River College professor Connor Lloyd advised:

> By increasing the ways in which we evaluate students, we are able to provide more comprehensive assessments and take the weight off of a single exam. Our ultimate goal with this approach is to discourage cheating online and ensuring our students can access resources and supports early on to help them with their programs this fall. (Grabish, 2020)

Another article reported that 100 first year UBC students were accused of cheating on a math midterm, with the professor posting: "I am extremely disappointed to tell you that there were over 100 cases of cheating…If confirmed, the students involved will receive a 0% for the course (not just the midterm) and I will recommend their expulsion from UBC" (*CBC News*, 2020).

In summary, there were numerous stories reported in the press on student misconduct from 2010–2020. Collectively, they highlight several areas of concern, including behaviours pertaining to sexual assault and harassment, as well as methods by which students may be cheating on their academic work. The latter included: wearable, wireless high-tech devices for communicating with accomplices; paying (bribing) TAs for answers and inflated grades; exam impersonation; and contract cheating (customized essay buying from freelance writers and essay sweatshops). The students in the stories were alleged to have cheated on a variety of assignments and tests, including admissions, English proficiency tests, skills-based certification exams, scholarly papers and exams. Consequences varied, from the opportunity to redo the assignment, to more punitive measures, such as grade reductions, expulsion, the rescinding of degrees, and even criminal charges (in the case of fraud and exam impersonation). Steps reportedly being taken to reduce student misconduct were also reported, including better education for students on what is expected, innovation in assignment design and exam invigilation. Two articles also raised the point that contract cheating in Canada may be particularly hard to combat, given the lack of legislation prohibiting essay writing services.

The last year of our review period (2020) also raised many issues associated with the ethics and effectiveness of remote exam monitoring procedures. As the impact of the Covid-19 pandemic hit Canadian campuses, and courses and examinations pivoted to online environments, 2020 saw a rash of news reports concerning questionable online invigilation practices. Many of these raised concerns with the rise of the "surveillance state" and student privacy, including mental health effects and discrimination against racialized students (see Eaton & Turner, 2020).

The fact that stories became increasingly easy to find and numerous over the course of this review, as the years progressed, may suggest that misconduct in the Canadian academy is becoming increasingly common. Certainly the sophistication and brazenness of cheating methods appears to be growing, including the use of wireless technology. Third parties also appear to be increasingly involved, such as exam impersonators, those employed as freelance writers by contract cheating firms, and organizations that promote such unethical services.

Conclusion and Call to Action

Much has transpired across the Canadian higher education landscape since Christensen Hughes and McCabe (2006a, b) conducted their study on academic misconduct and recommended:

> Revisiting the goals and values of higher education, recommitting to quality in teaching and assessment practice, establishing effective policies and invigilation practices, providing educational opportunities and support for all members of the university community, and using (modified) academic honour codes. (Christensen Hughes & McCabe, 2006a, p. 49)

While this work attracted significant attention from national and local media, and many university and colleges revisited their policies and procedures, some establishing academic integrity offices as well as developing workshops, on-line tutorials and orientation activities, our current review suggests if anything, the problem has become substantially worse. While students admitted to many questionable behaviours in the Christensen Hughes and McCabe study (2006b), buying a paper to submit as one's own, was not among them. Interestingly, we didn't even think to include exam impersonation amongst our list of 25 questionable behaviours. In contrast, the newspaper articles cited above, suggest a culture may be emerging in which some students—buoyed perhaps from the relatively low percentage of those disciplined—are pursuing more extreme forms of cheating, including using wireless communications technology, hiring exam impersonators or engaging with contract cheating services (academic sweat shops) for their written assignments.

Given the essentiality of integrity to the academy, it appears that more drastic measures need to be taken, in order to combat such behaviours, and ensure the integrity of both admissions and degrees conferred. Specifically, we suggest a campaign of advocacy for changing Canada's laws, to restrict the aggressive sales tactics of contract cheating firms, making it illegal to run such businesses in Canada.

Faculty also need to be much better educated in the temptations and opportunities their students are facing and provided with assistance in developing assessment strategies that can help to combat such practices. In fact, we suggest a fundamental rethink of assessment, placing much more focus on authentic approaches, such as requiring students to demonstrate what they can do, as a result of their learning. Such demonstrations could include a podcast on a topic, a debate, or the presentation of a recommendation to a community client, in which the students have the opportunity to demonstrate their breadth and depth of knowledge, as well as their skills in communication, and ability to respond to complex questions.

Exam invigilation also needs to be substantially revisited, vigorously defending against impersonation and the use of prohibited electronic devices, while ensuring that students are not writing under duress or falsely accused. Finally, we wonder if the time may be right to signal institutional commitment by having faculty and students adopt an honour pledge (in contrast to the traditional or modified honour codes used in the United States, see Eaton & Christensen Hughes, 2022). Such a pledge could help communicate institutional commitment to the highest standards of integrity, perhaps taken at an invocation ceremony for new students. Certainly, to have any meaning, it would need to be reinforced through a variety of educational programs and policies, for faculty and students alike.

Clearly, the time has more than come for all of Canada's post-secondary institutions to make an unequivocal commitment to academic integrity, and to put in place effective strategies to support its achievement. We are fortunate to have a press that continues to call out incidents of misconduct, hopefully helping to ensure that this essential issue receives the attention it deserves.

References

Allick, C. (2011, October 24). Cheating students get second chance in Newfoundland. *The Toronto Star*. https://www.thestar.com/news/canada/2011/10/24/cheating_students_get_second_chance_in_newfoundland.html

Bains, M. (2019, December 18). Woman allegedly paid to take exam arrested at SFU. *CBC News*. https://www.cbc.ca/news/canada/british-columbia/burnaby-rcmp-investigate-after-sfu-catches-alleged-paid-test-taker-1.5400400

Bernstien, J. (2016, October 21). Concordia student and tutor face criminal charges for allegedly cheating on exam. *CBC News*. https://www.cbc.ca/news/canada/montreal/concordia-student-charged-for-cheating-1.3815520

Brean, J. (2015, April 2). The death of the exam: Canada is at the leading edge of killing the dreaded annual 'final' for good. *The National Post*. https://nationalpost.com/news/canada/the-death-of-the-exam-canada-is-at-the-leading-edge-of-killing-the-final-for-good

Brown, L. (2010, September 11). Student cheaters have plenty of tricks up their sleeves. *The Toronto Star*. https://www.thestar.com/life/parent/2010/09/11/student_cheaters_have_plenty_of_tricks_up_their_sleeves.html

Caldwell, B. (2014, April 17). Alleged cheats arrested over math exam at University of Waterloo. *The Record*. Retrieved May 27, 2021, from https://www.therecord.com/news-story/5210859-alleged-cheats-arrested-over-math-exam-at-university-of-waterloo/

Canadian Council on Learning. (2010). *The 21st century cheater: Academic dishonesty in Canada's schools*. https://www.newswire.ca/news-releases/the-21st-century-cheater-academic-dishonesty-in-canadas-schools-544695482.html

CBC News. (2013a, September 17). *B.C. universities struggle to crack down on essay-buying*. https://www.cbc.ca/news/canada/british-columbia/b-c-universities-struggle-to-crack-down-on-essay-buying-1.1858433

CBC News. (2013b, September 7). *UBC investigates frosh students' pro-rape chant: Chant condoned non-consensual sex with underage girls*. https://www.cbc.ca/news/canada/british-columbia/ubc-investigates-frosh-students-pro-rape-chant-1.1699589

CBC News. (2013c, September 5). *Saint Mary's frosh sex chant sparks review*. https://www.cbc.ca/news/canada/nova-scotia/saint-mary-s-frosh-sex-chant-sparks-review-1.1399544

CBC News. (2014, December 18). *Alleged exam cheating leads to fraud charges against 2 students in Waterloo*. https://www.cbc.ca/news/canada/kitchener-waterloo/alleged-exam-cheating-leads-to-fraud-charges-against-2-students-in-waterloo-1.2877980

CBC News. (2018, September 19). *Alberta judge upholds university's right to rescind master's degree over plagiarism*. https://www.cbc.ca/news/canada/calgary/alberta-judge-university-plagiarism-masters-degree-1.4830594

CBC News. (2019, July 4). *22 electricians penalized after probe into cheating at Sask Polytechnic*. https://www.cbc.ca/news/canada/saskatchewan/construction-electricians-certificates-cancelled-suspended-1.5200227

CBC News. (2020, November 24). *100 UBC students accused of cheating on math midterm*. https://www.cbc.ca/news/canada/british-columbia/ubc-cheating-midterm-math-100-1.5814234

Christensen Hughes, J. M., & McCabe, D. L. (2006a). Academic misconduct within higher education in Canada. *The Canadian Journal of Higher Education, 36*(2), 1–21.

Christensen Hughes, J. M., & McCabe, D. L. (2006b). Understanding academic misconduct. *Canadian Journal of Higher Education, 36*(1), 49–63.

Counter, R. (2014, October 19). New frontiers in high-tech cheating: With shrinking wireless devices, online classes and the emergence of wearable technology, it's easier than ever to cheat. *MacLean's*. https://www.macleans.ca/education/uniandcollege/new-frontiers-in-high-tech-cheating/

Eaton, S. E. (2021). *Plagiarism in higher education: Tackling tough topics in academic integrity*. Libraries Unlimited.

Eaton, S. E. (2020a, January 13). *An inquiry into major academic integrity violations in Canada: 2010–2019*. http://hdl.handle.net/1880/111483

Eaton, S. E. (2020b). *Significant incidents of academic misconduct in Canada 2010–2019—Timeline Infographic*. http://hdl.handle.net/1880/111435

Eaton, S. E., & Christensen Hughes, J. (2022). Academic integrity in Canada: Historical perspectives and current trends. In S. E. Eaton & J. Christensen Hughes (Eds.), *Academic integrity in Canada: An enduring and essential challenge*. Springer.

Eaton, S. E., & Turner, K. L. (2020). Exploring academic integrity and mental health during COVID-19: Rapid review. *Journal of Contemporary Education Theory & Research, 4*(1), 35–41. https://doi.org/10.5281/zenodo.4256825

Francis, D. (2019, April 9). If you think cheating at universities is just an American problem, you're wrong, *Financial Post*. https://financialpost.com/diane-francis/if-you-think-cheating-at-universities-is-just-an-american-problem-youre-wrong

Gillis, A. (2015, March 23). Academic misconduct 'likely' on the rise in Canada. *University Affairs*. https://www.universityaffairs.ca/news/news-article/academic-misconduct-likely-on-the-rise-in-canada/

Grabish, A. (2020, August 18). University of Manitoba uses anti-cheating software to monitor remote exams. *CBC News*. https://www.cbc.ca/news/canada/manitoba/anti-cheating-software-university-of-manitoba-1.4223737

Gulli. (2017, February 26). Cheating? Who us? Most universities prefer to keep quiet on the topic of academic fraud. *MacLean's* (p. 41). https://archive.macleans.ca/article/20070226043/print

Gulli, C., Kohler, N., & Patriquin, M. (2007, February 12). The great university cheating scandal. *MacLean's*. https://archive.macleans.ca/article/2007/2/12/the-great-university-cheating-scandal

Juneau, J., & Drapeau, M. (2020, November 2). Royal military college, a dishonoured tradition. *The Hill Times*. https://www.hilltimes.com/2020/11/02/royal-military-college-a-dishonoured-tradition/269629

Keung, N. (2018, December 8). More than 400 students in India told to retake language tests after Niagara College flags concerns. *Toronto Star*. https://www.thestar.com/news/canada/2018/12/08/400-students-in-india-told-to-retake-language-tests-after-niagara-college-flags-concerns.html

Leo, G. (2017a, October 26). U of R engineering profs warned about teaching assistants taking bribes to increase grades. *CBC News*. http://www.cbc.ca/news/canada/saskatchewan/unviersity-of-regina-engineering-teaching-assistants-1.4369110

Leo, G. (2017b, October 24). U of R grades hacked through dean's computer account, according to internal email. *CBC News*. http://www.cbc.ca/news/canada/saskatchewan/university-of-regina-engineering-grades-hacked-dean-1.4368984

Leo, G. (2018a, March 23). Cheating incidents in the U of R faculty of arts have almost doubled in the past three years. *CBC News*. http://www.cbc.ca/news/canada/saskatchewan/cheating-incidents-in-the-u-of-r-faculty-of-arts-have-almost-doubled-in-the-past-three-years-1.4587953

Leo, G. (2018b, March 11). U of Regina suspects 'significant' number of students cheated in law and ethics class. *CBC News*. http://www.cbc.ca/news/canada/saskatchewan/university-regina-engineering-cheating-1.4567955

Leo, G. (2018c, April 12). U of R to record video in exam rooms to catch cheaters. *CBC News*. http://www.cbc.ca/news/canada/saskatchewan/u-of-r-to-record-video-in-exam-rooms-to-catch-cheaters-1.4617180

MacLean's. (2007a, February 12). *With more than half of Canadian university students cheating, all degrees are tainted. It's a national scandal. Why aren't schools doing more about it?* https://archive.macleans.ca/issue/20070212

MacLean's. (2007b, February 12). *Universities simply have to do better* (p. 4). https://archive.macleans.ca/issue/20070212

Maclean's. (2007c, Februray 19). *Go ahead and cheat* (p. 2). https://archive.macleans.ca/issue/20070219

MacLean's. (2007d, February 26). *Why not check out what's going on in high school? Most students don't get out of grade school without cheating.* https://archive.macleans.ca/issue/20070226

MacLean's. (2007e, March 5). *Students email essays to parents for editing or rewriting. Call it fraud lite.* March 5. https://archive.macleans.ca/issue/20070305

MacLean's. (2007f, March 12). *Vigilant on cheating* (pp. 4–5). https://archive.ma https://archive.macleans.ca/issue/20070312cleans.ca/issue/20070312

Meagher, J. (2016, October 21). Concordia student, tutor face criminal charges in exam cheating case. *Montreal Gazette*. https://montrealgazette.com/news/local-news/concordia-student-tutor-face-criminal-charges-in-exam-cheating-case

Moore, H. (2014, February 25). Cheating students punished by the 1000s, but many more go undetected: CBC survey shows 7,086 students disciplined for cheating at Canadian universities in 2011–12. *CBC News*. https://www.cbc.ca/news/canada/manitoba/cheating-students-punished-by-the-1000s-but-many-more-go-undetected-1.2549621

Osipian, A. (2007). Higher education corruption in world media, prevalence, patterns and forms. In *Proceedings of 32nd Annual Conference of the Association for the Study of Higher Education*

(ASHE), Louisville, Kentucky, MPRA Paper 8475, University Library of Munich. https://mpra.ub.uni-muenchen.de/8475/

Rivers, H. (2019, November 7). Surge in international students forcing colleges to step up anti-cheating campaigns. *The London Free Press*. https://lfpress.com/news/local-news/surge-in-international-students-forcing-colleges-to-step-up-anti-cheating-campaigns

Shah, M. (2013, September 7). Cheaters never prosper—If universities can catch them. *Toronto Sun*. https://torontosun.com/2013/09/07/cheaters-never-prosper--if-universities-can-catch-them)

Slark, C. (2020, January 9). BU nursing students punished after exam 'compromised'. *The Brandon Sun*. https://www.brandonsun.com/local/BU-nursing-students-punished-after-exam-compromised-566835141.html

Sutherland, T. (2018, March 22). Homework for hire: What schools can do about third-party essay writing services. *City News Toronto* (Producer). Rogers Media. https://youtu.be/2j9ZG7CA-e8

Sutherland, T. (2019, February 19). Exclusive investigation: Kenyan man says he wrote essays for Canadian students. *City News Toronto* (Producer). Rogers Media. https://toronto.citynews.ca/2019/02/19/cheating-at-u-of-t/

Julia Christensen Hughes, Ph.D. has long advocated for ensuring the highest standards of academic integrity in higher education—in teaching, research and administrative practice. Her article, Academic Misconduct within Higher Education in Canada, with the late Don McCabe (published in 2006, in the *Canadian Journal of Higher Education*), received the Sheffield Award for research excellence (2007), from the Canadian Society for Studies in Higher Education. As former and founding Dean of the Gordon S. Lang School of Business and Economics (2009–2019) at the University of Guelph, Julia was a champion of business ethics, corporate social responsibility and the need for business schools to be aligned with the UN's Sustainable Development Goals (SDG's). In her new role as President of Yorkville University, Julia is looking forward to enhancing the institution's long-standing commitment to integrity.

Sarah Elaine Eaton, Ph.D. is an Associate Professor in the Werklund School of Education and the inaugural Educational Leader in Residence, Academic Integrity, University of Calgary. She is also the Editor-in-Chief of the *International Journal for Educational Integrity* and the author of *Plagiarism in Higher Education: Tackling Tough Topics in Academic Integrity* (ABC Clio, 2021). Her research focuses on ethics and integrity in higher education and she has led numerous research teams and the local and national levels. Eaton advocates for pro-active and multi-stakeholder approaches to upholding and enacting integrity throughout the academy.

Chapter 4
Academic Misconduct in Higher Education: Beyond Student Cheating

Julia Christensen Hughes and Sarah Elaine Eaton

Abstract When people hear the term "academic misconduct", student cheating often comes to mind. In this chapter we provide a broader perspective, presenting formal definitions of the terms academic integrity and academic misconduct, arguing that such concepts should apply to all members of the academy. Unfortunately, research conducted in the UK and the US suggests that faculty and administrators engage in misconduct and unethical practice, in research as well as other domains. Here we review policy changes in Canada's approach to dealing with research misconduct, with the aim of strengthening "Canada's research integrity system" (HAL in Innov Policy Econ, 2009, i). We also present public accounts of academic transgressions by Canadian faculty and administrators, with a primary focus on research misconduct. A query of *Retraction Watch* found 321 retractions involving academics working in Canadian higher education institutions during the years 2010–2020. Articles in the press are then used to further highlight incidents of academic fraud and plagiarism, as well as questionable practices in student supervision, hiring practices, international student recruitment, and inappropriate interpersonal relationships. We conclude by calling for a comprehensive study of academic misconduct by faculty and administrators at Canadian higher education institutions as well as an assessment of how well the changes to Canada's policies on research misconduct are working, particularly with respect to public disclosure.

Keywords Faculty · Administrators · Academic Misconduct · Research Misconduct

J. Christensen Hughes (✉)
Yorkville University, Toronto, Canada
e-mail: jchristensen@yorkvilleu.ca

S. E. Eaton (✉)
University of Calgary, Calgary, Canada
e-mail: seaton@ucalgary.ca

S. E. Eaton and J. Christensen Hughes (eds.), *Academic Integrity in Canada*, Ethics and Integrity in Educational Contexts 1,
https://doi.org/10.1007/978-3-030-83255-1_4

Introduction

The term "academic misconduct" is often narrowly used in reference to various types of student violations of academic integrity such as plagiarism or exam cheating. In this chapter, we challenge this notion by providing a broader perspective. We begin with a discussion of the formal definitions of the terms academic integrity and academic misconduct, arguing that such concepts must apply to all members of the academy, and in particular, the behaviour of faculty and administrators who serve as important role models and set the moral tone. Unfortunately, and despite the essentiality of integrity to the academic mission, research suggests that some administrators and faculty do engage in misconduct, including in their scholarly pursuits, as well as administrative practices.

Next, we review calls made between 2007 and 2011 to strengthen "Canada's research integrity system" (HAL, 2009, i), as well as the policy changes that followed. Building on the work of Eaton (2020a, b; 2021), we then present examples of research misconduct as well as other transgressions by faculty and administrators, highlighting common themes. In particular, we present the results of a query to a data base maintained by *Retraction Watch*, which found 321 retractions involving academics working at Canadian higher education institutions between 2010–2020, as well as stories of misconduct in the Canadian media. We conclude by calling for a comprehensive study of academic misconduct by faculty and administrators at Canadian higher education institutions as well as an assessment of how well the changes to Canada's policies on research misconduct are working, particularly with respect to public disclosure.

Defining Academic Integrity and Academic Misconduct

In the *Handbook of Academic Integrity*, editor Tracey Bretag (2016) observed, "[a]cademic integrity is such a multifarious topic that authors around the globe report differing historical developments which have led to a variety of interpretations of it as a concept and a broad range of approaches to promulgating it in their own environments" (p. 3).

In 1999, the International Center for Academic Integrity (ICAI) advanced what has arguably become the most common definition of academic integrity in use in Canada today: "A commitment, even in the face of adversity, to five fundamental values: honesty, trust, fairness, respect and responsibility" (ICAI, 2021). A sixth value—"courage"—was added later, in recognition that doing the right thing, in the face of adversity, can require considerable personal courage.

Similar to many of the concepts embedded in this multi-faceted definition, the Merriam Webster (n.d. a) on-line dictionary, defines integrity as, "firm adherence to a code of especially moral or artistic values: incorruptibility. 2: an unimpaired condition: soundness. 3: the quality or state of being complete or undivided: completeness."

Its synonyms include, "character, decency, goodness, honesty, morality, probity, rectitude, righteousness, rightness, uprightness, virtue, virtuousness" (Merriam Webster n.d. a).

In contrast, misconduct—often mistakenly treated as an antonym to integrity—is defined much more narrowly. Merriam Webster (n.d. b) defines misconduct as, "1: mismanagement especially of governmental or military responsibilities. 2: intentional wrongdoing specifically: deliberate violation of a law or standard especially by a government official: MALFEASANCE. 3a: improper behavior…". Its synonyms include, "malfeasance, misbehavior, misdoing, wrongdoing" (Merriam Webster, n.d. b).

Applying these concepts to higher education in Canada, and writing in University Affairs, Mullens (2000, p. 23), lamented that "maintain[ing] a culture of academic integrity is now a considerable worry on campuses across Canada". Narrowly focusing on the behaviour of students, she defined academic dishonesty as, "anything that gives a student an unearned advantage over another."

Many Canadian institutions have drawn on one or more of these concepts in advancing their own definitions. As one example, Ryerson University's Senate documents draw explicitly from the ICAI's definition, applying academic integrity to all members of the university, yet define academic misconduct as a student-focused concern:

> This policy is premised on the commitment of the University to foster and uphold the highest standards of academic integrity, the fundamental values of which are honesty, trust, fairness, respect, responsibility, courage …All members of the University community, including faculty, students, graduate assistants (GAs), and staff, have a responsibility to adhere to and uphold [these values] in their teaching, learning, evaluation, research, and creative activity. This includes a responsibility to take action if they have reasonable grounds for thinking that academic misconduct has occurred.
>
> Academic Misconduct is any behaviour that undermines the university's ability to evaluate fairly students' academic achievements, or any behaviour that a student knew, or reasonably ought to have known, could gain them or others unearned academic advantage or benefit, counts as academic misconduct. (Policy 60, Ryerson, n.d.)

In its definition of academic integrity, the University of Waterloo similarly draws on the ICAI's definition, emphasizes that it applies to everyone, and explains why integrity in the awarding of degrees is important:

> Whether learning, teaching, researching or working, members of our community must conduct themselves honestly. Acting with integrity reinforces the university's reputation as a leading teaching and research institution.
>
> As a post-secondary institution, the value of the degrees the university awards deserving students at the end of their studies is dependent on the legitimacy of the education these students earn. A degree is valueless without integrity… . (University of Waterloo, n.d.)

Waterloo also cites the teachings of the *Seven Grandfathers in Academic Integrity* (Maracle, 2020), first adopted by the University of Toronto, which include: Respect, Bravery, Honesty, Wisdom, Humility, Truth, and Love.

Individual faculties and departments within Canada's higher education institutions have embraced similar approaches. As one example, the Faculty of Health

Sciences and Wellness at Humber College also draws on the ICAI's definition while encouraging students to take an academic integrity pledge; "Each year, approximately 1,500 students pledge to study with the values of honesty, trust, fairness, respect, and responsibility with courage even when faced with adversity" (Humber College, n.d.).

Academic associations in Canada have also advanced definitions and stated their commitment to upholding integrity. Universities Canada's statement on academic freedom, for example, includes the declaration that, "central to the mandate of Canadian universities has long been the pursuit of truth, the education of students and the dissemination of knowledge" (Dea, 2019). According to Dea, faculty are expected to uphold certain tenants while engaging in these pursuits, including:

> [C]onducting scholarship honestly, ethically, and according to the standards of your discipline or subdiscipline. That means performing your assigned teaching duties, grading student work fairly, subjecting one's work to peer review, reporting research results honestly, properly crediting other scholars' contributions, being careful not to misrepresent one's own expertise or position (for instance, being clear that one's extramural expression does not represent one's university), and so on. (Dea, 2019)

Colleges and Institutes Canada, which represents Canada's colleges, institutes, cegeps and polytechnics, recently produced a strategic plan (2019–2024), that similarly (but less specifically) acknowledges the organization's commitment to upholding "the principles of agility, inspiring others, and integrity in all that we do" (Colleges and Institutes Canada, 2021).

Upholding such values could not be more essential to the success of higher education institutions, whether conferring students with degrees, disseminating research findings in service to society, administering policies and practices, or providing strategic leadership, shaping institutional priorities and cultures. Indeed, higher education institutions have long been "perceived as epitomizing intellectual and social honesty, and they are expected to strive continually for that form of perfection" (Besvinick, 1983, p. 569). Yet evidence suggests—as presented in the next section and elsewhere—higher education has long fallen short of this promise (see for example Christensen Hughes 2022). We begin the next section with a brief review of faculty and administrator misconduct in the academy, in Britain, the US and elsewhere.

Misconduct in the Academy

Ten years ago Stone and Starkey (2011), provided a damning report on "doubtful ethics" in the British academy. Reflecting on their personal experience as instructors, and following a comprehensive literature review, the authors suggested that as a result of myriad factors, including economic pressures and government imposed performance metrics, many higher education institutions had become "self-serving, marketised, institutions, where students who pay increasingly high fees are subject to increasingly poor teaching and declining quality standards" (p. 156). They observed that the top priorities of higher education had become "money and research, while students come a poor third…Universities beckon students to come and learn, but are actually institutions primarily for maximising career opportunities for their staff, who teach decreasing hours and vie for promotion" (p. 158).

Corrupt, unethical and questionable practices they found evidence of pertained to a variety of domains, including (Stone & Starkey, 2011, 159–60):

- journal practices (poor quality refereeing, insider clubs, inappropriate credit—forced addition of senior names and suppression of junior names).
- access (favouring "well-connected" applicants and athletes; administrators taking bribes; students faking qualifications);
- falsified grades and degrees (bought through diploma mills, bribes, sexual favours);
- foreign student fees (attracting large numbers of unqualified students for tuition revenue);
- plagiarism and cheating (contract cheating, faculty not enforcing codes of conduct);
- quality issues (poor teaching, unclear/inappropriate assessment criteria, overly generous in marking to increase retention and student satisfaction scores, failure to update teaching material);
- faculty research (skimming funds, commercial funding influence, falsification of results, plagiarism); and,
- falsification of faculty records (falsification of CVs, representing faculty as employed and contributing to university when they are not, in order to drive rankings)

Ospian (2004, 2007) similarly explored corruption in higher education, which he concluded was related to issues of access, quality and equity (2007, p. 2). The examples he identified, based on his review of articles in the press in the US, UK and Russia, included "bribery, fraud, cheating, plagiarism, diploma mills, breach of contract and other forms of misconduct" as well as "credentials fraud and research fraud" (2007, p. 35).

Highlighting the difficulty of assessing the extent to which faculty research misconduct may be occurring, Smith (2006) observed:

> Most cases are probably not publicized. They are simply not recognized, covered up altogether, or the guilty researcher is urged to retrain, move to another institution or retire from research. (Smith, 2006, p. 4)

Further, Smith (2006) suggested that while some researchers are found guilty, fired and/or professionally disgraced, supervisors have treated such cases as "isolated incident[s]", and have been "slow to respond" (p. 1).

So concerning has research misconduct become, that explanations for its occurrence—in peer reviewed papers and faculty blogs alike—have shifted from the personal ("bad apples") to the systemic ("bad barrels" and "bad systems"), such as publication pressures and competition for research funding (Huistra & Paul, 2021, p. 2). Gervais (2021), for example, described a "toxic scientific ecosystem" in psychology (p. 15), evidenced by a "flurry of unsuccessful replications of prominent work, exposure of scientific fraud and negligence bordering on fraud, and publication of highly implausible research" (p. 1).

Another study investigated the practices of academic journal editors (Hamilton et al., 2020, p. 1). Despite its centrality to academic quality, they found wide variation in peer review processes, including that the majority allowed authors to recommend reviewers. Only half (49%) routinely checked for plagiarism.

Faculty are bemoaning the lack of standards and emerging pressures that are further eroding publishing system. Jones (2021) observed, "we are heading rather rapidly into a blizzard of material with no vetting or meaningful review" (para. 2). Specific concerns identified by Jones (2021) included: "open access upon publication"; "high levels of publication for tenure, promotion and funding"; "preprint servers"; "junk journals"; "reviewer fatigue"; and, "expansion of research into more of academia" (para. 3).

In keeping with these findings and perspectives, Smith (2006) observed, "All human activity is associated with misconduct. Indeed, misconduct may be easier for scientists because the system operates on trust" (p. 4). Further, junior researchers are often the whistleblowers, who can "encounter more problems than those on whom they blow the whistle—even when they are thoroughly vindicated" (p. 5). Recommendations from Smith (2006) included modernizing the accountability of journal editors, and creating "a national body to provide leadership" (p. 4).

Faculty and Administrator Misconduct in Canada

A comprehensive study has not yet been undertaken on misconduct by faculty and administrators at Canadian higher educational institutions. The types of behaviours, systemic pressures and potential solutions identified above, could provide a useful framework for such an undertaking. For now, in this section and building on the work of Eaton (2020a, b; 2021), we share examples of alleged academic misconduct by Canadian faculty and senior administrators available via *Retraction Watch* (n.d. a) and as reported in the Canadian press. While we have chosen to largely focus on research misconduct, other transgressions, such as those involving plagiarized speeches, questionable admissions practices, and inappropriate interpersonal relationships are also briefly highlighted.

Seemingly not as plentiful as media accounts of student cheating (see Christensen Hughes & Eaton, 2022), or misconduct by faculty and administrators in other countries (as reviewed above), we wondered if Canadian institutions are better at covering up transgressions (dealing with such issues confidentially as private, personnel matters), or if such incidents are in fact less prevalent than elsewhere. Regardless, cases of research misconduct by those working at Canada's higher education institutions became sufficiently concerning, that between 2007 and 2011 a concerted effort was made to review and strengthen the country's research integrity policies. We begin the next section by providing examples of the types of incidents that prompted this national response, as well as some of the key observations and recommendations that followed.

Efforts to Strengthen Canada's Integrity System

One of the most well-known Canadian cases of research misconduct involved R. K. Chandra, a faculty member at Memorial University, who was suspected of fabricating or falsifying data across multiple publications (Smith, 2006). While the university reportedly investigated and found no problem, Chandra ultimately left, moving to Switzerland. In 2005 the CBC produced a three part investigative series on Chandra, called *The Secret Life of Dr. Chandra* (CBC News, 2005), claiming that he had hundreds of bank accounts and suggesting that Chandra may have engaged in a number of fraudulent financial activities over many years.

Another high profile Canadian case involved Eric Poehlman, who was hired by the University of Montreal and awarded a Canada Research Chair, while being under investigation for numerous research violations in the US (Dalton, 2005). After resigning his faculty position, Poehlman "acknowledged falsifying 17 grant applications to the National Institutes of Health (NIH) for nearly $3 million, and fabricating data in ten published articles" (Dalton, 2005, para. 2).

Suggesting that other academics have quietly moved along once suspicions have been raised, Daniel Kwok, an engineering professor and Canada Research Chair at the University of Alberta was being investigated for misconduct, including inappropriately using research funds for personal benefit (purchasing car parts and entertainment systems) before he moved to the University of Calgary. Once there, he came under additional scrutiny and was eventually banned from future funding by Canada's National Sciences and Engineering Research Council (NSERC). Kwok was accused of plagiarism and the fraudulent use of research funds, also over many years (Hoag, 2010; Jerema, 2010; Munro, 2010).

Highlighting problems arising from the undue influence of industry partners, Barbara Sherwin, a psychology professor at McGill, is alleged to have been "part of a ghostwriting scheme paid for by drug giant Wyeth Pharmaceuticals to promote its products" (Laidlaw, 2009). Her compromised paper, published in the *Journal of the American Geriatrics Society,* suggested that estrogen could be effective for treating memory loss, cardiovascular disease, osteoporosis, and colorectal cancer.

Growing concern over cases such as these prompted the *Canadian Research Integrity Committee* (CRIC) to host a workshop on *Research Integrity: Towards a Canadian Approach* in 2007. Those involved included representatives from "16 Canadian research and academic institutions", the Association of Faculties of Medicine of Canada", and Canada's three national granting councils: the Canadian Institute of Health Research (CIHR), the Natural Sciences and Engineering Research Council of Canada (NSERC) and the Social Sciences and Humanities Research Council (SSHRC) (HAL, 2009, p. 1). The workshop resulted in the CRIC commissioning a study to review research integrity in Canada.

Consulting firm Hickling, Arthurs, Low (HAL), undertook the project, producing *The State of Research Integrity and Misconduct Policies in Canada* (HAL, 2009). The report's stated purpose was to "develop a comprehensive understanding of the organizations and policies that define how allegations of research misconduct are addressed in Canada and in other selected countries" and to "inform a discussion… about how best to strengthen Canada's research integrity system" (HAL, 2009, p. i).

The HAL (2009) report highlighted the damaging consequences of fraudulent research such as wasted resources (time, effort and money) as well as "potential harm to individuals and society" (p. i) including "unsafe products" and eroding "the public's trust in science" (p. ii). It also noted the importance of Canada's *Tri-council Policy Statement on Integrity in Research and Scholarship* (TCPS-IRS). In Canada, higher education institutions are responsible for responding to allegations of misconduct, in keeping with "the framework of the TCPS-IRS, and other institutional, international and, or, provincial policies" (p. ii).

Shortcomings of Canada's approach were found to be numerous, including: "a weakness in formal oversight; inadequate reporting requirements; inconsistent educational efforts; differing definitions as to what constitutes research misconduct; and poor whistleblower assistance" (HAL, 2009, p. iv). In terms of prevalence, the 29 institutions that participated in the study reported "dealing with some 39 cases per year" (p. iv). The report also acknowledged that these numbers likely understated the extent of the problem, given myriad factors including a tendency to sweep such issues "under the carpet" (p. iv).

While acknowledging variation in institution-specific definitions and policies, and the importance of exercising discretion in cases "based on misunderstanding or due to poor oversight" (HAL, 2009, p. iii), the HAL report underscored that "more needs to be done in Canada to address research integrity" (p. 4). This conclusion echoed a question raised in the Canadian Medical Association Journal; "Why has Canada lagged so far behind its Western counterparts in establishing comprehensive mechanisms and processes to deal with scientific misconduct?" (Kondro & Hebert, 2007).

Recommendations included the adoption of "an explicit national definition of research misconduct that identifies sanctionable behaviors in addition to the current definition of research integrity" (HAL, 2009, p. iii). They also recommended, "strengthened reporting requirements that necessitate the public reporting on an annual basis of all cases where research misconduct is found" (p. v). Other possible actions included the establishment of a "national system that gives well-meaning individuals with concern a place to go for information and assistance that is independent from their employer" (p. iv), such as an "Office of an Ombudsperson" or a "Canadian Office of Research Integrity" (p. vi).

Shortly after, a related study was undertaken at the request of Tony Clement, then Canada's Minister of Industry. An expert panel, under the auspices of the Council of Canadian Academies (CCA), and chaired by Paul Davenport, former president of Western University, produced a second report, *Honesty, Accountability and Trust: Fostering Research Integrity in Canada* (CCA, 2010). Amongst this report's recommendations was that "Canada must address the gaps in the existing research system that are undermining the system's transparency and accountability" (CCA, 2010, p. 2). Highlighting the panel's support for disclosing the names of "researchers and institutions convicted of breaching research integrity policy and the details of any imposed sanctions", Paul Davenport acknowledged, "There is a tension between society's desire to know quickly about allegations and to have strong privacy law" (Hoag, 2010).

Other recommendations included, "Canada needs a common, system-wide approach to research integrity that involves all actors"; "There is a need to foster a positive, values-based environment of research integrity in Canada", and "Canada needs a new entity, the Canadian Council for Research Integrity [CCRI], to serve as a central educational and advisory arm on issues of research integrity" (CCA, 2010, p. 2).

There were at least three significant outcomes from these undertakings. The first was the launch in 2011 of the Advisory Panel on Responsible Conduct of Research (PRCR). The PRCR's mandate is to:

> consider allegations of breaches of Tri-Agency policies by reviewing institutional investigation reports; recommend recourse, if appropriate, consistent with the Framework; provide advice to the Agencies on matters related to the responsible conduct of research; provide advice to the Agencies on revisions to the Framework; and review the Framework every five years. (PRCR, 2016)

The second, was that beginning November, 2011, under the auspices of the PRCR, researchers seeking funding from Canada's granting agencies were required to consent to having their names officially released, should a serious breach of research integrity be found to have occurred (Consent to Disclosure of Personal Information—Frequently Asked Questions, 2016):

> The Agencies may also publicly disclose information related to a serious breach without consent, if "in the opinion of the head of the institution, the public interest in disclosure clearly outweighs any invasion of privacy that could result from the disclosure" (Privacy Act, 8(2) (m) (i)). (PRCR, 2017)

The third was the publication of the *Tri-Agency Framework:Responsible Conduct of Research*, referred to in the PRCR mandate, which was updated in 2016 (see *RCR Framework*, 2016). In the spring of 2021, the PRCR undertook a second revision of the Framework, through a process of public consultation. Proposed revisions pertained to clarifying certain definitions such as "lack of rigour", "falsification", and "destruction of research records". Other revisions sought to clarify and expand the responsibilities of researchers and institutions, such as providing "adequate oversight of, and training to, their trainees and staff in responsible conduct of research", and being "proactive in supporting a healthy research environment". Other items pertained to process, including "guidance on what institutions should consider disclosing at the end of an RCR process" (*RCR Framework* (2016) – Proposed Revisions for Public Consultation, 2021). This last item was likely the most contentious of the recommendations.

Despite the existence of disclosure policy, it is noteworthy that only one case to date—that of Sophie Jamal—has been officially released (Oransky, 2016). In this particular case, the CIHR permanently banned Jamal from further funding. Jamal resigned from Women's College Hospital (WCH) and the University of Toronto, following an investigation in which she was found to have:

> Manipulated study data with the intention of supporting the underlying hypothesis of research studies; intentionally manipulated electronic datasets and presented them as raw data to investigators; falsely accused a research assistant of having carried out the manipulations; failed to correct the errors once the problems were discovered; shared manipulated rather than primary data with colleagues; deleted records that were to form part of WCH's forensic investigation; failed to retain research data to a standard appropriate to the discipline; and impeded an institutional investigation. (Oransky, 2016)

Responding to Canada's long standing practice of keeping such incidents private, James Turk, executive director of the Canadian Association of University Teachers, observed, "If someone is convicted of research misconduct, that should be known…if there is a finding of research misconduct then I think it should be made public" (Munro, 2011). The proposed 2021 revisions, do not make public disclosure any more likely, with its stated clarification that "Recourse against a Respondent should only be shared with the Respondent" (*RCR Framework* (2016) – Proposed Revisions for Public Consultation, 2021).

Retraction Watch

One organization dedicated to helping make serious incidents of research misconduct public is *Retraction Watch* (n.d. a). Supported by the MacArthur Foundation, the Arnold Foundation, and the Helmsley Trust, researchers Dr. Adam Marcus and Dr. Ivan Oransky founded *Retraction Watch* in 2010 as result of their growing concern about misconduct in medical research, the amount of time it was taking for retractions to occur, and the ongoing citation of discredited work. They concluded that engaging the media was essential for correcting the record; "If highlighting retractions will give journalists more tools to uncover fraud and misuse of funds, we're happy to help" (Oransky & Marcus, 2010).

Retraction Watch publishes daily accounts as well as weekly summaries of some of the most egregious practices, including fabricated data, doctored slides, and unreported conflicts of interest, particularly galling in pharmaceutical research published in medical journals. As one example, *Retraction Watch* is keeping a running tally of papers retracted concerning Covid-19. By April 2021, over 100 were on the list, with several other papers receiving "expressions of concern" (Retraction Watch, n.d. b).

In addition to highlighting recent publications, *Retraction Watch* also tracks papers published decades earlier that have been recently challenged on the basis of changing societal norms and evolving understandings of "bad" science. As one example, *Retraction Watch* (2020a) reported on the retraction of a paper on homosexuality and conversion therapy, published in 1951 in *the Journal of Nervous and Mental Disease*. Current journal editor John Talbott observed how social norms impact scientific findings:

> The 1951 Glover article supports long discredited beliefs, prejudices, and practices (conversion therapy) and will be retracted as requested. It will, however, be kept in the journal's archives for its historical value...But journals like this one, published papers in the past reflecting many other beliefs we find abhorrent today, such as those on eugenics, the disabled, women, Blacks, sexual problems, and yes, sexuality. (Retraction Watch, 2020a)

Highlighting the social harm such research can effect, *Retraction Watch* observed that the paper, "offered a medical rationale for President Eisenhower's 1953 declaration that homosexuals represented a threat to national security and were therefore to be removed or banned from federal employment" (Retraction Watch, 2020a). In Canada, work by J. Philippe Rushton (now deceased) on racial differences has similarly been retracted. Formerly on faculty at Western University, Rushton's work has been deemed "unethical, scientifically flawed, and based on racist ideas and agenda" (Retraction Watch, 2020b).

Retraction Watch also reports on stories on mass retractions, such as when *Springer* announced it was retracting over 100 papers on cancer research from one journal, *Tumor Biology,* now published by *Sage,* due to fraudulent reviews. In this case, false email accounts were allegedly used to misdirect papers to fake/favourable reviewers (Retraction Watch, 2017).

Most importantly for this chapter, *Retraction Watch* maintains a searchable database (by country, university etc.) of retracted papers (Retraction Watch, n.d. c). In fall, 2020 we requested a query of retractions involving academics with a Canadian university affiliation, for the years 2010–2020. The report found 397 Canadian university affiliations, pertaining to 321 retracted articles (Note: the number of institutional affiliations are higher than the number of articles, as an article may have more than one Canadian author). Annual rates of retracted papers varied from a low of 17 in 2013 to a high of 48 in 2019. The Canadian institutions that figured most prominently (with more than 10 author affiliations each) are listed in Table 4.1. Interestingly, all belong to Canada's prestigious "U-15 Group of Canadian Research Universities". Twenty-one other Canadian institutions had between two and nine affiliations each.

There were also 786 reasons provided for the 321 retracted papers (2.45 per paper on average). The most common are listed in Table 4.2 (i.e., those with a minimum of 20 instances):

> The most common reason for retraction was "Duplication of Articles (by journal)", meaning the article was mistakenly published more than once, as a result of journal error (Retraction Watch, n.d. d). Reasons where the authors clearly bore responsibility included: "Unreliable Results", "Error in Data", "Plagiarism of Article", "Manipulation of Images", and "Falsification/Fabrication of Data".

Incidents of Misconduct Highlighted by the Canadian Press

In addition to *Retraction Watch,* and as its founders envisioned, the press is another important source of information on misconduct by Canadian academics, as well as the effectiveness of national policies. In 2016, for example, the *Toronto Star* ran an article on research fraud in Canada, reporting that while the PRCR's Secretariat on

Table 4.1. Canadian universities with ten or more retraction affiliations (2010–2020). (*Source* Retraction Watch)

Institution	# Times affiliation appeared on retracted papers 2010–2020
University of Toronto	98
University of British Columbia	33
University of Calgary	26
McGill University	24
University of Ottawa	21
University of Alberta	19
McMaster University	17
University of Montreal	17
University of Saskatchewan	15
University of Western Ontario	15
Dalhousie University	11
University of Waterloo	11
Total	307

Table 4.2. Most common reasons for retractions of papers by Canadian academics, 2010–2020. (*Source* Retraction Watch)

Reason for retraction	Times used
Duplication of Article (by journal)	51
Investigation by Company/Institution	50
Notice—Limited or No Information	50
Investigation by Journal/Publisher	32
Unreliable Results	32
Withdrawal	29
Error in Data	28
Plagiarism of Article	26
Manipulation of Images	25
Concerns/Issues About Data	24
Error in Analyses	23
Date of Retraction/Other Unknown	22
Duplication of Image	22
Error by Journal/Publisher	22
Falsification/Fabrication of Data	22

Responsible Conduct of Research was tracking and reporting on cases, Canadian researchers were still not being named:

> Seventy-eight Canadian scientists have fabricated data, plagiarized, misused grants, or engaged in dodgy scientific practices in projects backed by public funds…

> But the publicly funded agency responsible for policing scientific fraud is keeping secret the details surrounding these researchers. The scientists' names, where they worked and what they did wrong is not made public because that information is protected under federal privacy laws… . (Robinson, 2016)

Robinson (2016) also explained, however, that "By law, the presidents who lead each of Canada's research funding agencies…have the power to release the findings of these investigations if it is deemed to be of significant public interest, defined as a concern of public health or national security."

One particularly egregious case involved fraudulent cancer research at the University of British Columbia (UBC), where "in 2014 investigators identified 29 instances of scholarly misconduct, 16 of them 'serious,' including falsification and fabrication of data…[The] tainted work had been included in 12 papers published in six journals between 2005 and 2012" (Komnenic, 2016). UBC did not release the results of their investigation or name the researcher, citing British Columbia's privacy laws and claiming that to do so was not "clearly" in the public interest.

Another example involved Dongqing Li, who held a prestigious Canada Research Chair at the University of Waterloo and a PhD student. Martin Bazant, a professor at the Massachusetts Institute of Technology accused Li of having plagiarized material from a "pre-published version" of an article he had submitted to the journal, *Microfluidics and Nanofluidics*, which Li founded and was serving as editor-in-chief (Brennan, 2012; CTV News, 2013). The article was retracted, Li resigned his editorship (Brennan, 2012) and he was also suspended from the University without pay for four months (CTV News, 2013).

One particularly notorious case involved Dr. Cory Toth, "former research director of the Calgary Chronic Pain Centre Clinic", who had received "more than $2.3 million in research funding in his nine years at the medical school" (Munro, 2014). Toth was the corresponding author on multiple published articles found to contain manipulated data and figures:

> [T]he journals Molecular Pain and Brain retracted two of Toth's team studies for data manipulation and two more studies in Diabetes were retracted for image doctoring, "fabricated" figures, and using "older data not representative of the cohorts (of mice) studied." Then this summer RETRACTED, in bold red type, was slapped on two papers in the journal Neurobiology of Disease, for data manipulation. The two most recent retractions, in the journal Neuroscience, are for "manipulated" figures and "faulty data"—bringing the total to nine. (Munro, 2014)

Commenting on the case, Dr. Ivan Oransky said, "I can't say whether it's an official record, but we haven't seen anyone else in Canada retract that many papers since we launched in 2010" (Munro, 2014).

Underscoring the particular vulnerabilities of graduate students, Shahid Azam, an engineering professor from the University of Regina, had a paper retracted after being found by the journal to not have given proper attribution to the thesis work of one of his master's students (Leo, 2014). Calling it a "grey area" and matter of "poor judgment", the journal said that Azam would not be banned from making future submissions. In his defense, the professor claimed to have written large parts of the student's thesis himself, suggesting that "in the field of engineering, it's common and acceptable for researchers to 'reuse' their own text from previous articles in subsequent papers". The graduate student Arjun Paul claimed "he wrote the papers and the thesis himself" (Leo, 2014). This case highlights the need to bring greater transparency to supervisor relationships and co-publishing practices.

As an example from the field of education, the University of Windsor suspended and demoted Clinton Beckford, its newly appointed dean of education after he was found to have engaged in plagiarism, following a formal investigation (CBC News, 2012; Chen, 2012). Another education leader who made the news was Chris Spence, the former director of the Toronto District School Board, who was found by the University of Toronto to have plagiarized large portions of his 1996 doctoral thesis (Alphonso, 2017). Spence resigned his position and his PhD was rescinded (Mandel, 2019).

Research misconduct—as previously suggested—is not the only type of academic integrity violation that has been in the Canadian press. One now infamous example of plagiarism in a convocation address involved Philip Baker, the former Dean of Medicine at the University of Alberta. Baker resigned after students discovered that his remarks were taken almost verbatim—including "personal stories about how medical science has helped his wife and children"—from an address previously made by "Atul Gawande, at Stanford University's 2010 medical school convocation" (CBC News, 2011). Class president Brittany Barber made a statement on behalf of students:

> To realize all this hard work may be marred by this unanticipated incident is very disheartening to the students. People should know that we will not stand for this academic dishonesty, and our deepest wish is that this incident does not reflect poorly on the integrity of our class, the medical school and, ultimately, the university. (CBC News, 2011)

Prior to coming to Canada, Baker had been at the heart of a medical scandal, where he was implicated in the death of a baby in Nottingham, England. A court ruling found Dr. Baker had provided "substandard and inappropriate" care (Weaver, 2000). This previous case was not mentioned in the 2011 Canadian press reports and raises questions concerning a potential lack of due diligence in academic appointments. Eaton (2020a; 2020b; 2021) questioned whether faculty should have to declare previous incidents in which findings of misconduct (academic, professional, personal) have been made. As of 2021, Baker is serving as the Pro-Vice-Chancellor and Head of College of Life Sciences, Dean of Medicine University of Leicester, in the UK.

Highlighting questionable practices in student recruitment, Broitman (2016), Director of Higher-Edge, which operates the Canadian University Application Centre, wrote about the impact of increasing financial pressures and competition:

> It is overwhelmingly evident that in the last two decades we have witnessed first-hand a remarkable and callous disregard for academic ethics and standards in a scramble by Canadian universities and colleges to sign up foreign students, who represent tens of millions of dollars to their bottom lines. (para. 3)

Specifically, Broitman (2016) called out "corrupt practices" and "contracted relationships between universities and colleges with education agents worldwide", suggesting that:

> Although Canadians typically think of their society and themselves as among the more honest and transparent found anywhere, how many Canadian institutions are engaging in activities that border on dishonest and are not entirely transparent around the world?. (Broitman, 2016, para. 2)

He also identified unsettling consequences of admitting students with poor English literacy skills, and/or those who are poorly academically prepared, such as undue pressure on faculty to ensure they pass regardless; "Some have reported failing students who later (somehow) manage to have passed. As we know, failing students is bad for business" (para. 5). Strikingly, Broitman (2016) concluded:

> Too few academic institutions are serious enough about screening and vetting applications…It's not just academic integrity that is lacking, academic quality is diminishing as cohorts of international students grow in number but not in ability...
>
> Most professors know what's going on. Yet, unless you listen carefully to low whispers on Canadian campuses you never hear of the academic compromises made in the interest of revenue… Ask any reporter how hard it is to get anyone to go on record. (Broitman, 2016, para. 10–11)

Inappropriate sexual relationships are yet another area of concern. As one example, Jim Pfaus, a psychology professor at Concordia University, retired after an internal investigation in which he was accused of inappropriate behavior with students, including that he had "pursued, dated or had sexual relationships with students in his classes or under his supervision" (Hendry, 2019). The article noted that at the time, Concordia did not have "a specific policy or guidelines discouraging professor-student romantic or sexual relationships". Following, Quebec's Ministry of Higher Education introduced Bill 151 (2017), "An Act to prevent and fight sexual violence in higher education institutions", requiring institutional policies on sexual violence. One of the outcomes, is that all new staff, faculty and students at Concordia must now complete "sexual violence awareness and prevention training" (It Takes All of Us, 2021).

Declining Trust in the Academy

Given these stories, perhaps it is not surprising that as identified as a concern in the HAL (2009) report, support for higher education and trust in academics and scientists in North America appears to be waning. In the US, a 2018 Gallup poll found a considerable decline, with less than half (48 percent) of American adults indicating they have "'a great deal' or 'quite a lot' of confidence in higher education" (Jaschik, 2018). According to Lawrence Bakow, President of Harvard University, "declining public support for higher education is one of the major challenges facing academe":

> For the first time in my lifetime, people are asking whether or not colleges and universities are worthy of public support. For the first time in my lifetime, people are expressing doubts about whether colleges and universities are even good for the nation. These questions force us to ask: What does higher education really contribute to the national life? (Jaschik, 2018, para. 9)

Another US study similarly found declining trust in scientists. Participants expressed particular concern about research misconduct (Funk, Hefferon, Kennedy & Johnson, 2019, p. 1):

> Most Americans are skeptical about key areas of scientific integrity. No more than two-in-ten Americans believe scientists across these groups are transparent about potential conflicts of interest with industry all or most of the time... Between about a quarter and half of Americans consider misconduct a "very big" or "moderately big" problem, with the public generally skeptical that those engaged in misconduct routinely face serious consequences.

More recently, the Annual Edelman Trust Barometer (2021) reported that trust in societal institutions fell in many countries around the world between May 2020 and January 2021, including amongst Canadian respondents, with business surprisingly emerging as the only institution perceived as being both competent and ethical (p. 7). The overall trust score found that just 56% of global respondents indicated they trust their social institutions (p. 9). Canada mirrored this result, up slightly from 53% in 2020 (p. 9). In terms of academics, their credibility as spokespeople was perceived as more trustworthy than CEO's, government officials and journalists, but the extent to which they were considered "very/extremely credible" declined considerably over 2020, down 8 points to 59% (p. 22). The authors concluded:

> After a year of unprecedented disaster and turbulence—the Covid-19 pandemic and economic crisis, the global outcry over systemic racism and political instability—the 2021 Edelman Trust Barometer reveals an epidemic of misinformation and widespread mistrust of societal institutions and leaders around the world. (Annual Edelman Trust Barometer, 2021, para. 1)

Within Canada, declining political trust in the academy has been reflected in increasing government oversight ("regulation and accountability measures"). One study of research-intensive Canadian universities (Eastman et al., 2018), observed that provincial governments are "seeking to align universities' activities or outcomes more closely with desired public policy goals" through enhanced "governance, transparency, accountability, value for money, and alignment with government's public policy priorities" (p. 72). While part of this distrust pertains to what students are learning, the academy is also clearly being challenged with respect to the value and impact of its research.

Recommendations and Conclusion

In summary, although we cannot say to what extent misconduct is occurring by faculty and administrators within Canada's higher education institutions, the aforementioned examples of research misconduct are deeply concerning. Reports of Canadian researchers fabricating and falsifying data and grant applications, doctoring images, fraudulently using research funds, failing to declare conflicts of interest, engaging with ghost writing services, and plagiarizing graduate work and in speeches, all serve to undermine public trust in science and the academy. While not the focus of this chapter, additional areas of concern beyond research misconduct were also briefly highlighted, including the quality of graduate student supervision, due diligence in hiring practices, ethics in international student recruitment, and inappropriate relationships between faculty and students. Each one of these themes has the potential to undermine institutional integrity, societal trust, and reputation.

In order to further strengthen Canadian higher education's culture of integrity, our first recommendation is that a comprehensive study of misconduct by Canadian academics and administrators be undertaken. As previously suggested, the categories identified by Stone and Starkey (2011) could provide a useful starting point for developing a survey of questionable behaviours and identifying suggested strategies for combatting them, as well as emerging systemic issues that may be catalyzing such behaviours. Data from such a study could be invaluable in informing policy and practice.

As Eaton (2021) pointed out, universities need effective policies and procedures to address scholarly and scientific misconduct among faculty, staff, and researchers. Moreover, such policies need to have a clear directive to address such misconduct in a clear and timely manner. Just as institutions produce annual reports regarding student academic misconduct, so too should they be transparent in their reporting of employee academic misconduct. The time has passed for dismissing misconduct among professors and other employees of the academy as "one off" incidents each time they occur. As we have shown, it is undeniable that faculty misconduct occurs in Canada, with some individuals engaging in numerous incidents over many years. Misconduct should not be ignored or trivialized, but instead addressed in ways that focus on accountability, transparency and prevention.

With respect to efforts to advance a national culture of research integrity, it has been several years since Canada's HAL (2009) and CCA (2010) comprehensive studies were commissioned and new oversight bodies and policies created. Perhaps it is time to revisit the original findings and recommendations, and where changes have been made, assess their effectiveness. While we appreciate the PRCR's commitment to engaging in a review every five years, including a process of public consultation, the proposed revisions for 2021 appear to be largely technical in nature. What we are proposing would be a more conceptual review, exploring the extent to which the original deficits have been resolved, such as the observation that Canada has lagged its Western counterparts in dealing with scientific misconduct. Most important, would be an assessment of the extent to which stated goals have been achieved, including the acknowledged need to "foster a positive, values-based environment of research integrity in Canada" (CCA, 2010, p. 2).

In closing, we offer this chapter as a reminder that academic integrity needs to be understood as pertaining to much more than student misconduct. We call for academic integrity to be valued as a broad-based institutional priority, involving all members. Only by having role models of integrity—faculty and administrators who bring the highest standards to their own work and deal with violations appropriately—will Canadian higher educational institutions have the moral authority to lead their students in their own academic journeys, and to earn the trust of the public, in the scholarly work we pursue.

References

21st Annual Edelman Trust Barometer. (2021). https://www.edelman.com/trust/2021-trust-barometer

Alphonso, C. (2017, June 20). Former TDSB director guilty of plagiarizing his PhD, panel says. *The Globe and Mail*. https://www.theglobeandmail.com/news/toronto/former-tdsb-director-guilty-of-plagiarizing-his-phd-panel-says/article35403977/

Besvinick, S. L. (1983). Integrity and the future of the university. *Journal of Higher Education, 51*(5), 566–573.

Bill 151 (2017). *Bill 151, An Act to prevent and fight sexual violence in higher education institutions*. National Assembly of Quebec. http://www.assnat.qc.ca/en/travaux-parlementaires/projets-loi/projet-loi-151-41-1.html

Brennan, R. J. (2012, September 12). Waterloo prof and student caught up in plagiarism scandal. *The Star*. https://www.thestar.com/news/canada/2012/09/12/waterloo_prof_and_student_caught_up_in_plagiarism_scandal.html

Bretag, T. (Ed.). (2016). *Handbook of academic integrity*. Springer.

Broitman, M. (2016). Corruption in higher ed: Canada in the crosshairs. *Inside Higher Ed*.https://www.insidehighered.com/blogs/world-view/corruption-higher-ed-canada-crosshairs

CBC News. (2011, June 12). *U of Alberta dean stole speech: Med students*. https://www.cbc.ca/news/canada/edmonton/u-of-alberta-dean-stole-speech-med-students-1.1047550

CBC News. (2012, December 10). University of Windsor suspends education dean over plagiarism. *CBC News Windsor*. http://www.cbc.ca/news/canada/windsor/university-of-windsor-suspends-education-dean-over-plagiarism-1.1256511

CBC News. (2005). *The secret life of Dr. Chandra*. https://www.youtube.com/watch?v=2R7-QM8eKCM

CBC News. (2019, July 4). *22 electricians penalized after probe into cheating at Sask Polytechnic*. https://www.cbc.ca/news/canada/saskatchewan/construction-electricians-certificates-cancelled-suspended-1.5200227

CCA. (2010). Honesty, accountability and trust: Fostering research integrity in Canada, Expert Panel on Research Integrity. *The Council of Canadian Academies*. https://cca-reports.ca/reports/honesty-accountability-and-trust-fostering-research-integrity-in-canada/

Chen, D. (2012, May 30). Dean of education at University of Windsor suspended over plagiarism. *Windsor Star*. http://windsorstar.com/news/local-news/dean-of-education-at-university-of-windsor-suspended-over-plagiarism

Colleges and Institutes Canada. (2021). https://www.collegesinstitutes.ca/stratplan/

CTV News. (2013, January 8). *Internal probe finds UW prof guilty of plagiarism*. https://kitchener.ctvnews.ca/internal-probe-finds-uw-prof-guilty-of-plagiarism-1.1105263

Christensen Hughes, J (2022). Academic integrity across time and place: Higher education's questionable moral calling. In S. E. Eaton & J. Christensen Hughes (Eds.), *Academic integrity in Canada: An enduring and essential challenge*. Springer.

Christensen Hughes, J., & Eaton, S. E. (2022). Student integrity violations in the academy: More than a decade of growing complexity and concern. In S. E. Eaton & J. Christensen Hughes (Eds.), *Academic integrity in Canada: An enduring and essential challenge*. Springer.

Consent to Disclosure of Personal Information—Frequently Asked Questions. (2016). *Natural Sciences and Engineering Research Council of Canada*. Retrieved May 28, 2021, from https://www.nserc-crsng.gc.ca/NSERC-CRSNG/governance-gouvernance/consentFAQ-consentementFAQ_eng.asp

Dalton, R. (2005, March 23). Obesity expert owns up to million-dollar crime. *Nature*, 434–424. https://doi.org/10.1038/434424a

Dea, S. (2019, January 18). The price of academic freedom.*University Affairs*. https://www.universityaffairs.ca/opinion/dispatches-academic-freedom/the-price-of-academic-freedom/

Dixon, B. (1989). Growing catalogue of fraud. *BMJ: British Medical Journal, 299*(6711), 1329–1330. https://www.jstor.org/stable/29706127

Eastman, J., Jones G., Bégin-Caouette, O., Li, S., Noumi, C., & Trottier, C. (2018). Autonomy in Canada: Findings of a comparative study of Canadian university governance. *Canadian Journal of Higher Education, 48*(3), 65–81. https://journals.sfu.ca/cjhe/index.php/cjhe/article/view/188165/186275

Eaton, S. E. (2021). *Plagiarism in higher education: Tackling tough topics in academic integrity*. Libraries Unlimited.

Eaton, S. E. (2020a, January 13). *An inquiry into major academic integrity violations in Canada: 2010–2019*. http://hdl.handle.net/1880/111483

Eaton, S. E. (2020b). Significant incidents of academic misconduct in Canada 2010–2019—*Timeline Infographic*. http://hdl.handle.net/1880/111435

Feith, J. (2020, July 5). Human Rights Commission says Concordia University should change how it deals with sexual assault complaints. *Montreal Gazette*. https://montrealgazette.com/news/local-news/human-rights-commission-says-concordia-university-should-change-how-it-deals-with-sexual-assault-complaints

Funk, C., Hefferon, M., Kennedy, B., & Johnson, C. (2019, August 2). *Trust and mistrust in Americans' views of scientific experts*. https://www.pewresearch.org/science/2019/08/02/trust-and-mistrust-in-americans-views-of-scientific-experts/

Gervais. (2021). Practical methodological reform needs good theory, perspectives on psychological science. *Sage*. https://doi.org/10.1177/1745691620977471

HAL. (2009). The state of research integrity and misconduct policies in Canada. Canadian Research Integrity Committee. *HAL Innovation Policy Economics*. https://www.nserc-crsng.gc.ca/_doc/NSERC-CRSNG/HAL_Report_e.pdf

Hamilton, D. G., Fraser, H., Hoekstra, R., Fidler, F. (2020, November 19). Meta-research: Journal policies and editors' opinions on peer review. *eLife*. https://elifesciences.org/articles/62529

Hendry, L. (2019, April 4), Students, staff left in the dark after Concordia's investigation of prof's behaviour. *CBC News*. https://www.cbc.ca/news/canada/montreal/students-staff-left-in-the-dark-after-concordia-s-investigation-of-prof-s-behaviour-1.5081527

Hoag, H. (2010, October 21). Canada urged to tackle research misconduct. *Nature*. https://www.nature.com/news/2010/101021/full/news.2010.555.html

Huistra, P., & Paul, H. (2021). Systemic explanations of scientific misconduct: Provoked by spectacular cases of norm violation? *Journal of Academic Ethics*. https://doi.org/10.1007/s10805-020-09389-8

Humber College. (n.d.). *Academic Integrity Policies & Resources*. https://healthsciences.humber.ca/current-students/academic-integrity.html

ICAI. (2021). *The fundamental values of academic integrity* (3rd ed.). *International Center for Academic Integrity*. https://academicintegrity.org/images/pdfs/20019_ICAI-Fundamental-Values_R12.pdf

It Takes All of Us. (2021). *Concordia University*. https://www.concordia.ca/conduct/sexual-violence/training.html

Jaschik, S. (2018). Falling confidence in higher ed: Gallup finds unusually large drop—primarily but not exclusively among republicans—between 2015 and 2018. *Inside Higher Ed*. https://www.insidehighered.com/news/2018/10/09/gallup-survey-finds-falling-confidence-higher-education

Jerema, C. (2010, March 15). NSERC bars scientist from receiving grants. *Maclean's*. https://www.macleans.ca/education/uniandcollege/nserc-bars-scientis-from-receiving-grants/

Jones, C. (2021, January 30). The coming publication apocalypse. *The Grumpy Geophysicist*. https://grumpygeophysicist.wordpress.com/2021/01/30/the-coming-publication-apocalypse/

Kondro, W., & Hebert, P. (2007). Research misconduct? What misconduct? *Canadian Medical Association Journal, 176*(7), 905.

Komnenic, A. (2016, December 14). In Canada, case spurs concern over misconduct secrecy. *Science*. https://www.sciencemag.org/news/2016/12/canada-case-spurs-concern-over-misconduct-secrecy

Laidlaw, S. (2009, August 22). Canadian named in HRT scandal. *The Toronto Star*. https://www.thestar.com/life/health_wellness/2009/08/22/canadian_named_in_hrt_scandal.html

Leo, G. (2014, November 13). University of Regina prof investigated for allegedly plagiarizing student's work. *CBC News*. https://www.cbc.ca/news/canada/saskatchewan/university-of-regina-prof-investigated-for-allegedly-plagiarizing-student-s-work-1.2832907

Mandel, M. (2019, February 26). Disgraced former TDSB chief loses bid to reclaim PhD. *Toronto Sun*. https://torontosun.com/news/local-news/mandel-disgraced-former-tdsb-chief-chris-spence-loses-bid-to-reclaim-phd

Maracle, I. B. J. (2020). Seven grandfathers in academic integrity. *Student Life, University of Toronto*. https://uwaterloo.ca/academic-integrity/sites/ca.academic-integrity/files/uploads/files/slc8581_7-grandfathers-in-academic-integrity-aoda.pdf

Merriam Webster. (n.d. a). *Integrity*. https://www.merriam-webster.com/dictionary/integrity

Merriam Webster. (n.d. b). *Misconduct*. https://www.merriam-webster.com/dictionary/misconduct

Mullens, A. (2000, December). Cheating to Win, *University Affairs* (pp. 22–28).

Munro, M. (2010, March 13). U of C Prof Hit by funding scandal. *Calgary Herald*. https://www.pressreader.com/canada/calgary-herald/20100313/296009146948158

Munro, M. (2011, September 19). Scientist fudges grant forms with fake research, studies. *Regina-Leader Post*. https://www.pressreader.com/canada/regina-leader-post/20110919/282376921308922

Munro, M. (2013, December 2). *China's academic 'black market' fooled Canadian journal, report says*. https://margaretmunro.wordpress.com/2013/12/02/chinas-academic-black-market-fooled-canadian-journal-report-says/#more-953

Munro, M. (2014, September 4). Prolific University of Calgary doctor heads to B.C. after his team caught faking data. *Post Media News*. https://margaretmunro.wordpress.com/2014/09/04/prolific-university-of-calgary-doctor-heads-to-b-c-after-his-team-caught-faking-data/#more-1198

Oransky, I. (2016, July 19). Canada funding agency bans researcher for fraud, and in first, reveals her name. *Retraction Watch*. https://retractionwatch.com/2016/07/19/canada-funding-agency-bans-researcher-for-fraud-and-in-first-reveals-her-name/

Oransky, I., & Markus, A. (2010, August 3). Why write a blog about retractions? *Retraction Watch*. https://retractionwatch.com/2010/08/03/why-write-a-blog-about-retractions/

Osipian, A. (2004). *Corruption as a legacy of the medieval university: Financial affairs*, MPRA Paper 8472. University Library of Munich. https://mpra.ub.uni-muenchen.de/8472/1/MPRA_paper_8472.pdf

Osipian, A. (2007). Higher education corruption in world media, prevalence, patterns and forms. In *Proceedings of 32nd Annual Conference of the Association for the Study of Higher Education (ASHE)*, Louisville, Kentucky, MPRA Paper 8475. University Library of Munich. https://mpra.ub.uni-muenchen.de/8475/

Policy 60, Ryerson University. (n.d.). *Academic Integrity*. Retrieved May 27, 2021, from https://www.ryerson.ca/senate/course-outline-policies/academic-integrity-policy-60/

Postmedia News. (2012, September 11). Top Canadian scientist and award-winning student caught in 'blatant plagiarism' of text. *National Post*. https://nationalpost.com/news/canada/university-of-waterloo-researchers-issue-retraction-and-apology-after-using-u-s-experts-text-and-information

PRCR. (2016). Mandate: Terms of reference. *Panel on Responsible Conduct of Research*. https://rcr.ethics.gc.ca/eng/about_us-propos_de_nous.html

PRCR. (2017). Disclosures. *Panel on Responsible Conduct of Research*. https://rcr.ethics.gc.ca/eng/disclosures-divulgations_backgrounder-document.html

RCR Framework. (2016). Tri-Agency Framework: Responsible Conduct of Research. (2016). *Panel on Responsible Conduct of Research*. Retrieved May 28, 2021, from https://rcr.ethics.gc.ca/eng/framework-cadre.html

RCR Framework – Proposed Revisions for Public Consultation. (2016/2021). Consultation. *Panel on Responsible Conduct of Research*. https://rcr.ethics.gc.ca/eng/consultations_proposed-revisions-to-rcr-framework-2016.html

Retraction Watch. (n.d. a). *Retraction Watch*. https://retractionwatch.com/

Retraction Watch. (n.d. b). Retracted coronavirus (COVID-19) papers. *Retraction Watch*. https://retractionwatch.com/retracted-coronavirus-covid-19-papers/

Retraction Watch. (n.d. c). Retraction watch database user guide. *Retraction Watch*. https://retractionwatch.com/retraction-watch-database-user-guide/

Retraction Watch. (n.d. d). *Retraction watch database user guide appendix B: Reasons*. https://retractionwatch.com/retraction-watch-database-user-guide/retraction-watch-database-user-guide-appendix-b-reasons/

Retraction Watch. (2017). A new record: Major publisher retracting more than 100 studies from cancer journal over fake peer reviews. *Retraction Watch*. https://retractionwatch.com/2017/04/20/new-record-major-publisher-retracting-100-studies-cancer-journal-fake-peer-reviews/

Retraction Watch. (2020a). Journal retracts 70-year-old article on homosexuality for "long discredited beliefs, prejudices, and practices". *Retraction Watch*. https://retractionwatch.com/2020/12/02/journal-retracts-70-year-old-article-on-homosexuality-for-long-discredited-beliefs-prejudices-and-practices/

Retraction Watch. (2020b). Psychology journal retracts two articles for being "unethical, scientifically flawed, and based on racist ideas and agenda". *Retraction Watch*. https://retractionwatch.com/2020/12/29/psychology-journal-retracts-two-articles-for-being-unethical-scientifically-flawed-and-based-on-racist-ideas-and-agenda/

Robinson. (2016, July 12). Canadian researchers who commit scientific fraud are protected by privacy laws. *Toronto Star*. https://www.thestar.com/news/canada/2016/07/12/canadian-researchers-who-commit-scientific-fraud-are-protected-by-privacy-laws.html

Smith, R. (2006). Research misconduct: The poisoning of the well. *Journal of the Royal Society of Medicine*, *99*(5), 232–237. https://www.ncbi.nlm.nih.gov/pmc/articles/PMC1457763/

Statistics Canada. (2018/2019). *Number and salaries of full-time teaching staff at Canadian universities (final), 2018/2019*. https://www150.statcan.gc.ca/n1/daily-quotidien/191125/dq191125b-eng.htm

Stone, M., & Starkey, M. (2011). The possible impact of university corruption on customers' ethical standards. *Journal of Database Marketing & Customer Strategy Management, 18*, 154–170. https://doi.org/10.1057/dbm.2011.18

University of Waterloo. (n.d.). *What is academic integrity?* https://uwaterloo.ca/academic-integrity/what-academic-integrity-0

Weaver, M. (2000, October 19). *Baby died after doctor ignored mother's pleas*. https://www.telegraph.co.uk/news/health/1370882/Baby-died-after-doctor-ignored-mothers-pleas.html

Julia Christensen Hughes, Ph.D. has long advocated for ensuring the highest standards of academic integrity in higher education. Her article, Academic Misconduct within Higher Education in Canada, with the late Don McCabe (published in 2006, in the *Canadian Journal of Higher Education*), received the Sheffield Award for research excellence (2007), from the Canadian Society for Studies in Higher Education. As former and founding Dean of the Gordon S. Lang School of Business and Economics (2009–2019) at the University of Guelph, Julia was a champion of business ethics, corporate social responsibility and the need for business schools to be aligned with the UN's Sustainable Development Goals (SDG's). In her new role as President of Yorkville University, Julia is looking forward to supporting the institution's long-standing commitment to integrity, that is at the core of its values.

Sarah Elaine Eaton, Ph.D. is an Associate Professor in the Werklund School of Education and the inaugural Educational Leader in Residence, Academic Integrity, University of Calgary. She is also the Editor-in-Chief of the *International Journal for Educational Integrity* and the author of *Plagiarism in Higher Education: Tackling Tough Topics in Academic Integrity* (ABC Clio, 2021). Her research focuses on ethics and integrity in higher education and she has led numerous research teams and the local and national levels. Eaton advocates for pro-active and multi-stakeholder approaches to upholding and enacting integrity throughout the academy.

BY

Chapter 5
Re-Defining Academic Integrity: Embracing Indigenous Truths

Yvonne Poitras Pratt and Keeta Gladue

Abstract Despite historical and ongoing challenges, Canada has been making promising strides towards reconciliation prompted in large part by the work of the Truth and Reconciliation Commission of Canada (2015). We honour our Indigenous Elders and Ancestors who have led social and educational movements that named and resisted the negative outcomes created and continued by a Canadian colonial history. The authors point to current institutional projects of decolonizing and Indigenizing the academy as holding the potential to re-define what academic integrity means. As a hopeful point of entry into how teaching and learning scholars might reconsider current conceptions of integrity, we see Indigenizing efforts across a number of Canadian universities as the basis from which to speak to a more inclusive and wholistic definition of academic integrity. The authors seek to problematize the current neoliberal and commercialized approaches to education where different forms of academic misconduct arise as inevitable outcomes. If education is viewed as the pursuit of truth, or more appropriately truths, then it is essential to nuance the scope of academic integrity to include Indigenous perspectives such as *wholism* and *interconnectedness*. In this chapter, we discuss these truths, challenging current conceptions, to propose a more inclusive definition of academic integrity by drawing upon Indigenous scholarship as well as dynamic forms of ancestral language to situate our work. In sum, sharing truths through the inclusion of Indigenous perspectives grounds the scholarly discussion in an equitable understanding of truth-telling as foundational to academic integrity.

Keywords Indigenizing · Decolonizing · Reconciliation · Truth-telling · Academic integrity

Y. Poitras Pratt (✉) · K. Gladue
University of Calgary, Calgary, AB, Canada
e-mail: yppratt@ucalgary.ca

K. Gladue
e-mail: kgladue@ucalgary.ca

S. E. Eaton and J. Christensen Hughes (eds.), *Academic Integrity in Canada*, Ethics and Integrity in Educational Contexts 1,
https://doi.org/10.1007/978-3-030-83255-1_5

Situating Ourselves

As Cree and Métis women, we situate ourselves within our ancestral and living communities as an authentic and community-centred practice in our scholarship. From this starting point, we begin the work of sharing Indigenous truths and connecting ideas in a good way. As a Métis scholar, Yvonne traces her known First Nations lineages from Cree, Haudenosaunee, Saulteaux, and Sioux Nations across Turtle Island since time immemorial; these lines joined more recently with those from Europe. The intertwining of these family lines formed the nation that would become her ancestors, the Métis. Their ancestral footsteps trace across eastern regions including Quebec, into the historic Red River Settlement, and scattered to lands near and far in the diaspora that followed the 1885 Resistance. More recent generations settled on the northern regions of Alberta in historic communities, some of which became Métis settlements.

Keeta brings two lines of Indigenous relations, the Sucker Creek Cree Nation and Métis ancestry reaching back to the historic homeland in the Red River Valley, to her scholarship. She also recognizes the Ehattesaht people of the Nuu Chah-Nulth, in whose territories she was raised on their unceded homelands, on an island traditionally known as Tlay Maak Tsu and now known as Esperanza, British Columbia. These nations and places inform who we are as Indigenous Peoples, scholars, and community members, and form the foundation of our work. It is with gratitude to our ancestors, the land, and those who share knowledge with us that we set out in a good way.

We engage with our ancestors through the learning, and revitalization, of Cree and Michif (Cree-Métis) words to ground our Indigenous ontological and epistemological locations. The use of ancestral languages, in both traditional and contemporary forms, provides a precision of meaning which we believe honours both the sacred purpose and the ideals of academic integrity. We work together to emphasize how the "more we assist and help each other with learning the language" (McLeod & Wolvengrey, 2016, p. xv), the stronger our collective efforts will be in redefining academic integrity. In *100 Days of Cree,* author and poet Neal McLeod reminds us: "It is by a collective effort that we can bring the power of the echo of the voices of the Old Ones, and the old stories, into the contemporary age" (McLeod & Wolvengrey, 2016, p. 1). McLeod implores those who believe in the power of collectivism to engage in wîcihitok, or to 'help one another!' Heeding the sage advice of the Old Ones, we work together to re-vision and re-define a renewed understanding of academic integrity through the sharing of Indigenous truths and contemporary realities.

According to the *Merriam-Webster* dictionary, integrity is defined as the quality of being honest and having strong moral principles; the dictionary further defines integrity as a state of being *whole* and *undivided*. Infusing these definitions of integrity with Indigenous principles transforms academic integrity into a *wholistic* and *interconnected* project premised on truth-telling in the academy. Through an Indigenous lens, shared beliefs held by Indigenous peoples around principles of relationality and interconnectedness represent a collectivist orientation through diverse ways of seeking and sharing knowledge (Absolon, 2010; Lindstrom, 2021; Smith, 2012; Wilson, 2001; Younging, 2018). To aid our discussion on academic integrity, we look to Opaskwayak Cree scholar Shawn Wilson (2001) who challenges mainstream approaches to decolonizing research by asserting: "A lot of people have tried to decolonize research methods ... but they are deconstructing a method *without looking at its underlying beliefs*" (p. 177, emphasis added). We maintain that a redefinition of academic integrity similarly requires the ability to unearth and critically analyze underlying assumptions inherent in essential academic terms as a wholistic approach. To achieve our aims, we provide a brief chronological overview of the ways in which the First Peoples of Canada have sought to have their voices heard and to share their historical truths over the years. In deconstructing a mainstream understanding of academic integrity as one laden with capitalist tones and the positioning of knowledge as a form of property, we offer Indigenous principles as a re-orientation towards interconnectedness, where honesty and a sense of responsibility to one another guides teaching and learning goals.

National Truths: A Foundation for Academic Integrity

> Universities are committed to the pursuit of truth and its communication to others, including students and the broader community. To do this, faculty must be free to take intellectual risks and tackle controversial subjects in their teaching, research and scholarship ... For Canadians, it is important to know that views expressed by faculty are based on solid research, data and evidence, and that universities are autonomous and responsible institutions committed to the principles of integrity. (Universities Canada, 2011, para. 4)

Academic integrity has long been held as a bastion within institutions of higher learning where principles of truth and academic freedom are seen as essential pillars in a healthy democracy (Universities Canada, 2011, para. 7). Scholars Alschuler and Blimling (1995) asked "why there is so little passion about this massive assault on the highest values of the academy," referring to a growing concern in the 1990s around breaches of academic integrity and what they perceived as a breakdown of the original values of integrity (p. 124). Seen as one of the major institutional responses to these concerns, the (now International) Center for Academic Integrity was set up in 1992 under Donald McCabe's leadership. This organization identified values of fairness, honesty, respect, responsibility, and trust as essential values to student conduct; courage was subsequently added. It is interesting to note that while Christensen Hughes and McCabe (2006a) proposed a modified honor code system as an American-inspired solution to growing Canadian concerns around academic misconduct, this system has not found mass appeal in Canadian post-secondary institutions (Eaton, 2021). Canadian universities have continued to navigate issues surrounding academic integrity from an eclectic, often punitive and deficit-based approach, devoid of its foundational values. Commodification of post-secondary knowledge has exacerbated these issues resulting in a fragmented approach which is largely ineffective, inequitable, and inconsistent. This shift to a market-driven educational model demonstrates a bypassing of fundamental values of academic integrity as institutions of higher learning transform into industries of credential mills, knowledge malls, and grade markets.

These dominant ideals of capitalism and individualism persist as societal norms in our nation; as a result, unethical and concerning behaviours such as contract cheating, plagiarism, and false credentials arise as natural and even inevitable outcomes within these highly competitive and hierarchical systems (Crossman, 2021; Eaton, 2021; Gray, 2021; Christensen Hughes & McCabe, 2006a; Lindstrom, 2021). A consumerist ideology pervades all institutional levels, including faculty, administration, researchers, as well as students, and ultimately results in a degradation of relationships (Crossman, 2021; Gray, 2021; Kier & Hunter, 2021; Lindstrom, 2021; Sopcak & Hood, 2021). Several scholars, including Bertram Gallant, point out the "moral panic" these ethical issues raise for citizens who believe in the higher good of universities. Contemporary scholars have shifted their focus from issues of academic misconduct to critically questioning how outdated teaching and learning approaches are implicated in matters of academic integrity (Bertram Gallant, 2008; Kenny & Eaton, 2021; Peters, Fontaine, & Frenette, 2021; Gray, 2021; Christensen Hughes & McCabe, 2006b; Rossi, 2021) and how a focus on faculty and departmental responses needs to be prioritized along with opportunities for informal learning (Kenny & Eaton, 2021). These various studies reveal fundamental cracks and flaws in how teaching and learning are both enacted, and experienced, in higher learning settings.

In taking a new approach to studying academic integrity from a teaching and learning lens, Tricia Bertram Gallant (2008) advises faculty and student affairs practitioners to reframe their central question from: "'How do we stop students from cheating?' to 'How do we ensure students are learning?'" (p. 6). As academic integrity scholar Sarah Eaton (2021) sees it, an over-reliance on outdated models of lectures and rote memorization has left students disengaged and removed from learning. By questioning how students are engaged in learning, these scholars have started to unearth the problematic foundations of an outdated approach to education.

To address these concerns, we draw on the principles of wholism and interconnectedness to instigate and elevate a more fulsome understanding of academic integrity within the national landscape of teaching and learning. In doing so, we honour that "[t]he Indigenous Voice is in dialogue with Oral Traditions and Traditional Knowledge—a process alive with connection and transformation" (Younging, 2018, p. 11). Taking up this endeavour, we offer the Cree term, ê-kwêskît, which, as McLeod (2016) defines it, is one way "to regain honour" (p. 9). In recognizing that mistakes are part of the human condition, the term also acknowledges that we can "turn our lives around, when we *atone*, then … [we] move towards regaining our honour" (p. 9–10, emphasis added). In this term resides the promise of reconciling relations through the act of learning and sharing previously untold truths as we work to rebuild ruptured relations between Indigenous and non-Indigenous Canadians through a collective will and commitment to do better.

We see academic integrity, a cornerstone of education, as implicated in nationwide efforts of decolonizing and Indigenizing, and ultimately extending to the national project of reconciliation. Decolonization being the work of critically considering western euro-centric hierarchical systems of colonization, oppression, and patriarchy, while Indigenization is the engagement of Indigenous ways of knowing, being and doing as parallel and valid means of constructing systems and practices. Namely, in the decolonizing act of identifying and challenging colonial assumptions within post-secondary spaces, an ethical space is created for shared truths inclusive of Indigenous perspectives (Ermine, 2007). This work also addresses the dilemma facing post-secondaries wherein students feel betrayed when they realize they have been taught a colonially biased and incomplete curriculum.

In response to this pressing need for Canadian educational reform, a growing number of studies reveal that too often institutional and professional commitments to Indigenizing the academy do not enact the structural shifts required (Battiste, 2018; Battiste, Bell, & Findlay, 2002; Gaudry & Lorenz, 2018; Held, 2019). In looking across Canada at the number of institutions who are initiating Indigenizing strategies, we call for a fundamental re-definition of what academic integrity is, and what a possible redefinition could mean, for those of us working within postsecondary settings. As the chapter topics within this handbook reveal, there are serious fault lines in the historical foundations of mainstream Eurocentric forms of schooling. Today, a highly commercialized model of education that markets and promotes the pursuit of wealth, profit-making, and efficiencies capsizes the noble pursuit of knowledge and plunges education into issues of plagiarism, essay mills, contract cheating, counterfeit credentials, and other deeply concerning tactics. These issues arise as inevitable outcomes of a corporate-driven agenda where individual interests precede that of the common good.[1] Further, unethical behaviours afflict the nature of our relations with one another. In an uber-competitive environment where top grades and outdoing one another forms the basis of our ongoing interactions, there is little room for collaboration and mutual respect. In these troubling times, what has become evident is that a neoliberal model of education that prioritizes economic interests over moral development has raised more issues than learning outcomes (Brimble, 2016; Kezar & Bernstein-Sierra, 2016). Nor does it honour Indigenous truths and perspectives around the purpose and practice of education.

We maintain that institutional projects of decolonizing and Indigenizing the academy hold the potential to re-define what academic integrity means from a wholistic and interconnected lens of truth-telling. We ground our scholarly discussion in the recognition of ethical considerations, including truth-telling, as foundational to understanding academic integrity (Christensen Hughes & Bertram Gallant, 2016). We maintain that it is only in recent times that Canadians are awakening to the hidden truths that surround Indigenous realities. As a hopeful point of entry into this work, we see Indigenizing efforts across a number of Canadian universities as the basis from which to speak to a more inclusive and wholistic definition of academic integrity through the integration of Indigenous principles. We share how the pedagogical innovations inherent in decolonizing and reconciliatory approaches serve as

---

[1] See David Callahan (2004), for a discussion of how American students translate 'the cheating culture' adopted in undergraduate and graduate schools into their future workplace settings.

markers of how educators might initiate discussions around the topic of ethics and shared values with a new generation of learners. In seeking an inclusive definition of academic integrity, we rely on Cree terminology within our discussion to expand the salient and ethical points of connection. Ultimately, we seek a wholistic redefinition of academic integrity that is challenged and deepened by the inclusion of Indigenous truths, values, and knowledge traditions that represent the truths of all Canadians.

Eurocentric Foundations: Understanding the Impacts of Neoliberalism and Capitalism in Post-secondary

As with other colonial nation-states, the contemporary focus within the scholarship of academic integrity in Canada is mired in a neoliberal model of education which reflects the colonial origins of our formalized educational systems (Battiste, Bell & Findlay, 2002; Kezar & Bernstein-Sierra, 2016; Lincoln, 2018; Schissel & Wotherspoon, 2002). Further reflecting its commonwealth origins, a largely Eurocentric definition of academic integrity appears to arise primarily from Judeo-Christian beliefs and values focused on ideals of progress, standardization, and honour codes (Bretag, 2016; Eaton & Christensen Hughes, 2021; Fishman, 2016; Thomas & Scott, 2016). In this type of system, scholars are expected to conquer, possess, and dominate knowledge within hierarchical structures that reward those who replicate and uphold the status quo.

Gaining knowledge of social justice issues, those that speak to the visibility or invisibility of structures and systems, is integral for engaging in and understanding the critical conversations that need to take place. When learners understand the systems that uphold societal inequities, they are empowered to not only name but also confront these barriers to learning. From an Indigenous perspective, Opaskwayak (Cree) scholar Greg Younging (2018) asserts that "in the past, Eurocentric knowledge has condescendingly associated Indigenous knowledge with the primitive, the wild, and the natural" making the process of intellectual domination another form of natural resource extraction (p. 111). The highly respected Maori scholar, Linda Tuhiwai Smith (2018), similarly regards the project of knowledge production within an imperialist-driven agenda to be hazardous to Indigenous knowledges. In her view: "Representation is important as a concept because it gives the impression of 'the truth'" (p. 37). In looking to collectively redefine academic integrity with the integration of Indigenous truths, we are claiming our right as Indigenous scholars to stand as equals in the co-creation of knowledge in the academy and to assert our collective truths.

Telling Truths in the Lands Now Known as Canada

> Our Indian legislation generally rests on the principle that the Aborigines are to be kept in a condition of tutelage and treated as wards or children of the state ... It is clearly our wisdom and our duty, through education and other means, to prepare him [sic] for a higher civilization by encouraging him [sic] to assume the privileges and responsibilities of full citizenship. (Annual Report of the Department of the Interior, 1876)

Despite a litany of historical and ongoing challenges, including forced assimilation and Christianization, across the lands now known as Canada, our nation has been making promising strides towards reconciliation. For most non-Indigenous Canadians, the residential school stories shared by the Truth and Reconciliation Commission (TRC) of Canada (2015) represent disturbing and shocking tales, ones they are often hearing for the first time. Today, Canadians are facing the atrocity of unmarked mass graves of Indigenous children unearthed in residential schoolyards. Yet, as Indigenous people can attest, these discoveries, the TRC Final Report (2015), and the 94 Calls to Action (2012) represent only the latest bid to improve relations between Indigenous and non-Indigenous peoples. This recent national initiative builds on a series of earlier attempts which sought to raise mainstream awareness around Canada's colonial history and its negative effects on the First Peoples of Canada (see, for instance, National Indian Brotherhood, 1972; Royal Commission on Aboriginal Peoples, 1996; United Nations Declaration on the Rights of Indigenous Peoples, 2008). In response to the TRC Calls to Action (2012), many post-secondary institutions, including national disciplinary entities such as deans' councils, have committed to Indigenizing and decolonizing aims thereby affirming education as key to improving relations between Indigenous and non-Indigenous peoples (Association of Canadian Deans of Education, 2010; Denzin & Spooner, 2018; Madden, 2019). For those working within higher education who are encountering dark truths and questioning previously upheld colonial assumptions, this awareness problematizes current manifestations of academic integrity.

Within a promising trend that carries the possibility of broader truth-telling, we are also cognizant that a distinct, and disturbing, pattern of raising hopes followed by failed outcomes typifies these national undertakings over the years. Moreover, this history can also be viewed as a storied way of understanding the current racial tensions and conflicts arising across Canada as steeped in a history of Indigenous distrust of non-Indigenous efforts to bring about societal change, fuelled by the frustrations of First Peoples not being heard despite continual efforts to engage in dialogue. In an attempt to foster improved relations between Indigenous and non-Indigenous, we once again look to the work of Neal McLeod as he proposes a new Cree term, kwéskî-âcimowina, to epitomize stories that can result in transformative learning, referring specifically to stories "where people change their lives around"' (p. 100).

In sharing kwéskî-âcimowina as transformative truths, we begin with the story of an early attempt to address educational issues impacting learners in what was then known as "Indian Country." This movement took form with the 1972 publication of *Indian Control of Indian Education*, issued by the National Indian Brotherhood (now the Assembly of First Nations), and brought a telling tale of the many ways in which mainstream education had failed Indigenous people through its imposition of a biased and colonial form of schooling which either vilified or erased the First Peoples of this land. In pointing out how this deficit in schooling had disadvantaged First Nations learners by privileging others, the Indigenous leaders set out three principles that they felt future generations should aspire to in pursuit of a good life and living as a person of moral character:

> Pride encourages us to recognize and use our talents, as well as to master the skills needed to make a living
>
> Understanding our fellowmen will enable us to meet other Canadians on an equal footing, respecting cultural differences while pooling resources for the common good.
>
> Living in harmony with nature will insure [sic] preservation of the balance between man and his environment which is necessary for the future of our planet, as well as for fostering the climate in which Indian Wisdom has always flourished. (National Indian Brotherhood, 1972, p. 1)

Specific aspects of these principles include respect for personal freedom and others' cultures, self-reliance, respect for nature and Indigenous wisdom, along with generosity in terms of sharing for the common good (NIB, 1972, p. 2). A significant cultural gap between Indigenous and non-Indigenous people was also noted by the authors and this gap was most evident in a largely irrelevant schooling curriculum and classroom teachers who lacked any knowledge of First Nations realities. Tellingly, their words ring distinctly true in our present-day: "To overcome this [gap], it is essential that Canadian children of every racial origin have the opportunity during their school days to learn about the history, customs and culture of this country's original inhabitants and first citizens" (p. 2). This historical recommendation is only now becoming manifest in some, but not all, learning institutions across our nation[2] (Kabatay & Johnson, CBC, 2019, October 2; Macdonald, 2016). Speaking to how a respectful approach to education might be realized through the integration of a full spectrum of Canadian truths, the authors noted that a blended curriculum drawing on the strengths of Indigenous and Western traditions would best support learners (p. 25). In re-imagining academic integrity as one that seeks wholism and interconnectedness as central tenets, this compelling manifesto holds key lessons around the importance of mandating Indigenous education and the inclusion of Indigenous perspectives within and across all curriculum areas as not only wholistic in nature but also as long overdue events. As history reveals, the impact of continually ignoring Indigenous counsel such as the NIB paper resulted in national turmoil such as that experienced in the Oka Crisis of 1990.

In 1996, the Royal Commission on Aboriginal Peoples (RCAP) released a 4000-page tome of truths that meticulously catalogued a variety of issues, including

[2] In Alberta, the mandating of First Nations, Métis, and Inuit perspectives within and across all subjects in the provincial curriculum arrived with Teaching Quality Standard #5 in 2019. This long-awaited moment is most welcome but is also facing challenges and critiques from those who see Indigenous education as "ideological brainwashing" and instead prefer to keep the colonial narrative intact (Aukerman, 2020).

education, impacting Indigenous peoples and the severe socioeconomic inequities resulting from a colonial past. This national commission was "[b]orn of conflict, [the] RCAP was established shortly after a 78-day armed standoff —known as the Oka Crisis—between the Mohawk community of Kanesatake, the Sûreté du Québec, and the Canadian army" (Troian, CBC, March 3, 2016). In setting out terms for a fair and honourable relationship between the Aboriginal and non-Aboriginal people of Canada, the seven commissioners concluded: "The main policy direction [of assimilation], pursued for more than 150 years, first by colonial then by Canadian governments, has been wrong" (Royal Commission on Aboriginal Peoples, 1996, para. 7). The truth of the attempted and failed assimilation of the First Peoples of Canada stands as a foundational pillar in our call for fellow educators to adhere to a national project of truth-telling:

> Successive governments have tried—sometimes intentionally, sometimes in ignorance—to absorb Aboriginal people into Canadian society, thus eliminating them as distinct peoples. Policies pursued over the decades have undermined—and almost erased—Aboriginal cultures and identities. This is assimilation. It is a denial of the principles of peace, harmony and justice for which this country stands—and it has failed. Aboriginal peoples remain proudly different. (Royal Commission on Aboriginal Peoples, 1996, para. 9–10)

Likewise, Mikmaw educator and scholar Marie Battiste (2018) identifies attempted assimilation as the impetus behind wronged relations and one that continues today in the form of cognitive imperialism in Canadian universities. By continuing to elevate a Eurocentric curriculum as the norm for all students, the "task of decolonizing education [that] requires multilateral processes of understanding and unpacking the central assumptions of domination, patriarchy, racism, and ethnocentrisms ... continue to glue the academy's privileges in place" (Battiste, Bell & Findlay, 2002, p. 84). Without the meaningful disruption of colonial terms and the inclusion of Indigenous ways, the goals of decolonizing and Indigenizing universities will remain unattainable and academic integrity will continue to be undermined as neo-colonial motives remain unchallenged.

Calling for Renewal in Relationships

In calling for a renewed relationship, the RCAP commissioners articulated a set of principles based on a robust set of data, including 178 public hearings, 96 community visits, multiple expert consultations, several commissioned research studies, alongside a thorough review of current and historical documentation (Royal Commission on Aboriginal Peoples, 1996, para. 5). The following four principles are re-presented here at length in the spirit of reframing academic integrity as conceptually grounded in a wholistic and interconnected project of truth-telling.

> *Recognition*: The principle of mutual recognition calls on non-Aboriginal Canadians to recognize that Aboriginal people are the original inhabitants and caretakers of this land and have distinctive rights and responsibilities flowing from that status. It calls on Aboriginal

> people to accept that non-Aboriginal people are also of this land now, by birth and by adoption, with strong ties of love and loyalty. It requires both sides to acknowledge and relate to one another as partners, respecting each other's laws and institutions and co-operating for mutual benefit.
>
> *Respect:* The principle of respect calls on all Canadians to create a climate of positive mutual regard between and among peoples. Respect provides a bulwark against attempts by one partner to dominate or rule over another. Respect for the unique rights and status of First Peoples, and for each Aboriginal person as an individual with a valuable culture and heritage, needs to become part of Canada's national character.
>
> *Sharing:* The principle of sharing calls for the giving and receiving of benefits in fair measure. It is the basis on which Canada was founded, for if Aboriginal peoples had been unwilling to share what they had and what they knew about the land, many of the newcomers would not have lived to prosper. The principle of sharing is central to the treaties and central to the possibility of real equality among the peoples of Canada in the future.
>
> *Responsibility:* Responsibility is the hallmark of a mature relationship. Partners in such a relationship must be accountable for the promises they have made, accountable for behaving honourably, and accountable for the impact of their actions on the well-being of the other. Because we do and always will share the land, the best interests of Aboriginal and non-Aboriginal people will be served if we act with the highest standards of responsibility, honesty and good faith toward one another. (Royal Commission on Aboriginal Peoples, 1996, para. 66–69)

In 2016, Canada formally adopted the United Nations Declaration on the Rights of Indigenous Peoples (UNDRIP) as a basis for recognizing the inherent rights of the First Peoples of Canada. The late adoption of this international covenant is not without its own story of resistance and racism here in Canada, exposing the colonial undertones of our nation-state, as national leaders debated the extent to which individual and collective rights could, or should, be equally recognized.

In the spirit of kwéskî-ácimowina, we ask readers to reflect on these Indigenous-led attempts to raise mainstream awareness of colonial injustices. Today, the horrific truths surrounding Indian Residential Schools are being amplified by the work of the Truth and Reconciliation Commission of Canada (2015). Some educational groups, such as *Facing History and Ourselves,* point out that the impelling force behind the formation of the TRC was "[b]ecause of the massive lawsuit it faced, the government was almost forced to focus on the Indian Residential Schools, and [in response] it set up a Truth and Reconciliation Commission (TRC) in 2008 to address those issues" (*Facing History,* Truth and Reconciliation, para. 1). From a social justice lens, it is revealing that the TRC arose only under threat of legal repercussions following another lengthy period of ignoring, or ignorance, of Indigenous ways. In setting out principles for moving forward, the TRC identified the need for all Canadians to recognize inherent Indigenous rights to self-determination, the exposing of colonial harms, the redressing of colonial harms at individual, leadership, and government levels, and finally the need for accountability within these areas. These principles comprise the foundations for respectful and ethical relations between Indigenous and non-Indigenous people moving forward; yet, as the recent backlash against the protests and community support for Indigenous and Black Lives Matter movements reveals, much work remains to be done.

Looking back at these moments in time, each has worked in some way to increase societal awareness around Indigenous realities yet it is also obvious that the same messages have been delivered time and again. If the act of telling truths, including Indigenous truths, is central to a reconfiguration of academic integrity focused on asking, "How do we ensure students are learning the full spectrum of truths?," then these historical initiatives should be viewed as foundational lessons in this work. In seeking to right the wrongs of a colonial past, those working within higher education—from faculty, students, to administration—are now being asked to confront previously unquestioned colonial assumptions that comprise the field of academic integrity. The consideration and inclusion of Indigenous principles and values within our institutions of higher learning holds the potential to re-define academic integrity from a more wholistic understanding replete with multiple truths and perspectives. Alternatively, we can wait for history and the inevitable lashback to repeat itself.

Decolonizing and Indigenizing As Forms of Academic Integrity

In a promising shift from multiple failed attempts to include Indigenous perspectives in the past, many post-secondary institutions, including national groups such as deans' councils, have recently announced their commitment to reconciliation through the formal adoption of Indigenizing and decolonizing goals. Several of these efforts preceded the TRC Calls to Action and "[t]hrough a process known as [I]ndigenization, many universities are making a conscious effort to bring [i]ndigenous people, as well as their philosophies and cultures, into strategic plans, governance roles, academics, research and recruitment" (MacDonald, 2016, para. 4). By affirming education as the key to improving relations between Indigenous and non-Indigenous peoples, these higher learning institutes are responding to the need for inclusion of Indigenous truths in the academy and, by extension, into the field of academic integrity. At the same time, "[p]robably the most complex, and contentious, aspect of [I]ndigenization is what it means for curricula, pedagogy and research..." (MacDonald, 2016, para. 10).

Over the years, Indigenous scholars have argued that decolonization, where critical examinations of power, privilege, and positionality are the basis for unlearning and examining colonially biased curriculum, form a precursor to the work of Indigenization (Battiste, 2013; George, 2019; Poitras Pratt, Louie, Hanson & Ottmann, 2018). The work of decolonization is one that applies to both Indigenous and non-Indigenous learners as together we work to understand how a colonial past has impacted the lives of all Canadians. In specific terms, "Decolonizing education entails identifying how colonization has impacted education and [how it is] working to unsettle colonial structures, systems, and dynamics in educational contexts" (Poitras Pratt et al., 2018, p. x). Through these efforts, Canadians have been asked to face the ways in which Indigenous peoples have suffered at the hands of colonial powers and how these neocolonial injustices continue today. As a precursor to Indigenization, the work of decolonization requires a willingness to sit in the discomfort of hard truths including how a colonial system has granted unearned benefits to many through the removal of resources, rights, and opportunities from Indigenous Peoples. Importantly, awareness is not enough as knowing better implicates doing better. As the Final Report from the TRC (2015) sets out, educators are asked to actively counter injustices through targeted action. It is also the case, as George (2019) asserts, that "[e]xploring Indigenous perspectives on reconciliation and decolonization often leaves me wondering if post-secondary institutions in Canada are willing and capable to effectively decolonize their own institutions because it means sacrificing privilege, power, and control" (p. X). As academic institutions that seek and share knowledge and truth as their raison d'être, universities are inherently implicated in the reproduction, or the unsettling, of how we ethically situate ourselves. In an ideal world, an increased level of awareness would prompt the deliberate and strategic prioritization of Indigenous perspectives in post-secondary settings. Here, the principles of academic integrity could be realized for all.

Despite undoubtedly good intentions, some commentators have noted that the onus for Indigenizing efforts tends to rest primarily on Indigenous scholars who have been recruited into what remains largely colonial institutions (Gaudry & Lorenz, 2018). By asking Indigenous scholars and staff members to make substantive change within the academy without considering what is required at a structural level to implement these shifts, post-secondaries are offering token gestures rather than true commitment to reconciliation. For those who have been assigned leadership roles in implementing Indigenizing effort in post-secondary institutions, the reconciliatory burden may be far too much for one person to manage, particularly given mounting pressures to enact change rapidly within an environment that holds no certainties (Gladue, 2021). One might even argue that the situation represents an ethical transgression if post-secondaries are not willing to invest the time, resources, and authority required to propel and sustain substantive changes in their respective houses of learning.

Another concerning and enduring truth that surrounds post-secondary institutions is the extent to which issues of inequities and racism persist in higher learning environments, particularly in the realities of how Indigenous students and faculty members are unfairly treated (Bailey, 2016; Henry et al., 2017; Mohamed & Beagan, 2019). As Senator Murray Sinclair points out to those who are willing to listen, colonial schooling systems that deliberately advanced the vilification and erasure of Indigenous peoples serve as the primary source of contemporary racism against Indigenous peoples. It might be argued that these injustices continue unabated due in large part to mainstream unknowingness, or what some term a pedagogy of ignorance, around Indigenous issues (Anwaruddin, 2015; Zembylas, 2005). This state of unknowing reflects the success of a colonial system that deliberately rendered Indigenous peoples invisible and voiceless but also signals the real outcomes of continuing to ignore Indigenous calls for reform.

It may also be the case that mainstream Canadians fear a loss of power and privilege in acknowledging the injustices that surround the lives of Indigenous peoples

(DiAngelo, 2011; Sensoy & DiAngelo, 2017; St Denis, 2007). We have only to recall former Prime Minister Stephen Harper's denial of Canada's colonial past, and Senator Beyak's more recent assertion that racism does not exist in Canada, to bear witness to how deeply entrenched mainstream resistance is to the hard truths of our nation's colonial past and present. And for those who may believe that resistance to Indigenous truths resides only in the political corridors of Canadian society, the comments section that follows any Indigenous media releases by our public broadcaster, the Canadian Broadcasting Corporation (CBC), reveals how widespread and deeply held the racist attitudes are across our oft-lauded "peaceable and tolerant" nation. Only recently have we seen Canadians willing to listen to how these lands and the original peoples have been exploited and mistreated since contact. In the midst of this admittedly complicated and difficult learning, the question of how academic integrity is defined within institutes of higher learning is central to the discussion of how we might ethically build and repair relationships with one another. But how do we disrupt the historical trend of ignoring and opposing Indigenous truths when apathy and opposition reify a mainstream investment in maintaining the status quo? And how do we engage others in the task of redefining academic integrity when post-secondaries are still struggling to deliver curriculum inclusive of shared colonial truths?

In seeking further inspiration around how we might work to redefine academic integrity, we look to the work of Smith (2012) whose work in decolonizing research has been highly influential and far-reaching. A series of 25 Indigenous projects arising from community research programmes and community-identified needs are grouped under themes of survival, self-determination, and control as central aims. More recent attempts by Indigenous peoples to speak to the responsibilities of the academy with specific reference to research and academic integrity include the *First Nations Ethics Guide on Research, Aboriginal Traditional Knowledge* (Assembly of First Nations, 2009); *Elements of Indigenous Style* (Younging, 2018), and *Research is Ceremony* (Wilson, 2008). These publications highlight the ways in which ethical considerations within Indigenous research can inform, contribute, and connect to the scholarship of teaching and learning with integrity.

In further promising initiatives, including *The Seven Grandfathers in Academic Integrity*, a two-page pamphlet issued by the University of Toronto, and the University of Calgary's Indigenous Academic Integrity multimodal resource, we see that Indigenous scholars are taking up the work of troubling the supremacy of neo-liberal western ethical and moral considerations of integrity in the academy. These parallel ways of expressing and centering truth are essential to the work of redefining academic integrity for all because they challenge the oft (consciously or unconsciously) held belief that western axiology and ethics are the pinnacle and definition of truth in academic culture. Additionally, these Indigenized resources seek to honour Indigenous paradigms, while also providing a basis for others to question the consumerist models which currently veil expectations of integrity in our institutions. This new foundation acknowledges Indigenous ways, honours Indigenous rigour, and validates the dedication to the caretaking of knowledge that is part of the *unquestionably* valuable and ancient inheritance of Indigenous traditions, languages, ceremonies, stories and practices. We bring forward this expansive knowledge to the academy as a transformative and reconciliatory way forward, provided that the academy is open and committed to ethical relations where the historical pattern of turning a blind eye to Indigenous truths that has caused harm and disconnection is ended.

As we see it, Indigenous knowledge/traditions must be acknowledged when post-secondaries take up Indigenizing and decolonizing practices/policies with respect to interrelatedness, interconnectedness, and wholistic ways. Again, the answer may rest in our willingness and ability to trouble the status quo, a social hierarchy of inequities that serves to subjugate some and provide power to others, in what we recognize as a neoliberal and capitalist-driven system that is showing signs of failing its own ideals.

Re-defining Academic Integrity Through Indigenous Values and Traditions

Indigenous perspectives highlight wholistic truths and the reality of our interconnectedness that could rightly form the basis of a new definition of academic integrity. In this section we bring forward Indigenous paradigms and principles which elucidate previously unexplored dimensions of academic integrity in the academy. In doing so, we align our understandings of academic integrity with the fundamental principles of Indigenous research methodologies that Smith (2012) shares: "Indigenous knowledge… has values and principles about human behaviour and ethics, about relationships, about wellness and leading a good life… knowledge has beauty and can make the world beautiful if used in a good way" (Smith, 2012, p. 161). By reconnecting to collectivist values that prioritize a sense of shared humanity, the spaces of learning and teaching can be transformed. What is transformative in this approach is the privileging of a sense of interconnectedness and community which empowers learners and educators alike to take positive risks and move into shared ethical spaces of knowledge creation. We explore the possibilities of this re-defined concept of academic integrity through the three central and interconnected principles of relationality, reciprocity and respect.[3]

Relationality

From an Indigenous perspective: "relationships do not merely shape reality, they are reality" (Wilson, 2008, p. 7). Relationships are integral to our identities, communities, and the ways in which we navigate the world around us. Relationships serve as

---

[3] We acknowledge there are multiple iterations of Indigenous principles related to integrity (see for example Kirkness & Barnhardt, 2001) but for the purposes of this discussion, we have focused on what we see as shared aims.

the connective tissue of the living organisms that are our societies, communities and the universe; it is good relations that allow us to function in a healthy, whole and undivided way. Relationships are complicated, they are not simple nor unchanging, and it is this inherent complexity which is also their strength. In considering relationality as a core concept within a discussion focused on academic integrity, we also acknowledge that, in the context of the academy, relationships encounter power dynamics, navigate ever-evolving circumstances, and bump up against highly individualistic tendencies. In truth, a collective orientation within learning and teaching environments is counterintuitive when matters of competitive grading, awards, and scholarships are those which learners, and educators, aspire to, within the current mainstream learning model. Yet, centralizing relationships is integral to the survivance, continuity and thriving of Indigenous Peoples and form the basis to our wholeness, knowledges, and integrity. The same could be said for all our relations.

Speaking to the challenge of navigating the realities of academia via the power of relationships, we bring the Cree concept of manâcihitowin advanced by Cree scholar McLeod and language-holder Arok Wolvengrey (2016) wherein "'respect; [is] where you think of someone highly without regard for yourself … we could use this as a term for ethics" (p. 178). The priority here is the communal and not the individual which ultimately speaks to the work of creating ethical spaces founded in academic integrity. Adopting relationality as a core value creates space for moving beyond the limits of an individualist approach and into the possibilities of a communally-informed academy (Donald, 2012). When we invoke the power of the collective in knowledge creation and sharing activities, we honour that "perhaps the single most important precept of the Indigenous world view is the notion that the world is alive, conscious, and flowing with knowledge and energy" (Younging, 2018, p. 114). We challenge our fellow educators to think about the possibilities of such a shift and how we might re-imagine the highly individualistic and hierarchical structure of learning where only a select few are recognized and rewarded. In a collective undertaking, benefits and responsibilities are equally shared by all in an ethos of ethical relationality and reciprocity.

Respect

To make space for the expansion of academic integrity with Indigenous truths, we invite you to engage in kâ-pê-isi-kiskêyihtahk iyinitowiyiniw-kiskêyihtamowin, or what McLeod (2016) explains is "the process of coming to know Indigenous Knowledge" (McLeod & Wolvengrey, 2016, p. 177). Within Indigenous models of teaching and learning all individuals are asked by the community to identify and serve their role in community. Collectivist pursuits of survival and flourishing are predicated on each member contributing to the whole. Thus the underpinning of the communities' relationships is respect. Respect for the work and role of each member as they strive towards your survival, your flourishing, your wholeness, wellness and equity. Indigenous peoples respect the knowledge that is being caretaken as it flows forward through time, the individuals who do the work of carrying this knowledge, and those who are new learners of the knowledge, who will someday take their place. This is, of course, the cycle of teaching and learning, and as the interconnectedness of this respect is learned and shared, ethical space is formed.

Reciprocity

The principle of respect is one that resides at the heart of reciprocity. When we recognize that "inherent in this commitment to the people is the understanding of the reciprocity of life and accountability to one another" (Hart, 2010, p. 9), we are moving from an individualistic pursuit of wealth, power, and prestige to considering those parameters that comprise collective wellness and wholeness. Reciprocity imbues us with a sense of responsibility, and as Indigenous peoples, this means we see ourselves as a link between past and future generations where our "responsibilities [are] connected to internal cultural imperatives, which include telling the truth, honesty with one another, mindfulness of impacts on the community, and mindfulness of continuity with history and heritage" (Younging, 2018, p. 18). We maintain these ethical commitments are universally shared values comprising the best of humanity.

Looking Ahead Seven Generations

In calling for a new definition of academic integrity where disparate worldviews encounter one another in a shared and ethical space, our hope is that we will build a shared understanding of what academic integrity could be, and indeed should be, within higher learning settings. We see a renewal of what academic integrity means arising from deep reflections on self and positionality, questioning how we interact with fellow citizens, and expressing itself most convincingly through ethical actions that serve the common good. We ask faculty members, as representatives of our institutions, if they are willing and prepared to engage with the entire spectrum of truths that are held by the complex nation of Canada. And more, are faculty, students, administrators, and researchers ready to acknowledge the validity and importance of other ways of knowing? We believe the onus for academic integrity resides with the institution, particularly faculty and administration who lead, design, and deliver appropriate content and effective pedagogical design. In other words, if education is viewed as the pursuit of truth, or more appropriately truths, then it is essential to expand the current definition of academic integrity to include Indigenous principles, truths, and perspectives across all institutional areas.

Working from an intersecting definition of integrity that is centred in wholism and interconnectedness, we invite fellow Indigenous scholars and the wider academic community into a shared ethical space to help us redefine these critical underpinnings of education (Held, 2019). To ensure ethically grounded and open discussions around what academic integrity entails, we must first be willing to engage in critical conversations such as those focused on problematizing the current neoliberal and commercialized approaches to education where commercial interests in teaching and learning mean academic misconduct runs rampant. If not commerce, what foundation should education then claim in the name of integrity? We offer a whole-minded values-driven approach where a biodiversity of knowledges flourishes and embraces alternative ways of knowing. It follows that institutional academic integrity could then be assessed on the extent to which Indigenous truths and principles are respectfully integrated into mainstream structures as equal paradigms of thought. This chapter is an invitation for others to join us in renewing relationships, with integrity, for the wellbeing of all our relations.

Points of Consideration

- Indigenization and decolonization are integral practices of academic integrity that all citizens need to embrace.
- Integrity demands that newcomers/settlers/colonizers instigate acts of atonement and actions of reconciliation which serve to intentionally disrupt the historical cycle of ignoring the injustices visited upon the First Peoples of Canada (Regan, 2010; TRC, 2015).
- Indigenous paradigms and practices provide a way forward for the academy to choose to re-center wholistic, respectful, reciprocal, and relational forms of academic integrity, but only if these ways of knowing and the scholarship which supports them are themselves treated with integrity.

References

Absolon, K. (2010). Indigenous wholistic theory: A knowledge set for practice. *First Peoples Child & Family Review, 5*(2), 74–87. https://doi.org/10.7202/1068933ar

Anwaruddin, S. M. (2015). Pedagogy of Ignorance. *Educational Philosophy and Theory, 47*(7), 734–746. https://doi.org/10.1080/00131857.2014.914879

Assembly of First Nations. (2009). *First Nations ethics guide on research and Aboriginal traditional knowledge.* Assembly of First Nations. https://www.afn.ca/uploads/files/env/atk_protocol_book.pdf

Association of Canadian Deans of Education. (2010). *Accord on Indigenous education.* http://www.csse-scee.ca/docs/acde/acde_accord_indigenousresearch_en.pdf

Alschuler, A. S., & Blimling, G. S. (1995). Curbing epidemic cheating through systemic change. *College Teaching, 43*(4), 123–126. https://doi.org/10.1080/87567555.1995.9925531

Aukerman, M. (2020, October 28). Opinion: Social studies curriculum should be based on research. *Edmonton Journal.* https://edmontonjournal.com/opinion/columnists/opinion-social-studies-curriculum-proposals-are-a-conceptual-mess

Bailey, K. A. (2016). Racism within the Canadian university: Indigenous students' experiences. *Ethnic and Racial Studies, 39*(7), 1261–1279. https://doi.org/10.1080/01419870.2015.1081961

Battiste, M. (2018). Reconciling Indigenous knowledge in education: Promises, possibilities, and imperatives. In M. Spooner & J. McNinch (Eds.), *Dissident knowledge in higher education* (pp. 123–148). University of Regina Press.

Battiste, M. (2013). *Decolonizing education: Nourishing the learning spirit*. Purich.

Battiste, M., Bell, L., & Findlay, L. M. (2002). Decolonizing education in Canadian universities: An interdisciplinary, international, indigenous research project. *Canadian Journal of Native Education, 26*(2), 82–95. https://ezproxy.lib.ucalgary.ca/login?url=https://www-proquest-com.ezproxy.lib.ucalgary.ca/docview/230305394?accountid=9838

Bertram Gallant, T. (2008). Moral panic: The contemporary context of academic integrity. *Academic Integrity in the Twenty-First Century, 33*, 1–143. https://doi.org/10.1002/aehe.3305

Bretag, T. (2016). Defining academic integrity: International perspectives–Introduction. In T. Bretag (Ed.), *Handbook of Academic Integrity* (pp. 3–6). Springer Reference.

Brimble, M. (2016). Why students cheat. An exploration of the motivators of student academic dishonesty in higher education. In T. Bretag (Ed.), *Handbook of Academic Integrity* (pp. 1–14). Springer. https://doi.org/10.1007/978-981-287-079-7

Callahan, D. (2004). The cheating culture: Why more Americans are doing wrong to get ahead. Houghton Mifflin Harcourt.

Christensen Hughes, J. M., & McCabe, D. L. (2006a). Academic misconduct within higher education in Canada. *The Canadian Journal of Higher Education, 36*(2), 1–21. https://doi.org/10.47678/cjhe.v36i2.183537

Christensen Hughes, J. M., & McCabe, D. L. (2006b). Understanding academic misconduct. *Canadian Journal of Higher Education, 36*(1), 49–63. https://doi.org/10.47678/cjhe.v36i1.183525

Christensen Hughes, J., & Bertram Gallant, T. (2016). Infusing ethics and ethical decision making into the curriculum. In T. Bretag (Ed.), *Handbook of Academic Integrity* (pp. 1055–1073). Springer.

Crossman, K. (2022). Education as a financial transaction: Contract employment and contract cheating. In S. E. Eaton & J. Christensen Hughes (Eds.), *Academic integrity in Canada: An enduring and essential challenge*. Springer.

Denzin, N. K., & Spooner, M. (2018). An interview with Dr. Norman K. Denzin on the politics of evidence, science, and research. In M. Spooner & J. McNinch (Eds.), *Dissident knowledge in higher education* (pp. 41–54). University of Regina Press.

Department of the Interior. (1876). *Annual report of the department of the interior for the year ended 30th June 1876*. Maclean, Roger & Co. https://central.bac-lac.gc.ca/.item/?id=1876-IAAR-RAAI&op=pdf&app=indianaffairs

DiAngelo, R. (2011). White fragility. *International Journal of Critical Pedagogy, 3*(3), 54–70.

Donald, D. (2012). Forts, curriculum, and ethical relationality. In N. Ng-A-Fook & J. Rottmann (Eds.), *Reconsidering Canadian curriculum studies: Curriculum studies worldwide*. Palgrave Macmillan. https://doi.org/10.1057/9781137008978_3

Eaton, S. E. (2022). Contract cheating in Canada: A comprehensive overview. In S. E. Eaton & J. Christensen Hughes (Eds.), *Academic integrity in Canada: An enduring and essential challenge*. Springer.

Eaton, S. E., & Christensen Hughes, J. (2022). Academic integrity in Canada: Historical perspectives and current trends In S. E. Eaton & J. Christensen Hughes (Eds.), *Academic integrity in Canada: An enduring and essential challenge*. Springer.

Ermine, W. (2007). The ethical space of engagement. *Indigenous Law Journal 6*(1), 193–203. https://tspace.library.utoronto.ca/bitstream/1807/17129/1/ILJ-6.1-Ermine.pdf

Fishman, T. (2016). Academic integrity as an educational concept, concern, and movement in US institutions of higher learning. In T. Bretag (Ed.), *Handbook of Academic Integrity* (pp. 7–21). Springer Reference.

Gaudry, A., & Lorenz, D. (2018). Indigenization as inclusion, reconciliation, and decolonization: Navigating the different visions for indigenizing the Canadian Academy. *AlterNative: An International Journal of Indigenous Peoples, 14*(3), 218–227. https://doi.org/10.1177/1177180118785382

George, C. T. (2019). Decolonize, then Indigenize: Critical insights on decolonizing education and Indigenous resurgence in Canada. *Antistasis, 9*(1), 73–95.

Gladue, K. (2021). Indigenous academic integrity. *Taylor Institute of Teaching and Learning Resource Library*. https://taylorinstitute.ucalgary.ca/resources/indigenous-academic-integrity

Gray, B. C. (2022). Ethics, ed tech, and the rise of contract cheating. In S. E. Eaton & J. Christensen Hughes (Eds.), *Academic integrity in Canada: An enduring and essential challenge*. Springer.

Hall, B. (2018). Beyond epistemicide: Knowledge democracy and higher education. In M. Spooner & J. McNinch (Eds.), *Dissident knowledge in higher education* (pp. 84–101). University of Regina Press.

Hart, M. (2010). Indigenous worldviews, knowledge, and research: The development of an indigenous research paradigm. *Journal of Indigenous Social Development, 1*(1A). 1–16. https://scholarspace.manoa.hawaii.edu/bitstream/10125/15117/v1i1_04hart.pdf

Held, M. B. E. (2019). Decolonizing research paradigms in the context of settler-colonialism: An unsettling, mutual and collaborative effort. *International Journal of Qualitative Methods, 18*, 1–16. https://doi.org/10.1177/1609406918821574

Henry, F., Dua, E., Kobayashi, A., James, C., Li, P., Ramos, H., & Smith, M. S. (2017). Race, racialization and indigeneity in Canadian universities. *Race Ethnicity and Education, 20*(3), 300–314. https://doi.org/10.1080/13613324.2016.1260226

Hunter, J. & Kier, C. (2022). Canadian open digital distance education universities and academic integrity. In S. E. Eaton & J. Christensen Hughes (Eds.), *Academic integrity in Canada: An enduring and essential challenge*. Springer.

Kabatay, J. & Johnson, R. (2019, October 2). *CBC News*. Charting progress on indigenous content in school curricula. https://www.cbc.ca/news/indigenous/indigenous-content-school-curriculums-trc-1.5300580

Kenny, N. & Eaton, S. (2022). Academic integrity through a SoTL lens and 4M framework: An institutional self-study. In S. E. Eaton & J. Christensen Hughes (Eds.), *Academic integrity in Canada: An enduring and essential challenge*. Springer.

Kezar, A., & Bernstein-Sierra, S. (2016). Commercialization of higher education. In T. Bretag (Ed.), *Handbook of Academic Integrity* (pp. 325–346). Springer Reference.

Kirkness, V., & Barnhardt, R. (2001). First nations and higher education: The four R's—respect, relevance, reciprocity, responsibility. *Journal of American Indian Education, 30*(3), 1–15. http://www.jstor.org/stable/24397980

Lincoln, Y. S. (2018). A dangerous accountability: Neoliberalism's veer toward accountancy in higher education. In M. Spooner & J. McNinch (Eds.), *Dissident knowledge in higher education* (pp. 3–20). University of Regina Press.

Lindstrom, G. (2022). Accountability, relationality and indigenous epistemology: Advancing an Indigenous perspective on academic integrity. In S. E. Eaton & J. Christensen Hughes (Eds.), *Academic integrity in Canada: An enduring and essential challenge*. Springer.

MacDonald, M. (2016, April 6). Indigenizing the academy. *Universities Affairs*. https://www.universityaffairs.ca/features/feature-article/indigenizing-the-academy/#:~:text=Through%20a%20process%20known%20as,%2C%20academics%2C%20research%20and%20recruitment

Madden, B. (2019). A de/colonizing theory of truth and reconciliation education. *Curriculum Inquiry, 49*(3), 284–312. https://doi.org/10.1080/03626784.2019.1624478

McLeod, N. & Wolvengrey, A. (2016). *100 days of Cree*. University of Regina Press.

Mohamed, T., & Beagan, B. L. (2019). 'Strange faces' in the academy: Experiences of racialized and indigenous faculty in Canadian universities. *Race Ethnicity and Education, 22*(3), 338–354. https://doi.org/10.1080/13613324.2018.1511532

National Indian Brotherhood/Assembly of First Nations. (1972). *Indian control of Indian education*. https://oneca.com/IndianControlofIndianEducation.pdf

Peters, M., Fontaine, S., & Frenette, E. (2022). Teaching the teachers: To what extent do preservice teachers cheat on exams and plagiarise in their written work? In S. E. Eaton & J. Christensen Hughes (Eds.), *Academic integrity in Canada: An enduring and essential challenge*. Springer.

Poitras Pratt, Y., & Danyluk, P. J. (2019). Exploring reconciliatory pedagogy and its possibilities through educator-led praxis. *The Canadian Journal for the Scholarship of Teaching and Learning, 10*(3). https://doi.org/10.5206/cjsotl-rcacea.2019.3.9479

Poitras Pratt, Y., Louie, D. W., Hanson, A. J., & Ottmann, J. (2018). "Indigenous Education and Decolonization." In G. Noblit (Ed.), *Oxford research encyclopedia of education*. Oxford University Press. https://doi.org/10.1093/acrefore/9780190264093.013.240

Regan, P. (2010). Peace warriors and settler allies. In *Unsettling the settler within: Indian residential schools, truth telling, and reconciliation in Canada*. UBC Press.

Rossi, S. L. (2022). Revisioning paraphrasing instruction. In S. E. Eaton & J. Christensen Hughes (Eds.), *Academic integrity in Canada: An enduring and essential challenge*. Springer.

Royal Commission on Aboriginal Peoples. (1996). *Highlights from the Report of the Royal Commission on Aboriginal Peoples*. https://www.bac-lac.gc.ca/eng/discover/aboriginal-heritage/royal-commission-aboriginal-peoples/Pages/final-report.aspx

Schissel, B., & Wotherspoon, T. (2002). *The legacy of school for Aboriginal people: Education, oppression, and emancipation*. Oxford University Press.

Sensoy, O., & DiAngelo, R. (2017). *Is everyone really equal?: An introduction to key concepts in social justice education*. Teachers College Press.

Smith, L. T. (2012). Decolonizing methodologies: Research and Indigenous peoples (pp. 114–175). Zed Books.

Smith, L. T. (2018). The art of the impossible—Defining and measuring indigenous research? In M. Spooner & J. McNinch (Eds.), *Dissident knowledge in higher education* (pp. 21–40). University of Regina Press.

Sopcak, P. & Hood. K. (2022). Building a culture of restorative practice and restorative responses to academic misconduct. In S. E. Eaton & J. Christensen Hughes (Eds.), *Academic integrity in Canada: An enduring and essential challenge*. Springer.

Spooner, M., & McNinch, J. (2018). Introduction. In M. Spooner & J. McNinch (Eds.), *Dissident knowledge in higher education* (pp. xxii–xxiii). University of Regina Press.

St Denis, V. (2007). Aboriginal education and anti-racist education: Building alliances across cultural and racial identity. *Canadian Journal of Education, 30*(4), 1068–1092. https://doi.org/10.2307/20466679

Thomas, J., & Scott, J. (2016). UK perspectives of academic integrity. In I. T. Bretag (Ed.), *Handbook of Academic Integrity* (pp. 39–54). Springer Reference.

Troian, M. (2016, March 3). CBC News. 20 years since Royal Commission on Aboriginal peoples, still waiting for change. *Canadian Broadcasting Corporation*. https://www.cbc.ca/news/indigenous/20-year-anniversary-of-rcap-report-1.3469759

Truth and Reconciliation Commission of Canada. (2012). *Truth and reconciliation commission of Canada: Calls to action*. https://ehprnh2mwo3.exactdn.com/wp-content/uploads/2021/01/Calls_to_Action_English2.pdf

Truth and Reconciliation Commission of Canada. (2015). *Honouring the truth, reconciling for the future: Summary of the Final Report of the Truth and Reconciliation Commission of Canada*. Government of Canada.

United Nations. (2008). United Nations declaration on the rights of Indigenous peoples. http://www.un.org/esa/socdev/unpfii/documents/DRIPS_en.pdf

MacDonald, M. (2016). Indigenizing the academy. *Universities Affairs*. https://www.universityaffairs.ca/features/feature-article/indigenizing-the-academy/

Universities Canada. (2011). Statement on academic freedom. https://www.univcan.ca/media-room/media-releases/statement-on-academic-freedom/

Universities Canada. (2015, June 29). Universities Canada principles on indigenous education. https://www.univcan.ca/media-room/media-releases/universities-canada-principles-on-indigenous-education/

Wilson, S. (2001). What is an Indigenous research methodology? *Canadian Journal of Native Education, 25*(2), 175–179. https://doi.org/10.1007/978-3-319-18395-4_8

Wilson, S. (2008). Research is ceremony: Indigenous research methods. Fernwood.

Younging, G. (2018). *Elements of Indigenous style: A guide for writing by and about Indigenous peoples*. Brush Education Inc.

Zembylas, M. A. (2005). Pedagogy of unknowing: Witnessing unknowability in teaching and learning. *Studies in Philosophy and Education, 24*, 139–160. https://doi.org/10.1007/s11217-005-1287-3

Yvonne Poitras Pratt As an Associate Professor at the Werklund School of Education, University of Calgary, Yvonne Poitras Pratt (Métis) has published on Indigenous education, social justice, media studies, Métis studies, reconciliatory pedagogy, service-learning, and the integration of arts in education. Yvonne traces her familial roots to the historic Red River community (now Winnipeg, Manitoba) with ancestral involvement in the fur trade and the 1869 Provisional Government, and more recently to Fishing Lake Métis Settlement in northeastern Alberta. Yvonne worked with members of the Fishing Lake Métis settlement community to create a series of 19 intergenerational digital stories as part of her doctoral research in 2009–10 and this decolonizing journey is detailed in the 2020 Routledge publication of *Digital Storytelling in Indigenous Education: A Decolonizing Journey for a Metis Community*. Serving as Director, Indigenous Education, Yvonne teaches at the graduate and undergraduate level and is the recipient of a 2016 Werklund Teaching Excellence Award and a 2017 Students Union Teaching Excellence Award. Dr. Poitras Pratt earned the Confederation of Alberta Faculty Associations (CAFA) Distinguished Academic Early Career Award in 2018 and, in 2021, was awarded the Alan Blizzard Award for collaborative teaching.

Keeta Gladue As a graduate student in the Faculty of Social Work at the University of Calgary, Keeta Gladue (Cree and Métis) is currently serving her communities as the Indigenous Student Program Advisor for Writing Symbols Lodge. Keeta is a registered social worker with degrees in multiple disciplines, and experience working in rural Indigenous communities and urban city-centres. In her current role, she supports diversity, equity, and inclusion as well as intercultural relationship building and anti-racism work. Keeta is an Indigenous researcher engaged in work focused on Indigenous wholistic mental health and wellbeing, academic integrity, and the decolonization and Indigenization of post-secondary institutions. She is the recipient of the Social Sciences and Humanities Research Council of Canada's Canada Graduate Scholarship—Master's.

Chapter 6
Accountability, Relationality and Indigenous Epistemology: Advancing an Indigenous Perspective on Academic Integrity

Gabrielle E. Lindstrom

Abstract Although the notion of academic integrity is advanced as a Western construct, Indigenous ways of conceptualising and mobilizing this construct represent a vast, diverse and enduring knowledge system that encompasses not only how sources of knowledge are attributed, but also serves as one of the ontological pillars that upholds honesty and truth-telling within a relationally oriented epistemology. Written from an Indigenous perspective, this chapter invites readers to critically reflect on the ways that academic integrity, as an ethical pillar of the Western academy, relies on institutionalized protocols that privilege a specific methodology of citation and referencing that elevates the written word whilst excluding Indigenous methodologies that are embedded within an ethic of truth-telling and relational accountability. Grounded in the scholarship that surrounds Indigenous knowledge as a participatory way of knowing and utilizing a values-based analysis, I highlight the conceptual parallels between Western understandings of academic integrity and an Indigenous relational epistemology that is rooted in accountability. In today's social climate of reconciliation, academic institutions across Canada are seeking avenues to decolonize their pedagogies and practices. One such avenue is in the area of academic integrity which is underlain with distinct and established ways of transmitting knowledge that have all too often left Indigenous knowledge systems to exist as alternative, or less rigorous, approaches to knowledge production. Movement towards a more equitable, critical and comprehensive understanding of how we, as scholars, are being accountable to those voices that inform and shape our own requires the consideration of a trans-systemic approach.

Keywords Academic integrity · Indigenous · Canada · Epistemology · Accountability · Relationality

---

G. E. Lindstrom (✉)
University of Calgary, Calgary, Canada
e-mail: gabrielle.lindstrom@ucalgary.ca

S. E. Eaton and J. Christensen Hughes (eds.), *Academic Integrity in Canada*, Ethics and Integrity in Educational Contexts 1,
https://doi.org/10.1007/978-3-030-83255-1_6

Introduction

Oki. Niisto nitanikkoo Tsapinaki nimok'tooto Kainaiawa. Greetings. My name is Gabrielle Lindstrom (nee Weasel Head) and I am from Kainaiwa. Niisto Siksikaitsitapi. I am from the Blackfoot-speaking tribes and a member of the Niitsitapi, Blackfoot Confederacy. I locate my identity within a Blackfoot tribal paradigm as part of a process of pushing back against the colonial forces that have shaped my worldview. The act of self-location, a common protocol in Indigenous research methodologies (Kovach, 2009), illuminates how my chapter is informed and interpreted from a distinct cultural worldview thus establishing my relationship and investment in the ideas that are contained herein.

As a Blackfoot woman and scholar who teaches and researches within the Western academic context, I am concerned with advancing the perspectives of a First Nations paradigm to highlight how many of the philosophies that shape Indigenous ways of knowing hold significant relevance for better understanding how the notion of integrity can buttress societal norms. An Indigenous paradigm is relationally-oriented. As such, the notion of integrity is holistic which means it is infused in all areas of life. As a Blackfoot scholar, I do not differentiate between academic integrity, social integrity or spiritual integrity. From a Euro-centric standpoint, the notion of integrity can be fragmented into a variety of social contexts and may be mobilized in equally fragmented ways. Academic integrity, a concept that is central to this chapter, is typically advanced and understood as a Western construct although it seems academic institutions rarely ascribe culturally defined roots to it. In contrast, Indigenous ways of conceptualising and mobilizing integrity are informed from vast, diverse and enduring knowledge systems that encompass not only how sources of knowledge are acknowledged but also places the notion of integrity as one of the ontological pillars that upholds honesty, transparency and truth-telling within a relationally oriented epistemology. Written from my perspective as a Blackfoot woman and scholar of Indigenous Studies, I invite readers to critically reflect on the ways that academic integrity, as an ethical pillar of the Western academy, relies on institutionalized protocols that privilege a specific methodology of citation and referencing that elevates the written word whilst excluding other ways of knowing. Moreover, discussions around academic integrity and the creation of an institutional culture of integrity within academia do very little in illuminating the power imbalances and hierarchical organization of knowledge that typify universities as sites of ongoing colonization.

The purpose of this chapter is to illuminate an Indigenous relational epistemology that is rooted in accountability in order to offer another way of understanding academic integrity. To this end and grounded in the literature, I first contextualize academic integrity and the problems associated with academic dishonesty through a critical values-based analysis. I then discuss Indigenous perspectives that surround the notion of academic integrity that include concepts such as tribal self-determination, Indigenous educational sovereignty, Indigenous values and knowledge, and briefly, the implications that Indigenous research methodologies hold in enacting Indigenous pedagogies. I also assert that the ways postsecondary institutions translate and mobilize academic integrity equates to complicity in ongoing colonization and disrupts institutional efforts aimed at indigenization and decolonization. Throughout this chapter, I argue that attempts to conceptualize and critically understand academic integrity from an Indigenous perspective require a paradigm shift and the visioning of differing but equally valid approaches. Movement towards a more equitable, critical and comprehensive understanding of how we, as scholars, are being accountable to those voices that inform and shape our own requires the consideration of a trans-systemic approach. Interwoven with critical reflections that emerge from an Indigenous tribal paradigm, I begin with a discussion of my understanding of academic integrity as drawn from the surrounding scholarship.

Conceptualization and Mobilization of Academic Integrity

To understand and appreciate the context within which Indigenous perspectives are advanced here, it is vital to establish how academic integrity is defined, conceptualized and mobilized in institutions of higher education. Bertram Gallant and Drinan (2008) have observed that academic integrity, although constituting broad contexts including financial aid corruption and research fraud, has been more associated with pedagogical concerns with a specific focus on how post-secondary institutions are addressing incidences of student plagiarism and cheating. In their recent annotated bibliography, Eaton et al. (2019) built on the work of others by outlining a set of previously identified fundamental values (International Center for Academic Integrity, 2021) that when taken together, comprise academic integrity as opposed to clear definitions. Earlier, Eaton and Edino (2018) highlighted the complications involved when attempting to arrive at a commonly understood definition of academic integrity. Instead, they pulled from the literature to conceptualize the broadened, related concept of educational integrity whilst issuing a plea to their readership to acknowledge "that complexities of educational integrity cross disciplinary boundaries and defy simplification" (p. 2). For the purposes of this chapter, I argue that to avoid simplification and open a space for Indigenous conceptualizations of academic integrity, this acknowledgement must also include culturally conceptualized notions that attend to the trans-systemic pedagogical contexts of Canadian universities. Moreover, a values-based understanding of academic integrity allows for broadening cultural relevance in ways that include Indigenous values. Yet, there must also be a critical understanding of what we place value upon. For example, in Western higher education, learning and knowledge are often understood within neoliberal contexts of monetary value and students' desire to not "waste" their money on irrelevant knowledges. By contrast, Indigenous learning and knowledge acquisition are conceptualized and embodied within a holistic (Battiste, 2002; Battiste et al., 2002) and relational epistemology (Bastien, 2016). Traditionally, meaning-making practices that were enacted prior to colonization but certainly ones that hold relevance today (Wilson & Restoule, 2010), reified the notion that all sources of knowledge added value to the human experience and taught people their responsibilities within a "framework of moral and ethical relationships" (Bastien, 2016, p. 15). The notion of integrity permeated Indigenous lifeways and members of society were expected to act with integrity in all facets of life. This is in stark contrast to how integrity is both conceptualized and mobilized in our institutes of higher learning which I expand on below.

To mobilize and strengthen academic integrity institutionally, Bertram Gallant and Drinan (2008) conceptualize a four-stage model that considers distinct academic institutional cultures. Further, by using a pendulum metaphor, they attend to the fluidity of organizational structures within the institutions such as leadership changes and strategic planning priorities. This model is not exclusively concerned with student behaviors. Importantly, Gallant and Drinan (2008) include faculty and administrative behaviors. Robinson and Glanzer's (2017) study drew on the model of an ethical culture (McCabe et al., 2012) to determine what aspects college students might deem as relevant factors that could possibly foster academic integrity. According to their examination, "The ethical culture can best be understood as a complex interplay among various formal and informal cultural systems that can promote either ethical or unethical behavior" (McCabe et al., 2012, p. 168). Robinson and Glanzer (2017) further identified certain codes used to define either academic honesty or dishonesty that are contained in student handbooks and other policy documents. These documents outline how a student is to behave in the learning milieu and the punishments that will be visited upon them if they transgress these codes. At the individual course level, the institutional codes are outlined as course codes that the instructor is free to create on their own or co-create with students. According to McCabe, et al. (2012), there is a need for building an ethical culture of academic honesty to minimize students' cheating.

In both studies outlined above (Bertram Gallant & Drinan, 2008; Robinson & Glanzer, 2017) there appears to be an underlying assumption that the institutional and ethical culture are relevant to an Indigenous paradigm. This is problematic given the pattern of how Western education has been complicit in assimilating Indigenous students into Eurocentric culture (Makokis, 2009; Schissel & Wotherspoon, 2003). The notion of an ethical culture must be based on a plurality of cultural systems which holds potential for considering how Indigenous perspectives on academic integrity can be conceptualized and mobilized within institutes of higher education. Within the discourse surrounding academic integrity, there is clearly an appeal to the moral values of students but given that students in Canadian universities are taught from a primarily Western paradigm, it becomes necessary to critically examine the moral values underlying Western society before such an appeal can be acted upon. Hence, exploring the culture of universities as shaped by students, administrators, faculty and staff helps us to better determine how academic dishonesty is expressed and the ramifications for students who engage in behaviors that compromise their integrity as growing scholars. The notion of culture, as it is used by Robinson and Glanzer (2017) and others (McCabe et al., 2012) in the context of academic integrity is rather narrowly defined as "the institutional environment that encourages the development and maintenance of an ethical community" (p. 210). Assumedly, the ethical culture of academia emerges from a Western paradigm that has, at its core, a competitive and individually driven philosophy that runs counter to Indigenous ways of knowing and relational accountability (Cote-Meek, 2014; Smith, 2012). Robinson and Glanzer (2017) further assert that "how a social context shapes moral reasoning, desires, and behaviors" (p. 210) must be taken into account. The current social context of academia utilizes a punitive approach to academic dishonesty encompassed in direct disciplinary actions such as student suspension or expulsion from the institution. These punishments work against intrinsic motivation for moral and responsible behavior which begs the question: how are we rewarded for doing what's right when the policies around academic integrity revolve around punishing students for doing wrong? A promising answer can be found in the notion of an ethical culture, yet Robinson and Glanzer (2017) appear to take a templated, universal approach to understanding academic culture and assume that all members of this culture should conform to a singular value system without interrogating both the nature and power of this value system. Rather than considering ethnicity or cultural positioning, student participants in their study were categorized as per gender and age only—categories which hinder a more nuanced understanding of the cultural elements at play.

In the same vein, Bertram Gallant et al. (2015) argue that rather than the looking at the institutional and ethical culture to determine risk factors involved in academic dishonesty, educational researchers should start with student populations. Specifically, they argue that male international students in high stakes programs like engineering or computer technologies tend to be more at-risk of cheating and/or engaging in academic dishonesty than others. This analysis, while perhaps warranted, tends to diminish the role of academia in students' academic dishonesty and reduces cheating to individual students—ultimately, the problem becomes the student and not the institutional values that work to foster competitive individualism within a punitive academic culture. Moreover, the authors adopt the view that cheating is intrinsic to student culture and part of psychological mechanisms that are impossible to change (Bertram Gallant et al., 2015). From an Indigenous perspective this is neither helpful nor hopeful since it not only essentializes students as inherently dishonest but assumes that negative qualities are beyond intervention. In an attempt to further analyze the factors involved, the authors surmise that "some cultures privilege the value of loyalty to peers and collaboration to navigate a difficult task" (Bertram Gallant, Binkin & Donohue 2015, p. 220). This assumption is also problematic since it further deflects responsibility from the institution and engages in a process of "othering" diverse ethnicities using culturally polarizing discourse. The authors suggest that it is up to the Western, Euro-centered academic institution to resolve difficulties presented by clashing cultural value systems. Bertram Gallant, Binkin and Donohue's (2015) solution is not to change the punitive structures of the academy, but instead to offer education focused on socializing at-risk students in conforming to the institution.

Nonetheless, Bertram Gallant, Binkin and Donohue (2015) provide a useful segue to consider students' standpoints. From a student perspective, fear of failing and feeling neither confident nor competent enough in their academic abilities to pass tests or write essays are all factors that must be considered especially in the context of assessment (Lindstrom et al., 2017). If the only reason a student does not engage in cheating behaviors is to avoid punishment, then this points to a concerning absence of both a deeper investment in their learning as well as intrinsic motivation to learn with integrity. From an Indigenous perspective, the qualities that encompass integrity are instilled in nation members from birth and reinforced throughout their lives via pedagogical strategies that nurture capacities for walking a life of integrity. Fear is not one of the motivating elements in Indigenous approaches to learning. Colonization and assimilation efforts have disrupted these capacities but for many Indigenous peoples, the qualities related to integrity are still passed on through Indigenous teachings. Today, fear culture is certainly a factor amongst all students, including Indigenous students, and one that institutions must consider as they mobilize strategies to strengthen academic integrity and work to quell the increasing number of post-secondary students engaging in academic dishonesty.

Rise in Academic Dishonesty

Robinson and Glanzer (2017) demonstrate that academic dishonesty is on the rise in college students with more than two-thirds reporting they've been involved in some form of academic dishonesty. In an earlier article focusing on academic integrity from an institutional standpoint, Bertram Gallant and Drinan (2008) argue that:

> Pervasive student academic misconduct (e.g., cheating on examinations, plagiarism, falsification, and fabrication) can challenge the value of the university degree and cast public doubt on the validity of teaching and assessment methods. At the faculty level, unchecked teacher or researcher misconduct (e.g., lecture unpreparedness, results manipulation) can corrupt the integrity of the institution and stimulate public doubt regarding postsecondary education accountability. (Braxton & Bayer, 2004, p. 27)

Implicating students, faculty and the administrative arm of the institution, Bertram Gallant and Drinan (2008) call attention to how academic integrity must not only be nurtured in students, particularly undergraduate students, but also in the broader context of pedagogy, research and administration. As an Indigenous educator teaching Indigenous Studies courses, I face unique challenges in attempting to address academic dishonesty amongst students given that there are few culturally appropriate resources or institutional supports to build learner confidence. Moreover, some of the factors as to why Indigenous students may cheat or plagiarize and the punitive outcomes brought to bear in cases of academic dishonesty are deeply nuanced and perhaps not widely understood by administrators and educators. For example, the role of trauma and colonization goes largely unexamined in the literature on academic integrity. Indeed, there is a dearth of literature that attends to a rigorous exploration of both the prevalence of Indigenous students engaging in academic dishonesty and the nuanced complexities that drive these behaviors. These silent areas in the scholarship prevent educators from gaining deepened insights into whether or not the general rise in academic dishonesty is also present in the Indigenous student population. Lack of evidence-based insights and clear data trails mean that institutional supports geared to strengthening academic integrity from an Indigenous perspective cannot possibly be implemented in ways that will have a positive impact on Indigenous students or be consistent with an Indigenous paradigm. From a philosophical standpoint that is shaped by my cultural positioning as a Blackfoot woman, addressing academic dishonesty within a punitive framework makes little sense because it does not enable me to draw on culturally appropriate models of academic integrity that would help students to feel confident or competent in their academic skills. Instead, I am forced to follow the institutional codes that, I argue, do not necessarily address the reasons why students cheat but focus on punishment for transgressing these codes. Complicating matters further is the fact that, as Bertram Gallant and Drinan (2008) point out, academic dishonesty is not just a problem with students.

Citing several high-profile plagiarism cases, Palermo's (2020) editorial and Eaton and Edino's (2018) extensive literature review also highlight how academic dishonesty is not only a problem with university students but within the ranks of both well-established scholars and public servants. Although Palermo (2020) argues that "when we fail to attend to academic detail, including ethical norms, we are wrong and, while not being unlawful, we are wronging someone. Common sense, integrity, and sound executive skills should suggest we acknowledge the work of others" (p. 297), I am also reminded that common sense and integrity do not always guide student or faculty behaviors. Indeed, within academia, this poses a unique problem and one that must be addressed especially if faculty are implicitly expected to model integrity in scholarly pursuits whether that be in ethical research practices or scholarly publishing and writing. Role modeling is a central practice in Indigenous pedagogy and one through which young people learn the social and moral value systems of their First Nation (Battiste, 2002; McLaughlin & Whatman, 2015). In order to ensure that the knowledge and histories of First Nations are transmitted to the next generation, adults must act with integrity lest they risk disrupting not only the fidelity of Indigenous knowledges but also the loss of confidence of their pupils. In parallel to this notion, Bertram Gallant and Drinan (2008) assert that, "Given the multifaceted and integral role played by postsecondary education in Canada and around the world, the integrity of the work performed by its members is critical" (p. 27). Whether we conceptualize integrity from a Western or Indigenous paradigm, congruencies exist between the two worldviews in that compromising integrity has serious and reverberating impacts on knowledge systems. How, then, are we to understand what can drive academic integrity beyond Western-based psycho-social models?

Indigenous Perspectives

Within an Indigenous paradigm, integrity is best conceptualized through an oral system of knowledge and transmitted via Elder teachings. These teachings contain moral and ethical guidelines for living a good life in-relation to self, other living entities and the natural world. Within the context of academic integrity, Indigenous perspectives may be understood through a critical and deepened exploration of the traditional purposes of learning both prior to Western colonial influences and enduring practices that remain as relevant pedagogies. Australian educator Karen O'Brien (2008) states that in academia, "learning involves not understanding the 'world itself' but others' views of the world" (p. 57) which is a world that holds little relevance for what Indigenous communities may value or what they may determine as meaningful knowledge. In other words, Indigenous students must learn about Western interpretations of our world which often lead students to struggle with the content which becomes reflected in poor grades and early school-leaving (Cote-Meek, 2014). These barriers are then seen as deficiencies of Indigenous students rather than inherent problems within the epistemological structures of academia. Learning within a Western context is underlain with notions of dominance and power. To be successful, one must be skilled at dominating highly complex vocabulary and discourses which in turn grants the learner the power to generate discrete knowledge that is often only accessible to others who wield similar power (O'Brien, 2008). Common assessments of student learning include written tests and essays yet these forms limit the myriad of ways that Indigenous students can demonstrate their new knowledge. By contrast, Indigenous learning takes a holistic approach by attending to the social, emotional, spiritual and mental aspects of the student in a culturally appropriate, collective context (McCarty & Lee, 2014). Indigenous learning also includes notions of autonomy, sovereignty and self-determination.

Indigenous Educational Sovereignty

McCarty and Lee (2014) advance the notion of educational sovereignty as part of both a culturally sustaining/revitalizing pedagogy (CSRP) and as a right of Native American students. CSRP attends to power imbalances by illuminating how the colonial legacy of schooling (Schissel & Wotherspoon, 2003) has led to asymmetrical power dynamics. For the purposes of this chapter, McCarty and Lee's (2014) model of CSRP enables us to see how power functions in various educational relationships including those between education and student and institution and student. However, educational sovereignty in the context of academic integrity does not operate as an external factor outside of Western state-run education systems. As McCarty and Lee (2014) assert, it must overlap with Western pedagogies and curriculum. A commitment to mobilizing educational sovereignty requires constant negotiation between Western and Indigenous thought systems as well as a critical understanding of the role of colonization within relationships. Moreover, reclaiming and revitalizing what has been lost due to colonization is another important component of CSRP (McCarty & Lee, 2014).

Institutional dialogues around post-secondary education institutes' accountability to historical antecedents and contemporary patterns of ongoing colonization within higher education set the stage for a praxis-based model that potentiates students' capacity to develop a deeper, intrinsic sense of efficacy in their academic abilities. In the context of academic integrity, building an academic integrity framework that acknowledges and incorporates Indigenous educational sovereignty can be a starting point for ensuring that Indigenous perspectives surrounding academic integrity are being included. Educational sovereignty as a component of self-determination has long been the vision of Indigenous Elders. Indeed, Elders have always supported Western education and the opportunities it brings to Indigenous youth but not at the expense of cultural sustainability. Instead, the notion of accountability underpins educational sovereignty which in turn can offer an alternative vision of academic integrity. However, as McCarty and Lee (2014) remind their readers, accountability is also "interlaced with ongoing legacies of colonization, ethnocide and linguicide" (p. 103). Understanding the conceptual role of academic integrity as being complicit in the ongoing cognitive imperialism (Battiste, 2002) of Indigenous students is a vital component of the decolonial process of imagining (Laenui, 2000) another way towards a model of academic integrity that is grounded in Indigenous values of accountability and truth-telling.

Academic Integrity and Ongoing Colonization

In her discussion outlining the importance of cultural studies to foster social justice oriented and ethically accountable students, Rossiter (2012) advances the notion of response-ability as a conceptual lens through which pedagogical approaches can be planned and enacted. Further arguing that response-ability transcends an individual's moral agency, Rossiter (2012) suggests that it encompasses a collective response to political and social consequences of colonial violence both in the historical and contemporary sense. This is important because it offers a useful bridge to reflect on the ways that academic integrity, as an ethical pillar of the Western academy, relies on institutionalized protocols that privilege a specific methodology of citation and referencing that elevates the written word whilst excluding Indigenous methodologies that are embedded within an ethic of truth-telling, orality and relational accountability.

While others (Bertram Gallant & Drinan, 2008; McCabe et al., 2012; Robinson & Glanzer, 2017) have argued for approaching issues related to academic integrity from a distinct institutional cultural ethos, Littlebear (2000) reminds us that "Culture comprises a society's philosophy about the nature of reality, the values that flow from this philosophy, and the social customs that embody these values" (n. p.). This reminder is significant because it highlights a need for administrators and educators within higher education to begin to critically reflect on the institutional culture as one that flows from a distinct Euro-centered philosophy out of which post-secondary institutional values and norms become positioned. Indeed, it is Euro-centric philosophy that drove colonization eventually pushing Indigenous ways of knowing to the very margins of society (Battiste, 2002; Cote-Meek, 2014; Daschuk, 2013; Ermine, 2007). The marginalized status of Indigenous knowledges is not only reflected in the debates surrounding their validity and utility when compared with Western empirical knowledge but also in the citation methodologies that are central to any model of academic integrity. Currently, as some university websites concede, academic referencing guides do not have a standardized method for citing Indigenous knowledges. Because Indigenous knowledges are "held in a variety of formats: on the page, through oral histories, in physical items, and on the land" (Bak, Bradford, Loyer & Walker, 2017, p. 13), they challenge conventional citation styles. While some universities such as Ryerson University and the University of Toronto in Toronto, Ontario, Canada (see https://learn.library.ryerson.ca/citationhelp/indigenousstyle; https://studentlife.utoronto.ca/wp-content/uploads/SLC8581_7-Grandfathers-in-Academic-Integrity-AODA.pdf) offer students citation options to support Indigenous students' academic success and assist all students in referencing traditional Indigenous knowledge sourced through Elder interviews, other institutions do not. Indeed, if students are wanting to reference Indigenous knowledges that are sourced from drum songs or land-based teachings, the current citation styles are insufficient for allowing students to reference them in accordance with academic guidelines. The inability to validate and reference Indigenous knowledges within the academic institution contributes to ongoing colonization in that it forces Indigenous faculty and students to limit sources of knowledge to those that can be most easily referenced as per current citation methodologies. In effect, Indigenous peoples and knowledges are being continuously assimilated into the Western system which has been a primary goal of colonization.

To counter ongoing colonization, our understandings of academic integrity must be broadened in order to make space for strategizing other ways of enacting models of academic integrity that are consistent with Indigenous ways of knowing. Movement towards institutional action requires a paradigm shift. To achieve this, we must ask different questions, pose alternate solutions, advance critical arguments that transform institutional priorities and incorporate Indigenous pedagogies in ways that meet all learners where they at. If this is to happen, then non-Indigenous faculty and university administrators must step into the humbling role of a learner and seek to understand Indigenous value-systems within a participatory and relational pedagogy.

Indigenous Core-Values and Teachings

As an educator teaching Indigenous Studies, connecting Indigenous values to students lives outside of the classroom has been a critical component of my pedagogy in emphasizing the relevancy of an Indigenous paradigm. Other Indigenous educators and scholars such McCarty and Lee (2014), in exploring Indigenous-led schools, identified how Indigenous nations' distinct core-values formed the schools' mission which guided the attitudes and behaviors of both students and teachers. Moreover, the values were incorporated into classroom pedagogies and curriculum in ways that fostered the students' sense of cultural identity whilst also nurturing a collective sense of accountability to Indigenous values. Although establishing practices around values can be an effective way of connecting Indigenous ways of knowing to academic integrity, McCarty and Lee (2014) caution that there is a risk of homogenizing Indigenous values as being the same across all Indigenous nations. There must be vigilance on the part of educators and administrators to avoid essentializing Indigenous values. This is a challenge given the diversity of Indigenous nations yet it is one that need not be thought of as impossible to negotiate. Rather, exploring and understanding this diversity should be embraced since it allows those of us working in higher education to decolonize how we think about academic integrity.

As a Blackfoot educator, I often draw on the work of other Blackfoot scholars such as Leroy Littlebear (2000) and Betty Bastien (2016) not only because their teachings are familiar to me, but they are also regionally specific. Indigenous knowledge is local knowledge and emerges from Indigenous peoples' reciprocal and participatory relationship with the lands (Simpson, 2017). By conceptualizing Indigenous knowledges within a local context, I am able to advance Indigenous values in the post-secondary classroom as a model for nurturing accountability and integrity in all areas on life.

In considering the value of honesty and how it is connected to integrity, Littlebear (2000) asserts, "For the purposes of social control, there is a strong expectation that everyone will share his or her truth (actually, "truthing" is a better concept) because people depend on each other's honesty" (n.p.) in order to maintain shared ontological understandings of a collective reality and the place of human beings within a web of relational alliances. As participatory members of society, we depend on each other to be truthful and honest in all that we do. For the Blackfoot and other Indigenous nations, to do otherwise would mean creating a society based on false understandings. Ceremonies such as the Smudge and Pipe ceremonies entrenched truth-telling as part of the sacred ways (Treaty 7 Elders, & Carter, 1995). Through both sacred and social customs, "truthing" (Littlebear, 2000) became a way of life for Indigenous peoples and is one that is carried forward today through Indigenous pedagogies and the teachings of the Elders (Bastien, 2016). Truthing fosters a sense of accountability to others which in turn nurtures a web of interdependencies within which human-beings become responsible for maintaining balance and harmony in all of their relations (Deloria et al., 1999; Littlebear, 2000). The value of humility ensures that human-beings know their place within these interdependent relational alliances. As Cree scholar Leona Makokis (2009) points out, no other living being is dependent on human beings for their survival. Rather, without the waters, living earth and the plant people and animal people, human-beings would perish. As a universal truth, our dependency requires we maintain balance and walk with integrity (Makokis, 2009).

The values of truth and humility demonstrate an understanding of Indigenous knowledges and pedagogy as existing within a distinct model of integrity that is buttressed by ancient ways of knowing that remain valid and relevant in today's world. Utilizing Indigenous research methodologies to further develop and cultivate Indigenous pedagogies offers a promising pathway for translating Indigenous perspectives on academic integrity into the university classroom and institutional culture.

Indigenous Research Methodologies, Pedagogies and Curriculum

Both Indigenous and Western scholars understand the importance of connecting research to classroom pedagogy (Louie et al., 2017; Macdonald et al., 2016; Maclaughlin & Whatman, 2015). Further, research has shown how restructuring assessments may help to deter cheating (Lindstrom et al., 2017). Robinson and Glanzer (2017) point to the role of the teacher and identify that "Teachers had one of the largest effects on students in our participants' perception of academic integrity" (p. 217). From an Indigenous perspective, Marchant's research (2009) demonstrates that teachers, regardless of whether they are Indigenous themselves, act as role models for Indigenous students. Easton et al. (2019) have shown how non-Indigenous faculty members may be consciously or unconsciously complicit in ongoing colonization through their curriculum choices which impact Indigenous students experiences in the classroom and hinder the advancement of the Truth and Reconciliation Commission of Canada's (2015) recommendations for addressing colonial violence in the classrooms of higher education.

Although the examples offered above have different foci, they highlight how research can help to illuminate shared priorities with respect to both direct and peripheral issues surrounding academic integrity in ways that integrate Western and Indigenous perspectives. Further, I argue here that there should be a greater emphasis on building institutional capacity for the incorporation of Indigenous research methodologies in order to explore and advance Indigenous pedagogies and curriculum designs. Given that Indigenous research flows from a relational epistemology (Drawson et al., 2017; Kurtz, 2013; Suárez-Krabbe, 2011; Wilson, 2008), theoretical approaches and philosophical positioning within Western methodologies that intersect with Indigenous research paradigms, such as autoethnographies for example (McIvor, 2010; Whitinui, 2014) potentiate pathways on which Indigenous and non-Indigenous researchers can explore the development of innovative and culturally relevant models of academic integrity.

Conclusion

The main argument central to this chapter advances the notion that a paradigm shift is required in order to critically and meaningfully understand and appreciate how Indigenous perspectives can be positioned within current constructions of academic integrity. I offered an analysis of both academic integrity and academy dishonesty in contrast with Indigenous truth-telling, relationality and accountability. I have clearly only skimmed the surfaces of Indigenous research methodologies and pedagogies. However, this chapter represents a starting point for dialogue around how Indigenous values systems can inform models of academic integrity in ways that move beyond punitive frameworks of enforcement. Focusing on how we, as educators, can reward students for their current knowledge and gifts can be a first step in improving learner motivation and confidence. The issues I have raised here not only point to a need for further dialogue around the potential for naturalizing the notion of accountability to others' voices but also how citation methodologies need to provide academic validation to Indigenous knowledges so students can reference these sources in accordance with academic procedures. The path ahead offers institutions an opportunity to discover how Indigenous perspectives on integrity can add a rich contribution to current understandings of academic integrity in ways that will empower students and build intercultural capacities within our institutes of higher education.

References

Bak, G., Bradford, T., Loyer, J., & Walker, E. (2017). Four Views on Archival Decolonization Inspired by the TRC's Calls to Action. *Fonds d'Archives, 1*. https://doi.org/10.29173/fa3

Bastien, B. (2004). *Blackfoot ways of knowing: The worldview of the Siksikaitsitapi*. University of Calgary Press.

Bastien, B. (2016). Indigenous pedagogy: A way out of dependence. In K. Burnett & G. Read (Eds.). *Aboriginal History: A reader*. Oxford University Press.

Battiste, M., Bell, L., & Findlay, L. M. (2002). Decolonizing education in Canadian universities: An interdisciplinary, international, Indigenous research project. *Canadian Journal of Native Education, 26*(2), 82–95.

Battiste, M. (2002). *Indigenous knowledge and pedagogy in First Nations education: A literature review with recommendations*. Indian and Northern Affairs Canada.

Bertram Gallant, T. B., & Drinan, P. (2008). Toward a model of academic integrity institutionalization: Informing practice in postsecondary education. *Canadian Journal of Higher Education, 38*(2), 25–43.

Bertram Gallant, T. B., Binkin, T., & Donohue, M. (2015). Students at risk for being reported for cheating. *Journal of Academic Ethics, 13*(3), 217–228. https://doi.org/10.1007/s10805-015-9235-5

Cote-Meek, S. (2014). *Colonized classrooms: Racism, trauma and resistance in post-secondary education*. Fernwood Publishing.

Daschuk, J. (2013). *Clearing the plains*. University of Regina Press.

Deloria, J., Scinta, S., Foehner, K., & Deloria, B. (1999). *Spirit and Reason: The Vine Deloria*. Colorado: Fulcrum Publishing.

Drawson, A. S., Toombs, E., & Mushquash, C. J. (2017). Indigenous research methods: A systematic review. *The International Indigenous Policy Journal, 8*(2). http://ir.lib.uwo.ca/iipj/vol8/iss2/5. https://doi.org/10.18584/iipj.2017.8.2.5

Easton, L., Lexier, R., Lindstrom, G., & Yeo, M. (2019). Uncovering the complicit: The Decoding Interview as a Decolonizing Practice. In L. Quinn (Ed.), *Reimagining curriculum: Spaces for disruption* (pp. 149–177). Stellenbosch: African SUNmedia.

Eaton, S. E., Crossman, K., & Edino, R. I. (2019). *Academic integrity in Canada: An annotated bibliography*. Canada: University of Calgary.

Eaton, S. E., & Edino, R. I. (2018). Strengthening the research agenda of educational integrity in Canada: A review of the research literature and call to action. *International Journal of Educational Integrity, 14*(1). https://doi.org/10.1007/s40979-018-0028-7

Ermine, W. (2007). Ethical space of engagement. *Indigenous Law Journal, 6*(1), 193–203.

Ermine, W. (1995). Aboriginal Epistemology. In M. Battiste & J. Barman (Eds.), *First Nation education in Canada: The circle unfolds*. UBC Press.

International Center for Academic Integrity (ICAI). (2021). *The fundamental values of academic integrity* (3rd ed.). https://www.academicintegrity.org/fundamental-values/

Kovach, M. (2009). *Indigenous methodologies: Characteristics, conversations, and contexts.* Canada: University of Toronto Press.

Kurtz, D. (2013). Indigenous Methodologies: Traversing Indigenous and Western worldviews in research. *AlterNative: An International Journal of Indigenous Peoples, 9*(3), 217–229. https://doi.org/10.1177/117718011300900303

Laenui, P. (2000). Processes of decolonization. In M. Battiste (Ed.), *Reclaiming Indigenous voice and vision,* (pp. 150–159). UBC Press.

Lindstrom, G., Taylor, L., & Weleschuk, A. (2017). *Guiding principles for student assessment.* Canada: University of Calgary.

Littlebear, L. (2000). Jagged worldviews colliding. http://www.learnalberta.ca/content/aswt/documents/fnmi_worldviews/jagged_worldviews_colliding.pdf

Louie, D., Poitras-Pratt, Y., Hanson, A. & Ottmann, J. (2017). Applying Indigenizing principles of decolonizing methodologies in University classrooms. *Canadian Journal of Higher Education, 47*(3), 16–33.

Makokis, L. (2009). Disordered dependencies: The impact of language loss and residential schooling on indigenous peoples. *Rural Social Work and Community Practice, 14*(2), 6–11.

Maracle, Iehnhotonkwas B. J. (2020). Seven grandfather in academic integrity. https://studentlife.utoronto.ca/wp-content/uploads/Seven_Grandfathers_in_Academic_Integrity.pdf.

Marchant, C. H. (2009). *Indigenous ways of learning, being and teaching: Implications for new teachers to first nations schools.* Unpublished Master's thesi, University of Victoria. https://dspace.library.uvic.ca/bitstream/handle/1828/1929/CMarchant2009h.pdf?sequence=3&isAllowed=y

McCabe, D. L., Butterfield, K. D., & Treviño, L. K. (2012). *Cheating in college: Why students do it and what educators can do about it.* United States: Johns Hopkins University Press.

McCarty, T. L., & Lee, T. S. (2014). Critical culturally sustaining/revitalizing pedagogy and indigenous education sovereignty. *Harvard Educational Review, 84*(1), 101–127.

McDonald, J., Kenny, N., Kustra, E., Dawson, D., Iqbal, I., Borin, P., & Chan, J. (2016). *Educational development guide series: No. 1. The educational developer's portfolio.* Ottawa, Canada: Educational Developers Caucus.

McIvor, O. (2010). I am my subject: Blending Indigenous research methodology and autoethnography through integrity-based, spirit-based research. *Canadian Journal of Native Education, 33*(1), 137–151.

McLaughlin, J., & Whatman, S. (2015). Recognising change and seeking affirmation: Themes for embedding Indigenous knowledges on teaching practicum. *International Education Journal, 14*(2), 113–124.

O'Brien, K. (2008). Academic language, power, and the impact of Western knowledge production on Indigenous student learning. *The Australiannon Journal of Indigenous Education, 37*, 56–60.

Palermo, M. T. (2020). Moral reasoning and academic integrity: Memory impairment, corrigenda, and the pursuit of knowledge. *International Journal of Offender Therapy and Comparative Criminology, 64*(4) 295–298.

Robinson, J. A., & Glanzer, P. L. (2017). Building a culture of academic integrity: What students perceive and need. *College Student Journal, 51*(2), 209–221.

Rossiter, P. (2012). Cultural Studies, Pedagogy, and Response-Ability. *Review of Education, Pedagogy, and Cultural Studies, 34*(1–2), 61–70. https://doi.org/10.1080/10714413.2012.643742

Ryerson University. (2020). Ryerson university library citation guides. https://learn.library.ryerson.ca/citationhelp/indigenousstyle.

Schissel, B., & Wotherspoon, T. (2003). *The legacy of school for aboriginal people : Education, oppression, and emancipation.* Oxford: Oxford University Press.

Simpson, L. B. (2017). Land as pedagogy. In *As We Have Always Done* (pp. 145–173). University of Minnesota Press. https://doi.org/10.5749/j.ctt1pwt77c.12

Smith, L. (2012). *Decolonizing methodologies: Research and Indigenous peoples* (Second edition.). Zed Books.

Suárez-Krabbe, J. (2011). Within reality: Towards de-colonial research methodologies. *Tabula Rasa, 14*, 183–204. http://search.proquest.com/docview/1017754759/.

Treaty 7 Elders, & Carter, S. (1995). *The true spirit and original intent of treaty 7*, (Vol. 149). McGill-Queen's University Press.

Truth and Reconciliation Commission of Canada. (2015). The final report of the truth and reconciliation commission of Canada, Canada's residential schools: Reconciliation. In *The final report of the truth and reconciliation commission of Canada, Canada's residential schools: Reconciliation, 6*. Truth and Reconciliation Commission of Canada.

Whitinui, P. (2014). Indigenous autoethnography: Exploring, engaging, and experiencing self as a Native method of inquiry. *Journal of Contemporary Ethnography, 43*(4), 456–487.

Wilson, D., & Restoule, J. P. (2010). Tobacco ties: The relationship of the sacred to research. *Canadian Journal of Native Education, 33*(1), 29–45.

Wilson, S. (2008). *Research is ceremony: Indigenous research methods*. Fernwood.

Dr. Gabrielle Lindstrom is an educational development consultant in Indigenous Ways of Knowing with the Taylor Institute of Teaching and Learning, University of Calgary. Dr. Lindstrom, a member of the Kainaiwa Nation and the Blackfoot Confederacy, works closely with the vice-provosts of teaching and learning and Indigenous engagement to advance Indigenous ways of knowing in campus teaching and learning communities, cultures and practices. Her teaching background includes instructing in topics around First Nation, Métis and Inuit history and current issues, Indigenous Studies (Canadian and International perspectives), and Indigenous research methods and ethics. Her dissertation research focused on the interplay between trauma and resilience in the postsecondary experiences of Indigenous adult learners. Other research interests include meaningful assessment in higher education, Indigenous homelessness, intercultural parallels in teaching and learning research, Indigenous lived experience of resilience, Indigenous community-based research, parenting assessment tools reform in child welfare, anti-colonial theory and anti-racist pedagogy.

Chapter 7
Understanding Provincial and Territorial Academic Integrity Policies for Elementary and Secondary Education in Canada

Brenda M. Stoesz

Abstract Research on academic integrity and misconduct in higher education is not difficult to locate, as work in this area has increased dramatically over the past several decades. Overall, findings reveal that cheating is a serious problem plaguing higher education with many institutions documenting various approaches to address the relevant issues. A careful look at this literature, however, exposes significant gaps in our understanding of academic integrity and misconduct in Canadian elementary and secondary (or K-12) education, which is problematic as behaviours practiced in these settings during the formative years may influence behaviours in later life stages. Furthermore, school policies, which reinforce expectations for students and teachers in the workplace are of particular importance as K-12 teachers arguably impact students' approaches to academic integrity. This chapter focuses on key questions related to K-12 education in Canada: Do provincial and territorial ministries of education address academic integrity through policy for K-12 education? If these policies exist, what evidence demonstrates their influence on the implementation of academic integrity education at the school level? To begin to examine these questions, I conducted an environmental scan of Canadian ministries of education websites to identify academic integrity and misconduct policies. I found that only a few education ministries outline student expectations for academic integrity and consequences for misconduct or describe teacher responsibilities for providing academic integrity education and responding to academic misconduct (i.e., Newfoundland and Labrador, Manitoba, and Saskatchewan). To conclude this chapter, I discuss the implications of the presence or absence of effective academic integrity and misconduct policies for K-12 education in Canada and beyond, the impact on higher education and advanced training, as well as avenues for future research in the field.

Keywords Academic integrity · Canada · Elementary school · Government · K-12 education · Policy implications · Secondary school

---

B. M. Stoesz (✉)
University of Manitoba, Winnipeg, Canada
e-mail: Brenda.Stoesz@umanitoba.ca

S. E. Eaton and J. Christensen Hughes (eds.), *Academic Integrity in Canada*, Ethics and Integrity in Educational Contexts 1,
https://doi.org/10.1007/978-3-030-83255-1_7

Understanding Provincial and Territorial Academic Integrity Policies for Elementary and Secondary Education in Canada

When I began my career in education as a certified K-12 general science and biology teacher in the province of Manitoba, Canada approximately 20 years ago, I had many hopes, questions, and concerns about the best ways to facilitate student engagement in the learning process. I wondered how students' interests, home lives and responsibilities, extra-curricular activities, nutrition and health, and social-emotional well-being influenced their learning. Although I was concerned about test and exam cheating, I did not consult relevant school policies (not sure these even existed), and I was generally unfamiliar with the broader concept of academic integrity. Other K-12 teachers may feel similarly when guidance is lacking, and when there are so many other pressing issues to consider when teaching children and adolescents. Consequently, I may have encouraged behaviours that I would now describe as violations of academic integrity.

As I began to write this chapter, I recalled past discussions with my students about the skills required in university, including the importance of having some exposure to writing and documenting sources while in high school. Some students commented that they were planning to enrol in science courses so there was no need to learn how to cite properly. I explained that, as a science major, I completed many science courses (e.g., plant sciences, genetics) requiring writing and citing, so these skills were relevant across disciplines. Because my students claimed to have little or no experience with documenting their sources (see also Crossman, 2014), I designed science assignments that required writing, searching for appropriate sources, and acknowledging other authors' ideas. I provided feedback on strengths and mistakes and opportunities to correct errors. My goal was not to create experts, but to expose my students to some expectations that they would encounter during their postsecondary studies and potentially help them to avoid plagiarism. This chapter was borne, in part, from these early experiences as an educator.

Background

Information about various aspects of academic integrity and academic misconduct in higher education are readily available as research in this field has increased dramatically over the past several decades (Ali & Aboelmaged, 2020). Cheating to gain an unfair advantage in academic work is a serious problem as it results in students who are less prepared for the next level in their education and are unable to apply knowledge and skills to workplace settings. Academic cheating is also linked to unethical workplace behaviour (Grimes, 2012; Lucas & Friedrich, 2005; Nonis & Swift, 2001). Because the consequences for engaging in academic misconduct can be detrimental to the individual and to society as a whole, many researchers, educators, and administrators in higher education are working to address the issue using a range of proactive and reactive approaches. A careful look at the academic integrity literature, however, exposes significant gaps in our understanding of academic integrity and misconduct in elementary and secondary education. One of those gaps relates to academic integrity policies. The goals of this chapter are to examine academic integrity in Canadian elementary and secondary education through a review of the literature and an examination of academic integrity policy at the provincial and territorial government level in Canada.

Academic Misconduct in Elementary and Secondary Education

Academic misconduct is not restricted to postsecondary education—students at every level are cheating (Davis et al., 2009) and the reported rates of academic cheating in K-12 levels may be increasing over time. The results from a survey conducted in the United States (US) revealed that 20%, 27%, and 30% of students in 1969, 1979, and 1989, respectively, believed that most of their high school peers had engaged in academic cheating (Schab, 1991). Furthermore, 34%, 60%, and 68% of high school students (during each of the three study periods) admitted to cheating on tests (Schab, 1991). In another US study, 93% of high school students admitted to cheating at least once, with students in larger schools cheating more often than students in smaller schools (Galloway, 2012). High cheating rates were also found in a national survey of >23,000 high school students from across the US showing that 38% admitted to copying an internet document to submit as part of an assignment, 58% admitted to cheating during tests, and 74% admitted to copying another student's homework (Josephson Institute Center for Youth Ethics, 2012). There is concern that "the problem of cheating is only increasing, that virtually nothing is being done currently about the problem (and students know that, too), and that students often lack explicit exposure to concepts related to academic integrity" (Cizek, 2003, p. 117).

American high school students are not the only ones making poor decisions regarding their schoolwork. When asked to reflect on their high school years, 58% and 73% of first year university students in Canada admitted to cheating on tests and written work, respectively (Christensen Hughes & McCabe, 2006). Similarly, 62% of students aged 12–18 years enrolled in private schools in Canada confessed to serious test cheating and 77% admitted to serious cheating in written work (Stoesz & Los, 2019). Further, 6–17% of junior high and high school students disclosed the turning in papers obtained from websites that did or did not charge fees (Stoesz & Los, 2019). In both studies, a significant proportion of students admitted to working on assignments with others when their teachers asked for individual work and helping their peers cheat on tests. Students who had engaged in academic misconduct were also more likely to report that these behaviours were not serious (Christensen Hughes & McCabe, 2006; Stoesz & Los, 2019).

When do cheating rates spike? High school students may be under the impression that cheating is a greater problem in high schools than it is in elementary schools or colleges (Schab, 1991). And there is some truth to this perception. Brandes (1986) explored the extent of cheating in 45 elementary schools ($n = 1{,}037$ sixth graders) and 105 secondary schools ($n = 2{,}265$ mostly eleventh graders) in California. The rates of all types of cheating were higher amongst high school students than amongst sixth graders. About 39% and 41% of sixth graders admitted to cheating on tests and plagiarizing, respectively, whereas 74% and 50% of high school students disclosed engagement in those cheating behaviours (Brandes, 1986). Similarly, self-reported cheating on math tests and assignments increased after transition to a midwestern US state high school; cheating rates were stable during the eighth grade but then increased significantly from the beginning to the end of the ninth grade (Anderman & Midgley, 2004). US high school students reported cheating on exams by looking at other students' exams or allowing others to view their exams more often than did college students (Jensen et al., 2002). In Canada, the trends appear similar in that the rates of academic misconduct in high schools are generally higher than the rates in post-secondary education (Christensen Hughes & McCabe, 2006).

Why do high school students cheat? Although 99% of US high school students agreed that it was important for them "to be a person with good character" and 93% indicated that their "parents/guardians always want [them] to do the ethically right thing, no matter what the cost", 36% of them feel that cheating may be necessary to succeed (Josephson Institute Center for Youth Ethics, 2012, pp. 4 & 6). If high school students believe that doing the right thing is important, then why are so many of them choosing to cheat in their academic work?

There are several possible predictors for cheating during high school. Peer culture, achievement pressures, fear of failure (Schab, 1991), lack of consequences (Christensen Hughes & McCabe, 2006), and failure to understand the actions that constitute plagiarism and other forms of academic misconduct are associated with increased rates of academic cheating in middle-school students (Wan & Gut, 2008; Wan & Scott, 2016). Parents may also facilitate the cheating behaviours of their children as they "have traditionally been encouraged by elementary and secondary schools to participate in their children's education" (Davis et al., 2009, p. 6). The COVID-19 pandemic has only served to increase this pressure on parents to spend more time assisting their children with their schoolwork and supporting learning. Parent involvement in education is also viewed as caring for their children (Galloway & Conner, 2015), but this caring may be misplaced in some circumstances. Some parents may not clearly understand the boundaries between helping their children and doing schoolwork for them and may inadvertently encourage behaviours that will later be viewed as inappropriate collaboration and contract cheating.

Increases in cheating from middle school to high school may also be attributed to changes in the goal structures of the learning environment, such that academic misconduct is more likely in classes with a perceived performance goal structure (emphasizing ability and competition) than mastery goal structure (emphasizing learning and effort) (Anderman & Midgley, 2004; Murdock et al., 2004). Regardless of the goal structure of the learning environment, the likelihood of cheating increases when a teacher's pedagogy is perceived as poor (Murdock et al., 2004). Overwhelming quantities of content, grading on curves, having to complete just one or two assessments (Evans & Craig, 1990; Galloway, 2012; Galloway & Conner, 2015), and uncaring teachers (Curtis & Clare, 2017; Murdock et al., 2004; Wangaard, 2016) increase the likelihood of cheating in middle school and high school. If teachers are perceived as uncaring, unfair, and discriminatory, "adolescents decide to cheat because" (Thorkildsen et al., 2007, p. 174) cheating is viewed "as a rational choice in a culture of warped values" (Kohn, 2007, p. xiv).

High school students also perceive that schools' academic integrity and misconduct policies lack clarity and are not enforced (Sisti, 2007; Stephens & Wangaard, 2013), and they are "forced to cheat in a school culture that promotes getting ahead over learning" (Galloway, 2012, p. 378). When policies are absent or unclear, it should come as no surprise that students, parents, and teachers may all be confused about expectations for writing and plagiarism and collaboration to complete schoolwork, and the long-term and short-term consequences of engaging in academic misconduct. Therefore, clear, thoughtful, and detailed academic integrity policy provides a solid foundation for which to create cultures of integrity within schools at all levels of the education system (Bretag et al., 2011, 2014; Stephens & Wangaard, 2013).

The Canadian Context

There is no federal ministry and no national oversight in Canadian education (see Bosetti et al., 2017; Capano, 2015; Eaton & Christensen Hughes, 2022); education is decentralised to Canada's ten provinces and three territories. In six provinces and territories, single ministries of education are responsible for K-12 and postsecondary education, and separate ministries of education are responsible for K-12 and postsecondary education in seven provinces (see Table 7.1). Despite decentralization, there are similarities in the education systems across the country (Volante & Ben Jaafar, 2008). For example, provincial and territorial governments have established partnerships to work toward common goals and align policies on curriculum design and assessment for primary and secondary education (see Capano, 2015). Historically, increased collaboration between provinces has been driven by reduced federal government funding especially during difficult economic times (Galway, 2012). Common education goals and financial constraints are argued to have fueled "a process of institutional isomorphism among provinces" (Capano, 2015, pp. 331–332), but the alignment of goals and policies across the country may also communicate areas of priority for education leaders to the public. Partnerships across Canadian education systems might be expected to lead to further collaboration in areas such as academic integrity because of the closely related link to fair assessment and curriculum design.

Based on the research literature and my professional experiences as an educator and researcher, I formulated two questions about elementary and secondary education in Canada. Do ministries of education address academic integrity and misconduct

Table 7.1 Academic integrity policy documents from provincial and territorial ministries of education

Province: Ministry of Education Responsible for K-12 Education	Dedicated academic integrity policy	Document Examined	Details
British Columbia (BC)**: Ministry of Education	No	Not found	Indication on website that academic integrity policies are created at lower district or school levels. Responsibility for academic integrity is placed on teachers and students, in particular, international students
Alberta (AB)**: Ministry of Education	No	The guiding framework for the design and development of kindergarten to grade 12 provincial curricula	Does not address academic integrity directly. Values (i.e., fairness, responsibility) deemed important in education, which overlap with the academic integrity values
Saskatchewan (SK)**: Ministry of Education	Yes	Academic integrity and student responsibility guidelines	Outlines school board, in-school administrator, teacher, and student, and parent responsibility. Template for model academic integrity policy at the division level provided
Manitoba (MB)**: Ministry of Education		Provincial assessment Policy Kindergarten to Grade 12: Academic responsibility, honesty, and promotion/retention	Each division and school must develop policies aligned with government policy
Ontario (ON)**: Ministry of Education	No	Ontario schools—kindergarten to grade 12: Policy and program requirements Growing success: Assessment, evaluation, and reporting in Ontario schools 2010	Integrity is mentioned in relation to the validity of student's performance on a test and modification/adaptations for students who experience challenges
Quebec (PQ): Ministère de l'Éducation et de l'Enseignement supérieur*	No	Policy on educational success: A love of learning, a chance to succeed	Ethics and religious culture are curriculum requirements. No mention of academic integrity
New Brunswick (NB)**: Department of Education and Early Childhood Development	No	10-year education plan: Everyone at their best (anglophone sector)	No mention of integrity, honesty, or other content related to academic integrity or academic misconduct

(continued)

Table 7.1 (continued)

Province: Ministry of Education Responsible for K-12 Education	Dedicated academic integrity policy	Document Examined	Details
Prince Edward Island (PEI)*: Department of Education and Lifelong Learning	No	Not found	
Nova Scotia (NS)**: Department of Education and early childhood development	No	Council to improve classroom conditions (two documents consisting of meeting minutes summarizing discussions) Provincial school code of conduct policy	Meeting goal was to build consensus on definition of academic integrity (e.g., plagiarism) Code of conduct policy neglects academic integrity and academic misconduct
Newfoundland and Labrador (NFLD)*: Department of Education	Yes	Assessment, evaluation and reporting policy (PROG-317)	States that students "work to the best of their abilities, in an academically honest manner and adhere to the classroom/school Code of Conduct" (p. 2). Short section on academic honesty for teachers, students, parents, and school administration. Document is non-academic misconduct centric
Yukon (YK)*: Department of Education	No		Focus of government level policies is on students' physical safety/risk management. Policies related to fair assessment, academic integrity, misconduct (or academic misconduct) were not found
Northwest Territories (NWT)*: Department of Education, Culture and Employment	No	Literacy with ICT Across the Curriculum	No policy on student academic integrity or academic misconduct, but sparse details on plagiarism, attribution, and ethical use of information within the IT literacy curriculum

(continued)

Table 7.1 (continued)

Province: Ministry of Education Responsible for K-12 Education	Dedicated academic integrity policy	Document Examined	Details
Nunavut (NU)*: Department of Education	No	Education Framework Inuit Aaujimajatuqangit for Nunavut Curriculum	Not a stand-alone academic integrity policy document. This framework document states that integrity is important. No details beyond this are provided

Note *Denotes provinces and territories with single ministries of education responsible for both K-12 and postsecondary education. **Denotes provinces with separate ministries of education for K-12 and for postsecondary education

through policy for elementary and secondary education? If these policies exist, what evidence demonstrates their influence on the implementation of academic integrity education at the school level? Academic integrity policy for K-12 education at the provincial and territorial level communicates the values that the community holds, provides a set of standards of quality, and guides the actions to uphold values and adhere to standards (Bretag & Mahmud, 2016), and would provide an important foundation for further policy development at the school level.

An Environmental Scan of Canadian Educational Policy for Academic Integrity

To begin to examine these questions, I conducted an environmental scan of Canadian provincial and territorial ministry of education websites to identify academic integrity or academic misconduct policies. Environmental scans are used widely in private and government sectors (Rowel et al., 2005) to inform policy development, and planning and strategic decision-making processes (Charlton et al., 2019; Choo, 2002), and are associated with improved organizational performance (Choo, 2002). Environmental scans are also useful when there is uncertainty in the extent of the information available (Charlton et al., 2019) as it enables one to broaden the search for information beyond the organization or the peer-reviewed literature. For this chapter, government level academic integrity policy for K-12 education in Canada is absent from the research literature, thus environmental scanning was deemed appropriate for collecting information on this topic.

Environmental scanning often involves the collection of administrative data, internal reports, and guidelines using informants, observation, internet searches (Albright, 2004; Charlton et al., 2019), and information about external events, trends, and other influences (Choo, 2002) but "there are no prescribed standard methods. [for] information collection" (Rathi et al., 2017, p. 79). The environmental scan for this chapter took the simple form of internet searches of Canadian ministry of education websites. The search strategy included terms such as "academic integrity," "academic honesty," "academic misconduct", "plagiarism," and "attribution" in addition to the name of a province or territory and "education department" or "education ministry". Where these terms were not located in a broad search of the ministries' websites using Google's search function, webpages listing policies were scanned for titles with these terms and documents with titles related to fair assessment, information literacy, and student misconduct. The initial search was conducted in February 2020 and repeated in June 2020 to confirm the results of the initial search.

Academic Integrity Policies at the Government Level

My search revealed that few provincial and territorial ministries of education appear to provide any statements regarding student expectations for academic integrity, consequences for misconduct, and teacher and principal responsibilities for providing academic integrity education and responding to academic misconduct. Manitoba and Saskatchewan have each published stand-alone, publicly accessible, online academic integrity policy documents. The Manitoba Education policy outlines two fundamental values of academic integrity (i.e., honesty and responsibility) and lists the expectations of school divisions and schools (e.g., specify a range of consequences for academic misconduct and invoke sanctions), principals (e.g., respond appropriately to academic misconduct, report behaviour on report card), and teachers (e.g., clear communication of assignment expectations, support students' time management, communicate with parents) (Manitoba Education and Advanced Learning, 2015). There are two unique aspects of Saskatchewan's policy document: (a) the inclusion of a template for a model academic integrity policy at the school division/district level, and (b) a statement that "actions such as cheating; plagiarism; having others complete the work (e.g., parents/guardians); buying papers from the internet; or re-submission of previously submitted work are all examples of actions that are not in keeping with academic integrity" (Ministry of Education Government of Saskatchewan, 2011, p. 2). Although not a dedicated document for academic integrity, Newfoundland and Labrador published an assessment policy, which include statements about academic honesty and the responsibility of students, parents, teachers, and school administration regarding academic misconduct (Newfoundland & Labrador English School District, 2013). This policy also emphasises the need for an educative approach and the importance of "second chance opportunities" when appropriate.

My environmental scan did not result in the identification of academic integrity or academic misconduct policies for any other region. This was somewhat surprising, particularly for the provinces of Ontario and Alberta as these provinces represent the most important cases of educational policy reforms, particularly in terms of the introduction of standardized assessments (Capano, 2015), which necessitates honesty, fairness, and trust in the processes and results of the evaluation in students' skills and abilities. Ontario's postsecondary sector is also extremely proactive in communicating the values of academic integrity by way of the Academic Integrity Council of Ontario (Ridgley et al., 2019), and similar networks are evolving in western Canadian provinces (McKenzie, 2018; Stoesz et al., 2020). The involvement of K-12 educators and administrators within these networks may facilitate a greater understanding of the importance of promoting academic integrity and in reducing academic misconduct in students' early education.

Academic Integrity Policies at the Secondary School Level

Next, I explored the extent to which government level academic integrity policy in Manitoba, Saskatchewan, and Newfoundland and Labrador may have impacted high school policy and practice. I randomly selected five high schools in each of Saskatchewan, Manitoba, and Newfoundland Labrador, and randomly selected five schools in each of three randomly-selected provinces that did not have a provincial level policy for academic integrity (i.e., British Columbia, Ontario, New Brunswick) using an online list randomizer (Random.Org, 2020). Next, I searched for academic integrity policies on the websites of the randomly selected high schools in each province from a publicly available list on each government's website. If the high school did not have a website, another school was randomly selected.

In Saskatchewan, only three of five high schools published academic integrity policies (within student handbooks) on their websites, which were limited in detail (e.g., few sentences, only described plagiarism). In Manitoba, two of five high schools had academic integrity statements, but details were also limited. Two of five high schools in Newfoundland and Labrador published academic integrity statements, and both referred to the government level policy. This appeared to communicate the message that academic integrity was important for stakeholders at all levels in the region's education system. Overall, only 47% of school handbooks examined referred to academic integrity policies. The selection of high schools and provinces for this set of analyses did not allow for the examination of the influence of the structure of ministries (i.e., ministries dedicated to K-12 education or those ministries that combined K-12 and higher education) on academic integrity policy development at the high school level. See Table 7.2.

Given the minimal information found on academic integrity policies in high schools, in those provinces that had government policies, I expected an even lower proportion of high schools to have academic integrity policies in those provinces without government-level policies. My hypothesis was not supported. Three, two, and three of the five high schools in British Columbia, Ontario, and New Brunswick (respectively) had academic integrity statements (overall 53%). My inspection also revealed significantly more detail on non-academic misconduct and its consequences in high school policies, suggesting a greater need to deal with disruptive and dangerous behaviour because it often has immediate negative impacts on others within the learning environment (e.g., increased peer disciplinary problems, reduced

Table 7.2 Academic integrity statements or policy documents from high schools in canada

Province School District/Division, School	Student Handbook Examined	Academic integrity statement or policy (Yes/No). Details of policy, if available
Saskatchewan**		
Creighton SD 111, Creighton Community School	Student Handbook (2019 –2020)	(Yes). Emphasis on plagiarism as an act of fraud. More consequences for late practices for assignments than for plagiarism
Good Spirit SD 204, Yorkton Regional High School	Policies and Procedures for Students and Parents: Academic integrity and plagiarism	(Yes). Teachers expected to use technology and collaboration to enhance teaching and learning. Students expected to be honest, complete coursework using their own efforts, and not to copy or plagiarize. Students may be required to redo the assessment honestly and/or attend an academic integrity seminar
Horizon SD 205, Lanigan Central High School	Not found	(No)
Saskatchewan Rivers SD 119, Carlton Comprehensive High School	Not found	(No)
South East Cornerstone SD 209, Estavan Comprehensive School	Student Handbook	(Yes). Values statements (respect, honesty) are provided. Plagiarism and copyright infringement are mentioned as well as inappropriate access to materials (but this is not about academic integrity). Final exam policy does not address academic misconduct, only exam scheduling
Manitoba**		
Beautiful Plains School Division, Neepawa Area Collegiate	N.A.C.I Policies	(No). Examination policy describes exemptions
Louis Riel School Division, Glenlawn Collegiate	Expectations for Students at Glenlawn Collegiate	(Yes). Emphasis on honesty and fairness in the school division and collegiate. Students expected to meet accepted academic honesty standards and consult teachers about expectations. Consequences for inappropriate collaboration, plagiarism, and cheating
Mountain View School Division, Gilbert Plains Collegiate Institute	Code of Conduct	(No)

(continued)

Table 7.2 (continued)

Province School District/Division, School	Student Handbook Examined	Academic integrity statement or policy (Yes/No). Details of policy, if available
River East Transcona School Division, Collège Miles MacDonell Collegiate	Assessment Beliefs, Strategies and Practices	(Yes). Defines academic dishonesty as "any submission of work that is not wholly the student's such as plagiarism, copying, cheating, not citing sources" (para. 6). Teachers determine if learning outcomes have been legitimately met and assign a "0" grade for compromised assessments
Western School Division, Morden Collegiate Institute Collégial Morden	Code of Conduct	(No). Single page devoted to student conduct with nothing further than general values statements, but no specifics related to academic integrity
Newfoundland and Labrador*		
Avalon Region, Gonzaga High School	Student Guidelines 2019–2020	(No). Nothing specific to academic integrity
Avalon Region, Queen Elizabeth Regional High School	2019–2020 Student Handbook	(Yes). Statements refer to the provincial policies on academic integrity
Central Region, J.M. Olds Collegiate	Principles of Success	(No). One statement on cheating: "Cheating: Deliberately using materials, information, or answers on an exam/assignment that is not your own" (p. 10)
Western Region, Indian River High School	Assessment, Evaluation and Reporting Policy Guidelines	(No). No specific details about academic integrity. Policy statement relates to late assignment submission
Labrador Region, Mealy Mountain	Assessment and Evaluation Guidelines (2018–2019)	(Yes). One-page outline of the expectations for students and teachers, and administration along with consequences. Details are limited
British Columbia**		
District 19, Revelstoke Secondary	Code of Conduct, Student Handbook, Athletic Handbook	(Yes). Academic misconduct is deemed an example of a behaviour that is moderately inappropriate. One statement about plagiarism
District 37, South Delta Secondary	Handbook/ Conduct	(Yes). Statement of academic integrity with a focus on plagiarism and cheating. Several examples are provided and a statement of the importance of integrity for school and personal reputation

(continued)

Table 7.2 (continued)

Province School District/Division, School	Student Handbook Examined	Academic integrity statement or policy (Yes/No). Details of policy, if available
District 51, Grand Forks Secondary	GFSS Student Code of Conduct	(No)
District 58, Merritt Secondary	Merritt Secondary Code of Conduct	(No)
District 33, Sardis Secondary	2019–2020 Student Planner	(Yes). At least a page of information on plagiarism and cheating; consequences are limited
Ontario**		
F E Madill Secondary School	Handbook/Code of Conduct Assessment Policy	(Yes). Some definitions, education, consequences included in the Assessment Policy
Sudbury Secondary School	Student Handbook	(Yes). Plagiarism is listed as an infraction and is defined. Distinct documentation styles are mentioned because of the expected use at postsecondary institutions. The approach to consequences for plagiarism are different for grades 9–10 and 11–12 and is partly dependent on intentionality of the offence
District School Board of Niagara (DSBN), Stamford Collegiate	DSBN Code of Conduct	(No). Simply states that integrity is important
Westmount Secondary School	Ownership and Authorship Procedure	(No). Detailed procedure about ownership, authorship, for all members of the learning community
Lakehead Public Schools, Hammarskjold High School	Not found	(No). Details non-academic misconduct
New Brunswick**		
A-East, Caledonia Regional	Student Handbook 2019–2020	(Yes). Plagiarism and cheating with consequences of re-doing the assignment or exam
A-South, St. Malachy's Memorial High School	Not found	(No)
A-North, Miramichi Valley High School	Student Handbook 2019–2020	(Yes). "Plagiarism is illegal." Provide tips on avoiding plagiarism and what plagiarism is. Second on cheating, and consequences
A-West, Central New Brunswick Academy	Student Handbook 2018–2019	(No)
Fredericton High	Student Handbook 2019–2020	(Yes). Plagiarism policy with definitions, details, and consequences; personal electronic devices in terms of cheating

Note *Denotes provinces and territories with single ministries of education responsible for both K-12 and postsecondary education. **Denotes provinces with separate ministries of education for K-12 and for postsecondary education peer test scores; Figlio, 2007). Unfortunately, even behaviour policies and the implementation of them are often described as ambiguous, superficial, and ineffective (Rowe, 2006).

The lack of policies and/or the inconsistent approaches to academic integrity education in K-12 education in Canada suggests several issues that require further investigation. First, structural changes that have occurred in education in an effort to increase efficiencies (Capano, 2015), including an overall shift in accountability such that schools have greater autonomy and locally elected school boards have reduced authority (Galway, 2012), may result in a communication gap between government level decisions and adoption of policy at the school level. Second, elected leaders may not have prioritized honesty, trustworthiness, and responsibility in student learning and assessment or in the education system as a whole, resulting in an inconsistency in the adoption of the values of academic integrity at the school level, potentially leading to a general apathy among students, parents, and teachers. The efforts of my colleagues and I to discuss academic integrity with high school educators have often been met with defensiveness, denial, and statements that academic integrity is not applicable to high school students because they are "just becoming scholars." My experiences are consistent with research demonstrating that teachers often underestimate or reject the idea that cheating is occurring in their classes, even when they admit that cheating is a significant problem in middle and high schools (Evans & Craig, 1990). Perhaps denial stems from teachers' lack of training and tools to promote academic integrity or deal with academic misconduct effectively.

Deprioritizing academic integrity education may have long-term implications for primary and secondary students, particularly as they transition to their postsecondary studies. Students are often expected to make a huge leap in understanding the rules and overall academic culture as they transition from high school to postsecondary and professors believe that students should have mastered skills, such as writing and citing, prior to their arrival at university (Peters & Cadieux, 2019). Students also perceive that postsecondary faculty take academic integrity and misconduct more seriously and implement strategies to discourage cheating more often than did their high school teachers (Christensen Hughes & McCabe, 2006). Thus, the enormous mismatch between the expectations for acting with integrity across educational levels is problematic and disadvantages students as they begin postsecondary studies. Although the majority of policies at the postsecondary level for academic integrity are imperfect and lack the level of detail (McKenzie et al., 2020; Stoesz et al., 2019; Stoesz & Eaton, 2020) recommended by leading academic integrity policy experts (Bretag et al., 2011), the contrast between K-12 and postsecondary policy for academic integrity in Canada is mindboggling.

Implications for K-12 Classrooms in Canada

As part of the development or revision of academic integrity policies, careful examination of how assessment policies and programs influence academic integrity or fuel academic cheating is essential. In Canadian K-12 education systems, high stakes assessments of provincial and territorial assessment programs have important consequences for secondary students—in some jurisdictions results from these assessments make up 30–50% of final grades and/or serve as graduation requirements (Volante & Ben Jaafar, 2008). Research data in the US suggests that high stakes exams contribute to academic misconduct by students in both K-12 education and postsecondary studies (Nichols & Berliner, 2007). Although provincial standardized assessments have been implemented to legitimize Canadian education on the global stage, improve teaching and learning systems, and to hold educators accountable (see Volante & Ben Jaafar, 2008), there has been substantial debate over the value of these assessments to serve these purposes (Cizek, 2001). Moreover, the link between high stakes standardized assessment and the pressure to cheat needs to be examined closely within the Canadian K-12 education context. Success in K-12 has traditionally been measured by achievement of high test scores, acceptance to postsecondary studies, and numerous accomplishments—when these are valued above the quality of learning, students may feel enormous pressure, and cheating may be seen as one way to both achieve and to alleviate the pressure (Galloway, 2012). Thus, exploring the association between standardized assessment and cheating may require that the definitions of success for elementary and secondary school students need to be reimagined (Galloway, 2012).

Changing current practice would arguably be enhanced if teacher training programs in postsecondary institutions were to provide preservice teachers with holistic education on academic integrity, including an understanding of the various perspectives and cultural traditions (e.g., First Nations perspectives; Lindstrom, 2022; Poitras Pratt & Gladue, 2022), and ethical assessment in K-12 education (Malone, 2020; Sisti, 2007; Wan & Scott, 2016). Such education would help to ensure that they are equipped to make professional decisions and can model the values of honesty, respect, and responsibility upon entry into the profession. This is necessary as teachers serve as important role models and are held to high standards in terms of their character and values (Lumpkin, 2008). Administrators in elementary and secondary schools should also ensure that teachers feel comfortable discussing school procedures with them (Yoannou, 2014) and have access to ongoing professional development to stay current with the latest developments in the field of academic integrity (Wan & Scott, 2016). Teachers who value, model, and practice academic integrity are more likely to provide direct instruction to students so that they can develop the appropriate skills to complete their assignments with integrity (Peters & Cadieux, 2019).

Teachers also need guidance from good policy and be prepared with the skills required to deal with cheating promptly, consistently, and effectively when it is identified (Davis et al., 2009). Effective intervention is possible only when the circumstances surrounding the cheating situation are understood. For example, if students have not been instructed or have not had time to practice learning with integrity, behaviours could be viewed as "teachable moments'" for building skills rather than executing a standardized punishment (McGowan, 2005; Wan & Scott, 2016). Moreover, because of the increasing rates of academic misconduct at the high school level, teaching relevant skills in the early elementary grades is necessary. Relevant education may be provided through the digital and information literacy curricula, however, the message that academic integrity is important in all schoolwork would be stronger if academic integrity education was woven throughout all core subject areas (Lampert, 2008). Finally, parents can support efforts to promote integrity "by talking to their children about the valuing of learning and honesty over grades, by tempering their own desire for their children to succeed at all costs, and by supporting the teacher in disciplining their children when they are caught cheating" (Davis et al., 2009, pp. 65–66).

Conclusion

My environmental scan revealed that few provincial and territorial ministries of education provided guidance to students on academic integrity and consequences for misconduct, or teacher and administrator responsibilities for providing academic integrity education and responding to academic misconduct. Interestingly, an association between the presence or absence of government and school level policies was not evident. Education leaders at the provincial, school division, and school levels in Canada should work together to develop holistic policies that are informed by research and the experiences of all stakeholders, including educators, parents, and students. Such policies must support teaching and learning environments where academic integrity is deemed valuable, is highly respected, and is consistently practiced, and that fosters the development of trusting relationships between students and teachers to support learning (Wan & Scott, 2016). Academic integrity policies must also provide guidance for appropriate consequences for academic misconduct, while at the same time avoiding the development of "... a climate of fear among students and a desire to challenge the system" (Bailey, 2010) by implementing zero tolerance policies, which may be flawed and ineffective (e.g., as shown for non-academic misconduct; Martinez, 2009). Policies must emphasize the values of academic integrity (International Center for Academic Integrity (ICAI), 2021), the importance of proper attribution, and strengthening information literacy skills (Wan & Scott, 2016), so that students in elementary and secondary education are not simply avoiding punishment but moving towards learning with integrity. Finally, postsecondary institutions must provide preservice K-12 teachers with holistic education on academic integrity, including various ways it is understood and expressed based on cultural traditions (e.g., Lindstrom, 2022; Poitras Pratt & Gladue, 2022) and ethical assessment (Malone, 2020; Sisti, 2007; Wan & Scott, 2016).

References

Albright, K. (2004). Environmental scanning: Radar for success. *Information Management, 38*(3), 38.

Ali, I., & Aboelmaged, M. (2020). A bibliometric analysis of academic misconduct research in higher education: Current status and future research opportunities. *Accountability in Research, 00*(00), 1–22. https://doi.org/10.1080/08989621.2020.1836620

Anderman, E. M., & Midgley, C. (2004). Changes in self-reported academic cheating across the transition from middle school to high school. *Contemporary Educational Psychology, 29*(4), 499–517. https://doi.org/10.1016/j.cedpsych.2004.02.002

Bailey, J. (2010). How schools are hurting the fight against plagiarism. *Plagiarism Today*. https://www.plagiarismtoday.com/2010/05/10/how-schools-are-hurting-the-fight-against-plagiarism/

Bosetti, L., Van Pelt, D., & Allison, D. (2017). The changing landscape of school choice in Canada: From pluralism to parental preference? *Education Policy Analysis Archives, 25*, 38. https://doi.org/10.14507/epaa.25.2685

Brandes, B. (1986). Academic honesty: A special study of California students. https://eric.ed.gov/?id=ED272533

Bretag, T., Mahmud, S., Wallace, M., Walker, R., McGowan, U., East, J., Green, M., Partridge, L., & James, C. (2014). Teach us how to do it properly! An Australian academic integrity student survey. *Studies in Higher Education, 39*(7), 1150–1169. https://doi.org/10.1080/03075079.2013.777406

Bretag, T., & Mahmud, S. (2016). A conceptual framework for implementing exemplary academic integrity policy in Australian higher education. In *Handbook of Academic Integrity* (pp. 463–480). https://doi.org/10.1007/978-981-287-098-8

Bretag, T., Mahmud, S., Wallace, M., Walker, R., James, C., Green, M., East, J., Mcgowan, U., & Partridge, L. (2011). Core elements of exemplary academic integrity policy in Australian higher education. *International Journal for Educational Integrity, 7*(2), 3–12. http://www.ojs.unisa.edu.au/journals/index.php/IJEI/

Capano, G. (2015). Federal dynamics of changing governance arrangements in education: A comparative perspective on Australia, Canada and Germany. *Journal of Comparative Policy Analysis: Research and Practice, 17*(4), 322–341. https://doi.org/10.1080/13876988.2014.952530

Charlton, P., Doucet, S., Azar, R., Nagel, D. A., Boulos, L., Luke, A., Mears, K., Kelly, K. J., & Montelpare, W. J. (2019). The use of the environmental scan in health services delivery research: A scoping review protocol. *BMJ Open, 9*(9). https://doi.org/10.1136/bmjopen-2019-029805

Choo, C. W. (2002). Environmental scanning as information seeking and environmental scanning as information seeking and organizational knowing. *PrimaVera, 2*(1), 2002.

Christensen Hughes, J. M., & McCabe, D. (2006). Academic misconduct within higher education in Canada. *Canadian Journal of Higher Education, 36*(2), 1–21.

Cizek, G. J. (2001). More unintended consequences of high-stakes testing. *Educational Measurement: Issues and Practice, 20*(4), 19–27. https://doi.org/10.1111/j.1745-3992.2001.tb00072.x

Cizek, G. J. (2003). *Detecting and preventing classroom cheating: Promoting integrity in assessment* (Vol. 3). Corwin Press, Inc.

Crossman, K. E. (2014). Intensive English for academic purposes: A curriculum designed and developed for local English language learners entering university. https://doi.org/10.11575/PRISM/26594

Curtis, G. J., & Clare, J. (2017). How prevalent is contract cheating and to what extent are students repeat offenders? *Journal of Academic Ethics, 15*(2), 115–124. https://doi.org/10.1007/s10805-017-9278-x

Davis, S. F., Drinan, P. F., & Bertram Gallant, T. (2009). Cheating in school: What we know and what we can do. *Wiley-Blackwell*. https://doi.org/10.1080/00098655.1966.11477001

Eaton, S. E., & Christensen Hughes, J. M. C. (2022). Academic integrity in Canada: Historical perspectives and current trends. In *Academic Integrity in Canada*. Springer.

Evans, E. D., & Craig, D. (1990). Teacher and student perceptions of academic cheating in middle and senior high schools. *The Journal of Educational Research, 84*(1), 44–53. https://doi.org/10.1080/00220671.1990.10885989

Figlio, D. N. (2007). Boys named Sue: Disruptive children and their peers. *Education Finance and Policy, 2*(4), 376–394. https://doi.org/10.1162/edfp.2007.2.4.376

Galloway, M. K. (2012). Cheating in advantaged high schools: Prevalence, justifications, and possibilities for change. *Ethics and Behavior, 22*(5), 378–399. https://doi.org/10.1080/10508422.2012.679143

Galloway, M. K., & Conner, J. (2015). Perpetuating privilege: Students' perspectives on the culture of a high-performing and high-pressure high school. *The Educational Forum, 79*(2), 99–115. https://doi.org/10.1080/00131725.2014.1002592

Galway, G. (2012). Lessons in leadership: Perspectives on corporate managerialism and educational reform. *Canadian Journal of Educational Administration and Policy*, 130, 32. https://www.umanitoba.ca/publications/cjeap/pdf_files/galway.pdf

Grimes, P. W. (2012). *Dishonesty Business: In Academics A Cross-Cultural and Evaluation of Student Attitudes, 49*(3), 273–290.

International Center for Academic Integrity (ICAI). (2021). *The fundamental values of academic integrity* (3rd ed.). www.academicintegrity.org/the-fundamental-valuesof-academic-integrity

Jensen, L. A., Arnett, J. J., Feldman, S. S., & Cauffman, E. (2002). It's wrong, but everybody does it: Academic dishonesty among high school and college students. *Contemporary Educational Psychology, 27*(2), 209–228. https://doi.org/10.1006/ceps.2001.1088

Josephson Institute Center for Youth Ethics. (2012). 2012 report card on the ethics of American youth—honesty. http://charactercounts.org/programs/reportcard/2012/installment_report-card_honesty-integrity.html

Kohn, A. (2007). Foreword. In E. M. Anderman & T. B. Murdock (Eds.), *Psychology of academic cheating* (pp. 11–19). Amsterdam: Elsevier.

Lampert, L. D. (2008). Student academic integrity. In Information Literacy Instruction Handbook (pp. 149–163). *American Library Association.* http://hdl.handle.net/10211.2/1998

Lindstrom, G. (2022). Accountability, relationality and Indigenous epistemology: Advancing an Indigenous perspective on academic integrity. In S. E. Eaton & J. Christensen Hughes (Eds.), *Academic Integrity in Canada*. Springer.

Lucas, G. M., & Friedrich, J. (2005). Individual differences in workplace deviance and integrity as predictors of academic dishonesty. *Ethics & Behavior, 15*(1), 15–35. https://doi.org/10.1207/s15327019eb1501_2

Lumpkin, A. (2008). Teachers as role models teaching character and moral virtues. *Journal of Physical Education, Recreation & Dance, 79*(2), 45–50. https://doi.org/10.1080/07303084.2008.10598134

Malone, D. M. (2020). Ethics education in teacher preparation: A case for stakeholder responsibility. *Ethics and Education, 15*(1), 77–97. https://doi.org/10.1080/17449642.2019.1700447

Manitoba Education and Advanced Learning. (2015). *Provincial assessment policy kindergarten to grade 12: Academic responsibility, honesty, and promotion/retention.* https://www.edu.gov.mb.ca/k12/assess/publications.html

Martinez, S. (2009). A system gone berserk: How are zero-tolerance policies really affecting schools? *Preventing School Failure: Alternative Education for Children and Youth, 53*(3), 153–158. https://doi.org/10.3200/psfl.53.3.153-158

McGowan, U. (2005). Academic integrity: An awareness and development issue for students and staff. *Journal of University Teaching and Learning Practice, 2*(3), 48–57. http://ro.uow.edu.au/jutlp/vol2/iss3/6

McKenzie, A. M., Miron, J. B., Eaton, S. E., Persaud, N., Steeves, M., Stoesz, B. M., & Thacker, E. (2020). Contract cheating language within academic integrity policies in the university sector in Ontario. In *International Center for Academic Integrity 2020 Conference.* Canada.

McKenzie, A. M. (2018). Academic integrity across the Canadian landscape. *Canadian Perspectives on Academic Integrity, 1*(2), 40–45. https://doi.org/10.11575/CPAI.V1I2.54599.G42964

Ministry of Education Government of Saskatchewan. (2011). Academic integrity and student responsibility guidelines.

Murdock, T. B., Miller, A., & Kohlhardt, J. (2004). Effects of classroom context variables on high school students' judgments of the acceptability and likelihood of cheating. *Journal of Educational Psychology, 96*(4), 765–777. https://doi.org/10.1037/0022-0663.96.4.765

Newfoundland & Labrador English School District. (2013). *Assessment, Evaluation and Reporting* (PROG-317).

Nichols, S. L., & Berliner, D. C. (2007). The pressure to cheat in a high-stakes testing environment. In *Psychology of academic cheating* (pp. 289–311). Elsevier Inc. https://doi.org/10.1016/B978-012372541-7/50016-4.

Nonis, S., & Swift, C. O. (2001). An examination of the relationship between academic dishonesty and workplace dishonesty: A multicampus investigation. *Journal of Education for Business, 77*(2), 69–77. https://doi.org/10.1080/08832320109599052

Peters, M., & Cadieux, A. (2019). Are Canadian professors teaching the skills and knowledge students need to prevent plagiarism? *International Journal for Educational Integrity, 15*(1), 1–16. https://doi.org/10.1007/s40979-019-0047-z

Poitras Pratt, Y., & Gladue, K. (2022). Re-defining academic integrity: Embracing Indigenous truths. In S. E. Eaton & J Christensen Hughes (Eds.), *Academic Integrity in Canada.* Springer.

Random.Org. (2020). List randomizer. Random.Org. https://www.random.org/lists/

Rathi, D., Shiri, A., & Cockney, C. (2017). Environmental scan: A methodological framework to initiate digital library development for communities in Canada's North. *Aslib Journal of Information Management, 69*(1), 76–94. https://doi.org/10.1108/AJIM-06-2016-0082

Ridgley, A., Miron, J. B., & McKenzie, A. (2019). *Building a regional academic integrity network: Profiling the growth and action of the Academic Integrity Council of Ontario.* Paper presented at the Canadian Symposium on Academic Integrity, Calgary, Canada. http://hdl.handle.net/1880/110308

Rowe, D. (2006). Taking responsibility: School behaviour policies in England, moral development and implications for citizenship education. *Journal of Moral Education, 35*(4), 519–531. https://doi.org/10.1080/03057240601026865

Rowel, R., Moore, N. D., Nowrojee, S., Memiah, P., & Bronner, Y. (2005). The utility of the environmental scan for public health practice: Lessons from an urban program to increase cancer screening. *Journal of the National Medical Association, 97*(4), 527–534.

Schab, F. (1991). Schooling without learning: Thirty years of cheating in high school. *Adolescence, 26*, 839–847.

Sisti, D. A. (2007). How do high school students justify internet plagiarism? *Ethics & Behavior, 17*(3), 215–231. https://doi.org/10.1080/10508420701519163

Stephens, J. M., & Wangaard, D. B. (2013). Using the epidemic of academic dishonesty as an opportunity for character education: A three-year mixed methods study (with mixed results). *Peabody Journal of Education, 88*(2), 159–179. https://doi.org/10.1080/0161956X.2013.775868

Stoesz, B. M., & Eaton, S. E. (2020). Academic integrity policies of publicly funded universities in western Canada. *Educational Policy*. https://doi.org/10.1177/0895904820983032

Stoesz, B. M., Eaton, S. E., Miron, J., & Thacker, E. J. (2019). Academic integrity and contract cheating policy analysis of colleges in Ontario Canada. *International Journal for Educational Integrity, 15*(1), 1–18. https://doi.org/10.1007/s40979-019-0042-4

Stoesz, B. M., & Los, R. (2019). Evaluation of a tutorial designed to promote academic integrity. *Canadian Perspectives on Academic Integrity, 2*(1), 3–26. https://doi.org/10.11575/cpai.v2i1

Stoesz, B. M., Gervais, L., Usick, B., Seeland, J., MacLeod, P., Vogt, L., Markovics, L., & Denham, T. (2020). Creating a collaborative network to promote cultures of academic integrity in Manitoba's postsecondary institutions [Practioner article]. *Canadian Perspectives on Academic Integrity*, 3, 39–48. https://doi.org/10.11575/cpai.v3i1.69763

Thorkildsen, T. A., Golant, C. J., & Richesin, L. D. (2007). Reaping what we sow: Cheating as a mechanism of moral engagement. In E. M. Anderman & T. B. Murdock (Eds.), *Psychology of academic cheating* (pp. 171–202). Elsevier. https://doi.org/10.1016/B978-012372541-7/50012-7

Volante, L., & Ben Jaafar, S. (2008). Educational assessment in Canada. *Assessment in Education: Principles, Policy and Practice, 15*(2), 201–210. https://doi.org/10.1080/09695940802164226

Wan, G., & Gut, D. (2008). Roles of media and media literacy education: Lives of Chinese and American adolescents. *New Horizons in Education, 56*(2), 28–42. http://www.ln.edu.hk/osl/new horizon/abstract/v56n2/3.pdf

Wan, G., & Scott, M. R. (2016). Start them early and right: Creating a culture of academic integrity in elementary schools. In T. Bretag (Ed.), *Handbook of Academic Integrity* (pp. 413–427). Singapore: Springer.

Wangaard, D. B. (2016). Practices to support developing academic integrity in secondary school students. In T. Bretag (Ed.), *Handbook of Academic Integrity* (pp. 429–448). Springer:Singapore. https://doi.org/10.1007/978-981-287-098-8_34

Yoannou, A. (2014). *Academic integrity: Perceptions and practices in secondary school humanities classes*. University of Toronto.

Brenda M. Stoesz In her role as a Senior Faculty Specialist (Academic Integrity Initiative), Dr. Brenda M. Stoesz provides support for instructors through the development and facilitation of workshops and other resources related to innovations in teaching and learning in higher education, most notably in the area of academic integrity. Stoesz also applies research and evaluation methods from various fields to examine holistic aspects of teaching and learning in higher education, including academic integrity broadly, contract cheating, and the perception and use of online learning environments.

Part II
Emerging and Prevalent Forms of Academic Misconduct

Chapter 8
Contract Cheating in Canada: A Comprehensive Overview

Sarah Elaine Eaton

Abstract In this chapter I present an overview of contract cheating in Canada over half a century, from 1970 to the early 2020s. I offer details about a failed attempt at legislation to make ghostwritten essays and exams illegal in Ontario in 1972. Then, I highlight a 1989 criminal case, noted as being the first of its kind in Canada, and possibly the Commonwealth, in which an essay mill owner and his wife were charged with fraud and conspiracy. The case was dismissed by the judge, leaving the contract cheating industry to flourish, which it has done. I synthesize the scant empirical data available for Canada and offer an educated estimate of the prevalence of contract cheating. Finally, I conclude with a call to action for educators, advocates, and policy makers. I conclude with a call to action for Canadians to take a stronger stance against contract cheating.

Keywords Essay mill · Term paper mill · Contract cheating · Canada · Academic integrity · Academic misconduct

Introduction

In this chapter, I present an overview of contract cheating in Canada, exploring its history and the extent of the problem today. Less is known about contract cheating in Canada compared with other countries such as Australia and the United Kingdom (UK), where contract cheating research and advocacy have matured since the early 2000s (Bretag, 2016, 2019; Lancaster & Clarke, 2007; Newton, 2018; Newton & Lang, 2016; Rogerson & Basanta, 2016). There are multiple reasons why Canada lags behind including the lack of: (a) widespread media coverage; (b) advocacy and education by quality assurance bodies; and (c) research funding and support.

To begin this chapter I point out that although the term "contract cheating" has been widely used internationally for more than a decade (Lancaster & Clarke, 2007), it is still gaining traction in Canada. Canadians may be more familiar with phrases such as

S. E. Eaton (✉)
University of Calgary, Calgary, Canada
e-mail: seaton@ucalgary.ca

S. E. Eaton and J. Christensen Hughes (eds.), *Academic Integrity in Canada*,
Ethics and Integrity in Educational Contexts 1,
https://doi.org/10.1007/978-3-030-83255-1_8

"term paper mill" or "essay mill", but the global community has recognized that the term "contract cheating" is more accurate, since it covers the outsourcing of all kinds of the academic work, encompassing both text-based and non-text based assessments, including for example, computer coding assignments (Lancaster & Clarke, 2017). It is essential to recognize that the contract cheating industry is global and operates on a massive scale, and has been estimated to be valued at $15 Billion USD (Eaton, 2021). The proliferation of early industry in the United States (US) in the 1970s is well-documented, leading to a naïve and erroneous assumption that early term paper mills flourished in America but that Canada was spared. There is ample evidence to show that commercial contract cheating was also active in Canada. In what is perhaps the most extensive and detailed history of the contract cheating industry in Canada, Buerger (2002) dedicated an entire chapter of his doctoral thesis to the topic, going to extensive lengths to conduct archival research, review legal documents and interview individuals involved in the industry, including key informants in a sting operation against an essay mill dealer in Toronto in the 1980s.

In this chapter, I synthesize what is known about the contract cheating in Canada. First, I provide a historical overview of the industry in Canada, including a failed attempt to make contract cheating illegal in Canada in the 1970s; and a subsequent landmark case to lay criminal charges against an essay mill in the 1980s. Following, I detail how the industry has grown and discuss why Canada continues to lag behind other countries in terms of research and advocacy. Next, I discuss what Canadians have been doing in recent years to catch up to other countries and how our efforts are becoming more systematic and organized across the country. I conclude with a call to action about what can be done to advance contract cheating advocacy, education, policy, and scholarship in Canada.

Canada's Connection to Early American Term-Paper Mills

The commercial essay mill industry began as early as the 1930s (Buerger, 2002), and was firmly established across the US and Canada in the 1960s and 1970s, with states along the Eastern Seaboard of the US being a hub for early term paper services (Buerger, 2002; Goodman, 1971a, b, c; Hechinger, 1972, Maeroff, 1971). As evidence of Canadian activity in the contract cheating industry, student newspapers, such as the *Varsity* at the University of Toronto, were running advertisements for ghost-written essays in the 1960s (Buerger, 2002).

American term-paper mills became hot news in the early 1970s, and reporters were quick to point out that Canadians were among those supplying services to the industry that was flourishing across the border (Goodman, 1971c; Shephard, 1972). In a six-page exposé in Cosmopolitan magazine in March 1973, journalist Jack Shepherd reported that:

> Termpapers Unlimited, Inc., [was] a nationwide operation run by Ward Warren, a self-made millionaire at twenty-three. The company employs some 3,000 ghosts [ghostwriters] during the academic year who toil in every major U.S. *and Canadian* city, cranking out,

> by Warren's own estimation, "90% of all the term papers now being disseminated in the country." (Shepherd, 1973, p. 172). (Emphasis added)

By 1972, US state judges were ordering term paper mills to close, effectively making it illegal for these businesses to operate in particular states (Waggoner, 1972). This merely prompted business owners to close down their business in one state and move to another where it was not illegal to operate, catalysing the growth of the industry across North America.

1970s: Canada's Commercial Term Paper Mills and "A Bill to Stop Essay Sellers"

Journalists began sounding the alarm about the commercial term paper mills in Canada in the 1970s in articles published by major newspapers, including in the *Calgary Herald* (Buchwald, 1972; Dallos, 1972) and in Canada's national newspaper, the *Globe and Mail* (O'Toole, 1974; Screening out the cheat, 1972; Would have to keep records: A bill to stop essay sellers, 1972; Wright, 1974). Since the 1970s, there have been repeated news reports of contract cheating companies operating openly in cities across Canada, including a television news story from CTV Edmonton, entitled "Essays for Sale", that won the Radio-Television News Directors Association Dan McArthur Award for in-depth and investigative journalism (RTNDA Canada announces, 2006 Prairie Regional Award Recipients, 2007).

The press has long served as an early alert system for unethical practices in education that merit the attention of the public, as well as those in decision-making roles who can effect change (Eaton, 2020c; Eaton & Turner, 2020). An analysis of historical newspaper records show that American suppliers were selling to Canadian customers, but that Canada also had its own home-grown essay mills owned and operated by and for Canadians. I elaborate on this point later.

Just as Americans were taking legal action against term paper mills operating on the Eastern Seaboard of the US, similar legislative initiatives were underway in at least one Canadian province, though with less success. In April 1972, the *Globe and Mail* reported that, "the Ontario Legislature is now toying with the idea of a law to stop firms from ghost-writing papers for students, perhaps by way of a charge of fraud or complicity, if a student were to testify that a paper was purchased and for what reasons" (Screening out the cheat, 1972, p. 6).

A few months later, the proposed bill made national news when it was reported on page five of the national newspaper, under the title "Would have to keep records: A bill to stop essay sellers" (1972). The report, with no author indicated, got a few of the details incorrect, and the correct details are archived online in legislative documents as a matter of public record. A review of the legislative documents shows that on June 14, 1972, a private member's bill was introduced by Member of the Provincial Parliament (MPP), the Honourable Albert Roy (Roy, 1972). Bill 174, An Act Respecting Ghost Written Term Papers and Examinations received a first reading in the legislature. The official report of the debate (i.e., the Hansard), recorded the introduction of the bill as follows:

> Mr. Roy moves first reading of bill intituled, An Act respecting Ghost-Written Term Papers and Examinations, 1972.
>
> Motion agreed to; first reading of the bill.
>
> Mr. Roy: Mr. Speaker, this bill enables the Attorney General, on the request of the Minister of Colleges and Universities (Mr. Kerr), or the Minister of Education (Mr. Wells), to bring a civil action in the Supreme Court to stop operations of a corporation, or business, which deals in ghost-written term papers or examinations.
>
> Mr. Shulman: It should also outlaw politicians' ghost-written speeches! (Legislative Assembly of Ontario Official report of debates (Hansard), 1972 p. 3651)

There is no evidence to suggest that the proposed legislation made it past a first reading (K. Laukys, personal communication, December 21, 2020). Although the bill was never passed, it is notable that it endeavoured to curb not only term papers written by third parties, but also examinations, which suggests that the practice of hiring impersonators to write one's exams in Canada has been a concern for many decades.

Early suppliers to the industry shared their experiences publicly, providing historical accounts of how the businesses operated, including costs and payments to suppliers. In an exposé published in Canada's national newspaper, the *Globe and Mail*, a writer who supplied services to the local industry in Toronto in the 1970s revealed that:

> The essay bank charges students according to their academic level (it's $4.95 a page for first, second and third year original papers and escalates after that; it's $2.75 a page for ready-made essays already in the bank). The student must supply all reference books and the writer must come in, pick them up and get the thing written for deadline. All business is done either by phone or in the essay bank's office. (O'Toole, 1974, p. 45)

Presumably, the prices indicated were in Canadian dollars, as the article was written in Canada about a term paper mill in Toronto. This may be the earliest available evidence regarding the prices of outsourced academic work in Canada. To put these prices in historical perspective, the average income for a family of two or more persons in Canada in 1974 was $16,147 CAD (Statistics Canada, 1977) and a pound of hamburger cost about $1.29 CAD (Stewart, 1974).

O'Toole (1974) indicated that term paper mills had walk-in stores operating in Toronto, similar to the ones operating in the US. In other words, the commercial contract cheating industry has been actively operating in Canada since the 1970s, and possibly even earlier; and it would be naïve and erroneous to claim that early term paper mills were exclusively an American phenomenon. A story in the *Globe and Mail* near the end of the decade declared that the essay mill business was "dying out" (Stead, 1978, p. 5), but evidence shows otherwise.

The 1980s: The Case of Custom Essay Service

The 1980s brought a landmark case against Custom Essay Service (CES), believed to be "Canada's oldest term paper mill" (Schmidt, 1998, C8), which had allegedly been operating since at least the 1970s. Buerger (2002) investigated the case in great detail, interviewing a number of individuals directly involved and conducting an analysis of primary documents never released to the public. Among those he interviewed were Detective Graham Hanlon at 31 Division and Sergeant Brian Dickson at 21 Division of the Metropolitan Toronto Police (now known as the Toronto Police Service), who led the sting operation that resulted in charges. Buerger (2002) also interviewed the Associate Dean of Students at York University, Mark Webber, who was instrumental in working with the police to have charges laid.

At the request of York University in 1988 the Toronto police began investigating CES, run by Derek and Marilyn Sim of Sunderland, Ontario (Buerger, 2002; Couple charged in essay scam, 1989). An initial investigation from the Fraud Division was unsuccessful, and the university "turned to attorney Neil Kosloff, who approached Crown Attorney Steven Leggett, who in turn convinced 31 Division that a prosecution on the grounds of uttering forged documents had merit" (Buerger, 2002, p. 302). The case was assigned to Dickson and Hanlon, who met with administrators at York in July of 1988 to determine how to proceed, and a sting operation was designed (Buerger, 2002).

Constable Suzanne Beauchamp was recruited to place an order with CES for Sociology 1010.06A, a course she had actually taken when she was a student at York herself, so she could speak legitimately about the course and the kind of paper required (Buerger, 2002). After successfully purchasing the essay, a Criminal Code search warrant was issued to the police. Based on interviews with individuals directly involved in the case, Buerger wrote that on "April 5 [1989], Dickson and Hanlon, accompanied by uniformed officers and Weber, raided the CES premises at 4 Collier Street and seized 'boxes and boxes and boxes' of term papers and, more significantly, order forms" (Buerger, 2002, p. 303).

The raided documents showed that during the three-month period from January to April 1989, approximately 530 order forms were on file, representing a gross income of $98,000 (CAD), about half of which was kept by co-owners Derek Robinson Sim and Marilyn Elizabeth Sim (Buerger, 2002). This is notable because if that three-month period was indicative of a typical business quarter, we can extrapolate this figure to estimate that the business was grossing revenues of about $392,000 (CAD) per year. It is not known how many essay mills were operating in Canada in the late 1980s but, based on evidence from this one police investigation, it is reasonable to estimate that essay mills in Toronto alone were taking in well over a million dollars per year by 1989.

The Sims were charged with one count of conspiracy to utter forged documents and seven counts of uttering forged documents (Beurger, 2002; Couple charged in essay scam, 1989) in what was believed be to be "the first case of its kind in Canada and in the Commonwealth" (Schmidt, 1998). The prosecution prepared a strong case and "were prepared to bring forward two dozen witnesses, including eight students who had purchased essays, university faculty who had received them, and even a disaffected former CES writer" (Beurger, 2002, pp. 304–305). The case was heard by Judge George E. Carter, who ultimately dismissed the charges on September 11, 1990, finding there was no intent to commit a criminal act (Beurger, 2002).

Although CES "escaped without penalty" (Beurger, 2002, p. 307), the students who were involved were not so lucky. Over 100 students faced academic misconduct disciplinary consequences, and all were found responsible and subjected to sanctions ranging from receiving a grade of zero on the assignment to a 10-year suspension from the university (Beurger, 2002). The contract cheating industry in Canada continued to flourish and there is evidence to suggest that CES itself continued to operate successfully well into the Internet era (see Schmidt, 1998).

The 1990s: An Exposé and the Impact of the Internet

In a nine-page exposé in *Harper's Magazine* in 1995, a writer supplying services to the contract cheating industry in Canada elaborated on her experiences. Writing under the pseudonym of Abigail Witherspoon, the writer provided extensive and exacting details about working for 'Tailormade', also a pseudonym, for an essay service in "a large Canadian city" (Witherspoon, 1995, p. 49), which was later determined to be written about CES (Buerger, 2002). The business was touted as being "Canada's foremost essay service" (p. 49) by the owner's wife, who answers the phone when calls come in. The writer explained how "orders came in from Vancouver, Calgary, Winnipeg" (p. 49) and how the crew of writers employed by the business "often wait at a bar around the corner" from the office, where the company has a regular table where writers gather to await their next assignment (Witherspoon, 1995, p. 50).

According to Witherspoon, writers supplying services to the company allegedly included "a professor who'd been fired from some school, we were never really sure where…" (p. 51) who eventually "started an essay-writing service of his own" (p. 51) and went on to become "Tailormade's main competition" (p. 51).

By 1995, Tailormade was allegedly charging "twenty dollars Canadian a page for first- and second-year course assignments, twenty-two a page for third- and fourth-year assignments, twenty four for 'technical, scientific, and advanced' topics." (p. 51), of which "the writers get half, in cash: ten and eleven bucks a page; twelve for the technical, scientific, and advanced" (p. 52). Students who allegedly did not bring in books and other reference materials to help the writers were charged an additional $2 per page (Witherspoon, 1995).

Witherspoon describes a life of pulling two to three all-nighters a week during peak times, fueled by licorice and extra strong coffee, eager to be assigned rush jobs, for which she was paid an extra dollar per page (Witherspoon, 1995). She reports that the assignments she disliked the most were from education students that "all involve writing up our customers' encounters in their 'practicum'"… including, "'reflections' on a 'lesson plan' for a seventh-grade English class" (p. 55). She then goes on to offer a direct quotation from a lesson plan she allegedly wrote for a teacher trainee.

Witherspoon further details how she wrote application essays for applicants to Canadian medical schools, describing her work as "academic prostitution" (p. 56) in what has been, to date, the most detailed account on record of a writer working for a Canadian essay mill. Three years after that exposé was published, Derek Sim was reported to be working from a "crammed, one-room office equipped with a fully-wired computer" (Schmidt, 1998, p. C8), having moved the business fully online in the age of the Internet.

The development of the Internet changed how contract cheating occurred all over the world, including in Canada. In the 1990s and early 2000s, there were numerous news stories, not only in Ontario, but across Canada about the term-paper industry moving online (Cribb, 1999; Ellingson, 2003; Gray, 2002; Mah, 1999; Maich, 2006; Pearson, 2002; Steffenhagen, 2001; Walker, 2001). There is at least one public account of students at the University of Alberta being disciplined for buying term papers from the Internet in the 1990s (Mah, 1999).

The 2000s: Research, Advocacy, and Collaboration

As in decades past, journalists across the country continued to publish stories about academic outsourcing, though by the turn of the millennium, most of the stories focused on Internet-based services (Ellingson, 2003; Maich, 2006; Steffenhagen, 2001; Walker, 2001).

A Focus on Research: Contract Cheating Data From Canada

The first decade of the new millennium brought research about academic outsourcing into sharper focus. Mentions of Internet term paper mill use among Canadian students began to appear in scholarly and professional journal articles (see Oliphant, 2002). Term paper mills were renamed when two computer science professors in England discovered that their students were outsourcing their coding assignments over the Internet. They proposed *contract cheating* as an umbrella term for all kinds of outsourced assignments (Clarke & Lancaster, 2006). News of their investigation was covered by the BBC (2006) and the two went on to systematically study the phenomenon of contract cheating, laying a foundation for researchers elsewhere to build similar programs of research. In Canada, TV coverage of term paper mills (e.g., Lee, 2012) happened at a local level and did not ignite large-scale action against contract cheating in the same way that news stories in Australia and the UK did.

Lancaster and Clarke repeatedly identified that Canada was among the top four countries from which students placed online orders for computer science assignments (Clarke & Lancaster, 2006; Lancaster & Clarke, 2007, 2009). The top three were the

US (#1), the UK (#2), and Australia (#3). Canadian computer science students were found to have ordered 6.8% of the total number of orders placed on the website, with orders originating from students at 19 different Canadian institutions (Lancaster & Clarke, 2007). One limitation to their data was that it was specific to computer science students but is nevertheless appropriate to establish from an empirical standpoint that Canada has been among the top countries from which students buy their academic work.

The seminal research by Christensen Hughes and McCabe (2006a, b) provided the most comprehensive data set about academic misconduct in Canadian higher education to date. Among respondents at 10 different institutions, 8% of undergraduate students and 3% of graduate students self-reported that they had turned in work completed by someone else (Christensen Hughes & McCabe, 2006a). Five percent of undergraduates and 4% of graduate students admitted to having written or providing a paper for another student (Christensen Hughes & McCabe, 2006a). Christensen Hughes and McCabe (2006a) found that 1% of undergraduate students and 1% of graduate students admitted to buying academic work from an online term paper mill or website in the early 2000s.

More than a decade later, Stoesz and Los (2019) replicated the survey administered by Christensen Hughes and McCabe in two different studies, both with students working towards high school completion. Their results revealed that as many as 17.9% of research participants self-reported having turned in papers obtained from a contact cheating company that charged a fee, though results varied across age groups.

A comparison between the two studies is not without its problems but is nevertheless a useful exercise. Focusing specifically on the question related to students to self-reported that they bought academic work from an online term paper mill or website, in the 13-year gap between the two studies, the number rose dramatically (see Table 8.1).

The Christensen Hughes and McCabe (2006a) study had a larger sample size and was conducted across Canada. They grouped results by the learning experiences students were reflecting on (i.e., high school, undergraduate, or graduate). Stoesz and Los's (2019) sample size was much smaller and focused only on students in the western Canadian province of Manitoba. In addition, their study focused on individuals taking junior high and high school courses (even the 28–32 year-olds studying at adult education centres). Stoesz and Los (2019) did not collect data from students enrolled in post-secondary courses.

What we know for certain at this point is that Canada lacks current accurate data about the prevalence of contract cheating on a national scale. Although there are indications that if we were to replicate the Christensen Hughes and McCabe (2006a) study (or parts of it) today the results might differ from what they were in the first few years of the new millennium when they collected their data, we cannot draw such a conclusion from a scientific standpoint. At best, we can make an educated guess. That is what I endeavoured to do a few years ago (Eaton, 2018). I created a model for understanding the probability of the extent of contract cheating in Canada that could be replicated over time.

Table 8.1 Comparative results of self-reported contract cheating violations among Canadian students

	Christensen Hughes & McCabe (2006a)			Stoesz and Los (2019)			
	Respondents from across Canada			Respondents from the province of Manitoba			
	Single study			Study #1			Study #2
	High school ($n = 1269$) %	Undergrad students ($n = 13\,644$) %	Graduate students ($n = 1318$) %	17–20 year-olds ($n = 28$) %	21–27 year-olds ($n = 31$) %	28–32 year olds ($n = 30$) %	12.8–17.9 year olds ($n = 28$) %
Turning in a paper obtained in large part from a term paper "mill" or website that did charge a fee	1	1	0	17.9	0	10.0	5.6

I drew from Curtis and Clare's (2017) meta-analysis of previously collected data sets ($N = 1{,}378$) from studies around the world. They found that 3.5% of students, on average, engaged in contact cheating, though they noted some variances among subgroups. I then mapped that percentage to Statistics Canada data about postsecondary enrollments across the country to arrive at an educated estimate that the number of post-secondary students engaging in contract cheating was 71,223 (see Eaton, 2018).

I selected Statistics Canada as the source of the post-secondary enrollments deliberately, as it is a reliable source of statistics with data collected in a consistent manner over time. Any changes in how they change their collection methods or presentation of the results is explained in detail and publicly available. This allows us to draw on the most statistically accurate data available. Since I conducted my initial estimate, Statistics Canada has updated their statistics for post-secondary enrollments in Canada to include data from the 2018–2019 academic year (Statistics Canada, 2021). Using these most recent statistics and Curtis and Clare's (2017) 3.5% figure as the average prevalence of contract cheating, I have estimated that over 75,000 post-secondary students engaged in contract cheating in the 2018–2019 academic year (see Table 8.2).

I emphasize that this is an estimate based on previously published scientific estimate and does not represent an estimate of actual rates of contract cheating based on Canadian data. These statistics were also published pre-COVID and at the time this book was published, we had no empirical data about the extent to which contract cheating may have increased during the pandemic in Canada. There remains a dearth of data about contract cheating in Canada and there is an urgent need to remedy this.

Table 8.2 An Estimation of the possible extent of contact cheating in canadian postsecondary institutions (based on 2018–2019 statistics Canada enrollment data)[1]

	Post-secondary enrollments in Canada (2018–2019)	3.5% who may engage in contract cheating
Full-time enrollments	1,655,286	57,935
Part-time enrollments	500,136	17,505
Totals	2,155,425[2]	75,440

[1] Values rounded up to the nearest whole number.

[2] Statistics Canada (2021) note: "All counts are randomly rounded to a multiple of 3 using the following procedure: counts which are already a multiple of 3 are not adjusted; counts one greater than a multiple of 3 are adjusted to the next lowest multiple of 3 with a probability of two-thirds and to the next highest multiple of 3 with a probability of one-third. The probabilities are reversed for counts that are one less than a multiple of 3." This resulted in a difference of 3 in the total number of enrollments. See Statistics Canada (2021) source data for further details.

A Focus on Advocacy and Collaboration

In 2008, the Academic Integrity Council of Ontario (AICO) was launched (McKenzie et al., 2020a), a provincial network that "has provided a forum for academic integrity practitioners and representatives from post-secondary institutions in Ontario to share information, and to facilitate the establishment and promotion of academic integrity best practices" (p. 25). In 2018, AICO launched a contract cheating sub-committee, which included representatives from six member institutions in the province and included a five-point action plan focused on building awareness, sharing resources and, engaging in advocacy (Academic Integrity Council of Ontario, 2018, 2019b; McKenzie et al., 2020a).

The first available evidence of Canadian collaboration with an international colleague is that of Corinne Hersey, a graduate student at the University of New Brunswick, who co-presented with Thomas Lancaster at a conference in the UK (Hersey & Lancaster, 2015). The emergence of graduate student research into contract cheating in Canada holds much promise for the future of academic integrity in Canada, but their work needs to be supported so they can develop sustained programs of research beyond graduation (Eaton & Edino, 2018).

In 2018, the Canadian Consortium of the International Center for Academic Integrity (ICAI, 2018a, b) focused on contract cheating at its annual meeting that year which is normally held as a pre-conference event prior to the centre's annual conference (Canadian Consortium—ICAI, 2018a, b; Miron & Ridgley, 2018). The following year, contract cheating continued to be a topic of interest, with AICO presenting a report of its sub-committee activities since it had been convened (AICO, 2019a).

The inaugural Canadian Symposium on Academic Integrity (2019) held at the University of Calgary provided a unique opportunity for scholars, students, and professionals to mobilize and share research and practical experience about contract cheating in Canada. Tracey Bretag focused on contract cheating in her keynote presentation (Bretag, 2019a) and Thomas Lancaster provided a feature session on the topic (Lancaster, 2019). In addition, there were a number of additional sessions presented on contract cheating (Blackburn, 2019; Eaton, 2019b; Hersey, 2019; Thacker et al., 2019; Usick et al., 2019, 2020). The symposium provided a unique opportunity for Canadians to dialogue about contract cheating in a way that no previous event had. During the symposium, AICO members facilitated a workshop on how to establish a regional academic integrity network (Ridgley et al., 2019). As a result, three new provincial networks were established in the six months following the symposium: the Alberta Council on Academic Integrity (ACAI); the British Columbia Academic Integrity Network (BC AIN); and the Manitoba Academic Integrity Network (MAIN) (see Stoesz et al., 2019b). The Manitoba group quickly established themselves as national leaders with a multi-institutional collaborative project to block the uniform resource locators (URLs) of contract cheating websites from being accessed on campuses (Seeland et al., 2020a; b). A few provinces to the west, the Alberta Council on Academic Integrity (Eaton et al., 2020a) established a working group (similar to AICO's sub-committee) to focus specifically on contract cheating. These initiatives demonstrate that contract cheating is an urgent and important issue in Canada.

Institutions across Canada have participated in the International Day of Action Against Contract Cheating since it began in 2016 (Mourelatos, 2020). Every year since, this global day of advocacy has been organized by the ICAI to promote awareness about contract cheating, with a variety of events being held on campuses and online. In 2020, Canadians collaborated on a national scale, when the entire event went virtual due to COVID-19, and the international program committee was chaired by a Canadian, Jennie Miron (Miron, 2020).

Developing a Canadian Research and Advocacy Agenda for Academic Integrity

Canadian researchers and practitioners have increased their momentum around contract cheating research and advocacy since about 2018, the year AICO launched its subcommittee on contract cheating and researchers and advocates began publishing about contract cheating in Canada specifically (Chang, 2018; Eaton, 2018; Flostrand, 2018). One observation of note about these initial research articles about contract cheating in Canada is that the authors were mostly unknown to one another, as they worked in different disciplines such as second languages (Chang, 2018), business (Flostrand, 2018) and education (Eaton, 2018). Canadians are now developing a strong and sustainable research community at a national level to address contract cheating. It is evident that Canada needs a robust community of scholars and advocates to build capacity and community if we are to make progress combatting contract cheating in Canada.

National Policy Analysis Project

In 2018, I developed a research project to better understand how contract cheating was addressed in academic misconduct policies across publicly funded Canadian postsecondary institutions (Eaton, 2019a). The project was modelled after research undertaken some years earlier in Australia (Bretag et al., 2011a, b; Grigg, 2010). I was fortunate to be mentored by Tracey Bretag on how to develop and implement the project (Eaton, 2020d; Eaton et al., 2020b). As a result of Bretag's advice, I divided the project into phases, based on region and institution type (e.g., universities and colleges).

At the time of this writing, different teams have undertaken an analysis of 67 institutional policies across five provinces (British Columbia, Alberta, Saskatchewan,

Manitoba, and Ontario) including colleges ($n = 22$) and universities ($n = 45$). We have three peer-reviewed conference presentations (McKenzie et al., 2020b; Thacker et al., 2019a, b) and two refereed articles (Stoesz et al., 2019a; Stoesz & Eaton, 2020), with another under development. As of mid-2021, we are in the midst of our academic integrity policy analysis of universities in Atlantic Canada, which will bring the total number of institutions included in this study up to 80. Through this project we are building a network of researchers across Canada who are developing experience and expertise collaborating on academic integrity and contract cheating research. Our intention is that we will be able to leverage this experience going forward to position ourselves for national-level research funding.

Development of Resources

In addition to research, Canadians are beginning to develop resources on contract cheating that can be shared among members of the academic integrity community. AICO created a student tip sheet, which they released in time for the International Day of Action Against Contract Cheating in 2020 (Miron & McKenzie, 2020). In addition, others have created resources to raise awareness about contract cheating in higher education (Stoesz et al., 2019c) and assist educators and administrators with recognizing and managing cases of it (Eaton, 2019c; 2020a). In 2021, members of the Alberta Council on Academic Integrity created a one-page synopsis of an analysis of the parallels between the contract cheating industry and organized crime (Grue et al., 2021).

The development of such resources is important because it means that Canadians must no longer rely on resources created in other countries, where educational systems differ. Although there can be value in using a variety of resource material as a reference point, it is nevertheless helpful to have country-specific support materials. A key point of note is that the resources created to date in Canada have been developed by individuals, often in collaboration with provincial networks, whereas in other countries such as Australia and the UK, quality assurance bodies have developed resources that they have made freely and publicly available and have put effort into promoting and sharing them widely (see, for example, TEQSA, 2017, 2020; QAA, 2020).

Role of Quality Assurance (QA) Bodies

As of 2021, bodies that oversee quality assurance in Canadian higher education had yet to produce resources related to contract cheating, or to play an active role in addressing it. The International Network for Quality Assurance Agencies in Higher Education (2020) highlighted the Alberta network as an international exemplar of excellence in their Toolkit to Support Quality Assurance Agencies to Address

Academic Integrity and Contract Cheating. "Assess the Sector" (see International Network for Quality Assurance Agencies in Higher Education, 2020). In the toolkit, quality assurance agencies are encouraged to connect with networks such as the Alberta Council "that will allow you to identify and respond to emerging issues" (p. 26).

Canada's lack of action stands in stark contrast to advocacy and education being led by quality assurance bodies in the United Kingdom (Quality Assurance Agency, 2020) and Australia (Tertiary Education Quality and Standards Agency, 2015, 2017, 2020). Efforts in Australia to act against contract cheating have been so successful that legislation to make it a criminal offense to supply academic cheating services came into effect in 2020 (Parliament of Australia, 2020). In the discouraging and enduring absence of legislation in Canada to combat this predatory industry, it is crucial for educational quality assurance agencies in Canada to take a strong stand against contract cheating and to bring about change. Further, it is evident that in countries where there is a national quality assurance body for higher education, such as Australia and the UK, significant progress has been made more quickly than in countries where educational quality assurance is addressed at a regional or state level. It is essential that quality assurance bodies across Canada coordinate their efforts and support one another in taking action, so the result is a national stance against contract cheating.

The Impact of COVID-19

The impact of the coronavirus pandemic on contract cheating has yet to be fully understood, given this book was written in 2020 and early 2021, with many of its contributors working or studying from their homes instead of from their campuses. COVID-19 revealed a variety of flaws in society in general, and education was not spared. Rates of academic misconduct increased around the world during the pandemic, and Canada was no exception (Basken, 2020; Eaton, 2020b).

Contract cheating, including commercial file-sharing companies and unethical tutoring, became amplified during the pandemic (Eaton, 2020c; Eaton & Turner, 2020), along with remote online proctoring (e-proctoring) of exams. Although online proctoring has nothing to do with contract cheating per se, one common feature between e-proctoring and contract cheating is the positioning of commercial entities as providing quick and easy solutions to academic misconduct during a moment of crisis. In turn, these third-party vendors collect student data on a massive scale, without students necessarily being aware of how their information is being used or who has access to it. Issues such as privacy and illicit use of students' data are questions beyond the scope of this chapter but suffice to say that they matter and neither educators nor students can afford to remain naïve to these issues (Gray, 2022).

Conclusion

In this chapter, I have endeavoured to synthesize what is known about contract cheating in Canada to date. It is a myth that contract cheating has not existed in Canada. Not only have commercial contract cheating vendors been actively operating in our country for more than half a century (and quite possibly even longer), but they also operate at scale and continue to prey on our students at every level, starting as young as elementary schools and in both official languages (Eaton & Dressler, 2019).

Limitations

COVID-19 resulted in particular limitations to this chapter, as access to original legislative and court documents was not permitted during this time. Much of what is known about the legal case in the 1980s against CES was meticulously documented by Geoffrey Buerger (2002) in his doctoral thesis. Nevertheless, consulting primary sources is preferable, but it was not possible during the coronavirus pandemic.

Due to my own limited language proficiency in French, all of the source materials I consulted were in English. Although there is strong evidence to suggest that contract cheating occurs in a variety of languages other than English (Eaton & Dressler, 2019), there is much work to be done to understand how contract cheating impacts those in Francophone regions of the country.

Call to Action

I conclude this chapter with an urgent call to action. We have much work to do in Canada not only raise awareness about contract cheating, but to take action against it. My recommendations include:

Student Advocacy

Because contract cheating companies prey on students, it is essential for students not only to be actively involved in advocacy efforts, but also to lead them. Student governments and provincial and national student leadership bodies are key stakeholders in the conversation about contract cheating specifically, and academic integrity generally. It is incumbent upon educators and administrators to include students in policy-making decisions about academic misconduct and involve them in advocacy work.

Research

Academic integrity research in Canada has lacked funding on a national scale (Eaton & Edino, 2018). The absence of federal research funding is one of the reasons that Canada lags behind countries such as Australia, where research programs on contract cheating have been well funded. It is imperative for funding bodies such as the Social Sciences and Humanities Research Council of Canada (SSHRC) and other national-level bodies to sponsor research on contract cheating.

Along the same vein, it is essential for Canadian researchers to undertake collaborative, multi-institutional, and multi-jurisdictional research projects. Although individual research projects are an excellent place to start, for research to have more impact, it is essential for researchers to work collaboratively on larger national-level projects.

Support for Graduate Students

It is essential to support graduate students who wish to study contract cheating in Canada. Only a handful of Canadians who have undertaken academic integrity study for their doctoral work have gone on to develop sustained programs of research on the topic. This must change in order for the field of academic integrity research to mature. Contract cheating continues to be an urgent issue and it is imperative for professors and university departments (particularly faculties of education) to actively support graduate student education and research.

Quality Assurance and Professional Bodies

As long as quality assurance bodies are not involved in efforts to address contract cheating, educational institutions may have little incentive or power to act. It is essential for the organizations responsible for the oversight of quality assurance of education in Canada to provide leadership and guidance regarding contract cheating, as well as to develop resources and supports to address it.

Professional regulatory bodies, such as those of engineering, nursing, and teaching, are key community stakeholders. When students engage in contract cheating, they are not earning their credentials legitimately. The result can be that graduates of reputable schools may lack the skills necessary to serve in the profession. Even worse, they may have developed habits of unethical and deceptive behaviour that they may carry forward into their professional practice. It is imperative for accrediting and professional bodies to hold schools accountable for the ways in which they uphold integrity. A particular focus on contract cheating is needed as part of that accountability.

Build Momentum and Sustain Our Actions

As I have shown in this chapter, Canada is not immune to contract cheating. Canadian educators, advocates and scholars have begun to mobilize and collaborate on a larger scale over since about 2018. It will be essential for us to ensure our efforts are sustainable over time. Although we have a few strong advocates working tirelessly to organize and encourage others, every community, every school, every quality assurance and professional body, and every political party needs individuals committed to tackling this contract cheating in Canada.

Legislation

As more countries take legislative action against contract cheating, Canada falls further behind. The issue of contract cheating needs to be on political agendas. To get it there, executive institutional leaders can help ensure that contract cheating is part of discussions with government. One approach that has been successfully used in countries such as Australia is to focus on the predatory nature of commercial third-party vendors who prey on our students.

2022 will mark 50 years since the first failed attempt to pass legislation to make it illegal to sell ghostwritten term papers (Roy, 1972). Even if that first effort was unsuccessful, it is not insignificant. It will be important to mark the 50th anniversary of that 1972 attempt to have legislation passed. We can celebrate the efforts of those who came before us and commit to carrying on the work they started until we are successful in legislating against contract cheating in Canada. More than ever before Canadians are poised to take a strong and united stance against contract cheating and now is the time to do so.

Acknowledgements I am grateful to Dr. Kim Clarke and Dr. Jonnette Watson Hamilton, from the Faculty of Law at the University of Calgary. They provided guidance on how to follow up on legal and legislative matters reported by the Canadian media. I further acknowledge Anna White, law student at the University of Calgary conducted some preliminary legal research and Serge Paquet, Reference Archivist, from the Archives of Ontario.

I extend special thanks to Dr. Geoffrey Buerger, whose doctoral thesis was particularly helpful to provide historical context. Dr. Buerger took the time to meet with me to share further details of his research via a video conference call as I was researching this chapter.

Finally, I owe a particular debt of gratitude to Ms. Kate Laukys, Index and Reference Officer of the House Publications and Language Services branch of the Legislative Assembly of Ontario. She located and sent me links to the original legislative documents for the proposed bill brought forward 1972 archived online, which I would never have found otherwise.

References

Academic Integrity Council of Ontario (AICO). (2019a). *AICO Contract Cheating Sub-Committee Report*. Paper presented at the Canadian Consortium—International Center for Academic Integrity. https://live-academicintegrity.pantheonsite.io/wp-content/uploads/2019/04/Contract-Cheating_ICAI-Canadian-Consortium_March-2019.pdf

Academic Integrity Council of Ontario (AICO). (2019b). AICO's Subcommittee on contract cheating. Retrieved January 3, 2021, from https://academicintegritycouncilofontario.wordpress.com/contract-cheating/

Academic Integrity Council of Ontario (AICO). (2018). Annual report 2017/2018. Retrieved from https://academicintegritycouncilofontario.files.wordpress.com/2018/10/academic-integrity-council-of-ontario-annual-report-2017-18.pdf

Basken, P. (2020, December 23). Universities say student cheating exploding in Covid era. *Times Higher Education*. https://www.timeshighereducation.com/news/universities-say-student-cheating-exploding-covid-era

BBC News. (2006). Student cheats contract out work. http://news.bbc.co.uk/2/hi/uk_news/education/5071886.stm

Blackburn, J. (2019). *A question of trust? Educators' views of contract cheating*. Paper presented at the Canadian Symposium on Academic Integrity. https://www.slideshare.net/JamesBlackburn7/a-question-of-trust-educators-views-of-contract-cheating

Bretag, T. (Ed.). (2016). *Handbook of academic integrity*. Springer.

Bretag, T. (2019). *Contract cheating research: Implications for Canadian universities*. Keynote presented at the Canadian Symposium on Academic Integrity. http://hdl.handle.net/1880/110279

Bretag, T., Mahmud, S., East, J., Green, M., & James, C. (2011). *Academic integrity standards: A preliminary analysis of the Academic integrity policies at Australian Universities*. Paper presented at the Proceedings of AuQF 2011 Demonstrating Quality.

Bretag, T., Mahmud, S., Wallace, M., Walker, R., James, C., Green, M., Partridge, L. (2011). Core elements of exemplary academic integrity policy in Australian higher education. *International Journal for Educational Integrity, 7*(2), 3–12. https://doi.org/10.21913/IJEI.v7i2.759

Buchwald, A. (1972, February 24). Art Buchwald—Commentary. *Calgary Herald*, p. 31. Retrieved from ProQuest Historical Newspapers: *The Calgary Herald*.

Buerger, G. E. (2002). The owl and the plagiarist: Academic misrepresentation in contemporary education. Unpublished Ph.D. dissertation, Dalhousie University. Retrieved from ProQuest Dissertations & Theses Global.

Canadian Consortium—International Center for Academic Integrity. (2018a). Agenda. Retrieved from https://live-academicintegrity.pantheonsite.io/wp-content/uploads/2018/10/FINAL-Cdn-Consortium-Day-Agenda-2018.pdf

Canadian Consortium—International Center for Academic Integrity. (2018b). Contract cheating facilitated discussion: Sarah Eaton. Retrieved January 6, 2021, from https://live-academicintegrity.pantheonsite.io/wp-content/uploads/2018/10/Contract-Cheating-facilitated-discussion-Sarah-Eaton-March-1-2018.pdf

Canadian Press. (1999, December 10). Cheaters are going high-tech. *Calgary Herald*. A3. Retrieved from ProQuest Historical Newspapers: *The Calgary Herald*.

Canadian Symposium on Academic Integrity: Program and Abstracts. (2019). In S. E. Eaton J. Lock & M. Schroeder (Eds.). University of Calgary. http://hdl.handle.net/1880/110293

Chang, D. H. (2018). Academic dishonesty in a post-secondary multilingual institution. *BC TEAL Journal, 3*(1), 49–62. https://ojs-o.library.ubc.ca/index.php/BCTJ/article/view/287

Clarke, R., & Lancaster, T. (2006, June19–21). Eliminating the successor to plagiarism: Identifying the usage of contract cheating sites. In *Second International Plagiarism Conference*. The Sage Gateshead, Tyne & Wear.

Couple charged in essay scam. (1989, May 30). *The Ottawa Citizen*, G15. Retrieved from ProQuest Historical Newspapers: *The Ottawa Citizen*.

Cribb, R. (1999, April 10). Term-paper mills thrive on Internet: Thousands of students mine 100 sites for cribbed essays to get out of academic work. *Toronto Star*, p. 1. Retrieved from ProQuest Historical Newspapers: *Toronto Star*.

Christensen Hughes, J. M., & McCabe, D. L. (2006a). Academic misconduct within higher education in Canada. *The Canadian Journal of Higher Education, 36*(2), 1–21. http://journals.sfu.ca/cjhe/index.php/cjhe/article/view/183537/183482

Christensen Hughes, J. M., & McCabe, D. L. (2006b). Understanding academic misconduct. *Canadian Journal of Higher Education, 36*(1), 49–63. https://journals.sfu.ca/cjhe/index.php/cjhe/article/view/183525

Curtis, G. J., & Clare, J. (2017). How prevalent is contract cheating and to what extent are students repeat offenders? *Journal of Academic Ethics, 15*(2), 115–124. https://doi.org/10.1007/s10805-017-9278-x

Dallos, R. (1972, February 14). Ghost-writing papers a lucrative business: A pass—but don't get caught. *Calgary Herald,* p. 51. Retrieved from ProQuest Historical Newspapers: *The Calgary Herald*.

Eaton, S. E. (2018). Contract cheating: A Canadian perspective. http://blogs.biomedcentral.com/bmcblog/2018/07/24/contract-cheating-a-canadian-perspective/

Eaton, S. E. (2019a). Contract cheating in Canada: National policy analysis. https://osf.io/n9kwt/

Eaton, S. E. (2019b). Reflections on the 2019 Canadian symposium on academic integrity. *Canadian Perspectives on Academic Integrity*, *2*(2), 1–6. https://doi.org/10.11575/cpai.v2i2.69454

Eaton, S. E. (2019c). U have integrity: Educator resource—How to lead a discovery interview about contract cheating. http://hdl.handle.net/1880/111077

Eaton, S. E., & Dressler, R. (2019). Multilingual essay mills: Implications for second language teaching and learning. *Notos, 14*(2), 4–14. http://hdl.handle.net/1880/110695

Eaton, S. E. (2020a). 15 Strategies to detect contract cheating. http://hdl.handle.net/1880/112660

Eaton, S. E. (2020b). Academic integrity during COVID-19: Reflections from the University of Calgary. *International Studies in Educational Administration, 48*(1), 80–85. https://prism.ucalgary.ca/handle/1880/112293

Eaton, S. E. (2020c). *An Inquiry into Major Academic Integrity Violations in Canada: 2010–2019.* University of Calgary. http://hdl.handle.net/1880/111483

Eaton, S. E. (2020d). *Academic Integrity Policy Development and Revision: A Canadian Perspective (Guest lecture).* Paper presented at the Çanakkale Onsekiz Mart University, YİDE6051—Academic Integrity Policies, PhD course. http://hdl.handle.net/1880/112907

Eaton, S. E. (2021, June 1). Academic Integrity in Canadian Higher Education: The Impact of COVID-19 and a Call to Action. Paper presented at the Canadian Society for the Study of Higher Education (CSSHE), University of Alberta [online]. http://hdl.handle.net/1880/113463

Eaton, S. E., Boisvert, S., Hamilton, M. J., Kier, C. A., Teymouri, N., & Toye, M. A. (2020a). *Alberta Council on Academic Integrity (ACAI) 2019–2020 Annual Report*. Retrieved from http://hdl.handle.net/1880/112970

Eaton, S. E., & Edino, R. I. (2018). Strengthening the research agenda of educational integrity in Canada: A review of the research literature and call to action. *International Journal of Educational Integrity, 14*(1). https://doi.org/10.1007/s40979-018-0028-7

Eaton, S. E., Stoesz, B., Thacker, E., & Miron, J. B. (2020b). Methodological decisions in undertaking academic integrity policy analysis: Considerations for future research. *Canadian Perspectives on Academic Integrity, 3*(1), 83–91. https://doi.org/10.11575/cpai.v3i1.69768

Eaton, S. E., & Turner, K. L. (2020). Exploring academic integrity and mental health during COVID-19: Rapid review. *Journal of Contemporary Education Theory & Research, 4*(2), 34–41. https://www.jcetr.gr/index.php/1308-2/

Ellingson, C. (2003, March 25). Teachers wage war against cyber-cheats: Schools deal with essays for sale on the Net. *Prince Albert Daily Herald*, p. 5. Retrieved from Canadian Newstream database.

Flostrand, A. (2018). Undergraduate student perceptions of academic misconduct in the business classroom. Simon Fraser University. https://www.sfu.ca/content/dam/sfu/tlgrants/documents/G0255_Flostrand_FinalReport.pdf

Goodman, E. (1971a, March 20). Term papers: Big business in Boston. *The Boston Globe*, pp. 1, 10. Retrieved from ProQuest Historical Newspapers: *The Boston Globe.*

Goodman, E. (1971b, March 27). Term papers still hot item. *The Boston Globe*, pp. 1, 7. Retrieved from ProQuest Historical Newspapers: *The Boston Globe.*

Goodman, E. (1971c, December 16). Term paper market flourishing. *The Boston Globe,* p. 47. Retrieved from ProQuest Historical Newspapers: *The Boston Globe.*

Gray, B. C. (2022). Ethics, ed tech, and the rise of contract cheating. In S. E. Eaton & J. Christensen Hughes (Eds.), *Academic integrity in Canada: An enduring and essential challenge*: Springer.

Gray, J. M. (2002, March 27). What's so creative about originality? *The Globe and Mail.* Retrieved from Canadian Newsstream database.

Grigg, G. A. (2010). *Plagiarism in higher education: Confronting the policy dilemma.* (Doctor of Philosophy). University of Melbourne.

Grue, D., Eaton, S. E., & Boisvert, S. (2021). Parallels between the contract cheating industry and organized crime. Alberta Council on Academic Integrity: Contract Cheating Working Group. http://hdl.handle.net/1880/113323

Hechinger, F. M. (1972, March 19). Passing grades for a price. *New York Times*, p. E11. Retrieved from ProQuest Historical Newspapers: *New York Times.*

Hersey, C. (2019). *"The struggle is real!" #Ineedapaperfast.* Paper presented at the Canadian Symposium on Academic Integrity.

Hersey, C., & Lancaster, T. (2015). *The Online Industry of Paper Mills, Contract Cheating Services, and Auction Sites.* Paper presented at the Clute Institute International Education Conference. https://www.researchgate.net/publication/280830577_The_Online_Industry_of_Paper_Mills_Contract_Cheating_Services_and_Auction_Sites

International Network for Quality Assurance Agencies in Higher Education (INQAAHE). (2020). Toolkit to support quality assurance agencies to address academic integrity and contract cheating. https://www.teqsa.gov.au/latest-news/publications/toolkit-support-quality-assurance-agencies-address-academic-integrity

Lancaster, T. (2019). Social media enabled contract cheating. *Canadian Perspectives on Academic Integrity, 2*(2), 7–24. https://doi.org/10.11575/cpai.v2i2.68053

Lancaster, T., & Clarke, R. (2007). Assessing contract cheating through auction sites: A computing perspective. *HE Academy for Information and Computer Sciences*, 1–6. http://citeseerx.ist.psu.edu/viewdoc/download?doi=10.1.1.453.8656&rep=rep1&type=pdf

Lancaster, T., & Clarke, R. (2009, June 4). *Contract cheating in UK Higher Education: Promoting a proactive approach.* ASKe Institutional Policies and Procedures for Managing Student Plagiarism Event, Oxford Brookes University. Retrieved from https://www.academia.edu/26594434/Contract_Cheating_in_UK_Higher_Education_promoting_a_proactive_approach

Lee, M.-J. (2012). Essays for sale: CTV hidden camera investigation. *CTV News Vancouver*. https://bc.ctvnews.ca/essays-for-sale-ctv-hidden-camera-investigation-1.952016

Legislative Assembly of Ontario. (1972, June 14). Official report of debates (Hansard). Ghost-written term papers and examinations, Vol. 4, p. 3651. https://archive.org/details/v4hansard1972ontauoft/page/3650/mode/2up

Mah, B. (1999, October 22). Professors on lookout for cyber-cheaters. *Calgary Herald*, p. 124. Retrieved from ProQuest Historical Newspapers: *Calgary Herald.*

Maeroff, G. I. (1971, July 10). Market in term papers is booming. *New York Times*, pp. 25, 27. Retrieved from ProQuest Historical Newspapers: *New York Times.*

Maich, S. (2006). Pornography, gambling, lies, theft and terrorism: The Internet sucks (Where did we go wrong?). *MacLean's, 119*(43), 44–49.

McKenzie, A., Miron, J. B., & Ridgley, A. (2020a). Building a regional academic integrity network: Profiling the growth and action of the academic integrity council of Ontario. *Canadian Perspectives on Academic Integrity, 3*(1). https://doi.org/10.11575/cpai.v3i1.69836

McKenzie, A., Miron, J. B., Devereaux, L., Eaton, S. E., Persaud, N., Rowbotham, K., Steeves, M., Stoesz, B., & Thacker, E. (2020b). *Contract cheating language within academic integrity policies in the university sector in Ontario, Canada*. Paper presented at the International Center for Academic Integrity (ICAI) 2020 Conference.

Miron, J. B. (2020). International Day of Action (IDoA) Against Contract Cheating 2020—Update from the chair of the IDoA planning committee. *Canadian Perspectives on Academic Integrity, 3*(2). https://doi.org/10.11575/cpai.v3i2.71473

Miron, J. B., & Ridgley, A. (2018). *Contract cheating*. Paper presented at the Canadian Consortium—International Center for Academic Integrity. https://live-academicintegrity.pantheonsite.io/wp-content/uploads/2018/10/March-1-Contract-Cheating-by-Jennie-Miron.pdf

Miron, J. B. & McKenzie, A. (2020). Academic Integrity Council of Ontario (AICO): Avoiding contract cheating student tip sheet. https://academicintegritycouncilofontario.files.wordpress.com/2020/10/student-tip-sheet-avoiding-contract-cheating-1.pdf

Mourelatos, E. (2020). The Birth of an Idea: The IDoA and Its early growth. https://www.academicintegrity.org/blog/spotlight/thethe-birth-of-an-idea-the-idoa-and-its-early-growth/

Newton, P. (2018). How common is commercial contract cheating in higher education? *Frontiers in Education, 3*(67), 1–18. https://doi.org/10.3389/feduc.2018.00067

Newton, P. M., & Lang, C. (2016). Custom essay writers, freelancers, and other paid third parties. In T. Bretag (Ed.), *Handbook of academic integrity* (pp. 249–271). Singapore, Springer.

O'Toole, L. (1974, September 19). The essay game. *The Globe and Mail*, p. 45. Retrieved from ProQuest Historical Newspapers: *Globe and Mail*.

Oliphant, T. (2002). Cyber-plagiarism: Plagiarism in a digital world. *Feliciter, 48*(2), 78.

Parliament of Australia. (2020). Tertiary Education Quality and Standards Agency Amendment (Prohibiting Academic Cheating Services) Bill 2019. Retrieved from https://www.aph.gov.au/Parliamentary_Business/Bills_Legislation/bd/bd1920a/20bd084

Pearson, C. (2002, October 26). Cyber cheats face U of W crackdown; Prosecutions on rise. *The Windsor Star*, A5. Retrieved from Canadian Newsstream database.

Quality Assurance Agency for Higher Education (UK) (QAA). (2020). *Contracting to cheat in higher education: How to address essay mills and contract cheating* (2nd. ed.). Retrieved from https://www.qaa.ac.uk/docs/qaa/guidance/contracting-to-cheat-in-higher-education-2nd-edition.pdf

Ridgley, A., Miron, J. B., & McKenzie, A. (2019). *Building a regional academic integrity network: Profiling the growth and action of the Academic Integrity Council of Ontario*. Paper presented at the Canadian Symposium on Academic Integrity. http://hdl.handle.net/1880/110308

Rogerson, A. M., & Basanta, G. (2016). Peer-to-peer file sharing and academic integrity in the Internet age. In T. Bretag (Ed.), *Handbook of Academic Integrity* (pp. 273–285). Springer.

Roy, A. (1972). Bill 174: An act respecting ghost written term papers and examinations. In *Legislative Assembly of Ontario: First and Second Sessions of the Twenty-Ninth Parliament*. https://archive.org/details/v5ontariobills1972ontauoft/page/n193/mode/2up

RTNDA Canada announces 2006 Prairie Regional Award Recipients. (2007, May 12). *Radio-Television News Directors Association (RNDA) Canada*. http://rtndacanada.mediaroom.com/index.php?s=18637&item=30340

Schmidt, S. (1998, June 22). Wired world gives cheating a new face. *Globe and Mail*, p. C8.

Screening out the cheat. (1972, April 22). *The Globe and Mail*, p. 6. Retrieved from ProQuest Historical Newspapers: *The Globe and Mail*.

Seeland, J., Stoesz, B. M., & Vogt, L. (2020a). Preventing online shopping for completed assessments: Protecting students by blocking access to contract cheating websites on institutional networks. *Canadian Perspectives on Academic Integrity, 3*(1). https://doi.org/10.11575/cpai.v3i1.70256

Seeland, J., Stoesz, B., & Vogt, L. (2020b). Shopping interrupted: Blocking access to contract cheating. https://www.academicintegrity.org/blog/research/shopping-interrupted-blocking-access-to-contract-cheating/

Shepard, L. R. (1972, February 12). War on term-paper racket. *The Christian Science Monitor*, pp. 1, 2. Retrieved from ProQuest Historical Newspapers: *The Christian Science Monitor.*

Shepherd, J. (1973). Who's the writer and who's the ghost? *Cosmopolitan, 174*(3), 172–173, 186–187, 239, 241.

Statistics Canada. (1977). *Canada Year Book 1976–1977*. Minister of Supply and Services Canada.

Statistics Canada. (2021, January 2). Table 37–10–0011–01 Postsecondary enrolments, by field of study, registration status, program type, credential type and gender. Retrieved January 5, 2021, from https://www150.statcan.gc.ca/t1/tbl1/en/tv.action?pid=3710001101. https://doi.org/10.25318/3710001101-eng

Stead, S. (1978, March 10). How's essay business? Dying at $5 a page. *The Globe and Mail (1936–2017)*, p. 4. Retrieved from ProQuest Historical Newspapers: *The Globe and Mail.*

Steffenhagen, J. (2001, October 17). Plagiarism detector to screen UBC essays: University subscribes to web service aimed at discouraging wrongful online borrowing of passages or entire assignments: [Final Edition]. *The Vancouver Sun*, B3. Retrieved from Canadian Newsstream database.

Stewart, W. (1974). How the cost of food split up one family. *MacLean's*. https://archive.macleans.ca/article/1974/4/1/how-the-cost-of-food-split-up-one-family

Stoesz, B., & Los, R. (2019). Evaluation of a tutorial designed to promote academic integrity. *Canadian Perspectives on Academic Integrity, 2*(1), 3–26. https://doi.org/10.11575/cpai.v2i1.61826

Stoesz, B. M., Eaton, S. E., Miron, J. B., Thacker, E. (2019a). Academic integrity and contract cheating policy analysis of colleges in Ontario Canada. *International Journal for Educational Integrity, 15*(4), 1–18. https://doi.org/10.1007/s40979-019-0042-4

Stoesz, B. M., Seeland, J., Vogt, L., Markovics, L., Denham, T., Gervais, L., & Usick, B. L. (2020b). Creating a collaborative network to promote cultures of academic integrity in Manitoba's Post-Secondary Institutions. *Canadian Perspectives on Academic Integrity, 3*(1). https://doi.org/10.11575/cpai.v3i1.69763

Stoesz, B. M., Usick, B., & Eaton, S. E. (2019c). Outsourcing assessments: The implications of contract cheating for teaching and learning in Canada. Paper presented at the Society for Teaching and Learning in Higher Education (STLHE). http://hdl.handle.net/1880/110489

Tertiary Education Quality and Standards Agency. (TESQA). (2015). Report on student academic integrity and allegations of contract cheating by university students. Retrieved from https://files.eric.ed.gov/fulltext/ED564140.pdf

Tertiary Education Quality and Standards Agency. (TEQSA). (2017). Good practice note: Addressing contract cheating to safeguard academic integrity. Retrieved from https://www.teqsa.gov.au/sites/g/files/net2046/f/good-practice-note-addressing-contract-cheating.pdf?v=1507082628

Tertiary Education Quality and Standards Agency. (TEQSA). (2020). Contract cheating and blackmail. Retrieved from https://www.teqsa.gov.au/sites/default/files/contract-cheating-blackmail.pdf?v=1591659442

Thacker, E., Eaton, S. E., Stoesz, B., & Miron, J. B. (2019a). *A deep dive into Canadian college policy: Findings from a provincial academic integrity and contract cheating policy analysis (updated)*. Paper presented at the Canadian Symposium on Academic Integrity.

Thacker, E., Miron, J. B., Eaton, S. E., & Stoesz, B. (2019b). *A deep dive into Canadian college policy: Findings from a provincial academic integrity and contract cheating policy analysis*. Paper presented at the International Center for Academic Integrity (ICAI) Annual Conference.

Thacker, E., Clark, A., & Ridgley, A. (2020). Applying a holistic approach to contract cheating: A Canadian response. *Canadian Perspectives on Academic Integrity*. https://doi.org/10.11575/cpai.v3i1.69811

University of Calgary. (2019). Canadian Symposium on Academic Integrity: Program and abstracts. In S. E. Eaton J. Lock & M. Schroeder (Eds.), University of Calgary. Retrieved from http://hdl.handle.net/1880/110293

Usick, B. L., Miron, J. B., & Stoesz, B. M. (2020). Further Contemplations: Inaugural Canadian Symposium on Academic Integrity. *Canadian Perspectives on Academic Integrity*, 3(2). https://doi.org/10.11575/cpai.v3i1.70480

Waggoner, W. H. (1972). State acts to outlaw companies selling theses. The *New York Times*, p. 46. ProQuest Historical Newspapers: *The New York Times*.

Walker, W. (2001, September 3). Teachers fight back against 'rampant' cyber-cheating; Web site lets schools check term papers for copied content. *Toronto Star*, A07. ProQuest Historical Newspapers: *Toronto Star*.

Witherspoon, A. (1995). This pen for hire: On grinding out papers for college students. *Harper's Magazine, 290*(June), 49–57.

Would have to keep records: A bill to stop essay sellers. (1972, June 16). *Globe and Mail,* p. 5. Retrieved from ProQuest Historical Newspapers: *Globe and Mail.*

Wright, C. (1974, March 23). Difficult to fulfil demand: Essay-selling business booming. *Globe and Mail,* p. 5. Retrieved from ProQuest Historical Newspapers: *Globe and Mail.*

Sarah Elaine Eaton Ph.D., is an Associate Professor in the Werklund School of Education and the inaugural Educational Leader in Residence, Academic Integrity, University of Calgary. She is also the Editor-in-Chief of the *International Journal for Educational Integrity* and the author of *Plagiarism in Higher Education: Tackling Tough Topics in Academic Integrity*. Her research focuses on ethics and integrity in higher education and she has led numerous research teams and the local and national levels. Eaton advocates for pro-active and multi-stakeholder approaches to upholding and enacting integrity throughout the academy.

Chapter 9
Ethics, EdTech, and the Rise of Contract Cheating

Brenna Clarke Gray

Abstract This chapter argues that establishing a "culture of academic integrity," in the era of digitally-situated plagiarism like contract cheating, begins with an institutional approach to student data and student work that is rooted in ethics. If "students cheat when they feel cheated" (Christensen Hughes, 2017, p. 57), then the ethical failures inherent in a system-wide move toward for-profit homework systems and plagiarism checkers sets a dangerous model for students to follow. Paper presented at the University of Calgary, Calgary http://hdl.handle.net/1880/110083), then the ethical failures inherent in a system-wide move toward for-profit homework systems and plagiarism checkers sets a dangerous model for students to follow. We are responsible for modelling for our students what it looks like to be a contributing member of an academic community, and we do so by taking seriously our students, their data, and their work, and not only when it comes time to run it through a plagiarism detector or check their IDs against a proctoring software. This chapter argues that a more responsible relationship to student data, and a less cozy relationship with for-profit educational technologies, is required if our institutions are serious about fostering a culture of academic integrity.

Keywords Academic integrity · Algorithm · Data · Canada · Contract cheating · Privacy

Introduction

When we introduce to our students the idea of establishing a "culture of academic integrity," we typically frame the discussion primarily around the responsibilities of students. In my own syllabi as an instructor, I talk about academic integrity embodying everything from explicit skills like correctly citing sources, to more intangible concepts like coming to class prepared and treating colleagues with respect. Faculty know that they, too—whether through scholarly associations, granting

B. C. Gray (✉)
Thompson Rivers University, Kamloops, Canada
e-mail: bgray@tru.ca

S. E. Eaton and J. Christensen Hughes (eds.), *Academic Integrity in Canada*,
Ethics and Integrity in Educational Contexts 1,
https://doi.org/10.1007/978-3-030-83255-1_9

agencies, or their own internal ethical compass—have a commitment to academic integrity. But when we frame academic integrity for students, that component is rarely discussed. It's common in higher education circles to hear about the notion of creating a culture of academic integrity (Hendershott et al, 2000), but definitions of what such an academic culture would look like vary widely (Macfarlane et. al., 2014). While most institutions focus on student responsibilities vis-à-vis academic integrity, it is rarer to see the conversation extend to the responsibilities of faculty, though the power of faculty modeling—such as with citations in slide decks and careful attention to reuse of content like images—is significant in helping students to understand the norms of their discipline regarding academic integrity (Robinson & Glanzer, 2017). Institutional policies and campus training programs focus on students. But modelling a culture of academic integrity begins with what happens in the classroom and across the institution, and as violations of academic integrity go high-tech with the rise of contract cheating, institutions must reckon with the way their data privacy and educational technology policies and practices fail to model academic integrity. In this chapter, I argue that the contract cheating epidemic can be insulated against with a renewed attention to ethical pedagogical strategies in the deployment of educational technologies. Given the explosive growth of the contract cheating problem and the huge money it makes for unethical players, it is imperative that post-secondary institutions protect students by all possible means, including examining their own cultures of academic integrity in the digital space. Canadian higher education—and indeed, higher education globally—has not to this point had a sector-wide conversation about ethics in educational technologies, and our institutions as a result often engage in practices and contracts with private, for-profit companies that include data agreements that would never pass an equivalent of a Research Ethics Board (Stewart, 2020).

This chapter focuses specifically on the failure of academic integrity known as contract cheating. This is cheating that takes the form of students hiring third parties—sometimes across the globe—to submit one or all of their assignments in a class for them. Contract cheating is not a situation of individual students in a course making poor choices: it's a business. There has always been opportunity for students with financial means to purchase coursework from colleagues, but now the gig economy and the easy ability to transfer data means that people—perhaps as far away as Kenya (Lancaster, 2019a)—are earning comparatively small amounts of money to produce intellectual labour which is then sold to desperate students in North America and Europe, particularly in English-speaking countries, for big profit (Rigby, 2014). It's hard to track by traditional means either pedagogical or technological; if every assignment in a course is created by someone else, the instructor has no grounds for comparison, and many of these companies proudly proclaim their high originality scores on Turnitin because, of course, the work is original—it just wasn't written by the student (Cadloff, 2018; Peterson, 2019). As a result, there is probably more of it happening even than we think (Eaton, 2020). And it makes a lot of money globally (Rigby, 2014; Ellis et al., 2018).

I am interested, though, in how the same practices we see engaged in by institutions and educational technology companies—a devaluing and de-prioritization of original work when it comes to the classroom space, predatory relationships between consumers and service providers, and a cavalier approach to handling data privacy—are echoed and magnified by contract cheating firms. I argue that a more responsible relationship to student data, and a less cozy relationship with for-profit educational technologies, is required if our institutions are serious about fostering a culture of academic integrity.

De-Valuing and De-Prioritizing Original Work in the Classroom

At the 2019 Academic Integrity Day held at Thompson Rivers University, student union groups repeatedly raised the issue of reciprocity and respect as critical to conversations about why students cheat. One student union representative specifically asked how students can be expected to feel a sense of responsibility over their own learning in courses increasingly taught using tools like for-profit homework systems or courseware[1] and publisher-provided lecture slides: "If you can buy your lectures and assignments," he asked the assembled professors and administrators, "why can't I buy my submissions?"[2] This echoes Julia Christensen Hughes' observation from reviewing student explanations of academic dishonesty that "students cheat when they feel cheated" (Christensen Hughes, 2017, p. 57). Added to this are the privacy and security issues enmeshed in homework systems, which at least in part monetize student data while simultaneously charging them for the opportunity to submit their coursework in classes for which they are already paying tuition (UNESCO IITE, 2020; Senack et al., 2016). Although there are good and compelling reasons why professors opt to use these kinds of tools, including an increasingly precarious professoriate, the pressures of producing research, and the additional stresses imposed by restructuring institutions in the wake of Covid-19, institutions, the message we send to students becomes deeply complicated. What does it mean to foster a culture of academic integrity across a university, and what does it mean to act with integrity—and does the responsibility only fall on students? If we truly wish to model academic integrity, the answer to the latter question must be no: if the stakes of academic integrity truly matter, our students should see us all embodying it (Morris, 2016).

As universities integrate ever more completely with large, for-profit educational technologies companies, they burrow ever deeper into troubling agreements where student data is monetized now or in perpetuity. In addition to troubling data practices, many of the solutions heralded as tools in the fight for academic integrity,

[1] Homework systems, courseware, and "course-in-a-box" are all synonyms for a class of edtech products provided primarily by textbook publishers, either as value-adds to traditional textbooks or stand-alone products. There is typically an added cost to students. Increasingly, we see courseware and homework systems as significant elements of the classroom experience for students; some of these tools are the primary means by which students submit homework, and these systems typically include exams, assignment prompts, and often even lecture materials.

[2] The identity of the student is kept confidential. Personal communication, 18 October 2019.

whether plagiarism detection software or e-proctoring platforms, engage in questionable ethical practices like profiling student behaviour (Swauger, 2020). Turnitin, for example, has access to wide swaths of student data in the form of essays and assignments, which they mine in order to be able to compare submissions to their database to assess whether student work has been copied. Their business model relies on receiving student intellectual property for free—students, of course, are not compensated for providing the content for their database—and has expanded to include a Revision Assistant tool for students that is also built from this massive amount of student data (Stommel & Morris, 2017). Revision Assistant, designed to help students identify errors in their writing prior to submission, is, in essence, a machine-taught tool to improve writing based on the vast swaths of student writing Turnitin's larger database can analyze. Are students fully informed about where their data is going, in this context, and who is profiting from it? Increasingly, we're seeing student groups advocate for more transparency in the use of Turnitin, and for opt-out policies to be made more explicit. Much of the way Turnitin is used in Canada—far less ubiquitously than elsewhere–is due to Jesse Rosenfeld's landmark legal action against Turnitin; Rosenfeld argued successfully that students should not be presumed guilty, which is the position from which all plagiarism detection software begins, but also that students should not be compelled to waive their copyright in order to be evaluated (Purdy, 2005). Instructors can ask to have the work their students submit deleted from the Turnitin database, but they have to know to ask. Turnitin has always downplayed the data mining they do, but it is the backbone of their ability to offer their service. It's also what makes them attractive to venture capitalists. In March 2019, Turnitin was acquired by a venture capital firm for US$1.75B, which gives you a sense of what all that uncompensated student intellectual property and mined data is worth (Luke, 2019).

And many of these companies impose on the central tenets at the core of university life, by holding institutions to restrictive non-disparagement clauses that limit the freedom of speech and critique of students, staff, and faculty alike, even sometimes when they are never party to the original agreement. The CEO of TopHat, for example, likes to talk about how much data they have access to, and that they can drill down into it enough to analyze individual student study habits (Zubair, 2017). But the End User License Agreement for TopHat includes provisions that students cannot link to TopHat in an article critical of its use, students are responsible for any data breeches that occur, and they offer no opt-outs for the collection of personal data beyond opting out of the service altogether (Rhinelander, 2017). When educational institutions contract with these firms, they believe the gain is greater that the loss; this is the same logic that drives desperate students to the essay mill, and it's equally misguided in both cases. If our integrity as institutions can be chipped away at through predatory agreements that disrupt the very mission of our institutions, can we be surprised when we see students engaging in the equivalent?

Predatory Relationships with For-Profit EdTech

For-profit educational technology companies—in contrast with open or publicly-funded edtech projects—can make money in a limited number of ways: they can sell an individual or an institution one-shot products, they can offer a subscription model that is institution-paid or student-paid, or they can sell the data they collect. Or some combination of the above. Many of the agreements our institutions sign with these companies give explicit rights to use student data for things like "targeted marketing," and opt-outs are complicated and Byzantine (American Association of University Professors, n.d.). In 2012, for example, the former textbook, now primarily data, company Pearson boasted that they have more access to student data in K-12 than anyone in the world (Office of EdTech, 2012). In the higher education space, Pearson is the biggest player, and they have some incredible access to student data, including everything from financial aid applications to interim and final grades. They say they don't sell student data, but they also publicly refused to sign the Student Privacy Pledge. And recently, the inevitable happened: a data breech, exposing data from 13,000 institutions and one million college students. The attack occurred in November of 2018, but Pearson waited to inform the FBI until the following March, and end users were not notified until August. While Pearson asserts that the breech was "limited" to first and last name, date of birth, and email address—enough to do a fair amount of damage!—it impacted data collected as early as 2001 (Olson, 2019). The roll out of the disclosure (and the disappearance of the statement from their website) suggests that the top priority in this instance wasn't ever student data, but brand management.

When students contract with cheating companies, they usually are required to hand over a lot of personal data, some of which should be specifically of concern to universities. Students give up credit card information, yes, and, distressingly, their social insurance numbers (SIN; the primary government identification number in Canada, similar to the SSN in the US); they also give up their student ID numbers and Learning Management System login information to companies with very limited privacy protections (Sutherland-Smith & Dullaghan, 2019). Certainly, giving up a credit card number and SIN can have far-reaching impacts for the student for years to come; handing over a student ID and login information is how contract cheating firms, once established at a university, experience exponential growth. Once a contract cheating firm has private student information, students become easily exploited; contract cheating companies have been reported to continue to extract money from students well after they have completed the course for which they contracted the service in the first place, and when students stop paying the extortion, the companies report the original act of plagiarism to the university (Yorke et al, 2020). The threat of this happening can keep a student in a cycle of contracting with the company, or recommending the service to their classmates, since they believe they will be reported if they do not. Further, I know from my own observation that once a contract cheating firm has access to the Learning Management System at an institution, their access to students grows rapidly: they can access course materials, view assignments, and directly message other students in the course in order to find new clients. They can access the data not only of the person for whom they are uploading assignments, but they can access class lists and steal the intellectual property of the class professor, too; this material will likely be reused and resold by the company. And depending on the practices of the company, it can be hard for IT Services to flag and block this activity.

Why do students feel comfortable sharing something as critical to the integrity of the university as their LMS login information in the first place? There is a lot of rhetoric about so-called digital native[3] students and their supposed disinterest in data privacy, but research does not support this assumption; on the contrary, students are increasingly concerned about these issues, but a lack of information and a lack of empowerment drives poor choices (Hargiatti & Marwick, 2016). Our traditional-age students have been raised in an informational ecosystem where companies like Google and Facebook know everything about them (and increasingly, they have had a presence on these networks before they were meaningfully able to consent to it) and then they go to university and interact daily with companies like Pearson, Turnitin, and TopHat who are monetizing their data with the express consent of their institutions. Perhaps instead of questioning their lack of care about their privacy and data, we might question whether they have ever felt empowered to resist these corporations, and it's worth considering whether institutions have treated seriously enough the fiduciary responsibility they hold over data when it comes to Big Tech.

Contract Cheating as Case Study

The practices by which contract cheating companies find our students are worth exploring as one example of this kind of shadowing between the emergence of practices in higher education and their exploitation by companies whose influence we seek to reduce. Algorithms are all around us, and they drive a substantial amount of decision-making. They also are not inherently bad or damaging: in its most basic form, it is a set of instructions that determines a series of outputs from a series of inputs. And we are surrounded by algorithmic processes all the time. It's an algorithm that drives what Netflix thinks you want to watch next, what Instagram thinks you might click-through to buy, and what Google anticipates you want from your search results. These experiences are sometimes creepy—like when a store you shop at knows before you do that you are pregnant (Hill, 2012)—and often aggressively capitalist, but they aren't necessarily explicitly harmful.

Algorithms are not neutral, however. Instead, algorithms reflect the old adage of "garbage in, garbage out," which is to say that whatever biases underwrite the

---

[3] Mark Prensky coined this term in 2001, but it has been rightly challenged conceptually. In particular, being raised with a tool and even using it extensively for social purposes does not train own to use the tool critically or in a manner commensurate with expectations of higher education. Erika Smith's (2012) review of the literature on the concept is a useful tool.

programming of an algorithm will be reflected in its outputs (Stinson, 2020). And, since we live in a society that wrestles with racism, sexism, classism, ableism, and many other inequities, we should not be surprised that algorithms are often built in a way that encompasses many of these inequities. Virginia Eubanks described the use of algorithms in the development of social programming as an "empathy override," a decision to outsource perceptions about who "deserves" care (Eubanks, 2018). This is a way of not having harder and more complex political conversations, and it relies on a scarcity model of resourcing social programs and care. Those are conversations that are important to have and will be shaped by individual values, but we have to have them, and not hide behind assumptions that these processes are somehow neutral.

What algorithms, for example, make decisions about who is a good bet for a mortgage or business loan, and what assumptions underlie those parameters? We see algorithms used to redraw community boundaries to further disenfranchise the poor and the marginalized. There's a term for this: digital redlining (Gilliard, 2017). Indeed, just as old-fashioned analog redlining worked in the service of segregation and reduced class mobility, digital redlining has a direct impact on socioeconomic mobility. Algorithmic processes are increasingly used by credit bureaus to analyze your social media connections, making judgements about financial solvency in part based on a subject's friends and relations (Waddell, 2016). Critically, a person's network is not a protected class, so while it may be illegal for an employer or lender to discriminate based on race, gender, or ability, it's not illegal to discriminate based on algorithmic assumptions made that are in turn based on a person's network (Boyd et al., 2014). Consider how much more of your network is documented and searchable now than ever before; your connection to a person the lender sees as undesirable is no longer theoretical or circumstantial, but instead comes with a lengthy data trail. Even though the realities of the people within a network may well be framed and circumscribed by those protected factors, nothing protects marginalized users from having this data turned against them. Which is to say: isn't this just a fancy way to get around traditionally racist and classist practices?

Contract cheating firms are very aware of the power of algorithms—it's how they find their clients. In Thomas Lancaster's work describing how social media is used by contract cheating firms, he's effectively describing an algorithmic process when he reflects on how "A single tweet by a student, even one expressing that they have an assignment due with no indication that they plan to cheat, can lead to them receiving 20 or more visible replies from contract cheating providers within an hour from when the tweet is made" (Lancaster, 2019b). These aren't human beings scanning social media: these are bots. They phish for students in incredibly predatory ways, using algorithmic processing of key words to track students on social media and pounce when they are most vulnerable. If your institution has a hashtag it uses to collect student posts on social media, you can see this for yourself by following it for a little while, especially around midterms and finals. You'll quickly find these companies using institutional hashtags to reach students, often cloaking their services in terms of "editing" or "tutoring" or "help." It's easy, especially if you're not versed in institutional branding—or you're just panicked and looking for any lifeline, and wanting it to be real—to see some of these posts and wonder if they're legitimately connected to the institution itself. And the companies also use these hashtags to track students as potential customers. They particularly like to use combinations of hashtags that pair a specific institution with words expressing affective experiences of student stress: #essaydue #finalsstress #essayhelp. So a student who is looking to commiserate with classmates on Instagram who uses the hashtag for her institution and, maybe, #freakingout #paperdue #needhelp, sends a bat signal not only for her classmates, but also for predatory contract cheating firms who sweep in to her direct messages at the last moment and offer "assistance."[4]

While it is never okay to purchase an essay, it's easy to imagine a situation where desperation combined with opportunity results in an individual making a choice they shouldn't. Given the spiralling rise in contract cheating, it doesn't seem likely that students are suddenly less ethical than they used to be, and research suggests that cheating is a highly contextual act, and even those students who seem to be predisposed to contract cheating typically do not engage in it for every assessment (Ramberg & Modin, 2019; Rundle et al., 2019). Students are targeted by predatory companies when they are at their most panicked and most stressed out, and it's a form of quote-unquote "help" that they can access when they are at that lowest point—say, 2 am the morning before a paper is due—when legitimate resources like learning centres and campus tutors and office hours aren't available. Contract cheating is wrong. Preying on vulnerable students, and profiting off their misery, is more wrong.[5]

Solutions

The barriers we place on learners, intentionally or not, can exacerbate the stakes and promote the fears and feelings that lead students to cheat. Whether it's a high-cost homework system that leaves a student financially vulnerable, or inaccessible technology that can't be accessed easily for students without stable internet connections, or a classroom environment that doesn't allow students to adapt content for their own learning, all of these unnecessary barriers impede the ability of a student to succeed in a course. Each barrier brings additional stress. These barriers can also damage the relationship between faculty and student—and this relationship, too, has

[4] In advance of Academic Integrity Day, we collected a large number of examples of these targeted ads in order to share the power of this imagery with our community. They have been archived with other artifacts from the day; see BC Academic Integrity Network in the references. Research in this area also includes Hersey, C. (2019). *"The struggle is real!" #Ineedapaperfast*. Paper presented at the Canadian Symposium on Academic Integrity, Calgary, Canada.

[5] This is an aside, but many for-profit EdTech companies prey on faculty at their most vulnerable moments, too, making inquiries at the beginning and end of semester when tensions are highest and demands are many. As the precarity of the academic workforce increases and demands on instructor time do, too, this practice is only on the rise. These pitches invariably promise miraculous time-saving measures or huge improvements in student engagement. And they come directly to faculty rather than to an office of educational technologies or faculty development, which might mean they encounter less resistance or fewer questions.

an insulating effect on student rates of cheating (Orosz et al., 2015). When students feel responsible to a class and valued by their instructor, they cheat less.

Many other writers in this collection will point to what we know about pedagogical strategy for reducing the temptation to cheat: scaffolded assignments, low-stakes practice, and reducing anxiety around performance. The research shows that these strategies work. We know that students are more likely to cheat on high stakes assignments where they have received little guidance. Conveniently, we also know that those same kinds of assignments do little to promote meaningful learning. Research suggests that we can both promote learning and reduce stress and anxiety for students by scaffolding assignments appropriately, checking in at multiple stages, and providing opportunities for questions and feedback (Rundle et al., 2019). Authentic assessments, too, that students can see reflect clearly the expectations of the world outside the university, have a meaningful impact in terms of lowering rates of academic dishonesty (Medway et al., 2018). In truth, the tools we know work for good instruction work to reduce the temptation for engaging a contract cheating company in the first place (ICAI, 2016).

I propose we can compound the efficacy of these pedagogical interventions by helping students understand the value of their data and privacy, and modeling our respect for it in the way we use theirs: give students a full understanding of why their data has value, and then don't sell it out to the highest bidder on their behalf and without their informed consent. Does everyone understand the seriousness of handing over your SIN, or the responsibility to other people in your classes inherent to keeping your login information secure? In this case, not sharing is caring: we protect ourselves and each other when we keep our learning tools secure. And it's worth talking about how we secure learning materials, as well. Textbook question banks and homework system assignments are incredibly useful, time-saving tools for faculty members. They're also incredibly insecure. If you use a question bank produced by a textbook manufacturer or other third-party, I encourage you to do an experiment: take a random question from your bank and Google it. If that resource is remotely popular, it's likely that searching out that one question will bring up the entire question bank. While it's certainly true that some students will use test banks as study tools, it's also not a far skip to cheating—and be certain, contract cheating companies already have access to all of that content, too. When a lot of users are drawing on the same resource, it only takes one bad decision by one person to have all that material available on the open web. It's a good reason to invest in building these tools on-site, particular to each unique context.

Conclusions

It may seem like an extreme leap to connect the dots from an efficiency practice like using anti-plagiarism software or class-in-a-box courseware systems to the nefarious rise of contract cheating within our institutions. But what do we really mean when we assert a commitment to a culture of academic integrity? Is it acting with integrity to allow student data to be monetized without compensation or to require students to subscribe to expensive services to submit assignments? Is it acting with integrity to offer no meaningful opt-out from or true informed consent for the use of these tools? And to return to that question from a student union representative at Academic Integrity Day, what do we model when it comes to the value of original work when institutional pressures like large class sizes and insufficient prep time lead us to lean on expensive—and, from an academic integrity perspective—wildly insecure tool like a homework system? We are responsible for modelling for our students what it looks like to be a contributing member of an academic community, and we do so by taking seriously our students, their data, and their work, and not only when it comes time to run it through a plagiarism detector or check their IDs against a proctoring software. When institution serve students "course-in-a-box" content solutions; require them to engage with third-party, for-profit entities to submit their assignments; treat their data as valueless while someone else earns a profit; and sign away their rights to critique tools they are forced to use, we do not model academic integrity. Instead, we demonstrate that their education has been commodified, with each component bought and sold by interested parties.

To return to the words of the student union representative: if an instructor works within institutional pressures so egregious that the reasonable solution is to buy the lectures and assessments—and charge the student a premium for the experience—we lose the moral ground to say they cannot buy their submissions in turn. Academic integrity collapses when we fail to uphold our moral and ethical obligations, long before a student chooses to cheat.

References

American Association of University Professors. (n.d.). *Primer on Privatization*. One Faculty, One Resistance. https://www.aaup.org/sites/default/files/Primer_on_Privatization%20%281%29.pdf

BC Academic Integrity Network. (2019). Academic integrity day memes. *BC Academic Integrity Day*. https://tru.arcabc.ca/islandora/object/tru:4954

Boyd, D., Levy, K., & Marwick, A. (2014). The networked nature of algorithmic discrimination. *Data and Discrimination: Collected Essays. Open Technology Institute*. http://www.danah.org/papers/2014/DataDiscrimination.pdf

Cadloff, E. B. (2018, April 4). How do you solve a problem like contract cheating? *University Affairs*. https://www.universityaffairs.ca/news/news-article/solve-problem-like-contract-cheating/

Christensen Hughes, J. (2017). *Understanding academic misconduct: Creating robust cultures of integrity*. Paper presented at the University of Calgary, Calgary. http://hdl.handle.net/1880/110083

Clarke, R., & Lancaster, T. (2006). *Eliminating the successor to plagiarism: Identifying the usage of contract cheating sites*. Paper presented at the Second International Plagiarism Conference, Gateshead, UK. https://citeseerx.ist.psu.edu/viewdoc/download?doi=10.1.1.120.5440&rep=rep1&type=pdf

Eaton, S. E. (2020, January 15). Cheating may be under-reported across Canada's universities and colleges. *The Conversation*. http://theconversation.com/cheating-may-be-under-reported-across-canadas-universities-and-colleges-129292

Ellis, C., Zucker I.M., & Randall D. (2018). The infernal business of contract cheating: understanding the business processes and models of academic custom writing sites. *International Journal for Educational Integrity, 14.* https://doi.org/10.1007/s40979-017-0024-3

Eubanks, V. (2018). *Automating inequality: How high-tech tools profile, police, and punish the poor.* St. Martin's Publishing Group.

Gilliard, C. (2017). Pedagogy and the Logic of Platforms. *Educause Review, July/August 2017.* https://er.educause.edu/articles/2017/7/pedagogy-and-the-logic-of-platforms

Hargittai, E., & Marwick, A. (2016). What Can I Really Do? Explaining the Privacy Paradox with Online Apathy. *International Journal of Communication, 10*(0), 21. https://ijoc.org/index.php/ijoc/article/view/4655

Hendershott, A., Drinan, P., & Cross, M. (2000). Toward Enhancing a Culture of Academic Integrity. *Journal of Student Affairs Research and Practice, 37*(4), 270–281. https://doi.org/10.2202/1949-6605.1119

Hill, K. (2012). How target figured out a teen girl was pregnant before her father did. *Forbes.* https://www.forbes.com/sites/kashmirhill/2012/02/16/how-target-figured-out-a-teen-girl-was-pregnant-before-her-father-did/

Huq, A. (2019). racial equity in algorithmic criminal justice. *Duke Law Journal, 68*(6), 1043–1134. https://scholarship.law.duke.edu/cgi/viewcontent.cgi?article=3972&context=dlj

International Center for Academic Integrity (ICAI). (2016). *Institutional Toolkit to Combat Contract Cheating.* http://integrity.fiu.edu/pdfs/Contract%20Cheating.pdf

Lancaster, T. (2019a). Profiling the international academic ghost writers who are providing low-cost essays and assignments for the contract cheating industry. *Journal of Information, Communication and Ethics in Society, 17*(1), 72–86. https://doi.org/10.1108/JICES-04-2018-0040

Lancaster, T. (2019b). Social Media Enabled Contract Cheating. *Canadian Perspectives on Academic Integrity, 2*(2), 7–24. https://doi.org/10.11575/cpai.v2i2.68053

Luke, J. (2019, March 13). That's No Plagiarism Checker. *EconProph.* https://econproph.com/2019/03/12/thats-no-plagiarism-checker/

Macfarlane, B., Zhang, J., & Pun, A. (2014). Academic integrity: A review of the literature. *Studies in Higher Education, 39*(2), 339–358. https://doi.org/10.1080/0307079.2012.709495

Medway, D., Roper, S., & Gillooly, L. (2018). Contract cheating in UK higher education: A covert investigation of essay mills. *British Educational Research Journal, 44*(3), 393–418. https://doi.org/10.1002/berj.3335

Morris, E. J. (2016). Academic Integrity Policy and Practice: Introduction. In T. Bretag (Ed.), *Handbook of Academic Integrity* (pp. 409–411). Singapore: Springer Singapore.

Newton, P.M. (2018). How common is commercial contract cheating in higher education and is it increasing? A systematic review. *Frontiers in Education.* https://doi.org/10.3389/feduc.2018.00067/full

Obermeyer, Z., Powers, B., Vogeli, C., & Mullainathan, S. (2019). Dissecting racial bias in an algorithm used to manage the health of populations. *Science, 366*(6464), 447–453. https://doi.org/10.1126/science.aax2342

Office of Ed Tech. (2012). *Pearson—Education Datapalooza.* https://www.youtube.com/watch?v=xgV9DssLsXg

Olson, P. (2019). Pearson Hack Exposed Details on Thousands of U.S. Students. *Wall Street Journal.* https://www.wsj.com/articles/pearson-hack-exposed-details-on-thousands-of-u-s-students-11564619001

Orosz, G. et al. (2015). Teacher enthusiasm: a potential cure of academic cheating. *Frontiers in Psychology, 6,* 318. https://www.ncbi.nlm.nih.gov/pmc/articles/PMC4379758/

Peters, M., Boies, T., & Morin, S. (2019) Teaching academic integrity in Queen universities: roles professors adopt. *Frontiers in Education.* https://doi.org/10.3389/feduc.2019.00099/full

Peterson, H. (2019, May 10). Millions of students are buying plagiarism-free essays for as little as $13—And it's nearly impossible for teachers to prove. *Business Insider.* https://www.businessinsider.com/students-buying-essays-impossible-to-prove-2019-5

Prensky, M. (2001). Digital Natives, Digital Immigrants Part 1. *On the Horizon, 9*(5), 1–6. https://doi.org/10.1108/10748120110424816

Purdy, J. P. (2005). Calling off the hounds: Technology and the visibility of plagiarism. *Pedagogy, 5*(2), 275–296. https://muse.jhu.edu/article/182339

Ramberg, J. & Modin, B. (2019). School effectiveness and student cheating: Do students' grades and moral standards matter for this relationship? *Social Psychology of Education, 22*, 517–538. https://doi.org/10.1007/s11218-019-09486-6

Rhinelander, J. (2017). Top Hat—Software to be avoided. *Imaginary Blog*. (n.d.). Retrieved November 20, 2020, from https://imaginary.ca/blog/2017/06/16/top-hat/

Rigby, D., et al. (2014). Contract cheating & the market in essays. *Journal of Economic Behaviour & Organization, 111*, 23–37. https://doi.org/10.1016/j.jebo.2014.12.019

Robinson, J. A., & Glanzer, P. L. (2017). Building a Culture of Academic Integrity: What Students Perceive and Need. *College Student Journal, 51*(2), 209–221.

Rowland, S., et al. (2017). Just turn to us: The persuasive features of contract cheating websites. *Assessment and Evaluation in Higher Education, 43*(4), 652–665. https://doi.org/10.1080/02602938.2017.1391948

Rundle, K., Curtis, G.J., & Clare, J. (2019). Why students do not engage in contract cheating. *Frontiers in Psychology*. https://doi.org/10.3389/fpsyg.2019.02229/full

Senack, E., Donoghue, R., O'Connor Grant, K. & Steen, K. (2016). *ACCESS DENIED: The new face of the textbook monopoly*. Student PRIGs. https://studentpirgs.org/assets/uploads/archive/sites/student/files/reports/Access%20Denied%20-%20Final%20Report.pdf

Smith, E. (2012). The Digital Native Debate in Higher Education: A Comparative Analysis of Recent Literature. *Canadian Journal of Learning and Technology, 38*. https://doi.org/10.1002/9781118326732.ch

Stewart, B. (2020, November 10). Why higher ed needs data ethics. *Inside Higher Ed*. https://www.insidehighered.com/blogs/university-venus/why-higher-ed-needs-data-ethics

Stinson, C. (2020, February 6). *Algorithms are not Neutral: Bias in recommendation systems*. The Department of Philosophy and School of Computing Colloquium Series presents, Queen's University, Kingston. https://www.catherinestinson.ca/Files/Papers/Algorithms_are_not_Neutral.pdf

Stommel, J., & Morris, S. M. (2017). A Guide for resisting edtech: The case against Turnitin. *Hybrid Pedagogy*. https://hybridpedagogy.org/resisting-edtech/

Sutherland-Smith, W., & Dullaghan, K. (2019). You don't always get what you pay for: User experiences of engaging with contract cheating sites. *Assessment & Evaluation in Higher Education, 44*(8), 1148–1162. https://doi.org/10.1080/02602938.2019.1576028

Swauger, S. (2020). Our bodies encoded: Algorithmic test proctoring in higher education. *Hybrid Pedagogy*. https://hybridpedagogy.org/our-bodies-encoded-algorithmic-test-proctoring-in-higher-education/

UNESCO IITE. (2020). *Personal data security technical guide for online education platforms*. UNESCO. https://iite.unesco.org/publications/personal-data-security-technical-guide-for-online-education-platforms/

Waddell, K. (2016, December 2). How algorithms can bring down minorities' credit scores. *The Atlantic*. https://www.theatlantic.com/technology/archive/2016/12/how-algorithms-can-bring-down-minorities-credit-scores/509333/

Yorke, J., Sefcik, L., & Veeran-Colton, T. (2020). Contract cheating and blackmail: A risky business? *Studies in Higher Education*, 1–14. https://doi.org/10.1080/03075079.2020.1730313

Zubairi, A. (2017, March 4). *CEO Mike Silagadze explains how data on Top Hat's platform can help struggling students*. Betakit. https://betakit.com/ceo-mike-silagadze-explains-how-data-on-top-hats-platform-can-help-struggling-students/

Zuboff, S. (2019). *The age of surveillance capitalism: the fight for a human future at the new frontier of power*. London: Profile Books.

Brenna Clarke Gray (MA Carleton, Ph.D. New Brunswick) is a literature scholar by training, a comics scholar by practice, and an educational technologist by trade. Her research interests include open pedagogies and ethical approaches to educational technologies. She is the Coordinator, Educational Technologies at Thompson Rivers University and is currently at work tracing the history and imagining the future of open tenure processes.

Chapter 10
Pay-To-Pass: Evolving Online Systems That Undermine the Integrity of Student Work

Nancy Chibry and Ebba U. Kurz

Abstract In an age where information is available at our fingertips, students in the post-secondary environment have equally ready access to resources that can be supportive of their academic development or academically questionable. In this chapter, we describe the pervasiveness of pay-to-pass websites in the Canadian post-secondary context. We distinguish pay-to-pass websites from other forms of contract cheating by defining them as sites encouraging students to share and access course material, assessments, and notes for academic and personal gain, as well as those providing real-time academic support. This chapter is a reflection on the nature and impact of these sites and explores a three-pronged approach to addressing the challenges posed by them on the upholding of academic integrity in post-secondary education.

Keywords Academic integrity · Canada · Contract cheating · File-sharing · Internet

The vast majority of university students today have never known life without the internet, and they have been taught to use it as the first source of information whenever a question arises. Technology is pervasive in their lives; as of 2018, 97.9% of Canadians aged 15–24 reported having a smartphone (Statistics Canada, 2019). Accustomed to connecting and sharing through social media and websites, Dyer (2010) refers to this generation as one living in an "age of collaboration" (p. 172). While some have viewed this as the democratization of knowledge, stripping universities of the role they have held for centuries, the proliferation of for-profit (pay-to-pass) websites for information and file sharing among university students has created an ecosystem or "sharing economy" (Richardson, 2015, p. 121) where knowledge has

---

N. Chibry (✉) · E. U. Kurz (✉)
University of Calgary, Calgary, Canada
e-mail: n.chibry@ucalgary.ca

E. U. Kurz
e-mail: kurz@ucalgary.ca

S. E. Eaton and J. Christensen Hughes (eds.), *Academic Integrity in Canada*, Ethics and Integrity in Educational Contexts 1,
https://doi.org/10.1007/978-3-030-83255-1_10

become an accessible commodity—for a price—eroding the foundation of academic integrity.

There is limited academic literature describing pay-to-pass websites and their impact on academic misconduct in the post-secondary context. Rogerson (2014) and Rogerson and Basanta (2016) recognized that these websites evolved conceptually from those developed to illegally share music and entertainment. They examined student motivation in using these sites (Rogerson, 2014; Rogerson & Basanta, 2016). Lieneck and Esparza (2018), in the context of a healthcare administration course, determined that 67% of students used online or social media tools outside the course learning management system to help with their work (Lieneck & Esparza, 2018).

In this chapter, we define pay-to-pass websites as those through which students upload and access course material, including past assessments, labs and class notes, for academic or personal advantage, as well as those offering online, instant access to 'experts' offering real-time academic support; often both of these features are offered. These sites represent a distinct subtype of contract cheating, a venue for "collaborative cheating" (Harrison et al., 2020, p. 2), which differs from vendors and web services through which students pay to have someone write their paper or take their tests. Among the most common in the Canadian context are Course Hero (coursehero.com), OneClass (oneclass.com), Studocu (studocu.com) and Chegg (chegg.com). This chapter is a reflection on the nature and impact of these sites in the context of our experiences as faculty administrators responsible for investigating allegations of academic misconduct amongst undergraduate students in our respective faculties at a Canadian post-secondary institution (University of Calgary). In addition, the chapter explores approaches that can be taken to address the challenges posed by these websites on the upholding of academic integrity in post-secondary education.

Questionable Practices and Big Profits

Pay-to-pass websites are big business. In late 2020, Course Hero was valued at $1.1 billion (US) (Mascarenhas, 2020), while in early 2021 Chegg's market value reached US$12 billion (Adams, 2021). Access to the content or services offered through these websites occurs primarily in two ways: by monthly (or yearly) subscription, or by students earning credits for uploading course materials, reminiscent of a barter economy. Some sites, including oneclass.com, offer a rewards and 'refer a friend' program, thereby incentivizing participation beyond the allure of academic gain (*Share Notes, Get Rewarded*, n.d.). In marketing to students, the sites promise better grades, reduced stress, and ready, round-the-clock access to personalized learning support. In some cases, sites offer scholarships (*Course Hero—Scholarships*, n.d.) and the quality of the service provided is backed by a guarantee that users will see improved grades (*How Does the Better Grades Guarantee Work?*, n.d.). Whether reflective of a perceived efficiency gain, time mismanagement or financial incentive (Amigud & Lancaster, 2019; Park, 2003), these promises are alluring. Using terms such as 'community', 'support' and 'collaboration', these companies create a façade that 'sharing is caring' in an academic context. Indeed, recent studies have identified that, compared to the view of instructors, students perceive these websites as far less problematic or dishonest and regard them as akin to unauthorized group work (Eaton et al., 2019; Harrison et al., 2020).

Using paid campus representatives, many of these sites market directly to students by gaining unauthorized access to course email distribution lists or by persistent text message-based marketing campaigns. The former typically occurs by bartering with a student by promising access to the site's resources in exchange for a copy of the class contact list from the course learning management system, even when this is in violation of campus information technology policies (New Policy for Acceptable Use of Electronic Resources & Information, 2019). The latter occurs after students initially register on a site, after which they receive persistent (often many times daily) text message reminders to upload documents or to return to the site. This is in violation of Canadian federal anti-spam legislation. In September 2020, the Canadian Radio-Television and Telecommunications Commission (CRTC), the federal tribunal charged with implementing laws and regulations pertaining to broadcasting and telecommunications, fined the parent company of oneclass.com for violations related to the use of unsolicited commercial electronic messages sent to Canadian post-secondary students between 2016 and 2020 (Government of Canada and the Canadian Radio-television and Telecommunications Commission (CRTC, 2020)). Together with their savvy marketing strategies, these companies have been diligent in ensuring their fine print indicates that students are expected to contribute and use resources in a manner consistent with their institutional academic integrity policy, essentially relieving the company from any culpability by transferring the burden of responsibility squarely onto their users. However, like many social media sites, most pay-to-pass sites do not review posted content, and only remove copyrighted content when a complaint is filed (Kolowich, 2009). Indeed, in our experience, many of these websites are responsive to faculty requests for removal of copyrighted information that has been posted by a user; however, this approach places the burden upon the instructor to monitor and report the uploading of protected course content.

In an effort to gain access to course material for their users, some pay-to-pass sites have also used questionable tactics to engage graduate teaching assistants. In early 2019 at the University of Calgary, under the apparent guise of a job interview for an online 'teaching opportunity', graduate students with experience as course teaching assistants were asked to share course material. It was only after realizing that no job was available, but course materials had been surrendered, that the graduate students recognized that they had been duped. Deceptively, the interviews were held on campus in space rented at the University's teaching and learning hub, perhaps as an attempt to underscore or obscure the illegitimacy of the opportunity (*What Is "Pay to Pass"?*, 2019).

Pay-to-pass companies have not only focused on attracting student users, but they aim to legitimize their approach through faculty recruitment (Lederman, 2020). Course Hero holds an annual education summit, provides educational grants, and invites faculty to join their faculty club, which is now over 30,000 members strong

(Lederman, 2020). Course Hero also encourages faculty members to create and share study resources online as a way to support student learning and earn extra income (*Help More Students, Earn Extra Income with Educator Exchange (Beta)*, n.d.), further feigning legitimacy and blurring the lines for students. Despite long-standing concerns about pay-to-pass sites, it is remarkable that they have entered into agreements with post-secondary institutions. In 2019, Purdue University joined forces with Chegg to integrate Chegg writing tools into the university's Online Writing Lab (Purdue News Service, 2019). These efforts are not without detractors (*Purdue Professors Criticize Writing Partnership with Chegg*, n.d.), and we are left to wonder what message this sends to post-secondary students who may view this as an endorsement of the totality of Chegg's offerings.

Prevalence in the Canadian Context

Among the earliest public descriptions of the incursion of pay-to-pass sites in the Canadian context was a 2014 article in the Ryerson University student newspaper, describing a professor's discovery of class notes on OneClass (Nemers, 2014). Since that time, there has been an explosion of websites offering students the opportunity to access completed assessments, class notes or expert assistance. It is challenging to quantify the penetrance of pay-to-pass services into the Canadian post-secondary sector. While there has been a documented increase in the use of contract cheating sites amongst Canadian post-secondary students between 2006 and 2018 (Clarke & Lancaster, 2006; Lancaster, 2018), no quantitative data have been published regarding rates of use of pay-to-pass sites. Nevertheless, posters advertising their services abound on university walls and social media campaigns flaunt the services. Some of these sites proudly boast of the size of their document repositories. In April 2019, when we presented at the Canadian Symposium for Academic Integrity (Chibry & Kurz, 2019), the oneclass.com repository for Western University was 90,000 documents, while McMaster University and York University were 60,000 each. As of November 2020, oneclass.com claimed to have over 105,000 documents available for classes at Western University, and over 70,000 each for McMaster University, York University and the University of Toronto St. George campus. Thus, over the course of 18 months, the repositories for each university grew by almost 17%. Perhaps reflective of their influence, the marked growth in the size of their document repositories suggest a similarly concerning rise in their use.

Although many of these websites have offered services to students for more than a decade, faculty across the country remain largely unaware of their presence. This was illustrated clearly in a live demonstration we held during a session at the 2019 Canadian Symposium on Academic Integrity (Chibry & Kurz, 2019). We invited a faculty member in the audience to share his university name and course number. Searching on Course Hero, he was shocked to discover both completed labs and copies of past exams posted for his engineering course. He, and many others in the audience, were unaware that such items were in circulation and so readily found.

As faculty administrators with responsibility for investigating potential breaches in academic integrity, we have observed an increase in student use of these sites in recent years. In some cases, students have submitted laboratory or course assignments bearing the answers to a preceding year's questions, leaving an obvious trail for the grader of the work. In other cases, students are identified by chance when documents still bearing their names or university identification numbers appear on a pay-to-pass website. While the former can be managed through existing academic misconduct procedures, the latter does not carry with it the same evidence of wrongdoing as required by many post-secondary academic misconduct policies. Nevertheless, in our experience it serves as an excellent opportunity for conversation and education. Students, many of whom have aspirations beyond their undergraduate studies, are often taken aback and embarrassed by the discovery. We approach this as an opportunity for them to reflect upon what this online behaviour may convey to an employer or professional/graduate degree program admission panel and to discuss the importance of acting with integrity in academics and beyond. Through these conversations, we have gained insight into the persistent marketing practices of these companies and their lucrative offers. In one case, a particularly prolific student contributor earned enough money to purchase a higher value laptop computer—all for sharing their personal sets of class notes. In all cases where we have been able to identify students, we have also asked them to request removal of posted material, which has occurred in all instances. Perhaps if a more concerted effort could be made across the country in the post-secondary sector, we would reduce the negative impact of these sites on academic integrity.

Pandemic Challenge: Online Learning and the Use of Pay-To-Pass Sites

With the rapid shift to online delivery of many courses due to the COVID-19 pandemic, there has been concern raised about observed increases in academic misconduct. In March 2020, educators worked quickly to redesign the delivery of the final weeks of their courses to offer them remotely. Since then, we and our colleagues across campus observed that this coincided with a marked jump in the number of academic misconduct cases, both reported and formally charged, over previous years. In large part, these cases were linked to pay-to-pass companies offering on-the-spot answers provided by their 'experts'. Indeed, this is comparable to the trend observed across Canada and around the world (Isai, 2020). With continued offering of online courses as a consequence of concerns due to the COVID-19 pandemic, the number of academic misconduct cases related to pay-to-pass companies now make up the majority of cases being reported for investigation. In one faculty at the University of Calgary, the number of academic misconduct cases related to Chegg and similar companies has risen from one or two cases per term to hundreds. While in the past we observed students finding or posting answers related to assignments and labs, it is now being observed that test questions are being posted (and answers received) in real time during the writing of tests (Isai, 2020). These companies are becoming so efficient at responding to posted questions that there have been cases where a student has uploaded questions during the writing of a quiz and received an 'expert' solution in under 15 min, allowing the student to submit the work for credit.

Prior to the COVID-19 pandemic, the majority of students at the University of Calgary had little to no experience with online courses. For the 2020–2021 academic year, the majority of courses were offered remotely. Although some students flourished with this new mode of delivery, and had adequate support structures, many students struggled with the self-discipline and time management skills required for remote learning. Students have indicated that social isolation, job loss and emotional strain made it particularly challenging to study and meet deadlines. These factors have created an environment that makes students more vulnerable than normal to these companies. Companies promising 'faster homework solutions' and 24/7 access to and support from experts are alluring to students who are struggling. Although academic misconduct cases in the past primarily consisted of unauthorized collaboration between students and the copying of answers from peers or older assessments, students recently under investigation for misconduct have claimed that it has been challenging to create the study groups that once helped them prosper and learn and they have been turning to these companies to fill this void.

Pedagogical Practice to Reduce Impact of Sites

The emergence and now widespread use of pay-to-pass websites among students points to the importance we must each place on reforming our pedagogical practice as it pertains to assessment design. A critical first step is to move away from the re-use of assessments (e.g., exams, labs, tests) across multiple terms. This can be challenging in circumstances where core material needs to be assessed and speaks more broadly for the need of a substantial shift in our approach to assessment design.

At our institution, this became abundantly evident in the weeks following the closure of our campus due to concerns for COVID-19. Many of the assessments used at the end of the Winter 2020 term, in the weeks after the pandemic was declared, were not redesigned for the unexpected shift to online delivery, leading to a spike in cases of academic misconduct. For many instructors, this brought to light for the first time the pervasive presence of pay-to-pass companies and their promises. It stimulated reflection and conversation within and across institutions and has led instructors to consider alternative ways of assessing student learning in a way that minimizes the likelihood of academic misconduct, or the usefulness of the instant 'experts' available on pay-to-pass websites. By way of example, one colleague piloted an exam that encouraged discussion and collaboration amongst students on breaks provided during the writing of their exam. In this, students wrote synchronously for a 20-min period, took a 20-min break, and repeated the sequence over a three-hour period. The instructor found that the marks for this exam were consistent with those received on 'pre-COVID' exams and, furthermore, assessment of individual student learning was not compromised. Other educators have integrated exam alternatives, such as summative projects that can be delivered in a variety of formats (e.g., YouTube video, animation, scrapbook) and that allow students to showcase their learning from the course. Not only does this approach reduce the likelihood of misconduct, but it also meets goals associated with Universal Design for Learning (La et al., 2018).

The late Tracey Bretag, a global leader in the area of academic integrity, identified that changes in assessment design alone are not a panacea for the rise in academic misconduct due to pay-to-pass websites and other digitally-based facilitation of cheating (Bretag, 2018). Lienack and Esparza (2018), who described a first-hand account of the impact of pay-to-pass sites on resource-sharing among students, created their own course-based study site to which both faculty and students provided content to aid learning, making it less tempting for students to visit third-party websites (Lieneck & Esparza, 2018). Considered together, these initiatives, and others limited only by our creativity, have the potential to reduce or eliminate the value and impact that pay-to-pass vendors have on university students. Many others in this volume discuss assessment design, but also point to the role of educating students as to the value and sanctity of their personal information (Gray, 2022).

A Three-Pronged Educational Approach to Student Integrity

Dyer (2010) has proposed a three-pronged approach to addressing the challenges to academic integrity in the age of collaboration, including proactive, reactive and adaptive steps (Dyer, 2010), while Stoesz and Eaton propose a "multi-pronged, multi-stakeholder" approach to promoting a culture of academic integrity in universities (Stoesz & Eaton, 2020). In this chapter, we elaborate upon Dyer's three-pronged approach, incorporating elements proposed by Stoesz and Eaton, to propose a strategy that can be implemented in the Canadian post-secondary context.

Proactive

Discussions of academic integrity need to occur long before students reach the post-secondary level; we need to be proactive in educating students, teachers and parents about academic integrity and pay-to-pass companies from the earliest levels of education. Promotion of academic integrity must be integrated into the curriculum starting throughout the K-12 level, setting the stage for more advanced discussion at the post-secondary level. Children and parents must understand the subtle differences between sites aimed at explaining concepts from those supporting inappropriate collusion and homework help. Messaging must be consistent and upholding and promoting academic integrity needs to be the norm and not the exception. In the post-secondary context, steps must be taken at the course, faculty and institutional levels to build a culture and model of academic integrity.

At the University of Calgary, proactive steps at the course level include such examples as having a statement of integrity on each assessment and, in some cases, requiring students to sign an acknowledgement that they understand the conditions of the assessment and promise to uphold principles of academic integrity during its completion. Other instructors have created course-specific modules that focus on academic integrity and the influence of pay-to-pass companies. The assessments associated with the module either contribute to the final grade or are a requirement for passing the course. The goal for the waiver, assessments, and modules is to educate students while holding them accountable should a violation of academic integrity take place.

Proactive educational approaches have also been used at the faculty-wide level. One faculty collaborated with the Student Success Centre at the University of Calgary to develop academic integrity modules for all first-year students in their faculty. University policies prevented the faculty from making the modules mandatory, as they had not been stipulated as degree requirements in the University's Academic Calendar. When pilots of these modules for incoming students in a number of faculties were launched, the participation rates were discouraging low (Lock et al., 2019). The faculty is now considering alternative approaches that might encourage enhanced participation with these modules. Most faculties include statements of academic integrity and explicit prohibiting of the sharing of course materials on course outlines with links to University statements and policies; however, this is by itself insufficient. Instructors not only need to draw students' attention to these statements but also embed opportunities for discussion about these pay-to-pass companies and highlight the importance of academic integrity throughout the course.

The Student Success Centre at the University of Calgary has created a series of interactive workshops available to all students, and commonly used in remediation for students identified to have breached the University's academic misconduct policy. These include sessions on plagiarism and strategies to avoid it, academic integrity in collaborating with peers, and steps to avoiding unintentional academic misconduct in online learning. The University of Calgary has also taken part in the International Day of Action Against Contract Cheating since 2017. This Day of Action began in Fall 2016 with 34 registered post-secondary institutions around the globe, including three Canadian institutions (Humber College, Humber Institute of Technology & Advanced Learning, University of Waterloo). Participation in the Day of Action continues to grow. In the Fall 2020, 300 institutions participated, including post-secondary institutions and high schools as well as education-focused companies; close to 40 Canadian post-secondary institutions were among this group. Although this event primarily focuses on contract cheating, the University of Calgary and many other institutions have taken the opportunity to expand this day to include discussions of pay-to-pass companies.

Since 2017, the University of Calgary has extended the International Day of Action into an Academic Integrity Week. During this week, events and workshops are offered both to and by faculty and students, including those with a focus on predatory companies, promoting of academic integrity and highlighting the supports available to instructors and students. In 2019, students played a major role in the planning, promotion and the hosting of events on campus. Empowering students to be active participants in all stages is integral in creating and promoting a culture of academic integrity. These student ambassadors facilitated discussion and educated their peers in fun, relatable and engaging ways.

Reactive

Universities must have institutional policies and procedures that support academic integrity by articulating the nature and consequences of academic misconduct. They must set clear expectations and the associated consequences must be universally applied (Dyer, 2010). The associated processes for reporting and handling of violations of academic integrity must not only be straightforward and transparent, but they must provide faculty with the necessary tools to aid in the prevention, detection and reporting of these breaches. Many institutions, including the University of Calgary, have either created or updated their statements on academic integrity as well as updated academic misconduct policies and procedures in an effort to clarify and promote academic integrity while also reacting to the growing number of cases of academic misconduct arising due to pay-to-pass websites.

In a study examining academic integrity policies and procedures from 23 publicly-funded universities in Western Canada, Stoesz and Eaton discovered that "nearly all documents described outsourcing behaviour and categorized it most often as a form of plagiarism", but did not specifically articulate these behaviours with the terms 'contract cheating' or 'pay-to-pass' (Stoesz & Eaton, 2020). While the University of Calgary policy neither addresses pay-to-pass companies nor contract cheating directly, the creation of Academic Integrity Week, an academic integrity website (https://www.ucalgary.ca/student-services/student-success/learning/academic-integrity), and a website that specifically addresses the dangers of paying for academic support (https://ucalgary.ca/current-students/paying-for-academic-support) guides students to uphold academic integrity.

Given how pervasive these sites are in the post-secondary context in Canada and around the world, it may be more appropriate to consider a broader response. For example, post-secondary institutions in Manitoba, Canada block access to these sites on campus computer networks, advising students that the websites are in violation of the institutional academic integrity policy and re-directing them to academic integrity resources (Seeland et al., 2020); the University of Calgary has recently taken similar action. In the United States, educational publishers have successfully used judicial paths to be awarded injunctions against websites posting textbooks, test answers and solution manuals (Pearson, 2020), reflecting another avenue for addressing these websites. While in Australia, legislation is now in place outlawing the provision or advertisement of academic cheating services (Cracking down on Cheating at Universities, 2020; Government of Australia, 2020). Convictions under the law can result in jail time and/or fines up to AUS$100,000 (CAD$95,000). More widespread implementation of such efforts in other jurisdictions could reduce the pervasiveness of pay-to-pass websites in the post-secondary context.

Adaptive

In their analysis, Stoesz and Eaton (2020) found that many of the academic integrity policies at Western Canadian universities tended to describe a punitive approach to breaches of integrity rather than taking an education-first perspective. This is in contrast to what Griffith (2013) found regarding academic integrity on the websites of 22 publicly-funded universities in Ontario, which predominantly reported an educative approach (Griffith, 2013). Griffith (2013) remarked that for websites to be impactful, they had to be easy to navigate, visually striking and with a strong focus on student-centred language, including the use of the pronoun *you* when addressing the student. These sites also took an approach that students were visiting this website to become better-informed and that they were educating themselves on preventing misconduct as opposed to assuming that misconduct had already taken place.

An educational approach is important when working directly with students who have committed academic misconduct. At the University of Calgary, in the majority of first-time academic integrity violations a grade penalty is assigned on the specific assessment and the student is given the opportunity to attend educational workshops in lieu of disciplinary probation. To track academic integrity violations, a neutral administrative indicator is placed on the student's file (but does not appear on the transcript), allowing administrators to identify potential 'repeat offenders', while allowing those who have had only a single episode to complete their program, and seek employment or experiential learning placements, without bias. This indicator is removed upon graduation.

Conversations with students who have committed academic misconduct typically reflect on the root cause(s) of why the misconduct took place, how it undermines academic integrity, and ways to avoid it from happening in the future. When the misconduct involves pay-to-pass companies, the conversation expands to not only the impact on the individual's learning but on the learning of others as well. These conversations are invaluable for shifting attitudes in an individual but remain woefully inadequate as an approach to changing the culture campus-wide.

Conclusion

The ubiquitous infiltration of pay-to-pass websites into the post-secondary landscape, with the lure of information accessible to all, has created a new challenge for upholding a culture of academic integrity. With the emergence of these sites in recent years, compounded by the rapid transition to online learning around the globe, proactive, reactive and adaptive responses are urgently needed to address the impact of these sites on academic integrity. These responses include but go beyond the scope of post-secondary institutions, requiring conversations that must begin at the earliest levels of education, while more concerted responses at the provincial or national level are equally essential. This ongoing problem represent a sizeable challenge as we look to the future of learning with integrity.

References

Adams, S. (2021). *This $12 billion company is getting rich off students cheating their way through covid*. Forbes. Retrieved February 26, 2021, from https://www.forbes.com/sites/susanadams/2021/01/28/this-12-billion-company-is-getting-rich-off-students-cheating-their-way-through-covid/

Amigud, A., & Lancaster, T. (2019). 246 reasons to cheat: An analysis of students reasons for seeking to outsource academic work. *Computers & Education, 134*, 98–107. https://doi.org/10.1016/j.compedu.2019.01.017

Bretag, T. (2018, April 26). *Academic Integrity*. Oxford Research Encyclopedia of Business and Management. https://doi.org/10.1093/acrefore/9780190224851.013.147

Clarke, R., & Lancaster, T. (2006). *Eliminating the successor to plagiarism: Identifying the usage of contract cheating sites*. Paper presented at the Second International Plagiarism Conference, The Sage Gateshead, Tyne & Wear, United Kingdom

Course Hero—Scholarships. (n.d.). Retrieved November 26, 2020, from https://www.coursehero.com/scholarships/

Cracking down on cheating at universities. (2020). https://www.theaustralian.com.au/news/latest-news/new-laws-passed-could-see-cheaters-who-sell-services-to-university-students-jailed/news-story/599e268e4e5ff39e0766544688274092

Chibry, N., & Kurz, E.U. (2019, April). Pay-to-Pass: Knowledge as a Commodity [Paper presentation]. *Canadian Symposium on Academic Integrity,* Calgary, AB.

Dyer, K. (2010). Challenges of maintaining academic integrity in an age of collaboration, sharing and social networking. In *Proceedings of TCC 2010* (pp. 168–195). TCCHawaii. Retrieved May 14, 2021 from https://www.learntechlib.org/p/43770/

Eaton, S. E., Chibry, N., Toye, M. A., & Rossi, S. (2019). Interinstitutional perspectives on contract cheating: A qualitative narrative exploration from Canada. *International Journal for Educational Integrity, 15*(1), 1–17. https://doi.org/10.1007/s40979-019-0046-0

Government of Australia (2020). *Tertiary Education Quality and Standards Agency Amendment (Prohibiting Academic Cheating Services) Bill 2019* (Australia) [Text]. Retrieved January 23, 2021, from https://www.aph.gov.au/Parliamentary_Business/Bills_Legislation/bd/bd1920a/20bd084

Government of Canada & CRTC. (2020). *Undertaking—File No.: 9109–2019–00522—Notesolution Inc. (OneClass)—Effective date of undertaking: 21 September 2020* [Undertakings]. https://crtc.gc.ca/eng/archive/2020/ut200921.htm

Gray, B. C. (2022). Ethics, ed tech, and the rise of contract cheating. In S. E. Eaton & J. Christensen Hughes (Eds.), *Academic integrity in Canada: An enduring and essential challenge*: Springer.

Griffith, J. (2013). Pedagogical or punitive?: The academic integrity websites of Ontario universities. *Canadian Journal of Higher Education, 43*(1), 1–22. https://doi.org/10.47678/cjhe.v43i1.2216

Harrison, D., Patch, A., McNally, D., & Harris, L. (2020). Student and faculty perceptions of study helper websites: A new practice in collaborative cheating. *Journal of Academic Ethics*. https://doi.org/10.1007/s10805-020-09373-2

Help more students, earn extra income with Educator Exchange (Beta). (n.d.). Share Your Study Resources with Our Community to Support Student Learning and Make Extra Income. Retrieved November 26, 2020, from https://educators.coursehero.com/educator-exchange

How does the Better Grades Guarantee Work? (n.d.). Customer Support—Course Hero. Retrieved November 26, 2020, from https://support.coursehero.com/hc/en-us/articles/218756988-How-does-the-Better-Grades-Guarantee-Work-Isai

Isai, V. (2020). The COVID-19 pandemic is changing how students cheat—and get caught. *National Observer*. https://www.nationalobserver.com/2020/09/28/news/covid-19-pandemic-changing-how-students-cheat-and-get-caught

Kolowich, S. (2009). *Course Hero or Course Villain?* https://www.insidehighered.com/news/2009/10/06/course-hero-or-course-villain

La, H., Dyjur, P., & Bair, H. (2018). *Universal Design for Learning in Higher Education*. University of Calgary Taylor Institute for Teaching and Learning. https://taylorinstitute.ucalgary.ca/resources/universal-design-learning-higher-education

Lancaster, T. (2018). *Turnitin DrSarahEaton Just reading comments from essay mill marketers in a blackhat forum in preparation for a talk next week. They put the US in first place for essays orders (not surprising), with the UK and Canada equal in second place.* Twitter. https://twitter.com/DrLancaster/status/1029014675198013440

Lederman, D. (2020). Course Hero Woos Professors. *Inside Higher Ed*. https://www.insidehighered.com/digital-learning/article/2020/02/19/course-hero-once-vilified-faculty-courts-professors-its

Lieneck, C., & Esparza, S. (2018). Collaboration or collusion? The new era of commercial online resources for students in the digital age: an opinion piece. *Internet Journal of Allied Health Sciences and Practice, 16*(3). https://nsuworks.nova.edu/ijahsp/vol16/iss3/7

Lock, J., Schroeder, M., & Eaton, S. E. (2019). Designing and implementing an online academic integrity tutorial: Identifying the challenges within a post-secondary context. *The Journal of Educational Thought, 52*(3), 193.

Mascarenhas, N. (2020). Course Hero, a profitable edtech unicorn, raises rare cash. *TechCrunch*. https://social.techcrunch.com/2020/08/26/course-hero-a-profitable-edtech-unicorn-raises-rare-cash/

Nemers, H. (2014, April 8). Profs nervous after finding lecture notes online. *Ryersonian.Ca*. https://ryersonian.ca/the-note-sharing-site-oneclass-allows-students-to-share-test-solutions-and-lecture-notes-online-for-credits/

New policy for Acceptable Use of Electronic Resources and Information. (2019). News. https://www.ucalgary.ca/news/new-policy-acceptable-use-electronic-resources-and-information

Park, C. (2003). In other (people's) words: Plagiarism by university students–literature and lessons. *Assessment & Evaluation in Higher Education, 28*(5), 471–488. https://doi.org/10.1080/02602930301677

Pearson. (2020). *Educational Publishers Obtain Preliminary Injunction Against 231 Websites Illegally Selling Test Answers and Solution Manuals*. Retrieved January 23, 2021, from https://www.prnewswire.com/news-releases/educational-publishers-obtain-preliminary-injunction-against-231-websites-illegally-selling-test-answers-and-solution-manuals-301177537.html

Purdue News Service (2019). *The Purdue University Online Writing Lab and Chegg Partner to Make World-Class Writing Education Tools More Accessible*. Retrieved November 26, 2020, from https://www.purdue.edu/newsroom/releases/2019/Q1/the-purdue-university-online-writing-lab-and-chegg-partner-to-make-world-class-writing-education-tools-more-accessible.html

Purdue professors criticize writing partnership with Chegg. (n.d.). Retrieved November 26, 2020, from https://www.insidehighered.com/news/2019/03/12/purdue-professors-criticize-writing-partnership-chegg

Richardson, L. (2015). Performing the sharing economy. *Geoforum, 67*, 121–129. https://doi.org/10.1016/j.geoforum.2015.11.004

Rogerson, A. M., & Basanta, G. (2016). Peer-to-peer file sharing and academic integrity in the internet age. In T. Bretag (Ed.), *Handbook of Academic Integrity* (pp. 273–285). Springer. https://doi.org/10.1007/978-981-287-098-8_55

Rogerson, A. M. (2014, June). *Detecting the work of essay mills and file swapping sites: some clues they leave behind*. Paper presented at the 6th International Integrity and Plagiarism Conference, Newcastle-on-Tyne, United Kingdom. https://www.ro.uow.edu.au/gsbpapers/434/

Seeland, J., Stoesz, B. M., & Vogt, L. (2020). Preventing online shopping for completed assessments: Protecting students by blocking access to contract cheating websites on institutional networks. *Canadian Perspectives on Academic Integrity*, *3*(1), 55–69. https://doi.org/10.11575/cpai.v3i1.70256

Share Notes, Get Rewarded. (n.d.). OneClass. Retrieved November 21, 2020, from https://oneclass.com/perks.en.html

Statistics Canada (2019, October 29). *Smartphone use and smartphone habits by gender and age group*. https://www150.statcan.gc.ca/t1/tbl1/en/tv.action?pid=2210011501

Stoesz, B. M., & Eaton, S. E. (2020). Academic integrity policies of publicly funded universities in Western Canada. *Educational Policy*, 0895904820983032. https://doi.org/10.1177/0895904820983032

What is pay to pass? (2019). News. https://www.ucalgary.ca/news/what-pay-pass

Nancy Chibry, M.Sc. is the Associate Dean, Undergraduate Programs and Student Affairs in the Faculty of Science at the University of Calgary. She is a Senior Instructor in the Department of Mathematics and Statistics and has always had a passion for showing others the beauty and stories behind numbers. She has helped promote academic integrity amongst students and faculty by serving on various academic committees, presenting at various conferences and co-publishing in the International Journal for Educational Integrity. She takes a student-centered approach in her teaching and interactions with students. She believes that through better understanding of how and when students are learning, educators can play a key role in guiding students to uphold academic integrity.

Ebba U. Kurz, Ph.D. is the Associate Dean (Undergraduate Health and Science Education) and Director for the O'Brien Centre for the Bachelor of Health Sciences Program. She is also a Professor in the Department of Physiology and Pharmacology and member of the Charbonneau Cancer Institute in the Cumming School of Medicine at the University of Calgary. Dr. Kurz is a passionate educator, mentor and leader in teaching and learning at the University of Calgary. She works closely with undergraduate students to create learning experiences that help them to think critically and to integrate complex information, while also supporting them in developing core transferable skills in oral communication, teamwork and academic writing. Dr. Kurz has a particularly keen interest in academic integrity—both fostering a culture of integrity in the classroom as well as understanding the impact of pay-to-pass websites of student learning. For her work in teaching and learning, Dr. Kurz has been honoured with the Killam Award for Undergraduate Mentorship, the McCaig-Killam Teaching Award, the University of Calgary Teaching Award for Excellence in Educational Leadership and the Students' Union Teaching Excellence Award.

Chapter 11
Education as a Financial Transaction: Contract Employment and Contract Cheating

Katherine Crossman

Abstract Over the last decade, high-profile cases of academic misconduct have surfaced across Canada (Eaton, 2020a). I argue that it is systemic issues that contribute to their ubiquity: knowledge is seen as a commodity, transcripts and credentials as products, and students as consumers. As provincial governments in Ontario and Alberta introduce funding models tied to graduate earnings and employment (Anderson, 2020; Weingarten et al., 2019), education becomes a financial transaction and academic integrity is threatened. Credentials hold more value than the process of learning, and when students pay for credentials, it is more palatable to pay for grades. This is exacerbated by a supply and demand for academically dishonest practices. File sharing websites that facilitate cheating are ubiquitous; coursehero.com alone is worth over one billion dollars (Schubarth, 2020). Targeted advertisements for essay mills abound. Meanwhile, academia increasingly relies on the labour of sessionals (Shaker & Pasma, 2018), who tend to underestimate the scope of misconduct (Hudd et al., 2009) and are less likely to report infractions (Blau et al., 2018). Furthermore, those with graduate degrees are increasing (Wall et al., 2018) while stable academic jobs are fewer (Kezar, 2013). Academics faced with precarious employment often supplement income in what Kezar et al. (2019) refer to as the "gig academy". They are well-positioned to meet the demand for ghost-written papers (Sivasubramaniam et al., 2016). Although many institutions have responded with well-articulated policies and procedures, when entrenched in a system that incentivises and facilitates dishonest practices, they are not lasting solutions to chronic problems.

Keywords Academic integrity · Neoliberalism · Contract cheating · Contract employment · Credentialism

---

K. Crossman (✉)
Bow Valley College, Calgary, Canada

S. E. Eaton and J. Christensen Hughes (eds.), *Academic Integrity in Canada*, Ethics and Integrity in Educational Contexts 1,
https://doi.org/10.1007/978-3-030-83255-1_11

Background

Over the last decade, high—profile cases of academic misconduct have surfaced across Canada (Eaton, 2020a) and the globe, implicating individuals in powerful positions, right up to the president of the United States, who was accused of hiring a proxy to sit his SAT exam, securing him entrance into Wharton School of Business (Trump, 2020). Closer to home, recent examples of academic misconduct in the Canadian news include the arrest of an impersonator during an exam (Bains, 2019), faculty degrees rescinded (Graveland, 2018), accusations of bribery in return for grades (Leo, 2017), the revocation of the Order of B.C. in response to a college admissions scandal (CBC News, 2020), and a questionable connection between the Alberta Minister of Advanced Education and a ghost-writing website (Siever, 2020). Although we see these types of cases with frequency in our newsfeeds, it is likely that the scope of academic misconduct is still more ubiquitous and undiscovered.

Post-secondary landscapes have changed since the seminal work of Christensen Hughes and McCabe (2006a, b) about academic misconduct in Canada. I argue that emerging and systemic issues in higher education and society as a whole have contributed to the ubiquity of academic misconduct and how it has shapeshifted in response to new pressures and technologies. A glance at the comments section of any news article about such cases and it is apparent that the public is quick to point fingers at individuals and their perceived moral failings; individuals are viewed to be solely responsible. Instead, in this chapter, I contend that neoliberalist pressures on post-secondary institutions have led to an academic landscape where knowledge is a commodity, transcripts and credentials are products, and students are consumers. This chapter argues that economic and employment precarity among instructors, disenfranchisement of students, and credentialism have created ideal conditions for academically dishonest behaviours, in particular contract cheating.

Education as a Transaction

Tensions between public education and government funding are not new. Earlier in this millennium, British Columbia faced massive cuts to education budgets under premier Gordon Campbell during a time of economic optimism (Millar, 2008). Years later, in the shadow of the economic downturn, such tensions persist and have heightened. Add to this the global pandemic and a resultant sea change in education, and the future of higher education is murky, with the only certainty being that financial tensions will endure.

In recent years, provincial governments have introduced new funding models tied to graduate earnings and employment (Anderson, 2020). Although delayed in Ontario due to COVID-19 (Friesen, 2020), the province's proposed plan will tie 60% of higher education funding (some 3 billion Canadian dollars) to a list of 10 metrics by 2024–25; the rate when this plan was released in 2019 was 1.4% for universities and 1.2% for colleges (Crawley, 2019). According to the Ontario model outlined by the Higher Education Quality Council of Ontario (Weingarten et al., 2019), educational outcomes are measured and quantified by tax-linked data, and faculty are compensated based on discrete research outputs and workloads. The overarching goal of these policies is to produce "outcomes-based funding mechanisms and meaningful, intentional performance agreements between government and providers" (Weingarten et al., 2019). The province of Alberta has proposed a model closely based on Ontario's; in fact, the lead author on the Higher Education Quality Council of Ontario's recommendation is a former University of Calgary president. Unlike Ontario, Alberta plans to push ahead with this proposed funding model despite the global pandemic (Friesen, 2020), as the provincial government focuses on economic recovery. Although these funding models have clear financial foci, what they lack is mention of the intangible benefits of higher education, such as the increase of knowledge or development of character. The gradual shift "from a mission of public knowledge and citizenship to a mission of job training and profitable patents" (Westheimer, 2018, p. 224) is notable.

The past decade has seen a marked shift from publicly-funded education to publicly-aided education (Usher, 2020, p. 33). Since 2008, post-secondary institutions across Canada have become increasingly dependent on tuition fees, the revenue from which doubled in the last 12 years from $8 billion to $16 billion CAD; much of it comes from international students who pay significantly higher tuition (Usher, 2020). It is unlikely that this recruitment of international students is a viable solution to funding woes, especially in the wake of COVID-19.

Unable to subsist on government funding and domestic student tuition, post-secondary institutions look to alumni and industry partners for donations. This is not specific to Canada; for example, Oxford University in the UK awarded a Chinese diplomat a created and meaningless credential in the hopes of securing donor dollars (Graham-Harrison, 2020). A quick look at almost any campus directory reveals where the money comes from. Buildings and faculties (now known as "schools") are often named for donors. I used to work in the Faculty of Education at the University of Calgary, which later became the Werklund School of Education and is colloquially referred to by faculty, staff, and students as "Werklund". It used to be called "Education."

Funding models based on discrete economic outcomes naturally lead to the unequal distribution of monies in higher education. Programs that demonstrate graduate employability and higher salaries simply receive more financial backing directly from individual donors and indirectly from provincial coffers, as universities direct more resources into programs that are best aligned with funding metrics. This is not limited only to funding, but also to prestige: Forbes ranks MBA programs by graduate salary increases (Financial Times, 2019).

Concomitant with such models of funding is credentialism: positions that previously did not require post-secondary education now demand it, despite unchanged job descriptions and responsibilities (Fuller & Raman, 2017) and lower graduate earnings (Usher, 2020, p. 67). This phenomenon is also known as "credential creep" or "qualification inflation" and a causal relationship between contract cheating and credentialism has been described (e.g., Walker & Townley, 2012; Bretag et al., 2018). It is also an unsurprising outcome of a job market where increasing numbers of post-secondary graduates are willing to accept jobs for which they had traditionally been over-qualified. As the goal posts have shifted, the number of business and STEM degrees conferred has increased dramatically while the number of humanities degrees has decreased over the last 15 years in the US and Canada (National Centre for Educational Statistics, 2019; Usher 2020), prompting some to call it the "death of the humanities" (i.e., Hanson, 2014). Similarly, business related post-secondary education is now the most popular major in Canada (Statistics Canada, 2017).

The increasing employer demand for higher education credentials has driven more people to turn to post-secondary programs to secure basic stable employment, despite having little interest or confidence in academia (Callahan, 2004). High school graduates realize that the jobs for which they will apply have artificial prerequisites; therefore they may see degrees as impediments standing between them and a living wage. It is only natural that they will try to remove obstacles from or shorten this path. This inevitably leads to what Westheimer (2018) refers to as the "shopping mall university" in which young people look for "the cheapest and fastest means for obtaining the basic skills and certification they need" and "courses not directly related to job training look more and more like useless dust to be eliminated" (p. 227).

Removing such "inefficiencies" from the system should not be the ultimate goal of higher education (Levidow, 2007). The path to deep knowledge is wending, unquantifiable, and inefficient by nature. Funding models that reduce knowledge to a job title or a figure on tax return is fundamentally at odds with institutional mission and value statements that cite the "advancement of learning and the creation and dissemination of knowledge" (McGill University, 2020), "embracing the power of curiosity, and continually seeking and sharing new knowledge" (University of Calgary, 2019), and "the pursuit, preservation, and dissemination of knowledge" (York University, 2020).

Education becomes a farcical transaction where the players pay lip service to the quest for knowledge while engaging in a transaction whereby time and money are exchanged for credentials, which are then exchanged for job opportunities. Research from the UK (Bunce et al., 2017) found that students who take a consumer-oriented approach to education tend to be in STEM fields of study, grade focused, and fee-paying (as opposed to students with scholarships or external funding). The current educational climate rewards all of these tendencies. The researchers found that such students were more likely to believe that grades should be assigned in exchange for tuition. In this scenario, grades and credentials are equated with currency: students are paid in points (Cleminshaw, 2019) in return for educational goods (assignments) and services (participation). When grades are akin to currency (Beatty, 2017), I argue that it becomes more acceptable to pay for them; for example, students who believe they are owed a certain grade because they have paid for it are more likely to exchange other currencies (money) for goods (ghost-written papers) and services (impersonation during an exam). This transactional model is exacerbated by both supply and demand for academically dishonest practices in general and contract cheating in particular. Contract cheating refers to the practice of students engaging in a transaction to have their schoolwork completed by a third party (Lancaster & Clarke, 2008). This typically involves the exchange of money, but can also include bartering.

Supply and Demand

As described earlier in this chapter, as more jobs require post-secondary education, the number of Canadians with university degrees has steadily increased over the last decades (Statistics Canada, 2017), and students are opting to enrol in more professional and career-focussed programs such as Business (Usher, 2020). One side effect of this is that, rather than a quest for knowledge, university has become a quest for a credential and an obstacle to be overcome. Students recognize this; they pay fees that have increased at rates that outstrip inflation (Usher, 2020) only to be stuffed together in huge theatre style classrooms and large online classes. They know they are being short changed and feel disenfranchised from universities; research has demonstrated that student dissatisfaction with their learning environment is a factor in contract cheating (Bretag et al., 2018).

Contract Instructors and Students

Meanwhile, increasing reliance on sessional labour in academia is a global phenomenon that is also occurring in Canada (Shaker & Pasma, 2018); these are also called contract or adjunct instructors, who teach under semesterly contracts. Although some sessional instructors in fields like law or medicine may be well-employed professionals, the vast majority of sessionals patch together small contracts to put food on their tables or pay off their student loans. They have no guarantee of continued employment beyond their contract and often receive meagre pay and no benefits. Although wages vary, $5000 CAD is not unusual, although $6000–7000 is more typical, depending on the institution and the instructor's place on the pay scale (Canadian Association of University Teachers, 2017), meaning that even with a full teaching load many sessionals live in poverty. In a national survey, sessional instructors rank job security is the most important concern followed closely by pay; over half of respondents reported that their ability to make long term plans to buy a home or have children has been negatively impacted by their job precarity (Foster & Birdsell Bauer, 2018).

Sessionals' precarious employment is compounded by the transactional nature of education and student disenfranchisement discussed earlier in this chapter. Threads on *Reddit* and online platforms for rating instructors commonly refer to how easy a course is, directing and encouraging students to choose courses based on the likelihood of getting a high mark for little work. They can review individual instructors on websites like *Rate My Professor*, much like they would review a pair of shoes they bought or meal they had. Likewise, institutional student evaluations, which are known to be flawed (Boring et al., 2016), are used as indicators of teaching efficacy and can impact a sessional instructor's chance of being rehired, although at least one Canadian institution has prohibited the use of student evaluations as factors influencing hiring and tenure (Farr, 2018). This system sets the stage for a consumer-oriented approach to education, where the customer is always right, even when they are doing wrong. When it comes to academic integrity, research has shown that sessional instructors tend to underestimate the scope of misconduct (Hudd et al., 2009) and are less likely to report infractions (Blau et al., 2018). It is possible that one reason for this reluctance to report is the precarious nature of their employment (Eaton, 2020c).

In fact, although sessional instructors are less likely to report academic misconduct, they are more likely to encounter it. It is sessionals who most often teach courses such as general writing and communications courses (Childress, 2019) that are taken by the majority of students across disciplines. These courses are typically large and often online, and the "large and growing workloads of many academics" is suggested by Walker & Townley (2012, p. 36) as causal factor in contract cheating. I recently taught a writing course that is taken by over 2000 students annually, in cohorts of 60 students. With no teaching assistants, the marking itself was punishing, but add to this communicating with students, preparing materials, and creating assignments, and instructors are left facing a choice "to a. teach for an embarrassingly small hourly rate, b. try to make their teaching something simpler and less time intensive, or c. not teach at all" (Childress, 2019, p. 277). Although there are many recommendations to prevent contract cheating and other forms of academic misconduct, such as changing assignments, alternative assessments, and individual tasks, they are often impractical given current workloads or curricular requirements. The COVID-19 pandemic and the subsequent transition to distance learning has exacerbated this.

The task of effectively teaching and assessing such large numbers of students is an almost impossible one without teaching assistance. Students may rightly feel unsupported and unheard. How can they all get individual attention and assistance when their instructor is over-extended? Certainly, there are proactive students that keep up with the materials and seek assistance of their own volition. But what happens to the students that cannot flag their struggles or articulate their needs to their instructor? With such large classes, especially in remote environments, it is not possible for instructors to know every individual student's writing style and to engage in the individual communication that is necessary to flagging many student issues. It is no surprise that private companies have stepped in to fill the vacuum of faculty and institutional support and mentorship by offering contract cheating services.

Students and Contract Cheating

In response to what Kaktiņš (2018, p. 272) refers to as the "fractured set of academic norms that have arisen in response to the new academic environment," students are often targeted by savvy companies. Advertisements for ghost-written papers and commissioned assignments are commonplace on campus bulletin boards and social media sites like Reddit and Instagram. Many contract cheating companies market to international students in other languages (Kaktiņš, 2018; Eaton & Dressler, 2019) and use deceitful techniques such as blackmail or extortion to threaten students who have purchased work (Sutherland-Smith & Dullagan, 2019). Recent large-scale research out of Swansea (Newton, 2018), demonstrated not only that contract cheating has increased rapidly in recent years, but also that as many as one in seven (or a mind-boggling 31 million students globally) have purchased assignments.

Besides purchasing assignments, students often use both formal and informal file sharing sites to share assignments and documents with other students. Like contract cheating, business is booming: Chegg is valued at over 12 billion US dollars, and its valuation increased threefold during the COVID-19 pandemic (Adams, 2021). Coursehero.com was worth over one billion dollars prior to the pandemic (Schubarth, 2020). This site purports to eschew plagiarism and academic misconduct (Course Hero, 2021) while supporting students, and the company has worked hard to create a brand that appears legitimate, even sponsoring educational events for faculty members (Course Hero, 2020). In reality, the company pays students to share their notes, assignments, and class files. Students can be paid with currency, or upload documents in return for access to other documents. Other, less formal ways of sharing assignments are also commonplace, with students sharing materials (i.e., lab reports, previous assignments, exam questions) within learning platforms that encourage collaboration and ePortfolios (Bollinger & Shepherd, 2010). In some cases, faculty encourage the sharing of previous materials such as exams or student collaboration on assignments, but much of what is uploaded onto file-sharing websites is done without instructor permission or knowledge and is used with the intention to misattribute work (Rogerson & Basanta, 2016). I believe that the lack of transparency and consistency among classes contributes to confusion about file sharing and file sharing companies capitalize on this opaqueness.

Contract Instructors and Contract Cheating

The services outlined above are borne of both supply and demand. It is relatively easy for an organization to compile a database of assignments by working with file sharing sites. Likewise, as graduate degree holders increase (Wall et al., 2018) and stable academic jobs decline (Kezar, 2013), those on the margins of academia, such as sessional instructors, are faced with precarious employment and often supplement income in what Kezar et al. (2019) refer to as the "gig academy." The precarity and scarcity of academic employment is expected to persist in Canada; Alberta's Occupational Outlook (Labour and Immigration, Government of Alberta, 2019) predicts a consistent and large surplus of job seekers compared to job openings for university professors and lecturers, with 874 fewer jobs than seekers predicted by 2028 in Alberta; for reference, the imbalance is 277 for 2020; these predictions were published in 2019 prior to the COVID-19 pandemic, and it is not clear how or if the pandemic will impact these forecasts. These academic job seekers are well-positioned to meet the demand for ghost-written papers (Sivasubramaniam et al., 2016). Much lower cost ghost writing is done overseas, particularly in Kenya, but former academics or unemployed academics have also been shown to produce commissioned assignments (Lancaster, 2019). Little research exists about this phenomenon because it is such a well-guarded industry (Lancaster, 2019).

One of the largest contract-cheating websites is exemplary of the issues discussed in this chapter; it is also the one implicated in the recent story that leaked wherein a ghost-writer's profile name and educational history shared many similarities with Alberta's minister of Advanced Education, Demetrios Nicolaides (Siever, 2020), although it is extremely unlikely he was actually the profile owner (Eaton, 2020b). This website's main commodities are custom essays written by "current and former academics… spit out or spit on by the system, [who] have become virtual mercenaries." (Unemployedprofessors.com, 2021b).

The FAQ section of this website further states that it is not illegal because the essay has been purchased and copyright transferred, so the customer can do whatever they want with it, and "that's the beauty of capitalism, baby!" Further down the page, the FAQ admits that it's "incredibly" unethical to purchase papers, but it is justified "because the academic system is already so corrupt" (Unemployed Professors, 2021a). As of February, 2021, this company claims to have completed 133,461 projects. I was a long-time sessional instructor with patchy employment and have also had targeted ads for this company pop up in my social media feeds.

This perfect storm of academic dishonesty is disheartening for those of us that value education and the creation of knowledge. Academia today has created a breeding ground for this situation—students who need university credentials for job opportunities but see the process of getting them as an obstacle to overcome, instructors that are overwhelmed and unable to give students the support and feedback necessary to facilitate deep learning, and an extremely competitive job market where graduate degree holders and those with academic writing skills find themselves unable to earn a living wage through traditional academic employment. So, what can be done, and how do we move forward? The next section outlines challenges and opportunities.

What to Do?

Although many institutions have responded with well-articulated policies and procedures, when entrenched in a system that incentivises and facilitates dishonest practices and situates academic integrity as an individual and moral issue, they are not lasting solutions to chronic problems. Similarly, in medicine, painkillers can make symptoms more bearable, but do little to treat the cause of an illness. Only by identifying and addressing the underlying factors that give rise to the symptoms will a truly effective treatment be possible.

Many go-to responses like workshops, punishments, and policy updates dull the pain of the academic integrity crisis but may also obscure or even exacerbate problems. For example, students may find themselves looking to policies, workshop information, or technological innovations like text matching software for loopholes or ways to hide dishonest practices. Instead, detailed and realistic policies, sound pedagogy, and educational opportunities for campus community members need to be seen for what they are: ways to enhance treatment and improve outcomes, but only when used thoughtfully and in conjunction with other more lasting measures. Otherwise, they are little more than palliative approaches. The following paragraphs outline areas in which changes need to take place in funding, grading, credentialing, and hiring. These are not easy solutions and they all entail a widespread and fundamental shift in approaches to higher education.

Discrete measurements like GPAs or letter grades are known to be ineffective for providing feedback that encourages learning. Students often look at the grade assigned for information about their work rather than instructor feedback about their work. Studies show (Harrison et al., 2015) that when grades are not included in the feedback, students are more likely to take it up. Grades motivate learners to meet a goal rather than benefit from the process of striving for that goal. One approach is to deemphasize grades or implement "ungrading" (Blum, 2020) to allow students and instructors the space to focus on improvement and learning rather than assigning grades. Grades are entrenched in the educational system, but instructors, administrators, and learners would be wise to question their wholesale value.

Similarly, funding models that look towards discrete measures like graduation and earnings should also be pushed back on. During a time when provincial governments in Canada build a system that favours private education and fosters a system where the privileged pay for credentials in order to maintain their privilege—those without the ability to pay will not have the opportunity to receive an education. Those of us that recognize the value of education as an opportunity to construct knowledge need to be vocal in our protests against models that reduce the value of education to a dollar figure.

Credential inflation also needs to be addressed. In many cases, university education is not necessary. Colleges and technical schools are better positioned to meet the needs of those who are looking for vocational programs. At the same time, colleges should focus on their mandate to provide students with career-track education or an alternative path to university. There has been a recent push in Ontario (Davidson & Ruparell, 2020) toward colleges granting degrees, while universities may find themselves offering career-track programs to placate funders and secure industry donors, both likely in a bid to compete for limited funds. In the same vein, employers need to recognize that a bachelor's degree is not a proxy for a better employee in many professions and should use other metrics when hiring.

Finally, the hiring practices in academia need to be addressed. It is unfair to those with advanced degrees to be treated as second class citizens, toiling away long hours in precarious, poorly remunerated work. It is unjust for sessional instructors who often find themselves with heavier workloads than their tenure track colleagues, while earning half (or less) their wages. To a lesser extent, it is unjust to teaching faculty who are officially hired to focus on instruction, while in practice are expected to engage in research and secure funding, all while teaching a heavier course load and earning a lower salary than their academic track counterparts. Sessionals in particular are often assigned large classes with heavy marking loads. A fairer redistribution of workloads and more equitable remuneration are crucial to addressing academic misconduct. Childress (2019), in his critique of contract employment in American academia, puts forth principles for post-secondary institutions and notes that a worthy institution ought to "foster and to respect its web of relationships. It is a culture shaped and steered by its faculty. It places everyone into a place of continual learning. It asks for regular public demonstration of that learning" he goes on to note that such an environment "would make contingency unthinkable" (p. 154).

I believe that in largely abandoning traditional grading and assessment practices, pushing back on metric-based funding models, reconsidering hiring practices and requisite credentials in industry, and making equitable hiring practices of faculty, academic dishonesty would also be unthinkable in the vast majority of cases. I recognize that these suggestions will be seen as unrealistic by administrators, but they are necessary if the academic integrity problems post-secondary institutions currently face are to be adequately addressed. Surely this would lead to decreased enrollment and revenue, but it would also lead to smaller classes, better pedagogy, knowledge creation, and it would allow universities to truly enact their value and mission statements.

The COVID-19 pandemic has demonstrated the vulnerabilities of the current higher education environment. As classes have moved online, the burden of responsive pedagogy has been revealed. When it was mostly sessionals teaching large online classes without teaching assistance, these concerns fell on deaf ears. Now that many tenure track faculty without fear of keeping their jobs find themselves teaching these classes, they are more able to speak out against the problems in the system. Likewise, students find themselves upset at paying the same tuition while purportedly receiving fewer benefits (Anthistle, 2020); however, academically speaking, little has changed. What students are not benefitting from in the time of the pandemic are the extracurriculars that have become part and parcel of university study. Only time will tell what the long-term impacts of the pandemic will be on higher education, but it has provided a good litmus test of problems that permeate the system.

It is clear that there are no easy solutions. Academic misconduct cannot be willed, punished, or defined away. It is borne of an academic environment steeped in neoliberal policies and funded by those with non-academic interests. It is unrealistic to expect that anything other than a sea change will have a lasting impact on academic integrity. All of us with a vested interest in ethical, just, and intelligent communities in academia and beyond need to recognize and take action against the toxic environment that perpetuates layers of unethical behaviour. It is my hope that the fissures in academia that the pandemic has revealed will catalyze a fundamental restructuring of academia where academic integrity will be the norm.

References

Adams, S. (2021). This $12 billion dollar company is getting rich off students cheating their way through Covid. *Forbes Magazine*. https://www.forbes.com/sites/susanadams/2021/01/28/this-12-billion-company-is-getting-rich-off-students-cheating-their-way-through-covid/?sh=6e5d6279363f

Anderson, D. (2020). Alberta post secondary funding will be tied to performance. *CBC News*. https://www.cbc.ca/news/canada/calgary/alberta-post-secondary-performance-funding-1.5433433

Anthistle, M. (2020). Coronavirus: Ontario students frustrated by full tuition fees for online classes. *Global News*. https://globalnews.ca/news/7298255/coronavirus-ontario-post-secondary-tuition-fees/

Bains, M. (2019). Woman allegedly paid to take exam arrested at SFU. *CBC News*. https://www.cbc.ca/news/canada/british-columbia/burnaby-rcmp-investigate-after-sfu-catches-alleged-paid-test-taker-1.5400400

Beatty, J. E. (2017). Grades as money and the role of the market metaphor in management education. *Academy of Management Learning & Education, 3*(2), 187–196.

Blau, G., Szewczuk, R., Fitzgerald, J., Paris, D. A., & Guglielmo, M. (2018). Comparing business school faculty classification for perceptions of student cheating. *Journal of Academic Ethics, 16*(4), 301–315. https://doi.org/10.1007/s10805-018-9315-4

Blum, S. D. (Ed.). (2020). *Ungrading: Why rating students undermines learning (and what to do instead)*. Morgantown, WV: West Virginia University Press.

Bolliger, D. U., & Shepherd, C. E. (2010). Student perceptions of ePortfolio integration in online courses. *Distance Education, 31*(3), 295–314.

Boring, A., Ottoboni, K., & Stark, P. (2016). Student evaluations of teaching (mostly) do not measure teaching effectiveness. *Science Open Research*. Retrieved from https://www.scienceopen.com/document_file/25ff22be-8a1b-4c97-9d88-084c8d98187a/ScienceOpen/3507_XE6680747344554310733.pdf

Bretag, T., Harper, R., Burton, M., Ellis, C., Newton, P., van Haeringen, K., Saddiqui, S., & Rozenbuerg, R. (2018). Contract cheating and assessment design: Exploring the relationship. *Assessment & Evaluation in Higher Education, 44*(5), 676–691. https://doi.org/10.1080/02602938.2018.1527892

Bunce, L., Baird, A., & Jones, S. E. (2017). The student-as-consumer approach in higher education and its effects on academic performance. *Studies in Higher Education, 42*(11), 1958–1978.

Callahan, D. (2004). *The cheating culture: Why more Americans are doing wrong to get ahead*. New York: Harcourt Inc.

Canadian Association of University Teachers. (2017). *CAUT Facts & Figures*. https://www.caut.ca/docs/default-source/Mailings-2017/caut---facts-and-figures-(2017-01).pdf?sfvrsn=0

Childress, H. (2019). *The adjunct underclass: How America's colleges betrayed their faculty, their students, and their mission*. Chicago: University of Chicago Press.

Christensen Hughes, J. M., & McCabe, D. L. (2006a). Academic misconduct within higher education in Canada. *The Canadian Journal of Higher Education, 36*(2), 1–21. http://journals.sfu.ca/cjhe/index.php/cjhe/article/view/183537/183482

Christensen Hughes, J. M., & McCabe, D. L. (2006b). Understanding academic misconduct. *Canadian Journal of Higher Education, 36*(1), 49–63. https://journals.sfu.ca/cjhe/index.php/cjhe/article/view/183525

Cleminshaw, A. (2019). Grades as currency or how many points is that worth? *Redesigning High School*. https://redesigningschool.org/grades-as-currency-or-how-many-points-is-that-worth/

Crawley, M. (2019). How the Ford government will decide on university, college funding. *CBC News*. https://www.cbc.ca/news/canada/toronto/ontario-doug-ford-university-college-post-secondary-grants-1.5121844

Davidson, M. & Ruparell, S. (2020). The future of Ontario's workers. *Strategycorp Institute of Public Policy and Economy*. https://strategycorp.com/wp-content/uploads/2020/06/Colleges-Ontario-The-Future-of-Ontarios-Workers-White-Paper-June-2020.pdf

Eaton, S. E. (2020a). *An inquiry into major academic integrity violations in Canada: 2010–2019.* Calgary, AB: University of Calgary. http://hdl.handle.net/1880/111483

Eaton, S. E. (2020b). *The intersection of contract academic work and contract cheating: Policy brief*. Calgary, Canada: University of Calgary. http://hdl.handle.net/1880/112662

Eaton, S.E. (2020c). *Is the Hon. Demetrios Nicolaides, Alberta Minister of Advanced Education involved with contract cheating? Teaching, learning and leadership: A blog for educators, researchers and other thinkers.* https://drsaraheaton.wordpress.com/2020/08/15/is-the-hon-demetrios-nicolaides-alberta-minister-of-advanced-education-involved-with-contract-cheating/

Eaton, S.E. & Dressler, R. (2019). Multilingual essay mills: Implications for second language teaching and learning. *Notos, 14*(2), 3–14. http://hdl.handle.net/1880/110695

Farr, M. (2018). Arbitration decisions on student evaluations of teaching applauded by faculty. *University Affairs.* https://www.universityaffairs.ca/news/news-article/arbitration-decision-on-student-evaluations-of-teaching-applauded-by-faculty/

Foster, K. & Birdsell Bauer, L. (2018). Out of the shadows: Experiences of contract academic staff. *Canadian Association of University Teachers.* https://www.caut.ca/sites/default/files/cas_report.pdf

Friesen, J. (2020). Ontario shelves plan for performance-based postsecondary funding, while Alberta pushes ahead. *The Globe and Mail.* https://www.theglobeandmail.com/canada/article-ontario-shelves-plan-for-performance-based-postsecondary-funding/

Fuller, J. B., & Raman, M. (2017). Dismissed by degrees: How degree inflation is undermining US competitiveness and hurting America's middle class. *Published by Accenture, Grads of Life, Harvard Business School.*

Graham-Harrison, E. (2020). How fake award for a tycoon left oxford university open to Chinese influence. *The Guardian.* https://www.theguardian.com/education/2020/aug/16/how-fake-award-for-a-tycoon-left-oxford-university-open-to-chinese-influence

Graveland, B. (2018). Judge upholds university's right to rescind master's degree over plagiarism. *The Canadian Press.* https://nationalpost.com/pmn/news-pmn/canada-news-pmn/judge-upholds-universitys-right-to-rescind-masters-degree-over-plagiarism

Hanson, V.D. (2014). The death of the humanities. *Hoover Institution.* https://www.hoover.org/research/death-humanities

Harrison, C. J., Könings, K. D., Schuwirth, L., Wass, V., & van der Vleuten, C. (2015). Barriers to the uptake and use of feedback in the context of summative assessment. *Advances in Health Sciences Education, 20*(1), 229–245.

Course Hero. (2020). Course Hero Virtual Education Summit '20. *Course Hero.* Retrieved February 21, 2021, from https://events.coursehero.com/education-summit/home

Course Hero. (2021). Academic integrity policies. *Course Hero.* Retrieved February 21, 2021, from https://www.coursehero.com/academic-integrity-policies/

Hudd, S., Apgar, C., Bronson, E. F., & Gravois Lee, R. (2009). Creating a campus culture of integrity: Comparing the perspectives of full- and part-time faculty. *The Journal of Higher Education, 80*(2), 146–177. https://doi.org/10.1353/jhe.0.0039

Kaktiņš, L. (2018). Contract cheating advertisements: What they tell us about international students' attitudes to academic integrity. *Ethics and Education, 13*(2), 268–284.

Kezar, A. (2013). Examining non-tenure track faculty perceptions of how departmental policies and practices shape their performance and ability to create student learning at four-year institutions. *Research in Higher Education, 54*(5), 571–598. https://doi.org/10.1007/s11162-013-9288-5

Kezar, A., DePaola, T., & Scott, D. T. (2019). *The gig academy: Mapping labor in the neoliberal university.*. Baltimore, U.S: Johns Hopkins University Press.

Lancaster, T. (2019). Profiling the international academic ghost writers who are providing low-cost essays and assignments for the contract cheating industry. *Journal of Information, Communication and Ethics in Society, 17*(1), 72–86. https://doi.org/10.1108/JICES-04-2018-0040

Lancaster, T., & Clarke, R. (2008). The phenomena of contract cheating. In *Student plagiarism in an online world: Problems and solutions* (pp. 144–159). Pennsylvania, U.S: IGI Global.

Labour and Immigration, Government of Alberta. (2019). *Alberta's occupational outlook 2019–2028.* https://open.alberta.ca/dataset/8987e228-9ffa-4a2e-9f79-a9b869df2ccb/resource/502659ff-47fb-4ce3-94db-6a0c2f1f722c/download/lbr-albertas-occupational-outlook-2019-2028.pdf

Leo, G. (2017). U of R engineering profs warned about teaching assistants taking bribes to increase grades. *CBC News.* https://www.cbc.ca/news/canada/saskatchewan/unviersity-of-regina-engineering-teaching-assistants-1.4369110

Levidow, L. (2007). Marketizing higher education: Neoliberal strategies and counter-strategies. In E. Wayne Ross & R. Gibson (Eds) *Neoliberalism and Educational Reform* (pp. 237–256). New York: Hampton Press Inc.

McGill University. (2020). *McGill University mission statement and principles.* https://www.mcgill.ca/secretariat/mission#:~:text=McGill%20University%20Mission%20Statement%20and%20Principles.%20MISSION.%20The,international%20standards%2C%20and%20by%20providing%20service%20to%20society

Millar, E. (2008). BC's cuts to universities, colleges much more than reported. *MacLean's.* https://www.macleans.ca/education/uniandcollege/campbell-govs-cuts-to-unis-colleges-much-more-than-reported/

National Center for Educational Statistics. (2019). Fast facts: Most popular majors. *NCES.* https://nces.ed.gov/fastfacts/display.asp?id=37

CBC News. (2020). David Sidoo stripped of order of B.C. over college admissions scandal. *CBC News.* https://www.cbc.ca/news/canada/british-columbia/david-sidoo-order-bc-college-admissions-scandal-1.5610450

Newton, P. M. (2018). How common is commercial contract cheating in higher education and is it increasing? A Systematic Review. *Frontiers in Education, 3*, 67. https://doi.org/10.3389/feduc.2018.00067

Rogerson, A. M., & Basanta, G. (2016). Peer-to-peer file sharing and academic integrity in the internet age. In *Handbook of academic integrity* (pp. 273–285).

Schubarth, C. (2020). The funded: Silicon Valley's newest unicorn flew in under the radar. *Silicon Valley Business Insider.* https://www.bizjournals.com/sanjose/news/2020/02/12/the-funded-silicon-valleys-newest-unicorn-flew-in.html

Shaker, C. & Pasma, E. (2018). Contract U: Contract faculty appointments at Canadian universities. *Canadian Centre for Policy Alternatives.* https://www.policyalternatives.ca/publications/reports/contract-u

Siever, K. (2020). Anyone know if this is the same Demetrios Nicolaides as @demetriosnAB? How many people with PhD's can there be with that name. Apparently, an MLA salary must not be enough if you have to write essays on the side for people. Weird. #ableg #abpoli https://unemployedprofessors.com/ProfessorProfile.aspx?ID=963 [Tweet]. Twitter. https://twitter.com/kim_siever/status/1294393014333259776

Sivasubramaniam, S., Kostelidou, K., & Ramachandran, S. (2016). A close encounter with ghost-writers: An initial exploration study on background, strategies and attitudes of independent essay providers. *International Journal for Educational Integrity, 12*(1), 1. https://doi.org/10.1007/s40979-016-0007-9

Statistics Canada. (2017). *Education in Canada: Key results from the 2016 census.* https://www150.statcan.gc.ca/n1/daily-quotidien/171129/dq171129a-eng.htm

Sutherland-Smith, W., & Dullaghan, K. (2019). You don't always get what you pay for: User experiences of engaging with contract cheating sites. *Assessment & Evaluation in Higher Education, 44*(8), 1148–1162.

Financial Times. (2019). Global MBA Rankings, 2019. *Business Education.* http://rankings.ft.com/businessschoolrankings/global-mba-ranking-2019

Trump, M. (2020). *Too much and never enough: How my family created the world's most dangerous man.* United States: Simon & Schuster.

Unemployedprofessors.com (2021a). *About Us.* Retrieved February 21, 2021, from https://unemployedprofessors.com/AboutUs.aspx

Unemployedprofessors.com. (2021b). *FAQ*. Retrieved February 21, 2021, from https://unemployedprofessors.com/Faq.aspx

University of Calgary. (2019). *Eyes High Strategy 2017–2022*. https://www.ucalgary.ca/live-d7-ucalgary-site/sites/default/files/ucgy/groups/Marketing/17-UNV-016-Eyes%20High%20strategy%20document-digital-FINAL.pdf

Usher, A., (2020). *The state of postsecondary education in Canada, 2020*. Toronto: Higher Education Strategy Associates. https://higheredstrategy.com/the-state-of-postsecondary-education-in-canada-2/

Walker, M., & Townley, C. (2012). Contract cheating: A new challenge for academic honesty? *Journal of Academic Ethics, 10*(1), 27–44. https://doi.org/10.1007/s10805-012-9150-y.

Wall, K., Zhao, J., Ferguson, S-J., & Rodriguez, C. (2018). Results from the 2016 Census: Is field of study a factor in the payoff of a graduate degree? *Insights on Canadian Society*. https://www150.statcan.gc.ca/n1/pub/75-006-x/2018001/article/54978-eng.htm

Weingarten, H.P., Hicks, M., Kaufman, A., Chatoor, K., MacKay, E. & Pichette, J. (2019). *Postsecondary education metrics for the 21st century*. Toronto: Higher Education Quality Council of Ontario. http://www.heqco.ca/SiteCollectionDocuments/Formatted%20Metrics%20for%20the%2021st%20Century_FINAL.pdf

Westheimer, J. (2018). Fatal distraction: Audit culture and accountability in the corporate university. In M. Spooner & J. McNinch (Eds.), *Dissident knowledge in higher education* (pp. 217–234). University of Regina Press.

York University. (2020). Mission and vision.*York University*. https://www.yorku.ca/about/mission-and-vision/

Dr. Katherine (Katie) Crossman earned her Ph.D. in Teaching English as a Second Language from the University of Calgary in 2014. She has lived and worked in Canada, Mexico, and Russia. Katie has taught language and education courses at the post-secondary level for over a decade and works as an instructor with a focus on academic research at Bow Valley College. Her research interests centre around language and settlement.

Part III
Integrity Within Specific Learning Environments and Professional Programs

Chapter 12
Academic Integrity in Work-Integrated Learning (WIL) Settings

Jennifer B. Miron

Abstract This chapter highlights the imperative for attention to, and action in, the promotion of academic integrity in work-integrated learning (WIL) settings across post-secondary programs. The importance of such efforts are closely tied to the efforts of strengthening ethical comportment with graduates who will go on to contribute to client care, client service, leadership, and research that will directly impact members of the public, hiring organizations, and global systems. WIL settings provide invaluable opportunities for students to learn essential skills and acculturate to professional ethical values through real world experiences. The experiential learning that happens in these settings helps influence the professionalization of students, encouraging safe, ethical practice that benefits those receiving care/service, future employers, and society. Since WIL is offered in both college and university settings and occurs across a number of professional and service programs, it has the potential to significantly influence a vast and varied number of professionals entering numerous career paths around the world. All members of learning communities in post-secondary organizations have a responsibility to understand their roles and opportunities in supporting, maintaining, and promoting academic integrity across WIL settings. While the narrative for the chapter is Canadian, the observations and recommendations may be relevant in other countries, where WIL plays a significant role in the education and development of professionals and service providers across a number of professions and trades.

Keywords Work-integrated learning · WIL · Academic integrity · Canadian · Ethics

J. B. Miron (✉)
Humber College, ITAL, Etobicoke, Canada
e-mail: Jennie.Miron@humber.ca

S. E. Eaton and J. Christensen Hughes (eds.), *Academic Integrity in Canada*, Ethics and Integrity in Educational Contexts 1,
https://doi.org/10.1007/978-3-030-83255-1_12

Introduction

The pandemic of 2020 challenged the world to rethink set approaches to public health and safety around the world. The ensuing chaos from CoVID-19 required rapid, appropriate responses from a number of different sectors. In Canada, higher education responded with an abrupt pivot to the delivery of online teaching and learning. Ensuring continued quality education and research experiences, combined with the pressing need to ensure the health and safety of all community members was a daunting task. One aspect of higher education that was particularly affected was student experiences based on work-integrated learning (WIL). In this chapter, WIL is discussed along with the various roles and opportunities we have to promote academic integrity within WIL settings. The relevance for promoting academic integrity within these settings is grounded in the need to support the development of ethical graduates who will be expected to practice in professional and service industries with integrity, and the opportunities we have as educators and leaders in post-secondary organizations to positively influence the ethical development of our graduates. In fact, all those in post-secondary organizations can and should play a central role in shaping students' sound ethical judgment and decision making skills when faced with real-world challenges (Christensen Hughes & Bertram Gallant, 2016).

Canadian Post-secondary

Currently, colleges and universities are two primary locations for post-secondary education in Canada. Universities have long histories associated with higher education and research. Younger college organizations offer a variety of educational experiences including certificate and diploma programs with the focus on vocational and trades programs. Some community colleges have continued to evolve into institutes of advanced technology and learning and polytechnic schools. These polytechnic schools are now able to provide additional programming at degree levels. While differences between universities and colleges remain in terms of mission, function, and foci, developing cultures of academic integrity and providing quality educational offerings are aspirations to both. Additionally, whether at university or college, learning can occur within multiple settings. Such settings include bricks-and-mortar classrooms, online, labs, libraries, study groups, tutorials, simulated sessions, apprenticeships, and work-integrated locations in external organizations. Many educational programs of study have required WIL experiences that support experiential learning within the professions such as like medicine, nursing, engineering, education, pharmacy, journalism, computer sciences, and various trades. Work-integrated settings provide invaluable opportunities for students to learn essential skills, develop professional identities, and acculturate to professional ethical values. The experiential learning that happens in these settings helps influence the acculturation of students to safe, ethical practice that benefits those receiving care/service, future employers, and society. It also situates our learners to be successful contributing members of their professional and vocational ethical communities.

Work-Integrated Learning (WIL)

As discussed, WIL in professional and service settings, vis a vis internships, field-placements, precepted partnerships, or other work-study placements, provide opportunities for experiential learning and the chance for learners to translate their theoretical knowledge to the work setting and develop transferable skills. Such knowledge translation happens through experience and reflections on past learning: "the field placement or work/study program is an empowering experience that allows them to capitalize on their practical strengths while testing the application of ideas discussed in the classroom" (Kolb, 2015, p. 5). These types of learning experiences are considered essential across many professional and service programs and are scaffolded as the student progresses in their learning and development.

WIL bridges theory to practical experience blending necessary knowledge with opportunities for specialized learning. Praxis, or the practical application of knowledge in practice and service settings, provide learners the opportunity to gain practice and work experience as they transition into the workforce (Valencia-Forrester, 2020). WIL is an appealing component of the educational journey for industry partners who welcome opportunities to build strong, stable, effective human capital (Smith et al., 2019). Of course, one of the main end goals for such learning includes assimilation of students to the ethical practice, and the assurance of safe care for clients. Such an approach to client care has benefits to future employers and is good for society at large. The importance of these learning experiences is irrefutable when you consider how our graduates go on to "undertake important roles in society: engineers, health professionals, lawyers etc. …higher education providers determine whether their students have achieved the learning required for those roles" (Newton, 2018, p. 1).

Academic Integrity in Work Integrated Learning Settings

Existing research suggests that academic dishonesty is indeed a problem within Canadian higher education (Christensen Hughes & McCabe, 2006; Eaton & Edino, 2018; Jurdi et al., 2011, 2012; Montuno et al., 2012). However research that examines academic integrity specifically within WIL settings is limited. Addressing this gap is of particular importance as dishonest behaviours and conduct within WIL settings can manifest in professional dishonesty and misconduct (Fida et al., 2018; Furutan, 2017; Guerrero-Dib et al., 2020; Johnstone, 2016; LaDuke, 2013; McClung & Schneider, 2018, Miron, 2016; Vandegrift et al., 2017). Much of the early literature that investigated this link, heralded from the business, engineering, and nursing professions. These three professions have contributed to our foundational understanding of issues related to academic integrity and WIL and serve as the basis for the literature review that follows. It is, however, important to note that other professional programs have also been studied in this regard. The following discussion highlights persisting concerns that have been identified with breaches to academic integrity in WIL settings, and the costs for future graduates in terms of lost learning and learned unethical behaviour. This in turn can contribute to unqualified or underqualified graduates; unqualified or underqualified members in the workforce; and the delivery of unsafe or suboptimal care and service. The end result is our graduates potentially are citizens that do not contribute to their professions and society to their fullest abilities. The early literature in business, engineering, and nursing is reviewed and contrasted to the more current literature in these programs of study. The intent of these comparisons is to illustrate the persisting worries about dishonesty in WIL settings.

Business—Academic Integrity and Student Work-Integrated Learning (WIL) Experiences

Nonis and Owens Swift (2001) reported that over 10% of the undergraduate and graduate business students they surveyed ($N = 1051$) across six different campuses minimized the seriousness of academic and workplace cheating behaviours. The researchers measured self-reports of students' perceptions of specific behaviours in both academic and workplace settings. Students were asked to rate if the behaviours were definitely cheating (1) or definitely not cheating (4) across a four point Likert scale. The students were then asked to self-report their participation in each of the behaviours in the academic setting using a 5 point Likert scale that ranged from never (1) to very often (5). Students who reported that they currently worked or had worked part-time or full-time in the past 5 years, were asked to report their participation in the same behaviours in their current or former workplace setting using the same 5 point Likert scale that ranged from never (1) to very often (5). The researchers noted that students who believed dishonest acts were acceptable were more likely to engage in acts of academic dishonesty ($p < 0.05$). The frequencies of academic dishonesty were also reported as positively correlated to work dishonesty ($p < 0.005$), although it is not clear of the sub-sample size for those students who reported working. Their findings suggested students who believed dishonest acts were acceptable were more likely to engage in academic dishonesty, normalizing dishonest behaviour and its acceptability. The researchers findings also suggest that those who cheat in school are more likely to cheat in their professional jobs.

This trend continues to persist in the field of business as reported through a more recent business study conducted across two separate schools in the United States ($n = 312$) and Slovakia ($n = 208$) (Furutan, 2017). Furutan (2017, p. 120) explored business students' levels of tolerance toward academic dishonesty and the correlation to their tolerance of workplace dishonesty using an adapted survey of 18 items that measured academic dishonesty and 19 items that measured workplace dishonesty. For both student groups the results revealed that students' ratings for academic dishonesty were positively correlated to their tolerance levels for dishonest workplace practices. Additionally, Furutan reported that students who were tolerant of academic dishonesty were 12 times more likely to tolerate dishonest workplace practices, compared to the Slovak students who were 20 times more likely to report the same pattern of tolerance. Furutan did not measure students' participation in academic or workplace dishonesty and focused solely on their perceptions related to the seriousness of different acts itemized in the administered survey. Like the earlier work of Nonis and Owens Swift who suggested carry-over features to dishonesty from academics to professional work, Furutan reported findings suggest that students' perspectives and tolerance for dishonesty would carry through from their academic experiences to their professional careers.

Engineering—Academic Integrity and Student Work-Integrated Learning (WIL) Experiences

Those researching relationships between academic and work dishonesty in the field of engineering have reported similar findings. Researchers in one exploratory mixed-method study, completed with engineering students ($N = 130$) across two private American universities, hypothesized that similarities existed in students' decision-making processes about whether or not to cheat in high school and, whether or not to cheat in college, and violate workplace policies (Harding et al., 2004, p. 313). They also hypothesized that self-reports of academic dishonesty in school would be an indicator for future dishonest behaviour in college and the workplace. The researchers explored students' temptations and pressures to engage in dishonest behaviour in high school and asked students to share factors that influenced their hesitation to act on these temptations. Finally, students were asked to report their actual engagement in acts of dishonesty in high school. Almost 64% reported cheating a few times in high school, and were most likely to cheat on homework, lab reports, and tests/quizzes. In the qualitative portion of the study, students reported lack of time as the biggest pressure to cheating (23%), followed by feeling underprepared for the assessment (14%). Hesitation to act on academic, dishonest behaviours (17%) was influenced by students feeling "shame, conscience, guilt, or loss of personal respect" (Harding et al., 2004, p. 315). The researchers also noted that almost 50% of the students reported feeling tempted to take company supplies, ignore workplace quality issues (22.4%), and falsify records (31.5%). Students felt pressured to act dishonestly in the workplace if they wanted or needed something (21.8%) or if the dishonest act seemed harmless (10.3%). Almost 14% of the respondents hesitated if they feared they would be fired or get caught. Of the respondents who felt tempted to violate conduct in the workplace, 30% reported they had indeed violated workplace policies in the past. The researchers could not establish statistical significance due to the small sample size, but trends in the data revealed respondents who admitted frequent cheating in high school were more likely to report they would cheat in college (61.5%). Additionally, 63.6% of students who reported cheating in high school, reported that they had violated workplace policies. The researchers concluded that cheating in high school was in fact a strong indicator of future college and workplace dishonesty. Their study would have been strengthened had they measured the incidence of student academic dishonesty within the college setting and had a larger sample size.

Equally distressing and similar findings were reported in another study of engineering students ten years later. Sixty-one students who had been charged with academic dishonesty, participated in a study that examined if students "could relate their academic behaviors to learning and working within the engineering field" (Bertram Gallant et al., 2014, p. 278). Students completed a required reaction paper that was then analyzed by four independent reviewers for common themes. Bertram Gallant and colleagues (2014, p. 288) found that 50% of the students had a "tempered acceptance" to their dishonesty and recognized their behaviour as a mistake. An additional 16% denied their culpability with their dishonesty. The researchers suggested that students were able to normalize their dishonest behaviour and blame external forces for their conduct. Bertram Gallant et al. (2014) concluded that conduct and behaviour becomes habit and is therefore a concern as students graduate and transition to professional practice with already set behaviours. Both these studies suggest that student behaviours in the academic setting may become learned behaviours that translate to professional settings with potential catastrophic complications to the care/service of clients and serious threats to the reputation of organizations that would employ our graduates.

Readers are encouraged to read deMontigny's (2022) chapter in this book that speaks to recent accreditation changes in Canada that now require engineering programs to report on academic integrity policies and procedures. deMontigny also shares his national survey findings about the state of engineering schools and their relation to academic integrity. These two current pieces speak to the relevance of promoting academic integrity in WIL since most engineering schools include WIL as part of their educational offerings.

Nursing—Academic Integrity and Student Work-Integrated Learning Experiences

Hilbert (1985) explored dishonest nursing student behaviours between the classroom and student clinical setting ($n = 101$; 1987; $n = 210$; 1988: $n = 63$). She reported significant positive relationships between self-reported classroom dishonesty and self-reported clinical setting dishonesty in all three of her studies ($p < 0.01$:1985; $p \leq 0.002$:1985; $p = \leq 0.01$:1988). Nursing students who self-reported classroom cheating behaviours were significantly more likely to report work-integrated clinical placement cheating behaviours. Dishonest behaviours in the work-integrated learning setting were manifested with students reporting they had engaged in breaching client confidentiality (73%), and falsely reporting the administration of required medications and treatments (26%). Nursing students rationalized their behaviours as socially acceptable (Hilbert, 1987). The detrimental effects of these actions for clients are especially concerning as they could affect client morbidity and mortality.

Hilbert (1988) also explored the relationship between moral development and departures of academic honesty in both the classroom and student clinical setting. She found a statistically significant inverse relationship between Kohlberg's higher moral development stages and the number of self-reported incidents of unethical clinical behaviour ($p = 0.027$). This was different for the relationship between moral development stage and the number of self-reported acts of classroom dishonesty ($p = 0.45$; Hilbert, 1988). Hilbert concluded that there was a disconnection for students between how they interpreted dishonesty in the two different learning settings. Twenty-five years later Miller Smith's (2010) doctoral study of 167 RNs completing an online course, showed that a positive relationship existed between departures from academic integrity and professional dishonesty ($r = 0.438$, $p = < 0.001$). Miller Smith used a survey to measure self-reported incidences of academic (16 items) or professional dishonest (21 items). She found that the nurses' attitudes, sense of what was considered normal for the environment (subjective norm), and their perceived behavioural control (what they could and couldn't do) were statistically significant and influenced whether they would or would not behave dishonestly. So, if nurses had a positive attitude, subjective norm (being honest was a good thing), perceived behavioural control (they could act honestly), then they reported having engaged in fewer incidents of dishonest acts in both academic and professional settings. Perhaps one of the largest studies heralds from the United States ($n = 973$) and sought to understand nursing students' perceptions, relationships, and neutralizing behaviours with academic dishonesty (McClung & Schneider, 2018). The researchers reported that some acts of dishonesty were reported as more egregious by students in both classroom and clinical settings, suggesting that students normalized certain cheating behaviours. Sixty percent of students in the study reported engaging in five or more dishonest behaviours in the classroom (e.g., sabotage—negatively affecting another student's work, accessing test banks for answers to questions) and clinical settings (e.g., failing to follow rules, clinical guidelines, stealing, creating false client information) although they reported cheating more in the classroom than clinical setting. Dishonesty in the clinical setting is of great concern when you consider that nurses are often part of an interprofessional care team. For example, other team members rely on the accuracy of nursing assessment and charting to plan additional care. False client information or failure to follow clinical guidelines could result in disaster for the client's health and welfare.

Strategies to Promote Integrity in Work-Related Learning Settings

One purpose of higher education is the continued development of students as global citizens with moral, personal, and societal responsibilities (Chickering, 2010; Liddell & Cooper, 2012; Pasquerella, 2019). In addition to the translation of theoretical knowledge to practice, we should be presumably leveraging WIL opportunities to acculturate students to the values consistent with academic integrity and ethical, professional work. WIL experiences can offer some invaluable opportunities for students in developing their knowledge, skills, judgement, and ethical comportment (Benner et al., 2008). The costs to doing nothing in leveraging such opportunities can quite literally mean life or death for those who will ultimately receive care and service from our graduates.

Acculturating students to values consistent with academic integrity (honesty, trust, fairness, respect, responsibility, courage) (International Center for Academic Integrity [ICAI], 2021) is foundational to ethical learning in the post-secondary setting and has been described as a twenty-first century teaching and learning imperative (Bertram Gallant, 2008). Efforts to incorporate and strengthen academic integrity within WIL requires a consistent and multi-layered approach. All members of post-secondary learning communities (students, faculty/staff, organizational leaders, external stakeholders) must be fully engaged and committed to WIL settings grounded in integrity.

Smith et al. (2019) note that WIL remains a focus for universities around the world. While WIL can offer invaluable learning experiences, it is also resource intensive, multidimensional and "requires teaching, facilitation, organizational, and interpersonal expertise for successful execution" (Smith et al., 2019, p. 1). Therefore creating and providing quality WIL placements that promote and exemplify integrity can present unique and complex challenges.

A review of the existing literature did not reveal content that speaks to practical approaches in addressing the need of promoting academic integrity within WIL settings. The following ideas for actions are original and based on past teaching experience, and my doctoral studies (Miron, 2016). Additionally, Bertram Gallant and Drinan (2008) proposed an evidence and research informed four stage model of institutionalization that could offer guidance to practical efforts. While their model was first used to describe a model of change for educational organizations related to creating cultures of academic integrity, the first three components of the model are transferable to addressing the gaps in WIL. They describe a four-stage model that includes: recognition and commitment; response generation; response implementation; and institutionalization (Bertram Gallant & Drinan, 2008). They liken the model to a pendulum in that the model offers fluidity and movement within the stages (Bertram Gallant & Drinan, 2008, p. 29). The first three components of the model are used to frame original ideas that are herein presented.

An important first step is to recognize and commit to the pressing issue of institutionalizing academic integrity across WIL settings. Describing a clear sense of urgency is part of this first stage which can prove challenging since WIL opportunities will include a number of people, from a number of organizations. For example, in working on securing clinical placements for WIL with nursing students, it is necessary to negotiate with various health care agencies and organizations. The challenge lies in engaging champions across different organizations to support the effort. One initial step would be to clearly articulate the need for such an effort in preparing career ready, competent, and ethically intact graduates who will contribute to the mission and vision of hiring organizations, and opportunities to build their human capital. Describing the educational organization's vision for WIL environments anchored in integrity is a start. The vision should be established and described by members of the educational organization and include participation and feedback from students, faculty, and industry advisors. Collaboration with industry partners will help bridge the goals and outcome of WIL endeavours so that the WIL experience becomes an "intentional pedagogy that blends theoretical content with workplace practises…whereby industry and universities nurture robust partnerships which inform curriculum and ensure an authentic student experience" (Jackson et al., 2017, p. 45). Bertram Gallant and Drinan (2008, p. 31) warn that while students can play an important role in this first stage, it is perhaps more important to include faculty champions, and those in power and authority to make change happen (Bertram Gallant and Drinan, 2008, p. 31). The vision should then be clearly communicated as a core component for the educational organization to all potential external partners important to WIL placements. Communication of the established vision must be clear, consistent, readily available, and obvious. Articulating and communicating what is meant by honesty, trust, fairness, respect, responsibility, and courage in words and actions is an important start and should be evident through the vision statement (Miron, 2016).

The second and third stages of the model are described as a response generation and the implementation phase (Bertram Gallant, 2008). In response generation educational organizations would identify and generate a response to the work of describing requirements to successfully promote WIL experiences that embody academic integrity. It would be important to include members of the learning community and industry to ensure that balanced and obtainable strategies are set to secure WIL settings that emulate ethics and the values consistent with academic integrity. Such placements will provide students the opportunity to interact and immerse with ethics in the workplace while gaining valuable workplace skills and knowledge. The implementation of such work would include describing a clear direction for the educational organization with action steps to achieve concrete results. Placement officers within post-secondary organizations, or staff who hold positions focused on securing placements, should be clear about what constitutes a desirable WIL location for students so that they source and secure appropriate placements. Organizational and professional program leaders, in collaboration with faculty/staff, must identify and articulate a gold standard for work-related student locations. The gold standard should be communicated clearly to those charged with finding WIL locations, and explicit to the processes they use to secure appropriate settings. Benchmarks like specific agency accreditation standards, professional codes of ethics, missions, visions, and values of targeted work-related locations can help inform the gold standard (Miron, 2016, 2019).

There is, however, a looming reality that despite best efforts, ethical issues will continue to arise in WIL situations and challenge students in their efforts to maintain practices consistent with academic integrity. This reality is unavoidable in considering that "organizational tensions and societal forces complicate the work of students and faculty" (Bertram Gallant, 2008, p.5). Faculty-supported experiences for learners, can mitigate or support learners to navigate such challenges. For example, that learner who is encouraged to be dishonest by their staff preceptor so that they both avoid potential disciplinary action can be both frightening and confusing for a learner. Having 24 h/7 day a week access to a faculty member that has the skills to navigate such a complex ethical situation and problem solve such a situation with the student is indispensable to the learner and can transform the learning opportunity into a positive experience that will allow the learner to learn and grow in building their ethical decision making and practice confidence.

It is important for organizational leaders to recruit and retain faculty and practice advisors who ascribe to the values that align with integrity. Miron (2016, 2019) reported that students relied on faculty to support their academic integrity efforts in the workplace. Those in academic roles play an important and influential role in setting the stage, modeling the desired behaviour, and addressing practice situations that deviate from integrity. Quite simply, students learn from what they see and experience. Ongoing development with faculty related to teaching and advising students in WIL settings is important and should be intentional and responsive to practice and industry changes so that faculty are able to provide the leadership students require and desire when learning in practice locations. The skill and expertise of faculty/practice advisors will support student integrity and motivation and support deeper learning (Bertram Gallant, 2017, p. 90).

Adopting strategies and learning resources that can prepare students for their WIL experiences are important. Active learning pedagogies are reported to positively influence the acculturation of students to integrity (Bertram Gallant, 2017, p. 89). For example, using case-based simulated scenarios that allow students to navigate real life situations they may experience provides safe and skilfully guided opportunities to problem solve those situations where integrity is challenged (Gropelli, 2010; Hagerdorn Wonder, 2017; Opsahl et al., 2020; Shoeb et al., 2014). Such controlled educational offerings provide safe opportunities for students to make the necessary and meaningful connections between behaviours consistent with academic and professional integrity. In turn, these connections can help to shape students' attitudes and behaviours related to conduct consistent with integrity, as well as prepare them for those situations in practice that may challenge their integrity (Miron, 2016).

Cultivating partnerships with organizations that host our students through their work-related experiences is an opportunity educational leaders must seize. Reciprocal educational and development for host organizations in specific fields of expertise or with current professional issues can create nurturing partnerships that benefit students, educational and host organizations (Miron, 2016). Cross-appointments, guest lecturers, shared research projects, and other tangible endeavours not only recognizes the expertise within host organizations but communicates respect and a collaborative spirit that will enhance student learning experiences (Miron, 2016). As well, these cultivated relationships may provide a competitive edge to organizations that are competing for quality WIL settings.

Preparing students through workshops or seminars focused on actions for success within WIL settings, and supporting their membership as students in professional bodies, are other invaluable undertakings. Practical educative sessions that include professional communication strategies, conflict resolution skills, ethical practice, leadership skills, emotional intelligence, assertiveness, and self-advocacy skills, are content topics that could be started through a workshop or seminar and be threaded through the WIL experience in meaningful ways. Engaging and strengthening these skills with students through regular student group discussions, personal reflections, or seminars will enable students to build ethical resilience and hardiness. Encouraging students to talk about breaches they have witnessed or experienced allows deeper more thoughtful reflection and deeper more thoughtful learning (Miron, 2016). Student memberships in professional organizations can expose students to their future professional communities and opportunities to build a deeper understanding of ethical practice. Often these organizations have a strong student to student opportunities that offer meaningful connections for students to explore and compare experiences with their ethics in practice.

Finally, educational organizations need to take a strong lead in formally preparing students through curriculum that teaches ethics, specifically how to "effectively deal with ethical dilemmas and misconduct" (Christensen Hughes & Bertram Gallant, 2016, p. 1057). In fact, this ethical content should be extended to and specialized for WIL experiences where learners are going to engage in practice that may very well challenge them ethically. Exposing students to professional ethical codes of conduct in combination with ethical philosophical frameworks may support their development as robust ethical practitioners (Bertram Gallant, 2011; Christensen Hughes & Bertram Gallant, 2016). In their chapter of the *Handbook of Academic Integrity* Christensen Hughes and Bertram Gallant make a strong case on the need for ethical education and while the chapter does not focus specifically on WIL it is an easy transition to make considering the nature, location, and intent of WIL experiences.

Final Thoughts

Many of the professional courses of study across the Canadian post-secondary setting incorporate WIL. While these opportunities are invaluable for students in translating their theoretical learning to practical application, there continues to be a need to highlight the importance of acculturating students to the values of academic integrity in their practice. There is a general agreement that all approaches to the promotion of learning cultures that herald integrity must be a holistic undertaking (Bretag et al., 2014). Promoting integrity "in every aspect of the academic enterprise" (Bretag et al., 2014, p. 1153) should include WIL for those programs that include WIL as part of the educational experience. Careful articulation of what such practice would look like along with thoughtful approaches to secure hallmark WIL opportunities for students are just two aspects worthy of consideration. Properly preparing students for this type of learning, offering ongoing education and development to students throughout the WIL experience as they build and strengthen their skills, are also important. Creating and cultivating respectful, meaningful, reciprocal relationships between academics sending students, and professional workers hosting students cannot be underestimated. Offering curriculum that includes specific ethics education should be incorporated into the WIL experience. There is also a great need for continued research in the area of WIL to continue to inform our understanding approaches to these settings in an evidence based manner so that positive, ethically grounded experiences are possible. While this chapter has largely approached WIL with a Canadian lens, the strategies offered are not limited to the Canadian experience and can be adopted to the subtleties of other countries and their learning settings.

Key Chapter Points

- Academic integrity is an underexplored and discussed topic for work-integrated learning (WIL) settings.
- Business, engineering, and nursing are key professional courses of study who have contributed to what we know about student behaviours in WIL settings and later professional practice.
- Attention to promoting integrity in WIL settings influences future behaviours and the care and service they will provide members of the public.
- It is important to describe hallmark features of WIL settings, secure these placement opportunities for students, recruit, retain, and professionally develop faculty/practice advisors in integrity and practice excellence.
- Students look to academics to mentor and model integrity.
- WIL prepares students for challenges they may see to ethical practice through the teaching of ethics.
- Cultivate reciprocal relationships with leaders and practitioners in organizations that host WIL.

References

Benner, P., Sutphen, M., Leonard-Kahn, V., & Day, L. (2008). Formation and everyday ethical comportment. *American Journal of Critical Care, 17*(5), 473–477.

Bertram Gallant, T. (2017). Academic integrity as a teaching & learning issue: From theory to practice. *Theory into Practice: Theoretical Approaches to Understanding and Promoting Academic Integrity, 56*(2), 88–94. https://doi.org/10.1080/00405841.2017.1308173

Bertram Gallant, T. (2008). Academic integrity in the 21st century: A teaching and learning imperative. *Association for Higher Education Report, 33*(5), 1–144.

Bertram Gallant, T. (Ed.). (2011). *Creating the ethical academy: A systems approach to understanding misconduct and empowering change in higher education.* New York, NY: Routledge.

Bertram Gallant, T., & Drinan, P. (2008). Toward a model of academic integrity institutionalization: Informing practice in higher education. *Canadian Journal of Higher Education, 38*(2), 25–44.

Bertram Gallant, T., Van Den Einde, L., Ouellette, S., & Lee, S. (2014). A systemic analysis of cheating in an undergraduate engineering mechanics course. *Science and Engineering Ethics, 20*(1), 277–298. https://doi.org/10.1007/s11948-013-9434-6

Bretag, T., Mahmud, S., Wallace, M., Walker, R., McGowan, U., East, J., Green, M., Partridge, L., & James, C. (2014). 'Teach us how to do it properly!' An Australian academic integrity student survey. *Studies in Higher Education, 39*(7), 1150–1169. https://doi.org/10.1080/03075079.2013.777406

Chickering, A. W. (2010). A retrospective on higher education's commitment to moral and civic education. *Journal of College and Character, 11*(3), 1–6.

Christensen Hughes, J. & Bertram Gallant, T. (2016). Infusing ethics and ethical decision making into the curriculum. In T. Bretag (Ed.) *The Handbook of Academic Integrity*. (pp. 1055–1073). Springer Reference. https://doi.org/10.1007/978-981-287-098-8

Christensen Hughes, J., & McCabe, D. (2006). Academic misconduct within higher education in Canada. *Canadian Journal of Higher Education, 36*(2), 1–21.

deMontigny, D. (2022). Managing academic integrity in Canadian engineering schools. In S. E. Eaton & J. Christensen Hughes (Eds.), *Academic integrity in Canada: An enduring and essential challenge*. Springer.

Eaton, S. E., Edino, R. I., (2018). Strengthening the research agenda of educational integrity in Canada: A review of the research literature and call to action. *International Journal for Educational Integrity, 14* (1). https://doi.org/10.1007/s40979-018-0028-7

Fida, R., Tramontano, C., Paciello, M., Ghezzi, V., & Barbaranelli, C. (2018). Understanding the interplay among regulatory self-efficacy, moral disengagement, and academic cheating behaviour during vocational education: A three-wave study. *Journal of Business Ethics, 153*(3), 725–740. https://doi.org/10.1007/s10551-01633-3373-6

Furutan, O. (2017). The relationship between tolerance for scholastic dishonesty and tolerance for dishonest workplace practices among university business management students. *San Diego: American Society of Business and Behavioral Sciences, 24*(1), 217–228.

Gropelli, T. (2010). Using active simulation to enhance learning of nursing ethics. *The Journal of Continuing Education in Nursing, 41*(3), 104–105.

Guerrero-Dib, J., Portales, L., & Heredia-Escorza, Y. (2020). Impact of academic integrity on workplace ethical behaviour. *International Journal for Educational Integrity, 16*(1), 1–18. https://doi.org/10.1007/240979-020-0051-3

Hagerdorn Wonder, A. (2017). Mock hospital ethics committee: An innovative simulation to teach prelicensure nursing students the complexities of ethics in practice. *Nurse Educator, 42*(2), 77–80. https://doi.org/10.1097/NNE.0000000000000320

Harding, T., Carpenter, D., Finelli, C., & Passow, H. (2004). Does academic dishonesty relate to unethical behavior in professional practice? An exploratory study. *Science and Engineering Ethics, 10*(2), 311–324. https://doi.org/10.1007/s11948-004-0027-3

Hilbert, G. (1985). Involvement of nursing students in unethical classroom and clinical behaviors. *Journal of Professional Nursing, 1*(4), 230–234.

Hilbert, G. (1987). Academic fraud: Prevalence, practices, and reasons. *Journal of Professional Nursing, 3*(1), 39–45.

Hilbert, G. (1988). Moral development and unethical behaviour among nursing students. *Journal of Professional Nursing, 4*(3), 163–167.

International Centre for Academic Integrity [ICAI]. (2021). The fundamental values of academic Integrity (3rd Ed.). http://www.academicintegrity.org/icai/assets/FV2013.pdf

Jackson, D., Rowbottom, D. Ferns, S., & McLaren, D. (2017). Employer understanding of work-integrated learning and the challenges of engaging in work placement opportunities. *Studies in Continuing Education*, 39(1), 35–51.

Johnstone, M. (2016). Academic dishonesty and unethical behaviour in the workplace. *Australian Nursing & Midwifery Journal, 23*(11), 33.

Jurdi, R., Hage, S., & Chow, H. (2011). Academic dishonesty in the Canadian classroom: Behaviours of a sample of university students. *Canadian Journal of Higher Education, 41*(3), 1–35.

Jurdi, R., Hage, S., & Chow, H. (2012). What behaviours do students consider academically dishonest? Findings from a survey of Canadian undergraduate students. *Social Psychology of Education, 15*, 1–23. https://doi.org/10.1007/s11218-011-9166-y

LaDuke, R. (2013). Academic dishonesty today, unethical practices tomorrow? *Journal of Professional Nursing, 29*(6), 402–406.

Kolb, D. (2015). *Experiential learning: Experience as the source of learning and development* (2nd ed.). New Jersey: Pearson Education Inc.

Liddell, D., & Cooper, D. (2012). Moral development in higher education. *New Directions for Student Services, 139*, 1–12.

McClung, E., & Schneider, J. (2018). Dishonest behavior in the classroom and clinical setting: Perceptions and engagement. *The Journal of Nursing Education, 57*(2), 79–87. https://doi.org/10.3928/01484834-20180123-04

Miller Smith, C. (2010). The relationship between academic and professional dishonesty in online RNBSN students. [Unpublished doctoral dissertation]. Medical University South Carolina.

Miron, J. (2016). Academic integrity and senior nursing undergraduate clinical practice [Unpublished doctoral dissertation]. Queen's University.

Miron, J. (2019). Academic integrity in a student placement environment–An elicitation study. *Journal of Educational Thought, 52*(3), 253–273.

Montuno, E., Davidson, A., Iwasaki, K., Jones, S., Martin, J., Brooks, D., Gibson, B., & Mori, B. (2012). Academic dishonesty among physical therapy students: A descriptive study. *University of Toronto Press, 64*(3), 245–254.

Newton, P. (2018). How common is commercial contract cheating in higher education and is it increasing? A Systematic Review. *Frontiers in Education, 3*(67), 1–18. https://doi.org/10.3389/FEDUC.2018.00067

Nonis, S., & Owens Swift, C. (2001). An examination of the relationship between academic dishonesty and workplace dishonesty: A multicampus investigation. *Journal of Education for Business, 77*(2), 69–77.

Opsahl, A., Nelson, T., Madeira, J., & Hagedorn Wonder, A. (2020). Evidence-based, ethical decision-making: Using simulation to teach the application of evidence and ethics in practice. *Worldviews on Evidence-Based Nursing, 17*(6), 412–417.

Pasquerella, L. (2019). The purpose of higher education and its future. *Association of American Colleges and Universities, 105*(3–4). https://www.aacu.org/liberaleducation/2019/summer-fall/president

Shoeb, M., Logar, T., Glass, M., Harrison, J., Brock, T., James-Ryan, S., Baralas, S., & Le, P. (2014). Teaching global health ethics using simulation: Interprofessional training. *The Lancet Global Health, 2*(1), S1. https://doi.org/10.1016/S2214-109X(15)70027-6

Smith, C., Ferns, S., & Russell, L. (2019). Placement quality has a greater impact on employability than placement structure or duration. *International Journal of Work-Integrated Learning, 20*(1), 15–29.

Valencia-Forrester, F. (2020). Models of work-integrated learning in journalism education. *Journalism Studies, 21*(5), 697–712.

Vandegrift, T., Dillon, H., & Camp, L. (2017). Changing the engineering student culture with respect to academic integrity and ethics. *Science and Engineering Ethics, 23*(4), 1159–1182.

Jennifer (Jennie) B. Miron, Humber College is a full-time professor in the Bachelor of Nursing Program at Humber College—ITAL. She completed her doctoral studies in 2016 and successfully defended her thesis titled Academic integrity and senior nursing undergraduate clinical practice. Jennie is currently the Co-chair of the Faculty of Health Sciences Academic Integrity Council, Chair of the Academic Integrity Council of Ontario (AICO), and Board Member at the International Centre for Academic Integrity (ICAI). She is currently a member of the editorial board of the Canadian Perspectives on Academic Integrity. Jennie continues to research and write on the topic of academic integrity across the post-secondary sector in Canada, and is currently part of a pan national Canadian team investigating contract cheating policy across Canadian post-secondary organizations.

Chapter 13
Canadian Open Digital Distance Education Universities and Academic Integrity

Jill Hunter and Cheryl A. Kier

Abstract This chapter highlights aspects of open digital distance education universities (ODDUs) that pose particular challenges for academic integrity promotion and academic misconduct prevention. It also provides insight into how these important issues might be addressed. This topic is especially relevant in light of the global shift to online instruction, in part, as a response to the COVID-19 pandemic. Using the 4M Model as a framework, this chapter describes how the macro and micro levels of the university need to work together to promote academic integrity. We provide evidence from the literature that demonstrates that academic integrity issues and solutions are more similar than different between ODDUs and traditional, campus-based institutions of higher learning. Although the context of this book is Canada, much of our discussion applies globally because academic integrity and the move to online education is a growing, global phenomenon.

Keywords Multi-faceted approach · 4M model · Academic integrity · Canada · Higher education · COVID-19 pandemic · Online

Introduction

In this chapter, we argue that despite the unique learning environment of Canadian open digital distance universities (ODDUs), the academic integrity issues and solutions are more similar than different between such institutions and traditional campus-based institutions. In both cases, similar actions at the macro and micro levels of the institution can help promote academic integrity and reduce misconduct. We identify the unique features of ODDUs, as well as the advantages and disadvantages these features pose for ensuring academic integrity. Beyond these features, we discuss challenges for the promotion of academic integrity, some of which apply specifically to ODDUs and others that apply more generally to traditional universities. We then make recommendations for both types of institutions. Where relevant

J. Hunter · C. A. Kier (✉)
Athabasca University, Athabasca, Canada
e-mail: cherylk@athabascau.ca

S. E. Eaton and J. Christensen Hughes (eds.), *Academic Integrity in Canada*,
Ethics and Integrity in Educational Contexts 1,
https://doi.org/10.1007/978-3-030-83255-1_13

we discuss how this applies to traditional institutions that have moved to online course delivery in response to the COVID-19 pandemic. Using the 4M model of the scholarship of teaching and learning as a framework we focus on the institutional (macro) and instructor (micro) levels (Friberg, 2016) and discuss how the institution and instructors must work together to effectively foster academic integrity and reduce misconduct (Christensen Hughes & McCabe, 2006a).

Features of ODDUs and Academic Integrity: Advantages and Disadvantages

Here we identify the unique features of ODDUs that provide the lens for our exploration of academic integrity. We outline specific advantages and disadvantages of these for ensuring academic integrity. The features include open, digital, distance and asynchronous course delivery that are common to Athabasca University undergraduate courses and programs; and those offered through Thompson Rivers University undergraduate Open Learning division (TRUOL, n.d.). Other Canadian institutions that specialize in online learning such as Teluq University (n.d.) and Royal Roads University (n.d.) have only some of these features (Bates, 2018). We briefly discuss online course delivery in response to the COVID-19 pandemic. Where this shares features with ODDUs it is reasonable to surmise it, too, will share some of the advantages and disadvantages for ensuring academic integrity outlined here.

Open. According to Bates (2019), the main characteristic of an open institutions is,

> the removal of barriers to learning. This means no prior qualifications to study, no discrimination by gender, age or religion, affordability for everyone, and for students with disabilities, a determined effort to provide education in a suitable form that overcomes the disability. (p. 377)

Disadvantage. Open universities have minimal admission requirements making it more likely that students are unprepared and do not have the requisite training in proper documentation or a clear understanding of what counts as academic misconduct. This student population is therefore vulnerable to accidental plagiarism and other forms of misconduct.

Digital. Digital, electronic or online delivery refers to a specific information and communication technology (ICT) that has become common in distance education. This could include the use of online platforms and the Internet and can be delivered synchronously or asynchronously (Qayyum & Zawacki-Richter, 2018).

Advantages. Despite a strong belief by some that online courses are more vulnerable to academic misconduct, the evidence suggests this is not the case (Harris et al., 2019; Peterson, 2019). Peterson (2019) states,

> [w]hile a review of the literature reveals that students may be cheating more in on-campus classes, the belief that online classes have a higher rate of cheating remains. In spite of the results found in these studies, many still believe that cheating is easier and is occurring more

> often in the online setting. This belief can negatively impact the perceived quality of online courses and the academic reputation of an institution. (p. 29)

"[C]urrent research shows the general assumption that online courses are worse off in terms of academic value or integrity is largely unsubstantiated" (Sterling & Farr, 2018, p. 4). Moreover, Bates (2018) identifies controls such as provincial standards and a centralized course development team, with course content and online pedagogical expertise, that ensure that online courses and programs are rigorous and of high quality. Even though the digital/online feature of ODDUs per se is not a disadvantage for ensuring academic integrity, the fact that students use and access digital technologies may make it easier for students to engage in academic misconduct. We discuss this later as it applies to both ODDUs and traditional universities.

Distance. Donovan et al. (2019) provide this description of distance education: "Distance education courses are those where no classes are held on campus—all instruction is conducted at a distance" (p. 23). To facilitate distance learning, each student is assigned a tutor/instructor who has advanced degrees and teaches in their discipline. Tutors provide instruction, course content support, encouragement, and mark student work. Communication with tutors can be asynchronous or synchronous.

Disadvantage. The distance between students and professors (physical and psychological) may make cheating more tempting for online students (Peterson, 2019). Distance and limited instructor/student contact may prevent development of a strong instructor/student relationship which can result in student anonymity. Further, without a strong connection to the instructor students may feel less guilty about cheating and more tempted to engage in misconduct. Students in on campus institutions with large classes, too, may experience anonymity but the online environment without face-to-face contact may exacerbate this situation (Adzima, 2020). Instructors and students do not have the ease of in-person discussions in asynchronous classroom settings with a student cohort as do traditional universities. It is likely that distance will be an issue for institutions that have been forced to move to the online environment in response to the pandemic. Though, unlike ODDUs, if courses are delivered synchronously, they may have the advantage of increased opportunities for contact, albeit virtual, with students, which may more closely mirror in-person instructor/student contact. Further, online course development and delivery because of the pandemic appear to be decentralized and individually driven by faculty, as well as inconsistent across and within Canadian post-secondary institutions. Some instructors pre-record lectures that are offered virtually at the same time as their in-person class would have taken place. Others have created "virtual" classrooms with the help of video conferencing technologies that students attend synchronously with their class cohorts that may or may not be recorded for later access (Professor A. Levey, University of Calgary personal communication, October 26, 2020). These virtual classrooms may allow for virtual synchronous discussions. Alternatively, discussions are offered through office hours via video conferencing or email communication in which students can expect an immediate response to their questions. Many use a hybrid model that includes a combination of components that may be delivered either synchronously or asynchronously (Professors A. Schmitter and J. Welchman, University of Alberta, personal communication, October 26, 2020). For those instructors who offer course content asynchronously only, with little instructor/student contact, student isolation and anonymity may be an issue that requires a similar response to that recommended for ODDUs. The quality of teaching, and whether students respect their teachers also relates to whether students decide to cheat (Christensen Hughes & McCabe, 2006b).

Asynchronous Delivery. Course content at ODDUs is delivered through online platforms via a learning management system (LMS) such as Moodle, Blackboard, and D2L and the Internet so it can be accessed when it is convenient to students. Email communication and discussion boards connect students who do not have to be on their computers or other devices simultaneously. As previously mentioned, course development is centralized and involves a team of experts to address quality assurance and the unique nature of asynchronous, digital and distance courses and program delivery (Bates, 2018). Further, continuous enrolment over a 12-month period allows students to take courses at different times, which generally means there are no student cohorts. Courses are not scheduled for a particular time (i.e., they are unpaced). This provides learners greater flexibility to complete course work at their own speed as long as they complete the course by the course end date. In essence, students study "anywhere, anytime" (Athabasca University website, 2020; TRUOL website, 2020).

The flexibility and convenience of ODDUs for transfer credits to student home institutions can result in a high number of visiting students, those who take only one or two courses. Some learners choose courses that their home institution does not offer or, because of limited capacity, are unavailable. Others want to accelerate their degree by taking additional courses at a digital distance institution or take one course to see if they are ready for post-secondary learning (Davis, 2001). As many as one-third of learners may be visiting students (Dr. S. Houry, Office of Institutional Studies, Athabasca University, personal communication, October 13, 2020).

Advantages. In digital distance institutions with asynchronous course delivery, when there is no student cohort there may be little interaction with other students, making in-course collusion less likely. Even when contact with other students is possible, such as an in-person invigilated exam, it would be nearly impossible to physically cheat as asynchronous course delivery means that students taking the same course would be writing exams at different times (Hunter, 2016). In contrast, students in classrooms generally have more opportunities to contact peers (Hollis, 2018), and engage in collusion (Harris et al., 2019). Moreover, the move from an in-person to online environment in response to the COVID-19 pandemic, if synchronous, may provide more opportunity to engage in collusion. Much of the evidence to date that points to an increase in unauthorized collaboration and cheating in those courses that have moved online is anecdotal (Jungic et al., 2020; Panico, 2020). However, Grant MacEwan University indicates there was a 38% increase in academic misconduct cases since the start of the pandemic in March to the end of the term (Rossiter, 2020), and CBC News reported that University of Waterloo experienced a doubling of academic misconduct cases over the past year, most of which was attributed to the upheaval and stress of the pandemic (Duhatschek, 2020). Further research is needed to determine whether academic misconduct is increasing in ODDUs during the pandemic despite its lack of student cohort. Perception of what peers are doing is a strong influence for cheating (Carrell et al., 2008; McCabe & Treviño, 1993), but online undergraduate students often have little access to this information because they are working at their own pace.

In addition, students choosing to study online tend to be older, and age is negatively correlated with cheating behaviour (Harris et al., 2019; Ison, 2014). Intrinsic motivation to learn is another possible reason to expect less misconduct among online learners (Peled et al., 2019). However, if students no longer have a choice about online learning because of the pandemic these factors may become obsolete.

Disadvantage. Although honour codes have been correlated with reduced student self-reports of academic misconduct (McCabe et al., 2012), these may be less effective in an online environment with asynchronous course delivery, for similar reasons that they are less effective in large institutions (LoSchiavo & Shatz, 2011). In both cases, the psychological and physical connection to instructors and peers is weaker, making the internalization of institutional values more difficult, which in turn may minimize the inhibition to cheat. Again, if this is accompanied with increased student anonymity students may be more tempted to cheat. Similarly, with a high visiting student population taking only one or two courses, students may experience anonymity and not identify or feel committed to the institutional academic integrity values making identification and commitment to these values more difficult to establish (Hunter, 2016). Without strong social connections, it seems that honour codes are less successful.

We have identified the unique features of ODDUs and discussed how they may serve as advantages or disadvantages to ensuring academic integrity. We have expanded our discussion to include traditional universities that have moved to the online environment in response to the pandemic. We now discuss some of the common challenges to academic integrity faced by both ODDUs and traditional universities. These include use of the Internet and digital technologies, the failure of faculty to report misconduct cases, and identity authentication.

Challenges for Both ODDUs and Traditional Universities

Internet and Digital Technologies

Access to the Internet and digital technologies can facilitate cheating (Bertram Gallant, 2008) regardless of the type of course delivery. In the case of plagiarism Ison (2014) explains that,

> students at both traditional and online institutions utilize the same types of sources—that is, online databases and literature-thus plagiarism should be expected to be comparable across

> institution types. As such, the cutting and pasting of material are equally accessible to both traditional and online students. (p. 278)

Learning management systems that are used by both kinds of institutions include functionality such as discussion forums that if left unmonitored may also provide opportunities for unauthorized collaboration. Social media platforms, chat rooms and instant messaging can connect students with each other and may provide opportunities for cheating and collusion. For example, students create Facebook pages that exclude anyone who is not a student thereby evading the oversight of instructors, and some websites sell previously written papers or test banks to learners so students can see potential questions and answers for quizzes and exams (Daffin & Jones, 2018).

Failure to Report

The literature suggests that faculty do not always cooperate in following academic integrity policy. There are a number of reasons why faculty may choose not to report misconduct when it occurs. Firstly, it may take time away from presenting content (Peters et al., 2019). Faculty may also feel that their job is not to police students (McCabe, 2005), or that teaching about academic integrity is not their responsibility (Peters et al., 2019). Others may believe that the infringement is not a serious enough issue to pursue, especially if they feel they are not sufficiently supported by their administration (de Maio et al., 2019). They may also view the institutional policy as too lenient or too harsh (McCabe et al., 2012). Finally, it can be time-consuming to follow-up on plagiarism or cheating cases (de Maio et al., 2019; Hamilton & Wolsky, 2021).

However, failure to comply undermines academic integrity (Lang, 2013). Instructors who are unwilling to apply the institutional academic integrity policy may then handle misconduct cases independently and informally. By doing so, students are at risk of being treated inconsistently and unfairly (Jendrek, 1989) as instructors may apply different sanctions from one another and from what is outlined in the academic integrity policy. Depending on the individual instructor's view of misconduct, students may be treated either more harshly or more leniently than the policy mandates. This is not only unfair to the students who are sanctioned by their instructors, but also students who are subject to the formal application of the institutional policy, and students who do not engage in any misconduct (Jendrek, 1989). Further, by investigating and sanctioning their own students, instructors may initiate a conflict of interest. Even if most instructors can remain objective and treat their students in an unbiased way, a perceived conflict of interest may be just as damaging as an "actual" conflict of interest. By failing to apply the institutional policy, serial offenders cannot be tracked and may go unpunished (Lang, 2013). Finally and perhaps most important, if instructors fail to comply with the institutional academic integrity policy this gives the impression that instructors do not value academic integrity. "If this is the message that is being conveyed, why should we expect students to value academic integrity?" (Hunter, 2016, p. 21).

Identity Authentication

With the development of online distance institutions, identity authentication (confirming that the individual registered in a digital distance course or program is the same individual who is submitting the work for credit) became an issue. There was concern students might cheat by registering in courses and programs and yet have someone else complete the work (Lee-Post & Hapke, 2017). With the introduction of the Higher Education Opportunities Act in the U.S., online distance education institutions were required to find ways to authenticate students' identity in order to retain accreditation (Lee-Post & Hapke, 2017). While this was originally identified as a problem for digital distance institutions, identity authentication is also a problem for traditional institutions insofar as students can contract out work for course assignments or download them from web sites purporting to provide "study resources" (Course Hero, 2020, para. 1) and submit them as their own. Such websites provide access to a wide range of assessments and course material in return for assessments uploaded by the student accessing the service.

While cultivating academic integrity and reducing misconduct can be challenging for traditional universities and open digital distance institutions, in the following sections, we offer recommendations on how these can be addressed at the macro and micro levels. First we note recommendations that are unique to ODDUs, followed by those that fit both types of institutions.

Promoting Academic Integrity at the Macro Level

Here, we discuss interventions that help to ensure academic integrity at the macro level, involving the senior executive and administration of the institution who have power to make institutional changes. These include recommendations for addressing the issues of distance, identity authentication, the promotion of academic integrity through a robust academic policy, and demonstrating a commitment to academic integrity. Institutions need to be responsible and provide resources necessary to promote academic integrity and prevent misconduct.

Recommendations Unique to ODDUs

Distance. There are a number of ways to address the physical and psychological distance between instructors and students. Despite the fact that learners and instructors are not in the same room, technologies such as video conferencing platforms and even older highly reliable technology such as the telephone are available that allow for increased synchronous one-to-one contact between instructor and student, and help facilitate virtual discussions. Furthermore, one-to-one instructor/student contact allows for individualized student instruction that could mitigate isolation and the experience of anonymity that have been attributed to an increase of academic misconduct (McGee, 2013). Also, ensuring that the ratio of instructor to students remains small may strengthen the instructor/student relationship. Institutions that have moved to the online environment in response to the pandemic, with limited opportunities for synchronous instructor/student contact will likely benefit from adopting some of these strategies as well.

Recommendations Common to ODDUs and Traditional Universities

Identity Authentication. Although identity authentication is an issue regardless of the mode of course delivery, one advantage of traditional institutions is that with in-person classes instructors usually have more direct personal contact and can monitor students more closely (McGee, 2013). This means they can have students complete course work in the classroom setting which ensures that the students are completing their own work. However, this kind of personal oversight may be duplicated to some degree in the online environment with oral examinations (Harris, 2000), student presentations via video conferencing platforms, and the telephone.

Another way to confirm student identity is through invigilated examinations that require students to produce government issued identification. These can be invigilated in-person or virtually through a remote proctor service (Lee-Post & Hapke, 2017). However, since the pandemic, in-person exam invigilation is not an option and is being replaced with alternative assessments and online exams that may or may not be proctored remotely. In the future, it may be possible to institute certain COVID-19 protocols to minimize health risks of in-person invigilation though synchronous exam invigilation would require large seating capacities which may be impractical.

Besides standard government identification, remote proctor services use technologies such as advanced biometric technology that use facial and voice recognition and fingerprint identification to confirm student identity, although the costs of such technology may be prohibitive to students and many post-secondary institutions (Lee-Post & Hapke, 2017) argue that the above technologies help establish the identity of students when they login but "presence or continuous" (p. 138) identity authentication is necessary to ensure it is the same student who completes the assessment.

Video monitoring, which may or may not be recorded, can accomplish this (Lee-Post & Hapke, 2017).

In addition to the costs associated with remote proctoring, student privacy is a concern (Lee-Post & Hapke, 2017). The issue revolves around the use of web cameras for monitoring students as they write their exams in the privacy of their own homes. Some have described the practice as invasive and Orwellian and that learners feel intimidated and spied upon (Hubler, 2020). However, when live proctoring is utilized via a web camera, one might question whether there is much difference between being monitored by a person remotely and being monitored by one in-person since they are both forms of surveillance.

Besides a concern about invasion of privacy, perhaps a more serious concern is the sharing of students' personal data by proctoring services (Hubler, 2020). Institutions should assess relevant policies on privacy and confidentiality before outsourcing proctoring. Even where alternative assessments can effectively replace exams, without procedures to establish student identity, it is possible that none of the student's course assessments are completed by the individual registered in the course. If institutions feel that identity authentication of students is integral to the prevention of misconduct, until in-person invigilation once again becomes viable, one alternative may be to offer at least one online assessment that makes use of remote proctoring. For professional degrees that require examinations for accreditation remote proctoring may be the only viable option. We have discussed some of the general concerns surrounding remote proctoring. Different types of remote proctoring services which use different technologies and processes will present other challenges, but technology may improve over time as well. When deciding whether to use a remote proctoring service, institutions should consider whether the advantages outweigh the disadvantages. These recommendations are imperfect but in a post-pandemic world, choices for preventing misconduct may be more limited.

Academic Integrity Policy

Honour Code. As previously mentioned, honour code systems may be less effective specifically as they apply to ODDUs but they are also less effective more generally within a Canadian context (see Eaton & Christensen Hughes, 2022). However, because it is not the honour code itself that reduces cheating but rather the values of academic integrity, honesty, trust, respect, fairness, courage, and responsibility (ICAI fundamental values, 2021) that are supported by the code, these can be facilitated in ways other than strict adherence to an honour code system (Lang, 2013). An institution needs to go beyond simple endorsement of those values and implement policy that supports academic integrity and enforcement of the rules when there are violations of academic misconduct. Even McCabe, a staunch supporter of the honour code system, supports the view that an honour culture is possible without an honour code and argues that the messages behind this would be meaningless without the enforcement of rules and policies (McCabe et al., 2012). Since the policy supporting academic integrity requires commitment from instructors and students, it is crucial that senior administrators consult with them when crafting or updating the policy. Student and instructor participation and ownership in a system of academic integrity are key for its sustainability (McCabe et al., 2012; Morris & Carroll, 2016). We now turn to the important characteristics of academic integrity policies.

Clear and Comprehensive Policy. Regardless whether a policy is created for digital distance institutions or face-to-face ones, it must clearly and comprehensively cover current categories of academic misconduct and be updated regularly for it to be effective. Researchers in Canada (Stoesz et al., 2019) reveal that many policies fail to use relevant language to address contract cheating and hence should be revised. Regular updating and revision ensures that the policy includes the most current methods of cheating and misconduct.

Since instructors have different views regarding what should be reported as academic misconduct, reporting procedures and the amount of individual instructor discretion must be made clear (Morris & Carroll, 2016; McNeill, 2022). This helps to eliminate inconsistent reporting of violations of the policy that confuse students. Further, if the policy permits instructors to handle minor infractions of misconduct on a discretionary basis, these cases should be documented for tracking purposes (Lang, 2013). Documentation ensures that the same students do not get multiple "teachable moments" without consequence. Keeping this record confidential and on a need-to-know basis until after a misconduct investigation is concluded is important to avoid bias against students based on their past behaviour.

Including a range of penalties may address faculty resistance to policy implementation on the grounds that the penalties are either too harsh or too lenient (Morris & Carroll, 2016). Penalties can be sufficiently severe to handle egregious cases (expulsion) but include softer penalties (reprimand) and education for minor cases (Morris & Carroll, 2016). To develop a culture of academic integrity further, interventions that enhance the moral education and character development of students could include participation in an academic integrity tutorial and some form of remediation. Elements of restorative justice (Benson et al., 2019) that address moral education and encourage offenders to take responsibility for their actions also could be included (Kara & MacAlister, 2010; see also Sopcak & Hood, 2022).

Demonstrating Commitment to Academic Integrity. In order to foster a culture of academic integrity effectively, the institution must itself serve as a model and demonstrate a commitment to academic integrity (Whitley & Keith-Spiegel, 2001). Not only is it important for the institution to do so, but it is equally important that it is perceived to have done so. Even if the institution is committed to upholding academic integrity, unless faculty, students and staff perceive this to be the case they may be less inclined to follow suit. Next we consider recommendations more applicable to ODDUs; then we present more general recommendations.

One way administrators can show commitment to academic integrity is to put words into action and provide the necessary resources to foster academic integrity. For example, professional development surrounding course and assignment design can help instructors create pedagogically sound courses and less cheatable assessments (Eaton et al., 2019). It is especially important for ODDUs that have a centralized team based course development system, asynchronous course delivery and continuous enrolment to support nimble course development and design systems. Unlike traditional universities, ODDUs can have different course start dates, which means learners complete assignments and take exams at different times, so assessments are not easily replaced. If several hundred students are enrolled in a single course over the year, it is not clear at what point assignments and exams should be changed. Nonetheless, nimble processes are necessary so new assessments can be created, especially when assessments become compromised.

For both ODDUs and traditional universities, there are many ways the institution can demonstrate to instructors a commitment to academic integrity. First, administrators can ensure that they follow through and support instructors when they come forward with legitimate cases of misconduct (Whitley & Keith-Spiegel, 2001). Even if faculty perceive their academic integrity policy as fair many are dissatisfied in the way it is applied and enforced (MacLeod & Eaton, 2020). Addressing the lack of confidence in the institution entails transparency and explanation if charges of misconduct are overturned when appealed by students. Adjudications of appeal cases must be seen to apply the policies and procedures accurately, fairly and consistently. Since many faculty members believe they have a responsibility to address misconduct when it occurs (MacLeod & Eaton, 2020), if instructors feel supported by the institution it is reasonable to surmise that they would be more willing to endorse the value of academic integrity themselves and apply institutional policy when it is appropriate. Some faculty members may not be familiar with the institutional policy or may prefer to give an informal warning and not report the infraction, so it is important that faculty are aware of the policy and potential consequences of not reporting (Christensen Hughes & McCabe, 2006a).

To demonstrate more generally a commitment to academic integrity, senior administrators can explicitly endorse academic integrity values (Whitley & Keith-Spiegel, 2001) by posting these prominently on the institutional web site and organizing institutional wide events that champion academic integrity. For ODDUs and traditional universities responding to the pandemic, events such as the annual "International Day Against Contract Cheating" created by the International Centre of Academic Integrity could be hosted as virtual events facilitated with online video conferencing technology. High student participation may help reduce academic misconduct through peer influence given that students who perceive that other students disapprove of cheating report cheating less (McCabe & Treviño, 1993).

Promoting Academic Integrity at the Micro Level

At the micro level, instructors play a major role in fostering a culture of academic integrity. They can help prevent misconduct through academic integrity education, skill development and course/assessment design as well as integrating tools to help students avoid misconduct. These strategies apply regardless of the mode of course delivery.

Academic Integrity Education

Faculty can play an important role in preventing misconduct through academic integrity skill development and education. A fundamental aspect of academic integrity education and a culture of integrity is to ensure students are familiar with the academic integrity policy and the reasons why academic integrity is a moral imperative for all academics. Since it is common for students to receive mixed messages within their own institution about what is acceptable writing behaviour (Eaton, 2017; Sutherland-Smith, 2018) instructors should seek clarification on any ambiguities in the policy to encourage a common understanding. In the end, instructors should uphold the academic integrity policy, and inform students that they, too, are expected to follow the institutional academic policy, why, and what that entails.

Further, instructors can teach students the documentation style of their discipline, including proper citation and paraphrasing (Rossi, 2022) so students have the necessary information and skills to avoid academic misconduct. Post-secondary students may not have been taught how to write papers using sources (Kashian et al., 2015; Peters & Cadieux, 2019), so it may not be surprising that when asked to do so they make mistakes such as forgetting to cite and paraphrasing poorly (Ison, 2017). Even when students are told that word-matching software will be used, cases of plagiarism still arise (Gomez-Espinosa et al., 2016), suggesting that some students are doing this inadvertently because they lack the necessary writing skills. In addition, some researchers suggest that faculty should provide their students with specific examples of cheating and how to avoid these (Eaton et al., 2019), although care in presentation is important so this does not become a lesson in how to cheat. Further, by discussing contract cheating (and other forms of misconduct), students will understand that their instructors are aware of how easy academic misconduct can occur from the Internet and other sources. Moreover, since many students believe their instructors are not aware of contract cheating (Eaton et al., 2019) by being proactive students may choose not to engage in it.

Academic integrity training and awareness is especially important in ODDUs with no academic admission requirements that can result in a student population who may not have been exposed to academic integrity standards.

Course and Assessment Design

Developing academic integrity skills applies to all types of institutions but may be more challenging within an asynchronous online context. For example, there is little opportunity to effectively discuss or present academic integrity content with a student cohort in real time, which is a common technique to promote academic integrity (e.g., Professor E. Gedajlovic, SFU, personal communication, Sept. 10, 2020). Stagg et al. (2013) stress the importance of resources that are self-paced and can be viewed at any time. Online tutorials have this advantage, and they can be viewed repeatedly for later reference (Owens & White, 2013). Some suggest that learning should be at the individual course level (Schrimsher et al., 2011), and embedded within the course (Greenwood et al., 2014). For ODDUs with asynchronous self-paced online course delivery and a high visiting student population, this approach may be the most effective. However, merely making this material available to students is insufficient for a number of reasons. Students rarely voluntarily access these materials (McKay, 2014; Stetter, 2013), possibly because they are not engaging (Kier, 2019). Greenwood et al. (2014) also found that students are not willing to make the time or effort to learn proper referencing because it is "a tedious, technical chore" (p. 450). Further, in light of the COVID-19 pandemic students are dealing with the multiple demands on their time. Based on this evidence, mandatory completion of these types of tutorials may be best (Benson et al., 2019). In addition, reinforcement of a single tutorial presented at the beginning of the course may increase effectiveness (Stetter, 2013). A few short activities and reminders of integrity increase academic honesty (Sterling & Farr, 2018). Although online tutorials meet the unique needs of asynchronous course delivery in ODDU, they are also beneficial for use in traditional institutions.

Instructors are responsible for assignments and exams in their courses and these can be adapted to reduce cheating. Assignments that are engaging, creative, and original are least likely to be plagiarized. For example, authentic or grounded assessments that tie students to time, place and the personal effectively engage students to learn and reduce misconduct (Lang, 2013; Bens, 2021). Along with assessment design, a number of different versions of the exam can be created by implementing automated randomized questions that are randomly distributed to students. This may help to minimize cheating opportunities (Krsak, 2007).

Course design can address time management challenges that affect all students regardless of the mode of course delivery. However, this may be more significant in ODDUs because there are no fixed deadlines for assignment submission beyond a course completion date. Providing sample schedules with suggested timelines for assignment submissions can serve as a useful guide for students. For both traditional institutions and ODDUs, providing an online tutorial with time management resources and information encourages students to develop time management skills. For ODDUs, an embedded tutorial enables students to produce an individualized study plan for the submission of assignments and the completion of their online course (Hunter, 2016). An individualized study plan can help prevent rushed work and possibly remove the need to engage in "panic cheating" (as opposed to planned cheating; Stuber et al., 2009, p. 5).

Conclusion

This chapter has used the 4M model to identify and review the roles of the institution at the macro level, and the instructor at the micro level, at ODDUs. By identifying the challenges to establishing a culture of academic integrity both more generally and specifically as they apply to ODDUs, we have offered recommendations on how these challenges might be addressed. While some barriers exist, engagement of individuals at both the macro level and the micro level can serve to create a culture that fosters the values of honesty, trust, respect, fairness, courage, and responsibility (ICAI fundamental values, 2021) and prevents misconduct in Canadian open digital distance education universities.

We have demonstrated that approaches to the promotion of academic integrity and prevention of academic misconduct are more similar than different between ODDUs and traditional universities. We have also tried to address, at least in a preliminary fashion, the complexities in connection to academic integrity that traditional universities face with the move to online course delivery because of the COVID-19 pandemic.

Further Research Opportunities and Unanswered Questions

As we move forward in a post pandemic world many questions arise, the answers of which will have significant effects on education environment and academic integrity, not only in Canada but also globally.

- How will the COVID-19 pandemic affect academic integrity for both ODDUs and traditional universities and how will institutions address academic misconduct?
- Will online education in the post-secondary sector become the norm?
  - If so, will universities adopt features from established ODDUs or will there be opportunities to develop innovative features that have not yet been considered?

What seems clear based on our research is that approaches to academic integrity and misconduct may vary to some degree based on course delivery but for the most part are equally applicable regardless of the delivery mode. Working together, the macro and micro levels of institutions can help cultivate a culture of academic integrity.

References

Athabasca University. (2020). *Benefits to fully online learning*. Retrieved October 10, 2020, from https://news.athabascau.ca/faculty/faculty-of-humanities-social-sciences/benefits-to-fully-online-learning

Adzima, K. (2020). Examining online cheating in higher education using traditional classroom cheating as a guide. *The Electronic Journal of e-Learning, 18*(6), 476–493. https://doi.org/10.34190/JEL.18.6.002

Bates, A. W. (2018). Canada. In A. Qayyum & O. Zawacki-Richter (Eds.), *Open and distance education in Australia, Europe and the Americas: National perspectives in a digital age* (pp. 49–62). Berlin: Springer.

Bates, A. W. (2019). *Teaching in a digital age*. Vancouver BC: Tony Bates Associates.

Bens, S. (2022). Helping students resolve the ambiguous expectations of academic integrity. In *Academic integrity in Canada: An enduring and essential challenge*. Berlin: Springer.

Benson, L., Rodier, K., Enström, R., & Bocatto, E. (2019). Developing a university-wide academic integrity E-learning tutorial: A Canadian case. *International Journal for Educational Integrity, 15*(1), 5. https://doi.org/10.1007/s40979-019-0045-1

Bertram Gallant, T. (2008). Academic integrity in the twenty-first century: A teaching and learning imperative. *ASHE Higher Education Report, 33*(5), 1–143. https://doi.org/10.1002/aehe.3S305

Carrell, S. E., Malmstrom, F. V., & West, J. E. (2008). Peer effects in academic cheating. *Journal of Human Resources, 43*(1), 173–207. https://doi.org/10.3368/jhr.43.1.173

Christensen Hughes, J. M., & McCabe, D. I. (2006a). Academic misconduct within higher education in Canada. *Canadian Journal of Higher Education, 36*(2), 1–21.

Christensen Hughes, J. M., & McCabe, D. I. (2006b). Understanding academic misconduct. *Canadian Journal of Higher Education, 36*(1), 49–63.

Course Hero. (2020). Retrieved November 3, 2020, from https://www.coursehero.com/about-us/.

Daffin, L. W., & Jones, A. A. (2018). Comparing student performance on proctored and non-proctored exams in online psychology courses. *Online Learning, 22*(1), 131–145.

Davis, A. (2001). Athabasca University: Conversion from traditional distance education to online courses, programs and services. *International Review of Research in Open and Distance Learning, 1*(2), 1–16.

de Maio, C., Dixon, K., & Yeo, S. (2019). Academic staff responses to student plagiarism in universities: A literature review from 1990 to 2019. *Issues in Educational Research, 29*(4), 1131.

Donovan, T., Bates, T., Seaman, J., Mayer, D., Martel, E., Paul, R., Desbiens, B., Forssman, V., & Poulin. R. (2019). Tracking online and distance education in canadian universities and colleges: 2018. Canadian National Survey of Online and Distance Education.

Duhatschek, P. (2020). https://www.cbc.ca/news/canada/kitchener-waterloo/university-of-waterloo-student-cheating-skyrockets-amid-pandemic-1.5836508

Eaton, S. E. (2017). Comparative analysis of institutional policy definitions of plagiarism: A pan-Canadian university study. *Interchange, 48*, 271–281. https://doi.org/10.1007/s10780-017-9300-7

Eaton, S. E., Chibry, N., Toye, M. A., & Rossi, S. (2019). Interinstitutional perspectives on contract cheating: A qualitative narrative exploration from Canada. *International Journal for Educational Integrity, 15*(1), 1–17. https://doi.org/10.1007/s40979-019-0046-0

Eaton, S. E., & Christensen Hughes, J. (2022). Academic integrity in Canada: Historical perspectives and current trends. In S. E. Eaton & J. Christensen Hughes (Eds.), *Academic integrity in Canada: An enduring and essential challenge*. Berlin: Springer.

Friberg, J. (2016, July 11). *Might the 4M Framework support SoTL advocacy?* The SOTL Advocate, https://illinoisstateuniversitysotl.wordpress.com/2016/07/11/might-the-4m-framework-support-sotl-advocacy/

Gómez-Espinosa, M., Francisco, V., & Moreno-Ger, P. (2016). The impact of activity design in Internet plagiarism in Higher Education. *Communicate, 48*, 39–48. https://doi.org/10.3916/C48-2016-044

Greenwood, M., Walkem, K., Smith, L. M., Shearer, T., & Stirling, C. (2014). Postgraduate nursing student knowledge, attitudes, skills, and confidence in appropriately referencing academic work. *Journal of Nursing Education, 53*(8), 447–452. https://doi.org/10.3928/01484834-20140725-01

Hamilton, M. J., & Wolsky, K. L. (2022). The barriers to faculty reporting incidences of academic misconduct at community colleges. In S. E. Eaton & J. Christensen Hughes (Eds.), *Academic integrity in Canada: An enduring and essential challenge*. Berlin: Springer.

Harris, R. (2000). Antiplagiarism strategies for research papers. In A Lathrop & K. Foss (Eds.) *Student cheating and plagiarism in the Internet era*. United States: Libraries Unlimited.

Harris, L., Harrison, D., McNally, D., & Ford, C. (2019). Academic integrity in an online culture: Do McCabe's findings hold true for online, adult learners? *Journal of Academic Ethics*. https://doi.org/10.1007/s10805-019-09335-3

Hollis, L. P. (2018). Ghost-students and the new wave of online cheating for community college students. *New Directions for Community Colleges, 183*, 25–34. https://doi.org/10.1002/cc.20314

Hubler, S. (2020). *Keeping online testing honest? Or an Orwellian overreach?* https://www.nytimes.com/2020/05/10/us/online-testing-cheating-universities-coronavirus.html.

Hunter, J. (2016). Academic integrity report. Canada: Athabasca University [unpublished report].

International Centre for Academic Integrity (ACAI) (2021). The fundamental values of academic integrity (3rd edition). https://www.academicintegrity.org/fundamental-values/

Ison, D. C. (2014). Does the online environment promote plagiarism? A comparative study of dissertations from brick-and-mortar versus online institutions. *Journal of Online Learning and Teaching, 10*(2), 272–281.

Ison, D. C. (2017). Academic misconduct and the internet. *Handbook of Research on Academic Misconduct in Higher Education*, 82–111. https://doi.org/10.4018/978-1-5225-1610-1.ch004

Jendrek, M. P. (1989). Faculty reactions to academic dishonesty. *Journal of College Student Development, 30*, 401–406.

Jungic, V., Burazin, A., & Lorvic, M. (2020). Let them cheat: Why it's tempting for college and university institutions to look the other way. https://www.cbc.ca/news/opinion/andie-burazin-1.5723960

Kashian, N., Cruz, S. M., Jang, J., & Silk, K. J. (2015). Evaluation of an instructional activity to reduce plagiarism in the communication classroom. *Journal of Academic Ethics, 13*(3), 239–258. https://doi.org/10.1007/s10805-015-9238-2

Kara, F., & MacAlister, D. (2010). Responding to academic dishonesty in universities: a restorative justice approach, *Contemporary Justice Review, 13*(4), 443–453. https://doi.org/10.1080/10282580.2010.517981

Kier, C. (2019). Plagiarism intervention using a game-based tutorial in an online distance education course. *Journal of Academic Ethics, 17*, 429–439.

Krsak, A. M. (2007). Curbing academic dishonesty in online courses. *Technology, Colleges, and Community Worldwide Online Conference Proceedings*, 159–170.

Lang, J. M. (2013). *Cheating lessons*. United States: Harvard University Press.

Lee-Post, A. & Hapke, H. (2017). Online learning integrity approaches: Current practices and future solutions, *Online Learning 21*(1), 135–145. https://doi.org/10.24059/olj.v21i1.843.

LoSchiavo, F. M., & Shatz, M. A. (2011). The impact of an honor code on cheating in online courses. *Journal of Online Learning and Teaching, 7*(2), 6.

MacLeod, P. D., & Eaton, S. E. (2020). The paradox of faculty attitudes toward student violations of academic integrity. *Journal of Academic Ethics*. https://doi.org/10.1007/s10805-020-09363-4

McCabe, D. L., & Treviño, L. K. (1993). Academic dishonesty: honor codes and other contextual influences. *The Journal of Higher Education, 64*(5), 522–538.

McCabe, D. L. (2005). It takes a village: Academic dishonesty & educational opportunity. *Liberal Education, 91*(3), 26–31.

McCabe, D. L., Butterfield, K. D., & Treviño, L. K. (2012). *Cheating in College: Why Students Do It and What Educators Can Do about It*. United States: John Hopkins University Press.

McGee, P. (2013). Supporting academic honesty in online courses. *Journal of Educators Online, 10*(1), 1–31. https://doi.org/10.9743/JEO.2013.1.6

McKay, T. M. (2014). Combating plagiarism using a community of practice approach. *South African Journal of Higher Education, 28*(4), 1315–1331.

McNeill, L. (2022). Changing "hearts" and minds: Pedagogical and institutional practices to foster academic integrity. In S. E. Eaton & J. Christensen Hughes (Eds.), *Academic integrity in Canada: An enduring and essential challenge*, Springer.

Morris, E. J., & Carroll, J. (2016). Developing a sustainable holistic institutional approach: Dealing with realities "on the ground" when implementing an academic integrity policy. In T. Bretag (Ed.), *Handbook of Academic Integrity* (pp. 449–462). Singapore: Springer Singapore.

Owens, C., & White, F. A. (2013). A 5-year systematic strategy to reduce plagiarism among first-year psychology university students. *Australian Journal of Psychology, 65*(1), 14–21. https://doi.org/10.1111/ajpy.12005

Panico, G. (2020), *University cheating might be up-but don't just blame the students*. Canada: CBC, Posted July 19, 2020. https://www.cbc.ca/news/canada/ottawa/giacomo-panico-1.2861706

Peled, Y., Eshet, Y., Barczyk, C., & Grinautski, K. (2019). Predictors of academic dishonesty among undergraduate students in online and face-to-face courses. *Computers & Education, 131*, 49–59. https://doi.org/10.1016/j.compedu.2018.05.012

Peters, M., & Cadieux, A. (2019). Are Canadian professors teaching the skills and knowledge students need to prevent plagiarism? *International Journal for Educational Integrity, 15*(1), 10. https://doi.org/10.1007/s40979-019-0047-z

Peters, M., Boies, T., & Morin, S. (2019). Teaching academic integrity in Quebec universities: Roles professors adopt. *Frontiers in Education, 4*, 1–13. https://doi.org/10.3389/feduc.2019.00099

Peterson, J. (2019). An analysis of academic dishonesty in online classes. *Mid-Western Educational Researcher, 31*(1), 13.

Probett, C. (2011). Plagiarism prevention. *Business Communication Quarterly, 74*(2), 170–172. https://doi.org/10.1177/1080569911404054

Qayyum, A., & Zawacki-Richter, O. (2018). Open and distance education in a digital age. In A. Qayyum & O. Zawacki-Richter (Eds.), *Open and distance education in Australia, Europe and the Americas: National perspectives in a digital age*, (pp. 1–8). Berlin: Springer

Rossi, S. L. (2022). Revisioning paraphrasing instruction. In S. E. Eaton & J. Christensen Hughes (Eds.), *Academic integrity in Canada: An enduring and essential challenge*. Berlin: Springer.

Rossiter, S. (2020). Retrieved November 14, 2020, from https://www.cbc.ca/news/canada/edmonton/cheating-becoming-an-unexpected-covid-19-side-effect-for-universities-1.5620442

Royal Roads University. (n.d.). https://www.royalroads.ca/?gclid=CjwKCAiAzNj9BRBDEiwAPsL0d1OFrHSngsx1oPRMJjsW-TH1RJtLuYYPOp397G4rlpEyeXS3vM8GgxoCXjsQAvD_BwE

Schrimsher, P. R. H., Northrup, L. A., & Alverson, S. P. (2011). A survey of Samford University students regarding plagiarism and academic misconduct. *International Journal for Educational Integrity, 7*(1), 3–17. https://doi.org/10.21913/IJEI.v7i1.740

Sopcak, P., & Hood, K. (2022). Building a culture of restorative practice and restorative responses to academic misconduct In S. E. Eaton & J. Christensen Hughes (Eds.), *Academic integrity in Canada: An enduring and essential challenge*, Springer.

Stagg, A., Kimmins, L., & Pavlovski, N. (2013). Academic style with substance: A collaborative screencasting project to support referencing skills. *The Electronic Library, 31*(4), 452–464. https://doi.org/10.1108/EL-01-2012-0005

Sterling, E., & Farr, D. (2018). Mix(ed/ing) messages: Online teaching, student success, and academic integrity in sociology. *The Journal of Public and Professional Sociology, 10*(1). https://digitalcommons.kennesaw.edu/jpps/vol10/iss1/8

Stetter, M. E. (2013). Teaching students about plagiarism using a web-based module. *Journal of Further and Higher Education, 37*(5), 675–693. https://doi.org/10.1080/0309877X.2012.684035

Stoesz, B. M., Eaton, S. E., Miron, J. B., & Thacker, E. (2019). Academic integrity and contract cheating policy analysis of colleges in Ontario Canada. *International Journal for Educational Integrity, 15*(4), 1–18. https://doi.org/10.1007/s40979-019-0042-4

Stuber-McEwen, D., Wiseley, P., & Hoggatt, S. (2009). Point, click, and cheat: Frequency and type of academic dishonesty in the virtual classroom. *Online Journal of Distance Learning Administration, 12*(3), 1–12.

Sutherland-Smith, W. (2018). Is student plagiarism still a serious problem in universities today? *Student Plagiarism in Higher Education*, 1–1.

Teluq University Website. (n.d.). https://www.teluq.ca/site/en/

Thompson Rivers University Website. (n.d.). https://www.tru.ca/distance.html?utm_source=google&utm_medium=cpc&utm_campaign=truol_canada_wide_branding&utm_term=thompson_rivers_university_open_learning&utm_content=ad_3&gclid=CjwKCAiA17P9BRB2EiwAMvwNyBwkRYlMIAC4Pqh1J5n5dDdHnFFMLRuY13FJZmkl2-9L_8wt5bDpHxoCrScQAvD_BwE

Whitley, B. E., & Keith-Spiegel, P. (2001). Academic integrity as an institutional issue. *Ethics & Behavior, 11*(3), 325–342. https://doi.org/10.1207/S15327019EB1103_9

Jill Hunter, BA Honours (University of Alberta), MA (University of Alberta) retired in 2020 from her positions as an Academic Coordinator in philosophy and the Bachelor of Arts Program Director at Athabasca University. She taught and coordinated courses on critical thinking and ethics. Her research interests include ethics, political philosophy and academic integrity. Her role as an academic integrity officer at Athabasca University provided the impetus for her research interest on academic integrity.

Cheryl Kier, BA (McGill University), MSc (University of Calgary), PhD (Reading University, UK) is an associate professor in psychology at Athabasca University, Canada's Open University. While she teaches and conducts research in the area of families, child development, and adolescent psychology, she also studies student success, particularly accidental plagiarism.

Chapter 14
Visual Plagiarism: Seeing the Forest and the Trees

John Paul Foxe, Allyson Miller, Glen Farrelly, Vincent Hui, Dianne Nubla, and Colleen Schindler-Lynch

Abstract Recent years have seen an increase in conversations in higher education around academic integrity. The subject of plagiarism in traditional written assessments has been much discussed and well researched. Considerably less is known about visual plagiarism. For the purposes of this chapter, we are defining "visuals" as mechanisms that convey meaning without articulation of, or dependence on language. Although some scholarly literature on visual plagiarism exists, there is a dearth of comprehensive literature on the topic and even less published are instructional or best-practice resources for instructors. Further complicating this topic are the differing ethical, legal, professional, and academic standards across fields. Here, we discuss practical ways to pre-emptively approach the topic of visual plagiarism through the education of faculty and students. We address prevention with suggestions for best practices in four distinct disciplines. Additionally, academic policy and administrative challenges are explored. Finally, we make recommendations for further research. This chapter will be of use both across Canada and globally, by providing a framework for defining and examining visual plagiarism in academic contexts and offering guidelines for pedagogical approaches to educate faculty, administration, and students on this important issue.

Keywords Visual plagiarism · Plagiarism · Presentation design · Illustration · Digital media · Architecture · Academic integrity · Canada

J. P. Foxe (✉) · A. Miller · G. Farrelly · V. Hui · D. Nubla · C. Schindler-Lynch
Ryerson University, Toronto, Canada
e-mail: johnpaul.foxe@ryerson.ca

A. Miller
e-mail: allyson.miller@ryerson.ca

V. Hui
e-mail: vincent.hui@ryerson.ca

D. Nubla
e-mail: dnubla@ryerson.ca

C. Schindler-Lynch
e-mail: cslynch@ryerson.ca

S. E. Eaton and J. Christensen Hughes (eds.), *Academic Integrity in Canada*, Ethics and Integrity in Educational Contexts 1,
https://doi.org/10.1007/978-3-030-83255-1_14

Introduction

A Canada-wide study examining university definitions of plagiarism identified only six of twenty institutions that explicitly include visual material in their policies (Eaton, 2017). Even within the academic integrity community, visual plagiarism, although a topic of great interest to some, remains a black box to others. Historically, text-based plagiarism has been the focus for academic integrity researchers, though that is changing with growing concern over contract cheating. Our goals for this chapter are threefold: (1) to raise awareness of visual plagiarism as a concern, (2) to recommend best practices for educating students on the use and creation of visuals for assessments, and (3) to encourage policy change at the institutional level. To achieve these goals, we brought together faculty from a variety of disciplines, to contribute to this paper, and to discuss visual plagiarism from their perspectives. The results highlight common issues as well as draw attention to the unique concerns within the respective disciplines.

For the purposes of this article, we are defining "visuals" as mechanisms that convey meaning without articulation of, or at least dependence on, language. Examples include, but are not limited to photography, architectural plans, fashion designs, computer code, and dance.

We will not be addressing issues of fraudulent manipulation of visuals for the purpose of misrepresenting scientific research results, although that too is a pressing concern.

Additionally, it is important to distinguish between copyright infringement and visual plagiarism. Copyright infringement is a violation of contract law, whereas visual plagiarism is a violation of institutional policy. As discussed below, in some disciplines, maintaining this distinction when educating students can be challenging given that students are learning the rules of academic engagement, while simultaneously preparing for entry into professional fields where expectations can be quite different.

Literature Review

Research on visual plagiarism is scant, but there have been a few attempts to lay the foundation for this important work. A UK-based study by Garrett and Robinson (2012) attempted to assess the frequency and scope of visual plagiarism in the arts through a survey where faculty and support staff responded to 27 questions to establish definitions of visual plagiarism, frequency of occurrence, detection methods, and methods of responding to incidents. Respondents' definitions were generally congruent with the standard definition of plagiarism, but several went further and included reference to unacknowledged appropriation, while some quantified boundaries by suggesting that, to be original, a work must be 80% the creator's own, or, the creator needs to have taken the idea through six mutations/variations in order to obtain originality. A relatively small number of participants reported encountering visual plagiarism but, interestingly, 42% reported encountering a lack of referencing on visuals, suggesting that participants' considerations of visual plagiarism, unlike written plagiarism, are not synonymous with considerations of citation. The respondents' strategies for prevention included the use of learning support services, online tutorials, as well as presentations from career advisors who can speak to professional expectations about creative work. At the heart of Garrett and Robinson's study is the exploration of similarity detection software for images, akin to the widely accepted and prolific use of text similarity detection software for written work. Although 65% of respondents indicated using technology to identify visual plagiarism (e.g., image search and/or reverse image search), when asked if they would support a visual version of similarity detection software they were, for the most part, doubtful about the benefit and or the effectiveness of such a tool.

Simon (2016), using computer code as the medium for exploring visual plagiarism, argued that non-text-based courses needed to consider different (creative) approaches to citation and detection and to recognize that the academic standards need to be developed with industry standards in mind. Acknowledging the collaborative practice that is fundamental in the tech industry, where coders are encouraged to share code and build on the work of others, Simon identified inappropriate collaboration as the primary source of plagiarism.

Alongside researchers who have explored how visual plagiarism is viewed and how it occurs, others have been demonstrating grassroots initiatives within and across institutions to fill in gaps in existing academic integrity policies and address some of the unique challenges in specific fields. One such initiative was the impetus to this chapter when Ryerson University's Academic Integrity Office (a unit within the Centre for Excellence in Teaching and Learning) partnered with a number of faculty from creative disciplines at Ryerson University to develop a guide called "Best Practices: Visual Plagiarism" (2019). In creating this guide, a review of practices elsewhere was undertaken.

Blythman, Orr and Mullin (2007) worked with two UK institutions to establish discipline specific guidelines that included a statement on the tradition of creation in the field, as well as instructional activities to explore these ideas with students. Another project out of the City University of Hong Kong's School of Creative Media, Hare and Choi (2019) created videos to teach visual integrity. Using a flipped classroom model, students watched short videos from home and explored discipline specific complexities via case studies in the classroom. Pre- and post-testing showed a significant improvement in student understanding of requirements for integrity when working with visuals.

To continue this work and build on this foundational research, Dianne Nubla (MPC, Professional Communications), Glen Farrelly (PhD, Professional Communications), Colleen Schindler-Lynch (Assistant Professor, School of Fashion, MFA) and Vincent Hui (Associate Chair, Architectural Science, MArch, MBA) address the challenges and best practices in their disciplines below.

Visual Plagiarism Across Disciplines

Visual Plagiarism in Standard Text-Based Presentation Courses (Dianne Nubla)

For both Canadian and international students, the realm of visual plagiarism in presentation slides is often a relatively foreign landscape, as guidelines on citing their visual sources in an academic setting can be easily ignored. Faculty are often pleased to see students playing with images, graphics, and illustrations in their presentations; however, they sometimes overlook the lack of citations for these creative additions (Huffman, 2010). To add to this uncertainty, students may see lecture/lab slides, as well as course handouts, where instructors omit visual citations when using internet-based images/graphics/illustrations, further encouraging the assumption that non-citation practice is acceptable.

When students are asked to create presentation slides, oftentimes textual research and its citations are prioritized. Although many Canadian post-secondary institutions use originality detection software that has been positively viewed as a helpful aid by instructors and teaching assistants to detect similarity with the software's text matching tool (Zaza & McKenzie, 2018), currently there is no equivalent formal visual plagiarism detection system. To fill this gap, manual substitutions have been employed, such as reverse image search, which are conducted by different means and methods. As a result, instructors do not have institutionally supported tools to detect visual plagiarism within visually rich submissions, such as presentation slides.

In an effort to find a solution, educators and students are increasingly using Creative Commons (CC) images sourced from content-delivery (e.g., Wikipedia) to image-based commercial (e.g., Shutterstock, Unsplash, and Flickr) websites. Creative Commons is a designated non-profit organization who seeks to "work closely with major institutions and governments to create, adopt and implement open licensing and ensure the correct use of CC licenses and CC-licensed content" (Creative Commons, 2020, para. 2). Educators and students should note that each website may contain a different framework for crediting their Creative Commons (and non-Creative Commons) image(s).

Navigating Through Visual Plagiarism Challenges in Presentation Design

Table 14.1 shows common visual plagiarism scenarios which can create confusion. Also provided are best practices for faculty and students when creating presentations in an educational environment.

The visual citation overview provided in Table 14.1 is based in educational, learning contexts, where the individual is not selling/renting their materials. If the produced slides are to be released commercially then the creator is advised to carefully consult the Canadian Copyright Act (Government of Canada, 2020) to ensure that their visuals are not in breach of the statute.

Table 14.1 Best practices in preventing visual plagiarism in presentation design

Challenges in presentation design	Best practices
Pre-loaded software, clipart, graphical elements e.g., use of graphics, such as tables, charts, diagrams, and infographics, within presentations	**Preparation** Educate students that "Shapes", "Table", "Chart", "Diagram", and "Word Art" creations do not need to be cited, as these are shells provided by the software to help creators input their data to create their own visual. Mention that the name of customizable graphics may differ, based on the software used. Though the graphics may not require citations, the raw materials in them will need a citation to properly credit the researcher(s) Emphasize that non-original content, even though personally modified, needs citations. **During Design Development** Students should be asked to track their image sources when working through the design process. In addition, it is important that students are clear on the citation expectations around their use of images. In a similar manner, industry professionals may want to read through the software's copyright policies found on their website on the legal uses of their content. Certain presentation software tools provide users with access to pre-loaded clipart images that can be embedded into the student's presentation which do not require citations. **After Deadline** Encourage students to take a visual inventory of their presentation to assess their original content and to check if external content (including inspiration pieces) were properly cited.
Images from websites added to presentations for aesthetic and/or functional purposes	**Preparation** Motivate students to build a habit of citing their visuals during the collection process. Provide different layout techniques on how to include image citations in a way that works with the slides' design layout. **During Design Development** Teach that when retrieving an image online, it is best to always provide a citation. Remind students that screenshots can also be categorized as images extracted from a website; therefore, these visuals will require a citation. **After Deadline** Review the presentation slides and make note of the visuals taken externally. It is easy to forget to cite when in a hurry; therefore, this can be used as a reflective exercise (for both students and faculty) to see how their slides can be improved in the future.

(continued)

Table 14.1 (continued)

Challenges in presentation design	Best practices
Personal creations	**Preparation** Remind students that images, illustrations, and graphics created by them do not need citations, as they own these creative materials. Encourage the use of shape and line tools in the presentation software as they empower the creator to customize their designs. **During Design Development** Schedule regular check-ins during the slide creation process to train students to assess if their personal creations were heavily inspired by an external source. Create a checklist (can be used in conjunction or substitution of the check-ins) to provide clear guidance on knowing what type of visuals to cite within the slides. **After Deadline** Advise that students place copyright or Creative Commons indicators on their custom visuals/slides in case they would like to share their work.

Discussion

Preventing visual plagiarism in presentation slides requires a mixture of institutional support, leadership from instructors, and student self-efficacy.

Macro Level Support:*Creating a Unified Visual Plagiarism Standard*. Guidance and deliverables from the post-secondary teaching support services help create a standardized practice for the institution to follow. For example, Ryerson University's Learning & Teaching Office, in partnership with the Academic Integrity Office and faculty members in the Faculty of Communication & Design (FCAD), created a "Best Practices: Preventing Visual Plagiarism" guidebook for its community. This guide encouraged further visual plagiarism discussions amongst its faculty, students, and teaching support departments to establish clearer academic integrity protocols for the university.

Micro Level Support: Instructors Leading by Example. With the mass movement of courses to an online platform due to COVID-19-related adjustments, instructors will be creating more educational resources and have an increasingly critical role. By using proper visual citation techniques in their own lecture and lab presentations, in addition to course handouts, in a consistent manner, they are demonstrating the usage of best practices.

Personal Empowerment: Student Self-Efficacy. A student's belief in their academic success will have a direct impact on the quality of their work. Students who experience challenges with time management and a lack of confidence in their academic studies are more inclined to omit details, such as visual citations.

Focusing on cultivating a student's self-efficacy by providing transparent guidelines and increasing support services (such as workshops and one-on-one assistance outside of the classroom) will have a positive impact on increasing their motivation to follow plagiarism prevention best practices.

For a formal, long-term visual plagiarism prevention strategy, educational institutions can consider the 4 M Framework. This approach was developed by the Scholarship of Teaching and Learning (SoTL) group to foster a symbiotic relationship "through four interrelated organizational lenses: (a) micro (individual); (b) meso (departmental); (c) macro (institutional); and (d) mega (community)" (Eaton, 2020, p. 1). Though this process will take years to develop, its benefits provide an environment that motivates buy-in to increase the likelihood of producing long-term sustainability in visual plagiarism education and detection.

Visual Plagiarism in Digital Media (Glen Farrelly)

Visual plagiarism is of particular importance in courses involving teaching about and creating digital media as copying digital work is so technically easy and as common digital media practice often entails no crediting of third-party content. Therefore, instructors are tasked with re-educating students on acceptable use of third-party visuals and helping prevent visual plagiarism in students' digital media projects. For educators in programs with a professional or applied focus, this issue intersects with copyright and trademark protections and artist permission and compensation, which are concerns for future practitioners in this area to help them avoid potentially litigious behaviour.

Digital media courses can include social media, web design & development, video game design, mobile application design, and emerging media (e.g., wearable technology, Internet of Things). Visual plagiarism in these courses can take the form of inappropriate use and attribution of digital versions of physical media, such as photographs, illustrations, comics, paintings, maps, videos, logos, and fonts as well as uniquely online visuals, such as social media posts, memes, emojis, collages, webpage and mobile app layouts and templates, banners and advertising graphics, machinima, mashups, mods, and skins. Students in digital media courses may use visual elements of digital media in conventional textual documents (e.g., essays, presentation slide decks, reports) as well as in the creation of digital media final products (e.g., websites, apps, games, social media accounts, e-books). Visual plagiarism in such work involves the issues covered in this chapter around inspiration and departure as well as attribution. The following table presents dimensions of visual plagiarism in digital media courses (Table 14.2).

Table 14.2 Best practices in preventing visual plagiarism in digital media

Challenges in digital media	Best practices
Instilling a concern in students that crediting creators is important. Students need to become aware first about the plagiarism aspects of common online behaviour and then understand the personal and social impact of using others' work without permission, credit, or compensation	Instructors can appeal to students as current and future artists and content creators. A class discussion can cover famous cases, such as the "Pepe the Frog" comic and its adoption as a meme by hate groups much to the concern of creator Matt Furie (Anderson & Revers, 2018). Ask students to comment on how they would feel if their creations were reused in such contexts.
Educating on differences between open-access, royalty-free, public domain, and copyrighted media e.g., Using a copyrighted photograph as an e-book cover image without creator attribution or embedding an open-access video in a blog post without creator attribution	Instructors should educate students on what permissions go along with different types of licences and the need to always cite/credit sources. Students can also be introduced to fair dealing provisions of copyrighted media.
How to credit in academic and professional contexts. For students seeking to properly cite image sources in their digital media work, there are a lack of standards and ability to credit. In digital media practice, there are few established norms or features for crediting (Simon, 2016) e.g., Inserting images found online into a website and not providing creator attribution or gaining permission; reposting a popular meme on social media with no creator attribution	The lack of conventions for crediting third-party digital media creators means the instructor will need to provide their own guidance. Note in many cases no one method of attribution may be sufficient and not all methods provide sufficient transparency. Some methods by medium include: *Digital image (generally) - watermark or superimposed credit line, file metadata in the Authors or Comments field, creator name used in file name * Digital image posted to social media - watermark or superimposed credit line, tagging the creator, credit in post or comment *Digital image used on website or app - watermark or superimposed credit line, file metadata in the Authors or Comments field, creator name used in file name, caption below photo or upon mouse hover (via CSS) *Video - superimposed credit line, opening or closing credits (written and/or spoken), credit in caption or comments, file metadata in the Authors or Comments field, creator name used in file name *Website, App, Blog, or Game Design - code comments, credit line in footer, credits page or list A class discussion or exercise could have students search for examples in digital media where credit has been provided.

(continued)

Table 14.2 (continued)

Challenges in digital media	Best practices
Use of third-party media as an element in a digital media design or using templates or themes. The creation of original digital media works may entail the student using third-party tools or content to build upon their own creation or entirely using other people's content and mashing it up into something new e.g., Using Google Maps tool with one's own customized icons to create an interactive map; taking images from another person's social media posts, adding text and then posting it to one's own social media account; paying a fee to use professionally designed layout template from a company such as Wix.com when building a website	The issue addressed in this paper regarding attribution and departure must be addressed here by instructors in assignment design. Instructors must establish and clearly state the parameters involving using third-party material or software. For example, stating the rules of a website design project on whether using templates or themes is permitted and how to credit (e.g., an HTML comment or a credit line in the footer).
Ascertaining proper re-use or sufficient departure for derivative works from established designs and iconography (assuming proper attribution, it can be difficult to know at what point third-party media are in common usage or when a layout is an established convention that no longer needs creator attribution) e.g., Using clipart arrow images in Microsoft software to create icons for a video game HUD; purchasing a font to use in a PDF brochure without attributing the font creator; copying an app layout from an industry leader when planning a new mobile app	Acceptable media reuse and departure are difficult areas to ascertain and will rely on the instructor's subject matter expertise. Instructors should be upfront to students about permissible use of such media and the degree of originality and innovation students must achieve. In general, students should always attribute all sources of third-party work in their academic creations, but this may not be necessary for commercial work.

Discussion

Educating students on the institutional rules of academic integrity and legal use of third-party visual media is a challenge given the lack of regulations and rampant violations in popular use of digital media. The educator must impress upon students the need to counter prevailing media use norms and instead practice responsible use of others' ideas and content. The culture of re-use and remix in digital media may help spread information and spur innovation, but it does not adequately give credit where credit is due. This issue is larger than educators and students, as many global digital powerhouses, such as Instagram and Twitter, thrive through the widespread reposting of third-party content with ease and rarely offer easy, elegant ways for users to provide credit.

Even for students who want to cite third-party media, this is not always simple, as there are often cases where tracking down essential credit information can be difficult to impossible, such as with finding who originated a meme. Viral, online content can be reposted rapidly by innumerable people, so tracking down the original creator can be impossible even with the help of archived databases of memes, such as Know Your Meme (n.d.). Also, people passing on memes may modify the original creation or add to it, so determining who the creator was through successive iterations can be further herculean. At present, there appears to be no academic or professional standards for what to do when one cannot determine the creator of a viral image. For example, is it sufficient to cite where one last saw a meme even if it is certainly not the originator?

An aspect of visual plagiarism that is of particular relevance to digital media educators is helping students prepare for professional practice in digital media jobs. Students in post-secondary, digital media development programs are likely to work in communication or arts related professions. Thus, it behooves educators in this area to teach students best practices for reusing and crediting media to help them either protect their own work as a future professional artist or entrepreneur or to avoid litigation as a future employee. Educators should inform students that work that is permitted for educational provisions of fair dealing may prove to be copyright infringement if the same work is used in business endeavours. Similarly, students who are permitted to use third-party templates or open access images in school assignments may find that they are not permitted to use them when they are no longer a student or the project is no longer non-profit.

In terms of detecting possible plagiarized visuals, there are a few tools or aids available to educators. There is as of yet no equivalent to Turnitin. However, reverse image search engines, such as Google's, will let one upload a suspect image and Google will check if there are similar images posted elsewhere on the web. However, this tool is not yet perfected and their database of images to check against is not exhaustive. In some instances, it is possible to find a suspected plagiarized digital image by looking at the file's metadata or code. But at this point, the best safeguard for educators is prevention. Through the use of scaffolding in assignments, either by having students begin their work in class or handing in preliminary or iterative designs, it can reduce the likelihood of cheating and provides transparency in the design process.

There are many related issues that are beyond the scope of this chapter but are nonetheless crucial. These include: model consent, subjects' privacy and children's security, trademarks (including colour), trade dress, design patents, and artists' moral rights. For students posting their work publicly, educators can also address how students can protect their own work from unauthorized use, such as via watermarks and Creative Commons licenses.

When courses involve digital media, it falls on educators to not only ensure that students are not visually plagiarizing but also to prepare students for acceptable practice in their future careers.

Visual Plagiarism in Illustration: Apparent Contradictions in Visual Practise and Two Case Studies in Illustration (Colleen Schindler-Lynch)

Visually dominant creative disciplines such as illustration and fashion are areas where it is easier to identify visual plagiarism. Iterative sketching is fundamental to the creation of images and development of designs, but the process of creation to fabrication, for images or designs, is not without contradictions and obstacles and visual plagiarism can occur at any stage of the process. In this component, I present considerations and concerns for visual plagiarism in illustration and fashion design along with two case studies, discussing apparent contradictions in these disciplines that might confuse students. For example, "Historically, some artists/designers have used copying as an analytical approach to learning. Investigating how an image/artefact was created involves a close reading of which media and methods were used, in which order, and how each was applied. By doing so, you gain material and compositional sensibilities etc. resulting in a technical exercise but not an original work. This practice will recreate the look and feel of something, but it is considered copying" (Ryerson University, 2019). Intended and accepted as a valid form of learning, its purpose is to gain knowledge rather than impart new meaning, and these types of mimetic assignments are still common in visual arts courses.

Further complications in the making and use of imagery are concepts like parody, satire, and appropriation. The Cambridge University dictionary (n.d.) defines parody as "writing, music, art, speech, etc.… that intentionally copies the style of someone famous or copies a particular situation, making the features or qualities of the original more noticeable in a way that is humorous" and satire as, "a way of criticizing people or ideas in a humorous way, especially in order to make a political point, or a piece of writing that uses this style." Additionally, the Museum of Modern Art (n.d.) (MoMA), defines appropriation as "…the intentional borrowing, copying and alteration of existing images and objects." Each of these are accepted modes of creating work that results in unique intellectual property built upon or as a deliberate derivative of the intellectual property of others, assuming the creator has departed from the original *enough*. Navigating that ambiguous *enough* can be challenging for professional artists, let alone for students who are still developing their skills and their personal artistic voice. One need only refer to the work of artists like Robert Rauschenberg, Shepard Fairey, or Sherrie Levine and Michael Mandiberg to see examples of well-known uses of appropriation.

When delving into the use of visual material, sometimes it is necessary to preserve an original image to some extent, but this must be coupled with visual or conceptual departure to avoid merely copying—further contributions should be made to an image to create a new version or new message. These are considerations that need to be discussed with students—it is imperative to speak about image making history alongside project expectations and the nuances of a particular field. Garrett and Robinson's (2012) research shows that some educators attempt to quantify *enough* by requiring a specific percentage of divergence from the original or a certain number of categorical shifts (e.g., colour, perspective, medium). This is not surprising given that students appreciate identifiable guidelines.

In Ryerson University's (2019) "Best Practices: Preventing Visual Plagiarism", faculty are encouraged to choose categories appropriate to their field and instruct students who are working with an inspirational work to change it in several categorical ways. Below are examples of possible categories:

- Colour
- Lighting
- Process
- Intention
- Setting
- Content
- Materials
- Proportion
- Pattern
- Feeling
- Context
- Meaning
- References
- Selection
- Motif
- Cropping
- Method
- Scale
- Fabric
- Juxtaposition

The case studies below illustrate some lessons learned and best practices for prevention.

Case Study: Styles, Styles Everywhere

Just as each person's written signature is distinct, so too is each person's artistic mark. In reviewing a submission from a student, I always refer to the work the student has completed in class for comparison. In this way, I learn the student's artistic voice and abilities and can identify inconsistencies that may indicate visual plagiarism and justify further investigation.

In one project, students were asked to create a suite of twelve original watercolour illustrations based on a given theme and they were required to include all references used in painting the work. Upon reviewing one student's submission, I immediately recognised inconsistencies in the illustrations, and they were dissimilar to the drawings I had observed in class. In fact, I identified five separate styles throughout the twelve watercolours as well as differing media applications.

Although I was unfamiliar with most of the original paintings, a few felt familiar and so I began the process of detection with a basic Google keyword search, such as fashion, watercolour, woman, and kitchen. This relatively quickly led me to the original artist. I was able to confirm the student had copied the layout, style, composition, and figure and had made only minor modifications such as a change of colour or a simplification of pattern.

Case Study: Process Makes Perfect

In this case, the project required that students design a croquis, which is a hand-drawn sketch of a live model. The student submitted process work that included a series of photos of themselves in various poses, and the photos seemed at first glance to match the sketched poses. As in the previous case, I noted inconsistencies in the drawings submitted by the student compared with their performance in class.

Upon closer inspection, I noted subtle differences between the self-photos presented as process work and the final project the student submitted. For example, the finger position in the photo versus the final was inconsistent, and, perhaps most telling, several of the sketches were mirrored versions of the self-photos: e.g., right knee bent in the photo and left knee bent in the sketch.

To investigate, I began with keyword searches such as "fashion" and "croquis" and discovered the exact figures the student had submitted in an online database. Through due diligence, I was able to detect and identify that the student found the figure drawings online first and sketched them, and then, in an attempt to deceive, faked the photos in the process-work.

It is key to understand that visual plagiarism is a broad area and there are many nuanced, discipline-specific concerns when considering prevention and detection strategies. Requiring process work from students to see the linear way they developed their work is a good practice but not failsafe. Communicating with students about the significant differences between inspiration and copying can help students understand that for their work to have been "inspired" by something, there must also be "departure." Detection may begin with intuition but is followed by basic keyword searches and online tools such as reverse image searches through companies like TinEye and Google, which are increasingly becoming more effective as their databases expand. A golden rule to impress upon students is that it is fine to use something as inspiration, but they must cite and change an original image/artefact in multiple significant ways so that the resulting work is new and communicates a different message (Table 14.3).

Visual Plagiarism in Architecture (Vincent Hui)

It's a Copy, Right? Visual plagiarism in architectural design is predicated on the notion that although there are commonalities in materials, methods, and models

Table 14.3 Best practices in preventing visual plagiarism in illustration

Challenges in digital media	Best practices
Work is aesthetically or stylistically similar to others e.g., Student replicated the style of a published illustrator/designer	**Prevention** Be clear about the expectations Emphasize the need for originality despite what the practices of industry or the discipline may be
Work formally similar to others e.g., Student copied composition/layout	Ensure ample discussion with students regarding the difference between inspiration and copying associated with the area/discipline
Work is technically similar to others e.g., Student traced figure drawings	Require process work and scaffold it into assignments. Students should cite and submit all references with their process work Schedule work-in-progress critiques where students' present and discuss their work in development
Work is conceptually similar to others e.g., Student used the same idea as another artist/designer	Review process work—although there is an impulse to simply confirm that process work was provided, attention to detail at each developmental stage will help you learn the artistic voice and mark of each student and, if necessary, help you identify possible plagiarism in the final work
Faked process work e.g., Student took photos to mimic the position of a figure reference	**Detection** Be familiar with the visual material associated with the area/discipline Actually, LOOK at and review the process work
Contract cheating e.g., Student hires a person or agency to execute a component of the work or the project in its entirety	If you suspect misconduct, do a reverse-image search through services like TinEye and Google to find and evaluate similarity

of the design of a building, the intentions, method of expression, and relationship to context factors will ultimately result in a unique design response. Plagiarism in architecture occurs when key characteristics of the design of a space bear a striking similarity to those found in a previous architectural work and fail to demonstrate an appropriate design response with a reasonable level of development. If the visuals of an architectural design (in drawings, digital or physical models, or renderings) fail to showcase a developed design response to design parameters, then it is a weak project. If asked to design a lab in the Arctic circle and a student presents imagery of a white house, then there is clearly an inability to propose an appropriate design response. If the suite of visual material fails to demonstrate a design response and heavily derives its formal expression from existing work, then it is architectural plagiarism. If asked to design a house and a student presented the imagery of the White House, then it is a clear example of focusing upon speed and form as opposed to development and response.

Despite iconic global architecture epitomizing cultures since the dawn of time, it was only in the 1950s when architecture emerged as a plagiarism case in California and was then formalized in the 1976 Copyright Act that curtailed the "*abuse of architectural documents*" in a Federal court decision (Giovannini, 1983). Though this law in architecture reflects a litigious era in architecture, it does not undermine the fundamental concept in architectural praxis that architecture is an evolutionary discipline that literally and figuratively builds upon its past precedents. From the architectural apprentices in medieval Europe to the digital designers producing bold architectural forms, architecture has been referential in its evolution. The critical step is to understand the line between developing upon precedent and outright plagiarism. Historically architects have not shied from heavy inspiration or outright copying of design elements, as seen in the resurgence of classical orders to recount the timelessness of ancient Greece at contemporary civic buildings or the callous copy/paste mentality of suburbia. Indeed, some famous architects have embraced the value of copying, from Robert A. M. Stern ("*As long as the source is good, I steal. Not in the sense of taking away from another architect- he is not poorer because of a theft but is in fact more influential.*") to Robert Venturi ("*There is nothing wrong with being influenced, or even with copying. Imitating is how children learn... Doing something good is better than doing something first.*") (Brainard, 1984).

To define architectural plagiarism, it is critical to understand a framework in establishing the similarities between architecture and other creative disciplines. Three differentiators in architectural praxis would be the extensive reliance on conventional commonalities, the nature of cascading changes, and the heavy reliance on collaboration.

Similar to how Western music has infinite outcomes with the same shared and limited notes, architectural pedagogy operates with baseline commonalities unique to the discipline including standards, convention, and shared components. A core component to architectural success is the ability to bring design innovation to operable, safe standards and within agreed upon conventions. To do anything less is sculpture. Architecture affords a range of aesthetic liberty, but all architects are beholden to regulatory standards and codes that may drive a similarity across projects with similar siting parameters (such as locations of fire exiting, window placement, or setbacks). Although regulatory constraints may initially seem confining, there remains a great deal of flexibility and interpretation that gives rise to design opportunity. As well, there are conventional dimensions in architecture that are effectively universal. To design a building with conventional level floors, vertical walls, or lights placed on ceiling would not be out of place in any given building and would be inherently expected in all architectural designs. To see commonalities like these across projects is expected. If convention and regulatory parameters create common guidelines for architects to operate within, another instance where commonalities among architectural work may emerge exist within the shared components used in contemporary design praxis. Building components (e.g., doors, furnishings, and lights) as well as supplemental entourage accessories (e.g., people, cars, vegetation) are available to students either as asset libraries in design software or online through manufacturer sites and asset repositories. That students can compose an entire architectural proposal with these assets without fear of committing plagiarism is a testament to the pedagogical imperative to prioritize the design of space as opposed to the value of commodity components.

Unlike some visual disciplines where changes may be quite immediate and simple to implement, within architecture, any adjustment, unless purely superficial, results in a cascade of changes throughout a project. It is not only a three-dimensional exercise, but visible and invisible changes often require multiple steps to integrate. Shifting a window in a building not only results in corresponding changes in building plans and section (a type of drawing that is a cut through of a building), but also mandates coordination with other Architecture, Engineering and Construction (AEC) facets (e.g., mechanical and structural systems). If architectural design projects were scaffolded with weekly design studio review sessions, any changes would result in multidimensional changes. Instructors should put forth design directions and precedents that students can use to demonstrate a robust knowledge of the challenges in architectural design, detailing, and delivery.

In the architectural industry, every work is a product of collaboration with a range of stakeholders. In academia, however, because of the difficulty of assessing collaborative work for individual contributions, and because the work generated may ultimately become part of the student's professional portfolio, students are generally expected to design alone. Through the use of precedents contextualized during design reviews, instructors can help mitigate that isolation and help students understand how to build upon the work of others while still creating work of their own.

Architectural Praxis: Everybody is doing it, just do it right. Architecture instructors must always bring precedents into discussion to make it clear that drawing upon them is not bad; however, indiscriminately copying them is. Like most creative disciplines, architecture is steeped in a tradition of looking at precedents for not only aesthetic inspiration, but also to expand a knowledge base on materials and methods others have developed as solutions to similar design challenges. Precedents must be conceptual, not literal. Instructors should use more than one example to make a concept clear as opposed to presenting a single "solution;" through multiple examples, a student is able to see the opportunities for appropriately responsive integration in their designs.

At design reviews, though, students are often overwhelmed with the feedback they receive including the litany of precedents presented to them. While a student pores through imagery, there is a tendency to focus less on the unique response and concepts at play and more on the formal design output to readily address the design challenge posed by reviewers. For example, at a studio review an instructor may suggest a student consider integrating sustainable design strategies and put forth some built precedents to examine, and the student may run the risk of plagiarism by hastily applying features from these precedents in a haphazard way often resulting in a "Frankenstein" or "Fruitcake" project—that is to say, a discordant amalgam of used or inappropriate parts that is either a monster or something nobody wants. To avoid creating Frankenstein, instructors can help students identify the concepts in the precedents (e.g., solar orientation, water reuse, limiting heat loss) and reinforce the importance of integrating them into their work within the programmatic and contextual parameters of the project as well as tempered with the student's aesthetic sensibilities. Asking students to identify a) the commonality and b) the applicability to their own design project can confirm that the student understands different ways at approaching a design response without undermining their own design intentions.

How to Copy Right

The following is an outline of some of the measures faculty may integrate in preventing visual plagiarism in the architecture design studio (Table 14.4).

Though visual plagiarism in architecture is unacceptable, integration of precedents to form a unique response to specific architectural conditions is not. This tradition is how architecture continuously evolves, and faculty should encourage students to understand this paradigm of operation. Faculty must inculcate in students a skill in developing a unique design response to an architectural challenge, a comfort in navigating, synthesizing, and presenting ideas from precedent, and an awareness of how to manage their resources to produce their unique design solutions. Building upon the work of past architects as well as drawing upon colleagues' work is core to success in architectural praxis.

Discussion

In each of the case studies described here, discipline-specific recommendations are made for preventing and addressing visual plagiarism. Despite the varied nature of the disciplines included in this chapter, several common themes emerge. Firstly, it takes a village. No sole instructor can be responsible for providing the required and necessary tools students need to succeed. Rather, a collective approach may be much more effective. Schools and departments across institutions in Canada (and abroad) routinely provide training to students on how to cite in written work and how to avoid text-based plagiarism. We are suggesting that a similar approach be taken to training students in visual plagiarism. Although an institutional standard may not be appropriate, departments of architecture or fashion (using two examples described here) in a given institution can take a departmental approach, where norms are established and clearly communicated to instructors and students. Of course, this requires institutional or departmental support as well as collaboration among instructors in a department. Although this may seem a daunting task, a close inspection of the best practices for preventing visual plagiarism in the four distinct areas presented here show significant overlap. For example, the practices presented for preventing visual plagiarism in presentation design and architecture can be applied, with little to no modification, in the field of digital media studies.

This collaborative approach in no way replaces the vital role of individual instructors in preventing visual plagiarism. As described in the case studies above, use of

Table 14.4 Best practices in preventing visual plagiarism in architecture

Challenges in architecture	Best practices
Precedent similarity e.g., Work formally similar to others; work aesthetically similar to others; work procedurally similar to others	**Preparation** Make a developmental document/booklet that showcases the evolution of the design throughout the duration of the project Have students outline their design intentions in a single sentence design statement and parti diagram and use that as the guide for each review **During Design Development** This essentially scaffolds subsequent reviews so student designs cannot copy/paste but instead synthesize solutions Have a strong vocabulary of precedents to showcase to students including hardcopy and digital/online media Find a venue to share and showcase precedents and student work (e.g., blogs, social media, pinup board) Encourage students to look at and share with the class precedents to ensure awareness of what is currently done as it deters direct copying Foster an understanding that architecture advances upon precedents and students are expected to do the same **After Deadline** Have students critically examine each other's work near the deadline and ask them to identify potential similarities with any precedents they encountered while doing in the project
Student work similarity e.g., Students have exhibited similar design ideas; students have similar stylistic methods of representation	**Preparation** Pre-emptively showcase to students all the notable current projects similar to what the students are doing **During Design Development** Students should have a venue to share their work with not only the instructor but their peers as well to ensure everyone can witness and learn from individual development Have students review each other (in pairs or small groups) so they can offer feedback and in cases where there are similarities, they can identify ways to differentiate **After Deadline** Post up all student work for others to see Allow students to comment on any similarities they have found from their classmates' work based upon their own work or precedents

(continued)

Table 14.4 (continued)

Challenges in architecture	Best practices
Layout similarity e.g., Presentation boards share the same organization or aesthetic; student architecture portfolios share the same layout and annotation styles	**Preparation** Assign a small component of the project assessment to layout, specifically its ability to align with the student's project **During Design Development** Make it a point to ask students at intermittent reviews to showcase a general layout of their work as it determines layout as well as anticipated volume of work to be produced Ask students for mock-up presentation boards/booklet layouts for pinup and make them assess their work against their peers before the deadline **After Deadline** Encourage students to post up their content online (such as portfolios) to a single repository for others to view Include the top layouts in an end of term gallery (online or physical)
Lack of citation e.g., Failure to reference precedent work in any given presentation; withholding evidence that the student had access to information/ resources others did not, like drawings from an architect's office	**Preparation** Mandate that students submit a citation sheet as part of the assessment; this may also be included in the aforementioned developmental booklet **During Design Development** Present multiple examples of precedents for a student to integrate into their design work and ask students to visually show how they integrated the ideas into their work in subsequent presentations Make a point of collecting all the precedents that the students have been drawing upon and ensure that there is a platform to share it so that there is a comfort in drawing upon design precedents **After Deadline** Remind students that if they wish, they can submit their citation sheet any time prior to their presentation as it allows them to take time to critically look at their own work without feeling rushed

(continued)

third-party images and designs can be addressed directly with students by requiring them to engage with these visuals as part of their assignments. Demonstrated knowledge of how to work with and cite other people's visuals can be an intended learning outcome. Asking students to demonstrate that they understand concepts of visual plagiarism and including a grade will help to communicate the importance of the issue. To that end, scaffolding assignments, asking students to provide drafts and

Table 14.4 (continued)

Challenges in architecture	Best practices
Group work citation e.g., Students using work produced by their colleagues for assignments or portfolio; students integrate work they did that overlaps with peers' content	**Preparation** Create a group agreement where every student acknowledges that they must cite each other for work produced including agreed methods of citation and methods of recourse Make it known that at the end of the term, all students' contributions will be shared with the team (or at a larger venue) **During Design Development** Keep in contact with students to remain abreast of which students are working on what part of an assignment Speak to those students whom other group members indicate may not be as active to ensure the student does their part and does not inappropriately draw upon their peers' work **After Deadline** Post up the final submission where students can see what others have claimed as their own work
Time management e.g., Student failed to manage their time and copied another project in desperation; student ran out of time and copied a technical component of another project	**Preparation** Set milestones with specific requirements and content demands (e.g., a structural analysis, interior perspectives) so that there will not be a need to haphazardly copy other work **During Design Development** Ask students to set a weekly schedule for themselves at the end of each design review to establish priorities, design goals, and feasibility to prevent copying in desperation **After Deadline** Allow students to submit any pertinent citation deliverables between the deadline for the principal design deliverables and presentation/assessment

process work gives instructors the opportunity to identify gaps in students' knowledge and the chance for students to learn from their mistakes.

As mentioned above, the dearth of published research on and institutional recognition of visual plagiarism is of particular interest (Eaton, 2017). Even within the academic integrity community, visual plagiarism, while a topic of great interest to some, remains a complete unknown to others. Historically, text-based plagiarism has been the go-to for academic integrity researchers, though that is changing with the global increase and awareness of contract cheating. Our hope with this chapter is to raise awareness of visual plagiarism as an issue. Through the use of four discipline-based case studies we have shown that visual plagiarism is an issue in a variety of fields, not all of which are necessarily dominated by visuals.

Conclusion

The dearth of literature on visual plagiarism can be seen as both a threat and an opportunity. There remains, in Canada, and globally, tremendous opportunity for research and growth in this important domain. We strongly recommend that institutional policies are amended to include visuals as part of their definition of plagiarism. In addition, we recommend that research looking at the prevalence of academic misconduct include visuals as part of their research. Finally, we recommend that departments and instructors embed learning outcomes concerning visual plagiarism into their curricula, explicitly recognizing it as an essential skill.

References

Anderson, C. W. & Revers, M. (2018). From counter-power to counter-Pepe: The vagaries of participatory epistemology in a digital age. *Media and Communication, 6*(4), 24–25. https://doi.org/10.17645/mac.v6i4.1492

Blythman, M., Orr, S., & Mullin, J. (2007). Reaching a consensus: Plagiarism in non-text based media. https://cpb-eu-w2.wpmucdn.com/blogs.brighton.ac.uk/dist/7/3977/files/2018/03/Reaching_A_Consensus_Plagiarism_In_Non-T-v0k6k9.pdf

Brainard, E. (1984). Innovation and imitation artistic advance and the legal protection of architectural works. *Cornell Law Review, 70*(1), 81–100.

Cambridge University Press. (n.d.). Parody. In *Cambridge dictionary*. https://dictionary.cambridge.org/dictionary/english/parody

Cambridge University Press. (n.d.). Satire. In *Cambridge dictionary*. https://dictionary.cambridge.org/dictionary/english/satire

Creative Commons. (2020). *What we do*. https://creativecommons.org/about/

Eaton, S. E. (2017). Comparative analysis of institutional policy definitions of plagiarism: A pan-Canadian university study. *Interchange, 48*(3), 271–281. https://doi.org/10.1007/s10780-017-9300-7

Eaton, S. E. (2020). Understanding academic integrity from a teaching and learning perspective: Engaging with the 4M framework. *Werklund School of Education Research & Publications*. https://prism.ucalgary.ca/handle/1880/112435

Garrett, L., & Robinson, A. (2012). Spot the difference! Visual plagiarism in the visual arts. Paper presented at the *Electronic Visualisation and the Arts (EVA 2012)*. https://doi.org/10.14236/EWIC/EVA2012.7

Giovannini, J. (1983, August 14). Today, more buildings are competitive creations. *New York Times*. https://www.nytimes.com/1983/08/14/arts/today-more-buildings-are-competitive-creations.html

Government of Canada. (2020). *Copyright Act (R.S.C., 1985, c.C-42)*. https://laws-lois.justice.gc.ca/eng/acts/C-42/Index.html

Hare, J., & Choi, K. (2019). Attribution and plagiarism in the creative arts. *Journal of Information Literacy, 13*(1), 62–75. https://doi.org/10.11645/13.1.2640

Huffman, S. (2010). The missing link: The lack of citations and copyright notices in multimedia presentations. *Tech Trends, 54*, 38–44. https://doi.org/10.1007/s11528-010-0401-8

Know your meme. (n.d.). https://knowyourmeme.com/

Museum of Modern Art. (n.d.). *MoMA Learning*. https://www.moma.org/learn/moma_learning/themes/pop-art/appropriation

Opar, B., & Havens, B. (2014). Plagiarism by design. *ACSA News*. https://www.acsa-arch.org/2014/03/17/plagiarism-by-design

Ryerson University. (2019). *Best practices: Preventing visual plagiarism*. https://www.ryerson.ca/content/dam/learning-teaching/teaching-resources/assessment/preventing-visual-plagiarism.pdf

Simon. (2016). Academic integrity in non-text based disciplines. In T. Bretag (Ed.), *Handbook of academic integrity* (pp. 763–782). Springer. https://doi.org/10.1007/978-981-287-098-8_61

Zaza, C. & McKenzie, A. (2018). Turnitin ® use at a Canadian University. *The Canadian Journal for the Scholarship of Teaching and Learning, 9*(1). https://doi.org/10.5206/cjsotl-rcacea.2018.2.4

John Paul Foxe is the Director of Ryerson University's Academic Integrity Office. Prior to this, he was the Manager of Ryerson's Learning & Teaching Office, where he managed the development and delivery of professional development in teaching programs. John Paul completed his undergraduate degree in genetics at Trinity College Dublin and holds an MSc in Molecular Evolution and a PhD in population genetics, both from York University. Most recently, he completed an MA in Public Policy at Ryerson. John Paul's interests include contract cheating prevention and awareness as well as the gamification of academic integrity education.

Allyson Miller is an Academic Integrity Specialist at Ryerson University. She holds a BA and MA in English Literature and has been working in the postsecondary environment supporting student writing for over 12 years. Although academic integrity has been an integral part of her work throughout her career, it was not until recently when she turned her full attention to this important topic. Her current research interests focus on detection of academic misconduct.

Glen Farrelly is Assistant Professor, Business Communications with the Faculty of Business at Athabasca University. He obtained a PhD in Information from the University of Toronto, a Master of Professional Communication from Royal Roads University, and Certificate in Internet Management from Humber College. He previously taught digital media courses for Ryerson University. Glen became focused on issues of visual plagiarism, originality of design, and copyright concerns as they uniquely apply to digital media through his prior professional career as a website producer. Glen researches and consults on user experience issues surrounding digital, social, and mobile media.

Vincent Hui holds several degrees including a Master of Architecture and Master of Business Administration. He has been awarded several teaching distinctions across different universities, most recently the 2015 OCUFA Teaching Award. As a faculty member in Ryerson's Department of Architectural Science, he teaches a variety of courses, from design studios to advanced architectural computing and digital fabrication. He has cultivated an extensive record of publications and research on design pedagogy, advanced simulation and rapid prototyping, and technological convergence in design praxis. A proponent of increasing connections to industry and the greater community, he has developed the Architectural co-op program as well as programming for aspiring young designers in elementary and high school.

Dianne Nubla has taught as a Lecturer for the School of Professional Communication at Ryerson University since 2011. She holds a Bachelor of Technology and Master of Professional Communication. She is the founder of DN Professional Communication where she delivers customized business writing and presentation seminars and workshops to industry professionals. Dianne's interests include combining her background in graphic design, technical communication, and adult education to assist post-secondary students and professionals in creating ethical and valuable deliverables to advance their personal and professional development.

Colleen Schindler-Lynch is an Associate Professor at Ryerson, where she has instructed Fashion Illustration and Accessory and Textile Design and Development for 19 years. She received a BFA from the University of Windsor and an MFA from Louisiana State University. Her research is in the form of scholarly, creative activity and is centred on autobiographical representations of personal narratives in non-linear ways, using fashion and textiles as modes of communication. She has exhibited both nationally and internationally. Colleen lectures on current trends in fashion, specifically relating to diversity and fashion illustration. She has presented at numerous conferences on these subjects and has authored the chapter, "Diversity in Fashion Illustration: An Oxymoron Don't You Think?" in the upcoming "Fashion Education: The Systemic Revolution". Colleen's interests in academic integrity are in the area of visual plagiarism and contract cheating dealing with visual material.

Chapter 15
Managing Academic Integrity in Canadian Engineering Schools

David deMontigny

Abstract This chapter explores what engineering schools across Canada are doing to address and advance academic integrity amongst their students, including how they are currently promoting academic integrity and managing related academic misconduct issues. Responses from a national survey are compared to identify the approaches and practices that are more widely adopted, as well as unique approaches that may warrant broader use. Input was also received from the twelve provincial and territorial engineering regulators that operate across the country. In addition to identifying areas of success, potential opportunities for additional progress are identified. This work serves as a starting point for dialogue among universities and regulators. All parties have a vested interest in strengthening the integrity of engineering students during their academic training and professional development. It is clear from this study that a collective effort is needed to develop solutions, educate faculty, and mentor students to achieve a higher standard of academic integrity. The successes and opportunities highlighted here may be helpful to other professional programs, such as nursing, medical, dentistry, law, and business schools, where integrity is also of extreme importance.

Keywords Engineering · Ethics · Professionalism · Integrity · Misconduct

Introduction

Academic integrity is a challenge for universities throughout the world, including professional schools here in Canada. There is a growing concern in many disciplines, including business, medicine, nursing, and engineering, that students who engage in academic misconduct may obtain unearned academic credentials that make them eligible for registration in professional associations. Given that professions are founded on honour, integrity, and ethics, this is highly problematic. In the case of engineering, the mandate is to serve society and ensure the protection of the public

D. deMontigny (✉)
University of Regina, Regina, Canada
e-mail: David.deMontigny@uregina.ca

S. E. Eaton and J. Christensen Hughes (eds.), *Academic Integrity in Canada*, Ethics and Integrity in Educational Contexts 1,
https://doi.org/10.1007/978-3-030-83255-1_15

and the environment. Therefore, it is critical that the engineering profession continues to have the confidence of the public. This level of confidence can be extended to the academic integrity of the engineering programs themselves. Engineering schools have an incredibly important role to play in both advancing academic integrity and mentoring students to behave as ethical professionals. This is of significant importance for provincial and territorial engineering regulators, who govern the practice of engineering in their region. Engineering regulators not only have a vested interest in what is being done within higher education to promote academic integrity, they also play an important role in supporting schools and student groups to promote professionalism and the engineering code of ethics.

Within the literature, very little has been reported about academic integrity in Canadian universities and there is even less reported from an engineering perspective. Christensen Hughes and McCabe (2006a) identified that cheating may be a serious problem at post-secondary institutions in Canada and they called for further research into strategies that could be used to help improve academic integrity in our schools. Smith et al. (2016) conducted an initial literature review on cheating in engineering schools, which was followed by Smith and Maw (2017) who completed a Canadian version of the P.A.C.E.S. study, which was originally developed by Carpenter et al. (2002). The results from Smith and Maw (2017) found that the academic misconduct situation in Canada appears to be very similar to what has been happening in the United States.

There have been a number of studies that examine whether or not academic dishonesty during undergraduate studies may lead to misconduct in the workplace. In the field of business, Sims (1993) found a positive relationship between academic dishonesty and dishonesty in the work environment. Similar findings were found by Nonis and Swift (2001) and Lawson (2004). In the field of nursing, Laduke (2013) found there may be a connection between academic dishonesty in school and unethical practices of nurses. Within engineering, Harding et al (2004a) found that unethical academic decisions are an indicator of potential poor behavior in the workplace. A related study by Harding et al. (2004b) found similar results and suggested that with the increasing trend of misconduct cases at engineering schools, it may be reasonable to expect to see an increase in disciplinary hearings of professional practice. This should be of significant concern for all professions. Within engineering, this illustrates the important role of educators, who are tasked with the academic training of future professional engineers.

In 2018 the Canadian Engineering Accreditation Board (CEAB) added a section under Criterion 3.3.2 in their accreditation questionnaire for schools to report on their academic integrity policies and procedures (Engineers Canada, 2018). This signaled an acknowledgment from the CEAB that engineering schools are expected to proactively address academic integrity issues and should therefore have effective policies and procedures in place for dealing with academic misconduct cases. Outside of that action, there has been very little discussion or coordination of efforts at the national level to promote and ensure academic integrity. This has changed slightly during the Covid-19 pandemic as instructors and institutions saw a rise in misconduct during non-proctored, online exams. Within Canada, there have recently been a few online forums to discuss misconduct challenges that have been occurring during this remote teaching and evaluation period. However, it is important to recognize that misconduct issues in engineering schools predate Covid-19. One of the respondents to this study observed that, "The Covid crisis will have been of tremendous help in shaking old teaching and testing habits."

Motivation

Christensen Hughes and McCabe (2006b) called for an understanding of how Canadian universities have been responding to academic misconduct. This chapter serves to answer that call by assessing how Canadian engineering schools are promoting academic integrity and managing academic misconduct, when it has been found to occur. Within the literature there have been numerous studies that explore why students cheat, the extent of cheating among the undergraduate population, the types of cheating, and more (Broeckelman-Post, 2008; Carpenter et al., 2006; Harding et al., 2012). Many of these studies provide recommendations on what can be done to try and reduce the instances of misconduct and mentor students to study and work with integrity (McCabe, 1997; Rettinger, 2017; Todd-Mancillas & Sisson, 1987). There does not appear to be an assessment of what is currently being done in practice, certainly within Canadian universities, to address and manage academic integrity at either the undergraduate or graduate level.

Engineering education in Canada will benefit from having a national dialogue on academic integrity and how it needs to be a part of the mentoring and training of young engineers. This chapter serves as a starting point for dialogue among universities, regulators, and students to account for what is currently being done with respect to academic integrity in Canadian engineering schools, and the handling of misconduct cases. Everyone has a vested interest in strengthening the integrity of engineering students during their academic training and professional development.

Engineering School Survey

In order to assess how engineering schools across the country address issues related to academic integrity and academic misconduct, a simple survey was prepared and distributed to all 43 engineering schools and campuses in Canada that offer an accredited CEAB program. The names of these schools and the programs they offer can be found on the Engineers Canada website. The survey was prepared in both English and French. Prior to distribution, the questions in the survey were reviewed by several associate deans from outside of the engineering discipline who regularly investigate allegations of misconduct. This was done to ensure the proposed questions covered a broad perspective of issues that arise when dealing with academic misconduct cases. Table 15.1 summarizes the ten questions that schools were asked in order to assess

Table 15.1 Academic integrity survey questions posed to Canadian engineering schools

Q1	Who investigates allegations of academic misconduct in your faculty?
Q2	How concerned are you about the academic integrity situation in Canadian engineering schools? Scale of 1 (not concerned) to 10 (very concerned)
Q3	Does your engineering school have a formalized system in place for instructors to report allegations of academic misconduct, or is the reporting informal? Explain
Q4	Does your engineering school have its own policies and procedures in place for investigating academic misconduct, or do you follow a policy set by your university?
Q5	What type of penalty system does your faculty/university use? Is it based on a principle of progressive discipline for repeat offenses, or does it depend on the nature of the offense?
Q6	Estimate the percentage of the types of misconduct cases that are investigated: Plagiarism in assignments; Copying assignments; Copying laboratories; Cheating on exams; Other
Q7	Does your faculty administration work with the undergraduate and graduate student associations to promote academic integrity and develop positive messaging and encourage reporting of misconduct?
Q8	Does your engineering school have a process in place for training graduate students to be exam invigilators?
Q9	Has your engineering school seen a trend (increase/decrease) in academic misconduct cases? If yes, is there any reason in particular that you could point to for the trend?
Q10	Has your engineering school or university taken on any major initiatives to combat misconduct in the past five years? If yes, report on its effectiveness

what is currently being done to address academic integrity and academic misconduct across the country. The surveys were directed to the engineering leadership at the schools including Associate Deans, Vice-Deans, and in some cases the Dean of the faculty.

In general, the questions in the survey were designed to determine what schools are currently doing to manage the challenges they faced with academic integrity. The questions were prepared in early 2020 prior to the Covid-19 pandemic, and the actual survey was conducted over the summer months when many universities were dealing with new challenges related to remote teaching and learning, particularly with online examinations. The stress and urgency of the situation at the time of the survey may have led to an increased interest, but at the same time some schools were too busy dealing with the remote teaching and learning challenges to respond.

In total, 25 schools responded to the survey. Table 15.2 outlines the distribution of the responses from across Canada. Responses were received from across the country in English and French that represented a diverse perspective from both small and large schools.

The 25 responses to the survey provided useful insight into how engineering schools in Canada are managing academic integrity and misconduct within their programs. Responses highlighted best practices while at the same time, identified

Table 15.2 Geographical survey responses from across Canada

Region	Number of responses	Number of schools/campuses
Western schools	7	11
Ontario	11	16
Quebec	4	11
Maritimes	3	5
Totals	25	43

opportunities for improvement and collaboration. Moreover, the feedback highlighted how important it is to have this type of data to support a national dialogue on the subject of academic integrity in our engineering schools. The generalized responses from the schools are summarized below in the order they were presented in the survey.

Q1. Who Investigates Allegations of Academic Misconduct in Your Faculty?

Approximately half of the schools ($n = 12$) indicated that an Associate Dean or Department Head is tasked with handling academic misconduct investigations. This appears to be the norm; however, several schools reported that a committee handles these investigations. Three schools indicated that the initial investigation is carried out by the instructor of the course and the investigation may proceed upwards to a Department Head (or equivalent) and eventually the Associate Dean, depending on the seriousness of the case or if the student is appealing any misconduct finding. Two schools reported that they have an Academic Integrity Officer within their faculty who handles the investigations.

In the cases where instructors conduct the initial investigation and assign penalties, it is unclear how these universities maintain a consistent process within the investigation process to ensure that the principles of natural justice are upheld. It is likely that instructors only handle minor and/or clear-cut cases, but such a process would need oversight to ensure misconduct penalties are consistent among cases, and that a formal record is kept in order to ensure that any subsequent violations by the same student are dealt with appropriately (progressive discipline).

Q2. How Concerned Are You About the Academic Integrity Situation in Canadian Engineering Schools? Scale of 1 (Not Concerned) to 10 (Very Concerned)

A strong majority of schools rated their concern for the current academic situation in Canada as high or very high. Twenty-four of the responses were at a 7 or higher, and 17 of the response were either a 9 or 10. The average among all 25 responses was a concerning 8.8 out of 10. Several respondents commented that academic misconduct is a serious problem in engineering schools, the situation is widespread, and misconduct is generally under-reported. One response stated, "Misconduct is a serious problem in Canadian engineering schools. Education is required for both students and faculty on the prevalence of this problem and collective efforts are needed to reduce its occurrence." Clearly there is a pressing need to address the issue so that the academic mission and the value of a Canadian engineering degree is not compromised.

Q3. Does Your Engineering School Have a Formalized System in Place for Instructors to Report Allegations of Academic Misconduct, or Is the Reporting Informal?

Almost all of the schools that responded ($n = 22$) have a formalized process in place for reporting allegations of academic misconduct, or if they did not have one yet they were in the process of creating one. One of the schools reported that they had an online submission system set up for instructors. Only a couple schools reported that they used an informal process for instructors to report allegations of misconduct.

Clearly there is a strong practice among schools to have a formal reporting mechanism in place, which facilitates the investigation. In hindsight, it would have been more useful to expand the question to include whether there was a process in place for students to report allegations of misconduct. Gynnild and Gotschalk (2008) found that 97% of undergraduate and 90% of graduate students had never reported a peer for cheating. Perhaps schools could benefit by developing systems that encouraged students to bring their concerns and observations about misconduct forward to the faculty leadership.

Q4. Does Your Engineering School Have Its Own Policies and Procedures in Place for Investigating Academic Misconduct, or Do You Follow a Policy Set by Your University?

Almost all of the responding engineering schools ($n = 21$) are following policies set by their university. In three cases schools have tailored the university policy for use within their faculty. Only one school reported using their very own faculty policy, which is separate from the governing policies of the university. This finding is not too surprising as most universities operate with an institution-wide framework. However, since some engineering schools have tailored their institution's policies for their situation, or have develop their own policy, it does raise the question whether the standard policies and procedures set by the university are functional for engineering schools. With misconduct being widely reported among engineering schools, it may be worth exploring whether customized policies and procedures for engineering schools would be more effective. Additionally, there may be an opportunity to have similar policies in place at engineering schools across the country in order to maintain consistent academic integrity expectations and consequences for acts of misconduct. One of the respondents commented that, "We need to have better systems in place for engineering, and maybe other professional faculties, than the rest of the university given the expectations for our students in their future careers."

Q5. What Type of Penalty System Does Your Faculty/University Use? Is It Based on a Principle of Progressive Discipline for Repeat Offenses, or Does It Depend on the Nature of the Offense?

Schools tend to have penalty systems that takes into account the nature of the offense and whether or not it is a first-time offense or a repeat offense. The suspension or expulsion of a student with a history of misconduct is a common practice. Most schools dismiss students on the third offense, but a few schools dismiss students on their second offense. In terms of consequences and training, a few schools currently assign students an ethics assignment or course as part of their penalty, or as a requirement for readmission into the faculty after a suspension or expulsion has been completed. This is something that could be adopted more broadly among engineering schools as it aligns with existing practices of some engineering regulators.

Q6. Estimate the Types of Misconduct Cases That Are Investigated: Plagiarism in Assignments; Copying Assignments; Copying Laboratories; Cheating on Exams; Other

Table 15.3 shows where engineering students tend to be investigated for allegations of misconduct in their academic assessments. Generally speaking, 60% of the misconduct cases are related to work on assignments and laboratories and the remaining 40% is misconduct on examinations. While the number of cases in term work is higher (assignments and laboratories), the grades available tend to be lower than the grades that can be achieved on exams. With roughly 40% of the misconduct investigations occurring on exams, there is an indication that students are willing to engage in exam misconduct for a shot at *"earning"* a lot of marks, since exams tend to be worth a large portion of the course grade. The risk of cheating on an exam may be higher, but the payoff is more substantial. With a large number of misconduct investigations coming from exams, there may be a need to either reassess assessment methods, or the manner in which exams are conducted.

Schools were not asked if their misconduct case statistics were made public to the student body, while protecting the identity of the individuals. It was not apparent from any of the responses if schools were doing this, and this was an oversight within the survey. Both Todd-Mancillas and Sisson (1987) and Lipson and McGavern (1993) reported on the importance of communicating the types of offences and subsequent punishments publicly. Their findings demonstrated that a secret sanction system provides no deterrent messaging to the student body. The engineering and university community benefits from knowing that students who engage in academic misconduct can be caught and sanctioned accordingly.

Table 15.3 Distribution of the types of academic misconduct investigations

Type of misconduct	Overall percentage (%)
Plagiarism in assignments	22
Copying assignments	23
Copying laboratories	15
Exam cheating	39
Other	1

Q7. Does Your Faculty Administration Work With the Undergraduate and Graduate Student Associations to Promote Academic Integrity and Develop Positive Messaging and Encourage Reporting of Misconduct?

Slightly over one-quarter ($n = 7$) of respondents indicated that they work with their student associations on academic integrity related matters during orientation week. Many schools, however, indicated that they are not doing much of anything, although there is some content in first year classes that encourage students to behave professionally. Schools also reported on requiring faculty members to include academic codes of conduct in course outlines. One school indicated that their first and second-year students take a workshop on intellectual integrity.

Student leadership at two schools developed ceremonies where participants received a pin to indicate their pledge to conduct their academic work with integrity. These ceremonies were student initiatives that were not led by the faculty or administration. One of the schools provided the script that their student society prepared for their so-called *honour pin ceremony*:

> I, as a student of engineering, shall recognize this code for guiding my conduct throughout my studies, personal life, and careers. I shall act at all times with honestly and trustworthiness towards my peers and society. Accordingly, I shall: hold paramount the safety, health and welfare of the public within the university and workplace by promoting a welcoming, respectful and ethical environment that values everyone equally; uphold the academic integrity of the university and faculty; complete and submit work that is founded on personal achievement and without plagiarism; conduct myself with fairness and avoid conflicts of interest; give credit where it is due and accept, as well as give, honest and fair professional comment; report any concerns to the appropriate governing body.

Overall, it appears as though engineering schools are underperforming in their work with student associations there are opportunities to do more direct work with the students. Schools would benefit from a more proactive approach to weave academic integrity learning and mentorship throughout the curriculum and not rely on introducing it only in orientation week and course outlines. One school indicated they are working hard to engage faculty and encourage them to promote academic integrity within their classroom. According to Gynnild and Gotschalk (2008), the most effective mechanism for learning about integrity is in the classroom. First year orientation ceremonies, advice from academic advisors, and the student handbook were found to have had little impact on students' academic integrity. Broeckelman-Post (2008) reported that explicit discussions led by the professor about his or her expectations for academic behavior is more effective. In other words, the tone and mentorship that the professor establishes in their classroom can have a huge impact in improving academic integrity and reducing the likelihood of misconduct.

Q8. Does Your Engineering School Have a Process in Place for Training Graduate Students to Be Exam Invigilators?

Forty percent of the schools ($n = 10$) indicated that their graduate students received training on how to invigilate exams, either from training offered by the faculty or by a centrally run unit of the university. This means that the majority of graduate student invigilators have received no training. Training programs for invigilators tend to outline the rights of the students, the rights of the invigilators, and how to report allegations of misconduct. Ultimately, they empower the invigilators to uphold the academic integrity of the institution. Given that so many schools lack such a program, this is an area where significant gains can potentially be made with relatively little effort or investment. Considering that 40% of the reported misconduct is on exams, invigilator training programs could play a strong role in reducing the number of misconduct cases.

Some schools expanded their feedback to suggest that junior faculty members would also benefit from invigilator training as well as training on how to properly report allegations of misconduct to the investigating officer. This is a valid point as the common assumption is that faculty members know how to do these sorts of tasks.

Q9. Has Your Engineering School Seen a Trend (Increase/Decrease) in Academic Misconduct Cases? If Yes, Is There Any Reason in Particular That You Could Point to for the Trend?

Eighty percent of the respondents ($n = 20$) reported seeing an increase in academic misconduct cases. About half of those schools felt the increase may be due to the Covid-19 pandemic, or partly due to improved reporting mechanisms. The general sentiment was that students engage in misconduct because they are under pressure to succeed and they are often overwhelmed with the workload, which is high in engineering programs. Some engineering administrators are starting to question if the traditional workload demands of an engineering program are realistic for today's world with all the pressures on students. In other words, are students cheating more because they do not have sufficient time to focus on their studies and cheating is the only way they can "survive" the program?

Q10. Has Your Engineering School or University Taken on Any Major Initiatives to Combat Misconduct in the Past Five Years? If Yes, Please Briefly Report on Its Effectiveness

Roughly half of the respondents (12) indicated that they have undertaken initiatives to address misconduct within their faculty, but little was offered in terms of perceived effectiveness which admittedly may be difficult to assess. A variety of initiatives have been taken, including the creation of invigilator training programs, misconduct reporting forms, student academic integrity pledges, and increased messaging on behaving professionally.

Similar to Question 7, it appears as though engineering schools/faculties and higher education institutions may be underperforming in this area. There may be different interpretations as to what constitutes a "major initiative", but the responses seemed to indicate that actions were in response to misconduct issues and there were few formalized strategic plans to address academic integrity. In other words, schools are tending to be reactionary rather than proactive. Given that concerns around academic integrity were rated high by the vast majority of schools, it would be noteworthy if addressing the issue was a part of any strategic planning efforts. This did not come through in any of the responses, but perhaps the question could have been expanded to specifically ask if integrity had been included in any strategic planning activity.

Input from Engineering Regulators

In addition to the survey results from the engineering schools, input was also sought from all of the provincial and territorial engineering regulators. These regulators govern the practice of engineering in their respective provinces and territories and include:

- Engineers and Geoscientists BC
- Association of Professional Engineers and Geoscientists of Alberta
- Association of Professional Engineers and Geoscientists of Saskatchewan
- Engineers Geoscientists Manitoba
- Professional Engineers Ontario
- Ordre des ingenieurs du Quebec
- Engineers Geoscientists New Brunswick
- Engineers PEI
- Engineers Nova Scotia
- Professional Engineers and Geoscientists Newfoundland and Labrador
- Engineers Yukon
- Northwest Territories Association of Professional Engineers and Geoscientists

Since graduates from accredited Canadian engineering programs are automatically eligible for registration as an engineer in training in any of these associations, it was important to highlight recent progress from the regulators in addressing and promoting academic integrity. The regulators were asked the following question:

Has your association done anything to address the issue of academic integrity in engineering schools? These actions may include:

- Changes in your application form and/or process.
- Working with universities or engineering student groups to promote integrity.
- Creating scholarships or awards to recognize and promote integrity.
- Advising Engineers Canada on academic integrity related matters.

Nine of the twelve regulators responded with feedback. In general, the regulators are concerned about academic integrity in Canadian engineering programs as well as in their own examination programs for graduates with non-Canadian degrees. Violations of academic integrity, including the falsification of marks or transcripts, are seen as a breach in the Code of Ethics and may require evidence of remorse and/or rehabilitation in order to be accepted for registration.

Many regulators have an assessment of "character" at the time of application, where applicants may disclose any disciplinary or criminal actions from their past. Being "of good character" is a licensing requirement and regulators reported that they have refused applications from people who have failed to adequately demonstrate good character. Applicants that have a history of academic misconduct could be subject to a negative "good character" assessment. One of the regulators recently changed their application form to specifically inquire about any academic discipline findings during the applicants' university studies. This was proactive on their part since universities tend to exclude academic misconduct findings on student transcripts. The view among many universities tends to be that young people make mistakes and it may not be appropriate to have a misconduct finding "haunt" them forever with a permanent record on their transcript. Student with repeat offences, on the other hand, may have a grade assigned that indicates misconduct has occurred. In cases when students with repeat misconduct offences are suspended or expelled, the nature of the suspension or expulsion is not always clear. Two schools reported that their university makes a specific notation regarding misconduct on a student's transcript in cases of suspension and expulsion.

There is a lot of positive work happening with the regulators and engineering schools across the country to promote professional behavior. Several regulators highlighted that they have worked and are working with engineering faculties and engineering student groups by providing course content and delivering guest lectures and seminars. Content from the regulators has a focus on topics within the profession related to ethics, discipline, risk management, safety, and professional practice. Regulators have also facilitated broader panel discussions with registered professional engineers that deliver content to engineering students on relevant topics of the day. In one jurisdiction the regulator offers a half-day ethics workshop that is facilitated by registered professional engineers who discuss ethics and discipline case studies. This workshop is done in partnership with the local Corporation of Seven

Wardens chapter, which conducts the Ritual of the Calling of an Engineer ceremony (or Iron Ring Ceremony) for new engineering graduates.

Lastly, a few regulators from smaller jurisdictions have established special awards and medals for students graduating from schools in their province. These awards typically recognize academic achievement, extra-curricular leadership, and ethics excellence. Currently, none of the awards specifically address academic integrity, which may be difficult to evaluate. That said, the referees of such awards could ask applicants to report on any instances of academic misconduct during their academic studies.

Summary and Conclusions

This work was initiated to assess what is being done by engineering schools and engineering regulators in Canada to promote and ensure academic integrity in engineering students. Overall, the level of concern about the current state of academic misconduct in Canadian engineering schools is high. Feedback from engineering schools and engineering regulators led to the following general conclusions:

- Roughly 40% of the reported misconduct is on examinations. Despite this behavior, less than half of the schools reported having invigilator training programs. This is an area where improvements can be made across the country. By training invigilators about student rights, invigilator rights, how to report allegations of misconduct, and how their service helps the institution maintain the integrity of its degrees, a lot of benefit can potentially be realized for relatively low administrative costs.
- Eighty percent of the schools reported seeing an increase in academic misconduct cases, especially during the move to remote teaching and learning as a result of the Covid-19 pandemic. This demonstrates that students can make poor decisions when exams are not properly proctored. However, the rise in misconduct cases started well before the Covid-19 pandemic and there are other issues at play.
- Only a quarter of the schools indicated they are working with undergraduate and graduate students' associations to help create a culture of academic integrity within their programs. Clearly more can be done in this area to foster professionalism and pride within the student body.
- On the engineering regulator side, the main contributions come in the form of lectures or seminars on engineering ethics. There is clearly an opportunity for the regulators to work more directly with engineering schools and student organizations on initiatives that specifically address academic integrity.
- Existing scholarships from regulators tend to evaluate academic achievement and leadership. While there was interest in scholarships for integrity, there is uncertainty about how such an award could be assessed.
- Some student associations took it upon themselves to create ceremonies to uphold academic integrity. Engineering regulators could support these types of initiatives

in order to make them more widespread at schools across the country. McCabe (1997) reported that honour codes have been shown to result in lower levels of self-reported cheating at engineering schools. The regulators could help this movement grow from a localized level to a national level, especially considering all regulators have a code of ethics for professional engineers that can be used to guide students to a higher standard.

Recommendations

The vast majority of engineering schools handle academic misconduct related issues by following the policies and procedures set by their university. There are concerns that those policies may not be suitable for professional schools, like engineering. It may be useful to explore the development of policies and procedures for professional programs. Doing so would allow programs like engineering to collectively establish the expected standards for academic integrity and acceptable sanctions in cases of academic misconduct.

Comments from schools indicated that the engineering curriculum is a heavy workload, and this may be contributing to academic misconduct issues. A formal study on the challenges engineering students face while attempting to balance their academic demands with their work and life commitments may yield some insight into the effort required to complete an engineering degree in today's hectic world. Times to completion, tuition rates, and credit hours required for the degree could be analyzed and evaluated against CEAB accreditation expectations.

Properly educating professors about the policies and procedures their engineering schools and institutions have in place for academic integrity and academic misconduct appears to be an issue. The literature indicates that professors can have a significant impact on the amount of misconduct in their classes by clearly outlining their expectations. Colby and Sullivan (2008) reported that faculty enthusiasm for the academic integrity agenda is important for succeeding at integrating ethics and professionalism into the curriculum. Additionally, Harding et al. (2012) encouraged faculty to encourage strong morals in students so they avoid cheating. The creation of a caring and nurturing classroom environment to mentor students can be more effective than stiff penalties. This approach would benefit from a wider strategic teaching and mentorship plan within the faculty.

Summary of Key Findings

- Canadian engineering schools and regulators are concerned about the level of academic misconduct in engineering programs.
- Engineering schools are actively working to try and address the issue and reduce misconduct, but the number of cases has been rising.

- Engineering schools have done a lot of good work, but a national dialogue is needed to discuss common issues and share effective strategies, policies, and procedures with each other.
- More can be done to work directly with students to promote professionalism and academic integrity. Professors can have a huge impact as mentors and engineering regulators can bring an outside perspective that may resonate with students.

References

Broeckelman-Post, M. A. (2008). Faculty and student classroom influences on academic dishonesty. *IEEE Transactions on Education, 51*(2), 206–211. https://doi.org/10.1109/TE.2007.910428

Carpenter, D. D., Harding, T. S., Montgomery, S. M., & Steneck, N. (2002). P.A.C.E.S.: A study on academic integrity among engineering undergraduates (preliminary conclusions). In *2006 Annual American Society for Engineering Education Conference and Exposition*, Montreal, Quebec (pp. 7.908.1–7.908.16). https://peer.asee.org/10591

Carpenter, D. D., Harding, T. S., Finelli, C. J., Montgomery, S. M., Passow, H. J. (2006). Engineering students' perceptions of and attitudes towards cheating. *Journal of Engineering Education, 95*(3), 181–194. https://doi.org/10.1002/j.2168-9830.2006.tb00891.x

Christensen Hughes, J. M., McCabe, D. L. (2006a). Academic misconduct within higher education in Canada. *The Canadian Journal of Higher Education, 36*(2), 1–21.

Christensen Hughes, J. M., McCabe, D. L. (2006b). Understanding academic misconduct. *The Canadian Journal of Higher Education, 36*(1), 49–63.

Colby, A., Sullivan, W. M. (2008). Ethics teaching in undergraduate engineering education. *Journal of Engineering Education, 97*(3), 327–338. https://doi.org/10.1002/j.2168-9830.2008.tb00982.x

Engineers Canada. (2018). Accreditation resources 2019–2020 accreditation cycle. Retrieved December 15, 2020, from https://engineerscanada.ca/accreditation/accreditation-resources/2019-2020-cycle

Gynnild, V., Gotschalk, P. (2008). Promoting academic integrity at a Midwestern university: Critical review and current challenges. *International Journal for Educational Integrity, 4*(2), 41–59.

Harding, T. S., Carpenter, D. D., Finelli, C. J. (2012). An exploratory investigation of the ethical behavior of engineering undergraduates. *Journal of Engineering Education, 101*(2), 346–374. https://doi.org/10.1002/j.2168-9830.2012.tb00053.x

Harding, T. S., Carpenter, D. D., Finelli, C. J., Passow, H. J. (2004a). Does academic dishonesty relate to unethical behavior in professional practice? An exploratory study. *Science and Engineering Ethics, 4*, 311–324.

Harding, T. S., Carpenter, D. D., Finelli, C. J., & Passow, H. J. (2004b). The influence of academic dishonesty on ethical decision-making in the workplace: A study of engineering students. In *2004 Annual American Society for Engineering Education Conference and Exposition*, Salt Lake City, Utah (pp. 9.1270.1–9.1270.11). https://peer.asee.org/13993

Laduke, R. (2013). Academic dishonesty today, unethical practices tomorrow? *Journal of Professional Nursing, 29*(6), 402–406. https://doi.org/10.1016/j.profnurs.2012.10.009

Lawson, R. A. (2004). Is classroom cheating related to business students' propensity to cheat in the "Real World"? *Journal of Business Ethics, 49*, 189–199. https://doi.org/10.1023/B:BUSI.0000015784.34148.cb

Lipson, A. & McGavern, N. (1993). Undergraduate academic dishonesty at MIT. Results of a study of attitudes and behavior of undergraduate, faculty, and graduate teaching assistants. Presented at the Annual Forum of the Association for Institutional Research, Chicago, Illinois. ERIC Number: ED368272.

McCabe, D. L. (1997). Classroom cheating among natural science and engineering majors. *Science and Engineering Ethics, 3*(4), 433–445. https://doi.org/10.1007/s11948-997-0046-y

Nonis, S., Swift, C. (2001). An examination of the relationship between academic dishonesty and workplace dishonesty: A multicampus investigation. *Journal of Education for Business, 77*(2), 69–77. https://doi.org/10.1080/08832320109599052

Rettinger, D. A. (2017). The role of emotions and attitudes in causing and preventing cheating. *Theory into Practice, 56*(2), 103–110. https://doi.org/10.1080/00405841.2017.1308174

Sims, R. (1993). The relationship between academic dishonesty and unethical business practices. *Journal of Education for Business, 68*(4), 207–211. https://doi-org.libproxy.uregina.ca/10.1080/08832323.1993.10117614

Smith, D. M., Bens, S., Wagner, D., & Maw, S. (2016). A literature review on the culture of cheating in undergraduate engineering programs. In *2016 Annual Canadian Engineering Education Association Conference*, Halifax, Nova Scotia. CEEA Paper 048.

Smith, D. M. & Maw, S. (2017). Supplementary results of the CAIS-1 survey on cheating in undergraduate engineering programs in Saskatchewan. In *2017 Annual Canadian Engineering Education Association Conference*, Toronto, Ontario. CEEA Paper 163.

Todd-Mancillas, W. R., & Sisson, E. (1987). Cheating among engineering students: An analysis. Presented at the Annual Meeting of the American Association for the Advancement of Science, Chicago, Illinois. https://eric.ed.gov/?id=ED281771

David deMontigny, University of Regina is an engineering professor at the University of Regina. In his role as Associate Dean Academic he is responsible for investigating academic misconduct cases and helping the faculty establish policies and procedures that promote academic integrity. His interest in academic integrity is closely tied to the ethics and integrity inherent in the engineering profession, and the need to mentor students on their pathway to becoming professional engineers.

Chapter 16
Teaching the Teachers: To What Extent Do Pre-service Teachers Cheat on Exams and Plagiarise in Their Written Work?

Martine Peters, Sylvie Fontaine, and Eric Frenette

Abstract Very little is known about preservice teachers' actions when it comes to plagiarizing and cheating in their university work. This is particularly the case in Quebec, Canada. It is important to know to what extent these students commit academic misconduct as they will ultimately become the role models who will shape future generations of learners. This chapter reports on a study of this important issue. An online questionnaire was used to survey preservice teachers ($n = 573$) in five Quebec universities in winter 2018. The majority of participants were between the ages of 18 to 25 and were studying to be kindergarten, primary, special education or high school teachers. The questionnaire contained items about demographic information as well as items on methods of cheating, peers' influence, perception of control, goal of performance and engaging in studying. Preservice teachers also answered questions that were used to control for social desirability bias. Results showed that some of them reported participating in academic misconduct. Fewer participants reported cheating on exams while studying at university (15.2%) than when they were in high school (34.9%). They believe that the best ways to plagiarise on written assignment are reusing one's previous work (47.6%), asking somebody else to do the assignment (38.6%), and collaborating with peers (37.2%) while the best ways to cheat on exams would be using hidden material (63%), looking at the neighbour's copy (55.7%) and using electronic devices (31.9%). Four interpretations for the preservice teacher actions are given: they commit academic misconduct because they want to succeed, because they have poor studying habits which lead them to make poor decisions, because of the cheating culture in which they evolve, and because of the cheating patterns they develop. Recommendations for teacher education programs conclude the article.

M. Peters (✉) · S. Fontaine
Université du Québec en Outaouais, Gatineau, Canada
e-mail: martine.peters@uqo.ca

S. Fontaine
e-mail: sylvie.fontaine@uqo.ca

E. Frenette
Université Laval, Québec, Canada
e-mail: eric.frenette@fse.ulaval.ca

S. E. Eaton and J. Christensen Hughes (eds.), *Academic Integrity in Canada*, Ethics and Integrity in Educational Contexts 1,
https://doi.org/10.1007/978-3-030-83255-1_16

Keywords Cheating · Plagiarism · University · Preservice teachers · Academic integrity · Canada

Introduction

According to many researchers, cheating on exams and plagiarism is rampant in universities all over the world. However, there is little known about these phenomena when it comes to preservice teachers. This study focused on examining academic misconduct in preservice teachers, a topic that has not been explored very much in the province of Quebec, or Canada as a whole.

In their review of the literature on academic integrity, Eaton and Edino (2018) thoroughly explore contributions from Canadian academics from 1992 to 2017. Their review is revealing in more than one way. Firstly, there has been little research on academic integrity in Canada, particularly in comparison to our American neighbours. Yet, it was demonstrated more than 10 years ago that academic dishonesty clearly occurs in the education system in Canada (Christensen Hughes & McCabe, 2006). Secondly, Eaton and Edino (2018) found that although graduate students in Canada are interested enough to study this area, as demonstrated by the number of masters and doctoral theses (Bens, 2010; Fredeen, 2013; MacLeod, 2014), few continue to publish on the topic later in their careers. Thirdly, Canadian studies conducted with students tend to focus on specific disciplines (health science, nursing, engineering and business) leaving a gap in other fields like education. Nonetheless, in their review, Eaton and Edino (2018, p. 7) revealed that there have been more publications in recent years, suggesting "that the issue of academic integrity is gaining some momentum as a research topic in Canada, though it remains limited".

The goal of this research with this specific group of university students was to obtain an overall picture of the amount of self-reported intentions to engage in plagiarism in written assignments and cheating on exams, and the reasons behind it. This understanding of students' perceptions of their behaviour should be helpful in designing learning environments that reduce opportunities for plagiarizing and cheating while promoting deeper and more meaningful learning (Lang, 2013; Scott, 2016).

Conceptual Framework

University diplomas are intended to represent acquisition of knowledge, skills and competency development within a specific domain of expertise. Yet, academic dishonesty, whether it be plagiarizing or cheating on exams, is a real concern in higher education, because it is jeopardizing the achievement of such outcomes (Lang, 2013; Scott, 2016) and consequently the validity of the grades and the credibility of the diplomas awarded (Desalegn & Berhan, 2014; Fendler et al., 2018).

A brief review of the literature is presented below, in which we define plagiarism and cheating, both of which are types of academic misconduct. Then, ways students perceived as being the best to plagiarize and cheat and why they would choose to do so are examined, with a focus on student teachers.

Definition and Types of Plagiarism and the Reasons Why Students Do It

Plagiarism is a major problem in education (Gullifer & Tyson, 2010; Vieyra & Weaver, 2016), as a high number of cases are detected each year in post-secondary institutions (Curtis & Vardanega, 2016). It can be defined as the appropriation of another person's words and ideas and presenting them as one's own, in order to obtain a benefit in an environment where originality is expected (Foltýnek et al., 2019; Kakkonen & Mozgovoy, 2010; Liddell, 2003; Walker, 2010).

Different types of plagiarism have been identified by various authors (Bretag & Mahmud, 2009; Curtis & Popal, 2011; Fish & Hura, 2013; Walker, 2010). Direct plagiarism (Louw, 2017) where a student copies and pastes another author's words without quoting is very popular with students (Kulathuramaiyer & Maurer, 2007). Idea plagiarism, also very present nowadays, according to Hossain (2019, p. 166) is "the representation of the author's ideas without attribution to those sources". Whether they are using direct or idea plagiarism, students can use words and ideas from published authors (Zwick et al., 2019), from friends (Ali et al., 2012), or even from themselves (Halupa & Bolliger, 2015). Student self-plagiarism has been defined as text recycling where a student will resubmit parts or a whole of an assignment previously submitted in another class to obtain a credit, thus obtaining grades twice for the same assignment (Halupa & Bolliger, 2015). Bruton (2014, p. 176) argues that while textual recycling does not involve stealing someone's words or ideas, it is still "unethical because it is deceptive and dishonest".

With the arrival of technologies in our universities, plagiarism has become easier and its very nature has changed (Jones & Sheridan, 2015). One type of plagiarism which is receiving a lot of attention, in the press and by researchers, is the use by students of essay mills to buy papers that are then submitted as their own (Bretag et al., 2019; Lancaster, 2020; Medway et al., 2018). Also known as contract cheating, this constitutes plagiarism because the students are handing in an assignment done completely by someone else (Bretag & Harper, 2020; Medway et al., 2018). Essay mills can easily be found on the web (Rundle et al., 2019), and ads are often posted on campus to attract students (Quality Assurance Agency for Higher Education, 2017). Students also buy assignments from other students (Lancaster & Clarke, 2016) or get them at no cost from friends and family (Harper et al., 2019).

Plagiarism can also be defined based on the intent of the students. Voluntary plagiarism is a deliberate act with the "intent" to deceive (Camara et al., 2017). A large number of researchers have shown that many students admit to intentional plagiarism (Carroll, 2005; Löfström & Kupila, 2013; McCabe et al., 2002; Selwyn, 2008). Involuntary plagiarism, on the other hand, is a gesture devoid of bad faith (Pereda et al., 2016) and can be explained by several reasons: the main ones being ignorance (Chen & Chou, 2017), including a lack of knowledge about the Copyright Act (Elander et al., 2010) and citation practices (Gravett & Kinchin, 2018) as well as students' popular beliefs and cultural values (Ison, 2018). Some will blame language difficulties (Zimitat, 2008), or lack of confidence in their writing skills (Strangfeld, 2019).

Numerous other reasons that are not linked to a lack of knowledge, have been given by students to justify their plagiarism. Many students will blame ambiguously defined institutional policies on plagiarism (Mahmud et al., 2019), or the lack of faculty support for academic integrity education (Peters et al., 2019).

Some students report a cheating culture which surrounds them (Crittenden et al., 2009). Callahan (2007) explains this culture by the normalization of cheating, the impression that everybody plagiarizes and that is a trivial action. Yet, other students will hold responsible the learning conditions which make plagiarizing so easy: the seemingly unlimited amount of information on the web (DeLong, 2012); the low probability that professors will detect and report the plagiarism (Eaton, 2020; Eaton et al., 2020); and their lack of interest/motivation for completing, the assignments given (Strangfeld, 2019). Finally, students justify their fraudulent actions based on all the pressures they feel: lack of time due to having an outside job (Amigud & Lancaster, 2019), high expectations from parents (Sarita, 2015) and their desire to obtain good grades (Camara et al., 2017).

Definition of Cheating, Methods and Reasons to Do It

Cheating on exams includes unpermitted behaviours students engage in, in order to increase their grades and chances of success at examination (Chaput de Saintonge & Pavlovic, 2004; Michaut, 2013; Pavlin-Bernardić et al., 2017). Cheaters are not all alike. Some are frequent, premeditated cheaters while others are occasional and spontaneous cheaters (Carrell et al., 2008). Although both types of cheaters will cheat on exams, the frequent cheater will have an elaborate plan for cheating (sitting next to a friend during exams, preparing unauthorized material to bring to the exam, etc.) while the occasional cheater, more prepared for the exam, may glance at a neighbour's copy for a few questions for which they do not have the answer (Fendler & Godbey, 2016).

Methods of Cheating

Students use a variety of ways to cheat during exams. Certain authors (Cizek, 1999; Faucher & Caves, 2009) group the methods used by students into three categories.

The first category includes the use of forbidden material during the exam period. Examples of this would be referring to notes written on pieces of paper, on oneself or on material authorized for the exam (calculator, etc.), or the usage of high-tech devices such as smartphones, smart watches, or earpieces (Michaut, 2013). The second category includes interactions with others in order to share information about the exam (Cizek, 1999; Faucher & Caves, 2009). For instance, students doing the exam first share the exam questions (and possibly the answers) with their friends who have not written the exam yet. Glancing at a classmate's exam with their consent, exchanging exams during the exam period or using codes to communicate the answers to a peer would all fall under this category. The third category (Cizek, 1999; Faucher & Caves, 2009) includes fabricating a reason to justify miss an exam. Of course, some excuses might be legitimate.

More recently, Chirumamilla et al. (2020) suggested that Cizek's (1999) categories are too broad and proposed six categories that are more focused. The first category, called *impersonation*, implies having somebody else write the exam. The second, called *forbidden aids*, includes the usage of all material or tools that should not be used during the exam. This second category is similar to Cizek's (1999) forbidden material category described above. *Peeking at the answer of the other candidate*, is Chirumamilla's et al. (2020) third category, which is considered distinct from *peer collaboration*, their fourth category, since a student can peek at a peer's examination paper without their consent (third) or with their collaboration (fourth). The fifth category includes students' efforts to find *outsider help* during the exam. A good example of behaviours within this category would be the use of earpieces allowing for an external person to provide answers during the exam. Finally, the last category, less documented in the literature, is called *student-staff collusion* (Trost, 2009) and involves the exchange of information between a student and a university employee during the examination. The examples of cheating behaviours within these categories are, of course, not comprehensive and new ways of cheating on exams, in class or online, are evolving as "cheating in school is growing" (Fendler & Godbey, 2016, p. 74).

Reasons for Cheating on Exams

The reasons students provide for cheating on exams are largely the same as the ones given for student plagiarism. For instance, the need to get a higher grade (Diego, 2017; Foudjio Tchouata et al., 2014; Olafson et al., 2013), the learning culture where the focus is on valuing grades more than learning (Christensen Hughes & McCabe, 2006), the lack of motivation (Ellahi et al., 2013), the lack of time to study (Dodeen, 2012; Guibert & Michaut, 2009) due to extracurricular activities like work (Makarova, 2019) or social activities (Yu et al., 2017). The influence of peers (Diego, 2017; McCabe & Trevino, 1997; Meng et al., 2014; Schuhmann et al., 2013) is also a factor that many researchers have concluded is at the forefront of the reasons students cheat. In a qualitative study conducted with 19 Cambodian students, Maeda (2019,

p. 13) found that "students who did not cooperate with their peers were labelled "unkind". Diego (2017, p. 123) also underscored the influence of peers. As one student observed, "I cheat with, from and for my friends".

While some students may not realize they are plagiarizing, this is not the case when cheating. There is no unintended cheating on an exam. Students report cheating for two reasons: 1) because they perceive the chance of getting caught as slim (Megehee & Spake, 2008) and 2) because they lack knowledge about the consequences of cheating (Meng et al., 2014; Murdock & Anderman, 2006; Schuhmann et al., 2013). In either case, student cheating on exams is not regarded as such a big thing and, as Fendler and Godbey (2016, p. 83) put it, "Students are well aware of the low probability of being punished, thus cheating continues to proliferate".

Academic Misconduct and the Age, Gender and Academic Major Variables

Research has been conducted around the world to better understand the variables that motivate students to plagiarize in their written assignments or to cheat on exams (Anderman & Won, 2019; Eaton, 2017; Guibert & Michaut, 2011; MacLeod & Eaton, 2020). An early meta-analysis (Borkowski & Ugras, 1998) of empirical studies conducted in the United States from 1985 to 1994 examined ethical behaviour with three independent variables: age, gender and academic majors. The authors reported that generally students became more ethical with age, women tended to report more ethical behaviours and that the program of study was not a significant factor. Has this changed some thirty years later?

Student's Gender and Academic Misconduct

Student gender and its link to academic misconduct have been studied extensively with various conclusions. For instance, some researchers (Baetz et al., 2011; Ellahi et al., 2013; Yu et al., 2017) concluded that male students tend to commit more academic misconduct than female students. However, recent research tends to suggest that gender may no longer be a variable of influence (Bokosmaty et al., 2019; Fass-Holmes, 2017; Kayışoğlu & Temel, 2017). That said, the reasons to cheat on exams might differ for male and female students. Male students are more likely to indicate that they cheat to avoid effort while female students are more likely to cheat if the perceived risk of being caught is low (Yang et al., 2013).

Student Age and Academic Misconduct

Student age has also been studied with results indicating that older students tend to commit less academic misconduct than younger students (Jurdi et al., 2011; Kisamore et al., 2007; Olafson et al., 2013). According to Jurdi et al. (2011), this may be due to a change in moral reasoning ability as suggested in Kohlberg's (1973) theory of moral development. Kohlberg suggested that younger individuals may be closer to the first stage of moral reasoning, focusing more on their personal needs and interests, than on universal moral principles like integrity. The categorization of stages in Kohlberg's theory has been questioned (Christensen Hughes & Bertram Gallant, 2016). However, the concept of maturity to explain academic misconduct is invoked by many authors. Indeed, Christensen Hughes and McCabe (2006) refer to student maturity in explaining their results, having found that university students cheat less than high school students and Bertram Gallant et al. (2015, p. 219) specify that "less mature students are more likely to self-report cheating (regardless of their year in college or their age)".

Academic Misconduct Within Various Programs of Study

Other studies have focused on academic dishonesty within various programs of study. For example, Crittenden et al. (2009), conducted a study with 1000 students in 115 universities from 36 countries and found student cheating in faculties of commerce worldwide. They explore three predictors of cheating in their study: gender, level of corruption in the country and socioeconomic environment. Without providing statistics, they conclude that women have a lower propensity to cheat than men and that the level of corruption and the socioeconomic conditions also have an influence on cheating. Teixeira and Rocha (2010) found similar results when conducting an international study with 7, 213 economics and business undergraduate students from 42 universities in 21 countries around the world. Their results indicate that 62% of business and economic undergrad students are cheating. Interestingly, they found differences within countries with Scandinavian countries cheating less (5%) than Eastern European countries (87%), Latin American (67.9%), Southern European (66.4%), New Zealand (20.7%) and the US and British Isles (17%). Klein et al. (2007), found that 86% of their respondents from business, criminal justice, engineering, biomedical sciences, nursing and social work programs reported academic misbehaviours during their college years. However, their research could not detect any significant differences between the programs of study although they mentioned that business students tend to have "attitudes on what constitutes cheating more lax than those of other professional school students" (Klein et al., 2007, p.197).

Academic Misconduct Within Teacher Education Programs

Very few researchers have examined academic misconduct of preservice teachers. The studies that examined gender differences in preservice teachers found that male teacher candidates had a tendency to plagiarize more than women (Eret & Gokmenoglu, 2010; Tasgin, 2018). As for a link between age and a tendency to engage in academic misconduct, one study by Tasgin (2018) found that older preservice teachers tend to plagiarize more, possibly because they need to maintain their high grades.

In Turkey, Eret and Ok (2014) used a questionnaire to examine a link between plagiarism and Internet use in preservice teachers. The researchers found that time constraints were a frequent reason given by the preservice teachers for plagiarism. They also reported that "the frequency of the plagiarism tendency was generally low and the percentages of the students never committing most of the plagiarism acts were generally high" (p. 10). Another interesting insight from this study is that preservice teachers who used computers more frequently and had a higher level of technological knowledge tended to plagiarize more.

Trushell et al. (2012) found similar results using a survey methodology with 42 women and five male students registered in undergraduate education programs. Approximately 45% of the students reported having engaged in academic misconduct. The authors report that education "students who had reported multiple infringements tended to rate their ICT capabilities higher than their peers" (p. 143) possibly because information communication technology (ICT) capabilities might facilitate academic misconduct.

The Crux of the Problem for Teacher Education Programs

It is particularly important to study preservice teachers during their university training because they are going to influence the behaviour of future generations, based on what they find acceptable in their own students' approaches to school work. Preservice teachers' values and habits when assessing assignments and proctoring exams will be passed down to their own students.

In Quebec, according to the Ministry of Education, preservice teachers must be able "To demonstrate ethical and responsible professional behaviours in the performance of his or her duties" (Ministère de l'Éducation du Québec, 2001, p. 55). And so, their role is twofold: they are to be leaders of integrity within the profession as well as models of integrity for their students (Boon, 2011; Cummings et al., 2007).

Unfortunately, according to Maxwell (2017, p. 323), "[e]ducation students are not leaving colleges and universities with a clear understanding of what is expected of them by society, their peers and the profession". Maxwell explains that there is more to being a "nice person" and that preservice teachers must comprehend and meet the ethical standards of their future profession.

Method

We used a questionnaire developed to explore the propensity to cheat among preservice teachers in five universities in the province of Quebec, Canada. The questionnaire included four sections: (1) demographic data; (2) questions related to the propensity to cheat in general, methods of cheating, institutional context, peers' influence, students' perception of control, their goals and their engagement in studying; (3) questions on the arguments for cheating; and (4) perceptions of risk related to cheating. Complete details about the development of the questionnaire can be found in a recent publication (Frenette et al., 2019).

For the purpose of this chapter, we concentrate on three areas of investigation: (1) reasons given for cheating by students, (2) the most prevalent dishonest behaviours in exams (high school and university), (3) the most prevalent dishonest behaviours in written assignments. For each question, students were required to choose two of the six options proposed. Differences between the variables were investigated using t-tests and ANOVA (with Bonferroni post hoc test) for frequent cheaters (versus. occasional cheaters), gender, working hours (15 h and more vs. lower than 15 h), age and programs. The research received ethics approval from all universities involved.

Participants

A link to the online questionnaire (LimeSurvey) was sent by email by the universities to a convenient sample of about 5,500 preservice teachers in the faculty of education of five universities in the province of Quebec at the beginning of 2018. A total of 573 students (486 females; 86 males; 1 other) completed the survey (~10.4%). In order to distinguish frequent cheaters (those who reported a high propensity for cheating) from occasional cheaters (those who reported a low propensity for cheating), respondents were asked to rate two items on cheating using a 4-point scale which ranged from 1 = "strongly disagree", indicating the absence of cheating, to 4 = "strongly agree" representing lots of cheating. Items used were: (1) I cheated in high school to get better grades and (2) I have cheated during my university degree. Frequent cheaters would be the students who chose "agree" or "strongly agree", indicating a high propensity for cheating. Participants that indicated they had been frequent cheaters during exams in high school represented 34.9% of the sample. In university they were less numerous (15.2%).

Approximately 27% of the students indicated they work more than 15 h per week. Other participants' characteristics are presented in Table 16.1.

Table 16.1 Characteristics of participants: age, year in program, and program

Age		Year in program (%)		Program (%)	
18–20	17.80%	1st	27.92	Kindergarten/primary	47.47
21–23	48.52%	2nd	24.26	Secondary	17.45
24–25	12.39%	3rd	23.91	Special education	19.55
26 and +	21.29%	4th	17.98	Other (arts, physical activity)	15.53
		Special case	5.93		

Results

A general profile of the *preservice teacher cheater* was established from the frequency of responses provided on three specific questions. One question requested that participants ranked the best two reasons, among a choice of six options, that would motivate them to cheat during exams: "I would cheat if…". For the other two questions, participants had to indicated their perception of the two best ways to cheat in exam "What would be the best way to cheat during an exam?" and the two best ways to plagiarize in written assignments "What would be the best way to plagiarize for an assignment?". In both cases, they were provided with six options to select from. The most frequent answers to each of the questions studied are presented in Table 16.2.

When asked what would be the specific characteristics of a student who decide to cheat or plagiarize, respondents selected two characteristics out of six: someone who spends little time studying (49.2%) and past experiences of academic misconduct (46.9%).

Table 16.2 Reasons preservice teachers would cheat during an exam and their preferred behaviours

I would cheat if (%)	
I do not think I can pass the exam	57.6
The chances of getting caught are low	43.1
I did not study enough	31.1
Dishonest behaviours in exams (%)	
Use notes hidden in my material	63
Look at my neighbour's copy	55.7
Use a cellphone or other electronic device	31.9
Dishonest behaviours in written assignments (plagiarism) (%)	
Reuse one of my existing assignment	47.6
Ask somebody else to do my assignment	38.6
Collaborate with peers	37.2

Results for Specific Characteristics of Cheaters in Preservice Teachers

As mentioned earlier, differences among variables were investigated using t-tests and ANOVA (with Bonferroni post hoc test) for frequent cheaters (vs. occasional) in exams in high school or in university, working hours (15 h and more vs. lower than 15 h), age and program. Frequency by options for each group are presented on Tables 16.3, 16.4 and 16.5. There were no significant differences between men and women participants so this will not be discussed in this chapter.

We can see that running out of time is evoked more often by students working more than 15 h than their peers working 15 h of less. It is also interesting to note on Table 16.3 that occasional cheaters in exams at university level are more influenced by their peers than frequent cheaters.

The age of the respondent also seemed to make a difference with younger students (18–20 years old) having a higher temptation to cheat if they have not studied enough when they are compared with the 24–25 years old as indicated on Table 16.4.

Table 16.3 Reasons to cheat: frequent cheaters (high school and university) and working hours

I would cheat if…	Frequent cheaters university (%)	Occasional cheaters university (%)	Frequent cheaters high school (%)	Occasional cheaters high school (%)	15 h and less (%)	More than 15 h (%)
The chances of getting caught are low	47.1	42.5	48.0	40.5	45.0	37.9
I need the highest possible mark	19.5	25.2	24.5	24.1	24.3	24.2
My peers cheat too	14.9	23.9*	21.0	23.3	23.3	20.3
I am running out of time	14.9	18.1	15.5	18.8	15.2	24.2*
I have not studied enough	40.2	29.5	33.0	30.0	31.0	31.4
I do not think I can pass the exam	56.3	57.9	54.0	59.5	57.9	56.9

*$p < 0.05$

Table 16.4 Reasons to cheat: age

I would cheat if…	18–20 (%)	21–23 (%)	24–25 (%)	26 + (%)
The chances of getting caught are low	45.1	44.6	40.8	39.3
I need the highest possible mark	27.5	23.3	31.0	22.1
My peers cheat too	21.6	21.2	21.1	27.0
I am running out of time	8.8	19.4	18.3	20.5
I have not studied enough	43.1*	29.9	22.5	28.7
I do not think I can pass the exam	53.9	59.0	60.6	55.7

$^{*}p < 0.05$

Table 16.5 Reasons to cheat: program

I would cheat if…	Kindergarten/primary (%)	Secondary (%)	Special education (%)	Other (%)
The chances of getting caught are low	41.5	58.0*	35.7	40.4
I need the highest possible mark	26.5	21.0	20.5	25.8
My peers cheat too	22.4	23.0	25.0	19.1
I am running out of time	13.6	18.0	22.3	23.6
I have not studied enough	35.7	25.0	31.3	23.6
I do not think I can pass the exam	58.1	55.0	59.8	56.2

$^{*}p < 0.05$

Preservice teachers that aim to teach in high school selected significantly more often the option the chances of getting caught are low than their peers from primary or special education programs as a justification for cheating.

Dishonest Behaviours in Exam and Assignments

In terms of dishonest behaviours for cheating on exams (Table 16.6), there are more significant differences. It seems that frequent cheaters at the university level would prefer *looking at their neighbour's copy* and *hide notes outside the classroom* as best ways to cheat while frequent cheaters at the high school level would select *use*

Table 16.6 Dishonest behaviours in exams

What are be the best ways to cheat on exams?	Frequent cheaters university (%)	Occasional cheaters university (%)	Frequent cheaters high school (%)	Occasional cheaters high school (%)
Use notes hidden in my material	59.8	63.7	70.5*	59.0
Look at my neighbour's copy	65.5*	54.0	60.0	53.4
Use a cellphone or other electronic device	18.4	34.4*	23.0	36.7*
Hide notes outside the classroom	18.4*	7.4	10.0	8.6
Exchange notes with other students	18.4	11.8	14.5	11.8
Talk to peers	14.9	25.8*	18.0	27.3*

$^{*}p < 0.05$

notes hidden in their material more than students from all other groups. Occasional cheaters, both at university and in high school, believe that *talking to peers* or *using cell phones or other electronic devices* are the best ways to cheat.

Although there were some differences between participants in the age groups and the programs, these two variables were not significant.

Table 16.7 presents the results for dishonest behaviours in written assignments. Once again, there are significant differences between frequent cheaters and occasional cheaters, the former considering copy-paste text from the Internet (high school and university) and buying assignment done by someone else (high school and university) as the best options for a student wanting to plagiarize while occasional cheaters chose more often the option reuse one of my existing assignments (high school and in university).

Significant differences were also present with age groups as shown in Table 16.8 where we could see that the older students (more than 26 years) choose significantly more often the options to *reuse one of my existing assignments* and to *ask somebody else to do my assignment* than younger ones. Younger students also chose the option *collaborate with peers* more often than the 26 + group.

Finally, the program of study made a difference with primary preservice teachers being more inclined to select the option *copy-paste parts of someone else's work* than preservice teachers studying to be special education teachers (Table 16.9).

Table 16.7 Dishonest behaviours in written assignments (plagiarism)

What are be the best ways to plagiarize?	Frequent cheaters university (%)	Occasional cheaters university (%)	Frequent cheaters high school (%)	Occasional cheater high school (%)
Reuse one of my existing assignments	21.8	41.6*	29.5	43.4*
Ask somebody else to do my assignment	9.2	18.1	15.0	17.7
Collaborate with peers	25.3	32.0	28.0	32.4
Copy-paste parts of someone else work	26.4	25.4	25.5	25.5
Copy-paste text from the Internet	55.2*	34.0	43.0*	34.0
Buy an assignment done by someone else	57.5*	46.0	55.0*	43.7

*$p < 0.05$

Table 16.8 Dishonest behaviours in written assignment: age

What are be the best ways to plagiarize?	18–20 (%)	21–23 (%)	24–25 (%)	26 and plus (%)
Reuse one of my existing assignments	33.3	34.2	43.7	50.0*
Ask somebody else to do my assignment	10.8	14.7	21.1	23.8*
Collaborate with peers	39.2*	34.2	23.9	20.5
Copy-paste parts of someone else work	24.5	24.1	29.6	27.0
Copy-paste text from the Internet	42.2	38.5	38.0	29.5
Buy an assignment done by someone else	50.0	50.7	38.0	44.3

*$p < 0.05$

Discussion

Before we examine the cheating and plagiarizing behaviours of our participants, it is important to note that students in teacher education programs do not have a reputation of plagiarizing and cheating as do business students for example (Crittenden et al., 2009; Lawson, 2004; Teixeira & Rocha, 2010). Statistics on preservice teachers' level of academic dishonesty were impossible to find other than Lancaster (2020) who reported that preservice teachers contract cheat less than other students. Our results show that 15.2% of our participants commit academic misconduct. While this is not a high percentage, it is still too high for professionals that will be role

Table 16.9 Dishonest behaviours in written assignment: program

What are be the best ways to plagiarize?	Kindergarten/primary (%)	Secondary (%)	Special education (%)	Other (%)
Reuse one of my existing assignments	40.1	32.0	38.4	41.6
Ask somebody else to do my assignment	17.6	20.0	10.7	18.0
Collaborate with peers	32.7	27.0	33.9	25.8
Copy-paste parts of someone else work	31.3*	20.0	26.8	12.4
Copy-paste text from the Internet	34.2	45.0	36.6	38.2
Buy an assignment done by someone else	42.6	56.0	48.2	52.8

*$p < 0.05$

models for future generations and will need to understand all the nuances of what is and isn't academic integrity. A possible explanation for this result is that once student teachers in Quebec are accepted in the program, as long as they pass their courses, they don't need high grades to find a job after they graduate (Fontaine et al., 2020). The low level of plagiarizing and cheating can also be explained by certain personal characteristics of preservice teachers, in Quebec and elsewhere. Firstly, in order to be admitted in most teacher education programs, students need a high-grade point average (Casey & Childs, 2007). This suggests that preservice teachers are usually students who invest time and effort in their studies, they are conscientious and achievement striving (Decker & Rimm-Kaufman, 2008). Secondly, they are also considered to be "nervous and concerned about their ability to succeed in relation to others" (Decker & Rimm-Kaufman, 2008, p. 58). These characteristics will be discussed in further details when interpreting our results.

Methods of Cheating on Exams

The perceived best methods of cheating on exams by preservice teachers are *hiding notes*. Frequent cheaters in high school would hide their notes *in the material* but once at university, they would choose to hide their notes *outside the classroom*. One plausible explanation is that high school students are not allowed to wander outside of class during school hours whereas there are always students in the hallways at the university, making it easier for cheaters to leave class to go and look at their hidden notes. There is also an element of preparedness to consider. In high school, students tried to peek at their notes, maybe on the spur of the moment when realizing that they do not know the exam content. In university, however, frequent cheaters chose to place their materials outside of the classroom, indicating that their cheating was intentional and premeditated. This brings up the question of intent to cheat which can be linked according to De Bruin and Rudnick (2007, p. 153) to "a lack of effort and a need for high excitement seeking".

Our results indicate that *using cell phones or other electronic devices* is not perceived as a very popular method of cheating by preservice teachers contradicting what Srikanth and Asmatulu (2014, p. 138) who confirm that "Smartphones are the most popular tools for cheating today". A possible interpretation for this difference is that in Quebec, students must leave their personal belongings in front of the class when writing an exam and so have no access to their phones.

Preferred Method of Plagiarizing

The three preferred methods that would be used to plagiarize are to *buy an assignment*, to *reuse one of their own assignments* or to *copy and paste from the Internet*. This can be linked very clearly to the amount of effort, and time put into an assignment by the students. *Buying a paper* and *reusing one* do not necessitate much effort, or as Amigud and Lancaster (2019, p. 106) explain, the students feel that the assignment is not "worthy of their efforts". On the other hand, *copying and pasting from the Internet* demands a web search and then some reformulating on the part of the student (Peters & Gervais, 2016). Many researchers (Bretag et al., 2019; Lancaster, 2020; Medway et al., 2018) have shown in last few years the rise of essay mills and it seems that preservice teachers are not an exception though they seem to contract cheat less than other students (Lancaster, 2020).

Older students tend to favor *reuse their old assignment* more, possibly because they have studied for a longer period of time and have a larger number of assignments to pick from. Recycling an assignment might also be considered less of an offence than buying a paper (Maxwell et al., 2008). These older students would also *ask someone else to write their assignments* more frequently than their younger counterparts, again having been longer at the university, they might know more students who have already gone through the program, making it easier to reach out and get an old assignment from a friend. Older students usually work while studying and have family commitments (Kasworm, 2003) which take time away from their studies and might tempt them into taking short cuts.

The younger students would be more apt to *collaborate with peers* to plagiarize. Suwantarathip and Wichadee's (2014) results confirm that this new generation of students prefers to use tools such as Google Docs to write collaboratively, which increases their motivation to study. The problem with working collaboratively is that often, because the limits of collaboration are not specified by the professors (McCabe, 2001), students will collaborate and cheat together. Unfortunately, Parameswaran and Devi's research (2006) has shown that students feel that helping peers with their assignments is not considered as academic dishonesty which is why Higbee and

Thomas (2002, p. 48) explain that "students may be accused of academic dishonesty when they believe they are using acceptable study strategies or seeking legitimate assistance". Furthermore, Wideman (2011, p. 38) specifies that students feel it is important that they display "loyalty to the group when they assisted each other in the completion of assignments and quizzes". Therefore, it is imperative that professors specify what is and what is not acceptable behaviour when collaborating on assignments or take-home exams.

Cheating in Order to Succeed

Preservice teachers' characteristics explain some of the reasons why our participants mentioned they would cheat. One reason is linked to their need to succeed. Preservice teachers would cheat if they do not think they *will pass the exam*. In that situation, their sense of self-confidence might be low when they are used to excelling in school and they wish to continue to have good grades. Decker and Rimm-Kaufman (2008, p. 58) explain it very well in their study on preservice teachers' characteristics: "Pre-service teachers educating themselves in such competitive settings may be more likely to experience feelings of stress and inferiority while competing with so many other high performing individuals". Other researchers have found similar results where the learning process and its newly acquired knowledge is less valued than the grades obtained (Heckler & Forde, 2015). Amua-Sekyi and Mensah (2016, p. 58) in their study found that preservice teachers' "fear of failure is the most frequent motivation cited by respondents" as the reason for academic misconduct. According to Pintrich (2003, p. 671), students who do not expect to succeed will be less "motivated in terms of effort, persistence, and behaviour". This might lead some students to dishonest behaviours.

Poor Studying Habits Lead to Bad Choices

Another reason preservice teachers give as a justification for cheating on exams is the fact that *they have not studied enough*. Age is one demographic factor that might explain this justification. Younger students are more likely to use this excuse than older students, possibly because they are more caught up with their social life than the older students who might have more responsibilities.

A contextual factor, working and studying at the same time might also explain why some preservice teachers would make bad choices. Students who reported working more than 15 h a week while studying would in fact be more likely to cheat on exams because they are *running out of time*. Trying to hold down a job and study at the same time can cause fatigue, stress, lack of preparedness for classes, all factors that can lead to poor decisions and academic dishonesty. Lack of time management skills was also a factor blamed for plagiarizing in Heckler and Forde's (2015) research.

The students in their study acknowledged that their own failings brought them to plagiarize.

Another possible explanation is the use of poor learning strategies. Jurdi et al. (2011) explain how using deep strategies for learning requires efforts and time from the students and usually result in better learning outcomes. The researchers found that "academic dishonesty was related negatively to the use of deep-level strategies and positively to the use of surface-level strategies" (Jurdi et al., 2011, p. 24). Unfortunately, *not studying enough* and *running out of time* would most certainly lead preservice teachers to adopt surface-level strategies which would lead to academic dishonesty.

Cheating Culture

Preservice teachers would cheat when they know the *chances of getting caught are low*. This is consistent with Christensen Hughes and McCabe's survey (2006, p. 16), in which they found that "the perceived low risk of being caught or penalized may lead students to conclude that a positive cost–benefit exists". It is possible that the preservice teachers in this study are aware of the low chances of getting caught and the relatively benign consequences, and this is why they would be willing to take a risk. Our results also show that the cheating culture in universities has consequences for occasional cheaters who said that they would be more likely to cheat if their peers were doing it. Jurdi et al., (2011, p. 23) explain "that observing peers' cheat or getting asked for help cheating sends the message that cheating is the "norm"". Other studies have shown that peer influence is a factor in the cheating culture at the university level (Crittenden et al., 2009; Heckler & Forde, 2015).

Cheating as a Pattern

One last reason why preservice teacher would cheat is perturbing. Our participants suggested that they would cheat because they *have cheated in the past*. This is perturbing because it indicates a pattern of bad behaviour in the preservice teachers. Has cheating become a habit for these students and will it continue to be a habit all through the program and into their professional life? Akbaşlı et al. (2019) in their study also found that preservice teachers who had a higher academic dishonesty tendency score would more often cheat on exams or plagiarize on assignments. This is very disturbing considering that "having a higher tendency towards academic dishonesty signals a lower moral obligation, moral accountability, and moral outrage scores" (Akbaşlı et al., 2019, p. 9). Teachers are expected to be examples and moral compasses for their students and this type of behaviour is certainly not what we want our primary and high school students to learn from their teachers.

Other authors (Klein et al., 2007; Lovett-Hooper et al., 2007) have shown that some students who cheated during their studies have continued to cheat in their work context. Though the participants in these studies were not preservice teachers, they came from fields of studies where there is a code of ethics, nursing, engineering, social work, etc., just like in education. These professionals, like our preservice teachers, are now in our workforce and are possibly repeating these dishonest behaviours.

Conclusion

It is imperative for our preservice teachers to follow their program of studies with integrity in order to show a high standard of integrity to their future students. The following recommendations are put forward to diminish the opportunities for cheating and plagiarizing in teacher education programs.

Our first recommendation is that professors should, on the first day of class and for each assignment repeatedly throughout the semester, state what is allowed and what is not for collaboration and what will be considered plagiarism. This should be explained and discussed with the students so that there is no ambiguity.

Our research has shown that preservice teachers would cheat when the risks of getting caught are low. Our second recommendation is to ensure that preservice teachers are made aware of the consequences of getting caught and of ways that their professors will enforce academic integrity. Professors should report all cases of academic infractions. If this is enforced and the message sent is clear, preservice teachers will think twice about committing academic misbehaviours.

In order to counteract a cheating culture, we recommend that all preservice teachers be made aware of the importance of the integrity qualities (International Center for Academic Integrity, 2021). Their role as future educators who will influence and model the next generations has to be emphasized during their teacher education program. The responsibilities and the ethic code of a teacher must be presented to the preservice teachers. They need to understand how studying with integrity is a habit to cultivate in themselves and their own students. Only then will we be able to establish an integrity culture in schools and higher education.

References

Akbaşlı, S., Erçetin, ŞŞ, & Kubilay, S. (2019). Relationship between prospective teachers' deontic justice attitudes and academic dishonesty tendencies. *South African Journal of Education, 39*(3), 1–12.

Ali, W. Z. W., Ismail, H., & Cheat, T. T. (2012). Plagiarism: To What Extent it is Understood? *Procedia—Social and Behavioral Sciences, 59*, 604–611.

Amigud, A., & Lancaster, T. (2019). 246 reasons to cheat: An analysis of students' reasons for seeking to outsource academic work. *Computers & Education, 134*, 98–107.

Amua-Sekyi, E. T., & Mensah, E. (2016). Guilty in whose eyes? Student-teachers' perspectives on cheating on examinations. *Journal of Education and Practice, 7*(21), 55–64.

Anderman, E. M., & Won, S. (2019). Academic cheating in disliked classes. *Ethics & Behavior, 29*(1), 1–22.

Baetz, M., Zivcakova, L., Wood, E., Nosko, A., De Pasquale, D., & Archer, K. (2011). Encouraging active classroom discussion of academic integrity and misconduct in higher education business contexts. *Journal of Academic Ethics, 9*(3), 217.

Bens, S. L. (2010). *Senior education students' understandings of academic honesty and dishonesty.* (Ph.D.). University of Saskatchewan, Saskatoon, Canada.

Bertram Gallant, T., Binkin, N., & Donohue, M. (2015). Students at risk for being reported for cheating. *Journal of Academic Ethics, 13*(3), 217–228.

Bokosmaty, S., Ehrich, J., Eady, M. J., & Bell, K. (2019). Canadian university students' gendered attitudes toward plagiarism. *Journal of Further and Higher Education, 43*(2), 276–290.

Boon, H. J. (2011). Raising the Bar: Ethics Education for Quality Teachers. *The Australian Journal of Teacher Education, 36*(7), 76–93.

Borkowski, S. C., & Ugras, Y. J. (1998). Business students and ethics: A meta-analysis. *Journal of Business Ethics, 17*(11), 1117–1127.

Bretag, T., & Mahmud, S. (2009). A model for determining student plagiarism: Electronic detection and academic judgment. *Journal of University Teaching and Learning Practice, 6*(1), 49–60.

Bretag, T., Harper, R., Burton, M., Ellis, C., Newton, P., van Haeringen, K., & Rozenberg, P. (2019). Contract cheating and assessment design: Exploring the relationship. *Assessment & Evaluation in Higher Education, 44*(5), 676–691.

Bretag, T., & Harper, R. (2020). Contract cheating at colleges and other non-university higher education providers. In T. Bretag (Ed.), *A research agenda for academic integrity* (pp. 127–137). Cheltenham, UK: Edward Elgar Publishing.

Bruton, S. V. (2014). Self-Plagiarism and textual recycling: legitimate forms of research misconduct. *Accountability in Research: Policies & Quality Assurance, 21*(3), 176–197.

Callahan, D. (2007). *The cheating culture: Why more Americans are doing wrong to get ahead*: Houghton Mifflin Harcourt.

Camara, S., Eng-Ziskin, S., Wimberley, L., Dabbour, K. S., & Lee, C. M. (2017). Predicting students' intention to plagiarize: An ethical theoretical framework. *Journal of Academic Ethics, 15*(1), 43–58.

Carrell, S. E., Malmstrom, F. V., & West, J. E. (2008). Peer effects in academic cheating. *The Journal of Human Resources, 43*(1), 173–207.

Carroll, J. (2005). Deterring, detecting and dealing with student plagiarism. Joint Information Systems Committee (JISC) Briefing Paper. http://www.jisc.ac.uk/media/documents/publications/plagiarismbp.pdf

Casey, C., & Childs, R. (2007). Teacher education program admission criteria and what beginning teachers need to know to be successful teachers. *Canadian Journal of Educational Administration and Policy, 6*, 1–24.

Chaput de Saintonge, D. M., & Pavlovic, A. (2004). Cheating. *Medical Education, 38*(1), 8–9.

Chen, Y., & Chou, C. (2017). Are we on the same page? College students' and faculty's perception of student plagiarism in Taiwan. *Ethics & Behavior, 27*(1), 53–73.

Chirumamilla, A., Sindre, G., & Nguyen-Duc, A. (2020). Cheating in e-exams and paper exams: The perceptions of engineering students and teachers in Norway. *Assessment and Evaluation in Higher Education, 45*(7), 1–18.

Christensen Hughes, J. M., & McCabe, D. L. (2006). Academic misconduct within higher education in Canada. *Canadian Journal of Higher Education, 36*, 1–21.

Christensen Hughes, J., & Bertram Gallant, T. (2016). Infusing ethics and ethical decision making into the curriculum. In T. Bretag (Ed.), *Handbook of Academic Integrity* (pp. 1055–1073). Singapore: Springer Singapore.

Cizek, G. J. (1999). *Cheating on tests: how to do it, detect it, and prevent it*. Mahwah, N.J: L. Erlbaum Associates.

Crittenden, V. L., Hanna, R. C., & Peterson, R. A. (2009). The cheating culture: A global societal phenomenon. *Business Horizons, 52*(4), 337–346.

Cummings, R., Harlow, S., & Maddux, C. D. (2007). Moral reasoning of in-service and pre-service teachers: A review of the research. *Journal of Moral Education, 36*(1), 67–78.

Curtis, G. J., & Vardanega, L. (2016). Is plagiarism changing over time? A 10-year time-lag study with three points of measurement. *Higher Education Research & Development*, 1–13.

Curtis, G. J., & Popal, R. (2011). An examination of factors related to plagiarism and a five-year follow-up of plagiarism at an Australian university. *International Journal for Educational Integrity, 7*(1), 30–42.

De Bruin, G. P., & Rudnick, H. (2007). Examining the cheats: The role of conscientiousness and excitement seeking in academic dishonesty. *South African Journal of Psychology, 37*(1), 153–164.

Decker, L. E., & Rimm-Kaufman, S. E. (2008). Personality characteristics and teacher beliefs among pre-service teachers. *Teacher Education Quarterly, 35*(2), 45–64.

DeLong, D. (2012). Propensity toward unintentional plagiarism. *Global Education Journal, 2012*(4), 136–154.

Desalegn, A. A., & Berhan, A. (2014). Cheating on examinations and its predictors among undergraduate students at Hawassa university college of medicine and health science, Hawassa Ethiopia. . *BMC Medical Education, 14*(1), 89–89.

Diego, L. (2017). Friends with benefits: Causes and effects of learners' cheating practices during examination. *IAFOR Journal of Education, 5.*

Dodeen, H. M. (2012). Undergraduate student cheating in exams. *Damascus University Journal, 28*(1), 37–55.

Eaton, S. E., & Edino, R. I. (2018). Strengthening the research agenda of educational integrity in Canada: A review of the research literature and call to action. *International Journal for Educational Integrity, 14*(1), 5. https://doi.org/10.1007/s40979-018-0028-7

Eaton, S. E., Fernåndez Conde, C., Rothschuh, S., Guglielmin, M., & Otoo, B. K. (2020). Plagiarism: A Canadian higher education case study of policy and practice gaps. *Alberta Journal of Educational Research, 66*(4), 471–488.

Eaton, S. E. (2017). Comparative analysis of institutional policy definitions of plagiarism: A pan-Canadian university study. *Interchange: A Quarterly Review of Education, 48*(3), 271–281. https://doi.org/10.1007/s10780-017-9300-7

Eaton, S. E. (2020). Cheating may be under-reported across Canada's universities and colleges. *The Conversation.* https://theconversation.com/cheating-may-be-under-reported-across-canadas-universities-and-colleges-129292

Elander, J., Pittam, G., Lusher, J., Fox, P., & Payne, N. (2010). Evaluation of an intervention to help students avoid unintentional plagiarism by improving their authorial identity. *Assessment & Evaluation in Higher Education, 35*(2), 157–171.

Ellahi, A., Mushtaq, R., & Bashir Khan, M. (2013). Multi campus investigation of academic dishonesty in higher education of Pakistan. *International Journal of Educational Management, 27*(6), 647–666.

Eret, E., & Ok, A. (2014). Internet plagiarism in higher education: tendencies, triggering factors and reasons among teacher candidates. *Assessment & Evaluation in Higher Education*, 1–15.

Eret, E., & Gokmenoglu, T. (2010). Plagiarism in higher education: A case study with prospective academicians. *Procedia - Social and Behavioral Sciences, 2*(2), 3303–3307.

Fass-Holmes, B. (2017). International students reported for academic integrity violations: Demographics, retention, and graduation. *Journal of International Students, 7*(3), 664–669.

Faucher, D., & Caves, S. (2009). Academic dishonesty: Innovative cheating techniques and the detection and prevention of them. *Teaching and Learning in Nursing, 4*, 37–41.

Fendler, R. J., Yates, M., & Godbey, J. (2018). Observing and deterring social cheating on college exams. *International Journal for the Scholarship of Teaching and Learning, 12*(1).

Fendler, R. J., & Godbey, J. M. (2016). Cheaters should never win: Eliminating the benefits of cheating. *Journal of Academic Ethics, 14*(1), 71–85.

Fish, R., & Hura, G. (2013). Students' perceptions of plagiarism. *Journal of the Scholarship of Teaching and Learning, 13*(5), 33–45.

Foltýnek, T., Meuschke, N., & Gipp, B. (2019). Academic plagiarism detection: A systematic literature review. *ACM Comput. Surv., 52*(6), Article 112.

Fontaine, S., Frenette, E., & Hébert, M.-H. (2020). Exam cheating among Quebec's preservice teachers: The influencing factors. *International Journal for Educational Integrity, 16*(14), 1–18. https://doi.org/10.1007/s40979-020-00062-6

Foudjio Tchouata, C., Lamago, M. F., & Singo Njabo, C. (2014). Fraude aux examens de formation des enseignants: Le cas de l'École normale supérieure de Yaoundé. *Formation Et Profession, 22*(3), 48–62.

Fredeen, S. M. (2013). Discourses of Im/possibility: International students at a Canadian university. (Ph.D.). University of Alberta, Edmonton, Alberta.

Frenette, E., Fontaine, S., Hébert, M.-H., & Éthier, M. (2019). Étude sur la propension à tricher aux examens à l'université : élaboration et processus de validation du Questionnaire sur la tricherie aux examens à l'université (QTEU). *Mesure Et Évaluation En Éducation, 42*(2), 1–33.

Gravett, K., & Kinchin, I. M. (2018). Referencing and empowerment: exploring barriers to agency in the higher education student experience. *Teaching in Higher Education*, 1–14.

Guibert, P., & Michaut, C. (2009). Les facteurs individuels et contextuels de la fraude aux examens universitaires.*Revue française de pédagogie, 169,* 43-52.

Guibert, P., & Michaut, C. (2011). Le plagiat étudiant.*Education et sociétés, 2*(28), 149-163.

Gullifer, J., & Tyson, G. A. (2010). Exploring university students perceptions of plagiarism: A focus group study. *Studies in Higher Education, 35*(4), 463–481.

Halupa, C., & Bolliger, D. U. (2015). Student perceptions of self-plagiarism: A multi-university exploratory study. *Journal of Academic Ethics, 13*(1), 91–105.

Harper, R., Bretag, T., Ellis, C., Newton, P., Rozenberg, P., Saddiqui, S., & van Haeringen, K. (2019). Contract cheating: A survey of Australian university staff. *Studies in Higher Education, 44*(11), 1857–1873.

Heckler, N. C., & Forde, D. R. (2015). The role of cultural values in plagiarism in higher education. *Journal of Academic Ethics, 13*(1), 61–75.

Higbee, J. L., & Thomas, P. V. (2002). Student and faculty perceptions of behaviors that constitute cheating. *NASPA Journal, 40*(1).

Hossain, M. A. (2019). Plagiarism in scholarly writing. *Research Journal Of English (RJOE).*

International Center for Academic Integrity (ICAI). (2021). *The fundamental values of academic integrity* (3rd ed). https://www.academicintegrity.org/fundamental-values/

Ison, D. C. (2018). An empirical analysis of differences in plagiarism among world cultures. *Journal of Higher Education Policy and Management, 40*(4), 291–304.

Jones, M., & Sheridan, L. (2015). Back translation: An emerging sophisticated cyber strategy to subvert advances in digital age plagiarism detection and prevention. *Assessment & Evaluation in Higher Education, 40*(5), 712–724.

Jurdi, R., Hage, H. S., & Chow, H. P. H. (2011). Academic dishonesty in the canadian classroom: Behaviours of a sample of university students. *Canadian journal of higher education (1975), 41*(3), 1.

Kakkonen, T., & Mozgovoy, M. (2010). Hermetic and web plagiarism detection systems for student essays—an evaluation of the state of the art. *Journal Educational Computing Research, 42*(2), 135–159.

Kasworm, C. E. (2003). Setting the stage: Adults in higher education. *New Directions for Student Services, 2003*(102), 3–10.

Kayışoğlu, N. B., & Temel, C. (2017). An examination of attitudes towards cheating in exams by physical education and sports high school students. *Universal Journal of Educational Research, 5*(8), 1396–1402.

Kisamore, J. L., Stone, T. H., & Jawahar, I. M. (2007). Academic Integrity: The relationship between individual and situational factors on misconduct contemplations. *Journal of Business Ethics, 75*(4), 381–394.

Klein, H., Levenburg, N. M., McKendall, M., & Mothersell, W. (2007). Cheating during the college years: How do business school students compare? *Journal of Business Ethics, 72*(2), 197–206.

Kohlberg, L. (1973). *Collected Papers on Moral Development and Moral Education*: Moral Education & Research Foundation.

Kulathuramaiyer, N., & Maurer, H. (2007). *Coping with the Copy-Paste-Syndrome*. Paper presented at the world conference on e-learning in corporate, Government, Healthcare, and Higher Education.

Lancaster, T. (2020). Academic discipline integration by contract cheating services and essay mills. *Journal of Academic Ethics, 18*(2), 115–127. https://doi.org/10.1007/s10805-019-09357-x

Lancaster, T., & Clarke, R. (2016). Contract cheating: The outsourcing of assessed student work. In T. Bretag (Ed.), *Handbook of academic integrity* (pp. 639–654). Singapore: Springer Reference.

Lang, J. M. (2013). *Cheating lessons: Learning from academic dishonesty*. United States: Harvard University Press.

Lawson, R. A. (2004). Is classroom cheating related to business students propensity to cheat in the real world? *Journal of Business Ethics, 49*(2), 189–199.

Liddell, J. (2003). A comprehensive definition of plagiarism. *Community & Junior College Libraries, 11*(3), 43–52.

Löfström, E., & Kupila, P. (2013). The instructional challenges of student plagiarism. *Journal of Academic Ethics, 11*(3), 231–242.

Louw, H. (2017). Defining plagiarism: Student and staff perceptions of a grey concept. *South African Journal of Higher Education, 31*(5), 16–135.

Lovett-Hooper, G., Komarraju, M., Weston, R., & Dollinger, S. J. (2007). Is plagiarism a forerunner of other deviance? Imagined futures of academically dishonest students. *Ethics & Behavior, 17*(3), 323–336.

MacLeod, P. D. (2014). *An exploration of faculty attitudes toward student academic dishonesty in selected Canadian universities*. Canada: University of Calgary.

MacLeod, P. D., & Eaton, S. E. (2020). The paradox of faculty attitudes toward student violations of academic integrity. *Journal of Academic Ethics, 18*(4), 347–362.

Maeda, M. (2019). Exam cheating among Cambodian students: When, how, and why it happens. *Compare: A Journal of Comparative and International Education*, 1–19.

Mahmud, S., Bretag, T., & Foltýnek, T. (2019). Students' perceptions of plagiarism policy in higher education: A comparison of the United Kingdom, Czechia, Poland and Romania. *Journal of Academic Ethics, 17*(3), 271–289.

Makarova, M. (2019). Factors of academic misconduct in a cross-cultural perspective and the role of integrity systems. *Journal of Academic Ethics, 17*(1), 51–71.

Maxwell, B. (2017). Codes of professional conduct and ethics education for future teachers. *Philosophical Inquiry in Education, 24*(4), 323–347.

Maxwell, A., Curtis, G. J., & Vardanega, L. (2008). Does culture influence understanding and perceived seriousness of plagiarism? *The International Journal for Educational Integrity, 4*(2), 25–40.

McCabe, D. L., & Trevino, L. K. (1997). Individual and contextual influences on academic dishonesty: A multicampus investigation. *Research in Higher Education, 38*(3), 379–396.

McCabe, D. L., Trevino, L. K., & Butterfield, K. D. (2002). Honor codes and other contextual influences on academic integrity: A replication and extension to modified honor code settings. *Research in Higher Education, 43*(3), 357–378.

McCabe, D. (2001). Cheating: Why students do it and how we can help them stop. *American Educator, 25*(4). http://www.aft.org/newspubs/periodicals/ae/winter2001/mccabe.cfm

Medway, D., Roper, S., & Gillooly, L. (2018). Contract cheating in UK higher education: A covert investigation of essay mills. *British Educational Research Journal, 44*(3), 393–418.

Megehee, C. M., & Spake, D. F. (2008). The impact of perceived peer behavior, probable detection and punishment severity on student cheating behavior. *Marketing Education Review, 18*(2), 5–20.

Meng, C. L., Othman, J., D'Silva, J. L., & Omar, Z. (2014). Influence of neutralization attitude in academic dishonesty among undergraduates. *International Education Studies, 7*(6).

Michaut, C. (2013). Les nouveaux outils de la tricherie scolaire au lycée. *Recherches en éducation*(16), 131–142.

Ministère de l'Éducation du Québec. (2001). *La formation à l'enseignement. Les orientations. Les compétences professionnelles*. Québec Ministère de l'Éducation, Gouvernement du Québec.

Murdock, T. B., & Anderman, E. M. (2006). Motivational perspectives on student cheating: Toward an integrated model of academic dishonesty. *Educational Psychologist, 41*(3), 129–145.

Olafson, L., Schraw, G., Nadelson, L., Nadelson, S., & Kehrwald, N. (2013). Exploring the judgment-action gap: College students and academic dishonesty. *Ethics & Behavior, 23*(2), 148–162.

Parameswaran, A., & Devi, P. (2006). Student plagiarism and faculty responsibility in undergraduate engineering labs. *Higher Education Research and Development, 25*(3), 263–276.

Pavlin-Bernardić, N., Rovan, D., & Pavlović, J. (2017). Academic cheating in mathematics classes: A motivational perspective. *Ethics & Behavior, 27*(6), 486–501.

Pereda, J. M., Lannelongue, G., & Benito, J. (2016). The antecedents of plagiarism in higher education: Support tools for teaching staff. *Arabian Journal of Business and or A Management Review, 6*, 1000227.

Peters, M., & Gervais, S. (2016). Littératies et créacollage numérique. *Language and Literacy, 18*(2), 62–78.

Peters, M., Boies, T., & Morin, S. (2019). Teaching academic integrity in Quebec universities: Roles professors adopt. *Frontiers, 4*(99), 1–13.

Pintrich, P. R. (2003). A motivational science perspective on the role of student motivation in learning and teaching contexts. *Journal of Educational Psychology, 95*(4), 667–686.

Quality Assurance Agency for Higher Education (2017). *Contracting to cheat in higher education: How to address contract cheating, the use of third-party services and essay mills*. The Quality Assurance Agency for Higher Education. www.qaa.ac.uk

Rundle, K., Curtis, G. J., & Clare, J. (2019). Why students do not engage in contract cheating. *Frontiers in psychology, 10*(2229).

Sarita, R. D. (2015). Academic cheating among students: Pressure of parents and teachers. *International Journal of Applied Research, 1*(10), 793–797.

Schuhmann, P. W., Burrus, R. T., Barber, P. D., Graham, J. E., & Elikai, M. F. (2013). Using the scenario method to analyze cheating behaviors. *Journal of Academic Ethics, 11*(1), 17–33.

Scott, G. (2016). The 36% problem. *Interchange, 47*(2), 133–156.

Selwyn, N. (2008). "Not necessarily a bad thing...": a study of online plagiarism amongst undergraduate students. *Assessment & Evaluation in Higher Education, 33*(5), 465–479.

Srikanth, M., & Asmatulu, R. (2014). Modern cheating techniques, their adverse effects on engineering education and preventions. *International Journal of Mechanical Engineering Education, 42*(2), 129–140.

Strangfeld, J. A. (2019). I just don't want to be judged: Cultural capital's impact on student plagiarism. *SAGE Open, 9*(1).

Suwantarathip, O., & Wichadee, S. (2014). The effects of collaborative writing activity using google docs on students' writing abilities. *Turkish Online Journal of Educational Technology - TOJET, 13*(2), 148–156.

Tasgin, A. (2018). The relationship between attitudes towards research and academic dishonesty tendencies of pre-service teachers. *International Journal of Progressive Education, 14*(4), 85–96.

Teixeira, A. A., & Rocha, M. F. (2010). Cheating by economics and business undergraduate students: An exploratory international assessment. *Higher Education, 59*(6), 663–701.

Trost, K. (2009). Psst, have you ever cheated? A study of academic dishonesty in Sweden. *Assessment & Evaluation in Higher Education, 34*, 367–376.

Trushell, J., Byrne, K., & Simpson, R. (2012). Cheating behaviours, the internet and education undergraduate students. *Journal of Computer Assisted Learning, 28*(2), 136–145.

Vieyra, M., & Weaver, K. (2016). The prevalence and quality of source attribution in middle and high school science papers. *Issues in Science and Technology Librarianship, 83*.

Walker, J. (2010). Measuring plagiarism: Researching what students do, not what they say they do. *Studies in Higher Education, 35*(1), 41–59.

Wideman, M. (2011). Caring or collusion? Academic dishonesty in a school of nursing. *Canadian Journal of Higher Education, 41*(2), 28–43.

Yang, S. C., Huang, C.-L., & Chen, A.-S. (2013). An investigation of college students' perceptions of academic dishonesty, reasons for dishonesty, achievement goals, and willingness to report dishonest behavior. *Ethics & Behavior, 23*(6), 501–522.

Yu, H., Glanzer, P. L., Sriram, R., Johnson, B. R., & Moore, B. (2017). What contributes to college students' cheating? A study of individual factors. *Ethics & Behavior, 27*(5), 401–422.

Zimitat, C. (2008). A student perspective of plagiarism. In T. S. Roberts (Ed.), *Student plagiarism in an online world problems and solutions* (pp. 10–22). Herchey PA: Information science reference.

Zwick, M., Springer, M. L., Guerrero, J. K., DiVentura, D., & York, K. P. (2019). An activity to promote recognition of unintentional plagiarism in scientific writing in undergraduate biology courses. *Journal of microbiology & biology education, 20*(2), 20.22.38.

Martine Peters is a Full Professor of Education at the Université du Québec en Outaouais. She teaches at the Department of Education at the graduate and undergraduate levels. Her research focuses on technopedagogy and the use of technology in the writing process. More specifically, she examines the use and the teaching of digital scrapbooking strategies as a means of preventing plagiarism in high school, college and university students. She can be contacted at martine.peters@uqo.ca.

Sylvie Fontaine Professor Fontaine has worked as Director of Teacher Education at the Université du Québec en Outaouais from 2012 to 2015 and Director of Graduate Study from 2006 to 2008 in the Faculty of Education. She is responsible for the assessment literacy course in the undergraduate education program and she also teaches research development courses at graduate level in the department of education. She has lead or collaborated to research projects on teacher preparation in New Zealand and in Quebec. Her current research interests focus on developing competencies in the assessment of students. She uses a learning community approach to work with teachers and school principals in the development of their competency in assessment literacy. Recently, she has been involved in research and partnerships concerned with academic misconduct, namely plagiarism and cheating. Sylvie can be contacted at sylvie.fontaine@uqo.ca.

Eric Frenette is a full Professor in Measurement and Evaluation at Université Laval in Québec City. He is responsible for the assessment of learning and the assessment for learning courses in the undergraduate education programs and he teaches Structural equation modeling course at the graduate level in Measurement and Evaluation. His current research interests include scale development, measurement model (IRT, CTT, generalizability), statistical analyses, validity and international studies. Eric Frenette can be contacted at eric.frenette@fse.ulaval.ca.

Chapter 17
The Distinctive Nature of Academic Integrity in Graduate Legal Education

Jonnette Watson Hamilton

Abstract This chapter examines the distinctive nature of academic integrity in graduate legal education in Canada, a nature rooted in the fact that almost all graduate students in law have practiced law. I consider the general acceptance of the unattributed copying of others' writing within the legal profession and the judiciary, contrasting that tolerance—even approval—with the unsympathetic reception given the same practices in the academy. I then turn to graduate legal education in common law Canada and the diversity among graduate students in law, including significant differences in their undergraduate legal education. Then, because many of the graduate students who have practiced outside Canada want to be admitted to practice law in Canada, I look at the impact that academic misconduct may have on their ability to be admitted to practice. In order to do so, I review all published Canadian court and tribunal admission decisions that considered academic misconduct committed while in law school. Lastly, in light of unique challenges of graduate legal education, I offer some suggestions for preventing academic misconduct and facilitating students' engagement with their own scholarship.

Keywords Graduate legal education · Academic integrity · Legal education · Bar admission · Good character

This chapter examines distinctive aspects of academic integrity in common law graduate legal education in Canada. I consider why and how educating graduate students in law about the norms of intellectual honesty should respond to this context.

Almost all graduate students in law have been admitted to the bar and have practiced law, some for many years. The unattributed copying of others' work is tolerated and even approved of within the legal profession and judiciary (Corbin & Carter, 2007). The contrast in positions between the practising and the academic branches of the profession—described as a "chasm" by Yarbrough (1996, p. 678)—makes it

---

J. Watson Hamilton (✉)
University of Calgary, Calgary, AB, Canada
e-mail: jwhamilt@ucalgary.ca

S. E. Eaton and J. Christensen Hughes (eds.), *Academic Integrity in Canada*, Ethics and Integrity in Educational Contexts 1,
https://doi.org/10.1007/978-3-030-83255-1_17

more challenging to bring home the serious nature of academic dishonesty in post-secondary education. The "copying is okay" attitude new graduate students bring with them from practice needs to be explicitly addressed. In addition, many graduate students in Canadian law schools are international students. In the context of law, this means that not only might English be an additional language for them, but they may come from jurisdictions with legal systems very different from Canada's common law system, with very different expectations about how law students ought to behave. Finally, many foreign-trained graduate students wish to be admitted to practice law in Canada, and must therefore meet law society fitness standards which require self-disclosure of academic misconduct. Once disclosed, an applicant bears the burden of proving their good character, and a public hearing into their suitability for the practice of law may be required. The perceived consequences of academic misconduct may therefore be greater for foreign-trained graduate students in law than they are for other students, due to the possible adverse impact on their desired careers.

I have taught or co-taught the compulsory graduate student course in our Master of Laws (LLM) program for all but five years since 1994. Since the program was expanded in 2007, that course has been a half-year graduate seminar on legal research and methodology taught to the ten to twenty new thesis-based (academic) and course-based (professional) LLM students admitted each year. The new seminar has always included instruction, practice, and evaluation on academic integrity. It has not always been successful at preventing instances of academic misconduct in the seminar itself or in other graduate courses. As a result, I have continued to revise the course, looking for the best way to reach this very diverse group of students.

In this chapter, I first consider the position of judges and practicing lawyers on unattributed copying in the profession because these are the professional norms that almost all graduate students in law bring with them to the academy, whether they are trained in Canada or not. Next, I look at Canadian common law graduate legal education and the diversity among graduate students in law, including significant differences in their undergraduate legal education. These parts of this chapter have been informed by the literature considering the teaching of legal research and writing to foreign-trained LLM students and the literature on plagiarism in legal practice. Both bodies of literature are primarily American and thus not entirely applicable to the Canadian context. Then, because many of the foreign-trained graduate students want to practice law in Canada, I consider the impact that academic misconduct may have on their ability to be admitted to practice here. In order to do so, I reviewed all published Canadian court and tribunal admission decisions that considered academic misconduct committed while in law school. Finally, in light of these distinctive aspects of graduate legal education, I offer some suggestions for preventing academic misconduct and facilitating students' engagement with their own scholarship.

Unattributed Copying in the Legal Profession

The common law legal system in which Canadian lawyers outside of Quebec practice is based on the doctrine of *stare decisis* (to stand on decided cases), which requires courts to consider and follow precedents set by higher courts on the basis that like cases should be treated alike.

Judges have law clerks and legal counsel who research and write memorandum and draft judgments for them, and they may adopt the written work of the lawyers who appear before them. The Supreme Court of Canada recently pronounced on the practice of unattributed copying by judges in *Cojocaru v BC Women's Hospital & Health Centre* (2013; see also Roussy, 2015). The trial judgment in that case copied 321 of a total of 368 paragraphs from the plaintiffs' written arguments. The court concluded that the wholesale word-for-word copying was not enough to overcome a strong presumption of judicial integrity and impartiality, stating:

> Judicial writing is highly derivative and copying a party's submissions without attribution is a widely accepted practice. The considerations that require attribution in academic, artistic and scientific spheres do not apply to reasons for judgment. The judge is not expected to be original. (*Cojocaru v BC Women's Hospital & Health Centre,* 2013, para. 65)

In addition, in legal practice, appropriation of a lawyer's work by a judge is seen as a "compliment of the highest order to counsel" (Wakeling, 2018, p. 848; see also Richmond, 2013; Roussy, 2015).

Although the judiciary's acceptance of unattributed copying has been made explicit, students are more likely to encounter similar, unarticulated practices in the legal profession. While undergraduate students may be exposed to these norms through summer work at law firms, those norms are more ingrained in graduate students who have usually practiced for a number of years.

Practising lawyers spend a great deal of their time and effort researching the law and writing a variety of documents such as memorandums, legal opinion letters, statements of claim, submissions to courts, and contracts. They often begin with work previously drafted by someone else. Also, much of what is written in legal practice is written collaboratively (Bast & Samuels, 2008; Hanson & Anderson, 2015). Lawyers have associates, articling students and paralegals who do research, write memorandum and draft documents. In the end, the written work is often the product of many people. As a result, scholars such as Corbin and Carter describe unattributed copying in legal practice as "systemic" and even "inherent" (2007, p. 60).

The norms surrounding unattributed copying in legal practice may appear to be similar to those concerning ghostwriting in politics, where speech writers are seldom acknowledged, or in government or corporate bureaucracies where work done by junior employees is signed by more senior officials (Martin, 1994). For example, the reinforcement of power and hierarchy in government and corporations is a feature shared by the legal setting (Martin, 1994). However, in legal practice, originality in writing is neither required, common, nor much valued; consistency and predictability are prized (Bast & Samuels, 2008; Richmond, 2013; Simon, 2019). Requiring originality would make lawyers' work more expensive and also create uncertainty and more legal disputes (Carter, 2019; Yarbrough, 1996).

This legal practice context is the context almost all graduate law students have become accustomed to before beginning graduate education. As several law professors have pointed out, it must be confusing to law students, and particularly international students from non-common law-based legal systems, to be required to rely on precedents and use the court's words as authoritative, and also to be told that they cannot copy without proper attribution (Simon, 2019; Thomas et al., 2017).

Graduate Students in Law

Canadian graduate legal education is typically absent from discussions about legal education (Jukier & Glover, 2014), although *Law and Learning*, the 1983 Report to the Social Sciences and Humanities Research Council of Canada by the Consultative Group on Research and Education in Law was an exception. Graduate education in law has also very rarely been the sole focus of scholarly inquiry (Anand, 2004). Nothing has changed since Anand wrote more than fifteen years ago, and their inquiry into the graduate legal education in Canada's common law faculties remains the only published work focused on the topic. None of this work mentions academic integrity as an issue. Looking at the literature outside Canada, few studies in the small body of scholarship looking at teaching foreign graduate students in law discuss academic integrity, with the work of Spanbauer (2007) being an exception in the American context.

Admission to a graduate program in law requires an undergraduate professional degree in law, formerly the Bachelor of Laws (LLB) and now the Juris Doctor (JD). Law degrees in common law Canada are post graduate degrees, in the sense that they must follow at least two years in another degree program. Very few JD students are admitted without at least one degree.

There are three general types of Canadian graduate students in law (Anand, 2004; see also Spanbauer, 2007). First, there are the practicing Canadian lawyers trained in the common law who are looking to develop specialized knowledge in particular practice areas. The second group are the foreign-trained lawyers who want a Canadian legal education. They may want a Canadian degree in order to enhance their practice back home, but they may also treat an LLM as a pathway to practice here, even though an LLM does not make its holders eligible for admission to the bar in Canada. The third and comparatively much smaller group are students who want an academic career.

It is the foreign-trained lawyers that I focus on in this part because their training often creates unique challenges in law as compared to many other areas of graduate education. In other disciplines, the focus may be on international students for whom English is an additional language (EAL). However, in law, it is the type of legal system from which graduate students received their undergraduate law degree that holds the most significance. Canadians often attend law school in England, the United States, and Australia and, less frequently, international students may obtain their undergraduate law degrees from Canadian law schools. In either case, it is where their legal training took place that is most significant, and not their citizenship.

As already noted, foreign-trained graduate students in law have usually been admitted to practice. The students in any cohort may have been trained in diverse jurisdictions, some with very different legal systems. Both teaching and learning can be much more difficult when students come from different legal traditions (Schukoske, 2011). The best-known classification, put forward by comparativist René David in their 1964 book, *Les grands systèmes de droit contemporain*, divided the world's legal systems into three large families based on legal techniques and concepts, worldview, and ideology: Romano-Germanic laws, Common Law, and Socialist Law (Pargendler, 2012). However, such traditional classifications cannot quickly convey why these differences matter to graduate students' training. Ugo Mattei's taxonomy, which is based on the role of the law as a tool of social organization with its patterns of social incentives and constraints, is more useful for this purpose (1997).

Mattei classifies the world's legal systems into three families: the rule of professional law, the rule of political law, and the rule of traditional law. The rule of professional law encompasses the western legal traditions, with the common law and civil law considered subdivisions. In the rule of professional law, the legitimacy of law has a technical nature, rather than a religious or political one: "the legal arena is clearly distinguishable from the political arena, and the legal process is largely secularized" (Mattei, 1997, p. 23). Jurisdictions within this family include the common law systems of Canada, United States, England, and Oceania, as well as the civil law systems of western Europe, the Scandinavian legal systems, and some "mixed" or hybrid systems such as those found in Quebec (Mattei, 1997, p. 36).

In contrast, in the rule of political law systems, the political and legal processes are not separate, and the idea of limiting political power by formal law is entirely inconsistent with how rules are made in these jurisdictions, especially when it comes to clashes between individual rights and government (Mattei, 1997, pp. 27–28). There is political involvement with the judiciary, high levels of police coercion and what the western legal tradition would call corruption, very little legal literature, limited publication of judicial opinions, and few legally-trained individuals (Mattei, 1997, p. 30). Russia epitomizes the rule of political law family, which also includes the majority of David's Socialist Law family, the less developed countries of Africa and Latin America where Islamic law is not strong, and Cuba (Mattei, 1997, p. 30).

As for the third family of legal systems, the rule of traditional law includes both Far Eastern systems (China and Japan) and Islamic systems where the source of legitimacy is supernatural (Mattei, 1997, p. 40). This legal tradition is characterized by a smaller role for lawyers compared to trusted individuals such as religious authorities, a focus on family groups and not individuals, the continued relevance of diversified local customs, a strongly hierarchical society, an emphasis on gender roles, and a social order based on duties rather than rights, among other distinguishing features (Mattei, 1997, p. 39).

Writing as a graduate student clearly requires acculturation into the relevant legal system (Newton, 2018), which is a formidable task. Foreign-trained graduate students are faced with very different understandings of what law is and what it is for, as well as more mundane differences in approaches to cases and statutes, interpretive methods, and ways of acting when resolving legal disputes (Picker, Lixinski & Fitzsimmons, 2016). The idea that writing about law as a Canadian common law graduate student requires analysis and critique, in addition to description, can be unfamiliar and even intimidating for students educated in jurisdictions where the state cannot safely be critiqued.

Of course, like many other international graduate students, those in law may be also be EAL students. Thus, for graduate students in law, the lack of language proficiency can raise many of the same issues that it does for other EAL graduate students, such as misconceptions about borrowing ideas, collaboration, and citation rules (Ahman et al., 2012; see also Palmer et al., 2019; Pecorari, 2010). However, Canadian common law requires a highly technical vocabulary, in part because its English was sourced in the law the French brought to England by the Norman invasion a thousand years ago, and its use of Latin comes from the dominant role of the early church and canon law in feudal England (Picker, Lixinski & Fitzsimmons, 2016). The common law's vocabulary is a stumbling block for students new to law even if English is their first language and this type of vocabulary is an additional barrier for EAL students, particularly if they were educated in the law of a different legal family which does not use the same or similar concepts.

As a result of these various differences, many Canadian law schools offer special graduate degrees for non-common law trained students. In some law schools, such as the University of British Columbia, students without common law degrees are funneled into special graduate programs designed exclusively for them (Anand, 2004). Elsewhere, as at the University of Calgary, students educated in very different legal systems are not admitted directly to the thesis-based program, but instead must begin in the course-based program and achieve success there before being able to transfer into a thesis-based program. Many Canadian law schools also offer special courses for non-common law-trained students, which introduce the common law method and focus on the differences between civil law and common law pedagogy and concepts (Anand, 2004).

However, it seems clear that graduate students in law also require explicit introduction to the principles and philosophy behind many western academic conventions (Handa & Power, 2005). The impact of transitioning from legal practice in what might have been a very different legal system to a university culture requires explicit academic skills orientation and instruction.

Good Character Requirements for Admission to Legal Practice

In my experience, a large percentage of foreign-trained graduate students in law do aspire to admission to practice in a Canadian jurisdiction. However, a graduate law degree is, at best, a round-about way to reach this goal; it is the undergraduate law degree that is required for admission to practice, supplemented by the Canadian undergraduate law courses that the National Committee on Accreditation requires applicants to successfully complete in order to receive a Certificate of Qualification (Federation of Law Societies of Canada, n.d.). Graduate students cannot enroll in those JD courses unless the law school has a special program for foreign-trained lawyers.

Two Australian professors have each argued that foreign-trained graduate law students may have extrinsic motivating factors to engage in academic dishonesty, such as obtaining a licence to practice law (Katkins, 2018; Saltmarsh, 2004). In other words, the fear is that the LLM degree may simply be a means to an end and, if an LLM is only a credential, then students may be motivated to take shortcuts (Katkins, 2018). This argument is a part of a larger controversy about credentialization in post-secondary education (Collins, 2019; Macdonald & McMorrow, 2013–2014) and a part of the scholarship on the role of motivation in academic dishonesty (Awdry & Sarre, 2013; Burke & Sanney, 2018; Moss et al., 2018).

But it is the fear that a finding of academic dishonesty might jeopardize the goal of some foreign-trained lawyers to be admitted to practice in Canada that is the focus of this part. How realistic are graduate law students' fears about the impact of academic dishonesty on their legal careers? It has been argued that the consequences for a law student of breaching the rules of academic integrity are unique because a breach may have long-term consequences for their reputation and their future in law (James & Mahmud, 2014). Law schools are also thought to apply academic integrity rules more strictly than other faculties (James, 2016), perhaps because many in the legal profession see plagiarism and cheating as "a serious breach of trust which is inconsistent with the values of the legal profession, particularly integrity, candour and honesty" (*Zhang v Law Society of Upper Canada,* 2015, para. 29).

The purpose of allowing academic misconduct to figure in admission decisions depends on a belief that an individual who is prepared to cheat in one institutional context is lacking in what some call "moral fibre" and will likely be inclined to do so in another (Corbin & Carter, 2007; Thomas, 2013). Legal academics who have studied the issue in Canada, Australia, and the United States have noted that there is no evidence of a correlation between past disclosed misconduct as a student and future conduct as a lawyer (Rhode, 1985; Thomas, 2013; Woolley, 2007). However, studies in other disciplines such as business, nursing and engineering do at least suggest there is a correlation, if not a causal link, between academic misconduct and workplace dishonesty, even if concerns about methodological flaws have been raised about these studies (Furutan, 2018; Harding et al., 2004; Hilbert, 1985; LaDuke, 2013; Miron, 2021; Nonis & Swift, 2001).

How and what to assess in making admission decisions is determined by each provincial or territorial law society, but each does require some version of "good character." Good character means something like "suitability" for practice, with suitability including "respect for the rule of law and the administration of justice, honesty, governability, and financial responsibility" (Federation of Law Societies of Canada, 2012, para. 24). All Canadian jurisdictions use one or more of the following criteria: suitability for practice, good character, good reputation or repute, fit to practise, or fit and proper person (e.g., *Legal Profession Act*, 1998).

All law societies require applicants to self-report conduct that might indicate a lack of good character, including academic misconduct (Woolley, 2007). They also accept third-party reports, but there is no information on whether Canadian law schools frequently or ever report to law societies when they find their students guilty of academic misconduct. There is at least one law school that appears to make it a practice to require law students to report themselves to the law society if they are found guilty of academic misconduct; see *Law Society of Ontario v Nsamba* (2020). The limited evidence suggests only that it is likely that law schools, as well as instructors, differ on whether and when they report (Thomas, 2013).

If there is an issue of an applicant's character, the law society will investigate and, if the issue is significant enough, there will be a hearing. The process model is thus a hybrid type, with features of both a traditional adversarial hearing and an investigative model (Zachariah & Morin, 2021). Once character is an issue, it is up to the applicant to prove that they are of good character at the time of the hearing (*Zoraik v Law Society of Ontario*, 2019).

As Woolley (2007, 2013) noted in her reviews of all published good character decisions up to 2012, until 2006 all law societies except Ontario's kept their hearings into good character closed to the public and their decisions unpublished. Today, all law societies except that of the Yukon make their decisions publicly available on CanLII, a web-based database maintained by the non-profit organization managed by the Federation of Law Societies of Canada with the goal of making Canadian law accessible for free.

In assessing the impact of misconduct on admission to practice, I was only interested in decisions that considered applicants' academic dishonesty while in university. For that purpose, I searched all CanLII law society databases for "academic integrity" or "academic honesty" or "academic misconduct" or "academic dishonesty" or "plagiarism" or "cheat". In order to locate appeals to the courts from refusals to admit that were not published, I repeated that search in "all courts and tribunals" for each province, adding "law society" ("barristers' society" in Nova Scotia; "barreau du Quebec" or "chamber of notaries of Quebec" in Quebec) to the search terms. "Academic integrity" and "plagiarism" turned up the most relevant cases, and searches using "cheat" revealed enough cases that had nothing to do with academic integrity to satisfy me that I had cast the net wide enough. I then repeated the searches in the commercial Lexis Advance Quicklaw database, and located three new cases.

No admission decisions considering applicants' academic misconduct in university were located in eight of the ten provinces nor in any of the territories. The only relevant decisions were from British Columbia and Ontario. There were a larger number of admission cases about plagiarism and unauthorized collaboration that occurred in the bar admission courses run by the law societies in Alberta, Saskatchewan, and Manitoba, as well as in British Columbia and Ontario. Ironically–sadly–most of the plagiarism occurred in the ethics evaluations (for example, *Law Society of Alberta v. Cattermole,* 2008; *Sahota v The Law Society of Manitoba,* 2018). While the consequences of cheating in bar admission ethics courses may be interesting, they are beyond the scope of this paper.

The twelve admission decisions that considered the academic misconduct of applicants for admission to the bar are summarized in the table below, which includes the factors the tribunals and courts considered most relevant to their decisions. None of the cases concern graduate students in a Canadian law school, although one was about a foreign-trained lawyer (*Olowolafe v Law Society of Ontario* (2019)). In all but two cases, the applicant's misconduct had occurred while they were in taking their law degree (*Olowolafe v Law Society of Ontario,* 2019; *Seifi v Law Society of Ontario,* 2019).

The first thing to note is how few cases have been reported. Only nine applicants were involved in these twelve decisions over the past twenty years. Clearly there were other relevant decisions that were not made publicly available; for example, the *Olowolafe v Law Society of Ontario* (2019) case notes that the applicant was denied admission to the bar in Alberta in 2016 but that decision is not available. The small number might be explained, in part, by the fact that law societies' internal review processes remain secret. We do not know why some applications that raise issues of good character proceed to a hearing and others do not. Woolley's research into good character hearings in general revealed that only 24 of the 575 Ontario applications that raised issues of good character went to hearings between 2006 and 2012 (Woolley, 2013). We also do not know how many applications were withdrawn once an investigation began or a hearing was scheduled but we do know some were (*Olowolafe v Law Society of Ontario,* 2019).

The number of cases is far too few to be the basis of much more than speculation. Nevertheless, it seems safe to say that graduate law students' fears about the impact of academic dishonesty on their legal careers are overblown. It appears to take a great deal of misconduct for admission to the bar to be denied or even delayed. If the results of the hearings in Table 17.1 seem lenient, Wooley (2013) also noted that between 2006 and 2012, only six applicants in all of Canada were denied admission to the bar on the basis of character. It also seems safe to say that genuine remorse and the passage of time appear to be the two most important positive factors, as illustrated by *Preyra v Law Society of Upper Canada* (2000) and *Preyra v Law Society of Upper Canada* (2003), as well as *Olowolafe v Law Society of Ontario* (2019).

Despite the small number of cases and smaller number of refusals of admission, plagiarism and other forms of academic misconduct can nevertheless impede or at least delay admission to practice because of the good character requirement (Latourette, 2010). Costs of the hearing may be awarded against applicants who are just starting their careers and who may still have large amounts of student loan debt. Hearings are increasingly made public, with the decision and reasons for decision

Table 17.1 Bar Admission hearings considering applicants' academic misconduct at university

Decision	Misconduct	Factors	Result
Preyra v Law Society of Upper Canada (2000)	Falsified 11 grades on JD transcripts and sent them to potential employers	Psychological expert evidence not supportive; lied about misconduct to employer, lawyer, family for 4 years; still lying 1 year before hearing	Refused admission But see Preyra 2003
Law Society of Upper Canada v D'Souza (2002)	Falsified JD transcripts and sent them to potential employers	Lied about why falsified; failed to admit misconduct	Refused admission
Preyra v Law Society of Upper Canada (2003)	Falsified JD transcripts; lied about that misconduct to employer, lawyer, family	Psychologist and employer evidence supportive; no dishonest behaviour in previous 4 years	Reapplication successful; granted admission
Law Society of Upper Canada v Burgess (2006)	Committed plagiarism while a 4th year undergraduate; accused of academic misconduct while a JD student	Lied about the type and extent of plagiarism to minimize it until law society investigated in 2005; blamed others; no psychological evidence; lying too recent to conclude of good character	Refused admission
Law Society of Upper Canada v Smith (2008)	While a law student, researched and wrote at least 5 papers that they sold to another student, and continued to write and sell papers after graduation; the misconduct was not discovered until after admission to the bar	Misconduct was for profit and made thousands of dollars; it was deliberate and extended over a period of years; but lawyer cooperated during investigation, was sanctioned by the law school (a note of the misconduct on their transcript for 5 years), accepted responsibility, and was remorseful	Reprimanded; granted admission

(continued)

Table 17.1 (continued)

Decision	Misconduct	Factors	Result
Mohan v Law Society of British Columbia (2013); overturning Law Society of British Columbia v Applicant 5 (2013); overturning Law Society of British Columbia v Applicant 5 (2012)	Cheated on math exam as an undergraduate (one year suspension); plagiarized an essay while a law student (18 month suspension); accused of plagiarizing significant portions of undergraduate honours thesis that was obtained in response to the law society's freedom of information request	Denied cheating on math exam for 9 years; failed to disclose exam cheating and suspension on application for admission; blamed math TA; credibility an issue re whether the plagiarized thesis was the one submitted for credit in question; but most recent incident was in 2002, more than 10 years prior to hearing; at hearing took full responsibility	Admitted by the initial hearing panel; denied admission by the review board; decision in favour of admission restored by the Court of Appeal
Zhang v Law Society of Upper Canada (2015)	Plagiarized papers in 6 courses in 3rd year of law school (suspended one year)	Admitted plagiarism when confronted; from China and lost support when Canadian mentor died; completed her 3rd year at same university; remorseful; strong support network; showed insight; law society did not oppose application	Granted admission
Seifi v Law Society of Ontario (2019)	Guilty of 2 instances of academic misconduct (cheating on exams) and 2 of assault before law school, while an undergraduate	Failed to disclose 2nd instance of academic misconduct, for which blamed professor and took 9 years to admit; plagiarized their good character essay in application for admission from a reported case; psychiatric evidence supportive; remorseful; last incident was 10 years before	Determined was of good character; directed a further hearing to decide if a conditional licence was appropriate

(continued)

Table 17.1 (continued)

Decision	Misconduct	Factors	Result
Olowolafe v Law Society of Ontario (2019)	Committed plagiarism in 2006, 2008 (suspended 12 months) and 2011 (suspended 3 years) while an undergraduate in Canada; studied at UK law school while suspended and graduated with a UK law degree in 2012; subsequently plagiarized while completing a philosophy degree	Failed to disclose misconduct when first applied; blamed others initially; denied admission in Alberta in 2016; but last plagiarism was in 2011; remorseful; rehabilitated; supportive network	Granted admission
Law Society of Ontario v Nsamba (2020)	Two separate charges of academic misconduct, the first involving plagiarism and cheating on a 2nd year law school exam, and then 4 instances of plagiarism on 4 papers in 3 courses in 3rd year, for which they failed the 3 courses, repeated 3rd year, apologized, and reported all matters to the law society	Misconduct continued after first disciplined, but while under extreme stress (orphaned refugee with dyslexia and little education supporting extended family in Uganda while in law school) and lacking a support system; initially blamed others; but now remorseful; strong supportive evidence; well-developed support network; contributing to profession and society	Granted admission, but under condition that they have a mentor for their first 2 years of practice

being made publicly available. While academic misconduct may not stop a foreign-trained graduate student from being admitted to legal practice in Canada, it still has consequences that can damage reputations and delay legal careers.

Should academic misconduct in university reverberate with negative consequences for years after graduation? It has been argued that, because of the conflict between what law students learn about plagiarism at university and what they will experience about unattributed copying during their legal practice, it is unfair for students to be held accountable on admission to practice for the much stricter rules of academic misconduct (Bast & Samuels, 2008; Wyburn, 2009). Along with those who have studied this issue in more depth (Rhode, 1985; Thomas, 2013; Woolley, 2007, 2013), I believe the answer to this question depends in part on whether there is any correlation between past academic misconduct and an individual's future conduct as a lawyer. The Federation of Law Societies of Canada seems convinced that a causal link must exist and unconcerned about whether there is any evidence to support that belief. However, as I have already noted, there is no available evidence of such a correlation in law. In addition, a law school is not simply a training school for the profession; it is also part of a university and shares the values of the academy as much as those of the profession. The divide between "town and gown" on plagiarism is only one of the many tensions between legal academics and legal practitioners that must be navigated. I see nothing unfair in holding law students to the academic standards of post-secondary education, even if they are held to different standards once they are no longer students. It is but one small example of the pluralism in Canadian legal norms and regulations that those in the profession deal with constantly.

Conclusions

The fear of punishment for committing plagiarism, not only within the academy but also within a profession that they may hope to join, seems likely to cause alienation and hamper the development of graduate students' voice and authority (Halasek, 2011; Pecorari, 2010). Emphasis on acquiring a credential and seeing a graduate degree simply as a means to an end can also make it difficult to engage some students. The factors that make graduate students in law unique means that prevention cannot be the only goal when teaching them about academic integrity. It is also necessary to try to engender and facilitate a genuine interest and excitement about their opportunity to conduct in-depth research on a subject that holds meaning in their life.

Burke and Sanney (2018) describe the components of the fraud triangle—a predictive instrument used by the accounting profession to explain what causes an individual to commit occupational fraud—as translated into the post-secondary education context. Those factors included financial, social, or academic pressure about grades without resorting to academic dishonesty; opportunities to cheat; and rationalization about the acceptability of taking advantage of those opportunities. They argue that eliminating or lessening one or more of those components can change the extent to which students may be tempted to engage in academic misconduct. For example, focusing on actual learning, rather than grades, can mitigate the pressure created by other demands on time or family. They also recommend safe spaces to learn from mistakes, exercises that provide formative feedback, and group work. In terms of eliminating or lessening opportunities, Burke and Sanney's recommendations include assignments requiring individual analysis, drafts, or the design of a unique project. As for rationalizations, they suggest the institution create an aggressively enforced zero-tolerance policy which the students are reminded of repeatedly. This conceptualization and these suggestions make sense in the context of graduate students in law.

Fostering an extrinsic interest in a particular legal area has been identified by others as one way to lessen extrinsic motivating factors such as the desire for permanent residence status or a licence to practise law (Katkins, 2018). Helping students to focus on actual learning and to feel excitement for their research projects is a lengthy process because, in my experience, it requires developing a relationship of trust between instructor and student. This requires many in-class discussions and practice work, and out-of-class collaboration with the student about the choice of topics for their theses or papers. I also believe that repeated explicit statements about the instructor's goals for the course and its students—goals of engendering excitement about their research opportunities and preventing plagiarism—are helpful as long as they are genuine. Both my own experience and the research indicates that students do better when they feel their instructor is on their side and wants them to succeed in a meaningful way (Christensen Hughes & McCabe, 2006, pp. 56–57).

In-class discussions about readings on academic integrity and in-class practice exercises—both individual and group work—are good ways to teach why academic integrity is valued, as well as practical skills. A comprehensive approach to teaching the accepted use of sources within law should include the hands-on learning of the skills of text comprehension, note taking, summarizing, and quoting, as well as paraphrasing and citation (Pecorari & Petric, 2014; Vance, 2009). Other research on helping EAL students succeed indicates that the more students identify as scholars with competence in a particular subject matter, the less likely they are to repeat the language of their sources (Pecorari, 2010). By working together in class and providing each other with formative feedback, students can learn to trust each other and can develop into a supportive cohort. It takes time to create numerous formative exercises that are appropriate to students' educational backgrounds and language skills. However, the reward lies in not simply preventing misconduct—which is a significant reward for both instructor and students—but even more so in facilitating an enjoyable group experience.

Requiring students to produce a short piece of analytical writing during one of their first classes can give the instructor a good indicator of the student's linguistic and analytical abilities. This allows prompt referral to an institution's writing and language support services (Picker, Lixinski & Fitzsimmons, 2016).

The last suggestion by Burke and Sanney (2018)—the institutional creation of an aggressively enforced zero-tolerance policy which the students are repeatedly reminded about—may seem harsh. However, the harshness is primarily at the institutional level and, if the instructor is successful, never reaches the students. Law graduate students, as practicing lawyers, are also accustomed to working and studying in an environment of statutes, regulations, by-laws and other rules that are enforceable and enforced.

The tension between legal academia and the legal profession has motivated suggestions specific to law undergraduate students. An academic misconduct policy that differentiates plagiarism standards for law students from standards for legal practitioners has been put forward as a way to educate law students about the need for attribution while they are students (LeClerq, 1999). Others have suggested there should be a code of conduct for law students that is focused on conduct relevant to professionalism (Baron & Corbin, 2012). Tanovich (2009) has argued that all Canadian law schools should have a code of conduct which resembles the rules of professional responsibility and which is separate and distinct from their university's academic regulations. One of the reasons invoked for their recommendation was the Law Society of Upper Canada v Smith (2008) case involving the law student who was found to have committed academic misconduct by selling papers that he had ghost-written (Tanovich, 2009, p. 78). Other similar suggestions include promoting academic integrity as emergent professional integrity among law students (James & Mahmud, 2014). If any of these types of suggestions are implemented for undergraduate students in law, care should be taken to consider the unique backgrounds and needs of graduate students.

References

Legislation

Legal Profession Act, SBC 1998, c 9.

Jurisprudence

Cojocau v BC Women's Hospital & Health Centre, 2013 SCC 30.
Law Society of Alberta v Cattermole, [2008] L.S.D.D. No. 168 (QL).
Law Society of British Columbia v Applicant 5, [2013] L.S.D.D. No. 78 (QL); 2013 LSBC 5 (CanLII).
Law Society of British Columbia v Applicant 5, [2012] L.S.D.D. No. 110 (QL), 2012 LSBC 24 (CanLII).
Law Society of Ontario v Nsamba, [2020] L.S.D.D. No. 83 (QL); 2020 ONLSTH 62 (CanLII).
Law Society of Upper Canada v Burgess, [2006] L.S.D.D. No. 81 (QL); 2006 ONLSHP 66 (CanLII).
Law Society of Upper Canada v D'Souza, [2002] L.S.D.D No. 62 (QL).
Law Society of Upper Canada v Smith, [2008] L.S.D.D. No. 57 (QL); 2008 ONLSHP 65 (CanLII).
Mohan v Law Society of British Columbia, [2013] B.C.J. No. 2487 (QL); 2013 BCCA 489 (CanLII).
Olowolafe v Law Society of Ontario, 2019 ONLSTH 155 (CanLII).
Preyra v Law Society of Upper Canada, [2000] L.S.D.D. No. 60 (QL).
Preyra v Law Society of Upper Canada, [2003] L.S.D.D. No. 25 (QL); 2003 CanLII 48959 (ON LST).
Sahota v The Law Society of Manitoba, 2018 MBLS 5 (CanLII).
Seifi v Law Society of Ontario, [2019] L.S.D.D. No. 82 (QL); 2019 ONLSTH 56 (CanLII).
Zhang v Law Society of Upper Canada, [2015] L.S.D.D. No. 251 (QL); 2015 ONLSTH 199 (CanLII).
Zoraik v Law Society of Ontario, 2019 ONLSTA 11 (CanLII).

Secondary Sources

Ahman, U. K., Mansourizadeh, K., & Ai, G. K. M. (2012). Non-native university students' perception of plagiarism. *Advances in Language and Literary Studies, 3*(1), 39–48. https://doi.org/10.7575/aiac.alls.v.3n.1p.39

Anand, S. S. (2004). Canadian graduate legal education: Past, present and future. *Dalhousie Law Journal, 27*(1), 55–162.

Awdry, R., & Sarre, R. T. (2013). An investigation into plagiarism motivations and prevention techniques: Can they be appropriately aligned? *International Journal for Educational Integrity, 9*(2), 35–49.

Baron, P., & Corbin, L. (2012). Thinking like lawyers/acting like professionals: Communities of practice as means of challenging orthodox legal education. *Law Teacher, 46*(2), 100–119.

Bast, C. M., & Samuels, L. B. (2008). Plagiarism and legal scholarship in the age of information sharing: The need for intellectual honesty. *Catholic University Law Review, 57*(3), 777–816.

Burke, D. D., & Sanney, K. J. (2018). Applying the fraud triangle to higher education: Ethical implications. *Journal of Legal Studies Education, 35*(1), 5–43.

Carter, A. M. (2019). The case for plagiarism. *UC Irvine Law Review, 9*(3), 531–556.

Collins, R. (2019). *The credential society: An historical sociology of education and stratification.* Columbia University Press. (Original work published 1979).

Consultative Group on Research and Education in Law. (1983). *Law and Learning*. Minister of Supply and Services Canada.

Corbin, L., & Carter, J. (2007). Is plagiarism indicative of prospective legal practice? *Legal Education Review, 17*(1 & 2), 53–66.

Christensen Hughes, J. M., & McCabe, D. L. (2006). Understanding academic misconduct. *Canadian Journal of Higher Education, 36*(1), 49–63.

David, R. (1964). Les grands systèmes de droit contemporains. Dalloz.

Federation of Law Societies of Canada. (2012). National admission standards project, Phase 1 Report. https://flsc.ca/wp-content/uploads/2014/10/admission3.pdf.

Federation of Law Societies of Canada. (n.d.). Lawyers trained outside of Canada. National Committee on Accreditation. https://nca.legal/

Furutan, O. (2018). The relationship between tolerance for scholastic dishonesty and tolerance for dishonest work place practices amongst university business management students. *Journal of Higher Education Theory and Practice, 18*(2), 116–127.

Halasek, K. (2011). Theorizing plagiarism in the university. *College English, 73*(5), 548–568.

Handa, N., & Power, C. (2005). Land and discover! A case study investigating the cultural context of plagiarism. *Journal of University Teaching & Learning Practice*, *2*(3), n.p.

Hansen, R. F., & Anderson, A. (2015). Law student plagiarism: Contemporary challenges and responses. *Journal of Legal Education, 64*(3), 416–427.

Harding, T. S., Carpenter, D. D., Finelli, C. J., & Passow, H. J. (2004). Does academic dishonesty relate to unethical behavior in professional practice? An exploratory study. *Science and Engineering Ethics, 10*, 311–324. https://doi.org/10.1007/s11948-004-0027-3

Hilbert, G. A. (1985). Involvement of nursing students in unethical classroom and clinical behaviors. *Journal of Professional Nursing, 1*(4), 230–234.

James, C. (2016). Academic integrity in legal education. In T. Bretag (Ed.), *Handbook of Academic Integrity* (pp. 695–711). Springer.

James, C., & Mahmud, S. (2014). Promoting academic integrity in legal education: 'Unanswered questions' on disclosure. *International Journal for Educational Integrity, 10*(2), 3–16.

Jukier, R., & Glover, K. (2014). Forgotten? The role of the graduate legal education in the future of the law faculty. *Alberta Law Review, 51*(4), 761–786.

Katkins, L. (2018). Contract cheating advertisements: What they tell us about international students' attitudes towards academic integrity. *Ethics and Education, 13*(2), 268–284. https://doi.org/10.1080/17449642.2017.1412178

LaDuke, R. D. (2013). Academic dishonesty today, unethical practices tomorrow? *Journal of Professional Nursing, 29*(6), 402–406.

Latourette, A. (2010). Plagiarism: Legal and ethical implications for the university. *Journal of College and University Law, 37*(1), 1–92.

Leclerq, T. (1999). Confusion and conflict about plagiarism in law school and law practice. In Burenen, L. & Roy, A.M. (Eds.), *Perspectives on plagiarism and intellectual property in a postmodern world* (pp. 195–203).

Macdonald, R. A., & McMorrow, T. B. (2013–2014). Decolonizing law school. *Alberta Law Review, 51*(4), 717–738.

Martin, B. (1994). Plagiarism: A misplaced emphasis. *Journal of Information Ethics, 3*(2), 36–47.

Mattei, U. (1997). Three patterns of law: Taxonomy and change in the world's legal systems. *American Journal of Comparative Law, 45*(1), 5–44. https://doi.org/10.2307/840958

Miron, J. B. (2022). Academic integrity in work-integrated learning (WIL) settings. In S. E. Eaton & J. Christensen Hughes (Eds.), *Academic Integrity in Canada: An enduring and essential challenge.*

Moss, S. A., White, B., & Lee, J. (2018). A systematic review into the psychological causes and correlates of plagiarism. *Ethics & Behaviour, 28*(4), 261–283.

Newton, P. M. (2018, August 30). How common is commercial contract cheating in higher education and is it increasing? A systematic review. *Frontiers in Education.* https://doi.org/10.3389/feduc.2018.00067.

Nonis, S., & Swift, C. O. (2001). An examination of the relationship between academic dishonesty and workplace dishonesty: A multicampus investigation. *The Journal of Education for Business, 77*, 69–77. https://doi.org/10.1080/08832320109599052

Palmer, A., Pegrum, M., & Oakley, G. (2019). A wake-up call? Issues with plagiarism in transnational higher education. *Ethics & Behavior, 29*(1), 23–50. https://doi.org/10.1080/10508422.2018.1466301

Pargendler, M. (2012). The rise and decline of legal families. *The American Journal of Comparative Law, 60*(4), 1043–1074.

Pecorari, D. (2010). *Academic writing and plagiarism: A linguistic analysis.* Bloomsbury Publishing.

Pecorari, D., & Petric, B. (2014). Plagiarism in second-language writing. *Language Teaching, 47*(3), 269–302. https://doi.org/10.1017/S0261444814000056

Philip Zachariah, P., & Morin, M. (2022). Academic integrity through a Canadian legal lens. In Eaton, S. E., & Hughes, J. C. (Eds.). *Academic integrity in Canada: An enduring and essential challenge.*

Picker, C., Lixinski, L., Steel, A., & Fitzsimmons, D. (2016). Comparative perspectives on teaching foreign students in law: Pedagogical, substantive, logistical and conceptual challenges. *Legal Education Review, 26*(1 & 2), 161–186.

Richmond, D. R. (2013). Unoriginal sin: The problem of judicial plagiarism. *Arizona State Law Journal, 45*(3), 1077–1106.

Rhode, D. L. (1985). Moral character as a professional credential. *Yale Law Journal, 94*, 491–603.

Roussy, A. (2015). Cut-and-paste justice: A case comment on Cojocaru v. British Columbia Women's Hospital and health centre. *Alberta Law Review, 52*(3), 761–778.

Saltmarsh, S. (2004). Graduating tactics: Theorizing plagiarism as consumptive practice. *Journal of Further and Higher Education, 28*(4), 445–454. https://doi.org/10.1080/0309877042000298911

Schukoske, J. E. (2011). Teaching across legal traditions: LLM students and the multi-legal cultural classroom in the United States. *University of Baltimore School of Law Legal Studies Research Paper*, 1–17. https://ssrn.com/abstract=1804250

Simon, D. J. (2019). Cross-cultural differences in plagiarism: Fact or fiction. *Duquesne Law Review, 57*(1), 73–91.

Spanbauer, J. M. (2007). Lost in translation in the law school classroom: Assessing required coursework in LLM programs for international students. *International Journal of Legal Information, 35*(3), 396–446.

Tanovich, D. M. (2009). Learning to act like a lawyer: A model code of professional responsibility for law students. *Windsor Yearbook on Access to Justice, 27*, 75–109.
Thomas, M. (2013). Admission as lawyer: The fearful spectre of academic misconduct. *QUT Law Review, 13*(1), 73–99.
Thomas, M., Cockburn, T., & Yule, J. (2017). Permissible plagiarism? Navigating normative expectations in the pre- and post-admission landscape. *International Journal of the Legal Profession, 24*(3), 295–317.
Vance, N. (2009). Cross-cultural perspectives on source referencing & plagiarism. *EBSCO Research Starters*, 1–7. http://connection.ebscohost.com/c/articles/45827562/cross-cultural-perspectives-source-referencing-plagiarism
Wakeling, T. W. (2018). Frederick A Laux, Q.C., Memorial Lecture. *Alberta Law Review, 55*(3), 839–851.
Woolley, A. (2007). Tending the bar: The good character requirement for law society admission. *Dalhousie Law Journal, 30*, 27–78.
Woolley, A. (2013). Can good character be made better? Assessing the federation of law societies' proposed reform of the good character requirement for law society admission. *Canadian Journal of Administrative Law & Practice, 26*(2), 115–139.
Wyburn, M. (2009). The confusion in defining plagiarism in legal education and legal practice in Australia. *Journal of Commonwealth Law and Legal Education, 7*(1), 37–63.
Yarbrough, M. K. (1996). Do as I say, not as I do: Mixed messages for law students. *Dickinson Law Review, 100*(3), 677–684.

Jonnette Watson Hamilton (BA UofA; LLB Dal; LLM Colum) focuses her research on access to justice, property law and theory, equality rights, and discourse analysis. She teaches property law, property theory, law & literature, and the graduate seminar in legal research and methodology. Before beginning her academic career, she practiced law in rural Alberta for 13 years, primarily in the areas of family, commercial, and dependent adult law. She received the 2016 Canadian Bar Association—Alberta Branch/Law Society of Alberta Distinguished Service Award for Legal Scholarship, a 2018 Students' Union Teaching Excellence Award, and the Howard Tidswell Memorial Award for Teaching Excellence in 2007 and 2011–2012.

Part IV
Barriers and Catalysts to Academic Integrity: Multiple Perspectives and Supports

Chapter 18
Student Insight on Academic Integrity

Kelley A. Packalen and Kate Rowbotham

Abstract Prior researchers have used surveys to identify frequencies and types of academic integrity violations among students and to identify factors correlated with academically dishonest behaviours. Some studies have also explored students' justifications for their behaviors. Comparatively little work, however, has explored students' opinions on academic integrity using more nuanced and conversational, but still rigorous, methodologies. To address this gap in the literature, we gathered written and oral comments from 44 Canadian undergraduate business students who participated in one of four year-specific computer-facilitated focus groups. Specifically, we analyzed students' responses to questions about the general attitudes among themselves and their peers with respect to academic integrity. We also analyzed students' suggestions of steps that both they and faculty could take to improve the culture of academic integrity in their program. Our contributions to the field of academic integrity were three-fold. First, we gave voice to students in an area in which historically their opinions had been lacking, namely in the generation of specific actions that students and faculty can take to improve academic integrity. Second, we connected students' opinions and suggestions to the broader literature on academic integrity, classroom pedagogy, and organizational culture to interpret our findings. Third, we introduced readers to an uncommon methodology, computer-facilitated focus groups, which is well suited to gathering rich and diverse insights on sensitive topics.

Keywords Methodology · Focus groups · Student viewpoint · Organizational culture · Classroom pedagogy · Academic integrity

---

Electronic Supplementary Material The online version of this chapter (https://doi.org/10.1007/978-3-030-83255-1_18) contains supplementary material, which is available to authorized users.

K. A. Packalen (✉) · K. Rowbotham
Smith School of Business, Queen's University, Kingston, Canada
e-mail: kelley.packalen@queensu.ca

K. Rowbotham
e-mail: kate.rowbotham@queensu.ca

S. E. Eaton and J. Christensen Hughes (eds.), *Academic Integrity in Canada*, Ethics and Integrity in Educational Contexts 1,
https://doi.org/10.1007/978-3-030-83255-1_18

Introduction

Academic administrators and faculty members have long lamented students' disrespect for academic integrity. Angell's (1928) description of students' academically dishonest behaviours is just as fitting today as it was when he wrote his book in the early twentieth century. There has also been no shortage of advice from administrators and faculty on ways educational institutions can improve their culture of academic integrity (e.g., Christensen Hughes & McCabe, 2006b; McCabe et al., 2012; Morris, 2018; Whitley & Keith-Spiegel, 2002). To put it bluntly, some percentage of students violate academic integrity, many faculty and administrators complain that they do, and at various points in an institution's history—often in response to a cheating scandal or a growing unease that the situation has gotten out of hand—faculty and administration introduce new programs, policies and/or pedagogical innovations designed to improve academic integrity (e.g., Raman & Ramlogan, 2020).

For these efforts to improve academic integrity to be successful, however, administration, faculty and students must recognize that there is a problem, be motivated to solve the problem, and be willing to change their attitudes and behaviours accordingly (Burnes & Jackson, 2011; Christensen Hughes & McCabe, 2006b; Vakola, 2013). Change is also more likely to be enduring when solutions incorporate the concerns and recommendations of all affected stakeholders (Eury & Treviño, 2019).

In our review of the literature we found that faculty members and university administrators frequently suggested ways to improve students' adherence to academic integrity. Many of the suggestions were valuable, particularly those related to best practices in pedagogy (e.g., Murdock & Anderman, 2006; Tammeleht et al., 2019) and those derived from students' self-reported behaviours and attitudes (e.g., Chapman et al., 2004; Fontaine et al., 2020). Largely missing from the discussion, however, was student-generated advice on ways to improve a school's culture of academic integrity (cf. Eury & Treviño, 2019; Hendershott et al., 2000; McCabe & Pavela, 2000). In short, students were frequently surveyed on what they do and why, but only sometimes consulted on whether they perceived their behaviour as problematic, and if yes, what they thought could be done to improve that behaviour.

Our research addressed this shortcoming in the literature by using a methodology—computer-facilitated or electronic focus groups—that to our knowledge had not been used previously to study academic integrity. Computer-facilitated focus groups combine anonymous written entries with oral conversation making it an ideal method for discussing confidential and sensitive issues. Students should have felt as comfortable supplying their honest opinions about their views on academic integrity as they would have in anonymous surveys. Unlike anonymous surveys, however, they also engaged in a conversation with their peers and the facilitator, which enabled a potentially deeper evaluation of the topic. The outcome was a window into conversations among students about how they viewed academic integrity and what they thought were the best ways to improve the culture of academic integrity in their program.

Sources of Student-Derived Insight on Academic Integrity

To encourage individuals to respond openly and honestly about stigmatized behaviours such as academic dishonesty, researchers have used several methods to maximize the likelihood of accurate responses. For example, many have used anonymous surveys with assurances of confidentiality to encourage truthful responses that have generated a reasonable, quantifiably-comparable, understanding of a population's attitudes toward and engagement in academic integrity violations. Bowers (1964, 1966) in his landmark census-style analysis of university students across the United States, McCabe, Treviño, Butterfield and colleagues in their 20-plus year longitudinal study of students' academic integrity behaviour around the world (e.g., Christensen Hughes & McCabe, 2006a; McCabe et al., 2012; McCabe & Bowers, 1994; McCabe & Treviño, 1997) and innumerable other researchers have used survey-based methods to provide us with a good understanding of the personal and situational factors which have influenced attitudes toward, and self-reported engagement in, academic dishonest behaviours (see e.g., Whitley (1998) and Lang (2013) for literature reviews).

To overcome some of the limitations of fixed answers, a hallmark of surveys, some authors have included open-ended questions to understand in a more nuanced way why students violated academic integrity (e.g., LaBeff et al., 1990; McCabe et al., 1999). For example, in related research, we used neutralization theory (Sykes & Matza, 1957) and moral disengagement (Bandura, 1999) to categorize students' volunteered rationales for violating academic integrity to demonstrate that students relied on different mechanisms to justify specific trivial violations (e.g., unauthorized collaboration) versus violations in general (Packalen & Rowbotham, 2021). Researchers have also asked students to predict how they would behave in scenarios where there was a potential to cheat, with key contextual factors modified among scenarios to enable systematic comparison of factors (Bernardi et al., 2004; Rettinger et al., 2004; Steininger et al., 1964).

A shortcoming of the scenario method, however, is that people, when asked "what would you do?", have tended to predict that they would behave more morally than they actually would in said circumstances (Kang & Glassman, 2010). As such, researchers have tried numerous creative approaches designed to capture rates of actual versus self-reported or predicted behaviour. One of these methods was to compare the self-graded and independent-graded scores on tests (Antion & Michael, 1983; Ward, 1986). More recently, behavioural economists have used experimental or quasi-experimental designs to record participants' tendencies to act dishonestly when put into tempting situations. Although each individual experiment has been limited to a narrow situation, as a group these experiments have provided us with information about which situations lend themselves to more dishonest behaviour and the extent to which individuals behave dishonestly.

Moving beyond surveys, scenarios, and (quasi-) experimental designs, a limited number of researchers have used methodologies designed to more fully engage with students. For example, Gullifer and Tyson (2010) used traditional focus groups to elicit students' perceptions on plagiarism; McCabe (1999) and Aljurf et al. (2020) used them to understand students' views on academic dishonesty more generally. Moreover, Blum's (2009) ethnography, which used semi-structured interviews, has been an exemplar for gaining an in-depth understanding of students' attitudes toward plagiarism specifically and conceptions of authorship and individualism more generally.

From these rich pools of data, faculty members and university administrators have made recommendations on how to improve adherence to academic integrity. These data driven recommendations, however, have tended to be top-down and may or may not have resonated with the students to which they have been directed. For example, McCabe et al. (2012) explained that the post-hoc investigation of the surprising failed vote among students at one school attempting to implement an honour code revealed that students were, in general, in favour of an academic honour code, but they were not in favour of adopting the code if it meant that they were required to report peers who they witnessed violating academic integrity. If the honour code had not included this one clause then the vote very likely would have passed; this suggested that students had not been adequately consulted during the development phase.

To address the dearth of student-driven recommendations in the prior literature, we asked a student population with diverse attitudes toward academic integrity not only how they thought about academic integrity but also what *they* perceived to be effective solutions for improving the culture of academic integrity in their institution.

Method

Research Setting and Context

Our participants were students in an undergraduate business program at a research-intensive Canadian university. The 1912 students in the 2018–2019 academic year were divided about equally among the four years. Most students in the program spent much of their time together whether it be in class, involved in extracurricular activities, socializing, and/or cohabiting in shared accommodations on or near campus.

In a companion study to this chapter we reported survey results from 852 students (45 percent of all students) in the same program in March 2019 (Packalen & Rowbotham, 2020). The results from that survey provided us with a general and representative understanding of the population and thus the environment in which our research participants were situated. Specifically, 85 percent of those surveyed self-reported engaging in at least one questionable behaviour in the 2018–2019 academic year and their average rate of academic misconduct was 7.05 (standard deviation

Table 18.1 Academic integrity (A.I.) related behaviours, perceptions and attitudes by year among the population from which our focus group participants were drawn (n = 852)

Variable	Year in Program				$\chi^2(3)$ w/ ties[b]
	First	Second	Third[a]	Fourth	
Rate of A.I. violations	5.87	8.14	5.11	8.04	32.09
Culture of A.I. scale	3.76	3.51	3.35	3.09	101.96
Estimated percent of peers who violate A.I	71.78	78.07	79.66	84.82	46.74

Note Table is adapted from Packalen and Rowbotham (2020)
[a]As explained in Packalen and Rowbotham (2020) we suspected that the lower rates of academic integrity violations among third year students, despite the linear decrease in the culture of academic integrity and linear increase in estimated percent of peers who violate academic integrity from first to fourth year, was a result of the fact that the third years who remained on campus during winter semester of their third year were students who were among the minority who did not go on exchange during the winter semester of third year and who, based on other survey measures, were generally less connected to the school and their classmates. [b]The Kruskal–Wallis equality-of-population rank test with ties indicated that for all three variables the averages per year values differed significantly across years at $p < 0.05$ (two-tailed)

= 6.50).[1] Respondents thought that on average 78 percent of their peers violated academic integrity and their assessment of the culture of academic integrity within the school, as measured by an 11-item scale, was just above neutral (3.46 on a five point Likert scale from *strongly disagree* to *strongly agree*, standard deviation = 0.73). Table 18.1, which was adapted from Packalen and Rowbotham (2020), highlights the differing behaviour, beliefs and attitudes in each of the four years of the program.

Recruitment

Following the methodology approved by our general research ethics board, in January 2019 we posted four separate recruitment ads on the research pool portal seeking up to 14 participants per pre-scheduled focus group.[2] To participate, students had to be available at the time the session for their year was scheduled and be members of the research pool affiliated with the business school. We restricted each focus group to a particular year because we assumed that students within the same year would both feel more comfortable participating among their peers and have similar

[1] For each of 24 questionable academic-related behaviours students were asked if they had *never engaged*, *engaged once or twice*, or *engaged more than* twice in the behaviour. We assigned a score of 0, 1 or 2 respectively to these choices. We then summed each student's score across the 24 behaviours to generate a rate of academic misconduct that ranged from 0 to 48.

[2] The maximum number of participants was determined in consultation with the computer-facilitated focus group facilitator who indicated that 10 to 12 was the ideal number of participants per session (although it was possible to accommodate more) and information from the coordinator of the Research Pool on average rates at which participants signed up to attend a session and then did not show.

cohort-related experiences on which to build.[3] In return for participating in three hours' worth of research studies students received a grade bump of one third of a letter grade in a maximum of one course per semester. Students who participated in our computer-facilitated focus groups received 1.5 hours of research credit. In the final week of January 2019, 10 first year, 13 second year, 10 third year and 11 fourth year students participated in their year-specific sessions for a total of 44 focus group participants.

From prior experience running sessions on academic integrity and being responsible for an anonymous email address to report questions, concerns and violations, we knew that gathering students voluntarily to discuss academic integrity tended to draw those who had strong opinions, particularly those who had not violated academic integrity themselves and who also thought that academic integrity was a very serious problem. While these students were vocal about their opinions, they may not have been representative of the student body overall. Thus, the main benefit of recruiting students through the research pool was that a little over two-thirds of the students, associated with 43 different courses in the program, participated in the research pool in Winter 2019 and students in the research pool tended to select studies primarily to obtain research credit and secondly because they were interested in the topic being studied. Importantly, this meant that we recruited students whose opinions on academic integrity were diverse.

Data Gathering and In-Situ Analysis Using Computer-Facilitated Focus Groups

To promote forthright and honest responses, numerous steps were taken to protect the confidentiality of the students who participated in the computer-facilitated or electronic focus groups. For example, we were not in the room during the sessions, we used a professional facilitator whose reputation was based on maintaining his clients' confidentiality, students anonymously typed their comments and we did not include any identifying information (e.g., names, gender, ethnicity) in the transcription of the oral component of the session. In short, the only identifying information that we retained about the students was the year in which they were enrolled in the program.

Computer-facilitated or electronic focus groups have combined the facilitator-led, discussion-based aspects of verbal discussion in traditional focus groups with computer-based written interactions using a group software-based decision support system (GDSS). We used the software ThinkTank 4.9 (GroupSystems, 2018), which enabled participants to type anonymous comments in response to open-ended survey-style questions and vote, rank and evaluate their agreement with participants' statements to gauge the (lack of) consensus among the group. ThinkTank was designed

[3] The significant differences in the survey responses of a representative sample of students in the program in Table 18.1 suggested that the assumption about cohort-related experiences was well founded.

to overcome many of the downsides of traditional group discussions such as domination by a select few members, interruptions, not getting a turn to speak until the topic has passed, evaluation apprehension and pressure to conform to a dominant idea (Nunamaker et al., 1991).

To enable post-hoc comparison and/or aggregation of responses across groups the facilitator used the same semi-structured format of questions in all sessions. Specific prompts that the facilitator used were:

1. What is the attitude among yourself and your peers with respect to academic integrity? Why?
2. Do you think academic integrity is a pressing problem?
3. What steps can students take to improve the culture of academic integrity?
4. What steps can faculty and administration take to improve the culture of academic integrity?

For prompt one the facilitator asked participants to anonymously electronically brainstorm a list and then clarify their comments with oral discussion and/or additional anonymous written explanation. For prompt two the facilitator set up a yes/no vote to which he asked students to respond.

For prompts three and four the facilitator asked participants to anonymously electronically brainstorm a list and then clarify their suggestions with oral discussion and/or additional anonymous written explanation. Next the facilitator engaged in in-situ analysis and combined similar options in the electronic file into higher order constructs in real time. This step was conducted with participant involvement to ensure agreement on how comments were aggregated. After aggregation was completed, the facilitator asked students to vote on the grouped suggestions that they thought could be most successfully implemented. Specifically, the facilitator asked students to select up to half of the grouped suggestions. For example, if there was a list of ten grouped suggestions, students would be asked to pick up to five suggestions.

Post-sessions Analysis

At the end of each session we received a text document that contained the record of all written comments, how they were aggregated and the results of any voting (12,086 words total for the four sessions). The software clearly distinguished original comments from later additions (such as the facilitator's additions to clarify a specific comment or headings used to label a group of comments). We also received an audio file which the first author transcribed (20,190 words total for the four sessions). Our transcripts of the oral discussion distinguished between the facilitator and students and between two students in a back-and-forth exchange. We were unable, however, to track a student's comments throughout the entire session (i.e., we could not reliability determine if the student who made comment 1 at the start of the session was the same student who made comment 15 three-quarters of the way through the session).

Next, we systematically read and manually categorized students' written responses to the open-ended question asked at the start of the session: "What is the attitude among yourself and your peers with respect to academic integrity? Why?" For example, we coded perceived level of adherence to academic integrity. When students provided a rationale for their attitude, we also coded the source of that rationale (e.g., competition). We applied the same process to the oral discussion that accompanied this first question and to the facilitator's ending question: "Is there anything else you want to add?".

Once we had finished coding within each year, we then compared responses across years; where appropriate we further aggregated the responses into themes. For example, we grouped the recommendations students made for themselves under themes of: perspective and attitude; foster and respect a culture of integrity; and proactive actions.

Results and Discussion

The first noticeable difference between the groups was that students in first year were unwillingly to speak and made all their comments electronically and anonymously. Only once did a student respond to a request for clarification from the facilitator and that was only after the student could no longer bear the awkward silence following the facilitator's repeated request for clarification. The second year students spoke a bit, the third year students more so and the fourth year students were very open in sharing their opinions verbally with the facilitator and their peers in the session. This was especially true with the prolonged conversation that followed the official end of the session and which provided further explanations for the low levels of adherence to academic integrity among themselves and their peers. In other work drawing on survey data from the same population we found that the students in fourth year as compared to those in first year were significantly more morally disengaged in that they viewed it acceptable to engage in trivial violations of academic integrity in many more scenarios (Packalen & Rowbotham, 2021). We didn't find it surprising, therefore, that these students who came from a cohort that perceived more trivial violations to be acceptable were also more willing to speak openly about those behaviours.

Student-Perceived Attitudes Toward Academic Integrity

Perceived Levels of Adherence

Many of the students answered the question "What is the attitude among yourself and your peers with respect to academic integrity? Why?" by writing about what they perceived to be the level of adherence to academic integrity in the program.

We summarized their responses and explanations for given levels of adherence in Fig. 18.1. Our first observation was that there were diverse opinions on the level

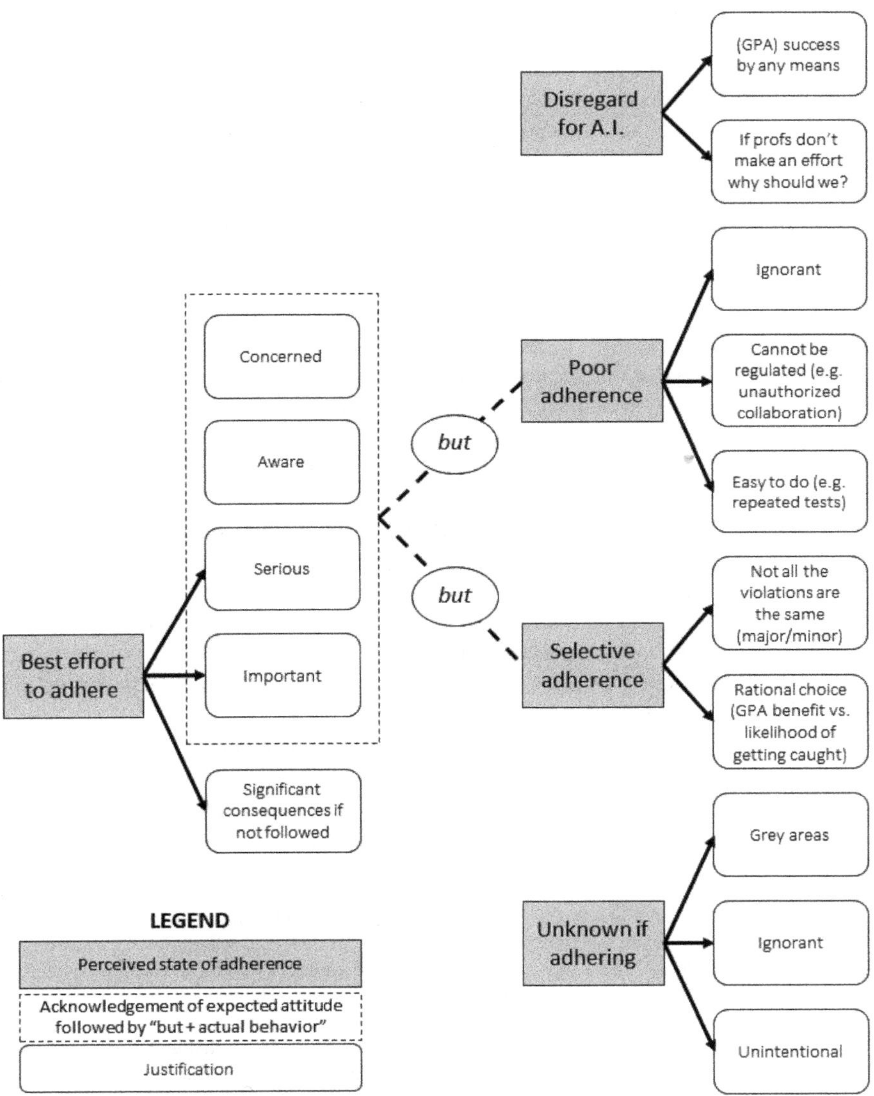

Fig. 18.1 Students' perceived attitudes towards academic integrity among themselves and their peers

of adherence, a fact which three students, including the following third year student noted when they wrote, "It seems as though there are three types of attitudes regarding academic integrity. People either don't know what exactly it is, completely disregard it or try to follow it."

These three individuals were the only students who spoke to there being a group of students who made their best effort to adhere to the policies and behave with academic integrity. As Fig. 18.1 demonstrates, those who made their best effort did so because they felt that academic integrity was serious, doing so was important and/or they were motivated by what they perceived to be significant consequences for not following academic integrity. These explanations were markedly different than the reasons that students in Miller's and colleague's (2011) study provided for what they would do if put in a situation where a professor left the answer key to an upcoming exam visible. In that situation about 94 percent of students said that they would not violate academic integrity and provided reasons that could be categorized into four main groups: they were afraid of the punishment or consequences; it was not in line with their moral character; it was simply wrong; or it undermined their goals of learning. The students in Miller et al.'s (2011) study, however, also had much lower rates of academic integrity violations when compared to the population from which our sample was drawn and also appeared to have a much stronger culture of academic integrity.[4]

Disregard for Academic Integrity. At the opposite end of the spectrum from those who did their best to adhere were those who perceived that they and their peers had a complete disregard for academic integrity. This viewpoint was shared by four students, all of whom were in fourth year. The main rationale for this disregard, as summed up by one fourth year student was: "Most people don't care about it or follow the rules. There's so much pressure to do well and get a high GPA that people will do whatever is necessary to get a high grade."

In their open-ended oral discussion, the fourth year students provided additional explanations for their disregard for academic integrity. Chief among these was their view that if professors did not make an effort to provide sufficient practice resources and new tests and assignments each year there was little reason for them to not copy resources from prior years. As another fourth year student noted:

> Something that bothers me at least. I find it very hard to find motivation to do what we are supposed to do when the professors are very lazy on their end when they repeat tests, assignments, questions. When they don't provide ample resources for you to learn the content on your own, not necessarily for an assignment, but for a test. They should have resources for you to be able to do that. And it's very frustrating on our part when we don't have those resources. When you see the laziness and then you don't feel motivated to not be lazy yourself. Like we pay a lot of money to be here and they shouldn't be doing that. So that's something I feel very strongly about.

[4] We came to this conclusion by visually comparing the very different rates at which students in the two populations (Miller et al., 2011 vs Packalen & Rowbotham, 2020, 2021) self-reported engaging in the same specific behaviours and the different values they assigned to similar items related to the culture of academic integrity.

The students in our focus groups were not unique in morally disengaging by euphemistically labelling (Bandura, 1999) their academically dishonest acts as laziness in light of their perception that their professors were lazy. Christensen Hughes (2017, p. 58) found similar explanations among the nearly 15,000 Canadian students that she and McCabe had surveyed (2006a, 2006b), noting that "students cheat when they feel cheated."

Poor Adherence to Academic Integrity. Five students, representing all four years of the program, perceived their peers and themselves to poorly adhere to academic integrity. Reasons given for poor adherence included that people frequently violated academic integrity because they were unaware of the rules, while others did so because "professors often make it easy to violate academic integrity as they reuse material year after year." (Third year student).

Although the aforementioned disregard for academic integrity and poor adherence had similar outcomes—frequent violations—the groups differed. Unlike those who had no regard for academic integrity, students often prefaced their statement about poor adherence with an ideal. Consider the difference between this fourth year student's response: "Academic integrity is a non-essential concept in terms of succeeding in this program as most students disregard any policies, warnings, or ideas given to us by the Program Office." with the following response from a first year whom we classified as believing they and their peers adhered poorly to academic integrity: "The majority of my peers appear to be very concerned with AI, but in reality there are AI violations being committed every day."

Selective Adherence to Academic Integrity. The most common attitude mentioned was selective adherence to academic integrity. This was the attitude described by 14 of the participants, half of whom were in second year. As one fourth year student noted, "I believe that there is almost an unwritten rule when it comes to academic integrity among students that outlines what is okay and what is not." As such, as another fourth year student told us, "I think we all care deeply about the grades on our transcript and if it is easy to get away with cheating then we will do it."

This group of students did not approach decisions about violating academic integrity as a moral decision, but as a rational cost–benefit decision not unlike the types of decision they were often encouraged to make when analyzing various case studies in their business courses. Again, these students were not unique in their approach. Christensen Hughes (2017) found a similar attitude among some of the nearly 15,000 Canadian students she and McCabe had surveyed (2006a, 2006b). This business, rather than ethical, mindset was also one of the blind spots that Bazerman and Tenbrunsel (2012) identified in their work on infamous business decisions in American corporate history.

Students may have thought that this selective adherence was a smart way to approach academic integrity; they knew that some of the most common types of violations, like unauthorized collaboration and use of material (e.g., textbook answer keys or case solutions), were the most difficult to "catch" and typically connected to less significant assignments (i.e., those worth a smaller percentage of the student's final grade) meaning that in the unlikely chance they were caught, sanctions tended to be minimal. Unfortunately, this process of moral disengagement where students convinced themselves that it was okay to violate academic integrity in some circumstances was found to be susceptible to turning into another one of the blind spots that Bazerman and Tenbrunsel (2012) identified, namely the slippery slope (Gino & Bazerman, 2009), whereby small violations led to more significant violations overtime. In other work, we demonstrated that unlike what the fourth year student above stated, all students did not share the same opinion of what was okay and what wasn't okay and the more situations in which students believed it was okay to violate academic integrity the higher rates of violations they had both in the specific trivial behaviours they were evaluating as well as minor and major violations more generally (Packalen & Rowbotham, 2021).

Unknown if Adhering. The last group, based on type of adherence, was mentioned by five students from first and second year. This group was distinguished by the fact that they generally had good intentions, but sometimes unknowingly violated academic integrity. As one second year student wrote, "Some people breach academic integrity because they do not know the rules rather than it being intentional."

These students were "nervous that they will break the rules without meaning to and get kicked out of the program" (first year student). They also spoke to the fact that "some forms of academic integrity are hard to distinguish. What is allowed vs what is not" (third year student), and that they thought "people don't intentionally commit academic integrity for the most part" (second year student).

Student-Written Recommendations for Students, Faculty and Administration

In the computer facilitated focus groups we also asked students for their suggestions of actions students could take to improve the culture of academic integrity and those that faculty and administration could take. Table 18.2 provides the summary of suggestions for students and Table 18.3 provides the summary of suggestions for faculty and administration.

We aggregated students' individual comments into representative ideas and grouped those ideas by themes. The original comments upon which the representative ideas were based are included in an online Appendix on SpringerLink's website for this book. Within each theme we grouped ideas roughly by years in which such ideas were mentioned. In this way we could see which themes were more predominant among different groups and how suggested actions within a theme changed by cohort. For example, as shown in Table 18.2, first year students tended to focus on changes in individual perspective and attitude as a way to improve the culture of academic integrity, while second year students largely made suggestions around proactive actions designed to limit the likelihood of both violating academic integrity themselves as well as acting as a facilitator in others' violations of academic integrity.

Table 18.2 Summary of students' suggestions of actions students can take to improve the culture of academic integrity and the percent of each year that agreed with the suggestion (n = 44)

Suggestions for students	1st year	2nd year	3rd year	4th year
Suggestions on Perspective and Attitude				
Spend time outside of the program to remind yourself why you are in the program	10%			
Be less competitive—there is more to life than getting the best grade in the class	80%			
Know your limits and don't take on more than you can handle	70%			
Remind yourself that success should be a measure of how much you have learned rather than the grade that you received	50%	46%		
Remind yourself that the only grade that you "deserve" to get is the one for which you did the work	60%		60%	
Suggestions to Foster and Respect a Culture of Integrity				
Just don't violate academic integrity and call your friends and teammates out if they do violate academic integrity	50%	54%	50%	36%
Really learn the academic integrity policy		62%	20%	
Report violations to the program office if you witness them		62%		45%
Talk about academic integrity. What are the issues? Why? Only once individuals acknowledge the "elephant in the room" will we begin to be able to address the underlying causes driving violations of academic integrity			60%	27%
Create a culture of academic integrity			60%	55%
Don't tell stories about when lots of people commit violations or about major scandals				64%
Suggestions of Proactive Actions				
To Prevent Yourself from Academic Dishonesty				
If you are struggling academically get help from legitimate sources (profs, tutors, academic advisors)	60%	38%		
Improve your time management. Create a schedule and start assignments well in advance of the deadline		92%		
Delete your old assignments off your computer so you won't be tempted to reuse them		15%		
To Prevent the Facilitation of Others' Academic Dishonesty				
Complete individual assignments at home instead of public gathering spots to avoid social pressure to collaborate		38%		

(continued)

Table 18.2 (continued)

Suggestions for students	1st year	2nd year	3rd year	4th year
Avoid social situations after taking a quiz where you will be tempted to share thoughts on it with people who haven't taken it yet		23%		
Don't share past assignments or tests with other students		54%		100%
Convince program extracurricular clubs to delete their shared electronic folders of past assignments and tests				45%

Note Students were asked to select up to half of the comments from the comments which they and their peers had generated and which they thought were actions that would help to improve the culture of academic integrity in their program. The theme of the comments is summarized in this table and if a year included comments related to that theme the percent that agreed with the comment is noted

Third and fourth year students took a more holistic view and provided suggestions meant to foster and respect a culture of academic integrity.

Such cohort patterns were not observed to the same extent among the suggestions to faculty and administration. Rather, we saw an increase in the overall number of suggestions as compared to the number of suggestions students had for themselves and some of the suggestions were mentioned by at least three of the four years. We grouped suggestions into those that addressed the policy, structure and culture of the program, those that were specific to the policy and its enforcement, and suggestions that addressed several aspects of assignments.

Reflections on Students' Recommendations

Recommendations for Themselves

Our initial reaction when reading through the recommendations that students provided was that they understood many of the drivers of the relatively poor culture of academic integrity in the program. These included a culture of competition, a pressure to excel in all aspects of life (academics, extracurricular activities, social and professional), and an academic environment that made the ease of violating academic integrity high and the likelihood of consequences low.

Our second reaction was that there was a big difference between knowing what you should do and doing the work needed to accomplish that task. For example, as one first year student suggested,

> There are different ways by which to measure success! Not just marks or people's opinions - maybe creativity, the interesting books you've read and learned from them, how much you learn in general, etc.

Table 18.3 Summary of students' suggestions of actions faculty and administration can take to improve the culture of academic integrity and the percent of each year that agreed with the suggestion (N = 44)

Suggestion for faculty and administration	1st year	2nd year	3rd year	4th year
Program-wide Suggestions				
Culture				
Stop focusing so much on grades and change the culture to one where learning is more important than grades			50%	64%
Ensure that students can speak to professors honestly and that their comments will be taken seriously	30%		30%	
Policy and Structure				
Coordinate across professors to better distribute deadlines		85%	40%	
Administration making goals of program more clear: they pride the program on the student conferences and how well students do in recruiting but provide little support to help students achieve this				18%
Have an official form or a request form to fill out for any absences related to recruiting				73%
Academic Integrity Policy Suggestions				
Explain the policy clearly, what is and is not okay so there are fewer grey areas. Also, clearly explain sanctions and how you discover violations	80%	15%		
Make sure students understand the reasoning behind certain academic integrity rules and the importance of them		8%		
Explain the policy at appropriate and critical junctures but don't force it upon us all the time and don't implement heavy controls on areas that cannot be properly managed (collaborating on assignments, handing down past exams, etc.). Pushing too often and/or too hard can lead to policy fatigue and/or pushback	50%		40%	
Enforcement				
Don't let students who breach AI make excuses and get off easy	50%			
Set up an online anonymous forum for students to discuss issues and anonymously report cases			40%	
Do not encourage snitching on assignments, do not punish one student when lots of people are engaging in the same activity and just weren't caught			20%	
Create incentives for students to come forward			10%	
Be consistent among professors and across faculties with respect to violations of academic integrity				45%

(continued)

Table 18.3 (continued)

Suggestion for faculty and administration	1st year	2nd year	3rd year	4th year
Assignment Suggestions				
Policy				
Allow more collaboration on assignments, particularly between groups working on assignments	50%	69%		
Be reasonable with assignment completion times and allow extensions when asked	20%		40%	45%
Have a flexible attendance policy and don't penalize for absence of extra-curricular activities or recruiting activities		92%	0%	9%
Learning Support				
Teach students how to properly cite their work	60%			
Hold tutorials		38%		
Provide lots of practice material (extra problems with solutions, samples of prior midterms and exams)		77%	50%	82%
Be more interactive and responsive to student questions rather than leaving these to the TA				36%
Logistics				
Have more and better proctors	50%	8%		
Create new material each year and never use the same exams or tests		31%	80%	100%
Create multiple versions of each test so that the person beside and someone writing the test at a different time have different versions		69%	60%	27%
Allow for sufficient space between desks during tests			70%	
Do not use online quizzes either in the classroom or outside of the classroom				64%
Evaluation				
Be more generous with grading so that cheating isn't seen as necessary to achieve a high GPA	50%	38%		
Focus on learning and assignments which emphasis learning rather than regurgitation of facts	50%	77%	40%	9%

Note Students were asked to select up to half of the comments from the comments which they and their peers had generated and which they thought were actions that they thought would help to improve the culture of academic integrity in their program. The theme of the comments are summarized in this table and if a year included comments related to that theme the percent that agreed with the comment is noted

Yet, while half the students in the first year focus group agreed with this statement as a means to help improve the culture of integrity in the program, and 80 percent agreed with another first year's comment to "Learn to accept failure and not be so competitive to prove yourself to others," without specific guidance on how to change their mindset and repeated messaging from their peers, faculty, and program administrators to help them improve their resilience, we suspect that students would struggle to appropriately change their mindset in this respect.

Perhaps this is why the first year students, who had the most frequent and reoccurring messaging about academic integrity and were relatively new to the program and its demands, were the cohort to take the most responsibility for their own perspective and attitudes. By the second year, students, who were in their most challenging year academically, were much more focused on the low hanging fruit as a means to improve academic integrity. These included suggestions like avoiding public spaces where they would be pressured to share information on quizzes and/or work together on individual assignments. While these suggestions might make a dent in the number of violations, they did not address the underlying culture of academic integrity.

In the third year, students were beginning to perceive that the system in which they were operating was broken and by the fourth year students were struggling to manage recruiting, interviewing and coursework (Packalen & Rowbotham, 2020). Thus, we saw a movement in the students' suggestions from suggestions that were individually-focused to suggestions on what they could do to improve the respect for and culture of academic integrity more broadly. For example, 60 percent of third year students agreed with their peer's suggestion to "Create an environment where breaches of academic integrity are looked down upon." Interestingly, several of the fourth year students' suggestions, including the three suggestions which received the most votes, were not suggestions on how to improve the culture among their own cohort, but what they as a cohort could do to improve the culture for those in lower years in the program. One interpretation of this finding was that the fourth year students viewed themselves as a lost cause and thus felt their efforts would be better directed to providing solutions that would improve the situation of those for whom all was not lost.

Recommendations for Faculty and Administration

Turning to the suggestions that students had for faculty and administration we saw a more consistent message across cohorts. First and foremost, students said faculty should do everything possible to eliminate the temptation for students to violate academic integrity. These suggestions spanned policy, attendance (which was often required in courses), providing ample supports for learning course material, logistics related to assignments and tests, and pedagogical best practices related to assignment design and evaluations. Faculty and administrators need not agree with all suggestions—we for one didn't think that being more generous with grades, as first and second year students suggested, was the answer—but instead of outright dismissing them we considered what might be driving these suggestions. In this case, the requests for easier grading and suggestions to faculty and administration to stop focusing so much on grades likely connected to the aforementioned pressure to succeed.

The first author of this chapter has repeatedly said "academic integrity violations are often a symptom of a larger problem." At the individual level the underlying problems have regularly been extenuating circumstances related to mental health and/or addiction concerns. At the program level, as students in our focus groups have identified, these have tied back to the issues around respect towards and the culture of academic integrity. Yet when we considered some of the other suggestions that students had for faculty and administration, particularly from those in later years as they attempted to manage school work, find a job post-graduation and do the right type and quantity of extracurricular activities to stand out among their peers and get that desired job, we were struck by a new possibility that we are excited to investigate more in future research.

At a preliminary level we wondered if one way to improve a culture of academic integrity was to better align expectations of both faculty and students. For example, for many faculty members, teaching is only one aspect of their job. Yet many of the students' suggestions and comments implied that they thought that the primary, if not exclusive, responsibility of faculty members was to teach. Their expectations for 100 percent new material each year was neither realistic nor sound from a pedagogical perspective. Certain lectures, cases and assignments have been repeated because those have been the material that best serve the learning goals of the course. At the same time, however, we thought students' recommendations to not use the same exams, midterms or problem sets from one year to next were some of the fastest and easiest ways to reduce students' abilities to violate academic integrity. We were also encouraged to see that students welcomed assignments designed to encourage learning rather than memorization of facts. In this respect they validated the advice that education specialists have shared with faculty members for years regarding ways to proactively decrease the likelihood of students violating academic integrity.

The idea of workload, however, was not just about improving students' understanding that faculty had other responsibilities than teaching, it was also about faculty having a better understanding of students' workload and competing demands. If we thought of students' school-related workload of comprising three or four main activities—coursework, job search and resume building undertakings such as extracurricular activities and/or part-time job(s)—we wondered how students would allocate the percentage of their time between the activities and how faculty would do the same. Although future research is required to answer this question we are quite confident many instructors view students' number one priority as coursework and as such they think students should allocate the greatest proportion of their school-related workload to said activity. In contrast, when we looked at students' suggestions for faculty and administration, such as allowing for extensions when asked, not penalizing students when they missed class for extracurricular or recruiting activities, and having an official form to fill out for recruiting absences, many of these suggested that students thought faculty were unsupportive or unwilling to help students manage these competing demands. If these tensions were clarified, not only in terms of priorities, as one fourth year student writes, "Administration making goals of program more clear: they pride the program on the student conferences and how well students do in recruiting but provide little support to help students achieve this.", but also in terms of percentage of reasonable time commitment, perhaps there would be more room both to implement the suggestions that students made for faculty and administration, but also for students to implement the suggestions made for themselves.

Limitations of Study and Computer-Facilitated Focus Group Methodology

Our sample size was small and we conducted a limited number of focus groups. In addition, the focus groups prioritized depth of discussion over standardized responses. For example, only one student explicitly distinguished between themselves and their peers, stating "I personally take academic integrity seriously but my friends think that it's a grey area where they can get away with it time to time" (second year student). As such, it was impossible to determine how much the statements reflected students' own attitudes or the attitude that they thought was prevalent among the student body. Lack of standardization was also evident when we looked at the guidance provided and then voted upon (Tables 18.2 and 18.3). These lists were generated first by students brainstorming possibilities and second with them voting on those options. Therefore, unless a student in a group offered a solution, their group could not vote on the suggestion. Practically this meant that while we could see agreement between years on certain features, the absence of a vote on a particular item did not mean that students would not have voted for the item if they had been given a chance to do so.

Closely related to the aforementioned limitations, the facilitator who ran the computer-facilitated focus groups was a professional who has been facilitating these types of sessions for well over a decade. Thus, he has developed a good sense of how to establish a level of trust and openness with the groups he has facilitated and with the group's help identify themes in the data to aid the aggregation of participants' comments for later voting. He was not, however, a subject matter expert. As such, some of the ideas that he combined were ones that we would not have combined given that we would expect students would react differently to specific comments within the grouped set. Thus, when students ranked or voted on these combined items we were unable to sort out whether they are reacting to what they perceived to be the most favourable, least favourable or averaged opinion in the group of combined ideas.

Finally, the demographic and socioeconomic profile of the student body was perhaps less diverse than programs in other universities and thus some of the attitudes, behaviours and suggestions could be less applicable to larger programs, those that rely more on commuter or part-time students, and/or those that have a more demographically diverse population. For example, in this program the passing of notes and assignments from one class to the next through membership in exclusive clubs has been an ongoing challenge that was acknowledged both in terms of suggestions of behaviours students should not do, but also in terms of advice to faculty. These shared cloud-based file folders have been the modern-day version of assignment filing cabinets in fraternities (Stannard & Bowers, 1970). Nevertheless, for schools that do not have such a tightknit group and/or strong connections between program years, we suspect that paid note sharing sites have become the digital era equivalent to assignment filing cabinets that are available to anyone who is willing and able to pay a fee to obtain them. Moreover, the similarity in behaviours and attitudes among our students and a larger Canadian population of students (Christensen Hughes, 2017; Christensen Hughes & McCabe 2006a, b) reassured us that the general trends we observed among our small group of students were more reflective of the larger population than not.

Conclusion

We undertook this study because we recognized the importance of obtaining the student voice not only as related to students' self-reported engagement in violations of academic integrity but also with respect to their attitude towards academic integrity and their own suggestions on what they, as well as faculty and administration, might do to improve the culture of academic integrity. Their responses revealed that students understood how the environment in which they were situated could foster a culture which undermined academic integrity; they also understood what they could do at both a macro- and micro-level to improve their own academic integrity and the culture of academic integrity in the program. Importantly, the students also reminded us that absent faculty and administration support and willingness to make macro- and micro-level changes such as the ones they suggested, their efforts would meet limited success. Academic integrity is not a student issue, but an institutional issue that requires administration, faculty and students alike to all do their part in fostering a culture of academic integrity.

Acknowledgements Funding for the research was provided by Smith School of Business Commerce Office. This study (reference number GBUS-595–18) received ethics clearance from the Queen's General Research Ethic Board (GREB). Thank you to the students who gave their time and shared their stories, without which this chapter would not be possible. We also thank Erik Lockhart for facilitating the focus groups and Gabrielle Lindstrom, Sarah Elaine Eaton, Julia Christensen Hughes and the attendees of the October 2020 Academic Integrity in Canada Virtual Symposium for their helpful comments and feedback.

References

Aljurf, S., Kemp, L. J., & Williams, P. (2020). Exploring academic dishonesty in the Middle East: A qualitative analysis of students' perceptions. *Studies in Higher Education, 45*(7), 1461–1473.

Angell, R. C. (1928). *The campus: A study of contemporary undergraduate life in the American university*. D. Appelton & Company.

Antion, D. L., & Michael, W. B. (1983). Short-term predictive validity of demographic, affective, personal, and cognitive variables in relation to 2 criterion measures of cheating behaviors. *Educational and Psychological Measurement, 43*, 467–483.

Bandura, A. (1999). Moral disengagement in the perpetration of inhumanities. *Personality and Social Psychology Review, 3*(3), 193–209.

Bazerman, M. H., & Tenbrunsel, A. E. (2012). *Blind spots: Why we fail to do what's right and what to do about it*. Princeton University Press.

Bernardi, R. A., Metzger, R. L., Bruno, R. G. S., Hoogkamp, M. A. W., Reyes, L. E., & Barnaby, G. H. (2004). Examining the decision process of students' cheating behavior: An empirical study. *Journal of Business Ethics, 50*(4), 397–414.

Blum, S. D. (2009). *My word!: Plagiarism and college culture*. Cornell University Press.

Bowers, W. J. (1964). *Student dishonesty and its control in college*. Columbia University.

Bowers, W. J. (1966). Student dishonesty and its control in college (doctoral dissertation). Columbia University, New York. Available from ProQuest Dissertations & Theses Global database. (UMI No. 6709326).

Burnes, B., & Jackson, P. (2011). Success and failure in organizational change: An exploration of the role of values. *Journal of Change Management, 11*(2), 133–162.

Caldwell, C. (2010). A ten-step model for academic integrity: A positive approach for business schools. *Journal of Business Ethics, 92*(1), 1–13.

Chapman, K. J., Davis, R., Toy, D., & Wright, L. (2004). Academic integrity in the business school environment: I'll get by with a little help from my friend. *Journal of Marketing Education, 26*(3), 236–249.

Christensen Hughes, J. (2017). *Understanding academic misconduct: Creating robust cultures of integrity*. [Paper Presentation] University of Calgary, Calgary, AB. http://hdl.handle.net/1880/110083

Christensen Hughes, J. M., & McCabe, D. L. (2006). Academic misconduct in higher education in Canada. *Canadian Journal of Higher Education, 36*(2), 1–21.

Christensen Hughes, J. M., & McCabe, D. L. (2006). Understanding academic misconduct. *Canadian Journal of Higher Education, 36*(1), 49–63.

Eury, J. L., & Treviño, L. K. (2019). Building a culture of honor and integrity in a business school. *Journal of Management Education, 43*(5), 484–508.

Fontaine, S., Frenette, E., & Hébert, M. H. (2020). Exam cheating among Quebec's preservice teachers: the influencing factors. *International Journal for Educational Integrity, 16*(14), https://doi.org/10.1007/s40979-020-00062-6.

Gino, F., & Bazerman, M. (2009). When misconduct goes unnoticed: The acceptability of gradual erosion in others' unethical behavior. *Journal of Experimental Social Psychology, 45*, 708–719.

GroupSystems. (2018). *ThinkTank* (Version 4.9) [Software]. ThinkTank website. https://thinktank.net

Gullifer, J., & Tyson, G. A. (2010). Exploring university students' perceptions of plagiarism: A focus group study. *Studies in Higher Education, 35*(4), 463–481.

Hendershott, A., Drinan, P., & Cross, M. (2000). Toward enhancing a culture of academic integrity. *Journal of Student Affairs Research and Practice, 37*(4), 270–281.

Kang, M. J., & Glassman, M. (2010). Moral action as social capital, moral thought as cultural capital. *Journal of Moral Education, 39*(1), 21–36.

LaBeff, E. E., Clark, R. E., Haines, V. J., & Diekhoff, G. M. (1990). Situational ethics and college student cheating. *Sociological Inquiry, 60*, 190–198.

Lang, J. M. (2013). *Cheating lessons*. Harvard University Press.

McCabe, D. L. (1999). Academic dishonesty among high school students. *Adolescence, 34*(136), 681–687.

McCabe, D. L., & Bowers, W. J. (1994). Academic dishonesty among males in college: A thirty year perspective. *Journal of College Student Development, 35*(1), 5–10.

McCabe, D. L., Butterfield, K. D., & Treviño, L. K. (2012). *Cheating in college: Why students do it and what educators can do about it*. Johns Hopkins University Press.

McCabe, D., & Pavela, G. (2000). Some good news about academic integrity. *Change, 32*(5), 32–38.

McCabe, D. L., & Treviño, L. K. (1997). Individual and contextual influences on academic dishonesty: A multi-campus investigation. *Research in Higher Education, 38*(3), 379–396.

McCabe, D. L., Treviño, L. K., & Butterfield, K. D. (1999). Academic integrity in honor code and non-honor code environments: A qualitative investigation. *Journal of Higher Education, 70*(2), 211–234.

Miller, A., Shoptaugh, C., & Wooldridge, J. (2011). Reasons not to cheat, academic-integrity responsibility, and frequency of cheating. *The Journal of Experimental Education, 79*(2), 169–184.

Morris, E. J. (2018). Academic integrity matters: Five considerations for addressing contract cheating. *International Journal for Educational Integrity,* 14(15), https://doi.org/10.1007/s40979-018-0038-5

Murdock, T. B., & Anderman, E. M. (2006). Motivational perspectives on student cheating: Toward an integrated model of academic dishonesty. *Educational Psychologist, 41*(3), 129–145.

Nunamaker, J. F., Dennis, A. R., Valacich, J. S., Vogel, D. R., & George, J. F. (1991). Electronic meeting systems to support group work. *Communications of the ACM, 34*(7), 40–61.

Packalen, K. A. & Rowbotham, K. (2020). *Clues to fostering a program culture of academic integrity: Findings from a multidimensional model* [Paper presentation]. Academy of Management Conference 2020, Virtual.

Packalen, K. A. & Rowbotham, K. (2021). *Down the slippery slope: Moral disengagement and academic integrity's grey areas.* [Paper presentation]. Academy of Management Conference 2020, Virtual.

Pavela, G. (1981). Cheating on campus: Who's really to blame? *Chronicle of Higher Education, 21*(22), 64.

Raman, V., & Ramlogan, S. (2020). Academic integrity and the implementation of the honour code in the clinical training of undergraduate dental students. *International Journal for Educational Integrity, 16*(9), https://doi.org/10.1007/s40979-020-00058-2.

Rettinger, D. A., Jordan, A. E., & Peschiera, F. (2004). Evaluating the motivation of other students to cheat: A vignette experiment. *Research in Higher Education, 45*, 873–890.

Stannard, C. I., & Bowers, W. J. (1970). The college fraternity as an opportunity structure for meeting academic demands. *Social Problems, 17*(3), 371–390.

Steininger, M., Johnson, R. E., & Kirts, D. K. (1964). Cheating on college examinations as a function of situationally aroused anxiety and hostility. *Journal of Educational Psychology, 55*(6), 317.

Sykes, G. M., & Matza, D. (1957). Techniques of neutralization: A theory of delinquency. *American Sociological Review, 22*(6), 664–670.

Tammeleht, A., Rodríguez-Triana, M. J., Koort, K., & Löfström, E. (2019). Collaborative case-based learning process in research ethics. *International Journal for Educational Integrity,* 15(6), https://doi.org/10.1007/s40979-019-0043-3

Vakola, M. (2013). Multilevel readiness to organizational change: A conceptual approach. *Journal of Change Management, 13*(1), 96–109.

Ward, D. A. (1986). Self-esteem and dishonest behaviour revisited. *Journal of Social Psychology, 126*(6), 709–713.

Whitley, B. E. (1998). Factors associated with cheating among college students: A review. *Research in Higher Education, 39*(3), 235–274.

Whitley, B. E., & Keith-Spiegel, P. (2002). *Academic dishonesty: An educator's guide.* Lawrence Erlbaum Associates.

Kelley A. Packalen Ph.D., is an Associate Professor at the Smith School of Business, Queen's University. She studies codes of conduct, moral disengagement and ethical cultures. She researches these topics in post-secondary education as well as in nascent entrepreneurs and their firms. She has also studied how career histories of founders may influence firm level outcomes and the evolution of multi-level organizational and industry networks over time. Dr. Packalen teaches courses in strategy, entrepreneurship, innovation and social innovation. Her research has been published in leading entrepreneurship journals and funded by the Kauffman Foundation, SSRC and SSHRC among others. She holds a BA (Honours) in psychology from Wellesley College and an MA in sociology and Ph.D. in industrial engineering from Stanford University.

Kate Rowbotham Ph.D., is an Adjunct Assistant Professor and Distinguished Faculty Fellow of Organizational Behaviour at the Smith School of Business, Queen's University. She researches integrity and how it's understood in different contexts. She has also studied inclusion and exclusion across different organizational and educational settings and deviance inside and outside of the workplace. She holds an BA (Honours) in political studies and French and an MSc in management from Queen's University and a Ph.D. in organizational behaviour and human resource management from the University of Toronto.

Chapter 19
Helping Students Resolve the Ambiguous Expectations of Academic Integrity

Susan L. Bens

Abstract Students find matters of academic integrity to be ambiguous. Many educators do not understand how this, and self-reported incidence of academic misconduct, can persist. Across Canadian higher education, students are alerted to policy via syllabus statements and awareness campaigns. Many faculty provide guidance and referrals to supports and resources. Yet, students report mixed messages that leave them unclear as to the real expectations. In this chapter, I offer an educational developer's perspective on how matters of academic integrity confuse students. I make the point, through story and review of selected research, that students encounter wide-ranging teaching and learning contexts and approaches, especially in early years of study. Next, I examine the practical limits of initiatives like standardized syllabus statements and campus awareness campaigns. I recommend contextualized course-based instruction approaches that occupy a teaching and learning space between policy awareness and general academic skill building. I conclude that instructors ought to target and reinforce areas of greatest concern with more explicit instruction in their courses.

Keywords Academic integrity · Ambiguity · Variability · Inconsistency · Disciplinary understanding

Students encounter wide-ranging teaching and learning contexts and approaches, especially in early years of postsecondary study. I make the case in this chapter that more can and should be done by educators to help students understand the contexts for academic integrity and the contextual nature of academic integrity. First, I introduce my perspective as an educational developer and then offer an invented story of "Alex", that provides a set of plausible settings and interactions in which students try to make sense of varied messages. Next, I discuss how the research corroborates and applies to the student story. I then acknowledge the practical limits of awareness initiatives and recommend instructional approaches that together emphasize a

S. L. Bens (✉)
University of Saskatchewan, Saskatoon, Canada
e-mail: susan.bens@usask.ca

S. E. Eaton and J. Christensen Hughes (eds.), *Academic Integrity in Canada*, Ethics and Integrity in Educational Contexts 1,
https://doi.org/10.1007/978-3-030-83255-1_19

contextual teaching and learning space between policy awareness and academic skill building. I conclude that instructors ought to target and reinforce areas of greatest concern with more explicit instruction about contextual and disciplinary differences where they exist. Throughout the chapter, I refer to faculty, professors, instructors, and educators interchangeably to mean those who teach in postsecondary institutions in Canada.

An Educational Developer's Perspective

In my work as an educational developer at the University of Saskatchewan, I interact with educators about ways to enhance teaching and learning at the course and program levels. Sometimes, my work includes advising on ways to prevent academic misconduct. Educators have a range of reactions when they encounter academic misconduct. Many I work with are disappointed and perplexed about the instances of academic misconduct they uncover; some ask, "Haven't students learned about *this* kind of academic misconduct before?" Over time, my answer has become, "Yes, I think many students have but maybe not in the context of your assessments or your subject area." I also add that some acts are interpreted differently or deemed less serious in other situations, and that these variations may contribute to students' misunderstandings. I go on to say that students may carry those other occasions with them and not anticipate another interpretation or different application of the same general rules. The differences students encounter may seem arbitrary and unpredictable to them. They need help to resolve the ambiguous expectations of academic integrity.

A Story of Mixed Messages

Alex is an 18 year-old, cisgender, male student who is enrolled in a general undergraduate first year with sights set on a career in a health profession. He aims for high grades, sees himself as intellectually capable, and expects to need to develop academic skills and work harder in the new learning environment. Alex is excited about university and is here to learn and achieve.

In English, the first assignment is to read the novel, The Great Gatsby. Alex recalls this title on his mom's bookshelf. He reads her book and quickly realizes it is not the novel, but something called "Coles Notes," which is a synopsis. He next learns there is also a 2013 movie starring Leonardo deCaprio and he watches it. The weeks go by, and while Alex fully intends to read the book he still has not on the day of the in-class essay. He writes the essay and gets a good mark. Since Alex made it seem like he read the book when he did not, he wonders if he has engaged in academic misconduct.

In Indigenous Studies, Alex learns about the importance of Elders in local First Nations communities. For a short paper in the course, Alex is told to use APA for citation. In passing, he wonders why the citation style for this course is different than the one for English. When he writes about an Elder's teaching received in his Grade 12 winter wilderness field trip, he uses the APA method for citing personal communication. He has marks deducted and a direct comment that these teachings are not his to share without permission of the Elder and that this is cultural appropriation and a form of plagiarism. Alex is very sure cultural appropriation is bad and certain plagiarism is academic misconduct, but he has no idea how to avoid both of these offences and feels embarrassed to ask because he is ashamed.

In Math, Alex learns students can work together on the weekly assignments worth 5% each. In fact, the instructor said they should work together, because it will help them learn. She asks that they show their work on the assignments and describe the steps in their own words so that "at least I know you did some independent thinking." She reminds the students that, when it comes time for the final exam, they need to do the work on their own. After class, Alex's friend recommends he get a subscription to a specific online tutoring service and adds that she has had one since high school for tutoring help and "for when I run out of time for getting assignments done." Seeing Alex's surprised reaction, she continues, "Oh, I think this is okay, she says we can collaborate on assignments." Alex wonders—is this what the professor meant by collaboration?

In Chemistry, Alex's lab partner is repeating the course because he broke his leg and had to withdraw mid-course last year. On the second lab of the term, their lab procedure fails, and the partners have no useable data. Alex says they need to start over. His lab partner, reaching into his backpack, says "Let's just use the data I got last year, I've still got these labs." Alex insists they instead talk to the lab coordinator. The lab coordinator asks a few questions about their procedure, then gives them a data set to use. Alex's lab partner, says "See I told you, we could have just used my data from last year." Alex wonders if you are only allowed to use fraudulent data when it is provided by a lab coordinator.

In Biology, Alex writes his first midterm exam in the same lecture theatre where he takes the course. Every seat is in use and Alex notices students one row in front of him sharing answers. Alex is distracted by this and thinks the professor has detected the cheating when she walks to their general vicinity and lingers there for the remainder of the exam. Alex expects the professor will speak with the students when they hand in their exams or set their exams aside for follow up. Alex does not see any response. He wonders if these students got away with it, or if the professor just turned a blind eye to avoid the hassle.

Alex has done some things in high school that he knows constitute academic misconduct, but he has no intention of such acts while in university. Every syllabus and instructor warn against academic misconduct and the penalties sound stiff. Now, he's nearly through his first term, and Alex is surprised by what has occurred so far and is trying to make sense of what the "real" rules are for getting by and getting good grades here.

This story is my own invention. I have composed it using my knowledge of policy, research, and students' experiences in the area of academic integrity. From an organization theory perspective, Czarniawska (1997) said that "the common way of understanding human action is by placing it in a narrative" (p. 14) and that "organizational stories capture organizational life in a way that no compilation of facts ever can; this is because they are carriers of life itself, not just "reports" on it" (p. 21). My account of Alex is meant to help us to see the wide-ranging experiences of our students and to illustrate the sources of potential confusion regarding academic misconduct.

Alex's experience makes it clear that there are many possible issues in how he is making sense of the expectations. Having good intentions and asking authorities may not provide sufficient guidance when messages take many forms and come from multiple sources. Students are left to wonder about the difference between what instructors communicate as serious and what our collective actions indicate we take seriously and why. Combined, these circumstances create an environment where misunderstanding is likely, instead of merely possible. Lack of consistency, in fact or appearance, contributes to ambiguity of expectations and even confusion for our students.

Origins of Ambiguous Expectations

Researchers have found diverse perspectives on what constitutes academic misconduct among educators. Differences in how students and faculty understand academic misconduct was an important finding in a landmark Canadian study (Christensen Hughes & McCabe, 2006a). Eaton and Edino (2018), in their review of Canadian literature, acknowledged the complexities of academic integrity across disciplinary boundaries and recommended more discipline-specific research. Disagreement on definition is a problem for researchers in this area as well. Definitions are "murky in reality" and guidelines have a "wobbliness" because of different meanings and histories of groups setting those definitions and guidelines, according to Blum (2009). For example, Barnhardt and Ginns (2017) chose to define cheating as an intentional academic deviance. Such a definition could be contested by many academic misconduct policy makers who frequently say a lack of awareness when a student reasonably ought to have known is not an acceptable defense, as is the case in the regulations at my own university (University of Saskatchewan, 2017).

In a study involving 24 academics from five distinct disciplinary areas, Borg (2009) found varying responses to what constitutes plagiarism and collusion, based in both personal experience and discipline. Different interpretations appeared to be rooted in thinking like a member of the discipline, valuing collaboration versus individual work, and norms for appropriate use of the work of others. In Susan Blum's (2009) multifaceted study of plagiarism, she observed that disciplinary assumptions underpin authorship and the subsequent rules of citation, adding that: "Different reasons govern each one, and different responses are appropriate for violations of each one" (p. 160).

Related to the matter of definition, faculty judgements about academic misconduct exist on a continuum of seriousness (Pincus & Schmelkin, 2003). In particular, matters of collaboration and collusion can be debated from a number of stances (Barrett & Cox, 2005; Sutton & Taylor, 2011). Collusion, also referred to as unpermitted or unauthorized collaboration in many policies, depends on context and intent may be a consideration (McGowan, 2016). How do students know what help *is* permitted? To Alex, it seems his professor has indicated collaboration on math assignments is permitted among classmates, but to his friend this seems extended to other collaborators. We can presume the professor did not mean to permit the outsourcing of assignment completion to a third-party commercial service, also called "contract cheating" (Lancaster, 2020). However, it could be asked what the reasons are to restrict the collaboration if students follow the same principles of learning communicated by the Math professor, that is, putting answers into their own words and, being prepared to work alone on a final exam? I have heard educators say their evaluation of seriousness depends on type, weighting, or importance of the assessment task in other respects. I have also heard seasoned faculty add that they know there is a divergent opinion on these topics in their own departmental hallways where the disciplinary culture is presumably shared at least to some extent. All of this is complicating and significant in terms of its implications as it leaves the new student, like Alex, uncertain and unprepared to meet a mix of standards.

I further explore the examples from Alex's experience using the notion of *signature pedagogies* (Shulman, 2005). Signature pedagogies are the teaching and learning practices based in assumptions about teaching and learning in different professions and subject areas. I depart here from Shulman's focus on the professions, and use his concepts of surface structures, deep structures, and implicit structures to illuminate the kinds of experiences for our students that allow ambiguity of expectations to occur.

Surface Structure Experiences

The surface structure of pedagogy "consists of concrete, operational acts of teaching and learning, of showing and demonstrating, of questioning and answering, of interacting and withholding, of approaching and withdrawing" (Shulman, 2005, pp. 54–55). It is common for first year students to take a breadth of introductory courses, meaning they interact with varied "operational acts" of multiple disciplines from the position of novice or newcomer. Alex is surprised in his first term. He is surprised because he is noting a difference between what was anticipated and what subsequently occurred (Louis, 1980) at an operational or surface level.

Surprise can illicit positive or negative emotions. Alex may feel embarrassed, ashamed, concerned, uncertain, pressured, worried, distracted, and even relieved that the rules are not as strict as he first thought. Alex has unmet and undermet expectations of instructors, peers, and self and these are often sources of surprise for newcomers in unfamiliar organizations (Louis, 1980). Alex expects an instructor to intervene during obvious exam cheating. He expects peers not to pay web-based third parties to complete their assignments or to want to copy last year's lab reports. He expects he, himself, is the kind of student who will in fact read the book before writing an essay as though he did and that he is someone who will cite, with sincere respect, the First Nation Elders whose teachings he values. The problem of mixed messages is greatest in early years of study where students meet the traditions of multiple disciplines or are new to postsecondary standards for what constitutes plagiarism. Surface structures are the first impressions that can form long lasting misunderstandings.

Deep Structure Experiences

The deep structure of pedagogy appears in the "assumptions about how to best impart a certain body of knowledge and know-how" (Shulman, 2005, p. 55). These assumptions exist in sequencing of content, selecting learning activities and assessing learning. They become implicit as time passes and the immersion in discipline deepens. For the educator who has achieved expert status, it is difficult to remember what it was like to be a novice for whom academic practices and expectations are not yet internalized. Relevant to matters of academic misconduct, use of certain assessment methods becomes an accepted practice. Professors who branch off into other types of assessment, even if known to provide better evidence of learning or improve academic integrity, may be breaking "rules of appropriateness, taken for granted understandings" (Knight & Trowler, 2001, p. 52) of their academic workgroup and with negative repercussions.

Alex needs to make sense of an overflow of varied experiences. Sensemaking is the way we create order in our organizational lives (Weick, 1995). Alex is accumulating experiences, reflecting to some extent as he goes, but he is not in a position to step out of the learning environments to recalibrate and resolve his uncertainty. From social cues and peer interactions, he is coming to understand that his concern for these matters is overinflated and unnecessary given the context. The next math assignment, the next in-class essay, the second citation protocol with or without guidance about citing Elders, the next lab report, and the next midterm exam are all around the corner for Alex. His sensemaking means he is determining what is okay and what is not, but any resolution or coherence is not coming from the collective expertise of his educators. Alex does not yet sufficiently understand or question the context in which a lab instructor recognizes students' missteps and supplies what they need (a useable data set) for the next step in their learning. Alex lives in his world as it is. In the absence of more explicit instruction, the ambiguity and confusion grow. This is a problem for postsecondary institutions that depend on clear expectations for academic integrity as a foundation for fair assessment and for scholarship more broadly.

Implicit Structure Experiences

The implicit structure of a signature pedagogy has "a moral dimension that comprises a set of beliefs about professional attitudes, values, and dispositions" (Shulman, 2005, p. 55). Extended, it is akin to the organizational culture (Schein, 1985) of a pedagogical community and may be known to members and also hidden from conscious view. How students come to grasp the system of shared assumptions, values and beliefs that govern how people behave is a matter of academic enculturation (Gilmore et al., 2010). For example, in some professional programs of study, it goes relatively unquestioned that students must handle fast-paced, high volume, high stakes expectations. When I have worked with such programs on curriculum renewal, a hidden curriculum has become apparent to me. Despite evidence that less content coverage, more active practice with priority learning outcomes, and better life balance for students could deliver improved retention of knowledge and achievement of most-valued skills, the faculty would not reduce curriculum load. This suggests an implicit structure for attitudes, values, and dispositions among graduates for handling extreme workloads and high-pressure situations. For Alex, at this point in his undergraduate career, we would not expect him to be grappling with implicit structures yet. But he is being introduced to these unstated or hidden expectations in each of his five courses where there may be subtle pulls exerted in five directions that may contribute to an overall sense of ambiguity.

In this section, I have explored the essence of teaching and learning relationships that create expectations for academic integrity and some of the potential origins of their ambiguity for students. Figure 19.1 positions the learner (possibly Alex) at the centre and depicts a cycle of diverse (especially in early years of study) course subjects (represented by icons related to the five courses in the story). Surrounding these course experiences are common kinds of general awareness building initiatives

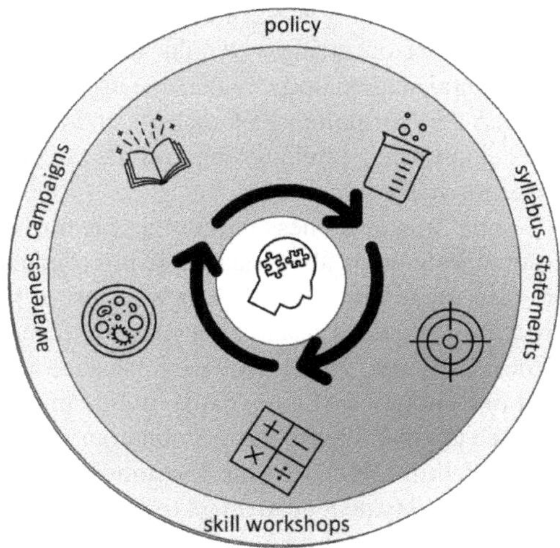

Fig. 19.1 A student experience of mixed academic integrity messages

that may also impact expectations, the practical limits of which is the topic of the next section.

Awareness Initiatives and Their Practical Limits

Awareness initiatives tend to be general by design, given the intended reach across an entire student body. Here, I argue that as a result of this general approach, awareness initiatives have practical limits that educators and policy-makers need to acknowledge.

Awareness initiatives or requirements are a common institutional level approach to try to reach all students with a consistent message regarding academic integrity. These are typically in place not only for the benefit of students but because academic integrity is important for institutional credibility and reputation writ large. Beyond institutional walls, there is a concerning relationship between academic misconduct and workplace misconduct (Nonis & Swift, 2001; Lucas & Friedrich, 2005). Thus, academic leaders want to be able to show internal and external institutional stakeholders that strategies are in place to address academic misconduct.

In the Canadian context some institutions present campaigns where academic integrity messages are broadcast through various venues to attract student attention and increase awareness (Lock et al., 2019). They can emphasize values (Benson et al., 2019), skill building and policies and penalties (Stoesz & Yudintseva, 2018). Often campaigns are strategically timed at a point in an academic term when students may be under some pressure and may benefit from the reminder to stay on the academic integrity track. Some campuses participate in awareness campaigns coordinated at the provincial level (McKenzie et al., 2020). Since 2015, the International Day of Action against Contract Cheating by the International Centre for Academic Integrity (ICAI, 2021) has been another opportunity for awareness specific to the problem of students outsourcing academic work to third parties. In my own institution, awareness initiatives are occurring at regular intervals and are designed for broad application to a general student body, with some aspects targeting the specific needs of first year or international students. Workshops and resources on topics like time management and paraphrasing explicitly incorporate the benefit of skills of this kind for avoiding academic misconduct.

A common awareness requirement is for instructors to include links to the institutional statements about academic misconduct in course syllabi or outlines. Called policies, regulations, or standards—these typically provide broad definitions and procedures that can reach across diverse contexts of study, research and authorship (Stoesz & Eaton, 2020). However, because a single definition of academic misconduct does not exist (Lang, 2013), policy makers may use definitions that are easier to agree upon and leave more ambiguous matters to be dealt with elsewhere (Pincus & Schmelkin, 2003). At the institutional level, as McGowan (2016) put it, "it is unrealistic to expect academics to be able to identify every type of action students may take that could compromise academic integrity, nor to identify every type of interaction that would be acceptable collaboration" (p. 238). Each institution must settle on its definitions, nonetheless, and these will usually leave instructors with the responsibility to apply the definitions in their contexts and according to their own judgment of seriousness. This is important to note, as it places responsibility squarely on the shoulders of instructors to educate students for academic integrity in their own course contexts. Despite this, some instructors admit to ignoring academic misconduct for because of insufficient evidence, seriousness, and time or emotional energy to do what is procedurally required (Coren, 2011).

As an educational developer, I fear some instructors conclude that providing links to policy information and other resources is sufficient, that is, they think they have done their duty with respect to making students aware. Likewise, I worry instructors note well-orchestrated awareness campaigns and centralized supports and think that these cover their students' specific needs. Instructor assumptions regarding the application of academic integrity principles in their own course or program may not be apparent even to themselves (Borg, 2009; Sutherland-Smith, 2013). This insufficiency has been studied with respect to matters of plagiarism in particular, including findings in one study that only half of students read the policy and that confusion remained (Gullifer & Tyson, 2014). For example, students at six Quebec universities said they expected to be taught the knowledge and skills to avoid plagiarism, while professors said they expected the students to already be competent in this respect (Peters & Cadieux, 2019).

Student actions should be seen as depending on more than their exposure to policy information. Just as "cheating" may have various definitions among students (Wei et al., 2014), personal definitions of plagiarism exist among faculty, often informed by disciplinary differences, and these impact judgment on what constitutes academic misconduct (Flint et al., 2006; Borg, 2009). It is important to recognize the impact of contextual factors like peer loyalty, class size, group learning, and alienation from the learning process (Ashworth et al., 1997). Pre-existing competencies and educational interventions aimed at building academic skills and awareness have received little attention in the research. Some studies conducted outside of Canada have found in-person instruction, web-based tutorials, and hybrid programs to improve awareness, attitudes toward integrity, and competence in key skills, but few have studied the effect on incidence of misconduct (Stoesz & Yudintseva, 2018).

I do not intend to be dismissive of these initiatives and requirements that focus on general awareness, skill-building, and student agency and responsibility when it comes to academic integrity. Rather, I caution that these have practical limits in terms of bringing clarity to students about what is expected in their individual courses. I argue that it is important to see these awareness initiatives as necessary but not sufficient when it comes to explaining the rules, equipping students to follow them, and enforcing the rules in the learning environments we create in postsecondary education. Recommendations for contextualized, in-course instruction appear in the next section.

Recommendations to Help Students Resolve Ambiguous Expectations

There is no silver bullet for the persistent problem of academic misconduct. Contextual factors related to academic misconduct rather than characteristics or dispositions of students is where educators can find the most influence, and the most hope. That is, many of the strategies known to promote and enable learning also reduce incidence of academic misconduct. The environment in which students engage in misconduct is, as Lang (2013) puts it, “the most relevant contextual factor of all” (p. 17).

In their comprehensive book, Ambrose et al. (2010) discuss how postsecondary educators may overestimate their students’ prior knowledge; or they may underestimate the range of experiences that may have distorted students’ interpretations about the learning environment. Addressing confusion on points of difficulty makes learning more effective and efficient while decreasing factors that may push students to consider misconduct to hide their own shortcomings. Thus, here I offer recommendations for contextualized, in-course instruction to explain rules and their application, to equip students to anticipate and recognize relevant academic misconduct errors, and to make the steps for enforcement predictable and transparent for students.

Explain

Rules for assessments and their rationale require explanation. Instructors can link them to the rules in a discipline and describe how the boundaries the rules provide are good for learning and assessment of learning. Explaining this early in a course in general terms to provide an overview, and then adding additional details when the assessment due dates are nearer at hand will provide specific information when students are more attuned to it.

A lesson that uses a concept from the subject area or discipline of the course can situate the importance of academic integrity in more relevant terms. Using a scenario-based exercise consisting of a sample of violations can allow students to think about the personal and public issues associated with academic misconduct. Trautner and Borland (2013) presented such an exercise in detail that includes disciplinary thinking and disciplinary relevance and they reported it clarified understanding among students. Current events in a discipline may provide examples of ethical breaches that can become important points of dialogue about pressures and poor decisions that translate directly to unwanted student experiences in a course. Being explicit about how these relate is important, otherwise students may not see the connection. In Alex’s Indigenous Studies course, this could be a lesson on how notions of academic integrity in higher education require decolonizing (Lindstrom, 2022) and that referencing conventions are only beginning to provide guidelines on teachings of Elders, community-based and sacred knowledge. This would be followed by instruction on “the interconnected principles of relationality, reciprocity and respect" (Poitras Pratt & Gladue, 2022) for academic integrity and under what conditions an Elder's teachings can be cited and the appropriate method to do so.

Equip

Students may need to develop their understandings and skills in the context of course assessments. This need is likely most apparent in matters of academic and professional writing and appropriate use of accepted referencing protocols. In early years, the referencing protocol expectations may, unfortunately, appear ad hoc to students. In later years, students are specializing and have the opportunity for more focused practice on the one or two protocols typical in their subject area. Some senior students may even come to understand how the disciplinary underpinnings and epistemologies are reflected in those conventions. Regardless of requirements, students need to feel comfortable to ask questions about the rules for academic integrity without repercussions or negative reactions. Practice allows students time to understand their errors and improve. In Alex's math course, this could look like allowing collaboration early on for weekly assignments, and then insisting students work more independently as the term progresses as explicit preparation for the individual work required of them on the final exam.

Reinforcing academic integrity expectations when students are most vulnerable to the temptations of misconduct is wise as are appropriate extensions or smaller late penalties to alleviate the pressure, where possible. It can help when instructors show that they know about the shortcuts students consider and the temptations they face and then give them the direction and tools they need to overcome them. This may include advising students on acceptable and unacceptable kinds of help.

A lesson that teaches students to recognize the more subtle or threshold differences in "rule-breaking" that tips the offence over into the realm of academic misconduct for an individual instructor makes the contextual nature of academic integrity explicit. For writing, using examples of effective and less effective paraphrasing or citing is common. Short situations or scenarios that point out the more subtle differences can contextualize this explicitly for students (see example in McGowan, 2016, p. 241 for situations used in a computing science context). For Alex's Chemistry lab, a lesson on what makes data fraudulent in research compared to the acceptable variations on lab data that can be provided in a lab experience to allow for learning objectives to be achieved would help.

Enforce

Students need to know under what circumstances and in what ways suspected academic misconduct, as governed by institutional policy will be addressed. While there are a range of approaches to enforcement used across Canada, instructors usually are responsible to set the rules for their assessments, flag suspected concerns, and engage with local policies and procedures for appropriate follow up. Students thereby learn what their professors find as acceptable by their action and by their inaction. Where consistent with policy, instructors can interact with students about the apparent misconduct and its causes to understand the nature and extent of the error.

It is important, however, to avoid treating all students as though they will cheat when given the opportunity because this contributes to mistrust and offends the majority of students. Rather, it is valuable to create an accurate expectation for vigilance and follow up. This way students can know where the policies ask instructors to apply their expert judgement as an educator and handle matters as teachable moments, and where it will be elevated to the procedures outlined by local policy. Walking students through what will occur when their instructor is faced with suspected academic misconduct can be another vivid deterrent. When instructors are clear on their follow up, it not only explicates the commitment, but will allow quick follow through because the personal steps have already been established. This can help with some of the fatigue, the frustration, the feelings of insult or self-doubt that are known barriers to instructors' follow up (Coren, 2011).

A lesson that requires students to rank the severity of several relevant forms of misconduct compared with the instructor's ranking allows for useful discussion of any differences that exist. Using a list of behaviours that is likely to generate "it depends" responses in determining whether they are academic misconduct or not can bring nuanced distinctions to light (see Christensen-Hughes & McCabe, 2006a, and Higbee et al., 2011 for examples of such lists). A lesson of this kind requires students to consider the relative seriousness and compare their responses to those of their instructor. Students, for example, may rank severity based on the amount of work or effort circumvented by the misconduct rather than other criteria like ethical norms (Colnerud & Rosander, 2009). Discrepancies in ranking should be discussed and the instructor's rating of seriousness must become clearly the one for students to adopt in the course. Acknowledging to students how personal thresholds for follow up may differ among instructors in the same program, or in other subject areas, or in earlier or later years of study situates multiple approaches to enforcement further. Helping students to see that the context of a course matters and the policy has different applications in different courses may help resolve the ambiguity.

In summary, faculty need to become aware themselves of the diverse practices and contexts that students encounter (McGowan, 2016) and provide the contextualized course-based instruction to explain the practices, equip the students with the knowledge and skills, and then enforce the rules (as depicted in Fig. 19.2 below). Looking back to Fig. 19.1, we can imagine contextualized instruction encircling each subject area icon, demonstrating that the students are learning about the context for academic integrity in all courses.

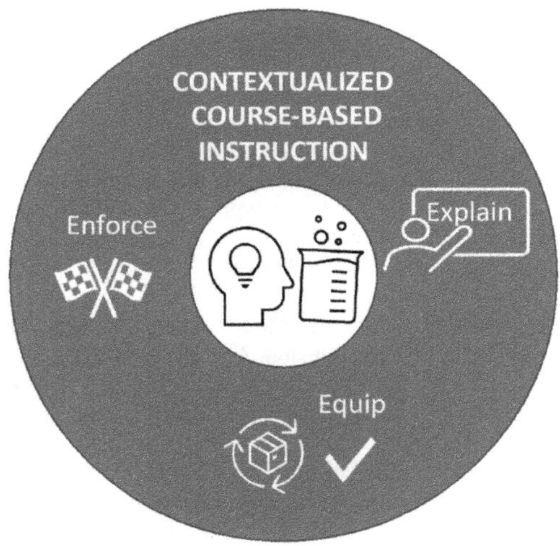

Fig. 19.2 Key actions for resolving ambiguous expectations of academic integrity at the course-level

Concluding Remarks

As an educational developer, I interact with and try to make sense myself of the disciplinary differences and diverse approaches for teaching and learning across my own university. There is a forgetting that happens by those of us immersed in the work of postsecondary institutions (Scutt & Hobson, 2013). We are also immersed in our own scholarship and teaching practices and life responsibilities. It is hard to step outside of our own years of experience to recall what it was like to be new to all of it. In my experience, returning to the multiple contexts of the student experience, inside and outside of our virtual and physical classrooms, usually allows a more grounded, holistic, and multi-faceted understanding.

The story of Alex is meant to situate the reader in the subjective lifeworld of the student who is a newcomer to the expectations of postsecondary study. Students are experiencing a range of courses and mix of messages from the institution, their instructors, their peers that include the messages that come from actions and inactions. Considering the potential origins of ambiguity of expectations, we see the need to contextualize the guidance from awareness campaigns, policy statements, and skill building resources and services explicitly through direct instruction. In this chapter, I call on postsecondary educators to recall the time and place when expectations for academic integrity were new for us and, now to do more to help students understand the context for academic integrity and the contextual nature of academic integrity.

References

Ambrose, S., Bridges, M., Dipietro, M., Lovett, M., & Norman, M. (2010). *How learning works: 7 research-based principles for smart teaching*. Hoboken: Wiley.

Ashworth, P., Bannister, P., & Thorne, P. (1997). Guilty in whose eyes? University students' perceptions of cheating and plagiarism in academic work and assessment. *Studies in Higher Education, 22*(2), 187–203. https://doi.org/10.1080/03075079712331381034

Barnhardt, B., & Ginns, P. (2017). Psychological teaching-learning contracts: Academic integrity and moral psychology. *Ethics & Behavior, 27*(4), 313–334. https://doi.org/10.1080/10508422.2016.1167604

Barrett, R., & Cox, A. L. (2005). 'At least they're learning something': The hazy line between collaboration and collusion. *Assessment & Evaluation in Higher Education, 30*(2), 107–122.

Benson, L., Rodier, K., Enström, R., & Bocatte, E. (2019). Developing a university-wide academic integrity E-learning tutorial: A Canadian case. *International Journal for Educational Integrity, 15*(5). https://doi.org/10.1007/s40979-019-0045-1

Blum, S. (2009). *My Word!* United States: Cornell University Press.

Borg, E. (2009). Local plagiarisms. *Assessment & Evaluation in Higher Education, 34*(4), 415–426.

Christensen Hughes, J. M., & McCabe, D. L. (2006a). Academic misconduct within higher education in Canada. *Canadian Journal of Higher Education, 36*(2), 1–21.

Christensen Hughes, J. M., & McCabe, D. L. (2006b). Understanding academic misconduct. *Canadian Journal of Higher Education, 36*(1), 49–63.

Colnerud, G., & Rosander, M. (2009). Academic dishonesty, ethical norms and learning. *Assessment & Evaluation in Higher Education, 34*(5), 505–517.

Coren, A. (2011). Turning a blind eye: Faculty who ignore student cheating. *Journal of Academic Ethics*, 9 (4), 291–305. https://doi-org.cyber.usask.ca/10.1007/s10805-011-9147-y

Czarniawska, B. (1997). *Narrating the organization: Dramas of institutional identity*. Chicago: University of Chicago Press.

Eaton, S.E., & Edino, R. I. (2018). Strengthening the research agenda of educational integrity in Canada: a review of the research literature and call to action, *International Journal for Educational Integrity, 14*(1). https://doi.org/10.1007/s40979-018-0028-7

Flint, A., Clegg, S., & Macdonald, R. (2006). Exploring staff perceptions of student plagiarism. *Journal of Further and Higher Education, 30*(2), 145–156. https://doi.org/10.1080/03098770600617562

Gilmore, J., Strickland, D., Timmerman, B., Maher, M., & Feldon, D. (2010). Weeds in the flower garden: An exploration of plagiarism in graduate students' research proposals and its connection to enculturation, ESL, and contextual factors. *International Journal for Educational Integrity, 6*(1), 13–28.

Gullifer, J. M., & Tyson, G. A. (2014). Who has read the policy on plagiarism? Unpacking students' understanding of plagiarism. *Studies in Higher Education, 39*(7), 1202–1218. https://doi.org/10.1080/03075079.2013.777412

Higbee, J. L., Schultz, J. L., & Sanford, T. (2011). Student perspectives on behaviours that constitute cheating. *Contemporary Issues in Education Research, 4*(10), 1–8.

International Center for Academic Integrity (ICAI). (2021). International day against contract cheating. Retrieved January 14, 2021 from https://www.academicintegrity.org/day-against-contract-cheating/

Knight, P. T., & Trowler, P. (2001). *Departmental leadership in higher education*. Society for Research into Higher Education and Open University Press.

Lancaster, T. (2020). Commercial contract cheating provision through micro-outsourcing websites. *International Journal for Educational Integrity, 16*(4). https://doi.org/10.1007/s40979-020-00053-7

Lang, J. (2013). *Cheating Lessons: Learning from Academic Dishonesty*. Harvard University Press.

Lindstrom, G. (2022). Accountability, relationality and Indigenous epistemology: Advancing an Indigenous perspective on academic integrity. In S. E. Eaton & J. Christensen Hughes (Eds.), *Academic integrity in Canada: An enduring and essential challenge.* Berlin: Springer.

Lock, J., Schroeder, M., & Eaton, S. E. (2019). Designing and implementing an online academic integrity tutorial: Identifying the challenges within a post-secondary context. *The Journal of Educational Thought, 52*(3), 193–208.

Louis, M. R. (1980). Surprise and sensemaking: What newcomers experiences in entering unfamiliar organizations. *Administrative Science Quarterly, 25*, 226–251.

Lucas, G. M., & Friedrich, J. (2005). Individual differences in workplace deviance and integrity as predictors of academic dishonesty. *Ethics and Behaviour, 15*(1), 15–35.

McGowan, S. (2016). Breaches of academic integrity using collusion. In T. Bretag (Ed.) *Handbook of Academic Integrity*, (pp. 222–245). Springer. https://doi.org/10.1007/978-981-287-098-8

McKenzie, A., Miron, J., & Ridgley, A. (2020). Building a regional academic integrity network: Profiling the growth and action of the Academic Integrity Council of Ontario. *Canadian Perspectives on Academic Integrity, 3*(01), 25–38.

Nonis, S., & Swift, C. O. (2001). An examination of the relationship between academic dishonesty and workplace dishonesty: A multicampus investigation. *The Journal of Education for Business, 77*(2), 69–77. https://doi.org/10.1080/08832320109599052

Peters, M. & Cadieux, A. (2019). Are Canadian professors teaching the skills and knowledge students need to prevent plagiarism? *International Journal for Educational Integrity, 15*(10). https://doi.org/10.1007/s40979-019-0047-z

Pincus, H. S., & Schmelkin, L. P. (2003). Faculty perceptions of academic dishonesty: A multidimensional scaling analysis. *The Journal of Higher Education, 74*(2), 196–209.

Poitras Pratt, Y., & Gladue, K. (2022). Re-defining academic integrity: Embracing Indigenous truths. In S. E. Eaton & J. Christensen Hughes (Eds.), *Academic integrity in Canada: An enduring and essential challenge.* Berlin: Springer.

Schein, E. (1985). *Organizational culture.* United States: Jossey-Bass.

Scutt, C., & Hobson, J. (2013). The stories we need: Anthropology, philosophy, narrative and higher education research. *Higher Education Research & Development, 32*(1), 17–29. https://doi.org/10.1080/07294360.2012.751088

Shulman, L. (2005). Signature Pedagogies in the Professions. *Daedalus, 134*(3), 52–59. http://www.jstor.org/stable/20027998

Stoesz, B. & Yudintseva, A. (2018). Effectiveness of tutorials for promoting education integrity: a synthesis paper. *International Journal for Educational Integrity, 14*(6). https://doi.org/10.1007/s40979-018-0030-0

Stoesz, B. M., & Eaton, S. E. (2020). Academic integrity policies of publicly funded universities in western Canada. *Educational Policy.* https://doi.org/10.1177/0895904820983032

Sutherland-Smith, W. (2013). Crossing the line: Collusion or collaboration in university group work? *Australian Universities Review, 55*(1), 51–58.

Sutton, A., & Taylor, D. (2011). Confusion about collusion: Working together and academic integrity. *Assessment and Evaluation in Higher Education, 36*(7), 831–841.

Trautner, M. N., & Borland, E. (2013). Using the sociological imagination to teach about academic integrity. *Teaching Sociology, 41*(4), 377–388. https://doi.org/10.1177/0092055X13490750

University of Saskatchewan (2017). Regulations on Student Academic Misconduct. Retrieved January 14, 2021 from https://governance.usask.ca/documents/student-conduct-appeals/StudentAcademicMisconduct.pdf

Wei, T., Chesnut, S. R., Barnaard-Brak, L., & Schmidt, M. (2014). University students' perceptions of academic cheating: Triangulating quantitative and qualitative findings, *Journal of Academic Ethics, 12*(4), 287–298. https://doi-org.cyber.usask.ca/10.1007/s10805-014-9219-x

Weick, K. (1995). *Sensemaking in Organizations.* United States: Sage.

Susan Bens Ph.D., has worked at the University of Saskatchewan, in Treaty 6 Territory and the Homeland of the Metis, since 1997. Building on an earlier career in student affairs, she has served as an educational developer for 10 years, working closely with faculty who want to improve their programs and their teaching. Susan's doctoral research was about how senior undergraduate students understand academic honesty and dishonesty, and this, along with experience, has allowed her the opportunity to develop teaching practices and to contribute to initiatives aimed at promoting academic integrity.

Chapter 20
How to Talk About Academic Integrity so Students Will Listen: Addressing Ethical Decision-Making Using Scenarios

Lee-Ann Penaluna and Roxanne Ross

Abstract The field of academic integrity in higher education has made significant gains in exploring the proliferation of integrity issues, the frequency of student misconduct behaviours, and in identifying strategies for embedding academic integrity education more broadly into the curriculum. Regardless of calls for institution-wide approaches which focus on preventing academic misconduct, those of us engaged in the field can attest that there will always be a need to address academic misconduct behaviours and support the development of those students who engage in them. As student affairs practitioners in a Canadian post-secondary institution, we present our approach to creating meaningful teaching and learning experiences that enable students with misconduct violations to critically explore potential misconduct situations and practice the skills needed to make alternative decisions. Utilising existing work that frames academic integrity as 'standards of practice', this chapter demonstrates our application of key themes from the academic integrity literature within our teaching and learning practice. Recognizing that mandated academic integrity education can be a challenging learning experience, we discuss our approach to engaging these students in analyzing the common situational factors that post-secondary students face that pose potential academic integrity conflicts and the way ethical decision-making frameworks can support their ability to navigate academic integrity concerns in the future. We conclude the chapter with our key learnings and recommendations for implementing an engaging experience with students who are mandated to attend instruction following an academic integrity violation.

Keywords Academic integrity · Canada · Decision making · Student affairs · Student misconduct

L.-A. Penaluna (✉) · R. Ross
University of Calgary, Calgary, Canada
e-mail: leeann.penaluna@ucalgary.ca

R. Ross
e-mail: rossr@ucalgary.ca

S. E. Eaton and J. Christensen Hughes (eds.), *Academic Integrity in Canada*, Ethics and Integrity in Educational Contexts 1,
https://doi.org/10.1007/978-3-030-83255-1_20

The predominant post-secondary institutional framing of academic integrity in ethical-legal terms has been widely critiqued as problematic (Adam et al., 2017; Bertram Gallant, 2008) with studies involving students illustrating the potential ways that this positioning can alienate students and ultimately hinder their learning (Ashworth et al., 1997; Gullifer & Tyson, 2010). Scholars argue that presenting academic misconduct as a student's moral failing or refusal to comply to rules situates the problem solely with the student (Bertram Gallant, 2008) and oversimplifies the nuances within academic integrity constructs such as plagiarism and collusion, for which studies have demonstrated that even faculty are challenged to arrive at unified definitions (Barrett & Cox, 2005). This has led for calls to move away from the punitive approaches that ensue from ethical-legal institutional discourses to a situating of academic integrity as a teaching and learning issue within the academy (Bertram Gallant, 2008; East & Donnelly, 2012). A teaching and learning focus allows for an understanding of students as learners, grappling with news ways of knowing and presenting knowledge, and thereby presents greater opportunities to engage students in discussions of academic integrity in all its complexities. In the context in which we teach academic integrity, mandated sessions for students who have experienced issues with our academic misconduct policy, a teaching and learning approach is essential. While there has been an increasing focus on teaching and learning approaches to academic integrity in the literature (East & Donnelly, 2012; Orr, 2018), very little discussion of theory and practice exists in relation to supporting the learning and development of students who have had academic misconduct breaches. In particular, there is a dearth of literature sharing practical approaches that address the challenges and sensitivities involved in engaging students who have experienced academic misconduct. This chapter focuses on our approach to delivering academic integrity education to those who have recently been found responsible for an academic misconduct and, have been mandated to attend an academic integrity workshop. In both shifting and deepening the conversation from the punitive to the developmental, we hope to contribute to the scarcity of literature that explores the methods by which those students that have been found responsible for an academic misconduct violation can be supported through educational programming to avoid recidivism. Taking direction from and offering critique of the existing literature, we present and critically assess our instructional approach. In sharing our experience, we aim to expand upon the scarcity of literature that informs practice with this population of students and seek to emphasize the necessity of a nuanced perspective of academic integrity, one that incorporates educational responses to, as East (2010) suggests, issues of "convention" (p. 69) and ethical dilemmas.

Context

As student affairs practitioners in academic support services, our work is situated within a student-facing unit in a large post-secondary institution in Western Canada. Our department provides a range of services broadly classified into three areas:

advising, learning, and writing. Academic integrity programming is situated within the learning classification. In addition to web-based educational resources including hyperlinks to the Student Academic Misconduct Policy and Procedure, the Student Academic Integrity Handbook, factsheets and other online resources, two core workshops are offered: Academic Integrity: Strategies to Avoid Plagiarism and Academic Integrity: Collaborating with Peers. Both workshops were developed in 2016 as a collaborative endeavour with faculties and Library staff for the primary purpose of providing academic integrity education for those students who had academic integrity breaches, and who had previously been required to attend individual meetings with a member of our unit's staff. In addition to addresses issues in scalability, we transitioned our one-on-one approach to academic integrity instruction to group sessions, in an effort to foster provide students with a more engaging and collaborative learning experience. Although the academic integrity workshops are open to all students, attendees are almost exclusively students who have been found responsible for academic integrity violations and have been mandated to attend by their faculty as part of sanctioning.

The Workshops

The workshops are delivered throughout the year, though we experience peak periods of demand that often coincide with mid-terms or the exam period at the end of each semester. Since their introduction in 2016, the number of attendees has increased which has resulted in an increase in the number of workshops offered. During peak periods up to six weekly workshops can be offered over the course of three weeks. After the peak period one workshop is delivered per week, alternating between the Plagiarism workshop and the Collaboration workshop.

The students self-register for the workshops by using the university's online booking system. If they have been mandated to attend, they are issued a deadline for completion by their Associate Dean. The duration of each workshop is 90 min with a maximum capacity for in-person delivery of 28 students. Each workshop is delivered by one facilitator.

Conversations surrounding the theme of academic misconduct can be highly emotive and negatively charged, even for those students who are not responsible for an academic misconduct violation but are answering to an accusation of one (Latopolski and Bertram Gallant, 2020). A students' emotional state can be adversely affected by the stress caused by the academic misconduct investigative process itself (Baird & Dooey, 2014). In our practice, we observe the outward expression of a students' prior experiences with the process. Students overtly display a range of emotions; distress, anxiety, vulnerability, sensitivity or embarrassment, anger and frustration. In the workshops, these emotions present in several ways in student behaviours. For example, some students will position themselves furthest away from the facilitator and other students, they may display defensive body language, avoiding eye contact with facilitator or with other students and appear closed to conversation.

We are intentional about framing each workshop as a learning opportunity for all students regardless of what their previous relationship with the academic integrity process may be, however based on institutional data and workshop participation, we can discern that approximately 95% of student attendees are mandated to attend. Although the decision to maintain an open workshop model poses challenges in that we are unable to determine the few students who are attending the session out of their own volition, this model provides us with an opportunity to protect student privacy, which we determined was of primary concern in establishing a safe learning environment for our mandated students. To further reinforce that anonymity, we do not ask for introductions in the room, taking attendance through student ID numbers. The relief in the room can be palpable. Students markedly change their body language, reacting in a way that suggests that they were anticipating a negative experience or were preparing for a combative session.

Students Reported for Academic Misconduct

Similar to our experience above, studies of students reported for academic integrity violations, though limited, demonstrate that these students experience a range of negative emotions as a direct result of their experience with the academic misconduct process (Pitt et al., 2020; Sutherland Smith, 2013). For instance, Pitt et al. report some students that have experienced academic misconduct allegations describe the experience as "the hardest, most challenging or worst experience of their lives" (2020, p. 5). That same study contains numerous impactful quotations from students who described the emotional impact of the accusation. Students comment that the experience "…was the worst phase of my life maybe" (2020, p. 5) and "If I could just describe that period, there's nothing darker than that, that I have experienced in my whole life. It was just a mixture of stress, embarrassment, mixture of losing my future, losing what I have been working for and towards. Honestly it was really bad" (Pitt et al., 2020, p. 5). Likewise, in Sutherland Smith's (2013) study engaging students who have been reported for academic integrity breaches related to collusion, shared that they "felt like a criminal" (p. 57). These previous negative interactions and the associated emotions illustrates why educating these students is unlike educating students who have yet to have a violation. As practitioners we may categorize the workshops as educational, realizing the intrinsic benefit of this developmental process, yet we must anticipate and acknowledge that to these students the workshop is not initially perceived as educational, it is simply an extension of the sanctions issued by faculty. In fact, mandatory attendance at academic integrity workshops is listed under 'educational sanctions' in our institutional policy. We acknowledge the place for formal academic integrity processes and the practice of sanctions. However, as we will discuss below, sanctioning practices framed within potentially alienating ethical-legal academic integrity discourses pose significant challenges in creating positive educational experiences for students who have had experiences with academic misconduct. A review of the broader academic integrity literature as well as the ethical decision-making scholarship related to academic integrity, demonstrates an increasing trend towards more nuanced understandings of how students encounter academic integrity. This literature described below, has been important in guiding our workshop development in response to the particular challenges of our teaching context. In the section below, we provide an overview of this scholarship.

Reframing Ethical-Legal Academic Integrity Discourses

In moving toward educational approaches for supporting students with reported instances of academic misconduct, we have sought to develop teaching and learning practices that reframe traditional ethical and legal academic integrity discourses and focus on developmental approaches. Much work has been done in problematizing the predominant academic integrity institutional frames of morality and rule compliance. In challenging these perspectives, Bertram Gallant (2008) emphasizes the binary nature of these perspectives and the failure to take into consideration broader "organizational, institutional [and] societal" (p. 49) contexts that impact of academic integrity issues. For instance, we have found in our discussions with students that there are significant disciplinary differences in relation to notions of groupwork and what constitutes a breach in academic integrity. Research on unauthorized collaboration confirms students lack clarity in distinguishing collusion violations from legitimate group learning (Sutherland-Smith, 2013). Our experience in our workshops confirms that students are often unable to identify differences between collusion and collaboration.

In addition, the "hazy nature of plagiarism" (Ashworth et al., 1997, p. 191) in particular, has been emphasized in several studies engaging students in discussions of academic integrity (Adam et al., 2017; Ashworth et al., 1997; Gullifer & Tyson, 2010). Price's (2002) analysis of integrity policies illustrates the complex and contextualized nature of plagiarism that defies institutions' attempts to present the construct as "fixed and absolute" (p. 89). This lack of clarity points to significant problems with the positioning of academic integrity as an immoral act or unwillingness to follow rules and raises issues of intention. However, in spite of recommendations to do so (Bertram Gallant, 2008), scholars point out that there is often little to no distinction given in academic integrity policies between intentional and unintentional plagiarism (Price, 2002).

Given the complexities of the skills needed in incorporating the voices of others in academic work and the nuanced understandings required in distinguishing when and how it is acceptable to work with others, framing academic integrity as part of students' overall development as learners seems much more appropriate. We would argue that this is particularly important in approaches to supporting students who have violated the academic integrity policies. As discussed above, our experience with engaging this student population is that those students who are on the receiving end of academic integrity processes framed as immoral or dishonest acts can come to us feeling alienated, vulnerable and somewhat let down by their institution. This is confirmed by Sutherland-Smith's (2013) study of students who went through the academic integrity process for collusion, with students expressing feelings of low academic self-worth, anger and continued confusion following their conduct experience.

This is not to ignore that there are academic integrity issues that do activate ethical questions, however. Although, we adopt a teaching and learning approach in our workshops rather than an overall ethical-legal framework, we follow East's (2010) view that there are times when students engage in behaviours that they themselves recognize as lapses in personal ethics and that as an academic community are more straightforwardly identified as unethical. As East points out, cheating may be one of those particular instances. In my own experience (Roxanne) as a former academic writing instructor, my assumptions that academic integrity was primarily an issue of convention were significantly challenged in the first meeting I encountered with a student who submitted a purchased paper. Important to academic integrity education for students who have been reported for academic misconduct issues in our view then, is the necessity of holding space for academic integrity as potentially an issue of "morality or convention" (East, 2010, p. 74). Our approach to supporting the learning of students who have been reported for academic misconduct, is therefore responsive to both possible origins of students' actions; that is, challenges in understanding institutional conventions, challenges with decision-making in alignment with the values of the institution or a blend of both. We now turn to the significant body of literature on the application of ethical decision-making frameworks that has emerged in response to the ethical implications of students' academic integrity decisions.

Ethical Decision-Making

Similar to conversations more broadly on academic integrity, ethical decision-making scholarship has also become increasingly more sophisticated in its depiction of students' academic integrity decision-making practices. Early literature tended to frame academic misconduct situations as an example of a moral situation or an ethical dilemma; where the student was expected to discern the correct from the incorrect decision. If the student were to make an incorrect decision, Dalton (2015) terms this an "ethical failure" (p. 72), a "moral situation[s] in which students act in unethical ways." (p. 74). For several decades scholars have attempted to explain how individuals respond to ethical dilemmas in a field of study known as ethical decision-making. Much of this early research utilized seminal work by Kohlberg and his theory of moral development which dominated the literature from the 1960s. Building on the early work of Piaget, Kohlberg was focused on the moral development of individuals, describing how they move unidirectionally through three levels of moral reasoning and six sub-stages. This was suggested as being predictive of an individual's ability to reason in a given situation (Kohlberg, 1984). Much emphasis is placed on a student's level of moral reasoning in relation to ethical decision-making with several studies concluding that students with a high level of moral reasoning are less likely to make poor ethical choices (Cummings et al., 2001; Malinowski & Smith, 1985). Despite critique of Kohlberg's research, the hierarchical nature of this research formed the basis for subsequent ethical decision-making theories, models and tests and its application across many situations and contexts, such as Ethics of Care (Gilligan, 1993), the Defining Issue Test (Rest, 1986), the Person-Situation Interactionist model (Trevino, 1986), the Issue-Contingency Model (Jones, 1991), the Action-Controlled model (Ferrell et al., 2016), the Moral Balance Model (Nisan, 1991), and the Moral Judgment Test (Lind, 2008). More recently, contemporary models highlight the influence of both individual and situational factors on the ethical decision-making process. In combining these two areas Schwartz (2016) proposed an Integrated Ethical Decision Making model that recognizes the complexity of the individual, noting that ethical behaviour is contingent on which individual is facing the dilemma. This offers reasoning as to why individuals do not respond identically and according to predetermined outcomes.

Despite the theoretical concepts, models and tests that outline what we expect the rationale behind ethical decision-making to be, students still make decisions that contradict theoretical expectations. The ethical decision-making process is multi-faceted; a complex consolidation of factors pertaining to the individual, the situational context and any issue-specific variables. No one theory is able to fully explain the intricacies and combinations of variables that converge in that moment of decision-making and influence a student's choice, however two themes associated with decision-making in misconduct breaches can be identified: a lack of awareness or error in understanding institutional rules leading to a question of intentionality, and the multicultural and diverse nature of the student population within post-secondary education.

One crucial element of the decision-making process requires the individual to identify that they are facing an ethical dilemma. This would be the basis of a discussion on intentionality; an individual making a conscious decision to violate a rule. Barnhardt (2016) argues that in some academic misconduct cases the student has been unable to distinguish intentionality and that interpreting the students' incorrect behavioral choice as a lack of morality is problematic. Certainly, it is noted by Christensen Hughes and McCabe (2006a) that "many students may engage in these behaviours simply because they don't believe they are wrong" (p. 18). Therefore, a student should not be deemed morally deficient when a decision breaches the academic misconduct policy if there was a lack of awareness that the situation presented is an ethical dilemma. Once the student has identified the situation as relating to academic integrity, the focus can then shift from a question of intentionality to one of decision-making.

In recognizing that even those individuals who demonstrate a high level of morality do still commit acts that are considered academically dishonest (Heriyati & Ekasari, 2020), we are drawn to consider the conflict that presents when prior experiences and personal values encounter institutional rules. Such differences are often the starkest between westernized and non-westernized cultures. For example, in China, students engage in copying behaviour, not to cheat, but to obtain their grade in the most efficient manner (Robinson & Kuin, 1999) and in Russia, not only is plagiarism considered normal practice, but students progressing into higher education are noted to be more vulnerable to collusion-based activities due to their extensive exposure to group work in early schooling (Frost & Hamlin, 2015). Christensen Hughes and McCabe (2006b) in their investigation of Canadian students also identify national culture as a contributing influence in students' academic integrity behaviours. These examples remind us that students are making decisions that are grounded in prior, culturally-influenced experiences. In addition to the complexities brought by prior experience and culture, the process of decision-making can also be influenced by their personal values (Weber, 2019). Academic misconduct may present as an ethical issue, but it is also combined with values that themselves are inextricably shaped by culture (Zhang & Yin, 2020). Students from different cultures and countries also have differing personal values and these personal values can be predictors of a student's decision-making (Arambewela & Hall, 2011). The increasingly nuanced perspectives that emerge from within both ethical decision-making literature and literature on academic integrity discourses, in addition to our own day to day engagement with students who share their encounters with academic integrity have led us to shape our practice in various ways. These practices, described below, include using a standards of practice frame in initiating academic integrity conversations (Bertram Gallant, 2008) and engaging students in applied decision-making practice through pedagogy centering on nuanced discussions and authentic scenarios.

A Standards of Practice Frame

In the recommendations section of Academic Integrity in the twenty-first century, Bertram Gallant advocates for adopting a standards of practice frame to "guide faculty and student behaviors for the enhancement of the teaching and learning environment" (2008, p. 98) similar to codes of conduct found in professional contexts. Although standards of practice models necessarily involve ethical considerations, they are tangible examples of contextualized ethical values, values that have been operationalized within a specific community. With this distinction from the traditional positioning of academic integrity as an expression of 'universal' values (East, 2010), introducing academic integrity to students as values that are shaped and enacted within the context of the institution, places a much greater emphasis on the newcomer's role as a learner. In her discussion of plagiarism, Price (2002) argues for the value of being transparent with students about its contextualized and shifting nature. She writes:

> We can explain that what we call plagiarism is located in a specific setting: *this* historical time, *this* academic community. We can demonstrate that ideas such as "common knowledge" and "original" are informed by their particular contexts. And once we have acknowledged to students and ourselves that plagiarism is part of an ongoing, evolving academic conversation, we can invite students to add their own voices to that conversation. (p. 90)

In the development of our workshops, we have found the standards of practice framing of academic integrity particularly helpful in engaging students who have been reported for academic misconduct in positive teaching and learning dialogues for several reasons which we elaborate on below. As an example of this in practice, one activity we begin a session with involves asking students to generate words that come to mind when they think of the word integrity, first on their own and then with a partner. After a short time of partner discussion, we ask each pair to share one word with the group and record each contribution, so they are visible to everyone. We then discuss the similarities in the words that were generated as a group, words such as honesty, respect, responsibility, etc. and compare those to definitions of academic integrity as well as professional codes of conduct found in Engineering and other disciplines. In addition to beginning the session interactively and in such a way that we hope validates students' prior knowledge, acknowledging the similarities in values that emerge within our classroom community and the definitions across different communities demonstrates the important 'integrity' learning that is required in order to understand the nuances of how integrity is operationalized within whatever communities we engage.

A standards of practice framing acknowledges integrity and thus, academic integrity as an ongoing learning process that students engage with as members of the community. It acknowledges that certain conventions that may seem arbitrary (East, 2010) initiate from particular values in the community and that as we encounter these conventions for the first time it is understandable to question their relevance and need support in their application. Setting up academic integrity as an ongoing learning process illustrates for students that asking questions about academic integrity is necessary to engaging in a community with integrity. This moves academic integrity understandings beyond rules to be memorized, to a recognition that students need to actively apply the general principles of academic integrity to ever new situations. This is important in particular for students who have had violations and may be extremely anxious about having another issue. When we position academic integrity from an ethical-legal perspective as simple rules within a policy and students who fail to apply these rules as lacking in morality, we effectively shut down a dialogue and inhibit students from asking good questions about how academic integrity principles apply in their day-to-day experience. This is significantly problematic for the future success of students who have experienced violations and for whom a second violation could potentially end their academic study.

In reviewing literature related to educational approaches involving the conventions of academic integrity, scholarship on teaching students to avoid plagiarism in the context of academic writing has been most prominent. This work has emphasized the need to move beyond sharing policy documents to instead focus on supporting students' understanding and development of skills associated with successful academic writing that incorporates the voices of others (Price, 2002). There is consensus in the literature that avoiding plagiarism, as embedded in the process of learning to write in academic contexts, involves a number of complex skills ranging from critical reading to shaping academic voices in support of an argument (Adam et al., 2017; Powell & Singh, 2016; Vardi, 2012). Powell & Singh (2016) distinguish between "conceptualisation" (p. 16) and "application" (p. 16) in relation to students' understanding of plagiarism, with conceptualisation involving naming and identification of plagiarism and application the ability to apply this understanding to new learning environments. Their study in which students experienced scaffolded instruction and practice, illustrated that educational interventions can support students' abilities in both conceptualizing and applying an understanding of plagiarism. Schuetze (2004) found a similar benefit in students' understanding in an evaluation of teaching strategies that allowed students to practice skills associated with the academic writing conventions of paraphrasing and citation.

Scholarship on plagiarism has also been the origin of most critical work on academic integrity, with scholars questioning "the assumptive stances taken by the institution" (Bertram Gallant, 2008, p. 57) and advocating for an emphasis on the contextualized nature of definitions of plagiarism as they are applied in Western institutions (Price, 2002). These critical perspectives have influenced academic integrity pedagogies that focus on presenting definitions of plagiarism as shifting and unstable and as such, necessitate students' involvement in a process of ongoing learning (Price, 2002). Situating notions of plagiarism as contextualized conventions, rather than traditional ethical discourses, provides an opportunity to openly discuss rationalizations and values that underpin current practices within Western academia (East, 2010), acknowledge that different historical and cultural practices exist (Howard, 1995) and invite students to engage actively in understanding and querying conventions as participants within a discourse community (Price, 2002). Overall, the practice of engaging students in discussion about conventions as important to supporting students' learning of academic integrity is emphasized in much of the literature on plagiarism (Price, 2002; Schuetze, 2004; Thomas & Sassi, 2017) and appears also in recommendations for supporting students' understanding of collusion (Sutton & Taylor, 2011).

Addressing Ethical Decision-Making: Scenarios

As discussed above, institutions may anticipate that ethical themes are universally understood and therefore, when presented with an ethical dilemma that contravenes institutional rules, an incorrect decision denotes a student that intended to breach the rule or one who has low morality. We challenge this notion of a decision being binary, rejecting the idea that decisions that result in a breach of the academic misconduct policy are wholly explained by a students' lack of morality or ethics, and should simply be punished. We have seen that the factors associated in making a decision in academic misconduct situations are multifaceted and complex. The diversity of students within individual post-secondary institutions results in a population that has extensively different personal values and ethical experiences that cannot simply be explained as a lack of morality. We must recognize that a student's prior ethical experience and personal values, which has the potential to be linked to a cultural component, has a role to play in ethical decision-making. Rather than a personal attack on their morality, students need support in understanding how the specific values of academic integrity are operationalized within the institution.

While issues of unintentionality, through misidentification of the situation presenting as an ethical dilemma, may be rectified through exposure to, and discussion of, the relevant academic integrity policies, the roles that culture and value conflicts play in decision-making necessitates a different approach. Scenarios are utilized widely in the literature to aid in the development of student ethical decision-making, and in particular, can be used to explore those situations that have the potential to lead to academic misconduct violations. These scenarios are not simply a case study designed to identify right or wrong actions, they are more a complex narrative identifying multiple factors that we recognize can influence decision-making. Embedding ethical dilemmas into morally themed scenarios, to highlight the grey areas in such situations, enables a deeper discussion to take place that can facilitate thinking and reasoning (Wong, 2020) and in turn, allow students to successfully understand and navigate the situation. The method by which the scenarios are explored with students is important. The learning outcome of the scenarios should not simply be identifying the ethical dilemma, but also to identify skills that can be used to implement their ethical choice, allowing the students to simulate, rehearse and practice their actual responses and master the skills necessary to navigate the potential academic misconduct situations (Basak & Cerit, 2019; Drumwright et al., 2015; Riemenschneider et al., 2016). In addition, we also propose that cultural themes and perspectives, prior experiences and personal values should form a major component of the decision-making conversation.

While the discussion of scenarios is frequented in the literature, the scenarios that are described above are used with students who have not yet had a misconduct violation. It is more difficult to identify scholarly pieces that focus specifically on our target population. Orr (2018) describes an academic integrity seminar that, similarly to ours, was not restricted to those that had an academic misconduct violation. Unfortunately, the seminar itself and the scenario-based activities were not described in detail. However, although we are unable to glean the specific activities that were used in the workshop, the student feedback obtained after the seminars shared by Orr allows us to conclude that those who have had a misconduct violation responded positively to this type of developmental education. This is also our experience in observing students' participation in scenario-based activities within our workshops. Below we present our practical approach to using scenario-based instruction to improve the ethical decision-making skills of students who have been mandated to attend academic integrity programing.

We use scenarios for the specific purpose of allowing students to practice their decision-making processes and skills to explore, propose and critique decisions without reprimand or judgement. The combination of factors that led to a violation are limitless and addressing each specific combination is impossible. In the workshops we encounter students that are keen to explore their own experiences of academic misconduct, but in that group programming setting accommodating the unique contextual situation of each student's academic misconduct violation is not possible. In an attempt to overcome this, we aim to combine an understanding of the academic integrity values and how they are operationalized in the institution, with specific delivery of related educational information and examples pertaining to the misconduct type of concern and then offer a range of scenarios to allow students to practice their decision-making skills. Similarly to Wong's (2020) description of moral stories, the scenarios produced for the academic integrity workshops are comprised of multiple characters (students, peers, friends, the university) which facilitate discussions of personal and societal perspectives on academic integrity situations. Intertwined with the characters are high stakes implications for not breaching the policy, e.g. failing a course, losing a scholarship, a friend not helped. Each scenario is framed by three main questions. Students are asked to comment on the behaviours within the case study that have the potential to lead to an academic misconduct, whether rationalizations are justified and what strategies could be adopted to avoid the situation. Students initially answer as anticipated, often very briefly, noting the obvious behaviours that put the student in the scenario at risk of an academic misconduct violation. Students can easily identify the rationalizations and very rarely accept them as valid justifications for the misconduct related behaviour. They are also able to offer basic strategies for avoiding the situation in the future.

This level of engagement and answering are witnessed more frequently in discussions around plagiarism, where the student can recite why citations and the requirement to paraphrase are important and how using reference management software, improving academic writing skills and addressing time management issues are potential strategies. However, scenarios concerning group work and helping a friend in need with an assignment are more complex to unpack with students. This is reflective of research in this area. Barrett & Cox (2005) found that students were able to identify plagiarism as unacceptable practice but struggled more so with the distinction between collaboration and collusion. The variations in uncertainty about what is acceptable collaboration when two students work together was noted as being especially problematic with the influence of disciplines of study, where the distinction and acceptance is nuanced. In framing the situation as "the 'mythical line' between collusion and collaboration" (p. 55), Sutherland Smith (2013) presents the difficulties faced by students in attempting to understand what constitutes collaboration and collusion. Students highlighted discipline differences: "I don't think collusion is seen the same way by all areas of the university. [...] How consistent is this across the university anyway?" (p.54), their personal values in helping friends; "[...] some of the younger Vietnamese students were struggling with all the readings [...] As an older student [...] it is my moral obligation to help. I mean, what kind of person would I be if I did not help?" (p.56) as well as continued confusion after a breach of the policy; "When I got the letter, I felt like a criminal. The worst thing was I didn't know what I'd done wrong. I still don't!" (p. 57). In these conversations the role of the facilitator is paramount.

The facilitator for the workshops does not accept superficial answers to complex scenarios. They probe the student into deeper, more critical thinking. This questioning aims to encourage the student to be completely open and honest when answering, encouraging the student to apply their personal values, ethical experience and cultural perspectives against the situation. Questioning strategies include: could you honestly say no to a friend in need? What would that look like, what wording would you use? What if the stakes were high not breaching the rules resulted in you/ your friend failing a course/ reducing your Grade Point Average (GPA)/ risked losing a scholarship? In this type of questioning, we notice immediate discomfort from students and consider this a visual manifestation of their colliding personal values and prior ethical experience and culture with the institutional rules. Students are less fluid with their answers. The difficulty they have with articulating the practical aspect of the scenarios reflects what we know from the literature; students need to practice the skills necessary, and that includes what wording to use. This practice can take the form of role play. The facilitator plays the role of the student in need. In mimicking the scenario, the facilitator asks a student in the group for help. The student is encouraged to formulate and give a response to the facilitator.

At the end of each workshop, students are asked to reflect upon the session. To guide their reflection they are asked to anonymously answer two brief questions: what was one thing that surprised you and what will you take away from the session. Students most often comment on a specific misconduct type that they were not aware of (such as self-plagiarism), an impactful news story (e.g. the Measles, Mumps and Rubella vaccination fabrication) and the breadth of resources that are available to them to help support their studies. We have used this feedback to make amendments to the content of the workshops and also to produce additional online resources.

Recommendations for Teaching and Learning

As Bertram Gallant points out, regardless of proactive teaching and learning approaches to academic integrity, which we also participate in, there will likely always be students who engage in academic misconduct (2017), the reasons for which stem from lapses in decision-making, lack of awareness of institutional policies, or incongruent values to name a few. Moving away from moral or legal binaries in academic integrity instruction to instead focus programming on a scenario-based curriculum alongside a standards of practice framework can provide student affairs practitioners with a flexible and responsive approach to the difficult task of responding to student audiences with have a variety of experiences with academic misconduct that we often find ourselves in.

In our situation the nature and specific details of the students' academic misconduct violation is unknown. This can present a problem with content design for the workshop. Students can become frustrated if their academic misconduct case was a violation of exam regulations and cheating and yet they are mandated to attend workshops on plagiarism or collusion. Therefore, we develop scenarios that incorporate a variety of potential academic misconduct themes. We also maintain an open dialogue with faculty so that common trends or themes in academic misconduct cases can be identified and utilized to continually update the scenarios.

Programming needs to be current and responsive in order to be effective. In developing academic integrity workshops or programming, consider workshops that focus on other academic misconduct types such as cheating. There is perhaps a tendency to focus on what are considered to be the most common types of academic misconduct, such as plagiarism and collusion, in offering programming, but as we are experiencing with the COVID-19 pandemic there is a shift in the types and nature of cases. In our practice, where additional workshops have not been created, we include content in both workshops that cover all misconduct types, current trends and themes and facilitate discussion in those areas.

Student timetables are often very busy and inflexible which can leave little time to attend a workshop. Students should not be forced to miss a normal lecture due to the need to attend a workshop. In planning the timetable for the workshops, we aim to offer a variety of different days and times, sometimes offering early morning or later evening slots. Where students have a full course load and have a short timeframe with which to attend a workshop, we may meet with the student on a one-to-one basis. It is worthwhile for student affairs providers to collaborate with Associate Deans to stay informed of cases so that additional workshops can be added to the schedule.

References

Adam, L., Anderson, V., & Spronken-Smith, R. (2017). It's not fair: Policy discourses and students' understandings of plagiarism in a New Zealand university. *Higher Education, 74*(1), 17–32. https://doi.org/10.1007/s10734-016-0025-9

Arambewela, R., & Hall, J. (2011). The role of personal values in enhancing student experience and satisfaction among International postgraduate students: An exploratory study. *Procedia—Social and Behavioral Sciences, 29*, 1807–1815. https://doi.org/10.1016/j.sbspro.2011.11.428

Ashworth, P., Bannister, P., & Thorne, P. (1997). Guilty in whose eyes? University students' perceptions of cheating and plagiarism in academic work and assessment. *Studies in Higher Education, 22*(2), 187–203. https://doi.org/10.1080/03075079712331381034

Baird, C., & Dooey, P. (2014). Ensuring effective student support in higher education alleged plagiarism cases. *Innovative Higher Education, 39*(5), 387–400. https://doi.org/10.1007/s10755-014-9285-4

Barnhardt, B. (2016). The epidemic of cheating depends on its definition: A critique of inferring the moral quality of cheating in any form. *Ethics & Behavior, 26*(4), 330–343. https://doi.org/10.1080/10508422.2015.1026595

Barrett, R., & Cox, A. L. (2005). At least they're learning something: The hazy line between collaboration and collusion. *Assessment and Evaluation in Higher Education, 30*(2), 107–122. https://doi.org/10.1080/0260293042000264226

Basak, T., & Cerit, B. (2019). Comparing two teaching methods on Nursing students ethical decision-making level. *Clinical Simulation in Nursing, 29*, 15–23. https://doi.org/10.1016/j.ecns.2019.02.003

Bertram Gallant, T. B. (2008). Academic integrity in the twenty-first century: A teaching and learning imperative. *ASHE Higher Education Report, 33*, 5. https://doi.org/10.1002/aehe.3305

Christensen Hughes, J. M., & McCabe, D. L. (2006a). Academic misconduct within higher education in Canada. *Canadian Journal of Higher Education, 36*(2), 1–21. https://doi.org/10.47678/cjhe.v36i1.183525.

Christensen Hughes, J. M., & McCabe, D. L. (2006b). Understanding academic misconduct. *Canadian Journal of Higher Education, 36*(1), 49–63. https://journals.sfu.ca/cjhe/index.php/cjhe/article/view/183525

Cummings, R., Dyas, L., Maddux, C. D., & Kochman, A. (2001). Principled moral reasoning and behavior of preservice teacher Education students. *American Educational Research Journal, 38*(1), 143–158. https://doi.org/10.3102/00028312038001143

Dalton, J. C. (2015). Making moral mistakes: What ethical failure can teach students about life and leadership: Making moral mistakes. *New Directions for Student Leadership, 2015*(146), 71–79. https://doi.org/10.1002/yd.20136

Drumwright, M., Prentice, R., & Biasucci, C. (2015). Behavioral ethics and teaching ethical decision making. *Decision Sciences Journal of Innovative Education, 13*(33), 431–458. https://doi.org/10.1111/dsji.12071

East, J. (2010). Judging plagiarism: A problem of morality and convention. *Higher Education, 59*(1), 69–83. https://doi.org/10.1007/s10734-009-9234-9

East, J., & Donnelly, L. (2012). Taking responsibility for academic integrity: A collaborative teaching and learning design. *Journal of University Teaching and Learning Practice, 9*(3), 1–11. https://ro.uow.edu.au/jutlp/vol9/iss3/2

Ferrell, O. C., Gresham, L. G., & Fraedrich, J. (2016). A synthesis of ethical decision models formarketing. *Journal of Macromarketing, 9*(2), 55–64. https://doi.org/10.1177/027614678900900207

Frost, J., & Hamlin, A. (2015). A comparison of international student attitudes concerning academic dishonesty. *Journal of International Business Research, 14*(2), 153–165. https://www.abacademies.org/articles/jibr_vol_14_no_2_2015.pdf

Gilligan, C. (1993). *In a different voice: Psychological theory and woman's development*. United States: Harvard University Press.

Gullifer, J., & Tyson, G. A. (2010). Exploring university students' perceptions of plagiarism: A focus group study. *Studies in Higher Education, 35*(4), 463–481. https://doi.org/10.1080/03075070903096508

Heriyati, D., & Ekasari, W. F. (2020). A study on academic dishonesty and moral reasoning. *International Journal of Education (12)*2, 63–72. https://doi.org/10.17509/ije.v12i2.18653

Howard, R. M. (1995). Plagiarisms, authorships, and the academic death penalty. *National Council of Teachers of English, 57*(7), 788–806. https://www.jstor.org/stable/378403.

Jones, T. M. (1991). Ethical decision making by individuals in organizations: An issue-contingent model. *The Academy of Management Review, 16*(2), 366–395. https://doi.org/10.2307/258867

Kohlberg, L. (1984). *The psychology of moral development*. Unites States: Harper & Row.

Latopolski, K.E. and Bertrum Gallant, T.L. (2020). Academic Integrity. In D. M. Waryold, & J. M. Lancaster (Eds.), *Student conduct practice: The complete guide for student affairs professionals* (2nd Edition). Stylus

Lind, G. (2008). The meaning and measurement of moral judgement competence. A dual-aspect model. In D. Fasko, Jr. & W. Willis, W. (Eds.), *Contemporary philosophical and psychological perspectives on moral development education.* Hampton Press.

Malinowski, C. I., & Smith, C. P. (1985). Moral reasoning and moral conduct: An investigation prompted by Kohlberg's theory. *Journal of Personality and Social Psychology, 49*(4), 1016–1027. https://doi.org/10.1037/0022-3514.49.4.1016

Nisan, M. (1991). The moral balance model: Theory and research extending our understanding of moral choice and deviation. In W. M. Kurtines & J. L. Gewirtz (Eds.), *Handbook of moral behavior and development*. L. Erlbaum.

Orr, J. (2018). Developing a campus academic integrity education seminar. *Journal of AcademicEthics, 16*(3), 195–209. https://doi.org/10.1007/s10805-018-9304-7

Pitt, P., Dullaghan, K., & Sutherland Smith, W. (2020). Mess, stress and trauma: Students experiences of formal contract cheating processes. Assessment and Evaluation in Higher Education, 1–14.https://doi.org/10.1080/02602938.2020.1787332

Powell, L., & Singh, N. (2016). An integrated academic literacy approach to improving students' understanding of plagiarism in an accounting course. *Accounting Education, 25*(1), 14–34. https://doi.org/10.1080/09639284.2015.1133311

Price, M. (2002). Beyond gotcha!: Situating plagiarism in policy and pedagogy. *National Council of Teachers of English, 54*(1), 88–115. http://www.jstor.org/stable/1512103

Rest, J. R. (1986). *Moral development: Advances in research and theory.* Praeger.

Riemenschneider, C. K., Manly, T. S., & Leonard, L. N. K. (2016). Using "giving voice to values" to improve student academic integrity in information technology contexts. *Journal of Information Systems Education, 27*(3), 183.

Robinson, V. M. J., & Kuin, L. M. E. I. (1999). The explanation of practice: Why Chinese students copy assignments. *International Journal of Qualitative Studies in Education, 12*(2), 193–210. https://doi.org/10.1080/095183999236259

Schuetze, P. (2004). Evaluation of a brief homework assignment designed to reduce citation problems. *Teaching of Psychology, 31*(4), 257–259. https://doi.org/10.1207/s15328023top3104_6

Schwartz, M. S. (2016). Ethical decision-making theory: An integrated approach. *Journal of Business Ethics, 139*(4), 755–776. https://doi.org/10.1007/s10551-015-2886-8

Sutherland-Smith, W. (2013). Crossing the line: Collusion or collaboration in university group work? *The Australian Universities Review, 55*(1), 51–58. https://files.eric.ed.gov/fulltext/EJ1004398.pdf

Sutton, A., & Taylor, D. (2011). Confusion about collusion: Working together and academic integrity. *Assessment and Evaluation in Higher Education, 36*(7), 831–841. https://doi.org/10.1080/02602938.2010.488797

Thomas, E. E., & Sassi, K. (2017). An ethical dilemma and academic integrity: It is every English teacher's dream. *The English Journal, 100*(6), 47–53. https://www.jstor.org/stable/23047881

Trevino, L. K. (1986). Ethical decision making in organizations: A person-situation interactionist model. *The Academy of Management Review, 11*(3), 601–661. https://doi.org/10.2307/258313

Vardi, I. (2012). Developing students' referencing skills: A matter of plagiarism, punishment and morality or of learning to write critically? *Higher Education Research and Development, 31*(6), 921–930. https://doi.org/10.1080/07294360.2012.673120

Weber, J. (2019). Understanding the millennials' integrated ethical decision-making process: Assessing the relationship between personal values and cognitive moral reasoning. *Business & Society, 58*(8), 1671–1706. https://doi.org/10.1177/0007650317726985

Wong, M.-Y. (2020). Beyond asking should and why questions: Contextualised questioning techniques for moral discussions in moral education classes. *Journal of Moral Education.* https://doi.org/10.1080/03057240.2020.1713066

Zhang, Y., & Yin, H. (2020). Collaborative cheating among Chinese college students: The effects of peer influence and Individualism-Collectivism orientations. *Assessment & Evaluation in Higher Education, 45*(1), 54–69. https://doi.org/10.1080/02602938.2019.1608504

Lee-Ann Penaluna is the Coordinator, Academic Integrity Programs at the University of Calgary. In addition to developing institution-wide initiatives that increase students understanding of academic integrity, she also provides educational support to students who have had academic misconduct violations. In her previous role as the Head of Higher Education at Abingdon and Witney College (UK), Lee-Ann was the Academic Misconduct Officer, responsible for the case management of academic integrity violations. Lee-Ann holds an MSc from Aberystwyth University and is currently studying for a PhD in the Department of Educational Research at Lancaster University.

Roxanne Ross is currently the Director, Student Success Centre at the University of Calgary. Her role involves working collaboratively within the institution to support the development and delivery of learning, writing and advising services for undergraduate and graduate students. Roxanne's previous professional work includes the Coordinator of Writing Support Services at Carleton University as well as teaching within the field of post-secondary English for Academic Purposes (EAP). Roxanne holds a Masters of Applied Language Studies from Carleton University and is currently studying in the Educational Doctorate program at the University of Calgary.

Chapter 21
Revisioning Paraphrasing Instruction

Silvia Luisa Rossi

Abstract Academic misconduct frequently occurs because developing academic writers lack both knowledge about the conventions for writing from sources and procedural skills for applying this knowledge. Paraphrasing is a particularly underdeveloped skill among students in higher education. This chapter illustrates how findings from existing quality assurance processes are supporting a revised approach to paraphrasing instruction by the writing strategist team at a Canadian undergraduate university. The new approach underlines the interpretive nature of paraphrasing and the agency of the student writer. By focusing less on the technical aspects of paraphrasing and more on its rhetorical purposes, we aim to foster among students a deeper level of engagement with texts, a more nuanced awareness of intertextuality, and recognition of the role disciplinary conventions play in writing from sources. Our vantage point as professionals working with students in a wide range of disciplines affords us unique opportunities to be campus changemakers. If we can encourage recognition that paraphrasing instruction must extend past first year composition courses and one-off workshops, and if we can help instructors seize opportunities to provide students with feedback on their paraphrasing, students will move beyond patchwriting and towards writing from sources with more confidence and integrity.

Keywords Paraphrasing · Patchwriting · Plagiarism · Academic integrity · Source use · Canada

The ability to effectively incorporate source information into one's work is a complex and essential skill for every academic writer. Although student writers quote, paraphrase, and summarise the work of others in their writing assignments long before they enter higher education, expectations around source use become more rigorous in post-secondary settings, and a common concern for university and college instructors is that their students' ability to use sources appropriately and in line with academic integrity standards is underdeveloped. One specific type of source use in which

S. L. Rossi (✉)
Mount Royal University, Calgary, Canada
e-mail: srossi@mtroyal.ca

S. E. Eaton and J. Christensen Hughes (eds.), *Academic Integrity in Canada*, Ethics and Integrity in Educational Contexts 1,
https://doi.org/10.1007/978-3-030-83255-1_21

students tend to lack confidence is paraphrasing, but since explicit instruction in and consistent feedback on paraphrasing are rare over the course of a student's undergraduate program, undergraduate writers have few opportunities to be guided in developing their paraphrasing skills. When these rare opportunities do occur, they tend to emphasise plagiarism avoidance, which can have the unintended effect of making students fear and even avoid paraphrasing. This chapter describes how writing specialists in the learning centre at one Canadian undergraduate university are using findings from existing quality assurance (QA) processes to support a new approach to teaching paraphrasing.

At Mount Royal University (MRU), a teaching and learning focused undergraduate institution with approximately 15,000 students (Mount Royal University [MRU], 2021), I am employed in the learning centre as one of five full-time professional writing strategists. Writing strategists mainly facilitate open workshops (i.e., workshops which students from any program, in any year, may attend) and in-class workshops (i.e., workshops tailored to an assignment in a particular course and facilitated during regular class time), consult with individual students and small groups of students, and develop learning resources in collaboration with faculty members. MRU is situated within the traditional territories of the Niitsitapi (Blackfoot), Îyârhe Nakoda, Tsuut'ina and Métis Nations, and just over 6% of students self-identify as Indigenous (MRU, 2021). Over 75% of MRU students are from Calgary, and international students make up less than 2% of the population (MRU, 2021).

In 2020, our writing strategist team revised its approach to teaching paraphrasing to prioritise contextualisation and writer agency. We shifted our attention away from plagiarism and towards the affordances of paraphrasing. Rather than leading students through mechanistic, decontextualised paraphrasing exercises, we found ways to emphasise not only the purpose of paraphrasing, but the broader purpose of source use, what research is and is not, and the responsibilities student writers have to their scholarly discourse communities. Importantly, we engaged with our faculty partners to generate opportunities for the integration of principled paraphrasing instruction into content classes. There are simple ways to bring nuanced paraphrasing instruction and feedback into disciplinary classes, and a collaborative approach between content instructors and writing specialists has the potential to make a positive impact on students' ability to write from sources with integrity.

Why Are Undergraduate Students' Paraphrasing Abilities Underdeveloped?

Lack of Explicit Instruction on Paraphrasing

Students rarely receive explicit instruction on how to paraphrase. In Shi et al.'s (2018) study of graduate students, 10 out of 18 participants had "never received any formal instruction but learnt how to paraphrase through reading published works" (p. 34).

Anecdotally, in the paraphrasing workshops I have facilitated since 2016, I have periodically asked undergraduate students how they learned to paraphrase, and no student has ever reported that they received explicit instruction on paraphrasing beyond the dictum "say it in your own words." Students report the dictum being followed by a caution: if they did not paraphrase well, they would risk committing plagiarism. This strong association between paraphrasing and plagiarism can lead students to avoid paraphrasing altogether—out of fear. In some cases, students even come to believe that the primary purpose of paraphrasing is to avoid plagiarism (Hirvela & Du, 2013). A participant in Shi et al.'s (2018) study reported that in high school, teachers did not provide instruction on paraphrasing; "they just [said] 'don't plagiarize'. And in university, they give you a paper about the policy about plagiarism" (p. 42). It seems that the focus is so strongly on avoiding plagiarism that students completely miss the point of paraphrasing and the benefits it confers on the writer. Rather than teaching students what paraphrasing can help them accomplish, the emphasis is too often on how paraphrasing can hurt them. When students are fearful of manipulating sources in any other way than safe quotation, getting excited about joining the academic conversation becomes difficult. As Jamieson and Howard (2019) noted, "the criminalization of missteps makes [writing from sources] a terrifying rather than satisfying learning experience for students" (p. 83).

Lack of Emphasis on the Purpose of Paraphrasing

The root of the problem may lie precisely in the "say it in your own words" conception of paraphrasing. Resources on post-secondary institutions' writing centre and library resource web pages typically describe paraphrasing as rendering an author's idea in one's own words. These descriptions of paraphrasing are consistent with knowledge telling as opposed to knowledge transforming (Scardamalia & Bereiter, 1987), or knowledge display as opposed to knowledge making (Abasi & Akbari, 2008). They imply an objective process of "linguistic reformulation" (Mori, 2018, p. 46). In scholarly writing, however, paraphrasing does more than recast the original author's idea. Writers paraphrase "to reconceptualize the source text coherently with [their] own authorial intentions" (Shi et al., 2018, p. 32). Interestingly, despite many university/college websites' definitions of paraphrasing corresponding to knowledge telling, the paraphrases they provide as models for students reveal processes of inferential thinking (Yamada, 2003). If paraphrasing involves inferential thinking, then it does more than simply recast an idea; it falls into the category of knowledge making. As Mori (2018) put it, "a paraphrase in its most basic sense is re-creation," (p. 51) not simple retelling. This function of paraphrasing is powerful, but students are rarely made aware of it, so they do not view paraphrasing as an empowering academic writing tool.

When student writers believe that the function of paraphrasing is only to recast what has been said by someone else, it is no wonder they have a difficult time finding the value in paraphrasing and feel resistance towards it. This undervaluing may even come directly from their instructors. One of the university professors interviewed by Pecorari and Shaw (2012) reported telling a student that "you have to somehow really write this and put it in your own words. I know that it isn't always so easy and sometimes it's silly but that's how it is" (p. 154). If the inherent value of paraphrasing is not made clear to students, then they are justified in asking themselves why their professors insist they go through the challenging, time-consuming and risky activity of paraphrasing when a quotation would serve to report the original author's idea more directly, quickly and safely. When students ask why they have to paraphrase, they are sometimes told that paraphrasing helps the instructor know whether the student has understood the source. Mori (2018) found that students were encouraged to paraphrase rather than quote because paraphrasing constitutes "proof of critical thinking and intellectual work" (p. 48). Although this may be one benefit of having students paraphrase information, it is not the reason paraphrasing exists in scholarly writing. Emphasising this purpose limits paraphrasing to a school-writing context, ultimately working against the goal of initiating students into the discourse community of their discipline (Abasi & Akbari, 2008). If the intention is that students begin to see themselves as members of and contributors to disciplinary communities, then it is vital that the tasks they complete, (academic writing-related or otherwise), be connected authentically to the real-world activities of those disciplinary communities.

Single-Sentence and/or Decontextualised Practice Activities

Where explicit instruction on paraphrasing does exist, instructional activities are too often based on single, decontextualised sentences that students are asked to transform into their own words (Pecorari & Petrić, 2014). Decontextualised activities deprive students of the opportunity to consider what they are using the information *for*. If paraphrasing involves recontextualisation, but neither the original context of the information nor the target context is provided, then the writer is faced with a simplistic, mechanistic and inauthentic task. In addition, single-sentence practice may lead student writers to believe that when they use sources, they should be on the lookout for individual sentences to extract and incorporate into their own writing. Although it could be argued that transforming single sentences is a suitable controlled practice activity—one that fits well within a scaffolded approach to paraphrasing instruction—the reality is that paraphrasing practice activities rarely go beyond this stage.

Lack of Feedback on Paraphrasing

Continuous feedback is essential to the development of complex skills, but post-secondary students rarely receive feedback on their paraphrasing. There are practical reasons for this. An instructor can easily miss a poor paraphrase if it does not contain red flags such as an abrupt change in style (Pecorari, 2013). More intentional approaches can be time-intensive. To provide feedback on a single paraphrase, an instructor would need to obtain the original source text, locate the exact passage in the text and compare it to the student's paraphrase. Since many research assignments require that students select sources themselves, each student will have used different sources, making this work of locating original passages prohibitively time-consuming. Even if students are required to provide the original passages, evaluating paraphrases takes time. Since the line between acceptable and unacceptable paraphrasing is difficult to draw (Roig 2001), a quick written comment may not be sufficient feedback; a conversation may be necessary.

In the absence of feedback, students are left to their own devices, and a sensible strategy some employ is imitating what they see in scholarly writing. The problem is that students draw incorrect conclusions from what they see (Pecorari, 2013), and when instructors do not alert them to textual missteps in their writing, they understandably conclude that their source use is appropriate, going on to potentially misuse sources unchecked for years (Pecorari, 2013). At my university, instructors regularly refer senior students to our team of writing strategists because of poor paraphrasing, and the instructors express surprise at the lack of understanding of paraphrasing basics. The conversation between the student and the instructor has usually revolved around plagiarism, so emotions run high on both sides. Students often feel angry that no one "called them on it" at an earlier stage of their undergraduate program.

Outsourcing Paraphrasing Instruction

The question of who is responsible for teaching students to paraphrase is part of the broader issue of responsibility for academic writing instruction. Instructors tend to believe that students should already have acquired academic writing skills such as paraphrasing by the time they enter higher education (Jamieson, 2013; Peters & Cadieux, 2019). As a result, "faculty often assign rather than teach research-based writing" (Serviss, 2016, p. 553). The Writing Across the Curriculum (WAC) and Writing in the Disciplines (WID) movements evolved in response to this problem, and WAC and WID proponents have advocated for a whole-institution approach to student writing development for decades. Still, a persistent belief on the part of many instructors is that it is not their responsibility to teach writing.

Perhaps if faculty conceived of writing not as a generic skill students should possess before entering higher education, but rather, as a discipline-specific mechanism for constructing knowledge, they would be more inclined to see writing instruction as integral to initiating students into their disciplinary community. As we work to decolonise the curriculum, educators have a responsibility to challenge the privileged position writing holds as a scholarly mode of communication, but for as long as writing retains such a vital role in the academy, we also have a responsibility to our students—to help them uncover the conventions of academic writing for their discipline. Writing is a manifestation of thinking, so if we accept that a central role of the university teacher is to guide students' "cognitive apprenticeship" (Brown et al., 1989)—that is, to help them learn how biologists think or how historians think—then it follows that we need to facilitate their learning to write in ways that are common in the discipline, too.

Even when instructors acknowledge the need to teach writing, real barriers exist. The first is time:

> Most instructors at Canadian universities would probably agree that the time and resources they have to effectively deliver their courses are either stretched to the limit or insufficient, so their reluctance to assume additional responsibility for instructing students in appropriate source use is understandable. (Evans-Tokaryk, 2014, p. 20)

Another barrier is that content instructors who are not writing specialists may feel ill-equipped to teach source use skills like paraphrasing. Because of these barriers, when student writing fails to meet expectations, many instructors refer students to first-year composition classes or writing centres.

Although writing experts on campus have an important role to play in supporting students' academic writing development, the discipline-specific aspects of writing need to be addressed by disciplinary experts. Paraphrasing conventions differ from discipline to discipline. In the hard sciences, it may be acceptable (indeed, necessary) to copy longer word strings from the original source than is acceptable in the humanities (Shi et al., 2018). Differences in citation practices also exist, and these differences have implications for the syntactic structure of paraphrases. In the social sciences and humanities, narrative (or integral) citations are more common than they are in the hard sciences and engineering (Hyland, 2004), and the reporting verbs necessary for the narrative citation structure are frequently the locus of the recontextualisation inherent in paraphrasing. Evans-Tokaryk (2014) concluded that "we need to make individual disciplines more accountable for the way they teach citation practices, source-use, and rhetorical strategies for engaging in the scholarly conversation" (pp. 20–21). A complicating factor, however, is that members of the same disciplinary community do not necessarily agree on the boundaries between acceptable and unacceptable paraphrasing (Roig, 2001). This reality makes it crucial for individual instructors to specify and illustrate expectations. As Susan Bens (2022) shows in her chapter in this volume, it is unfair to expect students to navigate the ambiguity of expectations related to academic integrity across courses on their own. Faculty members must address what they deem to be acceptable and unacceptable source use in their courses.

A Way Forward

Increased Content Instructor-Writing Specialist Collaboration

It is understandable that instructors who are not writing specialists may feel uncomfortable taking on the full responsibility for teaching source use skills such as paraphrasing. They, like our students, may never have experienced explicit paraphrasing instruction, and most disciplinary experts have not needed to think about how paraphrasing is used in their discipline as compared with other disciplines. In contrast, professional writing consultants meet with students from a variety of disciplines every day, giving us regular exposure to scholarly texts from many fields and a constant reminder that conventions differ by discipline. Writing centre professionals cannot deeply understand the conventions of every discipline, but the question is central to our day-to-day work. Collaboration allows both professionals to benefit: the instructor gains access to writing specialist knowledge, and the writing specialist gains access to disciplinary knowledge. A writing specialist could even be a partner in a Decoding the Disciplines style interview (Middendorf & Pace, 2004), where the writing consultant's role would be to ask questions to make explicit the paraphrasing conventions the faculty expert knows only implicitly. Serviss (2016) argued that instructors "need robust support as they design [writing] assignments for students, strategize ways to provide productive feedback, and ultimately evaluate and assess student work for both its course-specific content and its adherence to broader academic conventions such as academic integrity" (p. 553), and the specialists who work in writing centres are equipped to provide this very support.

At my institution, learning strategists developed and use an Intentional Model of Service Delivery (MRU, 2018) which prioritises embedding writing and learning strategies within content courses. The service model identifies four types of collaboration with our faculty partners: general (e.g., faculty partners offering students incentives for attending our open workshops), complementary (e.g., learning resources customised to specific assignments), integrated (e.g., co-created teaching materials) and embedded (e.g., consulting on curricular design).

Writing centre specialists across the country offer a similar range of collaborative support types (although they may not use the same labels), but it is not uncommon for writing centre professionals to feel that the potential for robust and sustained collaborations with faculty goes somewhat untapped. A perennial theme appearing in the conference programs of the Learning Specialists Association of Canada (LSAC) and the Canadian Writing Centres Association (CWCA) is generating and maintaining collaborations with content instructors. On these associations' 2019 conference programs were session titles such as "Now I Know You're Our Partners: Creating Embedded Learning Centre Services with Faculty" (LSAC), "Out of the Learning Centre and into the Classroom: Strategies for Embedding Writing Support" (CWCA) and "Supporting Sustainable Collaboration Between Writing Centres and Writing Instructors" (CWCA). Writing centre professionals are seeking opportunities to meaningfully and sustainably facilitate learning in partnership with faculty.

Projects at MRU, ranging from general workshops to integrated course-specific learning materials, have provided opportunities for our writing strategist team to approach teaching paraphrasing in new ways. Feedback from students and our faculty partners has been encouraging, and each of the sections below describes an aspect of this new approach.

Acknowledging Conflicting Notions of Authorship

When students enter college or university, they enter new discourse communities, and these scholarly communities conceive of authorship in ways that may conflict with students' notions of authorship. Many young adults entering our institutions are steeped in what Lawrence Lessig (2008) termed *remix culture*. They create memes and videos from multiple sources and share them freely without attribution. They quote from TV shows, films and songs, and *not* identifying the source is part of the appeal; the shared experience of watching or listening to the original makes explicit attribution unnecessary, and this implicit understanding is what sparks connection (Blum, 2009). When discussing source use, educators must be careful not to assume that students understand or agree with scholarly practices surrounding source use. Evans-Tokaryk (2014) advocated that when discussing source use, educators should "take remix culture as a point of (counter) reference" (p. 8). Using remix culture as a starting point allows us to build upon students' current experience and common practices and can make the contrast between what they know and the expectations of their new academic discourse communities clearer. Pecorari (2013) emphasised the importance of helping students understand their responsibility for transparent source use, and approaching this conversation by contrasting it with the way in which students engage in remix in their non-academic lives makes sense.

Contrasting remix culture with academic writing culture can be quick and easy. In a co-created asynchronous resource on academic integrity (including sections on paraphrasing and referencing), a nursing faculty partner and I included the slide reproduced in Fig. 21.1.

Fig. 21.1 Slide from asynchronous learning resource for nursing students

Note. This figure shows a slide whose purpose is to acknowledge that citation is expected within the cultural context of academic writing, but not within all contexts.

The inclusion of a slide like this one creates a quick opportunity to underline that citation is a cultural practice and to remind students that they are members of multiple cultures, each with unique norms.

Introducing Students to Paraphrasing As a Powerful Tool

Presenting paraphrasing as a tool which puts the writer in the powerful position of interpreting, evaluating and recontextualising information can help students view paraphrasing as valuable. In Mori's (2018) words, "a paraphrase in its rhetorical realisation may always involve some sort of evaluation or opinion, seeing that any writer has a reason for using a source, whether to support or refute a claim" (p. 46). When students recognise that they have the agency to shape information for a reason, and that reason is theirs to determine, they can begin to see paraphrasing as a useful tool rather than a burden.

The key may lie in orienting students to how scholarly discourse actually works and crucially, in helping them see themselves as active contributors to this discourse. As Hendricks and Quinn (2000) noted, many students enter higher education believing that knowledge is "something out there" (p. 451) rather than something that is constructed, that it is fixed rather than dynamic. Many approach writing from sources as a kind of reporting rather than the more creative and generative work of integrating ideas from sources with their own ideas. Faculty members could do more to unveil the rhetorical processes inherent in academic discourse and to guide students towards recognising the opportunities they have to participate in knowledge construction (Hendricks & Quinn, 2000), and the same goes for writing specialists.

For many years, the writing strategist team at MRU has offered a paraphrasing workshop as part of our Academic Success series. We commonly refer to workshops in this series as "open workshops" since they are open to students from any program, in any year of study. When I joined the team in 2015, the "Paraphrasing, Not Plagiarizing" workshop included no discussion of the reasons academic writers paraphrase or the benefits of paraphrasing. A later version included notes for the facilitator on the reasons paraphrasing is valuable, but the information did not appear on a slide or on the student handout. When I took over facilitation of the workshop, I moved the benefits of paraphrasing onto a slide: (1) [Paraphrasing] helps you to truly understand the original, (2) shows your instructor you understand, and (3) allows you to make complex ideas simple for your reader. Over time, I became dissatisfied with this list of benefits; if the point was to generate buy-in from students and break down their resistance to paraphrasing, the list felt flat and unconvincing.

I began to skip that benefits slide in favour of an approach that highlighted disciplinary conventions. I would ask students to generate an example of a discipline in which quoting is a common way to incorporate source information and a discipline where source incorporation occurs more commonly through paraphrasing (i.e., where quotation is uncommon). Students found this task challenging, leading me to conclude that most had never encountered the idea that the ratio of quoting to paraphrasing might vary by discipline. In the workshop, I would contrast Comparative Literature with Biology, exploring the reasons why, in general, the former would use more quotation than the latter. Although students generally reacted with interest, becoming curious about whether quoting was common or uncommon in their particular discipline, the explanation still seemed superficial. It fell short of a complete explanation of why paraphrasing is useful and sometimes preferable. Students came away with the idea that they should paraphrase, and that conventions differ by discipline, but they did not have a clear sense of why paraphrasing might *serve them better as writers*.

The 2021 version of the workshop retains the discussion of disciplinary conventions but also highlights that writers paraphrase because paraphrasing allows them greater flexibility for reformulating information to fit the point they are making in their own text. Our focus has shifted away from what students need to prove to their instructor, away from what the rules and conventions are, and towards the affordances paraphrasing provides the student writer, who is ultimately in charge. The idea that paraphrasing actually empowers the writer led one workshop participant to suggest that we refer to paraphrasing as "power-phrasing" (K. Toseland, personal communication, September 16, 2020). Not only did we immediately include the newly coined term in the workshop slide deck, but we incorporated it into the revised workshop title in January 2021: "From Paraphrasing to 'Power-Phrasing'."

Students who attend the paraphrasing workshop may choose to fill out a Reflection & Participation Form: an online form designed to take approximately 10–15 min to complete. (Each of the 15 workshops in our Academic Success series has a separate Reflection & Participation Form.) This assessment tool helps us determine whether learning outcomes are being met in the workshop and is a key quality assurance mechanism. The form for the paraphrasing workshop includes this question: "What's one strategy or concept you learned in this webinar that you'll apply in your future course work?" Responses from the Fall 2020 semester included:

> I learned a major benefit of paraphrasing. In some cases paraphrasing is better than quoting as it gives you more flexibility to shape your work.
>
> I learned the benefit of paraphrasing which is greater flexibility, incorporating the information more smoothly, shaping the information for specific purpose, and power phrasing.

The comments suggest that before the workshop, these students did not understand that paraphrasing grants the writer flexibility; they did not see that paraphrasing actually *serves* the writer.

Once students realise that paraphrasing serves them as writers, they are in a much better position to understand why they should avoid patchwriting, where the text "restates a phrase, clause, or one or more sentences while staying close to the language or syntax of the source" (Jamieson, 2018, p. 110). Students cannot truly understand why patchwriting is undesirable unless they first understand the purpose and benefits of paraphrasing. When they recognise that paraphrasing allows more flexibility in interpreting and re-shaping information, they can grasp why the mechanical "synonym substitution strategy" they may have thought of as paraphrasing misses the point. As a colleague explained to students, "when you patchwrite, you've essentially done a direct quote but made more work for yourself" (C. Willard, personal communication, September 28, 2020). Rebecca Moore Howard and others have argued that patchwriting represents a developmental phase in learning to write from sources and that the remedy is pedagogy, not punishment (Howard, 1993; Jamieson, 2016; Jamieson & Howard, 2019; Pecorari & Petrić, 2014). I wholeheartedly agree and believe that an emphasis on the purpose of paraphrasing is precisely the pedagogical starting point.

Evidence from an asynchronous learning module incorporated into a Fall 2020 first-year Health and Physical Education course revealed that for many learners, the idea that patchwriting is undesirable is new. After students completed the paraphrasing section of the module, they were asked to name one new thing they had learned about paraphrasing. Although only a fifth of the section focused specifically on patchwriting, 68/168 (40%) of students identified patchwriting (what it is, why they should avoid it, how to avoid it) as new to them.

A single workshop or learning module can only be a starting point on the road to competent paraphrasing, but as a starting point, it is gaining traction at our institution. Faculty members increasingly provide incentives (e.g., a small percentage of the final course grade) to their students to encourage them to participate in open workshops, and 69% of the students who registered for the paraphrasing workshop in Fall 2020 indicated either that an instructor was giving them some sort of incentive for participation and/or an instructor had recommended the webinar.

Avoiding Single-Sentence, Decontextualised Paraphrasing Activities

When modelling paraphrasing or creating practice activities, using a short passage from a source rather than a single sentence makes it possible to focus on the selection process so important to authentic paraphrasing. The educator can discuss with students which information to include in the paraphrase and which information to exclude so that the paraphrase best supports the writer's point. For the selection process to be remotely authentic, students must first have some context around the source (e.g., the author's main thesis) and some context around the text they are producing themselves (e.g., the topic sentence of the paragraph into which they are inserting their paraphrase). This target context helps students see that paraphrasing always has a rhetorical purpose. Another benefit of choosing a passage over a single sentence is that this practice aligns with the message that students should read sources thoroughly instead of mining sources for single sentences. Although any simulation is artificial to some degree, the more authentic the task, the more easily students will be able to transfer the knowledge and skills to a real situation.

In earlier versions of the open paraphrasing workshop, we used a single (albeit relatively complex) sentence from a scholarly journal article to walk students through our suggested steps in paraphrasing. We provided minimal context for the article itself, but no context for what students would be using the information *for*. We led students through the mostly decontextualised, mechanistic exercise of breaking the original sentence into lexical chunks, re-organising those chunks into a new sentence pattern, and finding new phrasing for each chunk. The workshop heavily emphasised a tool we called the "BIG-4 Checklist" for evaluating paraphrases: a plagiarism-free paraphrase must (1) have new words, (2) have new sentence structure, (3) have the same meaning as the original, and (4) be cited. Students evaluated a series of paraphrases as acceptable or unacceptable based on the BIG-4 criteria, and in our suggested set of steps to follow for successful paraphrasing, the final step was to "cross-check your paraphrase with the BIG-4." The learning assessment form students filled out at the end of the workshop asked them to identify one concrete idea/strategy they took away from the workshop, and the most frequent answers were the BIG-4 Checklist and, more specifically, a new awareness that changing sentence structure is a requirement for plagiarism-free paraphrases. What students were taking away from our workshop were techniques for avoiding plagiarism, but what we wanted them to come away with was something deeper, more positive, and more exciting: an understanding of how paraphrasing can make their writing stronger and how it is connected to writer agency.

The revised workshop uses a different source text (an article from *Canadian Business* magazine), and instead of providing students with a single sentence to work from, we use a passage:

> The company has been working to rapidly expand Tim Hortons beyond its Canadian roots. It signed a master franchise joint venture agreement with a private equity firm last year to open more than 1,500 of the coffee-and-doughnut shops in China—home to a burgeoning coffee culture and a hotbed of international coffee chain expansions. It also recently expanded into the Philippines, the United Kingdom and Spain. (Sagan, 2019, para. 10).

Using a three-sentence passage rather than a single sentence allows students the opportunity to consider which parts of the passage they would select to support a particular claim. And this step—selecting information according to the writer's purpose—is now central to the workshop.

We present two different scenarios to illustrate the importance of information selection in paraphrasing. In the first, students imagine they are taking a Sociology course and are writing a paper about coffee culture around the world. The topic sentence of the paragraph is, "China is another country where coffee culture has taken hold over the past decade." The students' task is to paraphrase the original passage to best support this topic sentence. In other words, they need to select only the parts of the original that are relevant to the point of the paragraph. Students need to ask themselves whether details such as "signed a master franchise joint venture agreement with a private equity firm" are useful for their purpose.

In the second scenario, students imagine they are taking a Management course and are writing a paper on international expansion. This time, the topic sentence is,

"Canadian food and beverage companies have been expanding into Asian markets through joint venture agreements of various types." In this scenario, students should realise that for this context, the specific type of joint venture agreement *is* significant and should probably be included in the paraphrase.

Logistically, the changes we have made to the paraphrasing practice activity are simple: (1) use a passage instead of a single sentence, and (2) provide context around what the writer is using the information *for*. Despite the simplicity of the adjustments, comments on learning assessment forms indicate that students are taking away deeper insights from the workshop.

> In my future work in paraphrasing, I will be focusing more on the context of my topic and taking the time to thoroughly decide which ideas are important. As shown in the webinar, I will highlight the sentences that pertain to my subject matter and focus on how I can include that information into my writing.

> I liked the idea of looking at what isn't important in the source so that you are able to focus on paraphrasing what is relevant. Compared to paraphrasing the entire quote or source. Looking at what parts of the source are relevant to my specific topic and how those important aspects might change depending on the topic. Especially taking a look at how that important information might change depending on if you are looking at it from a business perspective or a sociological perspective.

Although the above changes apply to the open paraphrasing workshop, we are making similar changes to paraphrasing-focused segments of our in-class workshops and asynchronous learning modules (i.e., more complementary and integrated types of support), and our faculty partners are expressing enthusiasm for the new direction. Faculty partners frequently report that our student learning materials are adding to their own understanding of paraphrasing. In reference to an asynchronous learning resource on paraphrasing for nursing students, one faculty partner commented, "I guess, I know how to do [paraphrasing], I have just never seen it so clearly delineated" (J. Harris, personal communication, October 14, 2020).

De-emphasising Plagiarism, But Teaching Paraphrasing in the Context of Academic Integrity

In paraphrasing instruction, plagiarism should cease to have such a central place. Students need a safe space in which to practice source use, one in which the fear of plagiarism is not a deterrent to exploration and experimentation. At the same time, Jamieson and Howard's (2019) assertion that "textual missteps commonly classified as 'plagiarism' do not belong in the category of academic integrity" (p. 74) is problematic. Academic writers have a responsibility to represent their sources fairly, accurately and transparently, and student writers are no exception. Jamieson and Howard (2019) argue that "like grammar, spelling, and punctuation, whose rules students may not know or may sometimes knowingly or carelessly neglect, careless source attribution and incorporation produces bad writing and should be addressed as such" (p. 72). Careless source incorporation results in more than bad writing, however. It represents a lack of respect for other members of the academic community, which makes it distinct from and more egregious than careless grammar, spelling or punctuation. Careless paraphrasing can result in a misrepresentation of the original author's position, and when this outcome is not connected to the values of academic integrity, specifically fairness, responsibility and respect (International Center for Academic Integrity, 2021), students miss out on the opportunity to see themselves as active members of disciplinary communities—members who have a responsibility to one another. Although I agree that single instances of patchwriting should not lead to punishment for the student writer, tying source use instruction to the values of fairness, responsibility and respect is essential.

An experience with senior students at my institution has strengthened my conviction that paraphrasing instruction must be tied to academic integrity. After the instructor identified source misuse in the work of a surprising number of their students' written assignments, I facilitated several small group sessions on referencing and paraphrasing. These sessions, along with reports of conversations the instructor had had with students, revealed that in some cases, the origin of source misuse was a lack of understanding of the purpose of paraphrasing and how to approach it. In other cases, however, the students admitted to "getting away with" sloppy paraphrasing and referencing for years. They were fully aware that they were taking shortcuts, but since no instructor had ever addressed the issue, the students had never felt the need to adjust their practice. These students did not recognise themselves as active, responsible members of their disciplinary community.

Expecting an undergraduate student to recognise a personal responsibility to their disciplinary discourse community is not unrealistic. At MRU, senior undergraduate students make public presentations, engage in primary research activities, and present their results at academic conferences. These students do contribute to the advancement of knowledge in their disciplines and need to understand how the misuse of sources can undermine scholarly discourse.

A collaboration with second-year clinical nursing instructors is providing an opportunity for students to receive feedback on their paraphrasing in a way that helps them make authentic connections between source use and their responsibilities to the communities they serve. Students in this community nursing course work in groups to complete a project in close partnership with a community agency, and one of the students' final tasks is to provide a written report to the agency. Agencies sometimes refer to these reports in funding proposals and/or their own stakeholder communications. Approximately one week before the due date, students can book a one-hour group consultation with a writing strategist, who reviews the report and prepares feedback. Although the feedback can range from matters of organisation to writing style to APA formatting, a key objective is to provide feedback on paraphrasing. Strategists consult the sources students have paraphrased and identify places where they have misunderstood the source, failed to delineate the source authors' conclusions from their own, misrepresented source authors' positions and/or patchwritten. Because all the students in the group and their instructor attend the appointment, the opportunities for discussion about what constitutes acceptable paraphrasing are rich and often nuanced. Over the course of our two-year collaboration, we have worked with approximately 10 different instructors who have consistently told us that (1) they come away from the appointments with new insights on paraphrasing, and (2) they would not have had time to compare students' paraphrases with the original sources and would not have caught many of the paraphrasing missteps we identify. Students are grateful for the feedback on their paraphrasing, especially because they know they will be presenting their report to their agency partner; the fact that their writing will go beyond the school-writing context enhances their sense of accountability.

The changes to our open paraphrasing workshop are also generating evidence that undergraduate students readily make the link between paraphrasing and academic integrity insofar as they recognise the importance of fairly representing the original source author's position. Whereas previous versions of the workshop dedicated little time to misrepresentation, the new version prominently lists misrepresentation as one of four paraphrasing pitfalls and uses a specific example to illustrate the link between the common practice of mining a source for a single useful sentence and unintentional misrepresentation. When asked (in the learning assessment form) to identify their main takeaway from the workshop, students are mentioning strategies for avoiding misrepresenting the original source:

> In order to avoid misrepresenting the original author, I will thoroughly read through sources in order to gain knowledge of the authors position accurately. Much of the time I find myself skimming through sources and sometimes this has resulted in me not fully understanding the main idea of the text and ultimately paraphrasing their position inaccurately.
>
> to make sure I read the source thoroughly so that I do not misinterpret what the author is saying. I need to make sure I know all the facts before paraphrasing a source, because I could potentially give the wrong interpretation, making it seem like I did not read the source, I just looked for what I wanted to find but did not go into depth with it.
>
> Before this workshop I wasn't really aware that it's very common to misinterpret an authors work by just reading small parts of their article. I just always assumed that all the parts of the article would specifically present their idea.

Students seem to be recognising the need for a deeper engagement with source texts—indeed, their *responsibility* to engage more deeply with source texts.

Future Directions

One-off workshops and learning modules are insufficient if our goal is to help students develop their ability to paraphrase competently and with integrity. Students need multiple opportunities, contextualised within their discipline, and spiralled throughout their program, to focus on source use, and crucially, to receive feedback on their paraphrasing. As writing strategists, we find ourselves working hard to dispel the notion that if all students participate in a paraphrasing and referencing workshop in the first year of their program, then they "should know it" and can be held accountable for source misuse in every course thereafter. We wholeheartedly support bringing key writing strategies like paraphrasing into first-year content classes, but we advocate for and can support next-level opportunities at subsequent stages of students' programs.

An approach analogous to Lang's (2016) "small teaching" may help make the integration of multiple learning opportunities more feasible. Small teaching activities "require minimal preparation and grading" (p. 8), and should take up only a small amount of class time. Instructors, in collaboration with writing specialists, could design and facilitate short paraphrasing activities so that students revisit key concepts and have chances to practice. A 15 minute block of time would be sufficient for educators to lead students through a side-by-side comparison of a paraphrase and the original passage from which it was derived, for example. Choosing a passage from a text students have already read for class would instantly provide authentic context, and if students evaluate the corresponding paraphrase in the context of a full paragraph rather than in isolation, the activity is more realistic and potentially illuminating. Even a simple comparison activity like this one can engender rich conversations about the line between interpretation and misinterpretation of an author's words/intent or the line between paraphrasing and patchwriting. Other quick classroom activities could include having students notice the balance between quotation and paraphrasing in a disciplinary text (Pecorari, 2013), comparing student-generated paraphrases of a passage from a text the whole class has read, or identifying the specific problem in each of several variations on a paraphrase. In all cases, writing specialists could be partners in co-creating the teaching materials and/or co-facilitating the activity.

Conclusion

To progress in their ability to use sources with integrity, students benefit from explicit instruction on the complex skill of paraphrasing and, importantly, feedback on their paraphrasing. When instruction and feedback focus more on what paraphrasing allows the writer to do and less on instilling fear of plagiarism, more on students' responsibilities as members of discourse communities and less on technicalities, students' confidence and abilities will grow. Sustained collaboration between content instructors and writing centre professionals may make it more feasible to weave paraphrasing instruction and feedback throughout a student's program.

Recommendations

- Leverage opportunities for instructor-writing specialist collaboration
- Acknowledge conflicting notions of authorship
- Help students see paraphrasing as a powerful tool
- Avoid single-sentence and/or decontextualised practice activities
- De-emphasise plagiarism, but link paraphrasing to the values of academic integrity

- Provide feedback to students on their paraphrasing
- Integrate short activities and feedback opportunities beyond the first year

References

Abasi, A. R., & Akbari, N. (2008). Are we encouraging patchwriting? Reconsidering the role of the pedagogical context in ESL student writers' transgressive intertextuality. *English for Specific Purposes, 27*(3), 267–284. https://doi.org/10.1016/j.esp.2008.02.001

Bens, S. (2022). Helping students resolve the ambiguous expectations of academic integrity. In *Academic Integrity in Canada: An Enduring and Essential Challenge.* Springer.

Blum, S. D. (2009). *My word! Plagiarism and college culture.* Cornell University Press.

Brown, J. S., Collins, A., & Duguid, P. (1989). Situated cognition and the culture of learning. *Educational Researcher, 18*(1), 32–42. https://doi.org/10.3102/0013189x018001032

Evans-Tokaryk, T. (2014). Academic integrity, remix culture, globalization: A Canadian case study of student and faculty perceptions of plagiarism. *Across the Disciplines, 11*(2). https://wac.colostate.edu/docs/atd/articles/evans-tokaryk2014.pdf

Hendricks, M., & Quinn, L. (2000). Teaching referencing as an introduction to epistemological empowerment. *Teaching in Higher Education, 5*(4), 447–457. https://doi.org/10.1080/713699175

Hirvela, A., & Du, Q. (2013). "Why am I paraphrasing?": Undergraduate ESL writers' engagement with source-based academic writing and reading. *Journal of English for Academic Purposes, 12*(2), 87–98. https://doi.org/10.1016/j.jeap.2012.11.005

Howard, R. M. (1993). A plagiarism pentimento. *Journal of Teaching Writing, 11*(2), 233–245.

Hyland, K. (2004). *Disciplinary discourses: Social interactions in academic writing.* The University of Michigan Press.

International Center for Academic Integrity. (2021). *The fundamental values of academic integrity* (3rd ed). https://www.academicintegrity.org/the-fundamental-values-of-academic-integrity/

Jamieson, S. (2013). Reading and engaging sources: What students' use of sources reveals about advanced reading skills. *Across the Disciplines, 10*(4). https://wac.colostate.edu/docs/atd/reading/jamieson.pdf

Jamieson, S. (2016). Is it plagiarism or patchwriting? Toward a nuanced definition. In T. Bretag (Ed.), *The handbook of academic integrity* (pp. 503–518). Springer. https://doi.org/10.1007/978-981-287-098-8_68

Jamieson, S. (2018). Shouldn't our expectations of students' and academics' intertextuality practices differ? In D. Pecorari & P. Shaw (Eds.), *Student plagiarism in higher education: Reflections on teaching practice* (pp. 105–122). Routledge. https://doi.org/10.4324/9781315166148-8

Jamieson, S., & Howard, R. M. (2019). Rethinking the relationship between plagiarism and academic integrity. *International Journal of Technologies in Higher Education, 16*(2), 69–85. https://doi.org/10.18162/ritpu-2019-v16n2-07

Lang, J. M. (2016). *Small teaching: Everyday lessons from the science of learning.* Jossey-Bass.

Lessig, L. (2008). *Remix: Making art and commerce thrive in the hybrid economy.* Bloomsbury Open Access. https://doi.org/10.5040/9781849662505

Middendorf, J., & Pace, D. (2004). Decoding the disciplines: A model for helping students learn disciplinary ways of thinking. *New Directions in Teaching and Learning, 2004*(98), 1–12. https://doi.org/10.1002/tl.142

Mori, M. (2018). Our speech is filled with others' words: Understanding university student and instructor opinions towards paraphrasing through a Bakhtinian lens. *Ampersand, 5*, 45–54. https://doi.org/10.1016/j.amper.2018.11.002

Mount Royal University. (2021, February 4). *Fast facts.* https://www.mtroyal.ca/AboutMountRoyal/FastFacts/index.htm

Mount Royal University. (2018). *Student Learning Services: Intentional model of service delivery*. https://docs.google.com/document/d/1aDlVFUO_I1AtBzfLnfE5jV9FPXj_E7IofjIpj9EJpbA/edit

Pecorari, D. (2013). *Teaching to avoid plagiarism: How to promote good source use*. Open University Press.

Pecorari, D., & Petrić, B. (2014). Plagiarism in second-language writing. *Language Teaching, 47*(3), 269–302. https://doi.org/10.1017/s0261444814000056

Pecorari, D., & Shaw, P. (2012). Types of student intertextuality and faculty attitudes. *Journal of Second Language Writing, 21*(2), 149–164. https://doi.org/10.1016/j.jslw.2012.03.006

Peters, M., & Cadieux, A. (2019). Are Canadian professors teaching the skills and knowledge students need to prevent plagiarism? *International Journal for Educational Integrity, 15*(1), 1–16. https://doi.org/10.1007/s40979-019-0047-z

Roig, M. (2001). Plagiarism and paraphrasing criteria of college and university professors. *Ethics and Behavior, 11*(3), 307–323. https://doi.org/10.1207/s15327019eb1103_8

Sagan, A. (2019, January 23). Restaurant Brands International announces executive changes and raises dividend. *Canadian Business*. https://www.canadianbusiness.com/business-news/restaurant-brands-international-announces-executive-changes-andraises-dividend/

Scardamalia, M., & Bereiter, C. (1987). Knowledge telling and knowledge transforming in written composition. In S. Rosenberg (Ed.), *Advances in applied psycholinguistics* (vol. 2, pp. 142–175). Cambridge University Press.

Serviss, T. (2016). Creating faculty development programming to prevent plagiarism: Three approaches. In T. Bretag (Ed.), *Handbook of academic integrity* (pp. 551–567). Springer. https://doi.org/10.1007/978-981-287-098-8_73

Shi, L., Fazel, I., & Kowkabi, N. (2018). Paraphrasing to transform knowledge in advanced graduate student writing. *English for Specific Purposes, 51*, 31–44. https://doi.org/10.1016/j.esp.2018.03.001

Yamada, K. (2003). What prevents ESL/EFL writers from avoiding plagiarism? Analyses of 10 North-American college websites. *System, 31*(2), 247–258. https://doi.org/10.1016/S0346-251X(03)00023-X

Silvia Luisa Rossi M.A., is a Writing and Learning Strategist at Mount Royal University in Calgary, Alberta. Her primary role is to support students in their development of academic writing and learning skills through group sessions and one-on-one consultations. In collaboration with faculty members in various disciplines, she develops course-specific workshops and instructional materials. Liaising with the university's centralised student conduct office, she provides customised programming for students requiring support around academic integrity. Silvia also designs educational development sessions for faculty on topics such as providing effective feedback on writing assignments and helping students learn referencing. She has co-published on academic integrity in the International Journal for Educational Integrity.

Chapter 22
Supporting Academic Integrity in the Writing Centre: Perspectives of Student Consultants

Kim Garwood

Abstract Writing centres are often described as safe spaces where students can explore their ideas and concerns, including questions about how to use and cite sources without plagiarizing. In many Canadian writing centres, these issues are addressed by student consultants who provide effective and influential peer-to-peer support in individual consultations. Little research, however, has directly examined the perspectives of student consultants in providing academic integrity support. This chapter provides a synthesis of what literature currently exists on the role of student consultants in supporting academic integrity before describing a case study with student writing consultants at the University of Guelph. Using data gathered through a survey, this chapter examines the experience and perceptions of student consultants in providing academic integrity support. The findings suggest that academic integrity conversations often arise indirectly, through conversations about referencing or paraphrasing. Student writing consultants consistently position themselves as intermediaries, helping protect students from academic misconduct by using a range of directive and non-directive strategies.

Keywords Canada · Academic integrity · Plagiarism · Writing centres · Student consultants · Peer-to-peer support · University of Guelph

K. Garwood (✉)
University of Guelph, Guelph, Canada
e-mail: kgarwood@uoguelph.ca

S. E. Eaton and J. Christensen Hughes (eds.), *Academic Integrity in Canada*, Ethics and Integrity in Educational Contexts 1,
https://doi.org/10.1007/978-3-030-83255-1_22

Introduction

A great deal of academic integrity research in higher education has focused on students' perceptions, attitudes, and behaviours related to plagiarism, and much of this research has concluded that most students are baffled by academic integrity policies and fearful of inadvertently contravening them (Adam et al., 2017; Gullifer & Tyson, 2010).[1] In response to these patterns, researchers assert that the best way to promote academic integrity and prevent plagiarism is to strengthen instructor–student relationships (Bluestein, 2015) and provide opportunities for students to ask questions and seek clarification about ethical source use (Broeckelman-Post, 2008; Buranen, 2009). At the same time, many students feel too intimidated to approach professors with these kinds of questions, fearing that they will expose themselves as incompetent or appear suspicious (Adam et al., 2017; Bluestein, 2015).

In this context, university writing centres can provide an alternative or complementary source of support for students to explore their ideas and concerns in a confidential, non-judgmental space. In many writing centres at Canadian universities, these issues are addressed by student consultants who provide effective and influential peer-to-peer support in individual consultations. These student staff play a key role in providing academic integrity guidance to many student writers.

How student staff perceive their roles in supporting academic integrity is an important but relatively understudied question. A considerable amount of North American research has examined peer-to-peer consultation practices in writing centres; however, there is comparatively little literature focused on how academic integrity is addressed in these consultations. Furthermore, it appears that no Canadian research to date has focused specifically on how student consultants in writing centres address plagiarism and academic integrity concerns in consultations.

To address this gap, the current study uses data gathered through a survey of student staff at a university writing centre to examine the following research questions: How often are plagiarism and academic integrity discussed in writing consultations with student staff, and what kinds of concerns are most common? How confident are student staff in addressing concerns and questions about academic integrity? What do the approaches of student staff suggest about the role of writing centres in supporting academic integrity? By focusing on the perspectives of student consultants at one Canadian institution's writing centre, this chapter will provide deeper insight, not only into current practices, but also into ways that we might further strengthen the role of peer-to-peer learning in supporting the academic integrity of individual students and the institution.

[1] I would like to thank the Writing Peers and Writing Support Teaching Assistants at the University of Guelph for participating in the study, and I would like to thank Sarah Elaine Eaton, Julia Christensen Hughes, Clare Bermingham, Sarah Gibbons, Lenore Latta, Kelley Packalen, Jodie Salter, and Ron Ward for their generous and helpful feedback.

Literature Review

Academic integrity has been well-described in the literature, and there is a growing body of Canadian research on this issue (Eaton, 2017; Eaton & Edino, 2018; Christensen Hughes & McCabe, 2006). However, despite the large body of literature, plagiarism, perhaps more so than other types of misconduct, remains difficult to define and address. In the literature review that follows, I briefly describe understandings of plagiarism from the literature and from the University of Guelph specifically before describing the role of writing centres and student staff in preventing plagiarism and supporting academic integrity more broadly.

The Challenge of Defining Plagiarism

At the University of Guelph, academic misconduct is defined as "behaviour that erodes the basis of mutual trust on which scholarly exchanges commonly rest, undermines the University's exercise of its responsibility to evaluate students' academic achievements, or restricts the University's ability to accomplish its learning objectives" (University of Guelph, 2020b). Plagiarism is considered a subset of academic misconduct and is defined as "misrepresenting the ideas, expression of ideas or work of others as one's own," with examples such as using portions of another work without properly quoting, paraphrasing, or citing; submitting work completed by a third party; or re-submitting work that was completed for another course (University of Guelph 2020b).

Institutional definitions such as the one provided by the University of Guelph make a concerted effort to clarify what plagiarism means, yet the literature demonstrates that a shared understanding of the term and its implications is elusive. Administrators, instructors, and students have a wide variety of understandings of the term (Blum, 2011), and when presented with examples, they often disagree about what constitutes plagiarism and about the seriousness of different types of plagiarism (Robinson-Zañartu et al., 2005).

The U.S.-based Writing Program Administrators' best practices document "Defining and Avoiding Plagiarism" argues that a key part of the problem is that definitions are too broad, lumping together deliberate attempts to plagiarize with unintentional citation errors or unskilled source use (Council of Writing Program Administrators, 2003). Because of the ambiguity of many plagiarism definitions and examples, many administrators and instructors have begun to treat plagiarism cases as teachable moments in which to discuss proper source use and integration. A strong proponent of this approach, Rebecca Moore Howard has argued for the "decriminalization" of plagiarism when it is the result of inadequate paraphrasing, a practice Howard refers to as "patchwriting" (Howard, 1992, p. 233).[2] In Howard's view, patchwriting represents a phase in skill development, in which students learn to incorporate the ideas of others into their writing. From this perspective, approaching the topic of plagiarism as an issue of process, practice, and development is a way to open more productive and supportive conversations about academic integrity.

Writing Centres as Spaces for Dialogue and Learning

Writing centres provide an ideal space for instruction and conversation about source integration and proper citation. In individual consultations, students can discuss their writing at any stage of the process, and most consultants approach this talk with a combination of indirect and direct questions and prompts that can encourage reflection and critical thinking. Though they are sometimes misidentified as "fix-it" shops where students should be sent for grammar correction or to have papers proofread, truly effective writing centres foster dialogue and deep engagement with the writing process.[3] Importantly, most writing centres in Canadian post-secondary institutions are located outside academic departments and strive to position themselves as neutral ground where students can explore ideas without risk or judgment.

The Role of Student Consultants

Research has shown that peer-to-peer learning has many advantages, such as promoting metacognition (Stigmar, 2016), supporting cognitive scaffolding (Mackiewicz & Thompson, 2014), and encouraging motivation and engagement (Topping, 1996). An early proponent of collaborative learning in writing instruction, Kenneth Bruffee (1984) described the key ingredient of peer learning as a conversation between students who are "status equals" (p. 642). In Bruffee's view, there is enormous learning potential in peer-to-peer conversations during the writing process: "[t]he way they talk with each other determines the way they will think and the way they will write" (p. 642). Given these benefits, student consultants have enormous potential to support students in navigating the often-challenging waters of academic

---

[2] In "A Plagiarism Pentimento," Howard defines patchwriting as "copying from a source text and deleting some words, altering grammatical structures, or plugging in one-to-one synonym substitutes" (p. 233).

[3] Stephen North, in the landmark essay "The Idea of a Writing Centre" (1984), asserts that the writing centre is not a place where writers should come (much less be sent to) for grammar correction or writing "first aid." In his view, writing centres are meant to provide the kind of supportive and insightful feedback that is essential to writers' growth, providing a much-needed source of conversation and intervention for writers in process. As he explains, "Writing centers are simply one manifestation—polished and highly visible—of a dialogue about writing that is central to higher education" (p. 440).

integrity; furthermore, writing consultations provide an opportunity for consultants to deepen their own knowledge and understanding of academic integrity concepts.

Writing Centre Approaches to Academic Integrity

The literature studying the role of writing centres in supporting academic integrity reflects the complicated position that writing centres occupy in relation to plagiarism and academic integrity. A significant portion of the writing centre literature on academic integrity (particularly in the United States) is devoted to confronting critics who misconstrue writing centres' work as unethical, viewing writing help as a form of plagiarism (Clark & Healy, 1996; Jurecka, 2004; Mackiewicz & Thompson, 2018). To steer clear of these accusations, most writing centre training guides focus on supporting the writer's learning and development, rather than directing a student about how to perfect a draft (e.g., Gillespie & Lerner, 2008; Ianetta & Fitzgerald 2016). As North explains, "[A writing centre's] job is to produce better writers, not better writing" (1984, p. 438). At the same time, many writing centre staff push back on the notion that consultants should be strictly non-directive. As Ianetta and Fitzgerald note, "Alongside the tradition of nondirective tutoring is one that honours modeling writing activities as a way of teaching writers how to eventually do them on their own" (p. 107). Others are even more forceful in their critiques of what they see as institutions chasing untenable notions of individual authorship despite the inherently social nature of writing. As Ginger Jurecka notes, "the concept of an unethical writing center has more to do with archaic notions of ownership within academia than actual moral faltering within the center" (2004, p. 2).

Most university and college writing centres, the majority of which are staffed by professionals without faculty status or tenure, must continually balance their commitment to providing a non-judgmental space for students with their responsibility to uphold the policies of the institution. Several writing centres have illustrated this complicated balance by sharing case studies of tutors encountering and addressing suspected plagiarism (Brown et al., 2007; Gruber, 1998; Pelzer, 2019). These experiences of addressing plagiarism can become moments of learning and reflection for tutors and administrators alike, as they wrestle with how to support students while maintaining institutional values. Writing centres still find ways to push boundaries and influence institutional policies, even in this "in-between" space. For example, Brown et al. (2007) describe the activist approach of their student consultant team, which, prompted by a student visit, delved into the research about Turnitin software, and were dismayed by the lack of information being shared with students about how the software works—and its limitations. They decided to share what they learned with students who visited the centre in order to empower students to initiate deeper conversations with their professors about how the use of Turnitin affected their learning in the classroom. A broader aim of this information sharing was to advocate that the university reconsider its use of similarity detection software and other policing strategies for addressing plagiarism. In another approach, writing centre director

Elizabeth Kleinfeld describes training student consultants to perform "close readings" of students' use of sources using the framework of the Citation Project[4] (2016, p. 56). By comparing citations to the original source material, student consultants learned how to recognize summarizing, copying, and patchwriting and were able to help writing centre visitors reflect their own source use strategies.

While most writing centres position themselves and their student consultants outside surveillance and policy enforcement, some have taken a more interventionist approach. In a case described by Sibylle Gruber (1998), the writing centre grappled with a student client who blatantly plagiarized and refused to heed a student writing consultant's warnings. The centre ultimately decided to have the student consultant contact the professor, breaking writing centre confidentiality in favour of supporting institutional integrity. As Gruber notes, "we considered ourselves to be in a no-win situation.... We would either fall short of our self-imposed policies and the trust that students put into their interactions with Writing Center staff, or we could be blamed for encouraging and perpetuating unacceptable behavior" (p. 54).

In another example, Pelzer (2019) describes how tutors' uncertainty about how to address possible plagiarism prompted the development of writing centre policies that included a three-strike model and the creation of a plagiarism-monitoring list. The guidelines aimed to guide tutors more clearly about how to "handle, record, and report plagiarism suspicions" (p. 5). Despite this responsibility for surveillance, tutors were also expected to project a non-judgmental stance in consultations and "not to judge a student's authenticity, but rather to educate and provide every resource available to help students improve in this area" (p. 5). In another interventionist approach, Bridgewater, Pounds, and Morley (2019) describe developing a program that required students charged with plagiarism to attend a series of consultations with writing peer tutors. As part of the program, the tutors were required to diagnose the student's plagiarism as intentional or accidental and shape their instruction and advice accordingly. This kind of policy enforcement role might be unpalatable to most writing centres; however, Bridgewater et al. describe it as an opportunity to strengthen the standing and profile of their centre, which "is seen as fulfilling a more academic role than most support centers because it now handles such a challenging issue" (p. 20).

These examples illustrate the complicated and often contradictory situations writing centres and student consultants negotiate in supporting academic integrity on campus. Despite a common desire to provide a judgment-free space for students to talk about plagiarism, writing centres are to varying degrees beholden to the academic integrity priorities and policies of their respective institutions. As Gruber notes, "We need to find the way that justifies our actions to our students, the instructors, the administration, and to ourselves. However, we need to be aware that our position as writing center administrators and writing center staff is a precarious one" (p. 60). In

---

[4] The Citation Project (http://www.citationproject.net/) is described as "a series of research studies on source use. Their purpose is to provide data and analyses that can help with educators' questions about plagiarism, information literacy, and the teaching of source-based writing."

the study that follows, I explore how student consultants approach their work within this complex web of relationships and responsibilities.

Methodology

In the summer of 2020, participants were recruited for the study from current and recent student writing consultants at the University of Guelph writing centre.[5] The University of Guelph is a mid-sized comprehensive university, with 29,000 undergraduate and graduate students, including 1,400 international students (University of Guelph, 2020a). The writing centre is located in the university's library and is staffed by 1 manager, 3 full-time professional staff, 10 graduate student writing support teaching assistants (TAs), and 15–20 undergraduate writing peer helpers (Peers). The team provides in-class instruction, specialized workshops and programs, English language support, and a variety of handouts and resources. The centre is best known for its individual writing consultations and provides more than 4,000 sessions (25- or 50-minute consultations) per year to students from all levels and disciplines. Students have the option of attending consultations in person or via an online platform; however, during the COVID-19 pandemic (when data were collected), all consultations were being conducted online.

TAs and Peers complete two days of training each September on conducting effective consultations; supporting writers who have English as an additional language; fostering diversity and inclusivity; writing in the disciplines; making referrals; and using resources. In addition to this, new undergraduate peer helpers receive a full semester of training which addresses similar topics in greater depth. Training of both TAs and Peers emphasizes the importance of students maintaining control over their papers. Consultants are encouraged to avoid writing on student papers other than to highlight areas of focus. Student visits are confidential, and the centre does not report suspected plagiarism, but consultants are encouraged to flag potential plagiarism for students and ensure that students are aware of how their source use may be interpreted by instructors.

To gather the perspectives of the student writing consultants, a 22-question survey was developed and mounted on the Qualtrics platform. The survey included a combination of multiple-choice and open-ended answers. Questions asked about consultants' experiences with supporting student clients with citation, paraphrasing, plagiarism, and academic integrity concerns. Survey results were collected in the Qualtrics platform. Multiple choice answers were analyzed using the report functionality in the Qualtrics software, which produces graphs and tables of responses. Ranking questions were further analyzed using Excel. Text answers were uploaded to NVivo software and analyzed for themes and patterns of language use.

---

[5] This study was reviewed by the University of Guelph Research Ethics Board for compliance with federal guidelines for research involving human participants (REB #20-04-004).

Results and Discussion

Twenty-two ($N = 22$) responses were gathered from 37 potential respondents over a six-week period, representing a response rate of 57%. Responses from TAs and Peers were evenly divided between TAs ($n = 11$) and Peers ($n = 11$); however, one TA response was excluded from the data set because the respondent did not answer any of the questions after Question 1 ("Please indicate your most recent role in Writing Services at U of G").

In the section that follows, I describe and interpret the survey results, focusing on key themes that emerge from the data.

Frequency of Topics Related to Plagiarism and Academic Integrity

One of the basic questions of the study was how often conversations about citing and referencing, paraphrasing, and plagiarism arise in student staff consultations. As shown in Fig. 22.1, conversations about citing and referencing were perceived to be the most common. This finding is not surprising; many students are drawn to our services to "check their references" or to learn how to cite in a particular style. What is interesting, however, is how these conversations can provide openings for student staff to initiate more substantive conversations about citing and referencing. As Peer 5 noted,

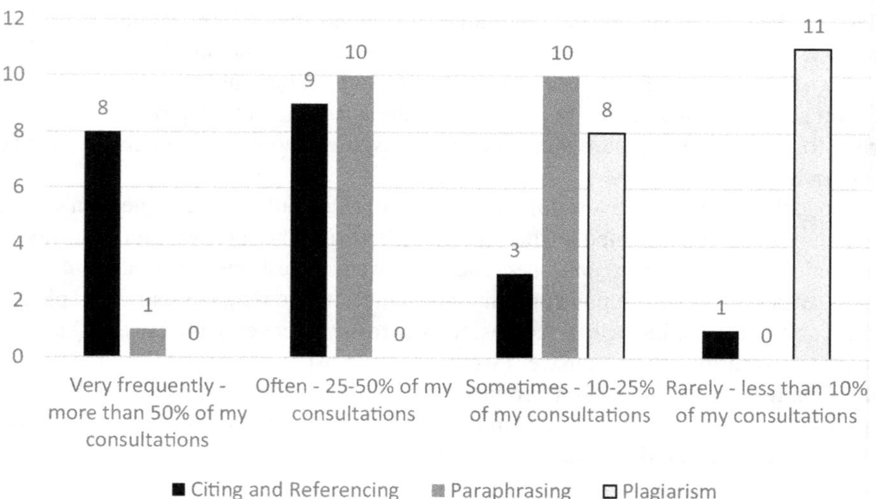

Fig. 22.1 Frequency of conversations about citing and referencing, paraphrasing, and plagiarism in consultations

> I used some of [the student's] citation-related queries as a segue into talking about citing and attribution…. The first angle I used was to say that it's important to tell the reader where the information comes from; one example I used was, "if you, [name], told me that A causes B [example from paper], and I want to write that in my paper, I need to write that you said it. And we can do that like this." That opened up the discussion of attribution, and we went from there.

Conversations about plagiarism, at least conversations that explicitly addressed this topic, were less common, with the majority of respondents reporting that it arose in less than 10% of their consultations. The consultants' comments suggest that rather than discussing plagiarism explicitly, they aim to help students avoid plagiarism by strengthening their skills in related areas, such as citing and paraphrasing. As Peer 11 explained,

> It is important not to accuse the student of plagiarizing. If I thought a sentence was not paraphrased adequately (or at all!) then I would ask the student to explain to me what the sentence meant (e.g., "Oh, I am not in science, can you just explain this to me so I understand"). If the student cannot explain the sentence then I would talk about paraphrasing and why it is important for their learning and so that they do not get in trouble (better to hear it from a writing peer, even if a little awkward, than to go through an academic integrity issue with the university).

The sentiments of Peer 11 were widely shared among survey respondents, who studiously avoided even the appearance of challenging or questioning a student's integrity, giving students the benefit of the doubt as much as possible. Shifting the conversation to related skills provided one common way to steer clear of confrontational conversations.

Another aim of the study was to examine more deeply what specific topics are discussed during conversations about citing and referencing, paraphrasing, and plagiarism. To gather this information, the survey asked consultants to rank the most common topics that arose in these discussions (Table 22.1).

Table 22.1 Most common citing and referencing topics reported by consultants (1 being most common)

Rank	Citing & referencing	Paraphrasing	Plagiarism
1	Formatting	How to	Fear of accidentally plagiarizing
2	What to cite	Thoroughness	Defining plagiarism
3	Placement	Defining	Why instructors care about plagiarism
4	Style guide	Importance	Contract cheating
5	Importance of citing	Accuracy	Penalties
6	Other[a]	Other	Other[b]

[a]"Other" text entries: "That/why both in-text citations and a reference list are needed"; "It was fairly common for students to want to discuss the distinctions between footnote/endnote citations and bibliographic citations; usually, the assignment specified which citation style was to be used"
[b]"Other" text entries: "How to avoid accidentally plagiarizing"; "The spirit of referencing"

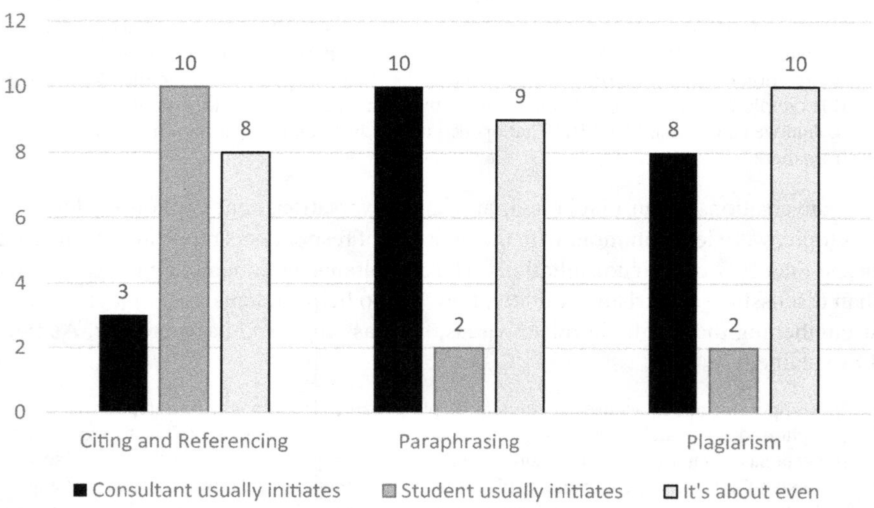

Fig. 22.2 Frequency of student and consultant initiation of conversations about academic integrity topics

Initiating Conversations About Academic Integrity

As Fig. 22.2 illustrates, in consultants' perceptions, initiation of conversations about plagiarism varied depending on specific topic: student clients were more likely than student consultants to begin conversations about citing and referencing, while student consultants were more likely to initiate conversations about paraphrasing or plagiarism. In all topic areas, there were many student consultants who indicated that clients and consultants were equally likely to initiate these conversations.

Student Staff Confidence in Addressing Academic Integrity Concerns

The data show that confidence in addressing academic integrity concerns was consistently high among the respondents. Across all academic integrity topics (citing and referencing, paraphrasing, and plagiarism), confidence was consistently high, with the majority of respondents agreeing or strongly agreeing that they felt confident having these conversations. On a five-point scale, the average confidence level was 4.7. Moreover, none of the respondents rated their confidence lower than 3 out of 5. It is reassuring to know that student staff feel comfortable initiating or responding to these issues, and this finding suggests in turn that training can focus on expanding consultants' strategies within these conversations.

Strategies for Supporting Academic Integrity

Valuable insights were found in consultants' strategies for supporting student skill development in the ethical and effective use of sources. Among the most prominent strategies were those that have been coded as asking curious questions; explaining the value of citing, referencing, and paraphrasing; oral paraphrasing; and using resources.

Curious Questions

Among the most common strategies cited by the consultants was the use of questions to begin conversations about academic integrity issues. In some cases, this approach dovetailed with the consultant's intention not to appear judgmental, such as in this advice shared by TA 8:

> Remember that plagiarism is a serious offence and accusation, so we want to make sure that we don't accuse someone of something that they've likely done inadvertently. I usually start with, "Where did you get that piece of information? Did you write that?" and have a conversation about the need to give credit where it's due.

As this example shows, questions enable consultants to keep students engaged in the consultation and help students think through their choices as writers. They also enable consultants to gather information before deciding what kinds of support are most needed.

Explaining Value

Another common strategy was to explain the value of citing and referencing, paraphrasing, and avoiding plagiarism ($n = 10$). In this strategy, consultants approached the topic by emphasizing the strategic importance or intrinsic usefulness of the conventions of source use. TA 10 also notes the importance of not promoting what they call "negative views about citing":

> I would try to relate to them in that citing can be tedious/annoying, but I would also be conscious about encouraging the negative views about citing. Crediting work is not only important for academic integrity but can also help students find other sources and be more critical about the sources they use.

TA 10's comment demonstrates the in-between place that student staff occupy, empathizing with students' experiences while also coaching students on how to adapt to the conventions and expectations of scholarship. Consistent with this example, student staff consistently asserted the authentic value of academic conventions of source use while at the same time acknowledging the challenge for new students of learning these practices.

Oral Paraphrasing

Several student consultants described asking students to explain source ideas out loud, a strategy coded as "oral paraphrasing." Peer 4 explained how they use this approach:

> Try to have the student explain to you what the literature is saying in words first without having it in front of them. Many students will paraphrase it well enough without realizing it, and then you can tell them that's all they have to write!

Similarly, TA 4 shared an example of taking a student from source to paraphrase:

> Once, I had a student that had trouble understanding how to avoid plagiarism in their paper. The student had a print-out of one of their sources and I asked them to locate the source of the information they were using in their paper. Next, I asked them to verbally explain to me that information. After that, I asked the student to write down what they had just told me. It took a bit of time, but we were able to paraphrase/summarize a small part of the content in a way that didn't incur in plagiarism and the student was able to understand the process of paraphrasing correctly.

These approaches reflect the usefulness of modeling writing strategies for students, as Ianetta and Fitzgerald (2016) note. In her article, "Revisioning Instructor-Writing Specialist Collaboration for Paraphrasing Instruction," Silvia Luisa Rossi (2022) describes the importance of providing paraphrasing instruction in a specific writing context. These examples demonstrate how peer-to-peer writing consultations provide an ideal opportunity for this kind of learning.

Using Resources

The writing centre provides a range of handouts on writing and referencing called "Fast Facts" and guidebooks for consultants and students, and there were many consultant responses ($n = 14$) that described using these as tools in their work with students. In one answer to "What advice would you provide to student consultants about helping students with citation and referencing?" TA 9 suggested:

> It's okay to grab a fast facts sheet or pull up the style guide online to help guide you as well. You can frame it as "Here is a resource that you can use even after the consultation ends; let's walk through how to find the information you'll need together."

By drawing on resources, student consultants provide another kind of modelling for students, demonstrating that source use and citation requires ongoing learning. These approaches emphasize that knowing how to find answers is as valuable as the answers themselves.

Additional Training Needs

As part of the survey, Peers and TAs were asked what additional training might be helpful to them in supporting students with academic integrity. Responses varied, including suggestions to cover referencing styles in greater detail; providing strategies for raising academic integrity concerns in consultations; instruction on how to teach paraphrasing strategies; and incorporating the university's academic integrity policy and website information into training materials.

Cultural Competence

The most common suggestion ($n = 6$) from student writing consultants was to increase the training about cultural differences in academic writing and how these might lead to unintentional plagiarism. TA 4 explains,

> I think that stronger training in cultural differences in academic writing will prove useful.... If the consultant is working with an international student and they find plagiarism in their paper, it's possible that a different writing culture is a reason why the student is (accidentally) plagiarizing. It shouldn't be assumed that they are plagiarizing on purpose!

There were several survey respondents who mentioned the importance of recognizing the additional challenges international students may face in adapting to academic norms in a Canadian academic context. Several noted, as TA 4 does, that international students may come from cultures where plagiarism is understood differently or not discussed at all.

Actively seeking to understand and engage with the diversity of our student population is critical to providing inclusive, welcoming, and accessible services. At the same time, scholars like Arabella Lyon argue that framing academic integrity as culturally rooted can lead to stereotyping international students as inherently "deficient" or "in need of remediation" (2009, p. 224). Similarly, Soni Adhikari (2018) argues that most international students, regardless of cultural background, already *do* know about plagiarism; problems of citation in their work are more often due to lack of citation skills, difficulties understanding content and context, or challenges with managing time. As Adhikari notes, "Instead of othering students based on how we believe their culture defines plagiarism and intellectual honesty, we can focus on teaching them practical skills that they need to learn" (p. 377). Revisiting our training with this perspective in mind could help our student staff avoid inadvertently othering students who are adapting to new academic and disciplinary conventions.

Role of the Consultant

An important theme that emerged from the survey responses was student consultants' perceptions of their roles. Consistent in the responses was the notion that consultants ought to be supportive insiders who help students learn to understand, negotiate, and apply academic conventions of source use. As Peer 5 explains, "You're helping them to understand the communicative framework they'll be working within for the next four years, and you're essentially providing insider tips!"

Consultants' commitment to being supportive and reassuring was tied to their perceptions of student writers' intent—specifically, consultants by and large interpreted students' lack of citations, patchwriting, or plagiarism as unintentional. Again, Peer 5: "Many students are simply concerned to get it right and not plagiarize accidentally; that's great. In my personal (and therefore anecdotal) experience, those who cheat deliberately are less likely to seek out writing help or guidance."

In consultants' perceptions, the plagiarism they observed was the result of an oversight, lack of knowledge or skill, or cultural differences. These positive beliefs about students' intent coincided, in my view, with consultants' commitment to intervening to protect students from the negative consequences of unintentional plagiarism, such as Peer 11, who noted, "better to hear it from a writing peer, even if a little awkward, than to go through an academic integrity issue with the university."

Conclusion

This study provides deeper insight into one Canadian writing centre's student consultant experiences of, approaches to, and beliefs about their roles in supporting academic integrity. Consistently throughout the data was the notion that the consultants see themselves as supportive, informed insiders who can intervene at a key point in students' learning and development as academic writers.

From an institutional perspective, these findings suggest that student consultants play important but largely unrecognized roles in supporting academic integrity in our universities. Their ability to relate to and empathize with students makes them an approachable source of information and skill development for anxious students who are concerned about accidentally plagiarizing; similarly, their knowledge and positionality makes them important role models and ambassadors for a wider culture of integrity on campus. By recognizing and promoting the role of these student staff, we may be able to contribute to the broader culture of integrity on our campus.

Key to writing centres' ability to contribute to a culture of integrity is our ability to navigate our complex positioning. Similar to many other university writing centres in Canada and the United States, the University of Guelph's writing centre plays a dual role of supporting students and promoting the values of the institution. Most of the time, these goals are mutually reinforcing; however, academic integrity and plagiarism bring with them a judicial aspect that complicates our role. How do we authentically support students who may be contravening the rules of the institution to which we are accountable? How do we uphold the values of the campus community without alienating individual students who come to us for support? The responses of student writing consultants suggest that they have found a way: by being informative and empathetic guides who are knowledgeable about guidelines and committed to understanding students' needs. By explicitly engaging student consultant teams in conversations about academic integrity and plagiarism, we can harness their insights and approaches to communicate our writing centre values to both the institution and our student clients in ways that are clear, respectful, and inclusive.

Two important limitations of this study are its single-institution focus and the small sample size. It is therefore important to understand the findings as informative themes and insights, rather than as predictive of future behaviours. However, future research could include more writing centres to explore the consistency of responses across institutions, allowing us to develop shared approaches to training and resource development. Another important dimension that could be explored in future research is the perspective of student visitors to the writing centre. Gathering these perspectives would help us better understand the experiences and beliefs of students and gauge the fit between consultant and student perspectives. Finally, in light of increasing use of online consultation formats, future research could explore how student consultants approach academic integrity support in a virtual environment.

References

Adam, L., Anderson, V., & Spronken-Smith, R. (2017). "It's not fair": Policy discourses and students' understandings of plagiarism in a New Zealand university. *Higher Education, 74*(1), 17–32.

Adhikari, S. (2018). Beyond culture: Helping international students avoid plagiarism. *Journal of International Students, 8*(1), 375–388.

Bluestein, S. A. (2015). Connecting student-faculty interaction to academic dishonesty. *Community College Journal of Research and Practice, 39*(2), 179–191.

Blum, S. D. (2011). *My word!: Plagiarism and college culture.* Cornell University Press.

Bridgewater, B., Pounds, E., & Morley, A. (2019). Designing a writing tutor-led plagiarism intervention program. *TLAR,* 11–27.

Broeckelman-Post, M. A. (2008). Faculty and student classroom influences on academic dishonesty. *IEEE Transactions on Education, 51*(2), 206–211.

Brown, R., Fallon, B., Lott, J., Matthews, E., & Mintie, E. (2007). Taking on Turnitin: Tutors advocating change. *Writing Center Journal, 27*(1), 7–29.

Bruffee, K. A. (1984). Collaborative learning and the "conversation of mankind." *College English, 46*(7), 635–652.

Buranen, L. (2009). A safe place: The role of librarians and writing centers in addressing citation practices and plagiarism. *Knowledge Quest, 37*(3), 24–33.

Christensen Hughes, J. M., & McCabe, D. (2006). Academic misconduct within higher education in Canada. *The Canadian Journal of Higher Education, 36*(2), 1–21. http://journals.sfu.ca/cjhe/index.php/cjhe/article/view/183537/183482

Clark, I. L., & Healy, D. (1996). Are writing centers ethical? *Writing Program Administration, 20*(1/2), 32–48.

Council of Writing Program Administrators. (2003). Defining and avoiding plagiarism: The WPA statement on best practices. http://wpacouncil.org

Eaton, S. E. (2017). Comparative analysis of institutional policy definitions of plagiarism: A pan-Canadian university study. *Interchange, 48*(3), 271–281. https://doi.org/10.1007/s10780-017-9300-7

Eaton, S. E., & Edino, R. I. (2018). Strengthening the research agenda of educational integrity in Canada: A review of the research literature and call to action. *International Journal for Educational Integrity, 14*(1), 5. https://doi.org/10.1007/s40979-018-0028-7
Gillespie, P., & Lerner, N. (2008). *The Longman guide to peer tutoring*. Longman.
Gruber, S. (1998). Coming to terms with contradictions: Online materials, plagiarism, and the writing center. *The Writing Center Journal, 19*(1), 49–71.
Gullifer, J., & Tyson, G. A. (2010). Exploring university students' perceptions of plagiarism: A focus group study. *Studies in Higher Education, 35*(4), 463–481.
Howard, R. M. (1992). A plagiarism pentimento. *Journal of Teaching Writing, 11*(2), 233–245.
Ianetta, M., & Fitzgerald, L. (2016). *The Oxford guide for writing tutors: Practice and research.*
Jurecka, G. (2004). Intellectual property paranoia and the writing center. *Praxis: A Writing Center Journal, 2*(1), 1–4.
Kleinfeld, E. (2016). Using citation analysis in writing center tutorials to encourage deeper engagement with sources. *Praxis: A Writing Center Journal, 13*(2), 52–58.
Lyon, A. (2009). "You Fail": Plagiarism, the ownership of writing, and transnational conflicts. *College Composition and Communication, 61*(2), W222–W239.
Mackiewicz, J., & Thompson, I. (2014). Instruction, cognitive scaffolding, and motivational scaffolding in writing center tutoring. *Composition Studies, 42*(1), 54–78.
Mackiewicz, J., & Thompson, I. (2018). Spoken written-language in writing center talk. *Linguistics and Education, 47*, 47–58.
North, S. M. (1984). The idea of a writing center. *College English, 46*(5), 433. https://doi.org/10.2307/377047
Pelzer, E. (2019). Writing center tutors take on plagiarism. *Praxis, 16*(3), 2–5.
Robinson-Zañartu, C., Peña, E. D., Cook-Morales, V., Peña, A. M., Afshani, R., & Nguyen, L. (2005). Academic crime and punishment: Faculty members' perceptions of and responses to plagiarism. *School Psychology Quarterly, 20*(3), 318–337.
Rossi, S. L. (2022). Revisioning instructor-writing specialist collaboration for paraphrasing instruction. *Academic Integrity in Canada*. Springer.
Stigmar, M. (2016). Peer-to-peer teaching in higher education: A critical literature review. *Mentoring & Tutoring: Partnership in Learning, 24*(2), 124–136.
Topping, K. J. (1996). The effectiveness of peer tutoring in further and higher education: A typology and review of the literature on JSTOR. *Higher Education, 32*(3), 321–345.
University of Guelph. (2020a). *About*. University of Guelph Website. https://www.uoguelph.ca/about
University of Guelph. (2020b). *Academic Misconduct—VIII. Undergraduate Degree Regulations and Procedures*. Undergraduate Calendar. https://www.uoguelph.ca/registrar/calendars

Kim Garwood has worked in academic support at the University of Guelph since 2007 and has collaborated on a national research project on academic integrity. She has a PhD from the University of Waterloo.

Chapter 23
Beyond the Traditional: Academic Integrity in Canadian Librarianship

Leeanne Morrow

Abstract Academic integrity and information literacy concepts are interwoven throughout academic processes. In Canada these are reflected in both secondary and postsecondary assessment environments. Academic librarians are well positioned within and beyond the academy to promote a culture of academic integrity to post-secondary and high school students. In 2008 authors Drinan and Bertram Gallant addressed the opportunity for librarians to take an active role in building a culture of integrity stating "The issue of plagiarism is one that cries out for the active participation of librarians not only in the academic integrity systems on their respective campuses, but also in the national and international academic integrity movement" (p. 137). The question is where are librarians in this movement in Canada? Beyond plagiarism, how far have librarians come in their involvement in academic integrity culture both on and off Canadian campuses? This chapter will look beyond the librarian's role in teaching information literacy and its principles in the classroom to further examine the inroads being made as an active partner with campus services and students in our communities. Connections between ACRL's six information literacy frames and academic integrity with a specific focus on "Scholarship as Conversation" and the role students' play in this process will be highlighted. Librarians have a pivotal role to play in moving the academic integrity conversation forward. Through their understanding of critical and ethical use of information they can be at the forefront of advocating for integrity in academic work and assisting in the success of students on and off campus.

Keywords Academic integrity · Information literacy · Outreach · Librarianship · Plagiarism · Citation · Canada

---

L. Morrow (✉)
University of Calgary, Calgary, Canada
e-mail: leeanne.morrow@ucalgary.ca

S. E. Eaton and J. Christensen Hughes (eds.), *Academic Integrity in Canada*, Ethics and Integrity in Educational Contexts 1,
https://doi.org/10.1007/978-3-030-83255-1_23

The professional work librarians do can often be a mystery to the campus community. The traditional perception of the library on campus is still often centered on its role as a research collection. Librarians have long been a profession that is well positioned to support the institutional goals of the university including supporting learners and researchers in navigating the vast information landscape of academic research. Combatting plagiarism and promoting proper attribution of sources is the one component of academic integrity that can be vital to both the research and teaching mission in post-secondary environments (Drinan & Bertram Gallant, 2008). This can easily be addressed by librarians through their information literacy instruction both inside the classroom and online. How do librarians in Canada support academic integrity in the academy? Are they adequately supporting the institutions priorities in this area? Are there any developments beyond librarians working solely in the area of teaching students about plagiarism and citation? This chapter will examine these question in addition to looking at opportunities for further development by research and learning library professionals across Canada.

Academic Integrity and Information Literacy

The International Centre for Academic Integrity has one of the most commonly accepted definition of academic integrity "as a commitment, even in the face of adversity, to six fundamental values: honesty, trust, fairness, respect, responsibility, and courage. From these values flow principles of behavior that enable academic communities to translate ideals to action." (International Centre for Academic Integrity, 2014).

The Association of College and Research Libraries (ACRL) has the most accepted and embraced definition for information literacy in North America:

> Information literacy is the set of integrated abilities encompassing the reflective discovery of information, the understanding of how information is produced and valued, and the use of information in creating new knowledge and participating ethically in communities of learning. (American Library Association, 2015)

The foundational framework built around this definition to guide when teaching learners has six frames. These frames include:

1. Authority Is Constructed and Contextual
2. Information Creation as a Process
3. Information Has Value
4. Research as Inquiry
5. Scholarship as Conversation
6. Searching as Strategic Exploration

Within this identified framework learning and modelling information literacy behaviours are further broken down to knowledge practices and dispositions. The core principles around academic integrity show up throughout these frames (American

Library Association, 2015). It is evident that these two definitions are connected and play an important role in the life of learners on campuses around the world. Academic integrity is most clearly embedded into the frame "Information Has Value". This frame and its dispositions indicate that learners will understand their role as "creators and users" of information particularly in a scholarly conversation (ACRL). The learner in this frame acknowledges the importance placed on citation and their responsibilities in respecting the ideas of others (ACRL). Frame number 5 centering on "Scholarship as Conversation" is another connection point where academic integrity values and practices appear in the information literacy framework. Here librarians can teach learners how to see themselves as active contributors to scholarly conversations through their work as researchers and writers. This is where researchers and writers will produce works that appropriately give credit to others in the field in which they are writing but also read in a discipline and identify works of knowledge that are authoritative and creditable in their field (American Library Association, 2015). The two definitions can exist nested together. It is important for learners and researchers to understand that you cannot consider a student population to be information literate unless they understand ethical knowledge creation. When our students of all ages can see they play a role in writing and citing in scholarly conversations where they contribute to knowledge creation, they can also see the importance placed on doing so with integrity.

As Lokse et al. (2017) share in their chapter on academic integrity in *Teaching Information Literacy in Higher Education* academic integrity not only helps to develop information literate students decision making skills it also helps ensure creditability in the future "production of new knowledge". Lokse et al. (2017) point out that helping students to understand they are not just empty vessels that are filled with new knowledge, but rather active participants in its production will further their motivation to comply with the "norms of academia" (p. 70). The authors build a strong connection between understanding academic integrity and its connections to research integrity.

"First, dealing with academic integrity is about the quality of student learning and formation. Second it is about the production of original, reliable and valid knowledge. The connection is that today's students are the future producers of new knowledge" (Lokse et al., 2017, p. 74). When librarians connect information literacy to academic integrity it strengthens students skill set. Thinking about the nesting of academic integrity within information literacy brings forth McCabe et al.'s (2012) notion of the "hidden curriculum". They address creating a "hidden curriculum" (p. 177) meaning offering student the opportunity to learn and practice academic integrity skills outside the classroom or outside obvious ethics courses. Often information literacy sessions offered by librarians give students the opportunity to discuss and explore issues related to whether a source is a "good" source, whether it's been created by an expert who can be trusted, or where and when we need to give credit to others in our research and writing. During these types of sessions students are developing their skills in a non-obvious, almost hidden way.

Plagiarism in the Canadian Context

In 2003 Christensen Hughes and McCabe conducted a study looking at the academic integrity behaviours and choices amongst Canadian post-secondary students. Based on an original survey conducted by the Center for Academic Integrity data was collected from eleven higher education institutions in Canada. This study was interesting in that it asked students to reflect on their experience in high school in addition to their experiences as an undergraduate or graduate student. One important finding from this critical work was that 73% of the participants admitted to cheating on written work (Christensen Hughes & McCabe, 2006, p. 8). Speaking to the role librarians can play around citing properly it should be noted that this study found that those students commonly reported improper citation or not citing at all while in high school. Christensen Hughes and McCabe (2006, p. 8) found similar results in the data from the undergraduate experience responses around citation but the number of students who admitted to this type of misconduct was much lower. The results from graduate students included the notable finding that 6% admitted to "fabrication or falsification of lab data" (p. 11). Librarians need to acknowledge that this happens in postsecondary environments to explain the implications on the breakdown of the scholarly conversation when data is manipulated as part of information literacy instruction.

The Librarian's Role

There is substantial literature centering on librarians' roles in advocating and educating around academic integrity, particularly coming from North American authors and researchers. In 1988 a foundational piece by Lorna Peterson (1988) examined traditional bibliographic instruction librarian's role in teaching about plagiarism. Lampert (2008) shares an overview of original research, including that of Peterson (1988), but with the addition of works by Auer and Krupar and Brandt that includes the early work around examining librarians, information literacy instruction and ethical use of information. Reviewing the developments over the last decade the major focus of the literature is on librarians work in preventing, detecting and educating around the topic of citation and plagiarism. Many authors have noted the critical (if often over looked) role a librarian can play in the integrity strategy of post-secondary institutions (Drinan & Bertram Gallant, 2008; Germek, 2009; Lampert, 2008; Synder Gibson & Chester-Fangman, 2011). As Synder Gibson and Chester-Fangman (2011) note librarians have been included in some of the broader literature around academic integrity but primarily the focus has been on plagiarism and the use of the librarians skills set in detecting possible plagiarized sources. Drinan and Bertram Gallant (2008) have a firm understanding of the role of librarians in helping students wade through the massive volume of information available to them in print and online. They point out the advantages the librarian has in being able to see and understand the skills it takes to navigate the twenty first century information landscape in a particular discipline (127). Germek (2009) suggests a laundry list of areas librarians should and could work in to improve the culture of integrity on campus. They specifically suggest that there should be a "comprehensive strategy" by the library to look at its role throughout the learning process around inhibiting plagiarism including using our online platforms like Libguides, our instruction sessions (moving beyond the one shot sessions), reference desk interactions addressing citations, and providing more workshops (p. 342).

Information Literacy and Academic Integrity Moving Beyond the Classroom

Synder Gibson and Chester-Fangman (2011) suggested that librarians partner with other units on campus to fully address academic integrity in the classroom and use these relationships to further their role at the institutional level. They suggest looking at building awareness of academic integrity policy on library websites and integrating into the information literacy instruction in the classroom. Both Germek (2009) and Greer et al. (2012) agreed that moving to an institutional approach to information literacy and academic integrity across all programs on campus, and extended information literacy sessions beyond the "one shot" that librarians normally offer should be a priority to help fix the problems of plagiarism. Germek (2009) claims ACRL's addressing of plagiarism is weak and could be improved. To test his theory that librarians are less likely to speak to students in their general instruction sessions about the importance of academic integrity and plagiarism he designed a survey for freshman composition teachers asking "is plagiarism commonly discussed by your librarian during instructional library sessions?". The results from this survey revealed that only 36.6% of librarians covered the topics of plagiarisms during class time. Germek (2009) found that often it was assumed that teaching about plagiarism was someone else's area of focus such as high school teachers or the instructors and not the librarians (Germek, 2009).

Synder Gibson and Chester-Fangman (2011) developed a survey sent to librarians and library staff in the United States asking them about their experience with plagiarism in the classroom. Three areas were of particular interest to the researchers:

1. Role that librarians are assuming in institution wide effort to combat plagiarism
2. Collaborations between librarians and instructors seeking to address this issue and
3. Approaches that librarians are using to teach students to avoid plagiarism. (p. 136)

610 librarians from across the United States completed the survey with participants primarily from post-secondary and a smaller percentage from school and public settings. The results were interesting in painting a clearer picture about libraries and their librarians' involvement with anti-plagiarism instruction in the US. Even a decade ago, when asked whether librarians should have a role in teaching about

plagiarism, 530 respondents indicated that it was a part of a librarian's role. Roughly a third of all respondents to the survey indicated they participated in the development of their institutions approach to plagiarism through policy development. 50% of those who responded said they had partnered with faculty or departments to address issues of plagiarism one to five times a year. And two thirds of the respondents indicated they had been asked to take part in an "investigation" around student plagiarism (Synder Gibson & Chester-Fangman, 2011). This makes sense when considering the literature around the commonly held belief that librarians are often considered as experts when it comes to taking on a detective role in plagiarism cases.

Appearing around 2004–2006 the possibility of taking academic integrity instruction online begins to emerge in the library literature. As Jackson (2006) notes in one of the first published articles looking specifically at online plagiarism tools "Web-based information literacy tutorials allow students to learn important research skills at their own pace, outside traditional class time and classrooms" (p. 419). The article describes a project at San Jose State University looking at the possibilities of the library and partners developing more tools to support students in their learning around plagiarism. Outside of the traditional class based instruction much of the literature has focused on building and sharing library led online plagiarism tutorials. Based on his analysis of the results from his 2009 study Germek suggested using library technology to not only define academic integrity but to produce tools that can show students first hand examples. One prominent early example from 2012 was the tutorial developed at the Oakland University Library and Writing Centre (Greer et al., 2012). This successful 6 part tutorial was developed by a collaborative task force specifically looking at building learning outcomes based interactive tutorials for all students at the University. It was one of the first articles to suggest the benefits of embedding the tutorials into the learning management software of institutions (Greer et al., 2012). Since these early developments tutorials have grown in numbers and can be found on library websites across North America. Building on the advice and research shared by these authors and researchers since 2006 librarians have often partnered with Writing Centre or Student Service units on campus to create add on tutorials when requested by the institution or when the librarians felt the one hour instruction session was not enough time to cover the topics of plagiarism and citation (Greer et al., 2012; Diamond, 2019; Park et al., 2011; Evers Ard & Ard, 2019; Creed-Dikeogu, 2018). Tutorial development seemed to be the next logical step in supporting students beyond the classroom.

Environmental Scan—Canadian context

Although there is not a great deal of literature around librarians' role in academic integrity systems in Canada, there are very good examples that highlight in roads and advancements that have been made by Canadian librarians in the last decade. Many institutions are working to enhance the student experience around academic integrity through the library. Liu and Pillon (2016) share their experience delivering in person workshops to international students at the University of Windsor and their move to building ACRL information literacy framework based online modules for further student learning around plagiarism. Sheridan College is a good example of an institution that has a strong in person and online support for academic integrity through their first-year librarian program (Goodfellow et al., 2018). Their partnership between the Library and Writing Centre allows for the integration of information literacy skills around plagiarism throughout their work with students. The University of Manitoba liaison librarians are working with students to provide post-discipline education around citing, reference style and managing sources effectively (Albrecht et al., 2020). Expansion of their work with students will include building more supports around critical reading, understanding sources and sharing the value of working with librarians. The author's own institution provides opportunities for librarians to work with students who have academic misconduct violations. Four librarians partner with the Academic Integrity Coordinator and the Student Success Centre to develop and teach sessions addressing plagiarism and how to avoid it as well as inappropriate collaboration. Additionally their work promoting an understanding of contract cheating around the International Day of Contract Cheating is a valuable contribution to campus discussions. This important day every October has become a regular occurrence on many campuses throughout Canada and around the world. A scan of Twitter and the hashtag #defeatthecheat shows libraries and their staff from across Canada taking an active role in this important academic integrity initiatives. Ideas range from workshops to interactive, learning displays to contests. Libraries often encourage their student peer volunteers to be involved in this day and have them engage one-to-one with students in the library around academic integrity.

Reviewing the websites of many Canadian post-secondary libraries and particularly the library websites of Canada's U15 can provide some context around the depth of support for academic integrity offered through the libraries. The U15 universities are a group of research intensive postsecondary institutions in Canada. The library websites of thirteen institutions of the U15 had strong content promoting academic integrity and as one might guess the focus was on citation and plagiarism. Almost every U15 library site displayed some formal connection to the University's academic integrity office, handbook or institutional definition through links from research support tools such as Libguides. Some libraries showed evidence of an expanded role around academic integrity such as UBC's Chapman Learning Commons. This unit within UBC's library system is taking the library lead on academic integrity and has developed extensive resources around various aspects of academic integrity including general citation, citing data and respecting copyright. Their role has developed over a long period of time as their work was noted in Drinan and Bertram Gallant in 2008.

It is evident when reviewing the U15 library sites that many librarians and library staff have contributed to the development of online academic integrity tutorials or videos. Most tutorials or videos explicitly highlight the library's contribution but are built in partnership with campus writing support services units. The Foundational Research Tutorials developed by the University of Alberta Libraries showcase a great example of the libraries contribution these types of learning tools. They scatter topics related to academic integrity throughout their series and finish with a plagiarism module. Beyond the U15 websites a simple Google search of "academic integrity and tutorials and library and Canada" will bring forth outstanding academic integrity contributions from libraries across the country. An example of cross unit collaboration based in a Learning Commons is York University's SPARK (Student Papers and Academic Research Kit) an e-learning tool which features material developed by the Learning Skills Centre, the Learning Commons and the Writing Department. University of Waterloo Library's "Academic integrity tutorial" features definitions and scenarios for students to work through around academic integrity. They feature the option to "chat" with the library on the tutorial page which is a great example of connecting services to modules for further learning. These are just a few examples of the work that libraries are taking part in on campuses throughout Canada.

Many Canadian librarians have begun to take part in the publishing stream around academic integrity. Of particular note is the 2020 Kwantlen Polytechnic University Pressbook "Academic Integrity" created by librarian Ulrike Kestler (see Kestler, 2020). This open access book covers topics like understanding academic integrity, understanding plagiarism, how to avoid plagiarism through both proper referencing and practicing proper writing skills. Within this interactive book you will find short readings, quizzes and other activities students can do to engage in these topics. This type of new resource can be shared and used by other institutions is an outstanding example of ways Canadian librarians can and should be contributing to the academic integrity conversation nationally. Another in-press title coming soon is Academic Plagiarism: Librarians' Solo and Collaborative Efforts to Curb Plagiarism. This title edited by Rysavy and Michalak will include multiple chapters from Canadian librarians working at institutions across the country.

Observations and Opportunities

Academic Librarians and High Schools

As many librarians and faculty members know writing and research can be a challenge for first year students entering post-secondary right out of high school. Many students come to university without having had experience in citing and writing. Many enter without highly developed information literacy skills. Rather than trying to place blame anywhere there is an opportunity for librarians to play a role in reaching out to local high schools. Highlights from McCabe's initial research in 1999 with junior high school students found that there were lessons to be learned from the self-reported academic integrity experiences. He found evidence to support the belief that cheating habits developed early. Initial results from the surveys included that 74% of junior high students admitted to cheating on a test. Initiating a second, larger survey in 2000 McCabe et al. (2012) found 81% of junior high students reported some form of test cheating or one or more instances of plagiarism.

With the knowledge that there are academic integrity challenges early in a student's life what role can libraries play in mitigating this? A recent article from Pennsylvania Libraries: Research and Practice reports on the decline of librarians in public schools in the United States and demonstrates how this loss of library expertise can negatively impact those entering their first year at a university or college (Lysiak, 2020). Various innovative projects are highlighted in this article to meet the needs of transitioning first year students including building modules around citing and writing and developing embedded mandatory modules across the curriculum. Seeing similar challenges at their institution in Louisana, Magale Library at Centenary College in 2012 began offering three different outreach opportunities to local high schools and their school librarians to help increase students comfort and familiarity with academic integrity and information literacy skills (Wrenn & Kohl, 2012). These community outreach programs included building professional development opportunities for local school and public librarians around academic integrity and offering supplemental instruction to student transitioning from high school to university. In reviewing Canadian academic library websites, it is evident that many post-secondary libraries offer spaces and collection access to high school students in Canada. There are institutions such as York University, University of Toronto, University of Victoria and University of Calgary which go a step further to offer on-campus information literacy instruction to their local high school student population. This extra preparation gives prospective students not only an introduction to campuses and spaces but also to introductory research experiences. Having some familiarity with information literacy and academic integrity before entering first year can definitely benefit students. Many universities and colleges in Canada include institutional goals of reaching out to the community. Many of their libraries have outreach librarians whose work it is to fulfill the library side of this community engagement. Providing opportunities for local high school students to experience researching, writing and citing through working with librarians on campuses is a great way to prepare student early for their post-secondary life. Christensen Hughes and McCabe (2006) suggested "Perhaps greater collaboration is needed between high schools and universities..." (p. 16). Time spent reaching out to high schools can lead to better academic integrity outcomes.

There is very little North American literature on post-secondary outreach programs to high schools on academic integrity. Wagg and McKinney (2020) researchers in the UK, investigated the value of outreach programs between higher education institutions and high schools specifically looking at aspects of information literacy programming. Their findings indicate that this kind of program "is an effective mechanism for bridging the social worlds of schools and higher education; for creating partnerships and knowledge sharing between institutions; for breaking down social barriers and inequalities; and for developing critically aware, independent learners" (p. 63).

Establishing an Effective Outreach Program

Often higher education institutions in Canada have strategic goals that focus on connections with surrounding communities. These goals are often met through strategic research partnerships. At the University of Calgary the Libraries and Cultural Resources unit implements community engagement strategic goal by supporting students and teachers in the K-12 environment through the delivery of a well-established outreach program. Students from eight high schools throughout the city of Calgary visit the Library at the University of Calgary at least twice a year, sometimes up to four times a year, to learn about and build hands-on skills in all aspects of information literacy. All classes are taught by librarians and staff who work with the students through the research process from finding a question, through looking for background information, to citation. Over the years of teaching in this outreach program visiting teachers and their school administration expressed a keen interest in having the librarians extend the information literacy focus to cover the interrelated topic of academic integrity. This opening allowed for the development of a more complete program around academic integrity for interested high schools, their students and their teachers. Schools now have the option to attend both the information literacy component of the program and the academic integrity piece. Some schools have requested the academic integrity piece be offered as a separate class which the librarians are able to deliver online.

What makes this an effective, accessible program at the University of Calgary? Part of the effectiveness is related to what Wagg and McKinney (2020) identify as barriers. In their research schools identified "taking time out of the curriculum, staffing and resources and cost of travel" as reasons for not taking part in outreach opportunities for their students in regard to building information literacy skills (61). The high school information literacy and academic integrity program at the University of Calgary works to eliminate as many of the barriers as possible. It has shifted entirely online during the COVID-19 pandemic and will remain as an online option for schools who may not be able to visit the campus due to transportation costs and logistics. Additionally the resources and staffing for this outreach program are entirely provided by the librarians and staff at the University. The librarians and staff work with the teachers to plan how the classes will relate to the curriculum. Addressing these barriers helps to ease the access to effective learning for students in both the information literacy arena as well as academic integrity.

To establish a program like this there are some key factors that will make success more likely. First, the initiative should support institutional goals such as engaging with the community and recruitment. Second library administration working with interested librarians should identify how the program can address those goals and their own priorities. A priority for the University of Calgary library is to give incoming students an advantage in understanding more about academic integrity and information literacy before entering first year. The goal at the University of Calgary is not only to build skill sets around research, critical thinking and integrity awareness but to showcase the University to the students and give them some idea of what the expectations will be for future work in a post-secondary environment. This can speak to the University's focus on recruitment. McCabe et al. (2012) suggest creating marketing material that can be used when promoting your institution during recruitment activities to high schools and highlighting the culture of integrity that is in place and the expectations required in your educational institution. Applying this lens to the creation of an academic integrity outreach program one might think of the instruction delivered by librarians to high school students as the marketing material and the opportunity to showcase the culture at your institution. Third, the initiative needs to address real needs in the community. In Calgary, there are very few professional librarians working in the school system, and therefore little formal information literacy instruction. Some schools have seen the program as a way to fill this gap in their students' education and give them advantages as graduates. Fourth, operationally it is helpful to identify both librarians and library staff interested in assisting with the program. Having more than one librarian able to teach academic integrity content allows for flexibility in program hours and offerings. Developing fluency in all aspects of academic integrity, beyond citation and plagiarisms is also crucial. Building from general cheating and plagiarism questions students will ask everything from "what happens if I have a violation"to very specific "how I can paraphrase better so I don't plagiarize". Having staff and librarians who can answer these questions is important. Having other administrative supports such as an online intake form is useful. This allows schools to share information in advance and works for the planning process. Building on what is offered for students, there is the potential to offer professional development opportunities for teachers in K-12 around academic integrity. This can be done by reaching out to the schools and school board administration to offer opportunities both in person and online to develop better awareness of academic integrity challenges. The University of Calgary has recently expanded its professional development offerings to include a full day workshop on academic integrity awareness in K-12 offered through a partnership between a librarian and faculty member in the school of education.

Considering the overall goals for your institution, staffing, community needs and what you need operationally is important to establishing a successful academic integrity outreach program. By doing this pre-first year preparation your library and librarians are contributing to recruitment and retention of students in first year.

Moving Beyond Plagiarism

The literature indicates librarians in Canada and North American are actively contributing to the areas of education around traditional definitions of plagiarism and citation on their campuses. But what about other aspects of academic integrity? There seems to be little evidence of librarians working with students to understand their role in academic misconduct like falsification or fabrication of data or collusion. As Drinan and Bertram Gallant (2008) suggest, because librarians critically evaluate, accumulate, store and share information and intellectual property they are well positioned to act as "key agents of coherence in the rapid flows of intellectual experience" (p. 127). This role beyond plagiarism and citation can be expanded to include more support for the foundational understanding of knowledge creation. In turn this can lead to embracing both academic integrity and information literacy. When working with students to help them understand the importance placed on producing data that is trust worthy and accurate, librarians can share their vast knowledge of the current and past "misinformation" or "fake news" world. When students can relate and see the impact misinformation has had on their own lives and how data that has been falsified can impact the planet, they seem to be able to value academic integrity more highly in their work. Both University of Calgary and University of Manitoba have librarians working with students who have been disciplined for academic misconduct. The University of Calgary librarians deliver the mandatory courses that are required to be completed after a violation occurs. These courses explore the student's role in creating knowledge and actively contributing to the truthful scholarly conversations in their field. The University of Manitoba librarians meet one-to-one with students who have been disciplined for academic misconduct to build their citation and research skills (L. Gervais, personal communication, December 14, 2020). Many librarians across the country are untapped resources when it comes to working with students as part of academic misconduct consequences. Their expertise in information literacy and citation band their understanding of knowledge creation itself to the role of educating those students who have encountered challenges.

Additional Programming

Libraries are intended to be a space for dialogue and engagement. There are opportunities to use library spaces as venues for more dialogue around academic integrity and as aspects related to this topic. The topic of building students' identity as authors is a crucial area more libraries could play a role in. "authorial identity" is defined by Elander et al. (2010) as "the sense a writer has of themselves as author and the textual identity they construct in their writing" (p. 159). According to Elander et al. there is evidence in the literature looking at the connection between accidental or unintentional plagiarism and lack of strong authorial identity. In their research, these scholars looked at implementing an intervention that explored building the confidence and identity of students as authors as well as providing instruction in some of the mechanics of avoiding plagiarism including proper paraphrasing. They measured using 6 different scales including: confidence in writing, understanding authorship and knowledge to avoid plagiarism. The results from this study indicated that educating students early in their learning journey around the topic of authorial identity and their specific role in writing as well as giving them some understanding of plagiarism had a positive impact in reducing unintentional plagiarism. From this research 66% of students reported they wrote better assignments and 86% of students reported they believed the interventions helped them avoid plagiarism (Elander et al., 2010).

So how would libraries contribute to building authorial identity? Cheung et al. (2018) explored this same topic but focused on the experiences and beliefs held around authorial identity by academics. Results from their qualitative exploration included a discussion of "authorial goals" or goals set out by the writer that focus on intention and communication rather than on writing for a grade. Results from this study suggested if students were able to understand writing as contributing to the construction of new knowledge rather than solely as mimicking models of academic writing in their discipline, then a more authentic, intentional voice would emerge. As one participant claimed "There's a huge difference between having writing skills and actually being a writer" (p. 1476). The finding also indicated that a possible way to indirectly support students' academic integrity goals of avoiding plagiarizing would be to emphasize respecting the community they are writing in. This could be done through embedding students in activities where they see themselves as active authors in their discipline community (Cheung et al., 2018). Librarians can explore options of more programming around providing opportunities for students to hear directly from academic writers about their experiences. The library could host events where students, both undergraduate and graduate, are offered the opportunity to present their writing and their research to others on campus. As Cheung et al. (2018) suggest this gives them the opportunity to perceive "oneself as part of the academic community" (p. 1480). Librarians can encourage this type of confidence building by working with discipline based classes to explore the non-academic literature in a subject. This could involve students reading and discussing not only the validity and truthfulness in say, a blog post, but also the writing style of the author (Cheung et al., 2018). Putting a focus on the priority of respecting themselves as authors, understanding the community in which they are writing both speaks to the ACRL frame of "Scholarship as a Conversation" and the disposition that students see themselves in as builders of new knowledge with a responsibility to enter into the conversation by respecting and valuing the contribution of others. (American Library Association, 2015). Librarians can build the skill sets of students as authors and in turn contribute to students writing better, more truthful assignments by seeing the connections and the opportunities they have in their role as educator both inside and outside the classroom.

Conclusion

Librarians understanding of the research process and how knowledge is created and shared give them the perfect perspective to take a leading role in the development of academic integrity in schools and on campuses everywhere. When offered a seat at the table both at the curriculum development level and the policy development level a librarian can contribute their unique perspective of helping dig into the value base around research and academic integrity (Lokse et al., 2017). Librarians can expand their role and share their expertise in understanding academic integrity at a broader institution-wide level as Drinan and Bertram Gallant state "librarians should see themselves as active, indeed proactive, participants in the design and operation of academic integrity systems" (2009). How can librarians become more involved in academic integrity? Reach out to the campus units involved in this area such as writing support services, teaching and learning centres or student services. Ask them to partner with the library on developing more in person and online supports. Make a connection with the units that do recruitment on campus to share information around classes that the library can offer to high schools to promote recruitment. Ensure the library's online guides and website always point to the institution's policies on academic integrity. Finally make sure the discipline-based instruction offered by liaison librarians embeds some elements of academic integrity into the curriculum and highlight this to faculty.

Academic librarians in Canada are taking a more proactive role both online and in person in contributing to the supports offered on campuses to students around academic integrity. They are offering workshops, building tutorials and becoming a central source of support and expertise for students and faculty. While their experience may lie in a more traditional role as educator around citation and information literacy, this can be expanded into assistance around other integrity topics like inappropriate collaboration or falsification and fabrication. There are untapped opportunities for Canadian librarians and libraries to contribute to the more holistic experience of academic integrity including offering outreach to the greater community to better prepare students for a post-secondary learning experience as well as expanding programming in libraries to cover broader skill development around research and writing. It is encouraging to see the expanding role librarians are taking in Canada and around the world in academic integrity. They bring a unique perspective to the academic integrity systems in post-secondary environments everywhere.

References

Albrecht, V., Clark, S., & Winkler, J. (2020). Sweet dreams? Librarians' roles in academic integrity. *OLA superconference.* http://accessola2.com/superconference2020/Sessions/2ThursJan30/OLASC_Sweet%20Dreams.pdf

American Library Association. (2015). Framework for information literacy for higher education. http://www.ala.org/acrl/standards/ilframework

Cheung, K. Y. F., Elander, J., Stupple, E. J. N., & Flay, M. (2018). Academics' understandings of the authorial academic writer: A qualitative analysis of authorial identity. *Studies in Higher Education, 43*(8), 1468–1483. https://doi.org/10.1080/03075079.2016.1264382

Christensen Hughes, J. M., & McCabe, D. L. (2006). Academic misconduct within higher education in Canada. *Canadian Journal of Higher Education, 36*(2), 1–21.

Creed-Dikeogu, G. F. (2018). The politics behind the library plagiarism tutorial: A case study. *Kansas Library Association College and University Libraries Section Proceedings, 8*(1), 1. https://doi.org/10.4148/2160-942X.1071

Diamond, K. (2019). Rejecting the criminal narrative: Designing a plagiarism avoidance tutorial. *Journal of Electronic Resources Librarianship, 31*(4), 232–240. https://doi.org/10.1080/1941126X.2019.1669962

Drinan, P. M., & Bertram Gallant, T. (2008). Plagiarism and academic integrity systems. *Journal of Library Administration, 47*(3–4), 125–140. https://doi.org/10.1080/01930820802186472

Elander, J., Pittam, G., Lusher, J., Fox, P., & Payne, N. (2010). Evaluation of an intervention to help students avoid unintentional plagiarism by improving their authorial identity. *Assessment and Evaluation in Higher Education, 35*(2), 157–171. https://doi.org/10.1080/02602930802687745

Evers Ard, S., & Ard, F. (2019). The library and the writing centre build a workshop: Exploring the impact of an asynchronous online academic integrity course. *New Review of Academic Librarianship, 25*(2–4), 218–243. https://doi.org/10.1080/13614533.2019.1644356

Germek, G. P. (2009). Imagine no possessions: Librarians, the net-generation student, and the imminent victory of plagiarism. *College & Undergraduate Libraries, 16*(4), 338–357. https://doi.org/10.1080/10691310903356000

Goodfellow, J., Traynor, M., Palombi, D., & Clark, A. (2018). Promoting and Supporting Academic Integrity at Sheridan College. Publications and Scholarship. 7. https://source.sheridancollege.ca/lls_publ/7

Greer, K., Swanberg, S., Hristova, M., & Switzer, A. T. (2012). Beyond the web tutorial: Development and implementation of an online, self-directed academic integrity course at Oakland University. *The Journal of Academic Librarianship, 38*(5), 251–258. https://doi.org/10.1016/j.acalib.2012.06.010

International Centre for Academic Integrity. (2014). *Fundamental Values*. https://www.academicintegrity.org/fundamental-values/

Jackson, P. A. (2006). Plagiarism instruction online: Assessing undergraduate students' ability to avoid plagiarism. *College & Research Libraries, 67*(5), 418–428. https://crl.acrl.org/index.php/crl/article/view/15820

Kestler, U. (2020). *Academic integrity*. Kwantlen Polytechnic University. https://kpu.pressbooks.pub/academicintegrity/

Lampert, L. D. (2008). Student academic integrity. In C. Cox & E. Blakesley Lindsay (Eds.), *Information literacy instruction handbook* (pp. 149–163). American Library Association.

Liu, G., & Pillon, K. (2016). Enhancing international students' library and academic skills at the University of Windsor, Canada. *International Leads, 30*(3), 7–8.

Lokse, M., Lag, T., Solberg, M., Andreassen, H. N., & Stenersen, M. (2017). Teaching information literacy in higher education: Effective teaching and active learning. Chandos Publishing.

Lysiak, L. (2020). Academic integrity: Developing an approach students can own! *Pennsylvania Libraries: Research & Practice, 8*(1), 58–63. https://www.palrap.org/ojs/index.php/palrap/article/viewFile/217/785

McCabe, D. L., Butterfield, K. D., & Trevino, L. K. (2012). *Cheating in college: Why students do it and what educators can do about it*. John Hopkins University Press.

Park, S., Mardis, L. A., & Ury, C. J. (2011). I've lost my identity-oh, there it is… in a style manual: Teaching citation styles and academic honesty. *Reference Services Review, 39*(1), 42–57. https://doi.org/10.1108/00907321111108105

Peterson, L. (1988). Teaching academic integrity: Opportunities in bibliographic instruction. *Research Strategies, 6*(4), 168–176.

Synder Gibson, N., & Chester-Fangman, C. (2011). The librarian's role in combating plagiarism. *Reference Services Review, 39*(1), 132–150. https://doi.org/10.1108/00907321111108169

University of Alberta (n.d.). Foundational Research Tutorial. https://www.library.ualberta.ca/tutorials/foundational

University of Waterloo (n.d.). Academic Integrity Tutorial. https://uwaterloo.ca/library/research-supports/academic-integrity/academic-integrity-tutorial

Wagg, S., & McKinney, P. (2020). Information literacy outreach between universities and schools: A case study. *Journal of Information Literacy, 14*(2). https://doi.org/10.11645/14.2.2692

Wrenn, C., & Kohl, K. (2012). Ensuring academic integrity through community and campus outreach. *Codex: The Journal of the Louisiana Chapter of the ACRL, 2*(1), 58–70. http://journal.acrlla.org/index.php/codex/article/view/64

York University (n.d.). Student papers and academic research kit. https://spark.library.yorku.ca/academic-integrity-using-and-citing-sources/

Leeanne Morrow is the Associate University Librarian, Student Learning and Engagement at the University of Calgary. She holds a Master's degree in Library and Information Studies from the University of Alberta and a Bachelor of Arts in Art History from the University of Calgary.

Part V
Institutional Responses

Chapter 24
The Barriers to Faculty Reporting Incidences of Academic Misconduct at Community Colleges

Melanie Hamilton and Karla Wolsky

Abstract Academic misconduct is a growing concern within Canadian higher education and around the world. Research suggests that university faculty have an extensive history of addressing academic misconduct, with an increased focus on detection and prevention. There has been little research, however, on faculty teaching in community colleges and their experiences with reporting and prevention, particularly within the Canadian context. As concern with academic misconduct continues to rise, we suggest that there needs to be more focus on these issues, particularly with respect to approaches that support a cultural shift with faculty that encompasses the fundamental values of academic integrity. For this to occur, it is essential for educational institutions to understand the forces that influence potential dishonest behaviors among students, create policies to address and support academic integrity, while creating a culture of academic integrity which supports both faculty and students alike. Faculty play a crucial role in creating environments that expound and uphold the values of academic integrity. Faculty are the frontline contact, espousing the values and expectations of their institution to students, monitoring, and reporting. Our scholarship of teaching and learning (SoTL) research was motivated by the aim to help community college faculty address the issue of academic misconduct within their classrooms and institutional environments. Barriers to reporting academic dishonesty, identified by faculty, include time and workload in reporting, a perceived lack of institutional support from administration and applicable institutional policies, as well as the perceived threat felt by faculty in reporting incidents.

Keywords Academic integrity · Faulty reporting · SoTL · Canada · College perspective

M. Hamilton (✉) · K. Wolsky
Lethbridge College, Lethbridge, Canada
e-mail: melanie.hamilton@lethbridgecollege.ca

K. Wolsky
e-mail: karla.wolsky@lethbridgecollege.ca

S. E. Eaton and J. Christensen Hughes (eds.), *Academic Integrity in Canada*, Ethics and Integrity in Educational Contexts 1,
https://doi.org/10.1007/978-3-030-83255-1_24

Introduction

The purpose of this chapter is to provide an understanding of the challenges and barriers perceived by faculty teaching within community colleges in Canada in identifying and responding to incidences of academic misconduct. Community colleges within Canada have a long-standing history of providing publicly funded, open-access educational programs; an education-for-all approach supporting individuals' edifying and workforce training needs. While programming varies from province to province and amongst institutions, the prevalence of academic misconduct remains a universal phenomenon. This is in part due to the complex nature of academic integrity and ambiguous roles in the ownership of and responsibility for upholding institutional cultures of integrity (Gottardello & Karabag, 2020).

As much of the literature examines this phenomenon from the lens of student responsibility, there is a gap in understanding faculty responsibilities for teaching and upholding the principles of academic integrity, particularly within Canadian community colleges. This chapter addresses this gap, presenting findings from our research on the perceived barriers identified by faculty in reporting academic misconduct. These hindrances include time and workload involved in reporting incidents; perceived lack of support by senior administration; faculty's lack of awareness of institutional policies related to academic integrity; and the perceived threats to faculty if they choose to report incidents.

It is essential to understand the faculty perspective within the community college environment and perceived barriers in order to provide appropriate and adequate support to address these impediments. This chapter will offer ways in which community colleges and, by extension, all post-secondary institutions can better equip their faculty to understand, communicate, teach, and uphold the fundamental principles of academic integrity; honesty, trust, respect, responsibility, and courage (International Center for Academic Integrity [ICAI] 2021). This includes advocating for clear and concise academic policies, professional development for faculty around an array of topics, and advocating for faculty support and resources.

We write this chapter wearing many hats. According to Eaton (2021), addressing academic integrity issues requires a multi-stakeholder approach. At the community college level, we work comfortably within the 4M Framework (Kenny & Eaton, 2022). At the micro level, we both have taught within nursing education for a combined total of over 30 years. We have seen many instances of academic integrity violations in the classroom including plagiarism, cheating on exams and projects, and contract cheating. Furthermore, we have seen instances of dishonesty in the clinical setting such as falsifying documents and assessments. We understand first-hand that faculty struggle with how to detect and whether to report academic integrity violations.

Wolsky has previously been the academic chair for the School of Health Sciences and Allied Health programs as well as the Bachelor of Nursing program where she was responsible to monitor and report academic integrity violations. She currently teaches within the Bachelor of Nursing program, working alongside faculty, and advocating for a culture of academic integrity. Hamilton is an educational developer and currently works at the meso level in the Centre for Teaching and Learning as the academic integrity lead. Along with a team, Hamilton ensures there is professional development for all college employees who teach and support students, related to academic integrity. We understand the barriers to reporting academic dishonesty as we have worked side by side with the faculty who have identified them. We chose to complete a scholarship of teaching and learning (SoTL) research project on academic integrity as "developing personal and informal networks of support is essential for supporting academic integrity" (Eaton, 2021, p. 77) in addition to the outcomes of the study.

Background

Despite faculty efforts to encourage students not to engage in academic misconduct, evidence suggests that academic misconduct remains rampant in higher education and is a growing concern on college and university campuses worldwide (Christensen Hughes & McCabe, 2006; Madara & Namango 2016). The continued advancement of technology-assisted educational practices has contributed to the continuing rise of academic misconduct (Anney & Mosha, 2015; Bristor & Burke, 2016) and while software for detecting plagiarism can help ease the burden of verifying referenced material, it is costly and not available at all educational institutions (Anney & Mosha, 2015). This has left faculty feeling frustrated and discouraged, as they attempt to stay one step ahead of new and innovative cheating methods (DiBartolo & Walsh, 2010).

Academic integrity polices are one-way institutions can address this emergent issue as part of a systemic approach. Bretag et al. (2011) undertook an analysis of 39 Australian universities' academic integrity policies to identify exemplar policies. This was done under the supposition that "a culture of academic integrity is central to all aspects of policy and practice" (p. 2). Additional research studies identified that even though institutional policies related to academic integrity exist, faculty are often reluctant to adhere to these policies (Bertram Gallant, 2008; Bertram Gallant & Drinan 2006) or choose at their discretion, a variety of ways in which to address the situation (Bristor & Burke, 2016). This may include a formal code of conduct reprimand, a one-on-one teaching opportunity with or without official reporting, or a chance to redo the assessment (Keener et al., 2019).

McCabe (1993) was one of the first authors to explore faculty reactions to suspected incidents of academic misconduct. He found that faculty were reluctant to report academic integrity violations formally, preferring instead to handle violations one-on-one, and depending on the severity of the event, give students a warning. Unfortunately, over 30 years later, faculty remain reluctant to address and report incidents of student academic misconduct. The International Centre for Academic Integrity (ICAI) espouses that academic integrity should be a fundamental component in education and is foundational in preparing students to succeed (ICAI, 2021). Whether students intentionally or unintentionally engage in unethical academic behavior, it is most often left to front-line faculty to educate and monitor students' academic activities. So why are faculty so resistant to report these incidents?

Faculty are concerned that reporting academic misconduct may negatively affect their employment in terms of professional reputations, application for tenure, and anxious whether their fellow peers would support them through the reporting process (Fontana, 2009; Tayan, 2017) in additional to potential litigation by the student. Faculty experience significant anxiety and stress related to the physiological discomfort experienced in reporting a student. They fear receiving poor student evaluations and are concerned with potentially damaging relationships with future students (Blau et al., 2018; Christensen Hughes & McCabe, 2006; Keith-Spiegel et al., 2010; Thomas, 2017).

The time required in reporting and attending a hearing is also perceived as a deterrent to reporting. Faculty are unenthusiastic to take on the enormous burden of reporting acts of academic misconduct, as faculty who had previously reported such incidents seemed unwilling to go through the arduous process again in the future (Eaton et al., 2020; Keith-Spiegel et al., 2010; Thomas 2017). According to Schneider (1999), a heavy teaching workload is one of the main reasons' faculty chose not to report academic misconduct. Grading huge volumes of scholarly papers can be daunting, without the onerous task of checking each student's references for acts of plagiarism.

The culture of academic integrity within the community college setting has been minimally explored within the literature but does present its own unique challenges. Many faculty hired by community colleges are employed on a short-term, contractual (hourly) basis. They are often employed elsewhere as well, resulting in an emotional and ethical detachment from the students and the institution (Bertram Gallant, 2018). Faculty hired to teach within community colleges often come from the industry in which they have been hired to teach—trades, policing, healthcare, agriculture—and do not have formal training related to teaching and learning. Contractual faculty also receive minimal orientation to the role of teacher, related explicitly to academic policies (Crossman, 2019) and may not feel adequately supported, or feel they have the required tools or knowledge to minimize cheating within their classroom (Garza Mitchell & Parnther, 2018). In addition, educational programs within community colleges are often short in duration; students can complete their program in under a year, providing faculty minimal time to cultivate professional, ethical practices in their students.

Context: Comprehensive Community Colleges and Academic Integrity

We situated our work within the Canadian community college context. Specifically, both educational institutions that participated in this study were from the province of Alberta. The Alberta post-secondary landscape has six publicly funded post-secondary institutions. The context of our research took place in the Comprehensive Community College (CCC) environment. According to the Alberta Government (n.d.), CCCs are responsible for preparing students for work in industry or providing them with the education needed for admission into other post-secondary programs. Comprehensive Community Colleges offer programming which includes academic upgrading, apprenticeship training programs, certificate and diploma programs, as well as some undergraduate degree programs. Comprehensive Community Colleges operate independently of one another but will often collaborate with other post-secondary institutions. Faculty who teach within CCC environments are expected to follow institutional policies and procedures.

Policies and Procedures

The literature provides information on developing effective policies and procedures (Clark et al., 2020; Stoesz et al., 2019). Many researchers and advocates of academic integrity suggest that it is essential for educational institutions to understand the motivations for academic misconduct, to create policies that address, enforce, and educate students and faculty, and to develop a culture of academic integrity which both faculty and students can understand and support (Orr, 2018; Shane et al., 2018). Institutional policies alone cannot address this complex issue. Instead as Morris (2018) explains, a "multi-pronged strategy is required for higher education institutions to promote and support academic integrity and effectively address its 'shadow'—student academic misconduct, particularly plagiarism, collusion, and contract cheating" (p. 2). Institutional policies on academic integrity should help guide students to adhere to the ICAI's six fundamental values, as students in post-secondary education are learning to develop their own moral compasses (ICAI, 2021; McCabe et al., 2012). Orr (2018) suggests that post-secondary faculty play a critical role by teaching their students values, including honesty and academic integrity, while schooling them on what constitutes academic misconduct and potential consequences.

Institutional Policies Are Imperative

Even though institutional policies and procedures that address academic integrity are essential, more is still needed. Stoesz et al. (2019) explain that "educational organizational policies are formal statements of principle that are used to establish boundaries, provide guidance, and outline best practices for educational institutions and should support their mission and values" (p. 1). Senior leaders need to explicitly demonstrate their support, reminding faculty about institutional policies on academic integrity, the expectation that they are followed, where to find the policies, and how to apply them. As noted in the work of Bretag and Harper (2017, slide #20), an institution-wide, holistic, and systemic approach is needed in addressing issues of academic integrity.

Academic policies are just one component of an institutional academic integrity strategy that includes supporting faculty and students. Proponents of such strategies suggest that programming should have an educational emphasis and should consist of topics and activities around professional development for all employees on academic integrity and misconduct (Bretag & Mahmud, 2016; Morris, 2018; Morris & Carroll, 2016). The topic of integrity should furthermore be woven into events such as "student recruitment, orientation and induction; policy and procedures, teaching and learning practices, working with students, the professional development of staff; and the use of technology" (Bretag & Harper, 2017, pp. 2–3).

Scholarship of Teaching and Learning Research Design

- Why do faculty within community colleges not report acts of known academic dishonesty among students?
- What perceived barriers exist to faculty in reporting acts of academic dishonesty among students?

Method

The overall aim of this study was to gain a better perspective of barriers perceived by faculty teaching at community colleges in reporting incidents of academic misconduct. Additionally, we explored to what extent faculty are reporting incidents of academic misconduct and influences impacting their decision to report or not report. We chose to situate our research from an interpretive lens, giving credence to the faculty's subjective experience and the institutional context wherein it occurred.

Data Collection

A quantitative non-experimental survey design was used, administered as an online digital distribution through Fluidsurvey. Our data collection tool included twenty-four questions using a five-point Likert-Scale questionnaire. Four of the questions allowed open-ended responses, so participants could give examples to support their answers. Participating institutions included two mid-sized community colleges from Alberta, Canada. An email communication inviting participation was distributed to all faculty at each institution via the faculty listserv. This included full-time and part-time continuing, term-certain, and contact (hourly) faculty (sometimes referred to as sessional). The email message provided information on assuring anonymity and contact information for the researchers.

Limitations

Limitations of the research study included using only two community colleges within Alberta, Canada. The findings in this study may not be generalizable to community colleges across Alberta or Canada. In addition, institutional culture at community colleges varies to that at research intensive universities (RIU), so we acknowledge faculty experiences between the two types of institutions may vary.

Results and Findings

We had a response rate of approximately 20% (n = 101), with 56 females and 44 males (1 response gender not indicated). Additional demographic information collected included the highest level of completed formal education (Table 24.1) and, years teaching in post-secondary education (Table 24.2).

Table 24.1 Highest level of completed formal education

Highest completed level of formal education		
Level of education	Frequency	Percentages
Diploma/certificate	3	3.0
Journeyman/person	17	16.8
Bachelor's degree	18	17.8
Master's degree	46	45.5
PhD	16	15.8

Table 24.2 Years teaching in post-secondary education

Number of years teaching in post-secondary education		
Years teaching	Frequency	Percentages
5 or fewer	27	26.7
6 to 10	26	25.7
11 to 15	13	12.9
16 to 20	8	7.9
21 to 25	9	8.9
26 to 30	7	6.9
31 or more	11	10.9

Table 24.3 Major academic disciplines

Academic discipline		
Teaching discipline	Frequency	Percentages
Sciences	20	19.8
Social sciences	26	25.7
Tech and trades	18	17.8
Health	30	29.7
Arts and humanities	7	6.9

Additional demographic information included which discipline of teaching was the respondent's primary area of instruction. The initial question included all programming areas among the two community colleges involved in the study. The data were then collated into five major academic disciplines as seen in Table 24.3.

While there is a breadth of literature on what faculty perceive as constituting academic misconduct and how faculty choose to address these events, there is less available literature on the barriers faculty face when trying to report, especially within the Canadian Comprehensive Community College context. While a significant percentage of participants identified that they would always report misconduct occurrences (24%), the remaining participants identified a plethora of reasons as to why they would not report.

We utilized an inductive approach to the coding the responses to the open-ended questions within the survey as we wanted the participants responses to determine the themes. From the open-ended questions in the survey the following four overarching themes emerged: time, knowledge, support, and fear. Figure 24.1, utilizing the sketchnote method, presents a visual representation of the four themes identified.

Discussion

For the purpose of the chapter, we have summarized the results of the open-end responses at a high level. It is our intention to use our initial findings to develop a second research project using a qualitative semi-structured interview approach to delve more deeply into participants views on community college faculty's perceptions of barriers to reporting academic integrity violations.

The Four Overarching Themes

Theme One: Time

There was significant agreement among the participants that reporting student incidents was too time-consuming (15%). This included the amount of time it took to

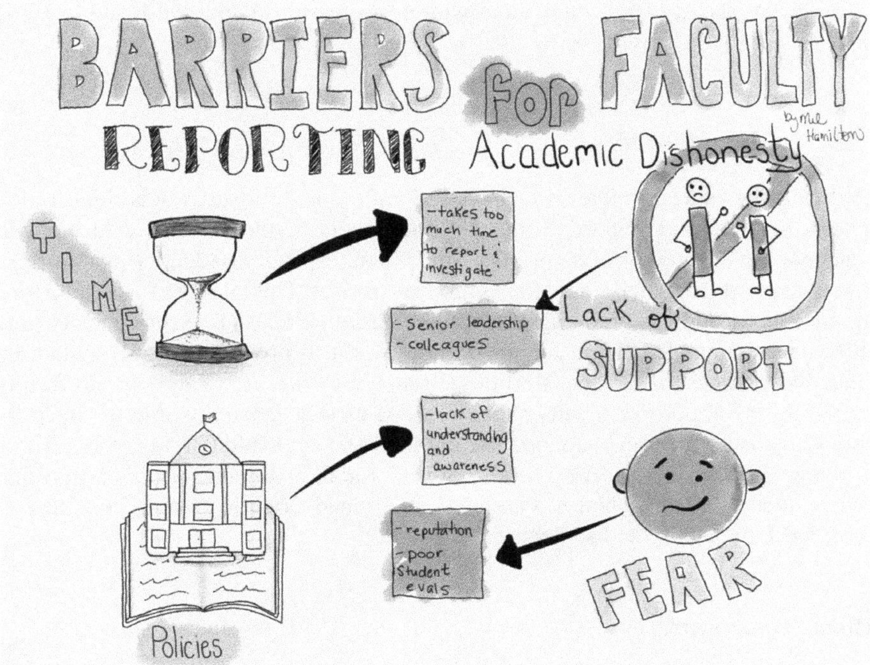

Fig. 24.1 Sketchnote of barriers to reporting academic integrity perceived by faculty

document the student's behavior, fill out the required forms, meet with the department heads, along with a general lack of time due to current teaching workload. This finding is congruent with existing literature (Bertram Gallant, 2018; Crossman, 2019; Thomas, 2017) in which both continuing and hourly contract faculty alike feel the encumbrance of time constraints. Crossman (2019) aligns with this view, recognizing that the extra time involved to address academic misconduct is not clearly identified within employment contracts, contributing to a culture of indifference.

Theme Two: Knowledge

An underlying assumption may be that all faculty are aware of intuitional academic policies and, as such, are able to act in accordance. Our findings identified that 14% of participants were unfamiliar with the institutional academic misconduct policies. This is consistent with other studies such as Eaton et al.'s (2020) study on the gap between institutional policy and educator practice in which 10.5% of respondents rated themselves as having a low understanding of their institution's policies on academic integrity. A lack of awareness around academic policies and institutional guidelines to assist faculty in dealing with transgressions can leave faculty feeling lost and unsupported (Crossman, 2019).

Theme Three: Support

To uphold the values, policies, and procedures of an institution, senior administration must be involved and supportive of faculty and students' alike. Otherwise, faculty will not engage in the process of reporting, with 19% of respondents identifying they felt a lack of support from their immediate senior supervisor. This can set a discerning tone of non-risk to students violating academic integrity policies. To ensure faculty hold students accountable, senior administration must also provide their accountability related to their assigned responsibilities (Bristor & Burke, 2016) and support faculty accordingly. Support for faculty should also be clearly enacted within the integrity policy to ensure practical supports are outlined and available (Bretag et al., 2011). A perceived lack of support by faculty of senior administration will deter reporting misconduct (Garza Mitchell & Parnther, 2018), inadvertently creating a culture of acceptance by faculty and students.

Theme Four: Fear

Overall, it seemed a sense of fear played a significant role in whether faculty reported academic misconduct. The fear felt by faculty encompassed several different aspects, including; fear of damaged relationships between the faculty member and their colleagues (9%); fear of negative impact from senior administration (8%); fear of negative student evaluations (6%); fear of confrontation (6%); fear of negative peer evaluations (4.5%); fear of verbal or physical assault by the student (4.5%); fear of damage to the relationship between student and the faculty member (4.5%); fear of damage to the faculty's reputation (4%); and fear of faculty losing their job (3%). These findings are substantiated by earlier research studies, ascertaining that faculty are fearful of repercussions if they identify and report incidents of academic misconduct (Crossman, 2019; Eaton et al., 2020; Keith-Spiegel et al., 1998).

While it is essential for community colleges to have comprehensive policies on academic integrity, it is equally important that faculty are aware of, understand the intricacies of the policy, and support a culture of integrity (Gottardello & Karabag, 2020). Faculty are key players who interact with students directly on a day-to-day basis and who are in the prime position to clearly communicate institutional expectations and policy information, including potential penalties (Bristor & Burke, 2016). Faculty's intrinsic beliefs regarding ethical and moral behaviors will influence how they choose to respond to incidents of academic misconduct. This can create a complicated situation on how to best respond to suspected incidents of academic misconduct.

Community College Faculty Profiles

From our research data, we developed three faculty profiles to clarify further the faculty's approach and position in how they identified they would handle academic misconduct among their students. These profiles were created based thematic analysis, and direct quotes have been included as further evidence. These typologies are useful in further understanding faculty's perspective and attitude in addressing academic misconduct.

Teaching Opportunity Faculty

Jane teaches classes that have a high number of international and ESL students. Jane has encountered several academic misconduct incidents this year already but has chosen not to report any of them. Instead, Jane feels that each of these incidents is a learning opportunity, thinks that none of her students are genuinely dishonest in their activities, and really wants each of them to graduate.

> "Some ESL students bring their cultural norms to the college, and on such occasions, this becomes a teaching moment."
> "It is a teaching opportunity. I sit down with the student and discuss academic dishonesty and teach them how to maintain academic integrity."
> "Used the incident as an opportunity to engage the student and correct/direct on a better approach to school."

Independent Faculty

Gurpreet is considered a senior faculty member, having taught in higher education for many years. Gurpreet chooses not to report incidents of academic misconduct but instead deals with it personally. This may result in a one-to-one conversation or a zero on the assignment. Gurpreet believes it is his responsibility to manage these incidents and not senior administration.

> "Prefer to handle it my own way."
> "I dealt with the matter with the student redoing the assignment but did not report it."
> "Failed student on the assignment rather than report it."
> "Personal policy of handling first-time, minor offences myself."
> "I dealt with it myself, I didn't report it to my Chair."

Fearful Faculty

Miya is passionate about the courses she teaches. She really enjoys the student interaction and works to make her classrooms fun. However, Miya believes that teaching and monitoring academic integrity are not her responsibility. She doesn't believe her students cheat or cheat intentionally. She wants them all to graduate and is afraid of what might happen if she does report.

> "Unsure if student truly intended to be dishonest—gave the student the benefit of the doubt."
> "Want the students to graduate."
> "I wasn't 100% sure it happened and if I could prove it."
> "Fear for the students future: i.e. losing scholarships or not being accepted to a grad school of their choice."
> "Difficult to prove the dishonesty."
> "Was accused of contributing to the student attrition rate in the program by the Dean by making waves and taking action."

Recommendations

We have noted numerous challenges when discussing faculty barriers related to reporting academic misconduct. However, there are some recommendations that we suggest will assist faculty in addressing and overcoming these barriers. Key stakeholders must work collaboratively in upholding the integrity of the institution. A multifaceted approach is crucial in creating an institutional academic community that upholds the institutional academic standards while promoting and cultivating a moral and ethical society. The following recommendations encompass the three perspectives in which academic integrity is largely studied: from a teaching and learning standpoint, from a policy issue, and from a moral perspective (see Fig. 24.2).

While there are several initiatives aimed at students, we will discuss supports and initiatives specifically focused on faculty, addressing the equated perceived barriers. In Fig. 24.3 we illustrate, via a sketchnote, there are many ways to assist faculty members and overcome these barriers. First and foremost, institutions must commit

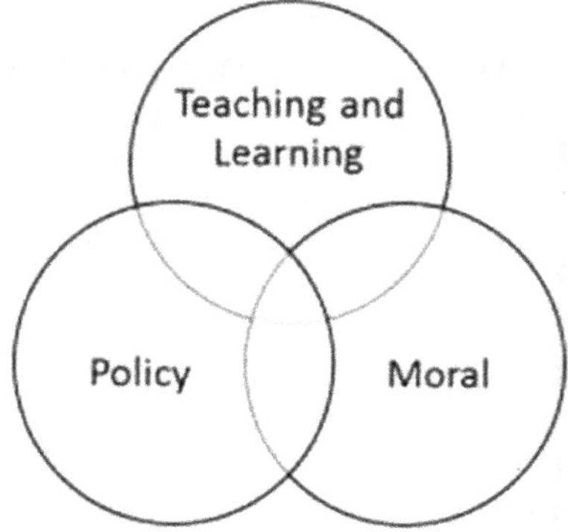

Fig. 24.2 Conceptual lenses for academic integrity inquiry. *Note* Adapted from *Student Perspectives on Plagiarism*, by L. Adam, 2016, In T. Bretag (Ed.), *Handbook of Academic Integrity* (pp. 519–535) and Plagiarism: A Canadian Higher Education Case Study of Policy and Practice Gaps by S. E. Eaton et al., 2020, *Alberta Journal of Educational Research*, 66(4)

Fig. 24.3 Sketchnote of required faculty support and resources

to creating a culture of integrity while supporting faculty in learning, upholding, and reporting academic misconduct. Each one of these aspects falls within each of the three conceptual lenses of academic integrity (see Fig. 24.2), intertwined and linked together, a multilayered approach.

Culture Change

Due to the very nature that cheating is so rampant in higher education, one could declare that higher education is inundated with a "cheating culture." If not addressed, the culture of cheating will extend beyond the borders of higher education and into student's professional lives (Caldwell, 2010). Faculty have a responsibility to assist students in developing their moral compass. A culture change is not merely about developing or adopting honor codes for students, but rather it is about supporting and teaching students to always act with integrity. Clear academic policies need to be in place to support faculty and students alike to help cultivate a culture of integrity. These policies are most effective, as identified by Stoesz and Eaton (2020), when they encompass more than one conceptual lens, incorporating an educational approach along with clear disciplinary outcomes. From a policy lens (see Fig. 24.2), institutions must include both formal institutional polices as well as guiding documents, procedures, and forms (Eaton, 2021) as ethical codification is an essential resource in fostering a culture of change.

Faculty Professional Development (Teaching and Learning)

Developing a space for faculty to learn about academic integrity is one of the most critical steps. Frequently faculty at the community college level are hired for their professional expertise (trades professions, nurses, police officers) and may not have the educational background or experiences specifically related to the discipline of teaching. Professional development related to the faculty's knowledge of and role pertaining to academic policies is a vital component. This includes addressing gaps in faculty's understanding on how to handle and manage their courses, the different measures by which students can violate academic policies, including what constitutes misconduct and preventable measures (Bristor & Burke, 2016).

The role of faculty within the college classroom is to convey to students the concept and values of academic integrity and to uphold their course's integrity. This can be accomplished through classroom discussions on integrity and plagiarism, developing and maintaining the integrity of authentic assessments, and having a clear understanding of institutional (Gottardello & Karabag, 2020). This knowledge is not inherent to faculty and therefore requires a means by which faculty can obtain this understanding. Professional development and faculty support can also address the disparity that occurs between "the rhetoric of policy documents and the actual practice of integrating academic integrity in the classroom" (Gottardello & Karabag, 2020, p. 1). Taking a developmental approach in closing the praxis gap of what is ideal within best-practice and policy to implementation within the student learning environment is most effective.

Professional development may facilitate a shared understanding of integrity and the shared values inherent to the institution's socio-cultural aspects (Gottardello & Karabag, 2020). One surprising finding in our research identified that 14% of respondents felt that academic integrity among students was not important. Edification may first need to begin with faculty to impart the importance of academic integrity related to the institution's mission and vision while contributing to society's moral well-being.

Modeling Behavior

As faculty have day-to-day interactions with students, it places them in a prime position to act as role models; to collaborate, teach, engage, and inspire. Within the conceptual lens of moral perspective (Eaton et al., 2020), modeling behavior around academic integrity is one of the most valuable ways that faculty can lead by example. Faculty are leaders, experts in their fields, and professional in nature due to their role as educators. Poor role modeling can lead to misinforming students and providing bad practice occurrences, resulting in negative outcomes (Morris & Carroll, 2016). Modeling of behavior would also align with Eaton et al.'s (2020) conceptual lens of teaching and learning (see Fig. 24.2), in that faculty should ensure their own academic integrity related to course documents and resources, class activities and handouts, as well as assessments. In addition, faculty can support and encourage principles of integrity by using educational approaches to help students learn and understand these principles. Aligning with Bertram Gallant's (2008) statement that academic integrity is a crucial component to teaching and learning imperative, we believe that modeling behavior for students is one of the key outcomes of our study. Fortuitously, our research collected data related to role modeling and academic integrity within the faculty by faculty. We had more than once incident where faculty were concerned with the behavior of their colleagues and their lack of integrity. We suggest future research would be valuable related to faculty incidences of academic dishonesty.

Support

Support of and for faculty is crucial to developing a culture of integrity. In addition to exemplar academic policies, the identification of specific supports for faculty must also be included (Bretag et al., 2011; Garza Mitchell & Parnther, 2018). Supports can refer to a multitude of endeavors such as academic integrity champions (Bretag & Mahmud, 2016) who are well versed in the academic integrity discourse and can educate and support faculty. Faculty also need to feel backed by senior administration (Bristor & Burke, 2016) as faculty who do not believe they will be supported by senior administration are less likely to address and report incidents, creating further disillusionment. This includes individuals in direct supervision of faculty as well as deans, provosts, and executive leadership (Bristor & Burke, 2016). Bristor and Burke reiterate that to create and sustain a culture of integrity, all members within the community must be committed and accountable for their assigned responsibilities.

Conclusion

This chapter presented perceived barriers faced by faculty when addressing academic integrity within their institutions. Time, knowledge, support, and fear all play a significant role in determining to what extent, if at all, faculty report and address incidents of academic misconduct within the community college setting. Faculty are the frontline workers who interact with students daily and are in a prime position to positively influence students' ethical and moral integrity while upholding the intrinsic values of academic integrity, their primary institution, and post-secondary education. The faculty's role not only includes edifying students on course content and engaging students within the learning process, but faculty must also encourage fair, honest practices, and promote and model a high standard of integrity (Gottardello & Karabag, 2020). This can be achieved through initiatives that support faculty and, by extension, students, through the conceptual lenses of academic integrity including teaching and learning, policy development, and from a moral development perspective (Eaton et al., 2020). Our research identified a disjuncture between faculty's perceptions and understanding about academic misconduct and institutional expectations and policies. It is essential that academic integrity is integrated into routine discourse in all matters related to post-secondary education. This will in return create a collective understanding and community that is dedicated to upholding the fundamental principles integral to academic integrity (ICAI, 2021). These fundamental values will support students not only in achieving their educational goals but will also assist them in developing an ethical perspective, contributing to the wellbeing of society.

References

Adam, L. (2016). Student perspectives on plagiarism. In T. Bretag (Ed.), *Handbook of academic integrity* (pp. 519–535). Springer.

Alberta Government. (n.d.). *Types of publicly funded institutions.* https://www.alberta.ca/types-publicly-funded-post-secondary-institutions.aspx#jumplinks-2

Anney, V. N., & Mosha, M. A. (2015). Student's plagiarisms in higher learning institutions in the era of improved internet access: Case study of developing countries. *Journal of Education and Practice, 6*(13), 203–216. https://eric.ed.gov/?id=EJ1080502

Bertram Gallant, T. (2008). *Academic integrity in the twenty-first century: A teaching and learning imperative.* Wiley.

Bertram Gallant, T. (2016). Leveraging institutional integrity for the betterment of education. In T. Bretag (Ed.), *Handbook of academic integrity* (pp. 979–993). Singapore.

Bertram Gallant, T. (2018). Part-time integrity? Contingent faculty and academic integrity. *New Directions for Community Colleges, 183*, 45–54. https://doi.org/10.1002/cc.20316

Bertram Gallant, T., & Drinan, T. (2006). Organizational theory and student cheating: Explanation, responses, and strategies. *The Journal of Higher Education, 77*(5), 839–860. https://doi.org/10.1353/jhe.2006.0041

Blau, G., Szewczuk, R., Fitzgerald, J., Paris, D. A., & Guglielmo, M. (2018). Comparing business school faculty classification for perceptions of student cheating. *Journal of Academic Ethics, 4*(16), 301–315. https://doi.org/10.1007/s10805-018-9315-4

Bretag, T., Mahmud, S., Wallace, M., Walker, R., James, C., Green, M., East, J., McGowan, U., & Partridge, L. (2011). Core elements of exemplar academic integrity policy in Australian higher education. *International Journal for Educational Integrity, 7*(2), 3–12. https://ro.uow.edu.au/asdpapers/341

Bretag, T., & Harper, R. (2017). *Addressing contract cheating: Local and global responses.* [PowerPoint slides]. Contract Cheating and Assessment Design. https://cheatingandassessment.edu.au/wp-content/uploads/2016/08/addressing-contract-cheating_local-and-global-responses.pdf

Bretag, T., & Mahmud, S. (2016). A conceptual framework for implementing exemplary academic integrity policy in Australian higher education. In T. Bretag (Ed.), *Handbook of academic integrity* (pp. 463–480). Springer.

Bristor, J., & Burke, M. M. (2016). Academic integrity policies: Has your institution implemented an effective policy? *The Accounting Educators' Journal, 26*, 1–10. https://www.aejournal.com/ojs/index.php/aej/article/view/338

Caldwell, C. (2010). A ten-step model for academic integrity: A positive approach to business schools. *Journal of Business Ethics, 92*, 1–13. https://link.springer.com/article/10.1007%2Fs10551-009-0144-7

Christensen Hughes, J. M., & McCabe, D. L. (2006). Academic misconduct within higher education in Canada. *The Canadian Journal of Higher Education, 36*(2), 1–21. http://journals.sfu.ca/cjhe/index.php/cjhe/article/view/183537/183482

Clark, A., Goodfellow, J., & Shoufani, S. (2020). Examining academic integrity using course-level learning outcomes. *The Canadian Journal For The Scholarship of Teaching And Learning, 11*(2). https://doi.org/10.5206/cjsotl-rcacea.2020.2.8508

Crossman, K. (2019). Is this in my contract? How part-time contract faculty face barriers to reporting academic integrity breaches. *Canadian Perspectives on Academic Integrity, 2*(1), 32–39. https://doi.org/10.11575/cpai.v2i1.68934

DiBartolo, M. C., & Walsh, C. M. (2010). Desperate times call for desperate measures: Where are we in addressing academic integrity? *Journal of Nursing Education, 49*(10), 543–544. https://doi.org/10.3928/01484834-20100921-01

Eaton, S. E., Fernandez Conde, C., Rothschuh, S., Guglielmin, M., & Kojo Otoo, B. (2020). Plagiarism: A Canadian higher education case study of policy and practice gaps. *Alberta Journal of Educational Research, 66*(4), 471–488. https://journalhosting.ucalgary.ca/index.php/ajer/article/view/69204

Eaton, S. E. (2021). *Plagiarism in higher education: Tackling tough topics in academic integrity.* Libraries Unlimited.

Fontana, J. S. (2009). Nursing faculty experiences of students' academic misconduct. *Journal of Nursing Education, 48*(4), 181–185. https://doi.org/10.3928/01484834-20090401-05

Garza Mitchell, R. L., & Parnther, C. (2018). The shared responsibility for academic integrity education. *New Directions for Community Colleges, 183*, 55–64. https://doi.org/10.1002/cc.20317

Gottardello, D., & Karabag, S. F. (2020). Ideal and actual roles of university professors in academic integrity management: A comparative study. *Studies in Higher Education.* https://doi.org/10.1080/03075079.2020.1767051

Hendricks, E., Young-Jones, A., & Foutch, J. (2011). To cheat or not to cheat: Academic misconduct in the college classroom. *LOGOS: A Journal of Undergraduate Research, 4*, 68–75. https://www.missouristate.edu/Assets/honorslogos/logos_vol4_full.pdf#page=76

International Center for Academic Integrity (ICAI). (2021). *The fundamental values of academic integrity* (3rd ed.). https://www.academicintegrity.org/fundamental-values/

Keener, T. A., Peralya, M. G., Smith, M., Swager, L., Ingles, J., Wen, S., & Barbier, M. (2019). Student and faculty perceptions: Appropriate consequences of lapses in academic integrity in health sciences education. *BMC Medical Education, 19*(209), 1–9. https://doi.org/10.1186/s12909-019-1645-4

Keith-Spiegel, P., Tabachnick, B. G., Whitley Jr, B. E., & Washburn, J. (1998). Why professors ignore cheating: Opinions of a national sample of psychology instructors. *Ethics and Behavior, 8*(3), 215-227.https://doi.org/10.1207/s15327019eb0803_3

Keith-Spiegel, P., Tabachnick, B. G., Whitley Jr., B. E., & Washburn, J. (2010). Why professors ignore cheating: Opinions of a national sample of psychology faculty. *Ethics and Behavior, 8*(3), 215–227. https://doi.org/10.1207/s15327019eb0803_3

Kenny, N., & Eaton, S. E. (2022). Academic integrity through a SoTL lens and 4M framework: An institutional self-study. In S. E. Eaton & J. Christensen Hughes (Eds.), *Academic integrity in Canada: An enduring and essential challenge.* Springer.

Madara, D. S., & Namango, S. (2016). Faculty perceptions on cheating in exams in undergraduate engineering. *Journal of Education and Practice, 7*(30), 70–86. https://files.eric.ed.gov/fulltext/EJ1118895.pdf

McCabe, D. L. (1993). Faculty responses to academic misconduct: The influence of student honor codes. *Research in Higher Education, 34*(5), 647–658. https://www.jstor.org/stable/40196116

McCabe, D. L., Butterfield, K., & Treviño, L. K. (2012). *Cheating in college: Why students do it and what educators can do about it.* John Hopkins University Press.

Morris, E. J., & Carroll, J. (2016). Developing a sustainable holistic institutional approach: Dealing with realities 'on the ground' when implementing an academic integrity policy. In T. Bretag (Ed.), *Handbook of academic integrity* (pp. 449–462). Singapore. https://doi.org/10.1007/978-981-287-098-8_23

Morris, E. J. (2018). Academic integrity matters: Five considerations for addressing contract cheating. *International Journal for Educational Integrity, 14*(15). https://doi.org/10.1007/s40979-018-0038-5

Orr, J. (2018). Developing a campus academic integrity education seminar. *Journal of Academic Ethics, 16*(3), 195–209. https://doi.org/10.1007/s10805-018-9304-7

Parnther, C. (2016). It's on us: A case study of academic integrity in a Mid-Western community college (Publication No. 2468) (Doctoral dissertation, Western Michigan University, 2016). *Scholarworks.* https://scholarworks.wmich.edu/cgi/viewcontent.cgi?article=3490&context=dissertations

Schneider, A. (1999). Why professors don't do more to stop students who cheat. *The Chronicle of Higher Education, 45*(20), 8–13. https://www.chronicle.com/article/why-professors-dont-do-more-to-stop-students-who-cheat-25673/

Shane, M. J., Carson, L., & Edwards, M. (2018). A case study in updating academic policies and procedures. *New Directions for Community Colleges, 2018*(183), 83–93. https://doi.org/10.1002/cc.20320

Stoesz, B. M., & Eaton, S. E. (2020). Academic integrity policies of publicly funded universities in western Canada. *Educational Policy.* https://doi.org/10.1177/0895904820983032

Stoesz, B. M., Eaton, S. E., Miron, J., & Thacker, E. J. (2019). Academic integrity and contract cheating policy analysis of colleges in Ontario, Canada. *International Journal for Educational Integrity, 15*(4), 2–18. https://doi.org/10.1007/s40979-019-0042-4

Tayan, B. M. (2017). Academic misconduct: An investigation into male students' perceptions, experiences & attitudes towards cheating and plagiarism in a Middle Eastern university context. *Journal of Education and Learning, 6*(1), 158–166. https://doi.org/10.5539/jel.v6n1p158

Thomas, A. (2017). Faculty reluctance to report student plagiarism. A case study. *African Journal of Business Ethics, 11*(1), 103–119. https://doi.org/10.15249/11-1-148

Melanie Hamilton MN, RN is an Educational Development Specialist at Lethbridge College. In that role, she is responsible for facilitating faculty professional development. Prior to her move to the Centre for Teaching, Learning, and Innovation, Melanie taught nursing in both the classroom and clinical setting for 20 years. Her research focuses on academic dishonesty and integrity in the college sector, K-12, and faculty reporting. In addition, Melanie is passionate about the Scholarship of Teaching and Learning (SoTL), facilitates and supports faculty with SoTL research, and is the current Chair of SoTL Canada and VP Canada for ISSOTL.

Dr. Karla Wolsky RN is a faculty member for the Bachelor Nursing program at Lethbridge College where she has taught within the theory, lab, simulation, and clinical environments for over 15 years. During this time, Dr. Wolsky undertook the role of Chair for the NESA BN programs subsequent to the Chair for the School of Health Sciences and Allied Health programs within the Centre for Health and Wellness. Dr. Wolsky's research focuses on academic integrity, specifically within the college sector and the K-12 system, as well as barriers to faculty reporting incidents of academic dishonesty. Additional scholarly activities surround student engagement and the benefits of using humor in the classroom.

Chapter 25
Changing "Hearts" and Minds: Pedagogical and Institutional Practices to Foster Academic Integrity

Laurie McNeill

Abstract This chapter shares findings of and recommendations from a three-year initiative at the University of British Columbia to develop and assess enhanced and explicit instruction in academic integrity in first-year writing courses, an enterprise that now involves 42 faculty members teaching up to 5000 students each year. This project began from the appreciation that, as an institution, we needed to close the gap between our expectations of academic integrity and students' understanding of those expectations, and to make explicit what is often treated as assumed understanding. This approach was intended to help students develop more robust knowledge and appreciation for academic integrity as a core element of the academic community to which they now belong. Drawing on the qualitative and quantitative data we gathered from students and faculty, including surveys, focus groups, misconduct reports, and interviews, I illustrate how what I call "pedagogies of integrity" have led to improved uptake by students (and instructors) of academic integrity as both theory and practice, resulting in a change in the number as well as type of academic misconduct cases, and have led to significant insights about the place of academic integrity in larger conversations about student belonging, wellness, and access. I share not only how the instructors in this project changed the conversation in their own courses, but also how these discussions are resonating across disciplines and faculties of our campus and beyond. Finally, I outline recommendations for next steps in policy and practice that these findings suggest.

Keywords Academic integrity · First-year students · Pedagogy · Policy · Writing courses · Faculty & student attitudes

First-year students' understanding of academic integrity (AI) is often unevenly distributed, unsophisticated, or overconfident (e.g., Brooks et al., 2011; Childers & Bruton, 2016; Howard, 1995; Jurdi et al., 2012; Locquiao & Ives, 2020; Newton, 2015; Power, 2009; Roig, 1997; Wilkinson, 2009), and undergraduate students more

L. McNeill (✉)
University of British Columbia, Vancouver, Canada
e-mail: laurie.mcneill@ubc.ca

S. E. Eaton and J. Christensen Hughes (eds.), *Academic Integrity in Canada*, Ethics and Integrity in Educational Contexts 1,
https://doi.org/10.1007/978-3-030-83255-1_25

generally show poor comprehension and/or uptake of AI, resulting in misconduct (e.g., Colella-Sandercock & Alahmadi, 2015; Dawson, 2004; Christensen Hughes & McCabe, 2006). Until recently, conversations about AI in higher education in response to these issues have taken a default model of deficiency and distrust, focusing on detection rather than education, and perpetuating assumptions about who commits misconduct (such as international students) without considering the systemic issues and biases that might account for disproportionate representation of those populations in misconduct cases.

This chapter shares findings of and recommendations from a three-year initiative at the University of British Columbia, Canada, to develop and assess enhanced and explicit instruction in academic integrity in first-year writing courses, an enterprise that now involves 42 faculty members teaching about 5000 students each year. This project began from the appreciation that, as an institution, we needed to close the gap between our expectations of academic integrity and students' understanding of those expectations, and to make explicit what is often treated as assumed understanding. This approach was intended to help students develop more robust knowledge and appreciation for AI as a core element of the academic community to which they now belong, and to advocate for pedagogical rather than punitive frameworks that support students as members of the academic community.

By outlining the design and implementation of a major project to change how academic integrity has been taught in a particular set of courses, with the broader goal of advocating for changes in undergraduate (and graduate) education that will help cultivate a "culture of integrity" (Eaton & Edino, 2018, p. 1), this discussion adds to existing literature on undergraduate understanding of AI and on pedagogical approaches to teaching it. I illustrate how what I call the "pedagogies of integrity" that we have developed and adopted in this project have led to improved uptake by students (and instructors) of AI as both theory and practice, resulting in a change in the number as well as type of academic misconduct cases, and have led to significant insights about the place of AI in larger conversations about student belonging, wellness, and access. In its attention to faculty experiences and insights, it addresses a gap in AI scholarship identified by Eaton and Edino (2018), and extends the considerations of AI institutionalization that Bertram Gallant and Drinan outline (2008). I provide an overview of the structure and organization of our project (its infrastructure, staffing, and funding), our practices, and our major findings. I conclude with next steps for developing pedagogies of integrity beyond first-year writing courses at UBC, and how these discussions are resonating across disciplines and faculties of our campus and beyond.

Starting Our "Hearts": Project Background

This project stems from my own "lightbulb" moment when, after almost two decades as an instructor in writing and English literature courses, I moved into an administrative role, one in which I had to meet with students for cases of alleged academic misconduct reported by their instructors. From this perspective—a step removed from the emotional aspects that a discovery of misconduct can provoke for the instructor—I had the opportunity to listen to and learn from our students about the ways we as an institution were clearly not doing a very good job of making academic integrity either understandable or desirable: the students in these meetings not only did not know how to meet the expectations of ethical research, they did not have much idea of why we cared about it so much, or, why they themselves should care, too. Instead, more often than not, we were taking the unproductive approach Rebecca Moore Howard (1992, 1995) and Cheryl Kier (2014) each categorize as punishing students for knowledge they did not have. I recognized that we were expecting students, even first-years, to know and understand how to apply a concept that even seasoned scholars sometimes struggle with. We weren't teaching it right, or in enough depth, yet we attached such weight to it—using it as a measure not of aptitude but moral fibre: student plagiarists are not typically thought as "bad citers," but as *cheaters*, or, as Mary Mulholland (2020) notes, as "dishonest" (p. 111) and "unethical" (p. 105).

Faculty, like students, can also have "teachable moments," and for me, this was mine. It had become clear that this "punitive" rather than "proactive" approach, in Sarah Elaine Eaton et al.'s words (2017, p. 29–30), was not the only option. We had opportunities to move from the default model of blaming and shaming that Ho (2015), Mulholland (2020) and others argue characterizes higher education's AI approach, with its dominant "judicio-moral paradigm" (Howard, 1992, p. 235), and see AI as a skill and way of knowing that—like all other concepts we think of as foundational to learning in our courses—we can and need to teach, explicitly, and with recognition of its complexity. With this new insight, and in collaboration with a similarly-minded Associate Dean Academic, I initiated a pilot project in 2016 that brought together eight full-time faculty members (both both tenure-track and lecturers, colleagues with multi-year contracts) who were teaching in Arts' First-Year Programs (FYP) to think with me about what we could do differently in our courses so that our students not only knew *how* to meet the expectations of academic integrity (itself a major learning curve), but also *why* they should care to do so, beyond just avoiding getting caught for violating it. Adopting an educative approach, framed by integrity, how could we equip students with the skills they need to meet the expectations of ethical knowledge production and a compelling rationale for doing so?

To support our shifting from a moralistic and affective approach to academic integrity to a theoretically-informed, evidence-based, and pedagogical one, we began with research into the state of misconduct in our courses. I reviewed the investigations I'd undertaken into reported cases to identify patterns in causes of misconduct, and held several workshops with FYP faculty to learn what "pain points" they were identifying (unsurprisingly, these skills included paraphrasing and citation, aptitudes commonly identified as challenging for students, as well as general research and note-taking practices (e.g., Colella-Sandercock & Alahmadi, 2015), as well as how they were teaching (or not teaching) the topic. To understand how other North American research universities were approaching this issue and identify best (and worst) practices as well as existing resources on which we might draw, we undertook an extensive literature and policy review. Having identified the most urgent gaps in student knowledge in our courses, and with a developing sense of the scholarly and policy conversation, we competed for funding from UBC's Teaching and Learning Enhancement Fund to support a larger initiative to implement and assess the effects of explicit and enhanced instruction on academic integrity in our first-year writing courses. Entitled "Our Cheating Hearts?: Changing the Conversation Through Academic Integrity Curriculum"—with the question mark signaling our interest in challenging the normative discourse about academic misconduct, who commits it, and why—the project was awarded $122,707 CAD in funding over three years. This funding included support for one teaching release in each of the first two years (requiring matching support from First-Year Programs), each taken by junior faculty members who were instrumental members of the working group and who had the heaviest teaching loads (this release allowed them to lead portions of the design and assessment components, including facilitating the focus groups) and renumeration and refreshments for student participants in focus groups. The majority of the funding was dedicated to hiring a project coordinator (full-time in the first two years, part-time in the last year) and graduate and undergraduate students in part-time work-learn positions. This staff support looked after data collection, cleaning, and analysis; meeting and workshop organization; poster and slide design; consultation on process (e.g., redesign of survey questions); draft reporting; and general troubleshooting. Given that I as principal investigator not only teach several classes a year but am a full-time administrator, this project support was essential to the project's success. Notably, however, we have been significantly under-budget throughout the project's tenure. Though certainly this illustrates good stewardship and judicious spending, it also demonstrates that similar projects could be done with much less investment, especially if in-kind support could be provided by the institution.

First-Year Programs courses—in the Arts One (100 students) and the Coordinated Arts Program (550 students) cohort learning communities, and in WRDS 150, a 13-week academic writing class (2020: 193 sections / 5628 students)—were well-situated for this project, since our curriculum was already implementing many of the best practices other scholars have identified as ideal for student understanding of ethical research (e.g., Childers & Bruton, 2016; Colella-Sandercock & Alahmadi, 2015; Eaton et al., 2017). For example, our courses include introductions to the theory and practice of citation, documentation, reporting expressions, summary and synthesis of sources, and assignments are scaffolded. Yet, as we charted causes of academic misconduct (both in "teachable moments"—issues at an early stage in the course, addressed directly with the student—and reportable cases), we noted the need for better grounding in core citation and research skills. In disciplinary meetings with me, students also indicated that they were getting so stuck on minor details of practice (e.g., how to cite a particular kind of source) that they missed the larger point of documentation; this experience reflects similar findings that students focus on the "mechanistic" elements of citation without consideration of AI more broadly (Brooks et al., 2011; Childers & Bruton, 2016; Howard, 1995; Newton, 2015). This pattern, as well as others that emerged in the misconduct meetings, highlighted that we needed not only to reinforce our instruction on how to meet the expectations of academic integrity, but—crucially—we were not being explicit enough about why it is important and has meaning to students themselves.

To evaluate the effect of the project, we surveyed students and faculty, initially in two groups ("working group" [WG] and "non-working group" [NWG]), and after the full-scale implementation in September 2018, without such division. We held follow-up interviews with faculty and focus groups with students and peer tutors, and presented findings for discussion at FYP meetings. A final series of focus groups and surveys planned for April 2020 was postponed due to the pandemic. We also tracked the number and type of misconduct cases reported to the FYP Chair.

Considerations and Project Principles

The question of making integrity meaningful and relevant presented a particular and additional challenge because our courses meet the first-year writing requirement, meaning that many students take them not by choice but under duress, and see a writing course as quite separate from the "real" work of their other courses and intended major or profession. If they associate "academic integrity" as a concern particular to that course, rather than a value and practice commonly-held across the university, then it becomes even more difficult for them to apply these principles to all of their work. Having identified these challenges, considerable as they were, we now had opportunity to address them. As we moved from the pilot to the first year of funding, we built on the following premises:

- We shifted our language to "academic integrity," what we aspired to rather than what we would punish or want to avoid. We saw this change in wording as not merely semantic but a commitment to a set of principles, and that resonated with students and faculty. For example, a student focus group participant noted in 2017, "[the term academic integrity]... gives people something to live up to. Cheating is just like, don't cheat, but then there are still a lot of things you could do that are like, not cheating but they're not exactly OK either." A respondent to our 2018 faculty survey ($n = 18$) noted not only their perception that student knowledge was different with the new approach but that it was also a lot more palatable: "I found that the focus on academic integrity—rather than misconduct—helped me reframe all this in a more positive light. Rather than making them fearful that they might accidentally do something wrong, it gives them something positive to aspire to."
- We recognized that students come to our courses with understandings of "academic integrity" that are unevenly distributed, often unsophisticated, and typically overconfident (Brooks et al., 2011; Childers & Bruton, 2016; Howard, 1992, 1995; Locquiao & Ives, 2020; Newton, 2015; Power, 2009), and therefore we should not assume any common understanding of either the concept or knowledge of how to apply it. Further, although this characterization is particularly true of first-year students (as Wilkinson, 2009, has similarly found), it is not exclusively so, and

so we should not assume that any members of our class would not benefit from explicit instruction in these expectations. In this approach, we aligned with the principles of Universal Design for Learning: accommodations for some members of a class result in improved learning for all (e.g., Scott et al., 2003). This recognition supports our shift from blaming students for what we are not teaching them, and counters dominant attitudes that students commit misconduct from wilfulness and dishonesty more often than ignorance (a finding not supported by our study of reportable cases in FYP). It also models an ethical pedagogy that addresses the needs of a diverse student body.

- Given that our curriculum already addressed many aspects of research and its production, we would focus on ways to extend those existing parts of the curriculum and make the instruction more explicit, with greater development of the rationale (the why) and targeted instruction in elements of application (the how). Since the intention was that, over the three years of the project, this enhanced curriculum would be included in all sections of our courses (at that time, with a combined enrolment of 2700 students), scalability and faculty buy-in were key considerations. Recognizing the significant new work this curriculum redesign involved, and the high number of contract sessional colleagues teaching in our units for whom such additional labour would be unpaid (and, as Ho argues, for whom such work can be "burdensome," 2015, p. 737), we determined to develop resources and materials that would be shared and that other instructors could adopt and adapt; we added a "sandbox" site for all FYP instructors on Canvas (UBC's learning management system) on which members could upload and access the exercises and materials we developed. This site has been an essential starting place for faculty (in our 2018 (n = 18) and 2019 (n = 17) faculty surveys, all instructors report using it), and is now mirrored in an open-access wiki hosted by UBC's Chapman Learning Commons.

Project Findings: Strategies for Building and Maintaining an AI Infrastructure

We accumulated a rich body of experiences and data from this project, and from them I outline the following seven key strategies that I argue were key to the success of creating an AI culture.

Get Faculty on Board

Faculty understanding of and attitudes towards academic integrity play an essential role in maintaining a proactive and educative AI culture (Childers & Bruton, 2016; Colella-Sandercock & Alahmadi, 2015; Löfström et al., 2015; Evans-Tokaryk,

2014; Brooks et al., 2011; Bertram Gallant & Drinan, 2008; Wang, 2008; Christensen Hughes & McCabe, 2006). Similarly, it was clear that our project would not succeed without faculty being able to perceive that it met their needs as well as their students. The ground-up approach we have taken, driven by instructors, based on practices in our own classrooms and our understanding of the needs of students in our courses, has led to widespread buy-in. In addition to taking a collaborative approach to curriculum development, other aspects of the project approach have helped us avoid the push-back that might be associated with curricular changes imposed from the administration. At the outset, from my position as both principal investigator and Chair of these units, as I considered the broader scale-up to all sections/course in FYP, I grappled with the challenges of how to implement this new expectation across not only a significant number of sections and instructors, but also different courses: how could we negotiate concerns about academic freedom and instructor autonomy, as well as the different cultures of the three distinct programs comprising FYP? I determined that it was more important that academic integrity (the aspirational value and practice) be taught in these courses, rather than mandate exactly how instructors did so. In other words, I aimed to "change the conversation" faculty were having with each other and in their courses, switching from misconduct to integrity, and taking up the responsibility of teaching what this term means, and I recognized that what that looked like might end up being a bit different in both scope and content. Our gradual implementation—a small number of sections and faculty in the pilot and first year—allowed us a long runway to gain cooperation, including the ability for the working group to report back to the wider group on the successes (and challenges) of the new approach.

By the time we were asking all faculty to participate, they were familiar with its premises, were provided with a "toolkit" to adapt, and presented with fairly persuasive findings that, even with relatively small changes to our curriculum, we could see significant differences in students' awareness and understanding of AI. Surveys run in October 2017 of students in the working group ($n = 86$) and non-working group ($n = 61$) sections were particularly compelling, with three questions in particular showing the project's promise: when asked if they had heard of the term "academic integrity" and that they knew what it meant, 100% of students in the working group (WG) had heard of the term AI and only 3.9% indicated that they were unsure of its meaning, while in the non-working group (NWG), 96% had heard of it but 19.6% were unsure of what it mean and 3.6% had never heard of it. Similarly, 83% of WG students responded that they knew about UBC's AI policy, in comparison to 50% of NWG. 93.5% of WG agreed or strongly agreed "the importance of AI is clearly communicated to students," versus 67.3% of NWG respondents; 32.7% of NWG students chose neutral or disagree to this statement, in comparison to 6.5% in the WG. Qualitative comments from student focus groups in November 2017 (WG = 3, NWG = 4) also indicated that WG students articulated a better understanding of AI as supporting the collective enterprise of the academic community versus the NWG's focus on individual effort.

Thus the change was not only feasible but highly productive for students and also for faculty, who would face fewer instances of academic misconduct. In the end, we were able to roll out implementation to all sections a full year ahead of schedule. Although the flexible versus standard approach does mean less certainty about uptake by individual faculty and potentially inconsistency in the scope of instruction, extended and explicit instruction in academic integrity, through an educative framework, is now a regular part of the curriculum in all three first-year programs.

Clarify Policy and Procedure

Part of the activity of building a culture of integrity in FYP was happening outside of the working group and curriculum design: it began with the very idea that academic integrity was a key and explicit value of our units, and that came with the expectation that faculty had an important role to play, and needed to participate in this shared enterprise. To do so, we needed a common understanding of policy and procedure, including when to report academic misconduct and how, since these practices were poorly articulated and inconsistently applied, and because we had a new organizational structure (the introduction of an FYP Chair in 2014). There was some initial reluctance or concerns by faculty that heightened attention to AI was in fact a commitment to a disciplinary or "law and order" approach rather than an educative one; the instructors of the WRDS course in particular drew on the work of Rebecca Moore Howard and others to defend patchwriting as developmental (Howard, 1992, 1995). These conversations helped push the conversation across FYP productively towards the theoretical framework the "Cheating Hearts" project had adopted, and identified an issue for us in conforming to Faculty of Arts' policy and procedure for reporting academic misconduct: in our first-year courses, with students new to the expectations of research writing and university practices, when was a "case" reportable, rather than a "teachable moment"? A sub-committee, with representation from the three FYP units, led a year-long process to produce clear guidelines that reflected faculty input and consensus about these elements. This process was invaluable in supporting the sea-change in our unit and laid the ground work for the pedagogical changes being developed.

Establishing AI Frameworks in Our Courses—Syllabus Language

In the pilot year, I identified our articulation of course policies in the syllabus as a low-hanging fruit ripe for signalling our new approach to AI. Adapting a practice James Orr articulates (2017), I created a course policy statement on AI that used the aspirational language of integrity—i.e., not on "cheating," misconduct," or "plagiarism"– and connected this concept to academic purpose and community, extending the finding by Löfström et al. (2015) that "integration into the academic community serves to prevent research misconduct" (p. 435).[1] Further, the statement takes an explicit and educative approach by clearly outlining examples of violations of AI, accurately noting the consequences for such violations, and linking to resources and materials students can consult to know more, including university policy documents and library guides, so that they know where to find the support and information they need to meet this community standard.

After widespread use by instructors in the project working group, this statement has been adopted at the unit level for First-Year Programs, and so appears on most syllabi in these units. Several instructors in the working group also embedded integrity in the syllabus by including a learning outcome and an evaluation criterion on ethical research practices. The explicit outlining of expectations reflects our premise that we do not assume that "everyone" knows about these expectations or how to meet them.

Explicit and Early Integration of AI in Course Content: The Definition Activity

We knew from experience that simply including the statement—no matter how intentionally designed—would not be sufficient for its uptake, even if we spent time in the first days of class discussing that statement, the practice reported by the majority of faculty in our non-working group (2017), and a recommendation frequently made in the literature on misconduct (e.g., Colella-Sandercock & Alahmadi, 2015; Wang, 2008). In the pilot year of the project, I designed a definition exercise[2] to foster this engagement and give students a clear understanding of what we mean, clarity that too often both policy and instructors fail to provide (e.g., Brooks et al., 2011; Jurdi et al., 2012). In this no- or low-stakes activity, students are assigned readings related to academic integrity (including materials from the syllabus statement, such as the UBC Calendar and library guides, institutional policy for researchers on ethical practice, and a popular article on some current instance of misconduct, such as Melania Trump's alleged plagiarism in 2016 of a speech by Michelle Obama). In class, they work with peers in small groups to produce a definition of AI based on these readings that must articulate not only what it means, but why it matters. After the class reviews these different definitions to identify the one or ones they find most accurate, we craft a composite definition of the concept that is posted on our course LMS page and referred to in the expectations for each of our formal assessments. We then revisit the definition at two points, mid-semester and just before the final research assignment, to reflect on how our ideas about integrity have changed, and to add any new insights or practices that they have subsequently understood. Through this collaborative process that requires personal investment and that reflects the particular community, creating a kind of group agreement or class integrity charter, students begin to take ownership of this concept and to establish it as a common value, an uptake I often see in my classes when students nudge each other during peer review about citation.

This activity is scheduled very early in the semester—often in the first sessions—and helps set up AI as the framework for the entire course. It requires students to review institutional policies and resources so that they know what they say and where to find them, and it allows them to confirm their understanding of these documents through working first with their peers and then as a class in conversation with the instructor. This opportunity to ask questions is essential: students see that working with AI takes effort—for all researchers. It is not something "everyone" already learned in high school, and it has complexities and nuances reflecting the array of research and professional practices in which it is applied and about which we can learn, together. Instructors can share their own experiences of difficulty in this area, from slip-ups while they were in university to issues in their own research (for example, I talk about my misreadings of "common knowledge" when I have published outside my field). In my own sections, we also typically produce our first "teachable moment," because, in their definitions, no groups ever cite their sources, and when we point this out, we can have a light-hearted reflection on collective failure and reset our practices.

Embed AI Learning Throughout the Course

We learned that, for AI to "live" as a concept and practice beyond the first couple of weeks, our explicit and enhanced instruction about the expectation and how to meet it needs to be a consistent thread throughout the course, and, ideally, integrated into the scaffolding for each formal assessment. The understanding of and ability to apply AI principles are dynamic aptitudes that continue to develop alongside "core" content. Gaps in comprehension will emerge over the semester and opportunities to ask questions can address not only frustrations but also help instructors learn their own assumptions about what is common knowledge. For example, I finally realized my students were failing to properly document online journal articles not out of duplicity, but because they didn't know where to find these sources in citation guides: the MLA category "scholarly articles in an online database" assumes that users already have a firm grounding in the language and infrastructure of research. Iterative instruction of AI also recognizes that different applications or situations will introduce complexities that students will need explicit help to navigate. This requirement will be particularly urgent in contexts that don't look like traditional assignments (e.g., a formal paper assignment or exam), perhaps because students are still internalizing the value and appreciating its significance outside of "schoolroom" rules and also because they may not yet associate novel assignments as additional forms that academic research can take. In my own courses, for instance, students typically stumble when they write their first blog post, forgetting to cite or link to sources, and not providing image credits, even though this assignment comes right after the definition activity. Since it is their first assessment for grades (upping the stakes) and is in a genre that most have not produced before, and that they associate with non-academic contexts, they don't know how to meet the expectation, or that they should. Although I include an explicit evaluation criteria about ethical research practices on every assignment, it clearly is something that needs not only reinforcement but opportunity for clarification.

With appreciation for this learning curve, instructors would incorporate opportunities for students to think together about what academic integrity will look like and require in *each* assignment, particularly those "untraditional" assessments: what might make it challenging to meet expectations in this particular application? What are solutions or strategies to address those challenges? For example, how do we cite sources in an oral presentation, or in genres such as websites or videos that typically don't document research in the same ways a formal paper might? What about collaborative projects—work that as Löfström et al. note, presents a "key academic integrity issue" about which instructors themselves may be "collectively confused" (2015, 9)? Similarly, instructors have noted issues—even before 2020's pandemic-related "pivot" to digital teaching—with online assessments such as midterms or quizzes that are being done together when they are not supposed to be. Assessment design can support and embed AI—for instance, implementing project reflections (in which group members outline what each person contributed) or "open-book" and explicitly collaborative online tests, but for students to develop their own savviness about and toolkit for ethical practices, we also need to involve them as partners in explicit conversation and problem-solving. Applications that illustrate "grey" areas or complexities of AI can be particularly productive to puzzle through together as a way to deepen both student and instructor understanding. As an FYP faculty member noted in the Fall 2018 instructor survey ($n = 18$), "Students went in thinking they knew what academic misconduct was but found (because the examples were borderline, complicated, unexpected etc.) that this was something they actually needed to learn about."

Reinforcing the Relevance of AI Beyond the Classroom

In addition to this attention to the "how" of academic integrity, we have deepened the discussion of the "why" by inviting students to consider what a commitment to working with integrity does in particular disciplines and professions. What are the consequences for us, in this class *and the field it represents*, of not doing our work with integrity? What harms will be done? For example, we might ask them to consider (in a class discussion, small group work, or individual reflection) why it matters if a psychology scholar falsifies data in a research publication, or a sociologist fails to protect the identities of community partners who have shared sensitive information, or a medical student copies answers on an exam. In "Teaching Integrity," John Dichtl (2003) similarly outlines the value of having students connect classroom and professional practice. He argues that instructors' discussions of integrity expectations need to take place "inside and outside the classroom, and be expanded outward to include conversations about the work of professional historians," including the American

Historical Association's "Statement on Standards of Professional Conduct" (p. 369). Similarly, an FYP instructor surveyed in 2018 suggested that students:

> Read the Tri-Councils' guidelines. Make a distinction for students between writing in most university classrooms where one must do one's own writing, and writing as a professional where there is often the availability of editors and others who can assist with revisions, etc., for both those whose first language is English and those for whom it is not. Much "real-world" writing involves boiler-plating, collaboration, copy-editing, etc.

This connection to professional standards and practices that Dichtl and the FYP instructor recommend is another way to focus on discipline-specific commitments to integrity (codes of conduct, ethics declarations) and helps shift the emphasis from consequences of cheating—a kind of schoolroom concern—to consequences of error, to thinking about the implications and risks of unethical research, because the work we do as scholars contributes in real ways to how the world works. There is harm that can be done. By framing academic integrity in connection to their scholarly identities—as members of particular discourse and research communities they now identify with—we lay the foundation for them to see AI as personally and collectively relevant and consequential.

Recognize AI as "Hidden Curriculum"

This project has necessarily also involved a shift in faculty attitudes and an understanding of the potential for our AI instruction to more broadly cultivate belonging for more students. The work we do in making explicit our expectations of AI—and the steps by which one meets those expectations—has become part of a larger effort to challenge the "hidden curriculum" that reflects and reinforces inequities and access in higher education. Conversations about AI, or more typically about misconduct, illuminate the many other, related knowledges about higher education and its practices that too often we assume are shared. My work both as an administrator and on this project has helped me understand that too often, violations of AI are "canary in the coalmine" moments for students who are struggling, often because of systemic inequities that undermine their sense of belonging and their understanding of "how to university." Many of the students I have interviewed for alleged academic misconduct ended up in disciplinary meetings because they did not understand how the university works: they didn't know they could ask for an extension, for example, or take a late penalty. Others were in significant personal crisis and did not know about campus resources or perhaps—more troublingly—they did not feel that they mattered enough to the institution to take advantage of such resources.

From the pilot year of "Cheating Hearts" on, we have extended our educative framework to connect explicit AI instruction to explicit discussions about reasons why students may struggle to meet these expectations, and the options and resources available to them to ease such struggles. As the project has continued, however, I have argued—within FYP and beyond—that we have a duty to be much more explicit about what we are asking students to do, and why, to normalize asking questions, and to check our assumptions about what we expect that "everyone already knows." Creating a framework of integrity seems to have had the additional benefit in our courses of encouraging students to talk to their instructors, giving us an opportunity to connect with and support them. A member of the 2017 working group ($n = 7$) noted a shift in the number and kind of these interactions: "if they are struggling with citation and issues of academic integrity, they tend to put it on the table, which is something that I've never seen before…They're extremely open about their struggles in general … I find it really refreshing."

"Cheating" Lessons: Overall Take-Aways

Although a final round of assessments planned for the "Cheating Hearts" project's scheduled conclusion in April 2020 has been delayed to the pandemic, we have met our major goals, so that, by 2018, all FYP courses and sections now include at least some explicit instruction on academic integrity and teach how to meet these expectations. Our 2017 pre-project surveys of working group ($n = 7$) and non-working group faculty ($n = 10$) document this change: working group faculty reported that "I didn't do anything with academic integrity in previous years" and "This was the first time we discussed it openly as a seminar," while the majority of non-working group instructors reported only discussing policy, early in the semester, and providing class time on avoiding plagiarism later in the course.

Significantly, the changes we made were transformative but actually quite small in scope and, as intended, built on our existing course content. The syllabus statement and variations on the definition activity were the most commonly used materials, as well as additional readings, paraphrase activities, discussions of patchwriting, discussion of student pressures and why students plagiarize, and quizzes. Instructors in 2018 ($n = 18$) and 2019 ($n = 17$) surveys reported that they spent 2–3 additional classes dedicated to introducing AI than they did before. Although we made space for this content in the courses (and addressed other pedagogical imperatives) by eliminating final exams, faculty continue to report that time is a continuous constraint. An initiative I led in 2020 to create an online "Introduction to academic integrity" module, embedded in the UBC orientations program Jump Start and available for instructors to use in any course, may give instructors a way to "flip" some of the preliminary grounding in this concept. (This module launched in August 2020, and has been used in undergraduate and graduate courses.)

One convincing point of data has emerged in the number and type of misconduct cases. While through 2018 the number of cases remained consistent with past years—unsurprisingly, given the greater scrutiny and expectation on faculty to report—in 2019, only five cases were reported to the Chair. Of those, three were deemed as minor infractions (patchwriting), and two were sent to the Dean's office as indicating academic dishonesty. In past years, the vast majority of cases reflected accidental misconduct, resulting from a genuinely poor understanding of expectations, or misconduct arising from students in crisis who made poor choices under exceptionally challenging circumstances—two groups that, ideally, would receive education and resources without having to come to the Chair's office. Given how acutely stressful a misconduct meeting is (for faculty, but particularly for students), this change in the demographics of reported cases is deeply gratifying.

Our "Hearts" Will Go on: Spreading the Conversation

This project has attracted intense interest from faculty and staff across UBC, with group members invited to create workshops and presentations on teaching with integrity in departments and units across campus and at other local institutions. These connections build out the conversation and reflect an increasing appetite to learn new ways to cultivate this foundational value and concept. As FYP's project illustrates, "changing the conversation" takes significant effort that benefits from collaboration to share the load. In taking up AI through an educational framework, UBC will need to make an ongoing commitment to invest—literally and figuratively—in the infrastructure this work requires so that we "achieve institutionalization," the fourth and final stage in Bertram Gallant and Drinan model of AI implementation (2008, p. 4). As this project wraps up, I have identified the following ways we need to keep changing the conversation about AI at UBC and beyond.

Incorporate AI Throughout the Degree

Our study was tied to first-year writing courses, representing a course and year level that too often is considered the default and only place that AI is be taught. AI instruction is not the sole responsibility of "composition" nor can it remain exclusively co-curricular, featured in orientations programming or library skills workshops. Although these additional learning contexts are crucial for reiteration and reinforcement, AI instruction needs to be a shared element of all curriculum: ideally, students would talk and learn about the expectations and practices of AI in every course they take, including senior-level classes designed for majors and in graduate work, since these students also come to our courses with gaps in their knowledge—from differences in culture, discipline, and /or training—and presumably the shame of "not knowing" will be even more keenly felt by those in advanced courses. An institution-wide and coherent program of AI instruction scaffolded to address increasing complexity and particular nuances, and supported by level-appropriate resources (e.g., library and learning centre) would more effectively foster a culture of integrity and allow all students access to meet these expectations.

Clarity and Consistent Application of Policy

This "integrity across the curriculum" approach should be buttressed by clear, student-centered policy that is consistently applied. As Sarah Elaine Eaton (2017) notes in her study of Canadian university policies on plagiarism, including UBC's, too often these documents speak about violations and misconduct in quite generic ways that, she argues, do little to support consistent understanding and uptake of AI practices by both faculty and students (278–9). Studies of student perceptions of AI point to the crucial need for consistent uptake and application of institutional policy in cultivating a culture of integrity: faculty must reflect a common understanding of and commitment to upholding the expectations that students do their work with integrity (Löfström et al., 2015; Evans-Tokaryk, 2014; Jurdi et al., 2012; 2011; Wang, 2008; Christensen Hughes & McCabe, 2006). Language is also an important consideration: Mulholland's analysis of Mount Royal University's plagiarism policy critiques the dominant "moralistic and ethical" discourses of academic dishonesty in which students are "categorized…as honorable or shameful" (p. 105) and that obfuscate the responsibilities of the institution to educate students (p. 113). We have opportunities at UBC to rewrite our policies so that they speak clearly to students as well as faculty and staff, and—like the syllabus statement modelled by the "Cheating Hearts" group—do so in educative and proactive ways that all parties will recognize and take up. Ideally, these policies would be located outside as well as inside the academic calendar, so that they were more easily accessible, and the process for reporting misconduct would be equally clear and accessible, at the level of the institution, faculties, and departments.

The COVID-19 pandemic has, perhaps ironically, created several spaces for this advocacy to be effective at UBC and, arguably beyond, since remote learning has made urgent the need for conversations about AI and assessment that have involved many more faculty than pre-pandemic initiatives would have. Discussions of "remote proctoring" platforms have, similarly, fuelled broader engagement with questions of ethics and equity, as instructors who wish to avoid such platforms have to rethink classroom practices. Faculty frustration with forms of academic misconduct such as peers' sharing of exam questions and course materials with each other and with "homework help" sites, apparent collaboration in online tests, and suspicions of contract cheating have bolstered calls for the institution to take a more explicit position on these issues—rather than leaving decisions up to individual departments or faculty members, which can then be seen as arbitrary and create perceptions of inequities—and provide support for staff and faculty to make the required pedagogical changes and to address issues such as copyright violations. Perhaps these challenges will result in a collective "teachable moment" about AI—and a change of heart.

Notes

1. This statement, and other teaching and learning materials developed by the "Cheating Hearts" project can be accessed at https://learningcommons.ubc.ca/faculty-resources/academic-integrity/.
2. For full assignment instructions, see https://learningcommons.ubc.ca/faculty-resources/academic-integrity/.

References

Bertram Gallant, T., & Drinan, P. (2008). Toward a model of academic integrity institutionalization: Informing practice in postsecondary education. *Canadian Journal of Higher Education, 38*(2), 25–43.

Brooks, T., Marini, Z., & Radue, J. (2011). Linking academic integrity and classroom civility: Student attitudes and institutional response. *Collected Essays on Learning and Teaching, 4,* 81–88. https://doi.org/10.22329/celt.v4i0.3277

Childers, D., & Bruton, S. (2016). "Should it be considered plagiarism?" Student perceptions of complex citation issues. *Journal of Academic Ethics, 14*(1), 1–17. https://doi.org/10.1007/s10805-015-9250-6

Christensen Hughes, J., & McCabe, D. (2006). Understanding academic misconduct. *The Canadian Journal of Higher Education, 36*(1), 49–63.

Colella-Sandercock, J., & Alahmadi, H. (2015). Plagiarism education: Strategies for instructors. *International Journal of Learning, Teaching and Educational Research, 13*(1), 76–84.

Dawson, J. (2004). Plagiarism: What's really going on? Teaching and Learning Forum (2004). https://litec.curtin.edu.au/events/conferences/tlf/tlf2004/dawson.html

Dichtl, J. (2003). Teaching integrity. *The History Teacher, 36*(3), 367–373. https://www.jstor.org/stable/1555693

Eaton, S. E. (2017). Comparative analysis of institutional policy definitions of plagiarism: A pan-Canadian university study. *Interchange: A Quarterly Review of Education, 48(3),* 271–281. https://doi.org/10.1007/s10780-017-9300-7

Eaton, S. E., & Edino, R. (2018). Strengthening the research agenda of educational integrity in Canada: A review of the research literature and call to action. *International Journal for Educational Integrity, 14*(5), 1–21. https://doi.org/10.1007/s40979-018-0028-7

Eaton, S. E., Guglielmin, M., & Otoo, B. (2017). Plagiarism: Moving from punitive to pro-active approaches. In A. P. Preciado Babb, L. Yeworiew, & S. Sabbaghan (Eds.), *Selected Proceedings of the IDEAS Conference 2017: Leading Educational Change Conference.* 28–36. Werklund School of Education, University of Calgary. https://prism.ucalgary.ca/handle/1880/52096

Evans-Tokaryk, T. (2014). Academic integrity, remix culture, globalization: A Canadian case study of student and faculty perceptions of plagiarism. *Across the Disciplines, 11*(2), 1–40.

Ho, J. K. (2015). An exploration of the problem of plagiarism with the cognitive mapping technique. *Systems Research and Behavioural Science, 32(6),* 735–742. https://doi.org/10.1002/sres.2296

Howard, R. M. (1992). A plagiarism pentimento. *Journal of Teaching Writing, 11*(2), 233–245.

Howard, R. M. (1995). Plagiarisms, authorships, and the academic death penalty. *College English, 57(7),* 788–806. https://doi.org/10.2307/378403

Jurdi, R., Hage, H. S., & Chow, H. P. (2012). What behaviours do students consider academically dishonest? Findings from a survey of Canadian undergraduate students. *Social Psychology of Education, 15*(1), 1–23. https://doi.org/10.1007/s11218-011-9166-y

Kier, C. A. (2014). How well do Canadian distance education students understand plagiarism? *The International Review of Research in Open and Distributed Learning, 15(1),* 227–248. https://doi.org/10.19173/irrodl.v15i1.1684

Löfström, E., Trotman, T., Furnari, M., & Shephard, K. (2015). Who teaches academic integrity and how do they do it? *Higher Education, 69*(3), 435–448. https://doi.org/10.1007/s10734-014-9784-3

Locquiao, J., & Ives, B. (2020). First-year university students' knowledge of academic misconduct and the association between goals for attending university and receptiveness to intervention. *International Journal for Educational Integrity, 16(5).* https://doi.org/10.1007/s40979-020-00054-6

Mulholland, M.-L. (2020). Honor and shame: Plagiarism and governing student morality. *Journal of College and Character, 21*(2), 104–115. https://doi.org/10.1080/2194587X.2020.1741394

Newton, P. (2015). Academic integrity: A quantitative study of confidence and understanding in students at the start of their higher education. *Assessment & Evaluation in Higher Education, 41*(3), 482–497. https://doi.org/10.1080/02602938.2015.1024199

Orr, J. (2017). Creating an academic integrity community through campus partnerships and educational initiatives. Webinar. *Turnitin.com.*

Power, L. G. (2009). University students' perceptions of plagiarism. *The Journal of Higher Education, 80(6),* 643–682. http://www.jstor.org/stable/27750755

Roig, M. (1997). Can undergraduate students determine whether text has been plagiarized? *The Psychological Record, 47*, 113–122.

Scott, S. S., Mcguire, J. M., & Shaw, S. F. (2003). Universal design for instruction: A new paradigm for adult instruction in postsecondary education. *Remedial and Special Education, 24*(6), 369–379. https://doi.org/10.1177/07419325030240060801

Wang, Y. (2008). University student online plagiarism. *International Journal on E-Learning, 7*(4), 743–757.

Wilkinson, J. (2009). Staff and student perceptions of plagiarism and cheating. *International Journal of Teaching and Learning in Higher Education, 20*(2), 98–105.

Dr. Laurie McNeill is Professor of Teaching in the Department of English Language and Literatures at UBC. Her research, publications, and teaching focus on two main fields: academic integrity studies, with a focus on pedagogies of integrity, and auto/biography studies, with particular interest in testimony, digital platforms, and archival life narratives. She has published on teaching and learning in auto/biography studies most recently in the journals *a/b: Autobiography Studies* and *English Studies in Canada*; with Kate Douglas (Flinders), she is co-editor of *Teaching Lives* (Routledge, 2017) and with John David Zuern, co-author of "Reading Digital Lives Generously," in *Research Methods for Auto/Biography Studies* (Routledge, 2019). She is the principal investigator on several SOTL research and teaching initiatives, including projects on academic integrity curricula and open-access writing resources for STEAM disciplines.

Chapter 26
Promotion of Academic Integrity Through a Marketing Lens for Canadian Post-secondary Institutions

Nazanin Teymouri, Sheryl Boisvert, and Katrina John-West

Abstract Although the study of academic integrity has addressed numerous perspectives on how to encourage, teach, and manage student behaviour, little has appeared on how to promote it beyond an educational or cultural lens. Though emphasis in the classroom through teaching is important to an overall understanding of academic integrity, the promotion—specifically through marketing tactics—may offer an entirely new and applicable approach to communication between academic institutions and students. Specific suggestions include gathering data on academic misconduct on a consistent basis, using data for institutional analysis of trends in misconduct so that a tailored approach to addressing specific challenges may be planned, and engaging students through relevant mediums and methods familiar to them.

Keywords Academic misconduct · Relationship marketing · Post-secondary · Higher education

Communicating with students about the importance of academic integrity occurs in a variety of ways, including through course outlines, faculty oral instruction, and via institutional websites, workshops and campaigns. The need to address academic integrity through such a holistic approach is well studied and documented (Bretag et al., 2014; East & Donnelly, 2012). A positive relationship between faculty and students is clearly demonstrated as a factor in how academic integrity is upheld and misconduct is addressed in higher education (Christensen Hughes and McCabe, 2006a). Christensen Hughes and McCabe (2006b) indicate that there is a general

N. Teymouri (✉)
Northern Alberta Institute of Technology, Edmonton, Canada
e-mail: NAZANINT@nait.ca

S. Boisvert · K. John-West
NorQuest College, Edmonton, Canada
e-mail: Sheryl.Boisvert@norquest.ca

K. John-West
e-mail: Katrina.john-west@norquest.ca

S. E. Eaton and J. Christensen Hughes (eds.), *Academic Integrity in Canada*, Ethics and Integrity in Educational Contexts 1,
https://doi.org/10.1007/978-3-030-83255-1_26

pervasiveness of misconduct in the Canadian education system from high school to post-secondary graduate programs and that there is a need for further exploration of the challenges relating to upholding academic integrity. Despite general agreement on what actions constitute academic misconduct, differences in opinion between faculty and students on the severity of these behaviours points to a disconnect in perspective that requires bridging (Christensen Hughes & McCabe, 2006b). Overcoming challenges to academic integrity cannot be achieved until there can be an alignment between faculty and student perceptions of not only what is considered academic integrity, but also the severity of different types of misconduct. The most effective way to create an understanding between educators and learners is to build meaningful relationships.

Though academic integrity is a key element in scholarship and education, the way students learn, receive information, and interact with one another has evolved beyond the traditional classroom. Digital tools and cultural diversity have changed the landscape of teaching and learning. The pervasive existence of misconduct across the post-secondary landscape is an indication that simply teaching students about academic integrity is not enough to mitigate inappropriate behaviour.

The focus of this chapter is on the potential of using marketing tactics to strengthen efforts in promoting academic integrity at Canadian post-secondary institutions. It is argued that current marketing efforts to recruit students and growing digital trends provide the means to leverage current communication practices for the promotion of academic integrity. Despite the highlighted use of marketing, the aim here is not to facilitate the perception of students as being clients or customers of post-secondary education. Instead, it is to encourage the incorporation of tools beyond the scope of an educational lens that may be relevant to the dynamic and complex challenges related to academic integrity.

To begin, the concept of relationship marketing and how it has evolved is explored. Following, an overview of current marketing efforts by the Canadian government and post-secondary institutions is provided to highlight the resources invested, and expertise demonstrated in the promotion of Canadian higher education. Parallel to a growing emphasis on marketing and communications universities, colleges, and technical institutes have progressively moved an increasing number of programs to online delivery (Bates, 2018). This trend not only offers greater learning options for students, but also broadens the prospect of expanded and diversified modes of communication between institutes and students.

Challenges to academic integrity are both complex and expand into areas beyond a teaching and learning lens. To overcome these challenges, it is necessary to think outside of educational concepts, mobilize the expertise of multiple stakeholders, and explore a range of disciplines relevant to the current environment in which post-secondary institutions operate (Bretag et al., 2014). Relationship marketing offers a space for the convergence of scholarship and operational practices, helping post-secondary institutions to shift towards creating cultures of academic integrity, rather the more simply endeavouring to manage academic misconduct (Bretag et al., 2014).

Overview of Relationship Marketing

The concept of relationship marketing has been discussed extensively since the 1990s. At a time well before the global ubiquity of connections and interactions through online platforms, marketers already had an acute realization of the benefits to understanding and caring for customers (Buttle, 1996). Buttle frames this as a shift away from a focus on timely transactions between firms and customers to one in which more long-term relationships are sought (1996). Sheth and Parvatiyar (1995) elaborate on this trend, describing the long-term value of mutual interdependence and cooperation fostered through relationship marketing practices. They explain that although transactional marketing approaches allow for greater independence and choice for customers, they are heavily based on the self-interest of marketers whose aim it is to maximize their return-on-investment (Sheth & Parvatiyar, 1995).

The shift away from a transactional approach has modified the emphasis on the traditional four P's of marketing—price, product, promotion, place—to a focus on customer retention (Buttle, 1996). With this focus, relationship marketing applies to tactics that encourage cooperation, interactive exchanges, and mutually beneficial bonds between actors within the business environment (Ashley et al., 2011; Buttle, 1996; Möller & Halinen, 2000; Sheth, 2002; Sheth & Parvatiyar, 1995). Of the models and concepts offering ways to optimize marketing efforts, it is particularly effective for achieving long-term, consistent behaviours in targeted groups (Ashley et al., 2011; Buttle, 1996; Möller & Halinen, 2000; Sheth, 2002; Sheth & Parvatiyar, 1995).

A key element of relationship marketing strategies focuses on the importance of customer retention over attracting new ones (Berry, 2002). Not only is retention important to sales, the practice of maintaining a customer base is a far more efficient allocation of marketing budgets (Berry, 2002). Ultimately, it is more efficient to engage and entice existing customers to continue their patronage than it is to convince new customers to purchase a product or service (Berry 2002). The use of data to develop personalized products and services aimed at meeting the specific needs of customers is one way to achieve this (Berry, 2002; Möller & Halinen, 2000; Sheth, 2002). The greater a company's ability to cater to their customers' needs, the better they are able to differentiate themselves among competitors. However, a key element of successful relationship marketing efforts is the longevity and strength of bonds created between firms and customers (Berry, 2002; Sheth & Parvatiyar, 1995). This outcome surpasses the notion of customer retention; thereby, through effective communication and customer satisfaction, companies earn the loyalty of their customers (Abeysekera & Wickramasinghe, 2013; Berry, 2002; Lewin & Johnston, 1997; Zakaria et al., 2018). Customer loyalty not only contributes to profitability but provides a basis from which companies can better predict and influence consumer behaviour (Lewin & Johnston, 1997; Zakaria et al., 2018). Thus, the defining principle of successful relationship marketing is an unwavering attention to customers and clients; whereby, elements of transactional marketing models—focused on the profitable exchange of goods—are secondary (Ashley et al., 2011; Buttle, 1996; Möller & Halinen, 2000; Sheth, 2002; Sheth & Parvatiyar, 1995).

The efficacy of targeted audience-centred approaches to communication practiced by governments to sway public behaviour is well documented (Abroms & Maibach, 2008). This is particularly evident in the management of public health (Abroms & Maibach, 2008). Similar to the efficacy of marketing campaigns aimed to retain customers, "the evidence is fairly compelling that interventions targeting individual-level factors can be a highly cost-effective way to promote population health" (Abroms & Maibach, 2008, p. 227). Also similar to relationship marketing is that in order to effectively and sustainably change public behaviour governments must also address the systemic challenges and barriers that compel individuals to make poor health decisions (Abroms & Maibach, 2008). It is with thorough knowledge of an audience, understanding of their behaviours, and an organizational approach to communication that governments are able to influence public behaviour in areas such as alcohol consumption and tobacco use (Abroms & Maibach, 2008). A company's approach to promoting a product or service operates through a different lens from that of government communications. However, the importance of knowing a customer and building a relationship with them to influence their choices follows a similar path to changing public behaviour.

Companies that understand their customers improve their ability to differentiate themselves in markets where diversity in products and services is difficult to achieve (Buttle, 1996). This facilitates both the initial attraction of customers and their retention. Modern database management systems, wide access to the internet, and social media provide countless tools for understanding customers more thoroughly than ever before. These tools provide companies with unprecedented insight into their customers' activities, interests and needs (Abeysekera & Wickramasinghe, 2013; Ashley et al., 2011; Buttle, 1996; Möller & Halinen, 2000; Sheth & Parvatiyar, 1995; Zakaria et al., 2018). Lewin and Johnston (1997) describe how a focal distribution firm in the lumber industry was able to differentiate itself within the market through a value added, customer service-oriented approach. By understanding their customers and meeting their needs effectively, the firm was able to distinguish themselves from competitors in a market where differentiation is difficult to achieve (Lewin & Johnston, 1997).

Similarly, Abeysekera and Wickramasinghe (2013) highlight the importance of "customer orientation," described as an understanding of customer behaviour and actions by salespeople as a key element in relationship marketing efforts. They attribute this not only to successful sales and retention, but also as a key element for achieving differentiation among competitors (Abeysekera & Wickramasinghe, 2013). Both global and local businesses that gather and use knowledge of their customers, develop personalized products, and communicate authentically with their customers, benefit from relationship marketing.

The value of customer retention within the banking industry is well documented and has been discussed for several decades (Murphy, 1996). Murphy describes how the use of relationship marketing by financial service providers has risen from the need for banks to differentiate themselves (1996). This combined with the realization that long-term relationships enhance profitability, made relationship marketing favourable among banks (1996). This is evident in Canada as all five major banks provide services in multiple languages and emphasize their ability to personalize their services to clients' various needs (Canadian Bank of Commerce, n.d.; Bank of Montreal, n.d.; Bank of Nova Scotia, n.d.; Royal Bank of Canada, n.d.; Toronto Dominion Bank, n.d.). Zakaria et al. (2018) also emphasize the value of customer orientation as a means to improving customer satisfaction. This they conclude contributes to both strong relationships and customer loyalty to businesses (Zakaria et al., 2018).

The notion of customer loyalty is particularly important to relationship marketing ventures and is more nuanced than the concept of retention. Retention can be seen as repeated business. In practice, it is a customer's return to a business to fulfill the need for a specific commodity. Loyalty in contrast demonstrates a deeper connection to a business—one that indicates an emotional bond.

Sheth and Parvatiyar explain that "when producers and consumers directly deal with each other, there is a greater potential for emotional bonding that transcends economical exchange" (1995, p. 389). Halimi et al. (2011) echo this notion explaining that loyalty is formed through "communication and personalization" (p.49). This concept aligns with the modern role of companies on social media. Successful firms can no longer focus primarily on advertising to communicate with customers. Instead, a steady stream of positive engagement is necessary for them to stay relevant. Without attention to the online activities of their customers, firms would disappear among the endless stream of digital communication customers and other companies engage in. Though technology has augmented the way firms learn about, interact with and communicate with customers, it remains that in order for them to stay relevant they must diligently focus on and consistently find ways to maintain their relationship with customers.

Möller and Halinen analyze the conceptual framework of relationship marketing as a general theory (2000). Their evaluation concludes that what is described loosely as relationship marketing is a combination of two theories they describe as being either "market-based" or "network-based" (Möller & Halinen, 2000, p. 29). Although Möller and Halinen provide valuable insight into relationship marketing as it relates to other theories within the marketing discipline, their analysis does not imply that there is a risk of reduced benefit for businesses that foster strong bonds with their customers. Rather, they note that the more complex the relationship is between businesses and their customers, the stronger the interdependence between them (Möller & Halinen, 2000). Despite the clear benefits, Ashley, Noble, Donthu, and Lemon explain that certain elements of relationship marketing activities can hinder efforts to build rapport with customers (2011). Programs that create inconveniences, do not provide meaningful benefits, present a privacy risk, or demand too much involvement from customers, are detrimental to creating sustainable relationships (Ashley et al., 2011).

What this indicates is that customer retention may be achieved through the benefits individuals experience from their patronage to a company. Though retention may lead to an increase in profits and market share, its longevity shares a negative correlation with competitors' ability to differentiate themselves beyond what has temporarily seized the attention of customers in the market. Loyalty implies a greater bond—one that is leveraged by emotional ties—than retention. Developing the emotional ties that lead to customer loyalty is a nuanced, fluid goal that requires consistent attention and positive communication. This is similar to personal interactions where the development of meaningful relationships is founded on authenticity and trust. In order for businesses to achieve this, there must be more than an intention to sell when interacting with customers. However counter intuitive this may appear and despite the absence of a concise theoretical framework, the positive implications of relationship marketing are worthy of attention.

Marketing Canadian Post-secondary Institutions

The promotion of programs and courses is a necessity for universities, colleges, and technical institutes. At a minimum, the information offered through academic calendars is required for students to plan their educational pursuits. Digital communication through websites and social media provides countless ways to reach out to students and to capture their attention. Although all Canadian post-secondary institutions have some form of a digital presence, there is potential to use existing marketing and communication expertise as well as effective modes of connecting with students to leverage the promotion of academic integrity. The emphasis being placed on marketing post-secondary institutions by federal and provincial bodies demonstrates a high level of will and expertise to connect with students.

Although these promotional efforts focus on international enrollment, they highlight the degree to which marketing education can be successful. Data collected for the academic years between 2007 and 2016 by Statistics Canada shows that Canadian post-secondary institutions experienced growth in international enrollment (Statistics Canada, 2020a; 2020b). During this time, though federal and provincial government funding decreased, the overall revenue of institutions increased—a result of increased private sponsorship and income from tuition (Statistics Canada, 2017; 2020a) (See Table 1). The increase in revenue outpaced enrollment across the country (Statistics Canada 2020a, 2020b). This is attributed in part to the significant increase in international student enrollment that accounts for a substantially higher proportion of total tuition revenue compared to that of domestic students (Statistics Canada, 2017).

This financial success is rooted in an unprecedented emphasis on marketing. Canada's latest national strategy for attracting international students includes plans to increase promotional efforts with both funding and sophisticated digital tactics (Global Affairs Canada, 2019). Much of this promotion is through EduCanada in collaboration with provincial governments (Global Affairs Canada, 2019). The Brand-Use Eligibility and Authorization Policy for EduCanada states that only institutions that have met the standards for quality of education may attend federally sponsored events and use its trademarks (EduCanada, n.d.). In order to allow for expanded use of the brand while ensuring the integrity of its standard for quality, eligibility for participation in and use of the EduCanada brand is largely determined by each institutions' home province (EduCanada, n.d.).

Corresponding to the growth in marketing is the increased digitization of education. A 2017 study indicates that between 2011–2016, online delivery of courses increased by 11% across Canadian institutions (Bates, 2018). This trend continues at a rate of approximately 2% per year (Bates, 2018). The movement towards online delivery of programs runs parallel to the rapid increase of online engagement among youth. A US study indicates that besides increasing engagement in digital communication, some individuals completing grade 12 can be reached effectively and solely through online mechanisms (Twenge et al., 2019). The evolving digital presence of institutions provides for the ideal environment to connect and communicate with students.

Although education remains at the core of post-secondary operations, the way students are drawn to programs has evolved along with the need for revenue generation (Eaton & Goddard, 2008; Guo & Guo, 2017; Marginson, 2002). Marketing and promotion are now a norm in educational discourse (Eaton & Goddard, 2008; Guo & Guo, 2017; Marginson, 2002). Data on revenue and enrollment demonstrates the value of marketing and promotion in maintaining Canada's educational institutions (Guo & Guo, 2017). Though some may resist the adoption of standard business practices within higher education, as complex organizations, the benefits of having a positive global and domestic brand, supported through savvy marketing is undeniable.

The Relevance of Relationship Marketing to the Promotion of Academic Integrity

Data Gathering and Use

A key element of marketing strategy is the collection and use of data. The more an organization knows about their targeted audience, the better they will be able to engage them. This practice is common in marketing but can quickly escalate to breaches of privacy and personal freedom. However, in the case of marketing academic integrity, there is no need to infringe upon students' privacy unless there is a justifiable reason such as is a risk of harm to themselves or someone else. Data gathering and effective targeting can be achieved ethically by several means.

For instance, information regarding cases of academic misconduct can provide insight on trends such as peak times that specific types of inappropriate behaviour occur, or courses prone to higher incidents of cheating. Knowing the timing of increased incidents of misconduct may point to gaps in student supports, instruction, or communication on academic policies. Similarly, awareness of courses indicating a higher rate of misconduct, may provide clues as to where focused attention may be needed, such as improving assessment design. Although this information may already be gathered by institutions and used by administrators to support students and instructors, institutional analysis of annual trends may provide more comprehensive insight into the factors initiating academic misconduct.

With this information, post-secondary institutions can proactively address challenges to academic integrity. However, organization-wide collaboration would be required for this to be possible. Though the goal may be to promote academic integrity to students, institution-wide communication would be necessary so that specific gaps are addressed. Co-ordination between academic departments as well as divisions responsible for handling cases of misconduct and communications would be necessary to ensure targeted and effective delivery of messages to students. Evidence of a concentrated and consistent effort to achieve this throughout post-secondary institutions is currently not available.

Relationship Marketing Tactics to Encourage Cooperation, Mutually Beneficial Bonds, and Interactive Exchanges

Co-operation, mutually beneficial bonds, and interactive exchanges are key elements of the learning environment. It is through these that students learn, educators teach, and scholarship advances. Through an educational lens, this is how the skills related to academic integrity can be taught. However, from a marketing perspective, co-operation, bonds and exchanges create relationships that foster loyalty to products, services, and brands. It is through loyalty that consumers are drawn to specific commodities. In this way consumer dedication parallels the way a culture guides traditions, habits, and perspectives. Used alongside teaching skills relevant to academic integrity, relationship marketing is one way of enhancing bonds and interactive exchanges within the educational environment between students and institutions.

Although the aim of promoting academic integrity through relationship marketing tactics is not to sell a product or service, actively reminding students of its importance may help to develop loyalty to the concept much like government campaigns to influence public behaviours. Similarly, certain commodities are a part of daily lives that can be discussed on social media and in entertainment, academic integrity must become a part of students' daily life for it to become a part of their culture.

Within the scope of post-secondary education institutional social media accounts can be used to carry out campaigns relating to academic integrity and misconduct. Data from cases of misconduct can be used in messaging to inform students and instructors on trending behaviours. For instance, if there is information that a copy of an assessment is being circulated among students, institutions may alert students that they are aware of the activity and remind students of instructional support to help them avoid cheating. Bringing this type of activity into the forefront of social media communication allows for conversations to develop, demonstrates a proactive approach to misconduct, and provides students with a reminder that they are supported to behave with integrity by their institutions.

Entertainment such as sports can also be used to encourage discussion about academic integrity. For many institutions sporting events are a source of entertainment and pride. Parallels between cheating in sports and academics can easily be drawn. Sportsmanship and dedication to fair play of athletic teams can be used as a way to demonstrate the importance of integrity within the culture of an institution. Although a sporting event may not be the ideal place to discuss academic integrity, highlighting how integrity in athletics and academics relate to one another through social media and institutional websites may promote positive habits, develop discussion, and integrate academic integrity into the culture of institutions.

Khan et al. (2020) highlight the importance of implementing institution-wide campaigns to raise awareness of academic integrity. With a specific interest in contract cheating, they describe how contract cheating is a social issue that is best addressed by interacting with students through familiar mediums such as social media (Khan et al., 2020). A particularly interesting finding from their study is that students enjoyed the interactions and discussions around academic integrity (Khan et al., 2020). Positive feedback and growth in participation throughout this study indicates the initiation of a mutually beneficial relationship between the institution and students (Khan et al., 2020).

Relationship marketing tactics are as diverse as institutional goals and modes of communication. Simply put, successful relationship marketing campaigns include ways to engage potential consumers through popular and relevant mediums. Although this discussion does not intend to suggest that students must be considered customers within higher education, there are certain proven methods of reaching individuals used by marketers that can be beneficial to awareness campaigns initiated by post-secondary institutions. As seen in Khan et al. (2020), the use of mediums does not have to be complex. Knowing enough about students to reach them through the use of common methods such as posting images and hashtags can have a significant and long-term impact on awareness (Khan et al., 2020). Khan et al. demonstrate that similar to marketing campaigns, attention and concern for students is an effective way to develop loyal relationships with them. Any activity that encourages academic integrity beyond the classroom has the potential to build institutional dedication to it. The key to creating co-operation, mutually beneficial bonds, and interactive exchanges is to highlight academic integrity as an element of institutional culture that relates to student life in positive way.

Conclusion

The management of academic integrity cannot be left to the classroom alone. Despite the efforts of educators to mitigate misconduct, students will face situations that will lead to inappropriate behaviours. Changes in technology and course delivery will pose new and continuously evolving challenges to upholding the integrity of assignments and assessments. Contributing to these factors, gaps in cultural understanding between educators and learners further complicate the matter.

Although providing supports for referencing and citation skills are an important part of coaching learners to behave appropriately within the educational environment, sustainable management of academic integrity requires a continuous and collaborative institution-wide approach. Where teaching skills provide tools to avoid misconduct, responsive attention to student behaviours, habits, and tendencies will facilitate more effective communication on and promotion of academic integrity. A relationship marketing lens may provide innovative ways to reach, engage, and interact with learners.

The concept of customer retention and influence on behaviour is as relevant to commerce as it is to communication with students in education. Post-secondary institutions and their supporting governmental bodies are already heavily engaged in communicating to students through marketing and promotions. Similarly, colleges, universities, and technical institutions alike are moving increasingly towards online delivery of courses and programs. Most importantly, students are highly engaged in communication through digital means as a way of information gathering and social connection. There is no lack of digital platforms with which to engage students, the technical expertise to do so exists, and marketers have well established methods to understand audiences.

However, the relationship between institutions and their students cannot be confused with that of companies and their customers. Though certain activities and initiatives, such as social media campaigns, taken from marketing practices can be utilized to communicate about academic integrity, certain factors must be considered. The most apparent is that, although consumers look to companies for commodities, students engage with their institutions primarily for their education.

With this comes a notable difference in power dynamics. As consumers, individuals have the power to make choices regarding their purchases and how they interact with companies. In contrast, students do not have the same flexibility in how they approach discussions regarding academic integrity with their instructors and institution. Nonetheless, further exploration in how communication and marketing tactics may facilitate the management of academic integrity may provide new and innovative ways to overcome the challenges faced by post-secondary institutions.

References

Abeysekera, N., & Wickramasinghe, A. (2013). Relationship marketing and customer orientation of sales people: Learning from banks. *International Journal of Financial Services Management, 6*(1), 79–91.

Abroms, L. C., & Maibach, E. W. (2008). The effectiveness of mass communication to change public behavior. Annual review of public health, 29. Chicago.

Ashley, C., Noble, S. M., Donthu, N., & Lemon, K. N. (2011). Why customers won't relate: Obstacles to relationship marketing engagement. *Journal of Business Research, 64*(7), 749–756.

Bank of Montreal. (n.d.). Accessibility at BMO. https://www.bmo.com/main/about-bmo/accessibility/

Bates, T. (2018). The 2017 national survey of online learning in Canadian post-secondary education: Methodology and results. *International Journal of Educational Technology in Higher Education, 15*(1), 1–17. https://doi.org/10.1186/s41239-018-0112-3

Berry, L. L., (2002). Relationship Marketing of Services Perspectives from 1983 and 2000. *Journal of relationship marketing (Binghamton, N.Y1.), 1*(1), 59-77. https://doi.org/10.1300/J366v01n01_05

Bretag, T., Mahmud, S., Wallace, M., Walker, R., McGowan, U., East, J., Green, M., Partridge, L., & James, C. (2014). 'Teach us how to do it properly!' An Australian academic integrity student survey. *Studies in Higher Education, 39*(7), 1150–1169. https://doi.org/10.1080/03075079.2013.777406

Buttle, F. (1996). Relationship marketing. In F. Buttle (Ed.), *Relationship marketing: Theory and practice* (pp. 1–16). Paul Chapman.

Christensen Hughes, J. M., & McCabe, D. L. (2006a). Academic misconduct within higher education in Canada. *The Canadian Journal of Higher Education, 36*(2), 1–21. http://journals.sfu.ca/cjhe/index.php/cjhe/article/view/183537/183482

Christensen Hughes, J. M., & McCabe, D. L. (2006b). Understanding academic misconduct. *Canadian Journal of Higher Education, 36*(1), 49–63.

East, J., & Donnelly, L. (2012). Taking responsibility for academic integrity: A collaborative teaching and learning design. *Journal of University Teaching & Learning Practice, 9*(3), 1–11.

Eaton, S. E., & Goddard, J. T. (2008, May). Revenue-generating language programs at Canadian post-secondary institutions. Paper presented at the Annual Congress for the Humanities and Social Sciences, Canadian Society for the Study of Education (CSSE), Vancouver, BC. https://files.eric.ed.gov/fulltext/ED508999.pdf

EduCanada. (n.d.). Brand-use eligibility and authorization policy for the EduCanada: A world of possibilities. https://www.extranet-educanada.ca/Styleguide/english/#page/BBAA680A-883A-4C0A-AA62FE98D11572A3

Global Affairs Canada. (2019). *Building on success: International education strategy 2019–2024.* https://www.international.gc.ca/education/assets/pdfs/ies-sei/Building-on-Success-International-Education-Strategy-2019-2024.pdf

Guo, Y., & Guo, S. (2017). Internationalization of Canadian higher education: Discrepancies between policies and international student experiences. *Studies in Higher Education, 42*(5), 851–868.

Halimi, A. B., Chavosh, A., & Choshali, S. H. (2011). The influence of relationship marketing tactics on customer's loyalty in B2C relationship–the role of communication and personalization. *European Journal of Economics, Finance and Administrative Science, 31*, 49–56.

Khan, Z. R., Hemnani, P., Raheja, S., & Joshy, J. (2020). Raising awareness on contract cheating–Lessons learned from running campus-wide campaigns. *Journal of Academic Ethics, 18*, 175–191.

Lewin, J. E., & Johnston, W. J. (1997). Relationship marketing theory in practice: A case study. *Journal of Business Research, 39*(1), 23–31.

Marginson, S. (2002). Education in the global market: lessons from Australia. *Academe, 88(3)*, 22–24. https://doi.org/10.2307/40252157

Möller, K., & Halinen, A. (2000). Relationship marketing theory: Its roots and direction. *Journal of Marketing Management, 16*(1–3), 29–54. https://doi.org/10.1362/026725700785100460

Murphy, J. A. (1996). Retail banking. In F. Buttle (Ed.), *Relationship marketing: Theory and practice* (pp. 74–90). Paul Chapman.

Royal Bank of Canada. (n.d.). Welcome to Canada: Business specialist locator. https://commercial.rbcroyalbank.com/culturalMarkets.en.asp

Sheth, J. N. (2002). The future of relationship marketing. *Journal of Services Marketing, 16*(7), 590–592. https://doi.org/10.1108/08876040210447324

Sheth, J. N., & Parvatiyar, A. (1995). The evolution of relationship marketing. *International Business Review, 4*(4), 397–418.

Statistics Canada. (2017). *Financial information of universities and degree-granting colleges, 2015/2016*. https://www150.statcan.gc.ca/n1/daily-quotidien/170713/dq170713c-eng.htm

Statistics Canada. (2018). Canadian postsecondary enrolments and graduates, 2016/2017. https://www150.statcan.gc.ca/n1/daily-quotidien/181128/dq181128c-eng.htm

Statistics Canada. (2020a). *Combined public and private expenditure on educational institutions, by level of education (x 1,000,000)*. (Statistics Canada; Table 37–10–0131–01). https://www150.statcan.gc.ca/t1/tbl1/en/tv.action?pid=3710013101&pickMembers%5B0%5D=1.1&cubeTimeFrame.startYear=2007+%2F+2008&cubeTimeFrame.endYear=2015+%2F+2016&referencePeriods=20070101%2C20150101

Statistics Canada. (2020b). Postsecondary enrolments, by registration status, institution type, status of student in Canada and gender. (Statistics Canada ; Table 37–10–0018–01). https://www150.statcan.gc.ca/t1/tbl1/en/tv.action?pid=3710001801&pickMembers%5B0%5D=2.1&pickMembers%5B1%5D=5.1&pickMembers%5B2%5D=7.1&pickMembers%5B3%5D=4.1&pickMembers%5B4%5D=6.1&cubeTimeFrame.startYear=2007+%2F+2008&cubeTimeFrame.endYear=2015+%2F+2016&referencePeriods=20070101%2C20150101

The Bank of Nova Scotia. (n.d.). However you say "home," we speak your language. https://www.scotiabank.com/startright/common/pdf/StartRight_Pamphlet_ENG_online.pdf

Toronto Dominion Bank Group. (n.d.). Diverse languages for diverse needs. https://www.td.com/corporate-responsibility/diversity/serving-diverse-needs/diverse-languages-for-diverse-needs.jsp

Twenge, J. M., Martin, G. N., & Spitzberg, B. H. (2019). Trends in US Adolescents' media use, 1976–2016: The rise of digital media, the decline of TV, and the (near) demise of print. *Psychology of Popular Media Culture, 8*(4), 329.

Zakaria, A., Ahmad, S. S., Omar, M. W., & Alhady, S. M. A. S. A. (2018). The effect of relationship marketing, customer satisfaction and service quality towards customer loyalty: A case study in xyz sdn bhd. *International Journal of Accounting, 3*(11), 98–104.

Nazanin Teymouri is a research specialist at the Northern Alberta Institute of Technology. Her interest in academic integrity began with her role as a college instructor teaching international students in businesses programs. With a background in communication and business administration, her focus is on analysis, cultural understanding, and collaboration aimed at improving the post-secondary learning environment.

Sheryl Boisvert B.Ed, CGA, CGA, is currently a full-time instructor at NorQuest College, located in Edmonton, Alberta, Canada. Sheryl originally studied accounting at Lakeland College and subsequently completed her designation with CGA Alberta. She later returned to the University of Alberta to complete her Bachelor of Education degree. Sheryl has always believed that students gain a better understanding of material when they can go beyond the textbook and put theories into practice. Sheryl always looks for opportunities to make students' learning more experiential and relevant as a way to keep them engaged and participating.

Katrina John-West is currently a project administrator and previously an instructional assistant at NorQuest College in the Faculty of Business, Environment, and Technology. She has completed her Bachelor of Commerce Degree, majoring in International Business at Grant MacEwan University. She comes from a background in the public sector, with experience in customer service and process management. Katrina is starting her career in research as a project manager coordinating activities for an internal project on Academic Integrity.

Chapter 27
Using Quality Assurance Frameworks to Support an Institutional Culture of Academic Integrity at Canadian Universities

Emma J. Thacker and Amanda McKenzie

Abstract In Canada, there is a national academic quality assurance framework—the Canadian Degree Qualifications Framework (CDQF) that guides quality assurance standards within universities across the provinces and territories. These standards exist to support the quality and consistency of postsecondary academic programming in Canada, and provide mechanisms for quality enhancement. The CDQF is supported by further quality assurance mechanisms at the provincial level. While the CDQF includes the notion of academic integrity as a learning outcome requirement, the implementation and review of this quality indicator across the sector is nebulous. The ongoing support for a culture of academic integrity requires a holistic approach, which includes the alignment of various policies and processes. It also involves the inclusion of academic integrity best practices into quality assurance processes, such as curriculum development and program review. In this chapter we discuss several quality assurance tools used in Canadian universities, with a focus on Ontario institutions, and discuss opportunities to leverage them to support academic integrity. The CDQF and provincial/territorial quality assurance frameworks should be better utilized for a holistic response to academic misconduct, to strengthen teaching and learning, and develop a culture of integrity in higher education. Opportunities within cyclical program review, curriculum mapping and educational development are discussed to highlight opportunities for academic integrity specialists, quality assurance staff, faculty, and policy makers to raise academic integrity awareness and weave best practices across an institution. Implications for the community college sector are also included. Recommendations can be applied to postsecondary institutions across Canada and integrated with quality assurance practices promoted by the Quality Assurance Agency (QAA) and others academic integrity advocates around the world.

E. J. Thacker (✉)
University of Toronto Scarborough, 1265 Military Trail, Toronto, ON M1C1A4, Canada
e-mail: em.thacker@utoronto.ca

A. McKenzie
University of Waterloo, 200 University Ave. West, Waterloo, ON N2L 3G1, Canada
e-mail: amanda.mckenzie@uwaterloo.ca

S. E. Eaton and J. Christensen Hughes (eds.), *Academic Integrity in Canada*,
Ethics and Integrity in Educational Contexts 1,
https://doi.org/10.1007/978-3-030-83255-1_27

Keywords Academic integrity · Canada · Curriculum mapping · Educational development · Learning outcomes · Program review · Quality assurance · Quality enhancement · University

Quality assurance frameworks require postsecondary institutions to engage in a variety of methods and approaches to ensure high quality academic programming. These frameworks and processes have been created in countries all over the globe (INQAAHE, 2020), and are viewed as critical to support the accountability of publicly assisted institutions. High quality programs require support and resources from many departments and areas of expertise in an institution. Staff and faculty across the institution work together to ensure that students receive educational experiences that not only positively impact their lives, but support the economy, local communities, and address global responsibilities. Quality educational experiences also uphold rigorous academic integrity to position graduates to move forward with high ethical standards in the next stage of their professional or academic lives. In this chapter we argue that quality assurance mechanisms can be used to promote and reinforce academic integrity, which results in long term positive impacts for students, higher educational institutions, and communities at large.

Academic integrity is critical to the education sector—without it credentials lack value and institutional reputation can be degraded. Academic misconduct also creates concern for the value of research itself and that research expertise is not trusted (Bretag, 2019a). Moreover, students may transition into employment without the skills and knowledge gained through rigorous academic programming and assessment. Students also risk their own reputations and credibility and may repeat academic misconduct (Curtis & Clare, 2017) or engage in similar misconduct behaviours later in their careers (Guerrero-Dib et al., 2020). Issues of academic dishonesty are not new, having persisted at institutions much longer than formal policy has existed to respond to it (Bertram Gallant, 2008b). Evolving forms of academic misconduct such as contract cheating (Clarke & Lancaster, 2007), also known as assignment outsourcing (Awdry, 2020), are exacerbated by socio-economic inequities, the commodification of education, and easy access to technology worldwide. This has required academic institutions to take a more active role in academic integrity education and implement preventative strategies. Some institutions are responding with the creation of dedicated academic integrity offices and committees, enhanced deterrence and detection initiatives, and robust policy revision. In Canada, academic integrity and quality assurance are not often regarded as interlinked processes and are typically located in separate departments, with little intersection. This chapter seeks to highlight how the overarching Canadian Degree Qualifications Framework (CDQF) allows for the two operations to overlap and work in concert to achieve their goals. Instead of having to build something completely new to help address academic integrity, we propose instead that institutions maximize and build upon pre-existing processes. In this chapter, we further offer recommendations to utilize the existing quality assurance framework as a mechanism to foster changes to the institutional academic integrity culture and reinforce academic quality and excellence.

Canadian Quality Assurance

In Canada, the oversight of higher education is decentralized (Weinrib & Jones, 2014), with each province and territory having responsibility for the quality assurance of its university programs. This education structure was determined in 1867 and is written into Canada's Constitution Act (Robson, 2012). Although oversight for the quality assurance frameworks differ in universities across Canada, their quality assurance processes are relatively homogenous with similar foundational principles and many of the same broad processes. The Canadian government does not have a federal ministry or department of education like the United States (U.S. Department of Education, n.d.), nor does it have a national higher education quality assurance agency, such as the United Kingdom's independent body: Quality Assurance Agency for Higher Education (QAA, n.d.) or the Australian Government's Tertiary Education Quality and Standards Agency (TEQSA, 2020). That said, Universities Canada, a national university advocacy association, requires that all institutional members adhere to a set of criteria, and commit to, "[a] quality assurance policy that results in cyclical or continuous assessment of all of its academic programs and support services, and which includes the participation by those directly involved in delivery of the program or service, as well as by other institutional colleagues and external experts and stakeholders" (Universities Canada, n.d., para. 5).

Universities Canada endorses the CDQF in the Ministerial Statement on Quality Assurance of Degree Education in Canada (CMEC, 2007). This Ministerial statement reinforces a common, national standard and clarifies aspects of institutional autonomy. The CDQF lays out the degree categories (i.e., Bachelors, Master's, Doctoral), their typical length, minimum admission requirements and qualification standards. These standards, often referred to as 'degree level expectations' (DLEs), describe competencies and general learning outcomes, including an outcome to support academic integrity. The CDQF also discusses institutional standards for becoming a degree granting institution and refers to 'Ethical Conduct' and 'Academic Freedom & Integrity' as a standard (CMEC, 2007, p. 12).

The overall CDQF is evident within each institutions degree criteria, however there are differences in how this is reflected across the provinces. In Ontario, for example, the Canadian Framework DLEs are for the most part reproduced in two quality assurance documents: 1) the Ontario Council of Academic Vice-Presidents (OCAV) Undergraduate and Graduate Degree Level Expectations (OUCQA, n.d.); and 2) the Ontario Qualifications Framework (OQF) (MCU, 2018). There is one notable exception in the OQF. Academic integrity is included as a learning outcome for all Bachelor, Master's, and Doctoral programs (see Tables 27.1 and 27.2), whereas, the CDQF only explicitly refers to academic integrity at the Bachelor's level, although it is implied that the standards are cumulative, "and each degree level presupposes the

Table 27.1 OCAV's Undergraduate Degree Level Expectations (DLE)

Degree Level Expectation	Baccalaureate/ Bachelor's Degree	Baccalaureate/ Bachelor's Degree (Honours)
Autonomy and Professional Capacity	"behaviour consistent with academic integrity and social responsibility" (OUCQA, n.d., p.3)	"behaviour consistent with academic integrity and social responsibility" (OUCQA, n.d., p. 3)

Note Table italics added. Table adapted from Ontario Universities Council on Quality Assurance (OUCQA, n.d.)

Table 27.2 OCAV's Graduate Degree Level Expectations (DLE)

Degree Level Expectation	Master's Degree	Doctoral Degree
Autonomy and Professional Capacity	"The ethical behaviour consistent with *academic integrity* and the use of appropriate guidelines and procedures for responsible conduct of research" (OUCQA, n.d., p. 5)	"The ethical behaviour consistent with *academic integrity* and the use of appropriate guidelines and procedures for responsible conduct of research" (OUCQA, n.d., p. 5)

Note Table italics added. Table adapted from Ontario Universities Council on Quality Assurance (OUCQA, n.d.)

accomplishment of an earlier one" (CMEC, 2007, p. 3). Ontario is not alone in its use of a provincial framework; for example, the Province of Alberta provides a qualifications framework which notes academic integrity at the Bachelor's level (Alberta Government, 2018, p. 8). In British Columbia, the 'Degree Program Review Criteria and Guidelines' include academic integrity as a degree level standard at the Bachelor level (BCMAEST, 2017, p. 16). The Maritime Provinces also provide a qualifications framework, and while adapted from the CDQF, does not provide a specific learning outcome for academic integrity (MPHEC, n.d.). It is worth considering how the CDQF and the other provincial frameworks or guidelines could be enhanced to ensure that an academic integrity outcome is included and required for all credentials (e.g., Diploma, Certificate). This would support academic integrity initiatives and curriculum enhancement across all postsecondary programming, particularly within the College sector.

The Ontario College sector (with the exception of Bachelor degrees offered by Colleges) relies on vocational program learning outcomes and essential employability skills (EES) to demonstrate program quality. While the EESs include learning outcomes related to information management, demonstrating personal responsibility, and communication, there is no direct reference to academic integrity (MCU, 2009a). Vocational program learning outcomes differ for each program, with no Ontario College Quality Assurance Service (OCQAS, 2020) requirement to include academic integrity at the program or course level.

Most Canadian postsecondary programs follow a continuous improvement (Jacobsen et al., 2018; Temponi, 2005) quality assurance approach, although compliance, audit, and accreditation models also exist (Harvey, 2008). The continuous improvement approach, typically modeled with cyclical program review, includes self and peer evaluation, leading to a set of recommendations for ongoing program enhancement. A compliance model would be seen during new degree development, and involves an external regulatory body with the authority to appraise a proposed new program and determines if it, "meets or exceeds minimum expectations" (Harvey, 2008, p. 13). The Ontario College sector provides an example of an institutional audit process where there is a "review of each college's quality assurance mechanisms" (OCQAS, 2020, para. 1) however it is not, "accompanied by any threshold judgement" (Harvey, 2008, p. 13). The Ontario College institutional audit process includes an audit panel, site visit and self-study audit report (OCQAS, 2016). Lastly, quality assurance for most professional programs with regulated designations such as Professional Engineer (P.Eng) or Registered Nurse (R.N.), would fall under an accreditation model (UNESCO, 2007), and would thus work with external accreditation bodies such as Engineers Canada (Engineers Canada, n.d.); however, they must also comply with the internal quality assurance processes of their institution. This can create tension throughout the review process; however, the inclusion of an academic integrity outcome in the CDQF supports the importance of these outcomes at the provincial and institutional levels. Research suggests that national academic standards, while serving to provide expectations, consistency, and transparency, make a "modest contribution to assuring academic standards" (Dill & Beerkins, 2013, p. 344). This suggests that while national frameworks are an essential foundation, local policy, procedure, and strategies must be utilized to enact real and lasting change.

Quality assurance frameworks have also been developed with an Indigenous perspective. The New Zealand Qualifications Authority for instance recognizes indigenous knowledge and education, and includes the 'Mātauranga Māori Evaluative Quality Assurance' approach (NZQA, n.d). In Ontario, Canada, the 'Indigenous Quality Assurance Standards in Ontario Colleges' framework, was developed by the Indigenous Knowledge Gifters' Council (IKGC, 2018). As of 2017, Indigenous Institutes in Ontario are included in the OQF. While Indigenous quality assurance approaches reflect an Indigenous context and vison, there are shared elements with the CDQF and the principles underlying academic integrity. The 'Indigenous Quality Assurance Standards in Ontario Colleges' framework notes a Seven Grandfathers Teaching, of "Gwekwaadziwin (Honesty)" (IKGC, 2018, p. 4). Another example is an academic integrity resource for Indigenous students entitled, "Seven Grandfathers in Academic Integrity" (Maracle, 2020) developed at the University of Toronto, First Nations House. Although the focus of this chapter is not Indigenous quality assurance or Indigenous perspectives on academic integrity (see Poitras Pratt & Gladue, 2022), the congruence of quality assurance and academic integrity principles across the Canadian postsecondary landscape is nevertheless noteworthy, regardless of the institutional and cultural approach. The implementation of a strong quality assurance framework and development of holistic approaches to academic integrity in Canada must be developed in the context of decolonization and the Truth and Reconciliation Commission of Canada: Calls to Action (2015). The integration of quality assurance, academic integrity and Indigenous "cultural standards" (Northern College, 2017, p. 5) are nicely reflected in the quality assurance policy at Ontario's Northern College (Northern College, 2017).

Academic Integrity in Canada

Academic institutions in Canada typically establish academic integrity or academic discipline policies, which outline academic expectations and provide a process for responding to academic misconduct, such as cheating or plagiarism (Stoesz et al., 2019). Over time, many institutions have moved away from the penalty focus of academic misconduct, to more pro-active, educative options (Christensen Hughes & McCabe, 2006; Bertram Gallant, 2008a; Bretag, 2019b). Educative options typically include instructional workshops, videos, tutorials, and online modules (Griffith, 2013), aimed to reduce intentional and unintentional plagiarism. Some institutions require completion of academic integrity education modules as part of student orientation, or as a result of a misconduct sanction (Penaluna & Ross, 2022).

Although other countries have quality assurance agencies that are actively engaged in academic integrity initiatives, such as the QAA's work on contract cheating (QAA, 2017; 2020), the Council for Higher Education Accreditation (CHEA, 2019), and TEQSA's Higher Education Integrity Unit (TEQSA, June 24, 2020), Canada does not have a national quality assurance body nor one that actively promotes academic integrity. The role of national quality assurance associations has been researched with regard to academic integrity and corruption (CHEA, 2015; Garwe, 2019; Glendinning, 2020), and although the resulting recommendations are valuable, without a national quality assurance agency in Canada, institutions must leverage alternative provincial and local strategies to support a culture of academic integrity. Canadian academic integrity practitioners and scholars are growing networks and these are bolstered through collective research and professional organizations (McKenzie et al., 2020; Stoesz et al., 2020). Several provinces in Canada also have organized associations or groups such as the Academic Integrity Council of Ontario (AICO, n.d.), the Manitoba Academic Integrity Network (MAIN, 2019), and the Alberta Council on Academic Integrity (ACAI, 2020). Many Canadian educational institutions are also members of the International Center for Academic Integrity (ICAI, 2020) as well as the ICAI Canadian Consortium, formed in 2014 (McKenzie, 2018). These organizations promote nation-wide networking, information sharing, research projects and innovative practices, including support for a holistic approach to nurture a culture of academic integrity.

Holistic approaches are promoted by many academic integrity scholars (Bertram Gallant, 2008a; Bretag, 2013; Morris & Carroll, 2015; Macdonald & Carroll, 2006), however institutions have been slow to adopt this approach. A holistic approach to academic integrity considers all stakeholders in an institution and works towards a shared understanding and responsibility for academic excellence to develop a culture of academic integrity. Although academic integrity policy, detection, and deterrence are critical, the holistic approach promoted by several academic integrity organizations in Canada moves away from a legalistic discourse (Sutherland-Smith, 2014), and a detection priority (QAA, 2020, p. 2), and leans more toward teaching and learning solutions.

Although this approach is promoted by several academic integrity organizations and scholars in Canada, there is still a great amount of work to be done to ensure that these approaches are supported by institutional leadership and administration. Developing a culture of integrity requires an institution to articulate their values into policy and practice, and reconsider euro-centric perspectives. The development of an institution-wide academic integrity strategy can be helpful to evaluate what academic integrity tools are available, what is working and what improvements can be made. Collaborative strategies require leadership, teamwork, authenticity, and a shared vision for onboarding new students, teachers, and staff into this institutional integrity culture. A culture of academic integrity also requires the weaving of academic integrity principles and processes into an institution's policy, teaching and learning practices. Each culture of academic integrity will look different in different institutions and must be grounded within an institution's values and promoted to all community stakeholders to flourish. Quality assurance policy, procedures, and continuous improvement activities can be a unifying mechanism to engage all stakeholders in the continual process of creating a culture of academic integrity and to raise the level of integrity across the board.

Quality Assurance Tools to Leverage Academic Integrity

Cyclical Program Review

Although each province, territory, and institution will differ slightly in process, cyclical program review is commonly understood to be the process to review academic programs for their strengths, challenges, and future direction (CMEC, 2007) leading to a set of recommendations and plans for improvement. Program review contains many elements, but common processes include a self-study or self-assessment, external review by disciplinary peer experts, a recommendations report with institutional response, and transparent reporting of the review outcomes. Self-studies combine quantitative and qualitative data for analysis and assessment. Qualitative examples include student focus groups or individual interviews; whereas, quantitative data may include performance indicators such as time-to-completion and attrition rates. A program review involves critical thinking about program challenges and opportunities, and developing action plans for short- and long-term improvement. Herein, lies the opportunity to highlight and promote academic integrity.

Many Canadian institutions, both college and university, have some flexibility over the content required in their program review 'self-study' report (Jacobsen et al., 2018; Liu, 2020; McKenzie, 2019; OUCQA, 2019). This flexibility allows institutions the chance to expand on specific enhancement goals and commitments such as Indigeneity, work-integrated learning, and academic integrity. To increase attention to academic integrity, a university could add questions to their self-study template such as, "what does your program currently do to enhance academic integrity?" or "what initiatives does your program plan to adopt in order to promote academic integrity?" (McKenzie, 2019). Inclusion of such questions in a self-study means that these questions must be revisited in subsequent program reviews, and there is therefore accountability for implementation of any improvement recommendations. It can also provide opportunities for programs to consider how to incorporate existing resources on campus such as the Library, Centre for Teaching and Learning (CTL), and Indigenous Centres for additional academic integrity support. Self-assessment is also a time to consider what academic integrity initiatives or supports are working well, and to ensure their continuity.

Self-study activities often include seeking student and alumni views. Students can provide valuable information to understand the existing culture of academic integrity within a program and make recommendations for academic integrity initiatives. Students can also be asked about how they were supported to learn about academic citation practices, their level of understanding about the academic integrity policy, their perception of academic misconduct in the program and the use of various academic integrity tools, such as text matching software (e.g., Turnitin) (Turnitin, 2020) or online proctoring services (e.g., Examity) (Examity, 2020), and opportunities to enhance student engagement in maintaining academic integrity. Program specific information can help to shore up pedagogical issues contributing to academic dishonesty, and curriculum related opportunities (e.g., course embedded library workshops related to research assignments or designing alternative assessments). Students can be engaged candidly to ask how they have navigated academic integrity throughout the program, and provide tangible tips to support assessment redesign, for example the inclusion of citation skills into assignment rubrics or iterative feedback (Barker & Pinard, 2014) with assignments. Alumni might also offer insights into areas that have long standing issues with academic integrity such as key programs or courses that were known to be difficult and where students were tempted to cheat. Moreover, alumni may be more willing to speak about academic integrity issues following graduation. Cyclical program reviews are comprehensive and can provide valuable space for academic integrity to be discussed, examined, and improved. The outcomes of a cyclical program review can lead to broader institutional initiatives, develop academic integrity champions across the campus, and inform academic integrity policy enhancements, or changes in process.

Curriculum Mapping and Educational Development

Curriculum mapping has become a common component and is often required as part of the cyclical program review in Canadian postsecondary institutions. Curriculum mapping is a collaborative process (Uchiyama & Radin, 2008) amongst faculty members and an educational developer to ensure curricular alignment. Curricular alignment typically refers to the mapping of course learning outcomes with program learning outcomes (PLO), and with the degree level expectations (DLEs). While mapping styles will differ across disciplines (Rawle et al., 2017), mapping ensures curricular alignment with other program elements such as assessment types, leveling, timing and volume of assessments, and that curriculum is scaffolded to address gaps and redundancies (Dyjur & Kenny, 2015). Mapping can confirm that the DLE regarding academic integrity is present throughout the curriculum, ensures that students are being taught and assessed on this content and the related research skills that align with their program and discipline across the years of study. In Canada, academic degrees must adhere to the CDQF, and in Ontario, the DLEs found in the OQF. Therefore, if all academic programs were required to include academic integrity as an element in the curriculum mapping session, each program and course would scaffold and support knowledge and skill development regarding academic integrity. Mapping also provides evidence and opportunity to assess if students are being exposed to citation style, writing skills, research best practices and resources for writing. When mapping, educational developers can guide instructors through questions such as: Is there a diversity of assessment types? Has Universal Design for Learning (UDL) been considered? Are certain assessment types more prone to cheating? Are instructors reusing the same assessment year after year? Is there a better way to assess the students? Can a number of smaller, formative assessments take the place of a high-stakes summative exam? CTLs can develop institutional guides which include questions and guide curricular change that support academic integrity. Given that academic integrity is embedded within national degree standards under the section of Professional Capacity/Autonomy (Council of Ministers of Education, 2007, p. 7), it should be evident in program and course learning outcomes to both faculty and students. We also recognize that assessment design is not a neutral endeavor. Faculty, especially part-time or sessional, face long-standing issues in the higher education system (Gagné, 2020) that challenge the ability to make academic integrity forward pedagogical choices (Crossman, 2019). A survey of sessional faculty concluded that some sessional instructors are concerned with a lack of access to teaching and learning resources, and professional development activities (Field & Jones, 2016). Part-time faculty members could be included in curriculum meetings and quality assurance activities; however, often they are not.

CTLs have the unique opportunity in an academic institution to work with both new teaching staff and experienced faculty. They are typically not considered to be spaces of formal quality assurance; however, they often support program review, curriculum mapping, and curriculum development. They also support a mission for ongoing educational and faculty development. Canadian CTLs are ever evolving in their scope of practice and this includes a role with policy and a shift to "quality improvement on a broader scale" (Forgie et al., 2018, p. 5). Canadian college CTLs provide a significant role with "implementing institutional processes that involve both quality assurance and curriculum development" (Liu, 2020, p. 63). CTLs are a rich resource and can integrate academic integrity best practices into faculty development sessions, such as course and assessment design, and positioning good course design as the foundation for academic integrity. Course and assessment design cannot eliminate cheating entirely (Bretag et al., 2019). That said, with what is known about why students cheat and how students learn, there are course and assessment design recommendations to be considered to minimize cheating and support learning (see Carroll, 2013; Christe, 2003).

Educational Developers (note, this role has several other titles (STLHE, n.d.)) can work with faculty and program teams, supporting decision-making regarding assessment design and how assignments that may reduce cheating can be implemented across a variety of disciplines, levels, and modes of delivery. CTLs can also offer professional development opportunities to discuss best practices as well as specific training on how to use text matching software to identify plagiarism and how technology can be used for and against cheating. Educational Developers can provide information to support UDL practices and inclusive assessment design. Inclusive excellence ensures all students have the tools and choices they need for academic success. Several Canadian CTLs also provide academic integrity specialists (e.g., University of Manitoba). Despite campus-wide CTL offerings and expertise, not every support unit, faculty, department, or program is aware of their resources. Therefore, connecting an institutional academic integrity point person with a program undergoing review can be effective, and encourages programs to learn what more they could do to maintain and promote academic integrity.

Engaging with Administration and Governance

Academic institutions offer governance structures that serve to provide oversight, transparency and a fiduciary duty to university administrative decisions and process (Jones et al., 2001). Governance is a mechanism for shared oversight. Governance bodies play a critical role in the oversight of quality assurance outcomes and upholding campus-wide policy. Governance structures are also a required standard in Canada for degree granting institutions (CMEC, 2007). Members of many Canadian university governance bodies are required to provide oversight and vote upon a variety of academic matters (Pennock et al, 2016). Quality assurance outcomes are typically reported to governance for information or for consideration. For example, educational institutions governance structures usually include a governance oversight body (e.g., Senate or similar delegated committee) whose mandate is to review or approve new program proposals and cyclical program reviews. Similarly, academic misconduct statistics are often reported up to Senate or a similar committee—usually on an annual basis (Neufeld & Dianda, 2007). Given that both quality assurance and academic integrity follow similar governance pathways, there is an opportunity for governance committees to ensure that quality assurance and academic integrity are being adequately addressed, not only from a program level perspective, but from a campus-wide or holistic perspective. At some Colleges, the results of program reviews are presented to Academic Council (e.g., Durham College, 2020, p. 4), to ensure accountability, but also to support the transfer of best practices to institutional stakeholders. The Ontario College system also requires each credential program to establish a Program Advisory Committee (PAC) (MCU, 2009b). PACs could be engaged in a similar way as governance bodies to support academic integrity accountability and initiatives.

Ensuring that members of governance bodies are familiar with the provincial and institutional DLEs, academic integrity policy, and their role to uphold academic integrity standards, raises the level of expectation for program proponents to be academic integrity forward in their program development. Members can also be presented with talks and workshops about quality assurance frameworks and its links to academic integrity (i.e., DLEs), which will raise the level of accountability for proposals moving through governance. Moreover, administration can consider how the annual academic misconduct reporting process can be expanded to include an update on academic integrity educational initiatives across campus. These processes weave both the quality assurance and academic integrity initiatives together and promote continuous educational improvement.

Conclusion

We have explored how quality assurance processes may not only be an effective tool for managing and assuring program quality, but can also be leveraged to support the continuous improvement of policies and practices, and the development of cultures, in keeping with academic integrity. Connecting quality assurance systems to teaching and learning accountabilities demonstrate that quality assurance and academic integrity are integrally linked—you cannot have one without the other. Colleges and universities are encouraged to explore how they can better integrate their quality assurance and academic integrity practices using examples outlined in cyclical program reviews, curriculum development, educational development, and through work with administration and governance. Highlighting academic integrity in the existing quality assurance processes in Canadian higher education institutions ensures that academic integrity will be considered and built upon from every cyclical program review and focuses on continuous improvement in this area into the future. As Canadian academic institutions continue to build local networks to build cultures of academic integrity, they may also consider advocating for more national support and collaboration to respond to postsecondary issues around academic misconduct, common to all institutions. While the CDQF supports academic integrity, provinces and institutions can weave additional accountability into existing processes and frameworks, to work towards a more holistic approach.

References

Academic Integrity Council of Ontario (AICO). (n.d.). Academic integrity council of Ontario. https://academicintegritycouncilofontario.wordpress.com/

Alberta Council on Academic Integrity (ACAI). (2020). Alberta council on academic integrity. https://albertaacademicintegrity.wordpress.com/

Alberta Government. (2018). Alberta credential framework. https://open.alberta.ca/publications/alberta-credential-framework

Awdry, R. (2020). Assignment outsourcing: Moving beyond contract cheating. *Journal of Assessment & Evaluation in Higher Education*, 1–17. https://doi.org/10.1080/02602938.2020.1765311

Barker, M., & Pinard, M. (2014). Closing the feedback loop? Iterative feedback between tutor and student in coursework assessments. *Journal of Assessment & Evaluation in Higher Education, 39*(8), 899–915. https://doi.org/10.1080/02602938.2013.875985

Bertram Gallant, T. (2008a). *Academic integrity in the twenty-first century: A teaching and learning imperative*. Jossey-Bass.

Bertram Gallant, T. (2008b). Revisiting the past: The historical context of academic integrity. *ASHE Higher Education Report, 33*(5), 13–31. https://doi.org/10.1002/aehe.3305

Bretag, T. (2013). Challenges in addressing plagiarism in education. *PLoS Medicine, 10*(12), 1–4. https://doi.org/10.1371/journal.pmed.1001574

Bretag, T. (2019a). Contract cheating will erode trust in science. *Nature, 574*, 599. https://www.nature.com/articles/d41586-019-03265-1

Bretag, T. (2019b). From 'perplexities of plagiarism' to 'building cultures of integrity': A reflection on fifteen years of academic integrity research, 2003–2018. *HERDSA Review of Higher Education, 6*, 5–35. http://www.herdsa.org.au/herdsa-review-higher-education-vol-6/5-35

Bretag, T., Harper, R., Burton, M., Ellis, C., Newton, P., van Haeringen, K., Saddiqui, S., & Rozenberg, P. (2019). Contract cheating and assessment design: Exploring the relationship. *Assessment & Evaluation in Higher Education, 44*(5), 676–691. https://doi.org/10.1080/02602938.2018.1527892

British Columbia, Minister of Advanced Education, Skills and Training (BCMAEST). (2017). Degree program review: Criteria and guidelines. https://www2.gov.bc.ca/assets/gov/education/post-secondary-education/institution-resources-administration/degree-authorization/degree-program-criteria.pdf

Carroll, J. (2013). *A handbook for deterring plagiarism in higher education*. Oxford Brookes University Press.

Christensen Hughes, J. M., & McCabe, D. L. (2006). Academic misconduct within higher education in Canada. *Canadian Journal of Higher Education, 36*(2), 1–21. https://doi.org/10.47678/cjhe.v36i2.183537

Christe, B. (2003). Designing online courses to discourage dishonesty. *Educause Quarterly*, 4, 54–58. https://er.educause.edu/articles/2003/1/designing-online-courses-to-discourage-dishonesty

Clarke, R., & Lancaster, T. (2007). Establishing a systematic six-stage process for detecting contract cheating. In*Proceedings of the 2nd International Conference on Pervasive Computing and Applications* (pp. 342–347). https://doi.org/10.1109/ICPCA.2007.4365466

Council for Higher Education Accreditation, International Quality Group (CHEA). (2015). Corruption in higher education: Can quality assurance make a difference? 5, 1–2. https://www.chea.org/corruption-higher-education-can-quality-assurance-make-difference

Council for Higher Education Accreditation (CHEA). (2019). Council for higher education accreditation–About. https://www.chea.org/about

Council of Ministers of Education Canada (CMEC). (2007). Ministerial statement on quality assurance of degree education in Canada. http://www.cmec.ca/Publications/Lists/Publications/Attachments/95/QA-Statement-2007.en.pdf

Crossman, K. (2019). Is this in my contract? How part-time contract faculty face barriers to reporting academic integrity breaches. *Canadian Perspectives on Academic Integrity*, *2*(1), 1–8. https://journalhosting.ucalgary.ca/index.php/ai/article/view/68934

Curtis, G. J., & Clare, J. (2017). How prevalent is contract cheating and to what extent are students repeat offenders? *Journal of Academic Ethics, 15*(2), 115–124. https://doi.org/10.1007/s10805-017-9278-x

Dill, D. D., & Beerkens, M. (2013). Designing the framework conditions for assuring academic standards: Lessons learned about professional, market, and government regulation of academic quality. *Higher Education, 65*(3), 341–357. https://doi.org/10.1007/s10734-012-9548-x

Durham College. (2020). Policy-Academic Program Review and Renewal–Quality Assurance. https://durhamcollege.ca/wp-content/uploads/academic-program-review-and-renewal-policy.pdf

Dyjur, P., & Kenny, N. (2015, May). Analyzing curriculum mapping data: Enhancing student learning through curriculum redesign. Paper presented at the 2015 University of Calgary Conference on Postsecondary Learning and Teaching, Calgary, AB. https://taylorinstitute.ucalgary.ca/sites/default/files/resources/handout_CR_5_analyzing_CM_data_2018_01_22.pdf

Engineers Canada. (n.d.). Engineers Canada-About accreditation. https://engineerscanada.ca/accreditation/about-accreditation

Examity. (2020). Examity–Online proctoring. https://examity.com/

Field, C. C. & Jones, G. A. (2016). A survey of sessional faculty in Ontario publicly-funded universities. Toronto: Centre for the Study of Canadian and International Higher Education, OISE-University of Toronto. https://www.oise.utoronto.ca/hec/UserFiles/File/Sessional_Faculty_-_OHCRIF_Final_Report_-_July_2016.pdf

Forgie, S. E., Yonge, O., & Luth, R. (2018). Centers for teaching and learning across Canada: What's going on? *Canadian Journal for the Scholarship of Teaching and Learning, 9*(1), 1–18. https://doi.org/10.5206/cjsotl-rcacea.2018.1.9

Gagné, A. (2020). *The Canadian precariat: Part-time faculty and the higher education system.* Universitas Press. https://www.ubcpress.ca/the-canadian-precariat

Garwe, E. C. (2019). Quality assurance agencies: Creating a conducive environment for academic integrity. *South African Journal of Science, 115*(11/12). 47–53. https://doi.org/10.17159/sajs.2019/6231

Glendinnning, I. (2020). The role of quality assurance and regulatory organizations to promote academic integrity. In T. Bretag (Ed.), *A research agenda for academic integrity*. Edward Elgar Publishing.

Griffith, J. (2013). Pedagogical over punitive: The academic integrity websites of Ontario Universities. *Canadian Journal of Higher Education, 43*(1), 1–22. https://files.eric.ed.gov/fulltext/EJ1007029.pdf

Guerrero-Dib, J. G., Portales, L., & Heredia-Escorza, Y. (2020). Impact of academic integrity on workplace ethical behaviour. *International Journal for Educational Integrity, 16*(2), 1–18. https://doi.org/10.1007/s40979-020-0051-3

Harvey, L. (2008). Placing Canadian quality assurance initiatives in an international context. In *Proceedings of CMEC Quality Assurance Symposium 2008*, (pp. 27–28). https://www.univcan.ca/wp-content/uploads/2015/07/qa-placing-canadian-qa-initiatives-in-international-context-2008.pdf

Indigenous Knowledge Gifters' Council (IKGC). (2018). Building a strong fire: Indigenous quality assurance standards in Ontario colleges. http://www.northernc.on.ca/indigenous/pdf/BuildingAStrongFire_WEB.pdf

International Centre for Academic Integrity (ICAI). (2020). ICAI—About. https://www.academicintegrity.org/about/

International Network for Quality Assurance Agencies in Higher Education (INQAAHE). (2020). INQAAHE—Membership. https://www.inqaahe.org/membership

Jacobsen, D. M., Eaton, S. E., Brown, B., Simmons, M., & McDermott, M. (2018). Action research for graduate program improvements: A response to curriculum mapping and review. *Canadian Journal of Higher Education, 48*(1), 82–98. https://doi.org/10.47678/cjhe.v48i1.188048

Jones, G., Shanahan, T., & Goyan, P. (2001). University governance in Canadian higher education. *Tertiary Education and Management, 7*(2), 135–148. https://doi.org/10.1080/13583883.2001.9967047

Liu, Q. (2020). The impact of quality assurance policies on curriculum development in Ontario postsecondary education. *Canadian Journal of Higher Education, 50*(1), 53–67. https://doi.org/10.47678/cjhe.v50i1.188301

Macdonald, R., & Carroll, J. (2006). Plagiarism - A complex issue requiring a holistic institutional approach. *Journal of Assessment & Evaluation in Higher Education, 31*(2), 233–245. https://doi.org/10.1080/02602930500262536

Manitoba Academic Integrity Network. (2019, MAIN). About—Manitoba academic integrity network. https://mbacademicintegrit.wixsite.com/main

Maracle, Bonnie Jane/Iehnhotonkwas. (2020). Seven grandfathers in academic integrity, University of Toronto, First Nations House. https://studentlife.utoronto.ca/wp-content/uploads/SLC8581_7-Grandfathers-in-Academic-Integrity-AODA.pdf

Maritime Provinces Higher Education Commission (MPHEC). (n.d.). Maritime degree level qualifications framework. http://www.mphec.ca/resources/DegreeLevelFrameworkEn.pdf

McKenzie, A. (2018). Academic integrity across the Canadian landscape. *Canadian Perspectives on Academic Integrity, 1*(2), 1–6. https://doi.org/10.11575/cpai.v1i2.54599

McKenzie, A. (2019). Enhancing academic integrity through quality assurance. Canadian Symposium on Academic Integrity. https://prism.ucalgary.ca/handle/1880/110296

McKenzie, A., Miron, J., & Ridgley, A. (2020). Building a regional academic integrity network: Profiling the growth and action of the academic integrity council of Ontario. *Canadian Perspectives on Academic Integrity, 3*(1), 25–38. https://doi.org/10.11575/cpai.v3i1.69836

MCU, Ministry of Colleges and Universities. (2018). Ontario qualifications framework (OQF). http://www.tcu.gov.on.ca/pepg/programs/oqf/

MCU, Ministry of College and Universities (MCU). (2009a). Essential employability skills. http://www.tcu.gov.on.ca/pepg/audiences/colleges/progstan/essential.html

MCU, Ministry of Colleges and Universities (MCU). (2009b). Minister's binding policy directive—Framework for programs of instruction. http://www.tcu.gov.on.ca/pepg/documents/FrameworkforPrograms.pdf

Morris E. J., & Carroll J. (2015). Developing a sustainable holistic institutional approach: Dealing with realities 'on the ground' when implementing an academic integrity policy. In T. Bretag (Ed.), *Handbook of academic integrity*. Springer.

New Zealand Quality Assurance (NZQA). (n.d.). Quality assurance division. https://www.nzqa.govt.nz/about-us/our-structure/quality-assurance-division/

Neufeld, J. & Dianda, J. (2007). Academic dishonesty: A survey of policies and procedures at Ontario universities. https://cou.ca/wp-content/uploads/2015/07/Academic-Colleagues-Academic%20Dishonesty-A-Survey-of-Policies-and-Procedures-at-Ontario-Universities.pdf

Northern College. (2017). Quality assurance policy. http://www.mynorthern.ca/wp-content/uploads/2018/08/VPA-1-Quality-Assurance-QA-Policy1.pdf

Ontario College Quality Assurance Service. (2016). Stages of the audit process. https://www.ocqas.org/wp-content/uploads/2015/08/CQAAP-Stages-of-the-Audit-Process-Revised-Feb-10-2016.pdf

Ontario College Quality Assurance Service. (2020). About college quality assurance audit process (CQAAP). https://www.ocqas.org/quality-assurance/about-cqaap/

Ontario Universities Council on Quality Assurance (OUCQA). (n.d). OCAV's undergraduate and graduate degree level expectations. https://oucqa.ca/wp-content/uploads/2013/06/APPENDIX-1.pdf

Penaluna, L., & Ross, R. (2022). How to talk about academic integrity so students will listen: Engaging students in ethical decision making. In S. E. Eaton & J. Christensen Hughes (Eds.), *Academic Integrity in Canada*. Springer.

Pennock, L., Jones, G. A., Leclerc, J. M., & Sharon, X. L. (2016). Challenges and opportunities for collegial governance at Canadian universities: Reflections on a survey of academic senates. *Canadian Journal of Higher Education, 46*(3), 73–89.

Poitras Pratt, Y., & Gladue, K. (2022). Re-defining academic integrity: Embracing indigenous truths. In S. E. Eaton & J. Christensen Hughes (Eds.), *Academic Integrity in Canada*. Springer.

Quality Assurance Association for Higher Education (QAA). (2017). Contracting to cheat in higher education: How to address contract cheating—the use of third-party services and essay mills. https://www.qaa.ac.uk/docs/qaa/quality-code/contracting-to-cheat-in-higher-education.pdf

Quality Assurance Association for Higher Education (QAA). (2020). Contracting to cheat in higher education: How to address essay mills and contract cheating–2nd Edition. https://www.qaa.ac.uk/docs/qaa/guidance/contracting-to-cheat-in-higher-education-2nd-edition.pdf

Quality Assurance Association for Higher Education (QAA). (n.d.). QAA—Academic integrity. https://www.qaa.ac.uk/about-us/what-we-do/academic-integrity

Robson, K. (2012). *Sociology of Education in Canada*. Pearson Canada.

Rawle, F., Bowen, T., Murck, B., & Hong, R. (2017). Curriculum mapping across the disciplines: Differences, approaches, and strategies. *Celt—Collected Essays on Learning and Teaching, STLHE*. https://doi.org/10.22329/celt.v10i0.4765

Society for Teaching and Learning in Higher Education (STLHE). (n.d.). Educational developers caucus—job descriptions. https://www.stlhe.ca/affiliated-groups/educational-developers-caucus/resources/job-descriptions/

Stoesz, B., Seeland, J., Vogt, L., & Markovics, L. (2020). Creating a collaborative network to promote cultures of academic integrity in Manitoba's post-secondary institutions. *Canadian Perspectives on Academic Integrity, 3*(1). 1–10. https://journalhosting.ucalgary.ca/index.php/ai/article/view/69763

Stoesz, B. M., Eaton, S. E., Miron, J., & Thacker, E. J. (2019). Academic integrity and contract cheating policy analysis of colleges in Ontario, Canada. *International Journal for Educational Integrity,15*(4), 1–18. https://doi.org/10.1007/s40979-019-0042-4

Sutherland-Smith, W. (2014). Legality, quality assurance and learning: Competing discourses of plagiarism management in higher education. *Journal of Higher Education Policy and Management, 36*(1), 29–42. https://doi.org/10.1080/1360080X.2013.844666

Temponi, C. (2005). Continuous improvement framework: Implications for academia. *Quality Assurance in Education., 13*(1), 17–36. https://doi.org/10.1108/09684880510578632

Tertiary Education Quality and Standards Agency (TEQSA). (2020). TEQSA—What we do. https://www.teqsa.gov.au/what-we-do

Tertiary Education Quality and Standards Agency (TEQSA). (2020, June 24). TEQSA to establish new higher education integrity unit. https://www.teqsa.gov.au/latest-news/articles/teqsa-establish-new-higher-education-integrity-unit

Truth and Reconciliation Commission of Canada (TRC). (2015). Truth and reconciliation commission of Canada: Calls to action. http://nctr.ca/assets/reports/Calls_to_Action_English2.pdf

Turnitin. (2020). Turnitin for higher education. https://www.turnitin.com/divisions/higher-education

Uchiyama, K. P., & Radin, J. L. (2008). Curriculum mapping in higher education: A vehicle for collaboration. *Journal for Innovative Higher Education, 33*, 271–280. https://doi.org/10.1007/s10755-008-9078-8.pdf

UNESCO. (2007). Quality assurance and accreditation: A glossary of basic terms and definitions. http://proiecte.aracis.ro/fileadmin/ARACIS/Publicatii_Aracis/Publicatii_ARACIS/Engleza/Glossary_07_05_2007.pdf

United States Department of Education. (n.d.). Federal role in education. https://www2.ed.gov/about/overview/fed/role.html

Universities Canada. (n.d.). Universities Canada—membership criteria. https://www.univcan.ca/about-us/membership-and-governance/membership-criteria/

Weinrib, J., & Jones, G. A. (2014). Largely a matter of degrees: Quality assurance and Canadian universities. *Policy and Society, 33*(3), 225–236. https://doi.org/10.1016/j.polsoc.2014.07.002

Emma Thacker M.A. is an administrator at the University of Toronto, specializing in governance, policy and ombuds work. She has held several positions to support institutional quality assurance, academic integrity and quasi-judicial affairs. Emma is a doctoral candidate in the School of Social, Political and Global Studies at Keele University, United Kingdom. Her doctoral research focuses on academic literacies and contract cheating. Emma is an active member of the Association of Canadian College and University Ombudspersons (ACCUO) and the Academic Integrity Council of Ontario (AICO). She has research interests in higher education policy and academic integrity education.

Amanda McKenzie M.A. is the Director of Quality Assurance (Academic Programs) and oversees quality assurance and academic integrity at the University of Waterloo. She is involved in academic integrity initiatives on a provincial, national and international level. Amanda is an active subject matter expert in this area and has spoken around the world. She has also published a number of articles and a book chapter in this field. Amanda has served as part of the International Center for Academic Integrity since 2016 and has been an Officer on the Board of Directors since 2018. She is also an active member of the Academic Integrity Council of Ontario (AICO) and currently serves as the Secretary/outreach Coordinator.

Chapter 28
Student Academic Misconduct Through a Canadian Legal Lens

Melissa Morrison and Philip Zachariah

Abstract The processes that post-secondary institutions use to detect, investigate, judge and discipline cases of academic misconduct are shaped by legislative and judicial requirements including procedural fairness. This chapter situates post-secondary institutions' options on addressing allegations of academic misconduct in the broader Canadian legal context. Reviewing leading Court cases, including those where students appealed findings of misconduct, this chapter analyses the key principals that post-secondary institutions should adhere to in order to provide sufficient procedural fairness. We conclude with practical considerations that post-secondary institutions can take to minimize decisions about academic misconduct being overturned by the Courts.

Keywords Academic integrity · Appeals · Administrative tribunals · Administrative law · Procedural fairness · Judicial review · Legal · Canada

Within this chapter, we discuss the overarching legal framework in Canada as it applies to student academic misconduct in post-secondary institutions. We also highlight some important cases in which academic misconduct decisions have been appealed to or judicially reviewed by the Courts. Our goal is to provide post-secondary institutions with the necessary information to create fair and sound policies, that would ultimately be supported by the post-secondary community and the Courts. This chapter does not examine in detail, although some examples are provided, the different approaches taken by post-secondary institutions across Canada, or make judgements on whether those approaches would be seen as fair and appropriate in law.

The number of cases in which findings of academic misconduct have been challenged in the Courts is small. However, these cases are illustrative of the balance

M. Morrison (✉) · P. Zachariah
University of Calgary, Calgary, AB T2N 1N4, Canada
e-mail: melissa.morrison@ucalgary.ca

P. Zachariah
e-mail: pzachari@ucalgary.ca

S. E. Eaton and J. Christensen Hughes (eds.), *Academic Integrity in Canada*, Ethics and Integrity in Educational Contexts 1,
https://doi.org/10.1007/978-3-030-83255-1_28

between the expertise and autonomy of post-secondary institutions to safeguard the academic integrity of the academy versus the duty of fairness and reasonability owed to their students. Post-secondary institutions must find an appropriate balance between deterrence and compassion, justice and education. The highly legal approach that post-secondary institutions have traditionally taken in Canada to dealing with academic misconduct may have kept the number of cases that get challenged in the Courts low. However, does such a dearth of cases imply that post-secondary institutions are finding the right balance? We are mindful of the alternatives to the traditional, adversarial approach to handling academic misconduct and the value of embracing the recommendations in the Truth and Reconciliation Commission[1] in order to facilitate the adoption of broader models of Justice.

Academic Misconduct: The Canadian Legislative and Policy Context

Canadian post-secondary institutions are for the most part creations of statute and the ability to oversee academics in general, including the power to discipline for issues like academic misconduct, flows from this legislation. As an example, Alberta's *Post-Secondary Learning Act* (Government of Alberta, 2020) speaks generically to the power of the General Faculties Council over "student affairs". It also specifically articulates the ability to discipline students, with such discipline including fines, suspension and expulsion. This power to discipline is subject only to the right of appeal to the institution's Board of Governors[2].

This governing legislation establishes the broad structure required for post-secondary institutions to govern themselves, along with some specific requirements around how to conduct their affairs. With that in mind, all decisions that result in discipline of a student because of academic misconduct must be made within the legislative governance framework established by the relevant statute or the post-secondary institution runs the risk of having a court find their action(s) or decision(s) beyond their authority or jurisdiction.

Post-Secondary learning is regulated under Provincial jurisdiction, as per the *Constitution Act, 1867s.93*[3]. The provinces exercise their jurisdiction over post-secondary learning institutions in a variety of ways.

For example, some provinces such as Ontario, have individual pieces of legislation which establish the governing structure of a specific post-secondary institution.

---

[1] Truth and Reconciliation Commission of Canada., United Nations., National Centre for Truth and Reconciliation., Truth and Reconciliation Commission of Canada & United Nations (2015). Truth & Reconciliation: Calls to Action.

[2] Post-Secondary Learning Act, Statutes of Alberta (2003, c.P-19.5) s.31. Retrieved from Alberta Government website: https://www.qp.alberta.ca/documents/acts/p19p5.pdf

[3] The Constitution Act, 1867 (UK), 30 & 31 Victoria, c 3.

Most other provinces have a single, overarching statute that provides for the governance of all post-secondary institutions[4]. However, what is mostly universal across the country (Kelleher, 2016) is the legislative establishment of a similar bicameral governance model with the creation of a Board of Governors and a Senate.[5] A Board of Governors, which is usually appointed by government and specific stakeholder groups within the institution, is typically responsible for the ongoing operational direction of the institution. The academic Senate, comprised of representation from the post-secondary community, is broadly responsible for the academic affairs of the institution. Legislation also identifies the senior officers of the institution e.g., President, Provost, Deans, etc.

Flowing from the enabling legislation, a post-secondary institution can create the structures and procedures to deal with allegations of academic misconduct involving students. Whatever structure or procedure is created, there must be clear jurisdiction granted by the appropriate governing authority as established by the legislation. Taking Alberta's legislation as an example once again, it would be important that post-secondary institutions in that province ensure that general policy and process around academic misconduct occur through General Faculties Council oversight, with a robust process to deal with student appeals of discipline to the Board of Governors. Alberta's *Post-Secondary Learning Act* speaks to the ability of the General Faculties Council to delegate its power to discipline to other bodies or persons allowing greater flexibility in process and structure to address issues.

There will be numerous campus entities with different roles and responsibilities, which collectively promote and support the institution's academic integrity, including faculty, academic units, Registrar, Secretariat, student services (i.e., Student Ombuds or Advocate). It is important that there are clear and coherent policies and procedures that delineate the different roles and responsibilities among these various entities. Typically, such policies also provide direction on what a suitable range of penalties might be for various types of infractions, depending on whether it is a first or subsequent offence, the severity of offence, etc. This is meant to encourage consistency across departments. Given faculty reluctance to bring cases forward, having a straightforward process that faculty view as reasonable can be helpful in encouraging the formal resolution of such incidents (see Christensen Hughes & McCabe, 2006).

---

[4] Examples include:

British Columbia: University Act, Revised Statues of British Columbia (1996, c.468). Retrieved from British Columbia Government website https://www.bclaws.gov.bc.ca/civix/document/id/complete/statreg/96468_01

Alberta: Post-Secondary Learning Act, Statutes of Alberta (2003, c.P-19.5) s.31. Retrieved from Alberta Government website: https://www.qp.alberta.ca/documents/acts/p19p5.pdf

[5] Kelleher, William Edward (2016). Canadian Laws Relevant to University Student Academic Discipline (ProQuest Number 10253968) [Doctoral Dissertation, Northcentral University]. Retrieved from ProQuest website https://search-proquest-com.ezproxy.lib.ucalgary.ca/docview/1867763133?pq-origsite=primo

When adjudicating academic misconduct, an institution's specific policies must also adhere to any provincial legislation that governs the functioning of administrative decision-making tribunals[6]. In provinces where such legislation is in force, a post-secondary institution needs to consider its application to their decision-making processes and ensure adherence to its requirements.

In addition to enabling legislation, provincial statute and institutional policy, the *Canadian Charter of Rights and Freedoms* (1982) may apply to certain decisions which exercise a post-secondary institution's authority to deal with academic misconduct allegations. Section 32 of the *Charter* states that it applies to actions of the Federal government, and "to the legislature and government of each province in respect of all matters within the authority of the legislature of each province". Therefore, the application of the *Charter* depends on the extent to which the prescribed action is determined by legislation or is the result of direct government action. The application of the *Charter* to the conduct of post-secondary institutions remains subject to contextual argument. However, in the case of *Prigden* v. *The University of Calgary* (2012)[7], the Alberta Court of Appeal found that the ability of the University to impose sanction pursuant to the *Post-Secondary Learning Act* was "beyond the authority held by private individuals or organizations"[8]. As such, the court rejected the University's position that the application of the *Charter* undermined academic freedom and found that "in exercising its statutory authority to discipline students for non-academic misconduct, it is incumbent on the Review Committee to interpret and apply the Student Misconduct Policy in light of the students' *Charter* rights, including their freedom of expression".[9] Thus, the potential application of the *Charter* to decisions of post-secondary institutions with respect to student academic misconduct remains contextual, with focus on the statutory framework at play, but still remains an important consideration. Post-secondary institutions should thus be mindful of how their actions and processes impact a student's *Charter* rights, which include freedom of expression, freedom of association and security from unreasonable search and seizure.

Addressing Academic Misconduct: Learning from the Courts

While the goal is for educational institutions to approach teaching, learning, and assessment in ways that foster academic integrity and minimize the potential for misconduct, there are circumstances that require a heavier response. If a post-secondary institution is seen as having ignored or brushed aside alleged instances of

[6] Example: Statutory Powers Procedure Act, Revised Statutes of Ontario (1990 c.S.22) Retrieved from Ontario Government website https://www.ontario.ca/laws/statute/90s22

[7] Pridgen v. University of Calgary (2012) ABCA 139.

[8] *Ibid.* at para. 105.

[9] *Ibid* at para. 112 and 113.

serious or repeated academic misconduct, the integrity of the school will be undermined and students may become ambivalent toward completing their work with integrity.

As such, post-secondary institutions need to have a fair and robust process to investigate and address alleged instances of academic misconduct. This process needs to accord with legislative requirements, if they exist, as well as mesh with the institution's values, policies, procedures, and practices. These processes also need to follow legal principles established by the courts as decisions about academic misconduct could have a significant impact on a student's life. Decisions about whether a student has committed academic misconduct and any resulting discipline or sanctions are administrative decisions that are subject to judicial scrutiny, primarily[10], though not exclusively, through the process of judicial review of the appropriateness of the decision, and whether the process followed in making the decision met the basic tenets of procedural fairness. "The fact that a decision is administrative and affects "the rights, privileges or interests of an individual" is sufficient to trigger the application of the duty of fairness."[11]

The degree of procedural fairness owed in a particular circumstance is a contextual analysis and involves the review of a number of factors [12], including: the nature of the decision being made, the statutory regime, the importance of the decision to the individuals affected, the legitimate expectations of those individuals, and the procedures chosen by the decision-maker.[13] While historically there has been a high degree of deference paid to decisions made by Universities, especially those decisions that directly relate to academics, decisions that have a larger impact on a person require a higher degree of procedural fairness.[14]

The Supreme Court of Canada, in the case of *Khan* v. *The University of Ottawa*, spoke to a requirement for a high level of procedural fairness for decisions that involve academic discipline. By extension, the more significant the discipline, the more procedural fairness will be required. In *Khan*, for example, the Supreme Court of Canada found that a "university student threatened with the loss of an academic year by a failing grade is also entitled to a high standard of justice".[15] Generally, the concept of procedural fairness and the underlying values that support this concept "relate to the principle that the individual or individuals affected should have the opportunity to present their case fully and fairly, and have decisions affecting

[10] The focus of this Chapter is on judicial review of academic misconduct decisions. However, actions in tort and breach of contract may be available to a student as well.

[11] Cardinal v. Director of Kent Institution, [1985] 2 SCR 643, para. 653. Retrieved from Supreme Court of Canada website https://scc-csc.lexum.com/scc-csc/scc-csc/en/item/106/index.do

[12] Baker v. Canada, [1999] 2 SCR 817, para. 21. Retrieved from Supreme Court of Canada website https://scc-csc.lexum.com/scc-csc/scc-csc/en/item/1717/index.do

[13] *Ibid.* at para. 23–27.

[14] Dunne v. Memorial University of Newfoundland, [2012]. NLTD(G) 41 at paras. 7 and 17.

[15] Khan v. University of Ottawa (1997) 34 OR 535 para. 9. Retrieved from CanLII https://www.canlii.org/en/on/onca/doc/1997/1997canlii941/1997canlii941.html

their rights, interests, or privileges made using a fair, impartial, and open process, appropriate to the statutory, institutional, and social context of the decision"[16].

In *Dunsmuir v New Brunswick*[17], the Supreme Court of Canada said the following about procedural fairness:

> Procedural fairness is a cornerstone of modern Canadian administrative law. Public decision makers are required to act fairly in coming to decisions that affect the rights, privileges or interests of an individual. Thus stated the principle is easy to grasp. It is not, however, always easy to apply.

The courts have further defined the basic hallmarks of procedural fairness and the degree to which decision makers have to ensure compliance with these requirements. While not all have considered them specifically in the context of academic misconduct, they have been reviewed in circumstances that similarly attract a higher degree of procedural fairness.

The Right to an Unbiased Decision Maker

It is important that decision makers view their role and the decision before them in a manner that is free from bias. The courts do not look at whether there is actual bias, but if there is a "reasonable apprehension of bias" in the circumstances. Particular caution must be paid to avoiding circumstances where decision makers have overlapping roles or jurisdiction over issues involving academics in general and academic misconduct decision making.[18] This can be particularly problematic in post-secondary institutions where leadership may have broad and intersecting oversight over multiple aspects of academic and student life. It is also important to prevent scenarios where a party in the process acts as both a complainant (accuser) and the decision maker or where their role as either may be influenced or reasonably seen as influenced by the other or other parties within the institution. In cases where individuals participate in multiple layers of the investigation and appeal process for academic misconduct, institutions must ensure their roles are insulated from bias or conflict.

In *Wilson v. The University of Calgary* (2014) at paragraph 69, the court highlighted this concern of overlapping roles, but was clear that there are always exceptions like in cases where it is specifically allowed by statute.

By extension, it is important for post-secondary institutions to put measures in place to avoid issues of reprisal in relation to findings of academic misconduct. For

---

[16] Alberta (Funeral Services Regulatory Board) v. Strong [2006] ABQB 873 para. 25. Retrieved from CanLii https://www.canlii.org/en/ab/abqb/doc/2006/2006abqb873/2006abqb873.html?resultIndex=1

[17] Dunsmuir v. New Brunswick (2008) 1 SCR 190 at para. 70. Retrieved from CanLii https://www.canlii.org/en/ca/scc/doc/2008/2008scc9/2008scc9.html?resultIndex=1

[18] Wilson v. University of Calgary (2014) ABQB 190 para. 67. Retrieved from Canlii https://www.canlii.org/en/ab/abqb/doc/2014/2014abqb190/2014abqb190.html?resultIndex=1

many students, committing academic misconduct is a singular transgression in their academic journey, which may be overcome through academic integrity education. Ensuring that the processes to address allegations of academic misconduct respect an accused student's privacy (i.e. confidentiality of process, minimize number of participants) is an important starting point. Students who have been found to have committed academic misconduct, or who have appealed a finding, may have legitimate concerns about whether they will be fairly evaluated by instructors in the future and post-secondary institutions need to be ready to respond to those issues.

The Requirement to Provide Notice, the Disclosure of the Case to Be Met and the Right to be Heard

While each of these terms appear to be easy to understand and common sense in their application, they are often the areas that decision makers have the most difficulty with in practice.

The requirement to provide notice, at its most basic level, means providing notice to affected parties that a decision is going to be made. Most obviously, this notice must be provided to the person who the decision is about. However, this may also extend to notice to other individuals who may be peripherally impacted by the decision.[19]

The notice provided must answer the who, what, where, why and how of the decision to be made or the issues that form the basis for the decision. It should outline the process that will be followed prior to a decision being made, as well as the potential outcomes.

The process leading up to a decision will require an opportunity for the student accused of academic misconduct to respond to the allegations. This is of critical importance. That may be in a formal hearing setting or more simply in a face to face discussion. Regardless, the accused student must be given enough time to prepare their response. The goal is not to ambush or to surprise them. The amount of time required for notice is once again dependent on the context and cases with a higher degree of complexity or with more serious potential outcomes or sanctions will require more notice.[20]

As part of the right to respond, someone accused of academic misconduct must be given the opportunity to review and respond to all evidence that the decision maker relied upon in making their decision. Again, this does not mean ambushing an accused student during the course of a hearing or in an interview, but giving this information to them in advance in order to be able to fully review and respond to this evidence. Decision makers often have a difficult time determining what evidence they

[19] Saskatchewan Ministry of Justice and Attorney General. Ombuds Saskatchewan: Practice Essentials for Administrative Tribunals. Regina, 2020. at pg. 17. Retrieved from Government of Saskatchewan website https://ombudsman.sk.ca/app/uploads/2020/03/Practice-Essentials-Final-with-Cover.pdf

[20] *Ibid.*

actually relied on and only provide evidence that supports the outcome or decision they made. However, they must disclose all relevant evidence even if it was discounted by the decision maker.

In cases where there are concerns around confidentiality or a desire for anonymity, the decision maker must weigh the competing interests in determining what should be disclosed. The default position should always be disclosure out of fairness to the individual accused of academic misconduct with holding back evidence happening in cases where there is very compelling reasons to do so, like the harm resulting from the disclosure outweighing any fairness achieved from its inclusion. "The fact that a person would prefer to have certain information kept confidential is not enough for non-disclosure."[21]

The Right to Counsel

The right to legal counsel is not absolute.[22] Again, a contextual analysis is required to determine whether the right to have the support of legal counsel is required to meet a post-secondary institution's procedural fairness obligations when it comes to academic misconduct decisions.

Generally, the more formality and complexity in the process and issues, the more likely it is that a student will require the support of legal counsel in order to fairly respond to the case against them. In *Wilson ibid*, the court did not find that the exclusion of legal counsel was a breach of the student's right to counsel and stated the following:

> This is not an instance where the talents of a lawyer were required in order to ensure adequate presentation of the Applicants' position. The facts were not in dispute. There were no witnesses called by either side. The nature of the proceedings was meant to be informal.[23]

With that in mind, cases where there are fundamental disputes on the facts that support the allegations of misconduct, the involvement of witnesses to speak to those facts, the formality of the process and the degree to which credibility must be assessed all weigh into the analysis around whether a student should be allowed to be supported, and the degree of the support provided, by legal counsel.

Across the country, post-secondary institutions have a variety of approaches when it comes to allowing counsel to assist a student. These include:

- No right to counsel whatsoever;
- The right to counsel or an advisor, but with some clear exceptions (advisor cannot be a family member);

---

[21] *Ibid*.

[22] Pridgen v. University of Calgary (2012) ABCA 139 para. 78. Retrieved at CanLII https://www.canlii.org/en/ab/abca/doc/2012/2012abca139/2012abca139.html?resultIndex=1

[23] *Ibid*. para. 82.

- Access to a student advocate;
- The right to an advisor, who may be legal counsel or anyone else, but who cannot take an active role in the process;
- The universal right to counsel, whether it be legal counsel or someone else of the student's choosing.

Given the contextual analysis required to determine whether a student should have the right to counsel or not, some of these may meet the threshold for procedural fairness in some cases, but not in others. Allowing for a more fluid position on the involvement of counsel which responds to the level of complexity of the case is best. This may be a formal request for counsel which can be decided on a case by case basis.

The Right to an Oral Hearing and to Cross Examine Witnesses

Much like many procedural fairness elements, the right to an oral hearing and to cross examine witnesses is not a standard requirement in all cases. The nature of the allegations of misconduct and the potential outcome help define whether a full oral hearing, with the ability to cross examine witnesses, is required or if a written hearing is sufficient. Additionally, it is important to determine whether governing legislation dictates the requirement to conduct an oral hearing.

As is generally the case with administrative decisions, the more serious the potential outcome, the higher degree of procedural fairness will be owed to a student. However, it is critically important to review the allegations against the student, as well the relevant evidence, when determining whether an oral hearing is required. Cases that have critical factual disputes, issues where credibility will need to be assessed, or matters that require oral submissions for a student to be able to sufficiently respond to the allegations, should have an oral hearing with an opportunity to cross examine witnesses.[24]

One challenging aspect is how to manage a student's access to witnesses or how to compel witnesses to participate in an academic misconduct process. Generally, a post-secondary institution will not have the ability to compel or force a witness to take part in an academic misconduct investigation or hearing. However, it is critically important that the post-secondary institution is seen to have done enough to facilitate access to witnesses or conversely not be seen to have obstructed that access. If key witnesses have not provided evidence or not been willing to be cross examined, the post-secondary institution will need to thoughtfully consider how to factor that in to the decision.

---

[24] Wilson v. University of Calgary (2014) ABQB 190 para. 84. Retrieved from Canlii https://www.canlii.org/en/ab/abqb/doc/2014/2014abqb190/2014abqb190.html?resultIndex=1

The Person Who Hears the Case Must Decide It

Decision making in educational institutions is often structured in a way that allows for someone in a senior leadership role to make the final decision on a matter (i.e., President, Provost, Dean), and it is sometimes the case that these individuals were not a part of the detailed review that took place. Commonly, this occurs through recommendations from the investigator(s) to the decision maker. While this is not necessarily wrong, it can be problematic in light of the very important concept in the duty of fairness that the person who hears the case should be the one who decides the case.

The purpose of this concept is to limit the influence of third parties on the decision making process.[25] It is best practice to have the party who has examined the evidence and made any credibility assessments to be the one responsible for the decision. In cases where a institution absolutely requires a senior official to make the final decision, ideally they would be directly involved in hearing and reviewing all of the relevant evidence. Where this is not possible, it should only be in the rarest of circumstances that the decision is contrary to those recommendations. In those cases, a court will want to see compelling reasons why the decision maker chose to deviate from the recommendations of the investigator(s).

The Right to Reasons

When a decision has a significant impact on a student's academic career and personal circumstances, they should be provided with the detailed written reasons in support of the decision. In considering what degree of procedural fairness should be afforded an individual who had applied for permanent residence for compassionate reasons, the Supreme Court of Canada found that "it would be unfair for a person subject to a decision such as this one which is so critical to their future not to be told why the result was reached".

Reasons foster better decision making and accord with principles of transparency and fairness.[26] Reasons should not be template, but responsive to the unique case before the decision maker. The reasons should support the decision arrived at while adequately explaining why evidence contrary to the decision was not accepted. Reasons are particularly important when there have been factual disputes or issues where credibility has been assessed in order to provide the decision maker's reconciliation of those pieces that are at odds.

---

[25] Saskatchewan Ministry of Justice and Attorney General. Ombuds Saskatchewan: Practice Essentials for Administrative Tribunals. Regina, 2020. Retrieved from Government of Saskatchewan website https://ombudsman.sk.ca/app/uploads/2020/03/Practice-Essentials-Final-with-Cover.pdf

[26] Baker v. Canada, [1999] 2 SCR 817, para. 38. Retrieved from Supreme Court of Canada website https://scc-csc.lexum.com/scc-csc/scc-csc/en/item/1717/index.do

Creating a Fair Process to Address Academic Misconduct

The jurisprudence on administrative decision making, and the specific cases dealing with decisions arising from the post-secondary environment, lay the foundation for creating a process that handles academic misconduct allegations and adheres to best practices.

In determining the best way to address academic misconduct allegations, the first step is to determine the style of process to follow. The following are the different models that a post-secondary institution can adopt to handle academic misconduct allegations:[27]

(1) Traditional Adversarial Hearing: this model is based on how the courts handle cases. It will feel more formal and adhere to stricter principles of conduct. The parties, who are in opposition with one another, present their cases to the decision maker. The decision maker relies on the parties to bring forward the evidence and argue the issues.

The Traditional Adversarial Hearing model is commonly used at the appeal stage. The appeal can be heard and determined either by an individual or a committee composed of a cross section of the post-secondary community and will convene when an appeal is brought against a finding of academic misconduct, or the penalty that is imposed. Some post-secondary institutions allow only a student to appeal findings of academic misconduct, while other institutions explicitly also allow administration to appeal findings as well. Most commonly it is left undefined as to which party may appeal a decision.

In this model, the right to appeal a decision is typically not absolute. Usually, the party wishing to bring an appeal of a decision must first demonstrate that they have proper grounds to support that there was a flaw in the decision. Common grounds include (a) that the decision was unreasonable based on the evidence before the original decision maker, (b) the original decision was made without procedural fairness, (c) the original decision maker showed bias or (d) that there is new evidence which was not available to the original decision maker, that has direct bearing on the reason for a finding of academic misconduct by the original decision maker.

While the format of a traditional adversarial hearing will differ across post-secondary institutions, a common feature is each side presenting their evidence in the presence of the other party. There is generally symmetry to a hearing, with each side taking turns presenting their evidence and fielding questions. Once one party has presented their case, the other party must have an identical opportunity to present and take questions. While it is common for the hearing panel to ask questions of the parties, the ability for a party to cross-examine the other is variable, with some institutions specifically not allowing cross examination.

---

[27] Saskatchewan Ministry of Justice and Attorney General. Ombuds Saskatchewan: Practice Essentials for Administrative Tribunals. Regina, 2020 at pg. 39. Retrieved from Government of Saskatchewan website https://ombudsman.sk.ca/app/uploads/2020/03/Practice-Essentials-Final-with-Cover.pdf

A fairly representative example of the Traditional Adversarial Hearing model is the University of Guelph. In that system, appeals are heard by the Senate Committee on Student Petitions[28], whose jurisdiction and powers are governed via Terms of Reference.

The challenges with this approach is the decision maker is entirely dependent on the parties to bring the issues and evidence to the hearing. This is especially deleterious where a party has an otherwise compelling case but is disorganized or incomplete in their presentation. The inability of either side to present relevant evidence, or to compel credible witnesses, can also hinder the efficacy of the Traditional Adversarial Model. The formality of this approach may also create significant stress on the parties.

(2) An Investigation Model: this model requires the decision maker to gather all of the evidence and question all parties who may have information about the allegations. The investigation is concluded with a decision being made.

In this model, the allegation of academic misconduct is usually made by an instructor or teaching assistant, who will report their suspicions and any supporting evidence to a designated investigator and/or decision maker. The decision maker will then review the relevant documents and interview the student or any other relevant witnesses to determine whether academic misconduct has occurred. Decisions are supported by the evidence gathered during the course of the investigation.

The decision maker has the authority and discretion to apply penalties. However, the decision maker is often constrained by directives which limit the range of penalties that can be applied in particular types of academic misconduct. For example, first time offenders may receive a warning or educational support, while subsequent findings of academic misconduct may invite greater penalties such as a failure of a course or suspension from the post-secondary institution.

The University of Calgary follows an Investigation Model when allegations of academic misconduct are raised. In the University of Calgary system, instructors must submit a written report of all incidents of suspected academic misconduct to faculty leadership. Students, or other individuals with evidence of academic misconduct, can also report allegations. Once leadership receives an allegation, there is a recommended time frame in which the student must be informed of the allegation and whether an investigation will be initiated. If an investigation is to be initiated, then the student must be informed of the nature of the allegation and all the evidence that has been collected. In addition, students are invited to meet to discuss the allegation in the presence of an advisor. There is a time limit for providing a written decision and if there is a finding of academic misconduct, the support for that finding and the consequences for the student.

The challenge with an investigation model is it does not typically offer an opportunity to either party to cross examine witnesses or challenge statements that may

[28] University of Guelph. (October 9th 2013) Senate Committee on Student Petitions, Committee By-Laws. Retrieved from https://www.uoguelph.ca/secretariat/office-services/senate/senate-boards-and-standing-committees/senate-committee-student-petitions

have been brought forward about the allegations. This model tends to work better in cases where the evidence is entirely documentary in nature (i.e., no witnesses) or where there in an internal right of appeal.

An Inquiry Model: similar to the investigation model, this approach entails the decision maker seeking out all of the evidence, but in the course of a hearing. The decision maker is the one responsible for asking the questions and gathering the evidence. This model has benefits which include putting the control of the process in the hands of the decision maker. However, with this control comes a significant amount of responsibility, which may make the process quite lengthy especially if a post-secondary institution has multiple cases of alleged academic misconduct.

This model is not typically seen in Canada's post-secondary environment with respect to academic misconduct.

(3) A Hybrid Model: There has been an increasing shift towards systems that incorporate features of both the Investigative model and Traditional Hearing model. Such systems are aimed at providing a more holistic approach to dealing with allegations of academic misconduct.

An example of a hybrid model is currently used by the Ryerson University. In the Ryerson system, allegations of academic misconduct are made to Designated Decision Makers, who are a pool of faculty who have been trained in investigations. Their process is unique as Designated Decision Makers have more flexibility in how they address findings of academic misconduct, which may include meeting with students through a "facilitated or non-facilitated discussion" to discuss possible outcomes such as attending an educational workshop or participating in an online quizzes to ensure the expectations of the institution are understood.[29]

Academic Misconduct Decisions: Judicial Review

Courts have a form of oversight. Because of the significant impact of these decisions on students, the Courts have typically found greater need for judicial intervention.

Judicial review will typically look at two aspects of the decision: 1. Was the decision made in a procedurally fair way?; and 2. Is the decision fair and reasonable? If the Court determines that the post-secondary institution did not meet its procedural fairness requirements, the decision will be overturned and one of a number of possible remedies will be ordered.

When assessing whether a post-secondary institution made a fair and reasonably justifiable decision, however, the Courts will first have to determine which standard of review they will apply to that decision. There are two potential standards of review that a Court will apply to the decision: correctness and reasonableness. The choice of the standard of review reflects how much judicial deference the Court should show

[29] Ryerson University (2019), Ryerson University Policy of Senate, Academic Integrity. Retrieved from Ryerson website https://www.ryerson.ca/content/dam/senate/policies/pol60.pdf

the decision maker. If the Court decides to show deference, then reasonableness is the standard. If the Court decides that no judicial deference is warranted, the standard will be correctness.

If the standard of review is correctness, "a reviewing court will not show deference to the decision maker's reasoning process; it will rather undertake its own analysis of the question."[30] Therefore, if the standard of correctness is applied to a decision of academic misconduct, the court can proceed to directly consider how it would have decided the matter if it was in the place of the decision maker.

The reasonableness standard recognizes that "certain questions that come before administrative tribunals do not lend themselves to one specific particular result and may "give rise to a number of possible, reasonable conclusions." Instead of proceeding directly to consider how it would have decided the matter, a reviewing court "is concerned mostly with the existence of justification, transparency and intelligibility within the decision-making process".[31]

Until recently, the leading case used to determine the applicable standard of review was *Dunsmuir v. New Brunswick*. In *Dunsmuir*, the Supreme Court of Canada established indicators to help determine the proper standard of review. This analysis could be described as challenging to navigate. The Supreme Court of Canada has tried to simplify and clarify how to determine the proper standard of review in the case of *Canada (Minister of Citizenship and Immigration)* v. *Vavilov,* 2019 SCC 65. In this case, the Supreme Court has held that there is a general presumption that the standard of review is reasonableness to any substantive decision made by a statutory decision maker. However, the presumption of reasonableness is rebutted if (1) the governing legislation indicates that a standard other than reasonableness that should apply, and (2) rule of law principles require that a different standard of review should apply to the decision. In the first instance, the analysis is prescriptive. In the second instance, the analysis is contextual.

While it is currently still too early to fully appreciate the effect that *Vavilov* will have on the practice of academic misconduct at post-secondary institutions, some general principles can be identified. The general presumption of reasonableness as a standard of review will in most cases apply to post-secondary institutions' decisions about academic misconduct. However, what constitutes reasonable remains contextual.

The specialized expertise of a decision maker is a relevant factor in determining whether a decision was reasonable. Arguably, a decision maker in an academic misconduct process has more specialized expertise in academic integrity than someone outside of a post-secondary institution. The application of this specialized knowledge may reveal why particular attention or preference was given to some evidence or issues over others (*Vavilov,* para. 93).

---

[30] Dunsmuir v. New Brunswick [2008] 1 SCR 190 at para. 50. Retrieved from CanLii https://www.canlii.org/en/ca/scc/doc/2008/2008scc9/2008scc9.html?resultIndex=1

[31] Dunsmuir v. New Brunswick [2008] 1 SCR 190 at para. 48. Retrieved from CanLii https://www.canlii.org/en/ca/scc/doc/2008/2008scc9/2008scc9.html?resultIndex=1

While the institutional context for the decision may attract judicial deference, the court cannot overlook non-transparency or gaps in logic in the process of the decision[32]. The decision maker must demonstrate in the reasons how the evidence before them was considered and how the outcome is supported by the evidence that was presented.[33] However, the reasons do not have to address each argument made by the parties.[34] The reasons must demonstrate a connection, or a path of analysis between the evidence and the decision. Reasons that merely set out the submissions made by the parties and then immediately arrive at conclusions will rarely be sufficient to demonstrate a path of analysis. Therefore, extreme care must be taken in how decisions are written. Decision makers are encouraged to consult with their institution's legal support to ensure that the written decision is sufficiently transparent, justified and intelligible. Failure to do so will make any decision, no matter how obvious on its face, appear unreasonable.

On judicial review, courts will rarely substitute their own decision for that of the original decision maker. Rather, courts can offer a variety of remedies to the applicant. Such remedies are meant to cure the underlying defect in natural justice or procedural fairness, such that the decision regarding the allegation of academic misconduct can be seen as 'fair'.

The general remedies available under judicial review are *certiorari* (an order voiding the decision under review), *prohibition* (barring an administrative act on jurisdictional grounds), *mandamus* (compelling an administrative act), and *quo warranto* (challenging the right of a decision maker to exercise its ability to make a decision).

Using the remedies available at judicial review, a student may be able to overturn a decision of the post-secondary institution that affects their standing or attendance at the institution. A student who has been found to have committed academic misconduct on clear evidence may nevertheless have that decision voided by a court if there were procedural defects in how the otherwise sound decision was reached. For example, a student who has been suspended from an institution may be re-admitted if the decision suspending the student was not made strictly in accordance with the enabling legislation.

The costs of judicial review can be high in terms of institutional resources, and time. In addition to the legal costs of defending an application in court, instructors and administrators will have to devote time in preparing the defense. Often, this outlay in resources will have to be made long after the actual events that form the basis of the academic misconduct allegation happened. If an applicant is successful at judicial review, the matter may be sent back to the post-secondary institution for re-adjudication.

---

[32] Canada (Minister of Citizenship and Immigration) v. Vavilov [2019] SCC 65 at para. 95. Retrieved from CanLii https://www.canlii.org/en/ca/scc/doc/2019/2019scc65/2019scc65.html

[33] *Ibid.* at paras. 125 and 126.

[34] *Ibid.* at paras. 127 and 128.

Practical Considerations

It is critically important to acknowledge that most students and academic leaders will not have a legal background and as a result, creating or participating in processes used to address academic integrity may be intimidating and overwhelming. Failure to support all stakeholders in the process could result in avoidance in addressing allegations of academic misconduct, as well as put students at a disadvantage when defending such allegations.

Students navigating academic misconduct policies, processes and investigations should be given access to knowledgeable support. This support does not necessarily need to have a legal background, but should be well versed in the post-secondary institution's policies, procedures, processes and be connected with key stakeholders. This may be a student advocate or student ombudsperson, or a law students advocacy organization on campus. This is commonly available in one form or another in post-secondary institutions across Canada. Additionally, access to explanatory literature about how the process typically unfolds and the respective rights of the parties can also be very beneficial.

Equally important is for academic leadership to have access to legal counsel as support in creating a fair and robust process for investigating and addressing academic misconduct, as well as to provide guidance in how to properly investigate and assess allegations as they come forward. Given the growing complexity of academic misconduct cases, legal counsel has an important role in ensuring fairness and in training academic leadership and faculty on investigation and decision making principles.

Fear of legal processes or the erroneous belief of the need for an "airtight case" can act to deter faculty from bringing forward allegations of academic misconduct. Additionally, historic processes that were overly arduous or slanted in the favour of students can also limit the number of cases which come to light. It is important to understand that academic misconduct need not be proven beyond a reasonable doubt. This is the standard of proof required for conviction in criminal cases. Academic misconduct must only be proven on the balance of probabilities standard of proof, meaning it is more likely than not to have occurred based on the evidence—a lower standard of proof than what is required for criminal charges.

The content in this Chapter highlights the complexity of the law when it comes to academic misconduct decisions and the importance of ensuring that all participants in the process are given access to the necessary support and guidance. It also underscores the need to examine alternate approaches to deal with academic misconduct, apart from just the traditional, highly legal approach taken by most post-secondary institutions. There remains mistrust by academic staff that traditional processes to address academic misconduct, which are often oppositional and adversarial, will lead to an unsatisfactory outcome. Final recourse to the courts is fraught with issues that stem from complex access to justice concerns (i.e., long times to get hearing dates, access to legal counsel etc.). This all speaks to the need to consider alternative dispute resolution, and varying perspectives on the concept of justice, and their place within the current post-secondary framework that responds to academic misconduct.

Finally, it is time to examine whether penalty-based sanctioning represents the best outcome or if there are different ways to deter conduct, while setting students up for academic success and integrity going forward.

References

Christensen Hughes, J. M., & McCabe, D. L. (2006). Academic misconduct within higher education in Canada. *The Canadian Journal of Higher Education, 36*(2), 1–21. http://journals.sfu.ca/cjhe/index.php/cjhe/article/view/183537/183482

Dunne v. Memorial University of Newfoundland. (2012). NLTD(G) 41.

Dunsmuir v. New Brunswick. (2008). 1 SCR 190 https://www.canlii.org/en/ca/scc/doc/2008/2008scc9/2008scc9.html?resultIndex=1

Government of Alberta. (2020). *Post-Secondary Learning Act*. https://www.qp.alberta.ca/documents/acts/p19p5.pdf

Government of British Columbia. (2020). *University Act*, RSBC 1996 C.468 https://www.bclaws.gov.bc.ca/civix/document/id/complete/statreg/96468_01

Government of Ontario. (1990). Statutory Powers Procedure Act, Revised Statutes of Ontario (1990 c.S.22) https://www.ontario.ca/laws/statute/90s22

Kelleher, W. E. (2016). Canadian Laws Relevant to University Student Academic Discipline (ProQuest Number 10253968) [Doctoral Dissertation, Northcentral University]. https://search-proquest-com.ezproxy.lib.ucalgary.ca/docview/1867763133?pq-origsite=primo

Khan v. University of Ottawa. (1997). 34 OR 535 https://www.canlii.org/en/on/onca/doc/1997/1997canlii941/1997canlii941.html

Pridgen v. University of Calgary. (2012). ABCA 139.

Ryerson University. (2019). Ryerson University Policy of Senate, Academic Integrity. https://www.ryerson.ca/content/dam/senate/policies/pol60.pdf

Saskatchewan Ministry of Justice and Attorney General. Ombuds Saskatchewan: Practice Essentials for Administrative Tribunals. (2020). https://ombudsman.sk.ca/app/uploads/2020/03/Practice-Essentials-Final-with-Cover.pdf.

University of Guelph. (2013). Senate Committee on Student Petitions, Committee By-Laws. https://www.uoguelph.ca/secretariat/office-services/senate/senate-boards-and-standing-committees/senate-committee-student-petitions

Wilson v. University of Calgary. (2014). ABQB 190 para. 67. https://www.canlii.org/en/ab/abqb/doc/2014/2014abqb190/2014abqb190.html?resultIndex=1

Melissa Morrison B.com, LLB is a mother, wife and practicing lawyer in the Province of Alberta. She currently works as the Student Appeals Officer for the University of Calgary and, as part of her role, she provides advice to internal hearing tribunals on appeals of a variety of decisions, including academic misconduct findings, and also offers guidance on appropriate investigation techniques. With over 17 years in practice, Melissa has gained significant experience in litigation, health and administrative law, as well as student appeals and professional regulatory processes.

Philip Zachariah MA, JD has over 15 years of experience in legal practice with post-secondary institutions. He is currently Legal Counsel for the University of Calgary where he provides advice on a wide variety of issues from student appeals to commercial procurement to privacy and data security. Before that, he was the Judicial Officer at the University of Guelph, where he did an MA on the applicability of alternative dispute resolution models to addressing breaches of academic integrity.

Chapter 29
Building a Culture of Restorative Practice and Restorative Responses to Academic Misconduct

Paul Sopcak and Kevin Hood

Abstract The *Universal Declaration of Human Rights'* Article 26 on education and more recently UNESCO's "World Declaration on Higher Education for the Twenty-First Century: Mission and Action" have called for civic and ethical education alongside academic education in postsecondary settings. Many post-secondary institutions have made fostering civic responsibility, engaged citizenship, and ethical decision making in students a strategic priority. What often remains ambiguous is how these priorities translate into action. A growing body of scholarly literature and research establishes the role Restorative Practice (RP) can play in pursuing these strategic priorities surrounding moral development, emotional intelligence, and engaged citizenship. Specifically, RP has been shown to prevent conflict and misconduct, while empowering marginalized individuals. Restorative practices demonstrate fairness; and foster empathy, compassion and accountability; through experiential learning opportunities. In light of these developments, MacEwan University, in Alberta, Canada, has been actively building a restorative culture. One aspect of this endeavour was the revision of its Academic Integrity Policy and Academic Misconduct Procedures to include the possibility of alternative resolutions to academic misconduct, based on restorative practices and principles. In our chapter, we will (a) provide a brief introduction to restorative practices that makes explicit its connection to universities' civic education mandate, integrity, and specifically, academic integrity; (b) describe the restorative practices model that is being established at MacEwan University; (c) discuss in detail the application of restorative practices to academic misconduct cases, including training of facilitators, as well as successes and challenges experienced in the first year since it became available; and, finally, (d) share feedback

P. Sopcak (✉)
Community Standards and Values, and Humanities Department, MacEwan University, Edmonton, AB T5J 4S2, Canada
e-mail: sopcakp@macewan.ca

K. Hood
Public Safety & Justice Studies Department, MacEwan University, Edmonton, AB T5J 4S2, Canada
e-mail: HoodK@macewan.ca

S. E. Eaton and J. Christensen Hughes (eds.), *Academic Integrity in Canada*, Ethics and Integrity in Educational Contexts 1,
https://doi.org/10.1007/978-3-030-83255-1_29

regarding its effectiveness received from students, staff, and faculty who participated in restorative resolutions.

Keywords Academic integrity · Academic misconduct · Restorative practices · Restorative justice · Citizenship education · Accountability · Canada

Academic Integrity and Post-Secondary's Civic Education Mandate

Although there will be some variation, when asked what the purpose and objectives of their work are, those with a formalized role related to promoting academic integrity in a post-secondary setting will mention the obvious, minimizing academic misconduct and ensuring the integrity and value of the degrees their institution grants. Perhaps after a pause, they might also mention those objectives that seem more lofty and are more closely related to the moral and civic education of students, such as promoting the values associated with academic integrity (Christensen Hughes & McCabe, 2006, p. 51). And indeed, post-secondary institutions have increasingly made fostering civic responsibility, engaged citizenship, and ethical decision making in students a priority in institutional strategic planning (Boyte, 2015; Jorgenson & Shultz, 2012; Stephens et al., 2000). This development is reflected in most institutions' mission and vision statements. Besides a long tradition of humanistic pedagogy, this priority finds support in the Universal Declaration of Human Rights, Article 26, as well as UNESCO's (1998) "World Declaration on Higher Education for the Twenty-First Century: Vision and Action." How this citizenship education is carried out varies, but integrity education—and ethical decision-making as part of it—is a key factor.

Imagine further that this same academic professional is asked what strategies they use to pursue those goals. In all likelihood, they will with some satisfaction state that traditional approaches to academic integrity that focused on rule compliance, deterrence and punishment, have been shown to be rather ineffective and that their institution has consequently adopted the strategy proposed by Tricia Bertram Gallant (2008) to treat academic integrity as a teaching and learning issue, emphasizing prevention and education over policing and punishment.

However, there seems to be an irreconcilable rift between prevention and education strategies and those governing *responses* to academic misconduct. It is as if there existed a divide and that the values and principles that guide our strategies in preventing misconduct no longer apply once a student crosses over to the dark side of misconduct, for the vast majority of university and college codes, policies, and procedures determining *responses* to academic and non-academic misconduct are quasi-judicial in nature. As such, they are structurally adversarial, with a focus on deterrence effects through engagement in an intimidating, formal and oppositional procedure resulting in punitive sanctions. Academic misconduct is treated first and foremost as a lack and violation of compliance with institutional codes and/or policies. Focusing on deterrence and punitive discipline, the response to academic misconduct follows a logic of escalating severity of punitive measures, which logically culminates in temporary or permanent exclusion from the university or college community (Bretag & Mahmud, 2016; Bretag et al., 2011a, b; Clark et al., 2012; Stoesz et al., 2019). This is not to say that educational/pedagogical outcomes are necessarily absent from this conventional approach; rather, the quasi-judicial, adversarial, framing of the codes, policies, and procedures is what determines the ground tenor and emphasis (Kara & MacAlister, 2010).

Support for this claim is available in an Australian study by Pitt et al. (2020), which found that students perceived their university's processes for dealing with academic misconduct (specifically contract cheating in this study) as a legal process (p. 9) and being involved in it as "the hardest, most challenging or worst experience of their lives" (p. 5). This perception was shared by students who were ultimately found to have been in violation of the policy and those whose cases were dismissed. Participants in the study further reported the negative impact their involvement in the university procedure had on relationships with family members, peers, and academics (Pitt et al., 2020, pp. 6–9). Faculty members are, of course, not blind to these effects of a quasi-legal approach to academic misconduct, which contributes to the widespread unwillingness to report academic misconduct according to institutional policy and procedure that research has found (e.g., Eaton et al., 2020).

Given this negative perception and impact, the standard, quasi-legal, adversarial process, emphasizing deterrence and punishment, must surely support the goals and objectives identified earlier then. Wachtel (2016), following Braithwaite (1989), argues that the opposite is true. He writes, "…reliance on punishment as a social regulator is problematic because it shames and stigmatizes wrongdoers, pushes them into a negative societal subculture and fails to change their behavior" (Wachtel, 2016, p. 3). James Lang (2013) provides historical and cites experimental evidence pertaining to (academic) misconduct which supports this view and shows that rule compliance models do a fair job, at best, at minimizing misconduct and consequently at protecting the integrity and value of university degrees (see also Bertram Gallant, 2008; and Clark, 2014). It is not surprising, then, that the ubiquity of academic misconduct remains a serious problem for post-secondary institutions (for an overview of the research, see Eaton et al., 2020).

Moreover, since these more pragmatic objectives are directly influenced by the loftier goals, such as promoting the fundamental values of academic integrity (ICAI, 2021), as well as the moral and civic education of our students, it is clear that the punitive, deterrence model also fails when it comes to these higher order, moral objectives. But why is that? Reflecting on the effectiveness of deterrence models in the criminal justice system, David A. Dana (2001) writes:

> …deterrence models of human decision-making do not fully describe how most people think in most contexts. People sometimes do not obey the law because their calculations indicate that expected penalties exceed expected gain… Instead, to a significant extent, people obey the law because they have internalized the belief that obeying the law is the right thing to do…And they respect the law because they perceive the law as embodying, as being in tune with, their own conception of what is just and unjust, right and wrong. (p. 777)

Clearly then, one of the reasons for their relative ineffectiveness is that compliance models primarily promote and reward rule following, not the moral reflection that is necessary to internalize the values underlying these rules. While rule-following may be a desirable outcome in regard to the two more pragmatic goals of academic integrity professionals, it is insufficient when it comes to the goal of moral and civic education, and at effecting the cultural shift necessary to address academic misconduct at its roots.

How, then, can this disconnect between academic integrity *prevention* work focused on values-based education, on the one hand, and procedures for *responding* to academic misconduct that are grounded in punitive, fear-based, rule-compliance, on the other, be rectified? Recently, Bertram Gallant (2017) revised her 2008 "teaching and learning approach" to academic integrity, which was entirely focused on *prevention*, by adding a strategy targeting the *response* to misconduct, namely, "leveraging the cheating moment as a teachable moment" (p. 88). Specifically, Bertram Gallant (2017) proposes the wider adoption of her institution's approach to require students who have engaged in academic misconduct to complete academic integrity seminars or courses focused on "activities and assessments that guide them through the experiential learning cycle to reach the learning objectives of developing ethical decision making skills, enhancing meta-cognition, and increasing student understanding of academic and professional integrity standards" (p. 92).

We wholeheartedly agree with Bertram Gallant on the value of such seminars and courses and thereby the extension of pedagogical goals and values to the *response* mechanisms. In fact, recent literature provides preliminary empirical support for their effectiveness (Stoesz & Los, 2019). However, what this approach does not address is the inconsistency in the value structure and guiding principles between prevention efforts on the one hand and response practices on the other, if these seminars are assigned as an "educational component" of an otherwise punitive, quasi-legal, and adversarial process. Unfortunately, in our experience, that is precisely how mandatory academic integrity seminars and tutorials are currently being assigned.

In what follows, we will first briefly define Restorative Practices (RP) and how they relate to Restorative Justice (RJ); we then present a restorative resolution process based on the principles of RP, followed by insights gained from its implementation at our home institution, MacEwan University in Canada; finally, we argue that having an RP approach as the default response to academic misconduct and the currently standard, quasi-legal, punitive approach as a secondary procedure to fall back on when conditions for the former are not met, ensures the *integrity* of an institutional strategy to academic integrity. It ensures that prevention and response remain firmly grounded in the goals, values, and principles pertaining not only to universities' pedagogical missions, but also those related to civic and moral education, as well as community building.

Brief Introduction to Restorative Practices

Definitions of restorative practices (RP) and restorative justice (RJ) vary, as well as descriptions of how one relates to the other. We adopt the International Institute for Restorative Practices and its founder Ted Wachtel's (2016) approach in considering RJ as a sub-category of RP, that is, as the application of restorative practices in matters pertaining specifically to criminal justice. This is helpful, since it highlights commonalities across disciplines in areas of research and practice that employ the same fundamental principles of RP, such as education, social work, etc. It also aligns with the preventative application of restorative principles to build community and social capital under the larger RP umbrella. Thus, since RJ is seen as one form of RP, the references to, and claims about, RJ presented in this chapter are considered to be representative of RP, in general.

So, what is distinctive about RP and RJ and how do its processes differ from other approaches to address wrongdoing, conflict, and harm? The following is a simple description by one of the most prominent RJ figures, Howard Zehr: "Restorative justice is a process to involve, to the extent possible, those who have a stake in a specific offense and to collectively identify and address harms, needs, and obligations, in order to heal and put things as right as possible" (Zehr, 2003, p. 40).

Tellingly, Zehr begins his influential *The Little Book of Restorative Justice* with a list of what RJ is *not*. It is telling because it is an indicator of the influence and persistence of some of the myths and misconceptions regarding RJ. We will merely provide a list of the points Zehr makes and send the reader to his short book for elaboration. First, *RJ "is not primarily about forgiveness or reconciliation*" (Zehr, 2003, p. 6). Although these might be byproducts of RJ/RP, they are not a primary goal or objective. Contrary to common belief, RJ/RP focuses first on the needs of the community and the harmed parties and then on those of the responsible party (for various reasons, including the separation from criminal justice proceedings, we will avoid the terms "victim" and "offender," and will instead refer to "harmed" and "responsible parties" throughout the chapter).

Second, *RJ is different from mediation.* Whereas in mediation the goal is to establish a mutually acceptable compromise between conflicting interests that are seen "on a level moral playing field, often with responsibilities shared on all sides" (Zehr, 2003, p. 7), in RJ at least one party must accept responsibility for the harm(s) they caused, if a case is to move forward to a facilitated encounter ("RJ/RP conference").

Third, *reducing recidivism is not a primary goal of RJ.* Although reduced recidivism has been documented in a number of projects and studies (e.g., Rodriguez, 2007), Zehr (2003) stresses that it is "an expected byproduct, but restorative justice is done first of all because it is the right thing to do: victims' needs *should* be addressed, offenders *should* be encouraged to take responsibility, those affected by an offense *should* be involved in the process, regardless of whether offenders 'get it' and reduce their offending" (p. 8).

Fourth, *RJ "is not a particular program or blueprint"* (Zehr, 2003, p. 8). Rather, it is a set of foundational principles that should be applied to institutions and situations in a way that is sensitive to particular contexts and needs. Fifth, although RJ may be applied to minor offenses, it *"is not primarily intended for minor offenses or first-time offenders"* (Zehr, 2003, p. 8). It is a widespread, seemingly intuitive, response to consider RJ/RP appropriate only to address these less severe cases. However, experience has shown that the processes work particularly well when there is a lot at stake for affected parties and they are invested.

Sixth, RJ "is not a new or North American development" (Zehr, 2003, p. 9). Zehr clarifies that despite the fact that RJ's current expression was first developed in the Mennonite community, many of the principles and practices have a long tradition and remain at play in Indigenous communities around the world. For an insightful analysis of some of the differences between Indigenous law and RJ in a Canadian context, and to assist in a differentiated discussion of the charge of appropriation, see Chartrand and Horn (2018).

Seventh, RJ "is neither a panacea nor necessarily a replacement for the legal system" (Zehr, 2003, p. 10). For reasons that will be addressed in a later section on the conditions for a RP/RJ process, to protect harmed parties, and to safeguard basic human rights, a functioning legal system is key, even if RP/RJ processes were to become the primary and default approaches to address harm. This also applies to the context of academic integrity, where the presence of RP options/processes does not render the quasi-legal, adversarial processes obsolete.

A further misconception we wish to address here is that RP/RJ is "soft on crime" and lets offenders off easy. In our experience this misconception is so persistent and widely accepted that it presents a serious obstacle to the implementation of RP/RJ processes. Exploring the harms one is responsible for and then meeting the obligations to repair them through active accountability is far more difficult than passively accepting a punitive sanction. Also, RJ/RP outcomes do not categorically preclude punitive measures.

Now that some of the common myths and misconceptions have been addressed, a look at some of the core principles of RJ/RP is in order. Although accounts vary, the most influential figures of RJ/RP agree on at least four underlying principles, namely "inclusive decision making," "active accountability," "repairing harm," and "rebuilding trust" (Karp, 2019, p. 9; see also Karp & Sacks, 2014). Rather than attempt to paraphrase Karp, we will reproduce his precise definition of RJ here in its entirety:

> Restorative Justice is a philosophical approach that embraces the reparation of harm, healing of trauma, reconciliation of interpersonal conflict, reduction of social inequality, and reintegration of people who have been marginalized and outcast. RJ embraces community empowerment and participation, multipartial facilitation, active accountability, and social support. A central practice of restorative justice is a collaborative decision-making process that includes harmed parties, offenders, and others who are seeking to hold offenders accountable by having them: Accept and acknowledge responsibility for their offenses; to the best of their ability, repair the harm they caused to harmed parties and the community; and work to rebuild trust by showing understanding of the harm, addressing personal issues, and building positive social connections. (Karp, 2019, p. 4)

These practices, applied not only in response to misconduct, but also as a proactive community building tool, have been shown to be an effective way of addressing bullying (Acosta et al., 2019), preventing conflict and misconduct by fostering a sense of trust and community, empowering marginalized individuals and communities (Ahlin et al., 2017; Cassel, 2014; Gal, 2016), pursuing and demonstrating fairness, as well as fostering empathy, compassion, and accountability (Kehoe et al., 2018; Winslade, 2018). Needless to say, these are all important aspects of civic and moral education, and minimize academic misconduct.

Restorative Resolutions of Academic Misconduct—MacEwan University's Model

In light of these insights and the rift we have observed between the desired outcomes regarding the culture of Academic Misconduct at our institution and the seeming inefficacy of a quasi-judicial procedure as the sole and/or default response to misconduct, paired with our institution's commitment to prioritizing prevention and education over policing and punishing, we have introduced a restorative resolution option based on the above RP principles into our procedures for dealing with academic misconduct. Our institution's Student Academic Misconduct Procedure defines Restorative Resolution as: "Any of a number of restorative processes involving the harmed parties, including representatives of the community, in reaching a resolution that repairs harms caused and rebuilds trust between the responsible party, the harmed parties, and the community" (MacEwan University, 2018, p. 1). Currently, roughly 25% of cases that require a formal hearing (severe and repeat misconduct) are resolved restoratively at MacEwan University, with a strong upward trend.

Context

At MacEwan University, instructing faculty members are the decision makers for suspected incidents of academic misconduct that occur in their courses. Based on policy and procedures that are grounded in procedural fairness (right to be heard, right to fair and impartial decision-making, etc.; Stoesz et al., 2019), faculty members decide on a balance of probabilities whether a given incident is academic misconduct or not and what the appropriate consequence should be. They have a list of consequences to choose from, including educational options. The maximum penalty an instructing faculty member can apply is a mark of zero on the assignment in question. Decisions related to cases of severe academic misconduct (e.g., contract cheating, impersonation, falsification) are made by trained faculty adjudicators after a formal hearing. MacEwan University has a centralized repository of reported incidents, and cases of repeat academic misconduct trigger a formal hearing presided over by faculty members who take on a role of adjudicator for 2–6 years, as part of their service load.

In the formalized sequence of steps listed in the Student Academic Misconduct Procedure document, as well as within resources available on MacEwan University's academic integrity website, faculty members are asked to consider the viability and appropriateness of a restorative resolution attempt prior to proceeding with a standard, quasi-judicial process. The severity of any given incident of academic misconduct, including whether it is a case of repeat misconduct, does not determine whether a restorative resolution attempt is an option. Rather, the following conditions must be met for an academic misconduct case to be considered for a restorative resolution:

1. There is no risk that the restorative resolution process could lead to additional harm.
2. The student must take full responsibility for their actions and show a willingness to reflect on the harms their action has caused, as well as on how that harm might be repaired. Any deflecting or minimizing of responsibility will normally make the case unsuitable for a restorative resolution attempt.
3. The affected parties voluntarily consent to participating in a restorative conference/resolution attempt.
4. The affected parties need to show a genuine interest in repairing harm and the situation. This includes the harmed parties' willingness to restrain retributive or vindictive urges.

If these conditions are not met or the restorative resolution attempt (restorative conference) is unsuccessful (e.g., the responsible party shifts blame or the affected/present parties cannot come to an agreement regarding the appropriate outcome), then the case goes back into the formal, quasi-judicial procedure stream.

Participants

The student who has engaged in academic misconduct is the responsible party and will be present during the restorative conference. For a first offense, a case will go to a restorative conference only if the faculty member in whose class the incident occurred is willing to participate. Since severe and repeat academic misconduct arguably have a greater impact on the wider university community, restorative conferences that respond to these involve further members as harmed parties. As such, a member of the Student Association of MacEwan University (SAMU) represents the student body as one of the harmed parties/communities, and a trained faculty adjudicator takes part to represent the University's body of faculty members. Although not present in their role as adjudicator, these faculty members have the necessary experience and training in matters pertaining to academic integrity and responses to academic misconduct that will ensure a fair outcome and that standards of academic integrity are maintained.

Pre-conference Meetings

One of the key elements in any RP response are the individual pre-conference meetings with the harmed and responsible parties. During these meetings, the facilitator assesses to what extent the conditions above are met, explains the procedure in detail, queries whether anyone else should be invited to attend the restorative conference, and can begin anticipating challenges that might occur.

Facilitators

At MacEwan University, we have adopted the facilitation model developed by the International Institute for Restorative Practices (IIRP) and have obtained training and license to, in turn, train and certify restorative conference facilitators. This has allowed us to build a pool of over 50 restorative conference facilitators and has supported consistency and quality facilitation. Faculty members who have completed the training facilitate restorative conferences in partial fulfilment of their service requirements. It is important to note that a facilitator's role in this context is different from that of a mediator or adjudicator. The facilitator guides the parties who have been affected by the incident(s) brought forward through a structured conversation. They ensure that it remains respectful and safe, and that it moves towards a tangible outcome.

Restorative Conferences

The conferences are highly structured, non-adversarial meetings. They are normally held in a circle formation with a carefully considered seating order, although we managed to successfully shift them to a video-conferencing format in 2020 to meet the COVID-19 public health requirements. All participants sign confidentiality forms prior to the conference and are reminded that no record will be kept of any information shared during the conference, except that which is included in the outcome agreement. A series of questions (Wachtel, 2016, p. 7), which all participants were made aware of prior to the conference, provides the structure. As these questions move the conversation from a focus on the past to one on the present and then the future, they explore the harms caused by the academic misconduct (emotional, material, to the community) and how those harms might be repaired through concrete actions (active accountability) on the part of the responsible party:

Restorative Conference Questions

(Questions marked with an asterisk* have been added to or slightly modified from Wachtel's (2016, p. 7)).

To responsible parties:

- What happened?
- What were you thinking of at the time?
- What have you thought about since?
- Who has been affected by what you have done?
- In what way have they been affected?*
- What do you think are the obligations resulting from your action?* What are appropriate consequences?* What do you think could be put in place to ensure it doesn't happen again?*

To harmed parties:

- What did you think when you realized what had happened?
- What impact has this incident had on you and others?
- What has been the hardest thing for you?
- What do you think needs to happen to make things right? What are appropriate consequences?* What do you think could be put in place to ensure it doesn't happen again?*

(Wachtel, 2016, p. 7).

Through the structure these questions provide, the restorative conference focuses on the harms resulting from academic misconduct in a collaborative process that holds students accountable and collaboratively explores how harms can be repaired, as well as what needs to be put in place to avoid future misconduct by the student. It provides an opportunity for students who engaged in academic misconduct to listen to the impact of their actions (material, emotional, on the community) in a non-adversarial environment and supports them in taking responsibility for their actions, as well as the resulting obligations.

Outcomes

After an exploration of the impact a given incident of academic misconduct has had in terms of emotional and material harm, as well as harm to the community, the conversation turns to what an appropriate outcome of the restorative conference might be. Specifically, the parties present discuss what actions the student might take to repair each of the harms caused, what appropriate sanctions might look like, and what might be put in place to ensure it doesn't happen again. This part of the restorative conference is an opportunity not only for the student who engaged in academic misconduct to reflect on their obligations and how to avoid future misconduct, but also for the student body representative and the faculty member(s) to consider whether in the concrete case before them any altered teaching strategies, additional institutional resources, or different forms of peer support might have supported the student in question more fully and minimized the incentive to engage in misconduct. If any of these latter considerations are verbalized, it is done without minimizing or shifting responsibility.

Although these outcomes need not be *identical* to outcomes of adversarial, "model code," disciplinary hearings, they must be *equitable* and *fair*. To protect fairness, as well as the reputation and integrity of the restorative resolution procedure, it must not be (nor run the danger of being perceived as) an "easy way out." Choosing appropriate harmed party representatives of the student and faculty bodies, respectively, and the university community, in general, is critical in this regard. In our experience, the presence of a students' union member with knowledge and experience related to appropriate outcomes, whether through student advocacy activities or prior participation in restorative conferences, as well as a trained faculty adjudicator as representative of the faculty body has proved effective.

In order to set the stage for a fair and equitable outcome, the harmed parties are asked what in their experience the outcome of a "model code" hearing for a comparable case would be. This then forms the point of comparison during the collaborative discussion of an appropriate outcomes. These outcomes often include some punitive measures but mostly focus on constructive actions students take to repair the harm they caused, and if appropriate to the situation, students are also asked to reflect on what they might do to help their peers avoid engaging in academic misconduct.

The facilitator does not provide suggestions regarding the substance of the outcome but does assist in clarifying questions of fact and ensuring that the tasks agreed upon are captured in sufficient detail, including deadlines, as well as consequences should the agreement be breached. Since signing of the outcome agreement is voluntary, it cannot be appealed.

To provide some concrete examples, the outcomes of restorative resolutions of academic misconduct at MacEwan University have included grade reductions with and without transcript notations, in addition to the requirement to successfully complete an online academic integrity tutorial and write a reflective paper. These papers have targeted students' experiences related to engaging in academic misconduct, including the restorative conference; their reflection on the harms of their actions and academic misconduct, in general, as well as on what could have been done differently; and the development of a strategy to avoid misconduct should the student find themselves in a similar situation in the future that includes a list of available supports and resources. Despite the fact that these are common elements of outcome agreements, each will address the specific needs and obligations of the particular case and context.

Responses to Restorative Resolutions of Academic Misconduct at MacEwan University

The following "testimonials" capture how the RP procedure described above is perceived by MacEwan students and faculty members who have participated in restorative resolutions of academic misconduct.

Student's Comments on Experience of Participating in a Restorative Resolution of their Academic Misconduct (Anonymized):

> For starters the restorative resolution was a relief for me because I wanted to right the wrong that I had done not only to [professor] but to myself and the greater school community. The restorative resolution was a great choice for me because I was so stressed at the time to be persecuted and ridiculed for my mistake, instead in the restorative resolution meeting I was given a chance to state my point clearly without blame and to just talk about mistakes and how to go forward with the resolution. I was glad that I could come clean and work towards a solution that would be a positive to everyone involved. A learning to take away is that I will use the checklist that was made by me (...) to reinforce the research that I have done on the topic of academic integrity.

One thing that stands out for you when you reflect on your experiences of participating in restorative conferences?

Sean Waddingham, President, Students' Association of MacEwan University.

> So, one I guess trend that I saw that stood out for me when we worked with students in these restorative resolution conferences was that they learn from their mistakes, that they're remorseful and that students that really take this in, take it seriously, and have a bit of a progression from the time when we first meet with them to the end of the process … There's a lot to be said for how much they start to take responsibility for the mistakes they've made, how much they learn along the way. I noticed they often go from a place of being kind of fearful, trying to figure out what happens next (what do I do about this?), to a place of understanding, where they think okay now I'm equipped with the information on what it means to commit academic misconduct and how I can avoid it, and most importantly why that matters. So, they end up understanding why it's critical to the university that they conduct themselves well in academic matters in the future, and students take that seriously, and I was very happy to see that and have any skepticism remedied by that.

Joanne Loh, Faculty Member (Assistant Professor), Department of Accounting and Finance, MacEwan University.

> One really interesting thing that stands out for me is that, I know that the students know that cheating or misconduct is wrong, but a lot of times they do not really know until we go through the process, when we explain the harm that is done, you know, to whether it's the faculty, the university or students as a whole or even to themselves, that they truly understand the harm that has been done. I think people know it's wrong to cheat, but they may not know the extent of how that will impact and with the restorative process, you know, the process itself incorporates that as part of the resolution.

Michelle B., Sessional Instructor, Department of Communication, MacEwan University.

> I still reflect back and think that we accomplished something more than we would have if we had just doled out a punishment or a change of grade and not addressed anything.

When I look back, I think it was worth it, that maybe I changed, or together we changed the trajectory of what was into something more positive, something my student will remember and reflect back on. I think this process changed her sentiment about her own behaviour, but also about the academic setting, and about why these values are important. There was a lot of reflection on her part that probably wouldn't have happened otherwise, or maybe would have happened, but wouldn't have been reconciled into something that moved us forward.

How do Restorative Resolutions align with your personal or professional values? Michelle R. Andrews, Associate Professor, Department of Public Safety & Justice Studies, MacEwan University.

I make mistakes all the time. I live in a position of privilege where I get to fix it most of the time. I think so often with students, they don't have that opportunity. Sometimes it because they don't know how, sometimes it's because we don't give them that opportunity, but restorative practices which are rooted in that notion of relationship give the opportunity for the person who made the mistake, in this case a student and the person who experienced that mistake, in this case me as a faculty member to come together and talk that through and sort it, sort it out. I also know that that takes time, and restorative practices provide a process to work it through in a way that's unhurried and unforced. I think that's important too. In criminal justice so often, well we call assembly line justice right, we move people through the system, but restorative processes give that space, gives that time to listen, to carefully, carefully listen…to the story, to the narrative…how did we get here? And just as importantly, what are we going to do about it? Where are we going to go from that? In this case, the student was given the opportunity to explain how we got to this place. I think it surprised her. It surprised me as well. But, what I do know as a person, as a professional, as an academic, is that the restorative process that I was involved in was so authentic, was so genuine…almost revolutionary in ways, for both the student and for myself, that it re-affirmed that which I know to be true about restorative processes…is that they can make things right. I was there. I saw it.

Michelle B., Sessional Instructor, Department of Communication, MacEwan University.

For me, this entire process can be summed up in one word or sentiment, which is authenticity. And that is one of my highest values, this pursuit of truth, of what actually is or what actually happened, and being honest about that. Authenticity and honesty and truth were all enabled by this process. Instead of just covering up what happened, or addressing it with a punishment, we were actually able to address the situation. To find out what really happened. To talk through why it happened. To look beyond what had actually happened in the classroom to other factors that were driving those behaviours. To honestly work through that. And then we were able to move forward, with this authenticity in how we actually felt about what had happened and what we could actually do to address it.

How do Restorative Resolutions align with MacEwan's Mission and Vision? Sean Waddingham, President, Students' Association of MacEwan University.

[Faculty members] are willing to take the time and sit down with students and work out what may have caused the students' lapse of judgement when it came to academic conduct, or the ways in which they might mitigate this in the future, and really helping them understand what impact is had when misconduct is committed. So, for a university that cares about students and always talks about students first, I think it fits into MacEwan's strategic planning, MacEwan's culture and everything quite nicely.

What differences between a restorative process and a disciplinary process did you perceive?

Tom van Seters, Associate Professor, Department of Music, MacEwan University.

> I thought it was great that there was a procedure in place in which both parties are asked a series of questions that prompts them to verbalize the nuances of their experiences, and I think this led to deeper reflections on their respective experiences. I guess another thing that was different was that there was an opportunity to discuss what actions could be taken to repair any harm that was done …There was a more complete sense of resolution, when compared with the more traditional disciplinary process.

What made you want to engage in RP?

Michelle R. Andrews, Associate Professor, Department of Public Safety & Justice Studies, MacEwan University.

> I was reluctant, and I'll tell you why. It was a timing issue more than anything else. It was the end of term. I was very tired. I was annoyed, as well, because it was not the first time that this had happened with this student, not in a course that I taught, but I coordinate a program and so I am sometimes aware of other issues that students have, and I just wanted it to be over and done with and make the decision, pass it over to the Office of Academic Integrity and be done with it. And then it was one of those moments where you go…ohh, so this is what hypocrisy looks like, and so what I decided was, it's time for you to step up Michelle and to…I actually reframed it is what I did, and so instead of thinking of it as an obligation, I saw it as an opportunity and again, to be fully participatory in a process that I supported, from an intellectual level, and now in a very personal level, that's what got me to that point.

Additional Comments:

Sean Waddingham, President, Students' Association of MacEwan University.

> I am really impressed by MacEwan's faculty buy-in. There was great reception at the annual adjudicator meeting for academic misconduct adjudication around this kind of idea, and the support from faculty is critical because it's a volunteer-only kind of program, so everyone engaging in a restorative practice has to do so willingly…that includes the student, and includes the faculty as well. So, these faculty members – and in some cases…these incidences of academic misconduct are happening in their own classrooms… – they're willing to come to the restorative conferences and let the student know what impact that has, and that's critical. My experience at MacEwan has made me realize that our professors are available and are willing to talk to students and this is a further example of that. This really stood out to me at one of the sessions I participated in where quite a few professors were affected and nearly all of them came. I think we had six or seven faculty volunteering to be in that room at one time and it's really uplifting and hopeful to see the faculty buy-in because, with a process like this, where students are showing up and faculty are showing up, it's a more long term solution to academic misconduct. It's a real cultural shift, rather than you know, simple punishments on a sporadic basis, so that was great to see…faculty really buy in and care about the process.

Discussion and Conclusion

The responses from both responsible and harmed parties above are representative of the overwhelmingly positive reception of restorative resolutions of academic misconduct, and they aptly demonstrate the effectiveness of restorative practices to provide a *response* to academic misconduct that is consistent and coherent with a *prevention* approach focusing on teaching and learning as well as ethical decision making skills and meta-cognition (Bertram Gallant, 2008, 2017). What is more, it provides an experiential learning opportunity to all involved that highlights the rootedness of ethical decision-making in relationships and community.

For instance, the contrast could hardly be starker between responses reported in Pitt et al.'s (2020) study of how students experience going through a quasi-legal, disciplinary procedure in response to contract cheating allegations and the MacEwan University student's response to participating in a restorative resolution provided above. Whereas the students in Pitt et al.'s study perceived the process as legalistic, extremely challenging, and as having a strong negative impact on their relationships with their university, professors, peers, and family members, respectively, (Pitt et al., 2020, p. 5–9), the student quoted above who participated in a restorative resolution expressed his thankfulness to having been given the opportunity to "right the wrong that [they] had done not only to [professor] but to [them]self and the greater school community" (MacEwan student, anonymous). Particularly worth noting here is the insight that in violating academic integrity they had also wronged themselves and the school *community*. For this student, the restorative resolution in effect removed the barriers to self-reflection, learning, and growth that stress and stigmatizing shame present, and allowed them to become actively accountable in addressing the harm done, as well as to participate in a future- and solution-oriented collaborative effort, in which the student felt supported by the university community.

Also, the responses of those who participated in restorative resolutions presented above demonstrate the perception that the process was governed by and in turn promoted values that, unbeknownst to them, form part of the *fundamental values of academic integrity* (ICAI, 2021). In particular, participants explicitly associated honesty (authenticity, truth) and responsibility with the process, and the values of trust, fairness, respect, and courage were implicit in many of their responses. Moreover, participants mentioned that the restorative process facilitated a deepened and "memorable" reflection on the underlying causes of the misconduct as well as the resulting harms, and, importantly, on why academic integrity matters. Worth highlighting, also, is the mention that restorative practices led to a "more complete sense of resolution" (see van Seters' comments above) and a "real cultural shift" (see Waddingham's comments above).

Integrity is sometimes described as doing the right thing when no one is looking. What this implies, of course is that true integrity requires the internalization of values and principles. The drastic surge in academic misconduct cases, particularly contract cheating cases, during the COVID-related scramble to move courses and assessments online with limited ability to invigilate has been a sobering experience in that regard. It has made abundantly clear that much work remains to be done when it comes to promoting integrity, rather than mere rule-compliance.

If only anecdotally, participants in MacEwan University's restorative resolutions support the RP research literature in their perception that the process promoted an internalization of ethical values and not only constitute a more effective tool for the moral and civic education of our students than compliance and discipline models, but also for effecting the more general cultural shift necessary to address academic misconduct at its roots and as a community issue. They do so by "fostering remorse, not fear" (Sherman & Strang, 2007, p. 12) and by encouraging the "[k]eeping [of] promises versus following orders" (Sherman & Strang, 2007, p. 58).

The increased attention academic integrity has been receiving in Canada (Eaton, 2018) presents an opportunity to explore the implementation of restorative resolutions more broadly. For instance, due to the clear alignment with its institutional values, vision, and mission, and because of the promising early outcomes of the incorporation of a restorative resolution option for academic misconduct cases, MacEwan University has recently modified its non-academic misconduct procedure to include a restorative resolution option and is carefully considering the option of using a restorative justice approach to sexual violence on campus. Although the academic and non-academic misconduct procedures present the restorative resolution as the default approach, there remains work to be done to turn this into reality.

At the close of this chapter, a remark is in place to avoid feeding into the myth that restorative practices are "soft on crime" or wrongdoing. Some might argue that the negative experiences related to compliance and discipline-based procedures described by Pitt et al. are unfortunate, but unavoidable, consequences of students' actions, if universities are to promote and protect academic integrity and the value of their degrees. Because it is such an important point, we reiterate it here: responses to academic misconduct based on the principles of RP do not make the conventional, quasi-legal policies and procedures obsolete. The latter will be appropriate and necessary in some cases. The question that we asked in this chapter, however, is how well these in fact a) promote and protect academic integrity; b) align with the objectives, vision, and mission of postsecondary educational institutions; and c) whether, in light of these considerations, they must necessarily be the sole or default response to academic misconduct.

What we hope to have successfully argued is that having a RP approach as the default response to academic misconduct and the currently standard, quasi-legal, punitive approach as a secondary procedure to fall back on when conditions for the former are not met, ensures the *integrity* of an institutional strategy to academic integrity. It ensures that prevention *and* response remain firmly grounded in the goals, values, and principles pertaining not only to universities' pedagogical missions related to academics, but also those related to civic and moral education, as well as community building. Doing the right thing when no one is looking requires honesty, trust, respect, fairness, responsibility, and courage (ICAI, 2021). These values are to a large degree relational and presuppose a sense of community. Restorative Practices help make these values tangible and concrete within relationships.

Quick Tips:

- Examine and invite discussion on how well your institution's responses to academic misconduct align with:

  - the stated strategy to promote academic integrity (and the objectives related to this strategy); and
  - its strategic goals, and mission and vision, including its commitment to civic education;

- Explore the possibility of adding a restorative resolution approach to the standard, quasi-judicial procedure;
- Attend restorative justice/restorative practices training (e.g., International Center for Restorative Practices; San Diego University's Center for Restorative Justice)
- Collaborate with your Indigenous centres; offices of human rights, diversity and inclusion; and colleagues with expertise in RJ/RP (e.g., in correctional services, law, social work, sociology, etc.);
- Contact the chapter authors for further information and resources.

References

Acosta, J., Chinman, M., Ebener, P., Malone, P. S., Phillips, A., & Wilks, A. (2019). Evaluation of a whole-school change intervention: Findings from a two-year cluster-randomized trial of the Restorative Practices intervention. *Journal of Youth and Adolescence, 48*(5), 876–890. https://doi.org/10.1007/s10964-019-01013-2

Ahlin, E. M., Gibbs, J. C., Kavanaugh, P. R., & Lee, J. (2017). Support for restorative justice in a sample of U.S. university students. *International Journal of Offender Therapy and Comparative Criminology, 61*(2), 229–245. https://doi.org/10.1177/0306624X15596386

Bertram Gallant, T. (2008). *Academic integrity in the twenty-first century: A teaching and learning imperative*. Jossey-Bass.

Bertram Gallant, T. (2017). Academic integrity as a teaching & learning issue: From theory to practice. *Theory into Practice, 56*(2), 88–94. https://doi.org/10.1080/00405841.2017.1308173

Boyte, H. C. (Ed.). (2015). *Democracy's education: public work, citizenship, & the future of higher education*. Vanderbilt University Press.

Braithwaite, J. (1989). *Crime, shame and reintegration*. Cambridge University Press.

Bretag T., Mahmud S. (2016). A conceptual framework for implementing exemplary academic integrity policy in Australian higher education. In: Bretag T. (eds) *Handbook of Academic Integrity*. Springer. https://doi.org/10.1007/978-981-287-098-8_24

Bretag, T., Mahmud, S., East, J., Green, M., James, C., McGowan, U., Partridge, L., Walker, R., & Wallace, M. (2011a). Academic integrity standards: A preliminary analysis of the academic integrity policies at Australian Universities. Paper presented at the Australian Universities Quality Forum (AUQF), Melbourne, 29 June–1 July 2011.

Bretag, T., Mahmud, S., Wallace, M., Walker, R., Green, M., East, J., James, C., McGowan, U., & Partridge, L. (2011). Core elements of exemplary academic integrity policy in Australian higher education. *International Journal for Educational Integrity, 7*(2), 3–12.

Chartrand, L. N., Horn, K., Canada, & Department of Justice. (2018). *A report on the relationship between restorative justice and Indigenous legal traditions in Canada*. Department of Justice Canada. https://www.deslibris.ca/ID/10099014

Cassel, J. (2014). *Impacts of restorative justice on youth in conflict with the law : A narrative approach*. [Master's Thesis, Ryerson University]. Ryerson University Digital Repository. https://digital.library.ryerson.ca/islandora/object/RULA%3A3546

Christensen Hughes, J. M., & McCabe, D. L. (2006). Academic misconduct within higher education in Canada. *The Canadian Journal of Higher Education, 36*(2), 1–21. http://journals.sfu.ca/cjhe/index.php/cjhe/article/view/183537/183482

Clark, K. L. (2014). A call for restorative justice in higher education judicial affairs. *College Student Journal, 48*(4), 707–715.

Clark, S. C., Griffin, R. A., & Martin, C. K. (2012). Alleviating the policy paradox through improved institutional policy systems: A case study. *Innovative Higher Education, 37*(1),11-26.

Dana, D. (2001). Rethinking the Puzzle of Escalating Penalties for Repeat Offenders. *The Yale Law Journal, 110*(5), 733–783. https://doi.org/10.2307/797607

Eaton, S. E. (2018). Editorial: Academic integrity gaining increased attention in Canada. *Canadian Perspectives on Academic Integrity, 1*(2). https://doi.org/10.11575/CPAI.V1I2.56931

Eaton, S. E., Fernández Conde, C., Rothschuh, S., Guglielmin, M., & Otoo, B. K. (2020). Plagiarism: A Canadian higher education case study of policy and practice gaps. *Alberta Journal of Educational Research, 66*(4), 471–488. https://journalhosting.ucalgary.ca/index.php/ajer/article/view/69204

Gal, T. (2016). 'The conflict is ours': Community involvement in restorative justice. *Contemporary Justice Review, 19*(3), 289–306. https://doi.org/10.1080/10282580.2016.1185950

International Center for Academic Integrity (ICAI). (2021). *The fundamental values of academic integrity* (3rd ed.). https://academicintegrity.org/images/pdfs/20019_ICAI-Fundamental-Values_R12.pdf

Jorgenson, S., & Shultz, L. (2012). Global citizenship education (GCE) in post-secondary institutions: What is protected and what is hidden under the umbrella of GCE? *Journal of Global Citizenship & Equity Education, 2*(1).

Kara, F., & MacAlister, D. (2010). Responding to academic dishonesty in universities: A restorative justice approach. *Contemporary Justice Review, 13*(4), 443–453. https://doi.org/10.1080/10282580.2010.517981

Karp, D. R. (2019). *The little book of restorative justice for colleges and universities: Repairing harm and rebuilding trust in response to student misconduct*, 2nd edn. Good Books.

Karp, D. R., & Sacks, C. (2014). Student conduct, restorative justice, and student development: Findings from the STARR project: A student accountability and restorative research project. *Contemporary Justice Review, 17*(2), 154–172. https://doi.org/10.1080/10282580.2014.915140

Kehoe, M., Bourke-Taylor, H., & Broderick, D. (2018). Developing student social skills using restorative practices: A new framework called H.E.A.R.T. *Social Psychology of Education, 21*(1), 189–207. https://doi.org/10.1007/s11218-017-9402-1

Lang, J. M. (2013). *Cheating lessons: Learning from academic dishonesty.* Harvard University Press.

MacEwan University (2018). Student Academic Misconduct Procedure. https://www.macewan.ca/contribute/groups/public/documents/policy/student_acad_misconduct_proc.pdf

Pitt, P., Dullaghan, K., Sutherland-Smith, W. (2020) 'Mess, stress and trauma': Students' experiences of formal contract cheating processes. *Assessment & Evaluation in Higher Education*: 1–14. https://doi.org/10.1080/02602938.2020.1787332

Rodriguez, N. (2007). Restorative justice at work: Examining the impact of restorative justice resolutions on juvenile recidivism. *Crime & Delinquency, 53*(3), 355–379. https://doi.org/10.1177/0011128705285983

Sherman, L. W., Strang, H., & Smith Institute. (2007). *Restorative justice: The evidence.* The Smith Institute.

Stephens, J. M., Colby, A., Ehrlich, T., & Beaumont, E. (2000). *Higher Education and the Development of Moral and Civic Responsibility: Vision and Practice in Three Contexts.* http://eric.ed.gov/?id=ED443325

Stoesz, B. M., & Los, R. (2019). Evaluation of a tutorial designed to promote academic integrity.*Canadian Perspectives on Academic Integrity, 2*(1), 3–26. https://doi.org/10.11575/cpai.v2i1.61826

Stoesz, B. M., Eaton, S. E., Miron, J., & Thacker, E. J. (2019). Academic integrity and contract cheating policy analysis of colleges in Ontario Canada. *International Journal for Educational Integrity, 15*(1), 1–18. https://doi.org/10.1007/s40979-019-0042-4

UNESCO. (1998). World Declaration on Higher Education for the Twenty-First Century: Mission and Action. http://www.unesco.org/education/educprog/wche/declaration_eng.htm

Wachtel, T. (2016). Defining Restorative. *International Institute for Restorative Practices.* Retrieved from https://www.iirp.edu/images/pdf/Defining-Restorative_Nov-2016.pdf

Winslade, J. M. (2018). Restorative justice and social justice. *Wisdom in Education 8*(1), Article 5. https://scholarworks.lib.csusb.edu/wie/vol8/iss1/5

Zehr. (2003). *Little book of restorative justice.* Good Books.

Paul Sopcak is Coordinator of the Office of Student Conduct, Community Standards and Values at MacEwan University. He holds a Ph.D. in Comparative Literature and teaches English literature, comparative literature, and philosophy. As an International Institute of Restorative Practices certified trainer, he has trained and certified over 50 Restorative Conference Facilitators at MacEwan University. He is responsible for Academic Integrity and Restorative Practices at MacEwan University and has recently developed restorative resolution policy and procedures in response to academic and non-academic misconduct.

Garfield Kevin Hood is an Associate Professor at MacEwan University. He has been a faculty member with the Department of Public Safety and Justice Studies' Correctional Services program since 1991. Kevin was Department Chair from 2011 to 2019. In his professional career, Kevin worked in a variety of roles, including child abuse investigations and social work with youth involved in high risk behaviours. He managed the Protection of Children Involved in Prostitution program for Alberta Children's Services and was senior manager responsible for Crime Prevention and Restorative Justice with Alberta Solicitor General during his time with the Alberta public service. Kevin has worked and taught in the area of restorative practice since 2004. His current research interests in the area of restorative practice focus on community engagement, relational truth and socially engaged art. Kevin has also worked on research projects examining truth and reconciliation processes with Canada's Indigenous peoples.

Chapter 30
Academic Integrity Through a SoTL Lens and 4M Framework: An Institutional Self-Study

Natasha Kenny and Sarah Elaine Eaton

Abstract Institutions are placing increased emphasis on the importance of academic integrity. Suffusing a culture of integrity is complex work. Influencing academic cultures (including the shared norms, values, behaviours and assumptions we hold) requires impact across multiple organization levels, stakeholders, structures and systems. These dimensions can be influenced by working with individual instructors, learners and staff (micro), across departments, faculties, networks and working groups (meso), through to the institution (macro), and disciplinary, national and international levels (mega). Akin to nurturing strong teaching and learning cultures communities and practices, institutions tend to support change at the institutional (vision, policies, structures) and individual levels (targeted programs to develop expertise). Less focus has been placed on how we establish strong networks of support and knowledge-sharing to influence decision-making, action, and change at the meso and mega levels. In this chapter we offer an institutional self-study of academic integrity through a scholarship of teaching and learning (SoTL) lens. Informed by the 4M (micro, meso, macro, mega) framework, we examine how integrity is upheld and enacted at each level. We examine both formal and informal approaches to academic integrity, looking at how a systematic, multi-stakeholder networked approach has helped to establish a culture of integrity at our institution, and make recommendations for others, wishing to do the same.

Keywords Academic integrity · Canada · Higher education · SoTL · Scholarship of Teaching and Learning

N. Kenny (✉) · S. E. Eaton
University of Calgary, Calgary, AB T2N 1N4, Canada
e-mail: nakenny@ucalgary.ca

S. E. Eaton
e-mail: seaton@ucalgary.ca

S. E. Eaton and J. Christensen Hughes (eds.), *Academic Integrity in Canada*, Ethics and Integrity in Educational Contexts 1,
https://doi.org/10.1007/978-3-030-83255-1_30

Introduction

The purpose of this chapter is to examine academic integrity through a teaching and learning lens, using the University of Calgary as an institutional case study. We begin with a brief background on how and why it is essential to understand—and advocate for—academic integrity as part of the teaching and learning activities in education. We ground our inquiry in workplace learning theory and systems thinking. Then, we present the 4M Framework (Eaton, 2020c; Friberg, 2016; Kalu et al., 2018; Kenny et al., 2016; Miller-Young, 2016; Poole & Simmons, 2013; Simmons, 2016; Williams et al., 2013) as a model to disentangle some of the complexities inherent in systems and organizational theory. The model offers a simplified way to situate academic integrity within broader contexts.

From there, we bring together theory and practice through a conceptual model for supporting academic integrity at the University of Calgary. We expand on our initial simplified model to show how formal and informal networks, local-level leadership and microcultures play a role in institutional advancement of academic integrity. We highlight specific examples from the University of Calgary to show how our institution continues to develop with regards to academic integrity.

We discuss some challenges and limitations of this work, including (a) ensuring its sustainability; (b) how misunderstandings related to the evolution of an academic integrity culture within the university can impact institutional development; and (c) the invisible nature of much of the work. We conclude with concrete recommendations for how to continue to advance this work, advocating for a sustained focus on teaching and learning as being integral to academic integrity over the long term.

Background

Until about the twenty-first century, academic integrity was often viewed through a punitive lens, with a focus on student academic misconduct, and with students primarily being held responsible for preventing misconduct. Since the turn of the millennium, a shift has occurred to re-focus academic integrity as a multi-stakeholder responsibility (Carroll, 2007; Eaton, 2021; Macdonald & Carroll, 2006; McCabe et al., 2012; Morris, 2016; Tertiary Education Quality and Standards Agency (TEQSA), 2017). In a multi-stakeholder approach to academic integrity, students, educators, staff, and administrators have designated responsibilities within the learning organization.

This shift towards a shared responsibility model led to changing views from applying policy and sanctions after misconduct had occurred to a stronger focus on education and prevention. Although policy remains an important aspect of academic integrity to address breaches in fair and equitable ways, there is much educators and other members of our educational communities can do to help students build the skills associated with academic integrity, such as citing and referencing, as well as an understanding of ethical-decision making for learning. It has long been recognized that academic integrity in educational contexts is related to ethical conduct in professional life (Austin et al., 2006; Guerrero-Dib et al., 2020; Yıldırım et al., 2019). It is important that students and educators understand that academic integrity is more than rule-compliance, but rather that it serves as a foundation for a lifelong practice of ethical decision-making, action and knowledge creation.

Academic Integrity Through a Teaching and Learning Lens

Academic integrity has been deemed to be a teaching and learning imperative (Bertram Gallant, 2008). Advocates promote proactive pedagogy and supports to help students learn the skills and expectations to uphold and enact integrity in their learning (Eaton et al., 2017; Eaton et al., 2019a, b; Howard, 1995, 2002; Morris, 2016; Williams et al., 2013). Further, academic integrity is not only the responsibility of students, but requires a commitment from all members of the campus community embedded throughout the organization. This multi-stakeholder approach to integrity ensures that a commitment to upholding ethical standards is shared across the institution (Morris, 2019; TEQSA, 2017).

Theoretical Foundations

We draw from workplace learning and organizational development theories to frame our discussion of a multi-level, multi-stakeholder approach to academic integrity.

Workplace Learning Theory

As we consider these multi-level approaches, it is important to explore how learning occurs in an organization. While many calls to action related to academic integrity emphasize increased focus on the training and development of academic staff, graduate students and staff supporting instruction, as well as providing educational programming for students (e.g., Christensen Hughes & McCabe, 2006b), there are many formal and informal processes which facilitate learning. Jarvis (2010) describes that learning must involve understanding, and that learning can happen through a range of formal education courses, programs and training that are intentionally planned, and through informal learning that occurs through everyday life, is often unplanned, unintended or *incidental*. He further suggests that learning is cyclical and occurs as we individually internalize local and global cultures, and then externally process this learning through social interaction. Importantly learning, "...must always be seen within the wider cultural context" (Jarvis, 2010, p.68).

Although we often privilege the learning that is planned and occurs in formal contexts, research has suggested that much of what we learn about our teaching and learning practices and approaches happens through small, but significant conversations with colleagues, which occur through relationships bound by trust, privacy and intellectual intrigue (Roxå & Mårtensson, 2009). These significant networks and conversations can have important influence on teaching and learning cultures, especially at the local level (Roxå et al., 2011). Individual learning is impacted by the cultural contexts within an institution (Jarvis, 2010), and these same cultures are influenced by conversational patterns and networks that guide shared sense-making and action (Roxå et al., 2011). In order to ensure learning related to academic integrity is meaningful, we must provide both formal and informal opportunities that are contextually based, that are embedded in practice, and that facilitate on-going reflection and action (Webster-Wright, 2009).

As it relates to professional learning for educators, these informal and formal opportunities may be conceptualized around a cycle of academic integrity that can guide conversation and practice (Fig. 30.1).

Building upon the work of authors such as Bertram Gallant (2017), Christensen Hughes and McCabe (2006), McCabe and Pavela (2004), and Morris (2016), this cycle includes the following dimensions:

- **Modelling:** modelling and affirming the values of integrity through our everyday academic practices (including teaching, research, scholarship, leadership and service).
- **Designing:** meaningfully designing learning activities that uphold the values of integrity and foster a love of learning, developing fair and relevant forms of assessment, and reducing opportunities for students to engage in misconduct.

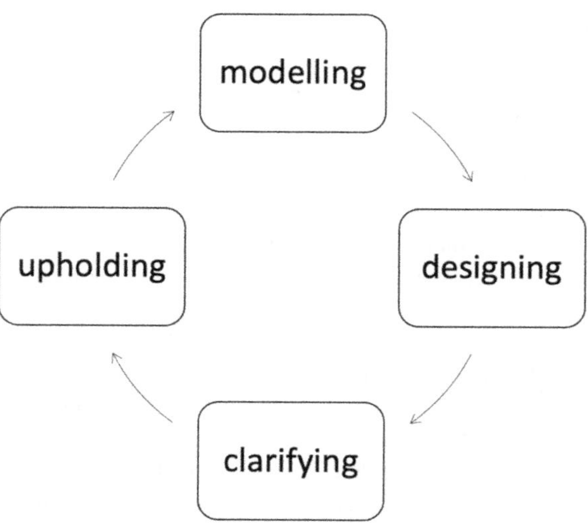

Fig. 30.1 Professional learning cycle for academic integrity as a framework for conversation and practice for educators in postsecondary education

- **Clarifying:** clarifying expectations related to academic integrity in all forms of communication as it relates to teaching and learning activities and assessments, including helping to develop awareness of institutional and departmental policies and procedures related to academic integrity.
- **Upholding**: upholding the values of academic integrity by affirming actions that promote academic integrity and taking appropriate action on activities that contradict these values.

Organizational Learning Theory and Systems Thinking

Impacting organizational change and learning is complex. Shifting postsecondary teaching and learning cultures, communities and practices related to academic integrity requires change across multiple organizational levels. The idea of systems thinking is not new. It has existed for decades, or even longer, across a variety of disciplines. General systems theory (von Bertalanffy, 1968) and ecological systems theory (Bronfenbrenner, 1976, 1981) are two of the foundational theories that were later developed into other fields, including education. Approaching academic integrity from a systems perspective can provide a useful way to talk about this complex topic (Bertram Gallant, 2011; Bertram Gallant & Kalichman, 2011; Drinan & Bertram Gallant, 2008; Eaton, 2020c).

A Model of Integrity: The 4M Framework

The need for taking a multi-stakeholder, multi-level, systems-approach to fostering academic integrity in higher education has been highlighted by numerous academic integrity scholars (Bertram Gallant & Drinan, 2008; Bertram Gallant & Kalichman, 2011; Bretag, 2019; Christensen Hughes & McCabe, 2006a; Eaton, 2021)

Overview of the Model

Within the field of the scholarship of teaching and learning (SoTL), the 4M framework offers such an approach to understanding how the practices of teaching and learning, as well as inquiry around these practices, are connected to the broader educational landscape (Eaton, 2020c; Friberg, 2016; Kalu et al., 2018; Kenny et al., 2016; Miller-Young, 2016; Poole & Simmons, 2013; Simmons, 2016; Williams et al., 2013). The framework consists of four nested organizational levels: micro, meso, macro, and mega. Each level represents a particular lens through which an opportunity, issue or problem of practice can be framed (see Fig. 30.2).

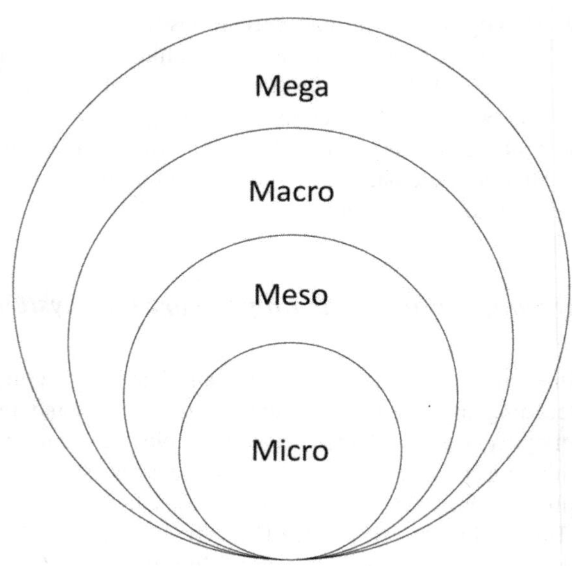

Fig. 30.2 Simplified 4M Model highlighting micro, meso, macro, and mega levels

Hannah and Lester (2009) suggest that this multi-level approach to organizational learning occurs when leaders set the conditions for change to emerge through shared learning and knowledge flow. They propose that programs, resources and strategies must be provided to support targeted learning experiences for individual knowledge catalysts at the *micro* level. At the *meso* level, they emphasize the importance of creating learning networks, with embedded knowledge catalysts. Here, both informal (or *emergent*) and formal leaders play a critical role in influencing and championing change, especially at the local level (i.e., within and across university departments and faculties) (Mårtensson & Roxå, 2016; Verwoord & Poole, 2016; Williams et al., 2013; Fields et al., 2019). At the *macro* level, senior leaders influence the vision, policies, resources and infrastructure to support and champion change, as well as to allow for system-wide knowledge flow and diffusion (Hannah & Lester, 2009).

Translating their work through the lens of academic integrity, this work highlights the importance of: (a) establishing institutional policies, standards and procedures that uphold and affirm the importance of academic integrity (*macro*), (b) ensuring that faculties and departments have the appropriate committees, leadership and cultures to translate policies into academic practice and that cross-unit working groups are established to share information and knowledge related to academic integrity within and across faculties and departments (*meso*), and (c) supporting instructors, staff and learners in developing the skills, knowledge and behaviours to model and implement strategies to promote academic integrity in their teaching, learning, research, assessment and academic practices (*micro*). Bertram Gallant and Kalichman (2011) also emphasize the importance of academic integrity at the societal level, where political, society, economic and technological "factors can operate as models of accepted, or at least unacceptable, behaviors" (p.41). Within the context of fostering organizational change in the scholarship, leadership and practice of teaching and learning, Simmons (2016) describes factors at this level as having influence at the *mega* level.

The Meso-Level Gap

When considering a multi-level approach to change, it is interesting to note that the primary focus for change related to teaching, learning and academic integrity has been put on implementing macro-level vision, policies, and procedures and establishing training and development at the individual or micro-level. Less emphasis has been placed on the importance of influencing change through faculties, departments and working groups *(meso-level).* Trowler et al. (2005) and Kenny et al. (2016) refer to the importance of addressing this *meso-level gap*, especially as it relates to supporting change in teaching and learning cultures, communities and practices. At the meso-level individual and collective actions are influenced by the microcultures, norms and structures which surround them (Roxå & Mårtensson, 2015; Trowler et al., 2005). These microcultures are, in turn, influenced by the behaviours, norms, decisions, actions and values of local leaders, as well as those that are established through social networks and working groups (Fields et al., 2019; Kenny et al., 2016; Mårtensson & Roxå, 2016). It is at the meso-level that action or change can either be "blocked or facilitated" by local microcultures (Trowler et al., 2005, p. 435). Christensen Hughes and Mighty (2010) reinforce that local leadership may be "one of the most significant barriers to academic change" (p. 269). Moving forward, local-level norms, cultures, values, behaviours, and political structures must become a critical component in catalysing, supporting and sustaining change in academic integrity.

Bringing Together Theory and Practice: A Conceptual Model for Supporting Academic Integrity at the University of Calgary

At the core of the model are four key elements for change (High-Impact Professional Learning; Local-level Leadership and microcultures; Scholarship, research and inquiry; and Learning spaces, pedagogies and technologies). Each of these elements is supported through Informal and Formal Processes that occur across multiple organizational levels (Micro, Meso, Macro and Mega). The core of the model highlights that academic integrity is influenced by:

- **High-impact Professional Learning for Individuals and Groups.** Professional learning activities are provided through formal and informal opportunities that are contextual, embedded in practice, and that facilitate on-going reflection and action (Webster-Wright, 2009). These professional learning activities are often focused on the values, and principles of academic integrity, associated policies, and teaching, learning and assessment practices that most directly influence academic integrity.

- **Local-level Leadership and Microcultures:** At the local-level (i.e., faculties, departments, working groups, student leadership groups), informal and formal leaders act as catalysts to inspire action and change, and to help influence the development of microcultures that either support or hinder academic integrity (Fields et al., 2019; Hannah & Lester, 2009; Kenny et al., 2016; Mårtensson & Roxå, 2016). Change in local-level climates for teaching and learning, including academic integrity, must be visibly reinforced through the expectations, actions, and decisions of those who hold formal leadership roles (i.e., Deans and Heads); leadership must also be distributed through the actions, behaviours, norms and values held by several educators within a faculty or department (Christensen Hughes & Mighty, 2010; Knapper, 2010).
- **Scholarship, Research and Inquiry**: Scholarship, research and inquiry in teaching and learning (Felten, 2013; Trigwell, 2013) provide a lens for systematically investigating, disseminating and strengthening knowledge and practices that relate to academic integrity in postsecondary education, including the opportunities, challenges, issues and impacts of academic integrity on the academic community, as well as the factors that support or hinder academic integrity across multiple organizational levels (Hubball et al., 2013; Kenny et al., 2017).
- **Learning Spaces, Pedagogies, and Technologies**: Physical and digital learning spaces, pedagogies and technologies can have an enormous influence on academic integrity (Bertram Gallant, 2017; Sotiriadou et al., 2020). Never has the importance of the relationship between learning spaces, pedagogies and technologies and academic integrity been more apparent than through the rapid transition to remote and online learning during the COVID19 pandemic, as issues related to ethical assessment, contract cheating, collaboration and corroboration, online proctoring, and teaching and learning in remote spaces proliferated across the globe (Eaton, 2020a).

These core elements are consistently influenced informally through significant conversations, relationships, communities and networks, and formally through policies, committees, programs and resources that influence academic integrity across multiple organizational and societal levels (*micro, meso, macro, mega*) (Hannah & Lester, 2009; Kenny et al., 2016; Roxå & Mårtensson, 2009; Simmons, 2016). For example, at the macro level senior leaders, such as Presidents and Provosts and institutional committees, must reiterate the importance of academic integrity by articulating a compelling vision, modelling through action, setting guidelines for success, and providing the necessary structural, organizational, governance, procedural, strategic, and financial resources to catalyse and sustain change (Hannah & Lester, 2009; Kenny et al., 2016). At the meso level integrated networks of knowledge sharing must be established and maintained within and across disciplinary boundaries and local-level leaders must provide visible support for each of these elements (Hannah & Lester, 2009). At the micro level tangible resources and incentives must be provided to ensure individuals are supported, recognized and rewarded for their work in advancing academic integrity as it relates to each element (Hannah & Lester, 2009; Kenny et al., 2016). It is critical to note the importance of ensuring the student voice and leadership are included in decisions and discussions related to academic integrity, especially as policies, procedures and practices are enacted at the macro (institutional) and meso (faculty, department) levels (Bertram Gallant & Drinan, 2008).

4M Model in Action: A Case Study of the University of Calgary

In 2019, the University of Calgary launched the Educational Leaders in Residence (ELR) program, designed to create leadership opportunities for faculty members focused on priority areas that aligned with the university's strategic academic and research plans (University Relations Staff, 2019). The roles were situated as two-year part-time secondments to the Taylor Institute for Teaching and Learning offered in partnership between various Vice-Provosts' portfolios, including the Vice-Provost Teaching and Learning, Graduate Studies and Student Enrolment Services. The first cohort of educational leaders in residence three distinct, but interrelated portfolios: (a) academic integrity; (b) online learning; and (c) graduate supervision and mentorship.

The ELR for academic integrity portfolio included objectives such as further building awareness of academic integrity across the university; advising on and contributing to the development of resources and supports; and developing local, regional, and national partnerships to connect practice and scholarship relating to academic integrity, as well as maintaining an active connection to other ELRs to share learning and further advance through collaboration.

Specific ELR Academic Integrity Projects

Within the broad terms of reference for the role, the ELR for academic integrity (Eaton) developed a work plan that aligned specific activities with the institutional academic and research strategies. The work plan was reviewed and approved by the Vice Provost Teaching and Learning, as well as the Senior Director for the Taylor Institute of Teaching and Learning (Kenny), with further endorsement from the Vice Provost, Student Experience, as well as the dean and vice dean of the school of education. The work plan reflected a systematic approach to activities to support institutional goals at a variety of levels.

Example #1: Research Project, "Academic Integrity: Faculty Development Needs for Canadian Higher Education"

One major project subsumed into this role was a major national research project, "Academic Integrity: Faculty Development Needs for Canadian Higher Education" (Eaton et al., 2019). This project involved a partnership with industry through the D2L Innovation Guild, as well as partners from the University of Manitoba, the University of Waterloo, and the University of Guelph. At the time of this writing, data collection was underway at all four universities to understand faculty perceptions and needs related to academic integrity in Canadian higher education. This project is an example of how the various levels of the 4M framework intersect. Through the micro lens, this project benefited the PI (Eaton) individually, as her research program focuses on educational ethics and academic integrity. Through the meso lens, the Senior Director of the Taylor Institute for Teaching and Learning (Kenny) served as the institutional (macro) representative to the broader steering committee, which operated at a mega level, including partners from various post-secondary institutions, along with D2L as a corporate partner. Because the project included collaborators from multiple universities, as well as industry, it also reached into the mega level.

This was the first research project in Canadian history on academic integrity to actively engage industry partners. From a networked perspective, the relationships built from this project have had a lasting impact, as evidenced by the fact that all the research team members from various universities involved in the project have also contributed unique chapters to this volume (see the individual chapters authored or co-authored by, Crossman, Stoesz, McKenzie, and Garwood). This project not only offered individual researchers an opportunity to collaborate on this particular study, but it also provided an opportunity for individuals to deepen their networked connections and strengthen their own professional learning and relationships beyond the project.

Example #2: Institutional Policy, Procedure, and Statement on Academic Integrity

In 2019, the University of Calgary launched its first academic misconduct policy and procedure. Prior to that, academic misconduct had been addressed in the university calendar as regulations. From a governance perspective, there is a difference between regulations which are intended to direct student conduct, and policies which articulate responsibilities and institutional expectations for a variety of stakeholders. The policy and procedure took several years to develop, as the process involved a number of drafts which were reviewed by both formal (e.g., councils, committees), as well as informally by student groups, and other stakeholders. Through various revisions, different stakeholders had an opportunity to provide input and feedback, including administrators, faculty, staff, and students. The policy and procedure became effective on July 1, 2019, the same day as the ELR Academic Integrity role was launched.

In the first year of the role, the Educational Leader in Residence for Academic Integrity supported the rollout and implementation of the policy and procedure, as well as offered informal support to faculties and departments at the meso level, by engaging in consultations and significant conversations with those who were responsible for developing unit-level processes for reporting and investigating breaches of academic integrity.

One aspect of the policy development work that remained unfinished was the institutional Statement on Intellectual Honesty, which had remained constant in the university calendar for longer than many administrators and faculty members could remember. With nothing to replace it, the statement remained in the calendar during the 2019-2020 academic year, but it became increasingly apparent that this statement reflected outdated ways of thinking about academic integrity and required revision. The ELR provided institutional-level guidance on how the statement might be revised. As with the policy, consultation was undertaken at various levels, led by the Provost and Vice Provost Student Experience, to recraft the statement so that it reflected current approaches and research related to academic integrity.

The process was accelerated during the COVID-19 crisis when members of the university community quickly pivoted to remote teaching and learning. This revised statement was officially written into the 2020–2021 academic calendar as follows:

Academic integrity is the foundation of the development and acquisition of knowledge and is based on values of honesty, trust, responsibility, and respect. We expect members of our community to act with integrity.

Research integrity, ethics, and principles of conduct are key to academic integrity. Members of our campus community are required to abide by our institutional code of conduct and promote academic integrity in upholding the University of Calgary's reputation of excellence. (University of Calgary, 2020–2021 Academic Calendar, n.p.).

This institutional statement served to reshape the narrative away from misconduct and towards integrity and served to anchor conversations around ethical teaching, learning, and assessment during the COVID-19 pandemic.

Example #3: Integrity Hour: Informal Online Community of Practice

An informal community of practice for academic integrity had been initiated at the University of Calgary some years earlier to help advance conversations related to academic integrity and misconduct across faculties by another professor, with one or two meetings happening each academic year. Stewardship of the group was passed on to the ELR, Academic Integrity in 2019. Seeing a need to build capacity and knowledge beyond what was happening on our own campus, particularly during the COVID-19 crisis when requests were coming in regularly for assistance both from on-campus faculty and off-campus colleagues, she reconceptualized and redesigned the community of practice to take place in a weekly format, via Zoom (Eaton, 2020b). Integrity Hour was launched in the last week of March 2020 creating an informal network of knowledge sharing and support.

Colleagues within the academic integrity community in Canada were invited to join in to the weekly one-hour meetings. Over the first six months of Integrity Hour (March-August 2020), a total of 255 attendees (including regular participants) joined in over the course of 21 meetings. This included attendees from an average of eight institutions (in addition to the University of Calgary) and four provinces each week.

During the coronavirus pandemic, Integrity Hour provided scholars, administrators and practitioners an informal opportunity to learn with and from one another. Participants repeatedly remarked that the value in this online community of practice was information and resource sharing, particularly around hot topics such as e-proctoring, case management, contract cheating, file sharing and academic labour issues related to academic misconduct during the coronavirus pandemic. Although institutional data regarding academic misconduct were not formally available through official means until much later, through a crowd-sourcing approach to information seeking and sharing, participants were able to engage in meso- and macro-level conversations at their own institutions about what was consistently being reported by colleagues on a regular basis in the community of practice. Integrity Hour continues to serve as a mega-level online community of practice many months later.

Example #4: Webinar Series: Urgent and Emerging Topics in Academic Integrity

The Educational Leader in Residence for academic integrity developed a webinar series to address topics relating to academic integrity that had been previously under discussed in the literature. Topics such as equity, diversity and inclusion as related to academic integrity and Indigenous perspectives on academic integrity were highlighted. Each webinar served not only to raise awareness, but also to promote public scholarship and community engagement at the macro level.

Each webinar typically attracted more than 100 registrants from a variety of countries. The ELR served as the series convener and host of each session, with guest speakers invited to address particular topics such as equity, diversity, and inclusion as they relate to academic integrity, admissions fraud, and contract cheating.

Example #5: Internal Educational Development

The ELR for academic integrity provided educational development for colleagues across campus in a variety of ways. This included collaborating with colleagues at the Taylor Institute for Teaching and Learning to present sessions such as "Academic Integrity for Emerging Academics." In addition, she led departmental discussions and guest lectures upon request and provided individual consultations with academic staff, teaching assistants, department heads and other administrators. This aspect of the work was sometimes planned in advance, but was often conducted in a responsive "just in time" way to address immediate needs as they arose.

The Educational Leader in Residence for Academic Integrity provided support to individuals (micro level), departments and other units on campus (meso level), the institution (macro level) and also involved advocacy and outreach to the broader community (mega level). Some of the work was visible and more formalized, such as webinars and workshops, but much of it was less visible, including informal activities such as individual conversations and consultations with members of the campus community, ad hoc meetings and special projects.

Challenges and Limitations

The Educational Leader in Residence program is not without its challenges. In this section we highlight three main limitations of this initiative through the lens of the ELR for academic integrity: (a) sustainability; (b) misunderstandings related to the evolution of an academic integrity culture within the university; and (c) the invisible nature of much of the work.

We address the issue of sustainability first. The Educational Leader in Residence Program was initiated as a special two-year initiative. "Soft funding" was provided to allow for part-time secondments. This means that project funds, rather than operating funds, were allocated to the program. Project funding is enough to start an initiative, but not to sustain it over the long term. In terms of the sustainability of the work, specific short-term projects were undertaken for which the scope could be contained within the two-year duration of the role. Longer-term initiatives that would have required more than two years to complete could not be undertaken within this role.

Next, we address the issue of misunderstandings related to the evolution of an academic integrity culture within the university. When an institution commits to developing a culture of academic integrity, one of the outcomes can be an increase in the number of academic misconduct cases reported. Reports of misconduct can increase when systems are in place to facilitate reporting. Also, when members of the campus community are aware of the processes involved with reporting and feel comfortable doing so, then more cases may be reported. The number of cases reported does not equal the total number of cases, so when reporting increases it does not necessarily indicate an increase in the incidence or rates of misconduct. Communicating this message is of the utmost importance when a campus community is actively undertaking a process to develop a stronger culture of academic integrity.

The third limitation is the invisible nature of academic integrity work itself. Although some of the work related to this portfolio is public or visible in nature, there are aspects of it that would be considered less visible. These include individual consultations, attendance at meso-level and macro-level meetings, document review, and so on. Evaluating the work done in the ELR portfolio remains ongoing, however, capturing and communicating the impact of this work in terms of contribution to the institution and beyond, remains complex. Akin to the work of educational developers, this work of connecting individuals, fostering relationships, creating communities and opportunities for collaboration, and sharing knowledge across once disparate networks has been contextualized within social network theory as acting as, "weak ties connecting across disciplines, infusing new ideas about teaching and learning, and enabling the translation of innovations across these academic networks" (Matthews et al., 2015. p. 248). This work is often difficult to track, evaluate and communicate within the context of traditional academic structures and reporting processes, and its impact needs to be made more visible and explicit (Kenny et al., 2017; Matthews et al., 2015; Timmermans, 2014).

Implications and Recommendations

We conclude by offering concrete recommendations about how to support academic integrity work within the institution at a variety of levels. We then contemplate how what we have learned may have applicability beyond our own institution.

Recommendations

Based on our experience undertaking this work thus far, we can offer a number of recommendations:

Recommendation #1: Recognize that a Systematic Approach to Addressing Academic Integrity Is Needed

Institutional leaders must recognize and implement strategies that recognize the importance of addressing academic integrity across multiple levels, by engaging multiple stakeholders, and by establishing and influencing formal and informal activities, policies, processes and practices that impact professional learning and training, local-level leadership and microcultures, learning spaces, pedagogies and technologies, as well as research and scholarship related to academic integrity.

Recommendation #2: Provide Ongoing Training and Support to Various Institutional Stakeholders Across Multiple Levels

Academic integrity training is essential for academic staff, as well as those working in management and support staff roles. Because of the meso-level gap, those serving as leaders of departments, units, and other groups within an institution may benefit from opportunities designed specifically for those at that level. This might include both formal training, such as courses, but also informal opportunities for growth such as communities of practice.

Recommendation #3: Intentionally create informal and formal networked knowledge-sharing within and across units

When it comes to matters related to academic integrity, there is a need for informal and formal knowledge sharing within and across units. This may occur through formal governance and committees, as well as informal communities of practice, working groups, scholarly networks and conversations.

Recommendation #4: Recognize academic integrity as legitimate leadership and scholarly contributions

As long as academic integrity work is done "off the side of one's desk" it will continue to be marginalized or dismissed as administrative work. This can lead to decision-making that is neither informed nor evidence-based. Academic integrity work must be recognized as an important aspect of teaching and leadership at various levels of the learning organization.

Conclusions

Academic integrity work is situated within the broader context of applied ethics in educational contexts. The word integrity comes from the same Latin root, "*integritas*". The word "integrate", meaning to make something whole, is derived from the same root. When we think about academic integrity as something that makes our learning communities whole, we see that it goes beyond student conduct; it extends to teaching and learning, ethical assessment practices, ethical decision-making by individuals in a variety of roles, working in different units across the institution. Academic integrity is not just about students; it is about everyone working in a learning ecosystem.

Academic integrity work is inherently messy. The nature of academic integrity work is both systematic and complex. Systematic aspects are articulated through policies, procedures, and regulations, but as are realized in the broader academic culture. In and of themselves, these are insufficient to make our learning communities, and the experiences of those who learn, teach, and work within those communities—whole.

We began our chapter by presenting a simplified model of the 4M model (Fig. 30.2). The purpose of this was to provide a basic framework to understand how individuals are situated within units that are part of a learning organization, that then connects to society more broadly. After presenting this foundational framework of how individuals are part of a community, we went on to show how connections, networks, and relationships connect individuals in formal and informal ways (Fig. 30.3). We conclude by emphasizing the importance of taking a systemic approach to addressing academic integrity engaging multiple stakeholders across

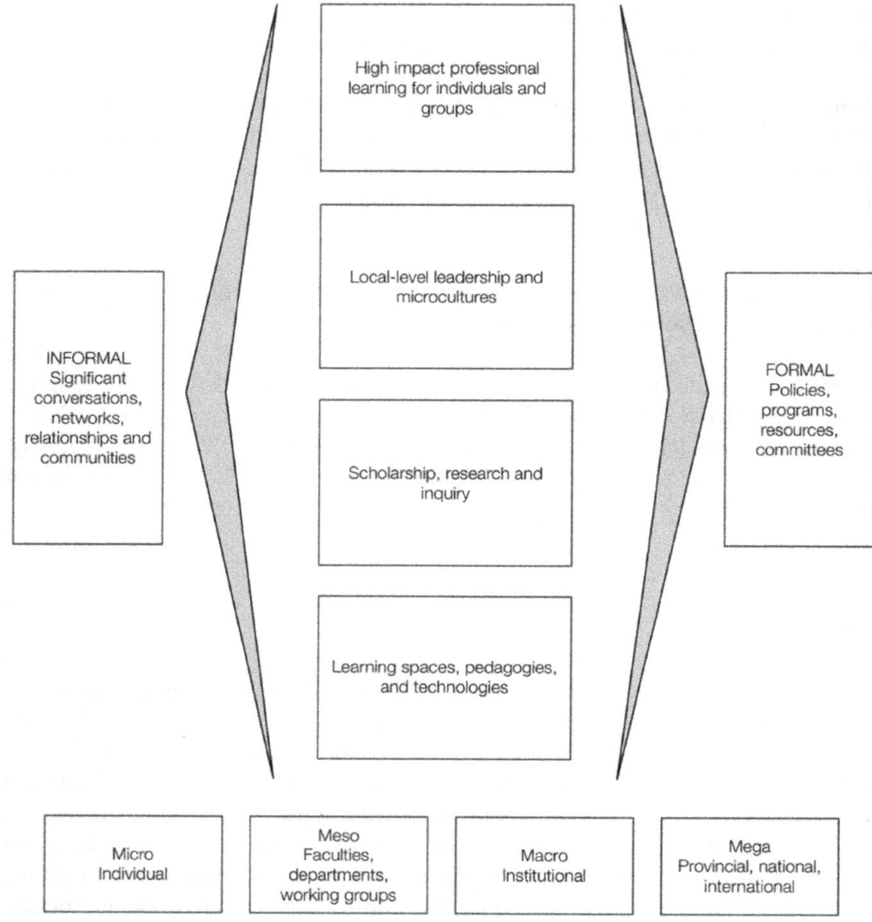

Fig. 30.3 Integrated model for academic integrity through a SoTL lens

multiple levels. We call on academic leaders to consider this systematic approach to addressing academic integrity: (a) by focussing efforts across multiple-levels (i.e., individuals, working groups, departments, faculties, institutions, society); (b) by engaging multiple stakeholders (i.e., students, faculty, teaching assistants, support staff, postdoctoral scholars), and (c) by establishing and influencing formal and informal activities, policies, processes and practices that impact high-impact professional learning, local-level leadership and microcultures, scholarship, research and inquiry related to academic integrity, and learning spaces, pedagogies and technologies.

We have shown how the University of Calgary established the Educational Leader in Residence roles to engage in boundary-spanning work to address complex phenomena within a learning organization. We recognize the need for this work to continue to evolve, for relationships to be nurtured, and networks sustained through ongoing and committed efforts over time.

References

Bertram Gallant, T. (2008). *Academic integrity in the twenty-first century: A teaching and learning imperative*. Wiley.

Bertram Gallant, T. (Ed.). (2011). *Creating the ethical academy: A systems approach to understanding misconduct and empowering change in higher education*. Routledge.

Bertram Gallant, T., & Kalichman, M. (2011). Academic ethics: A systems approach to understanding misconduct and empowering change in the academy. In T. Bertram Gallant (Ed.), *Creating the ethical academy: A systems approach to understanding misconduct and empowering change in higher education* (pp. 27–44). New York: Routledge.

Bertram Gallant, T., & Drinan, P. (2008). Toward a model of academic integrity institutionalization: Informing practice in postsecondary education. *Canadian Journal of Higher Education*, 38(2).

Bertram Gallant, T. (2017). Academic integrity as a teaching & learning issue: From theory to practice. *Theory into Practice, 56*(2), 88–94. https://doi.org/10.1080/00405841.2017.1308173

Bretag, T. (2019). Contract cheating research: Implications for Canadian universities. Keynote address presented at the Canadian Symposium on Academic Integrity, Calgary, Canada. http://hdl.handle.net/1880/110279

Bronfenbrenner, U. (1976). The Experimental Ecology of Education. Paper presented at the American Educational Research Association (AERA), San Francisco, CA.

Bronfenbrenner, U. (1981). *The Ecology of Human Development: Experiments by Nature and Design*. Harvard University Press.

Carroll, J. (2007). *A handbook for deterring plagiarism in higher education* (2nd ed.). Oxford Centre for Staff and Learning Development.

Christensen Hughes, J. M., & McCabe, D. L. (2006a). Academic misconduct within higher education in Canada. *The Canadian Journal of Higher Education*, 36(2), 1–21. https://doi.org/10.47678/cjhe.v36i2.183537

Christensen Hughes, J. M., & McCabe, D. L. (2006b). Understanding academic misconduct. *Canadian Journal of Higher Education*, 36(1), 49–63. https://doi.org/10.47678/cjhe.v36i1.183525

Christensen Hughes, J., & Mighty, J. (2010). A call to action: Barriers to pedagogical innovation and how to overcome them. In J. Christensen Hughes & J. Mighty (Eds).*Taking stock: Research on teaching and learning in higher education* (pp. 261–277). Queens School of Policy Studies.

Drinan, P. M., & Bertram Gallant, T. (2008). Plagiarism and academic integrity systems. *Journal of Library Administration, 47*(3–4), 125–140. https://doi.org/10.1080/01930820802186472

Eaton, S. E. (2020a). Academic Integrity During COVID-19: Reflections from the University of Calgary. *International Studies in Educational Administration*, 48(1), 80–85. https://prism.ucalgary.ca/handle/1880/112293

Eaton, S. E. (2020b). Integrity Hour: A Guide to Developing and Facilitating an Online Community of Practice for Academic Integrity. University of Calgary. http://hdl.handle.net/1880/112347

Eaton, S. E. (2020c). Understanding Academic Integrity from a Teaching and Learning Perspective: Engaging with the 4M Framework. Calgary: University of Calgary. http://hdl.handle.net/1880/112435

Eaton, S. E. (2021). *Plagiarism in higher education: Tackling tough topics in academic integrity*. Santa Barbara, CA: Libraries Unlimited.

Eaton, S. E., Chibry, N., Toye, M. A., & Rossi, S. (2019a). Interinstitutional perspectives on contract cheating: A qualitative narrative exploration from Canada. *International Journal for Educational Integrity*, 15(9). https://doi.org/10.1007/s40979-019-0046-0

Eaton, S. E., Crossman, K., Stoesz, B. M., McKenzie, A., Garwood, K., Cepuran, B., & Kocher, R. (2019b). Academic Integrity: Faculty Development Needs for Canadian Higher Education. Calgary: University of Calgary. https://doi.org/10.17605/OSF.IO/X2VA3

Eaton, S. E., Guglielmin, M., & Otoo, B. (2017). Plagiarism: Moving from punitive to pro-active approaches. In A. P. Preciado Babb, L. Yeworiew, & S. Sabbaghan (Eds.), Selected Proceedings of the IDEAS Conference 2017: Leading Educational Change Conference (pp. 28–36). Calgary, Canada: Werklund School of Education, University of Calgary. https://prism.ucalgary.ca/handle/1880/52096

Felten, P. (2013). Principles of good practice in SoTL. *Teaching and Learning Inquiry, 1*(1), 121–125. https://doi.org/10.2979/teachlearninqu.1.1.121

Fields, J., Kenny, N. A., & Mueller, R. A. (2019). Conceptualizing educational leadership in an academic development program. *International Journal for Academic Development, 24*(3), 218–231. https://doi.org/10.1080/1360144X.2019.1570211

Friberg, J. C. (2016). Might the 4M Framework Support SoTL Advocacy? (July 11). https://illinoisstateuniversitysotl.wordpress.com/2016/07/11/might-the-4m-framework-support-sotl-advocacy/

Guerrero-Dib, J. G., Portales, L., & Heredia-Escorza, Y. (2020). Impact of academic integrity on workplace ethical behaviour. *International Journal for Educational Integrity, 16*(1), 2. https://doi.org/10.1007/s40979-020-0051-3

Hannah, S. T., & Lester, P. B. (2009). A multilevel approach to building and leading learning organizations. *The Leadership Quarterly, 20*(1), 34–48. https://doi.org/10.1016/j.leaqua.2008.11.003

Howard, R. M. (1995). Plagiarisms, authorships, and the academic death penalty. *College English, 57*(7), 788–806. https://doi.org/10.2307/378403

Howard, R. M. (2002). Don't Police Plagiarism: Just TEACH! *The Education Digest, 67*(5), 46–49.

Hubball, H., Pearson, M. L., & Clarke, A. (2013). SoTL inquiry in broader curricular and institutional contexts: Theoretical underpinnings and emerging trends. *Teaching and Learning Inquiry, 1*(1), 41–57. https://doi.org/10.2979/teachlearninqu.1.1.41

Jarvis, P. (2010). *Adult Education and Lifelong Learning* (4th ed.). Routledge.

Kalu, F., Dyjur, P., Berenson, C., Grant, K. A., Jeffs, C., Kenny, N., & Mueller, R. (2018). Seven voices, seven developers, seven one things that guide our practice. *To Improve the Academy, 37*(1), 111–127. https://doi.org/10.1002/tia2.20066

Kenny, N., Watson, G. P. L., & Desmarais, S. (2016). Building sustained action: Supporting an institutional practice of SoTL at the University of Guelph. *New Directions for Teaching and Learning, 2016*(146), 87–94. https://doi.org/10.1002/tl.20191

Kenny, N., Popovic, C., McSweeney, J., Knorr, K., Hoessler, C., Hall, S., Fujita, N., & El Khoury, E. (2017). Drawing on the Principles of SoTL to Illuminate a Path Forward for the Scholarship of Educational Development. *The Canadian Journal for the Scholarship of Teaching and Learning*, 8 (2). https://doi.org/10.5206/cjsotl-rcacea.2017.2.10

Knapper, C. (2010). Changing teaching practice: Barriers and strategies. Taking stock. Research on teaching and learning in higher education. In J. Christensen Hughes & J. Mighty (Eds).Taking stock: Research on teaching and learning in higher education (pp. 229–242). Queens School of Policy Studies.

Macdonald, R., & Carroll, J. (2006). Plagiarism: A complex issue requiring a holistic institutional approach. *Assessment & Evaluation in Higher Education, 31*(2), 233–245. https://doi.org/10.1080/02602930500262536

Mårtensson, K., & Roxå, T. (2016). Leadership at a local level–Enhancing educational development. *Educational Management Administration & Leadership, 44*(2), 247–262. https://doi.org/10.1177/1741143214549977

Matthews, K. E., Crampton, A., Hill, M., Johnson, E. D., Sharma, M. D., & Varsavsky, C. (2015). Social network perspectives reveal strength of academic developers as weak ties. *International*

Journal for Academic Development, 20(3), 238–251. https://doi.org/10.1080/1360144X.2015.1065495

McCabe D.L., & Pavela, G. (2004) Ten (Updated) principles of academic integrity: How faculty can foster student honesty. *Change: The Magazine of Higher Learning*, 36:3, 10–15. https://doi.org/https://doi.org/10.1080/00091380409605574

McCabe, D. L., Butterfield, K. D., & Treviño, L. K. (2012). *Cheating in college: Why students do it and what educators can do about it*. Johns Hopkins University Press.

Miller-Young, J. (2016). Using the Micro-Meso-Macro-Mega (4M) framework for annual reporting and strategic planning. Retrieved from https://sotlcanada.wordpress.com/2016/07/25/using-the-micro-meso-macro-mega-4m-framework-for-annual-reporting-and-strategic-planning/

Morris, E. J. (2016). Academic Integrity: A Teaching and Learning Approach. In T. Bretag (Ed.), *Handbook of Academic Integrity* (pp. 1037–1053). Springer Singapore. https://doi.org/10.1007/978-981-287-098-8_11

Poole, G., & Simmons, N. (2013). Contributions of the scholarship of teaching and learning to quality enhancement in Canada. In R. Land & G. Gordon (Eds.), *Enhancing quality in higher education: International perspectives* (pp. 278–298). Routledge.

Roxå, T., & Mårtensson, K. (2009). Significant conversations and significant networks–exploring the backstage of the teaching arena. *Studies in Higher Education, 34*(5), 547–559. https://doi.org/10.1080/03075070802597200

Roxå, T., Mårtensson, K., & Alveteg, M. (2011). Understanding and influencing teaching and learning cultures at university: A network approach. *Higher Education*, 62(1), 99–111. https://doi.org/10.1007/s10734-010-9368-9

Roxå, T., & Mårtensson, K. (2015). Microcultures and informal learning: A heuristic guiding analysis of conditions for informal learning in local higher education workplaces. *International Journal for Academic Development, 20*(2), 193–205. https://doi.org/10.1080/1360144X.2015.1029929

Simmons, N. (2016). Synthesizing SoTL institutional initiatives toward national impact. *New Directions for Teaching and Learning, 2016*(146), 95–102. https://doi.org/10.1002/tl.20192

Sotiriadou, P., Logan, D., Daly, A., & Guest. R. (2020). The role of authentic assessment to preserve academic integrity and promote skill development and employability. *Studies in Higher Education,(45)*11, 2132–2148 https://doi.org/10.1080/03075079.2019.1582015

Tertiary Education Quality and Standards Agency (TEQSA). (2017). Good Practice Note: Addressing contract cheating to safeguard academic integrity. https://www.teqsa.gov.au/sites/g/files/net2046/f/good-practice-note-addressing-contract-cheating.pdf?v=1507082628

Timmermans, J. A. (2014). Identifying threshold concepts in the careers of educational developers. *International Journal for Academic Development, 19*(4), 305–317. https://doi.org/10.1080/1360144X.2014.895731

Trigwell, K. (2013). Evidence of the impact of scholarship of teaching and learning purposes. *Teaching and Learning Inquiry, 1*(1), 95–105. https://doi.org/10.2979/teachlearninqu.1.1.95

Trowler, P., Fanghanel, J., & Wareham, T. (2005). Freeing the chi of change: The Higher Education Academy and enhancing teaching and learning in higher education. *Studies in Higher Education, 30*(4), 427–444. https://doi.org/10.1080/03075070500160111

University Relations Staff. (2019, May 13). New initiative seeks teaching and learning experts across campus: Educational Leaders in Residence program starts this fall. UToday. https://www.ucalgary.ca/utoday/issue/2019-05-14/new-initiative-seeks-teaching-and-learning-experts-across-campus

Verwoord, R., & Poole, G. (2016). The role of small significant networks and leadership in the institutional embedding of SoTL. *New Directions for Teaching and Learning, 2016*(146), 79–86. https://doi.org/10.1002/tl.20190

von Bertalanffy, L. (1968). *General system theory: Foundations, development, applications*. George Braziller.

Webster-Wright, A. (2009). Reframing professional development through understanding authentic professional learning. *Review of Educational Research, 79*(2), 702–739. https://doi.org/10.3102/0034654308330970

Williams, A. L., Verwoord, R., Beery, T. A., Dalton, H., McKinnon, J., Strickland, K., Pace, J., & Poole, G. (2013). The Power of social networks: A model for weaving the scholarship of teaching and learning into institutional culture. *Teaching & Learning Inquiry: the ISSOTL Journal, 1*(2), 49–62. https://doi.org/10.2979/teachlearninqu.1.2.49

Yıldırım, D., Kırşan, M., Kıray, S., Korhan, E. A., Üstün, Ç., & Aykar, F. Ş. (2019). Nurse Academicians' Attitudes Related to Academic Ethical Values and Related Factors. *Journal of Academic Ethics, 17*, 363–373. https://doi.org/10.1007/s10805-019-09339-z

Natasha Kenny holds a PhD in Land Resource Science and is Senior Director of the University of Calgary's Taylor Institute for Teaching and Learning (TI). In her role, Natasha leads and collaborates with colleagues across the TI and university to strengthen teaching and learning practices, cultures and communities. In 2018, she was awarded the Educational Developers Caucus of Canada Distinguished Educational Development Career Award for helping to advance the field of educational development locally and nationally. Her research interests relate to educational leadership, well-being in higher education, organizational learning and change, and the scholarship and practice of educational development, and the scholarship of teaching and learning (SoTL).

Sarah Elaine Eaton PhD, is an Associate Professor in the Werklund School of Education and the inaugural Educational Leader in Residence, Academic Integrity, University of Calgary. She is also the Editor-in-Chief of the *International Journal for Educational Integrity.* Her research focuses on ethics and integrity in higher education and she has led research teams and the local and national levels. Eaton advocates for pro-active and multi-stakeholder approaches to upholding and enacting integrity throughout the academy.

Chapter 31
Conclusions and Future Directions for Academic Integrity in Canada

Sarah Elaine Eaton and Julia Christensen Hughes

Abstract In the conclusion to this edited volume, we highlight key themes from the book, making reference to the particular chapters that address them. We discuss the symbolic importance of the work by situating previous work and celebrating milestones related to academic integrity in Canada. We acknowledge the limitations of the book and offer recommendations for future directions for research, practice, and policy.

We chose the title of this volume, "Academic Integrity in Canada: An Enduring and Essential Challenge" (Eaton & Christensen Hughes, eds., 2022) intentionally. Contributors from across the country have shared new perspectives on enduring problems, but do so in a way that has been uniquely and exclusively Canadian. Contributors also bring new insights on important and essential topics, such as Indigenous perspectives on academic integrity (see Lindstrom, 2022; Poitras Pratt & Gladue, 2022) that until now, have not been part of the broader discourse.

Symbolic Importance of this Volume: Situating Previous Work and Celebrating Milestones

This book began with the idea of marking the fifteenth anniversary of the seminal articles by Julia Christensen Hughes and Donald (Don) McCabe (2006a, b) and demonstrating how far Canada has come since this work was published. Despite Christensen Hughes and McCabe's work receiving extensive media attention and even an award from the *Canadian Journal of Higher Education* for the year it was

S. E. Eaton (✉)
University of Calgary, Calgary, AB T2N 1N4, Canada
e-mail: seaton@ucalgary.ca

J. Christensen Hughes
Yorkville University, Toronto, ON M4Y 1W9, Canada

S. E. Eaton and J. Christensen Hughes (eds.), *Academic Integrity in Canada*, Ethics and Integrity in Educational Contexts 1,
https://doi.org/10.1007/978-3-030-83255-1_31

published (see Christensen Hughes & Eaton, 2022b), it remained, for many years, the only major study on the topic in Canada.

As research on educational integrity was flourishing in other countries, Canada lagged behind (see Eaton & Edino, 2018). Canadians working in the field of academic integrity often found themselves turning to research and guidance from other countries and attempting to apply those findings to our own context. Although transferring findings from elsewhere can be helpful to an extent, such applications are limited in many ways. Even in the widely referenced *Handbook of Academic Integrity* (Bretag, ed., 2016), a volume spanning more than 1000 pages, there was one chapter that included a focus on Canada, and even then it was done in comparison with another country (see Foeger & Zimmerman, 2016). Although there were other contributors to the handbook who were Canadian (see: Christensen Hughes & Bertram Gallant, 2016; Newton & Lang, 2016; Rogerson & Basanta, 2016), there were no chapters exclusively about Canada.

This book showcases how far Canadians have come in terms of their contributions to the field in the fifteen years since Christensen Hughes & McCabe (2006a, b) published their work. It also highlights unique aspects of the Canadian higher education context. In doing so, it demonstrates how far we have come in the five years since the internationally acclaimed *Handbook on Academic Integrity was published* (Bretag, 2016).

The Significance of Contributions in This Volume

In this volume, contributors share empirical findings (see deMontigny, 2022; Garwood, 2022; Hamilton & Wolsky, 2022; McNeill, 2022; Packalen & Rowbotham, 2022; Peters et al., 2022; Rossi, 2022), as well as conceptual and other forms of scholarly expertise and insights (see Christensen Hughes, 2022; Christensen Hughes & Eaton, 2022a, b; Crossman, 2022; Eaton & Christensen Hughes, 2022; Foxe et al., 2022; Hunter & Kier, 2022, Miron, 2022; Teymouri et al., 2022, Watson Hamilton, 2022) and perspectives from leadership and professional practice (see Kenny & Eaton, 2022; Morrison & Zachariah, 2022; Morrow, 2022; Penaluna & Ross, 2022; Thacker & McKenzie, 2022). Of particular note are the chapters that broaden understanding of academic integrity beyond the questionable behaviours of students, to include that of faculty, administrators and the history and cultures of institutions of higher learning, as well as those that extend the dialogue around the Scholarship of Teaching and Learning (SoTL) (see Bens, 2022; Kenny & Eaton, 2022; Hamilton & Wolsky, 2022), signalling that academic integrity inquiry can fit within SoTL when the focus is on learning and teaching.

This book builds on previous scholarship in the field, but also brings new insights on topics that have previously received limited or no treatment in the literature. For example, to the best of our knowledge, this is the first time Indigenous voices have been included in scholarly discourse on academic integrity (Lindstrom, 2022; Poitras Pratt & Gladue, 2022). Similarly, although restorative practices have been discussed as one approach to addressing breaches of integrity, Sopcak and Hood's (2022) chapter brings new depth to the discussion. We also know that academic integrity at the K-12 level has received inadequate treatment, which Stoesz (2022) addresses in her chapter.

Brenna Clark Gray (2022) addresses questions around the ethics of educational technology, signalling that educators, policy makers and others must pay attention to the ways in which technology will continue to shape education and the ethical complexities that will no doubt bring. Eaton (2022a) presents a historical account of contract cheating in Canada going back more than half a century. These contributions are essential, given the dramatic shift to on-line learning and assessment, as well as the increasingly brazen behaviour of contract cheating companies that have flourished in Canada, becoming billion dollar businesses.

Limitations and Future Directions

As with any book, ours is not without its limitations. We recognize that although Indigenous contributors have begun an important dialogue about the need to decolonize and Indigenize academic integrity and approaches to educational ethics broadly, the voices of Indigenous scholars included in this volume are from Western Canada. We know that First Nations, Inuit, and Métis peoples are not a singular monolithic group. We recognize the need to extend the dialogue about how to decolonize ethics and integrity in educational contexts further and engage with others from historically marginalized groups; we see the chapters in this book by Poitras Pratt and Gladue (2022) and Lindstrom (2022) as a starting point, not an end.

As contributors were in the early stages of drafting their chapters in 2020, we heard news of George Floyd's murder in Minneapolis (see Hill et al., 2020) and subsequent news stories of continued racism against Black people and other persons of colour. These occurrences are not limited to the United States, and also happen in Canada and elsewhere. During this time period, the Alberta Council on Academic Integrity (2020) released its Statement Against Racism in Matters Relating to Academic Integrity and others began advancing the dialogue about equity, diversity and inclusion as they relate specifically to academic integrity (see Boisvert et al., 2020; Eaton, 2020; Parnther, 2020); we have yet to fully address the ways in which minoritized students are overrepresented in the reporting of misconduct behaviours or sanctioned differently from White peers. These are important topics that must continue to be addressed through research, policy, practice, and advocacy.

We recognize the invaluable role that higher education professionals play in contributing to cultures of integrity and to the learning supports for students. We are delighted to have chapters that include perspectives from those working in academic integrity offices, student affairs, the library, academic writing centres, quality assurance and other non-academic units within learning institutions (see, for example, Bens, 2022; Foxe et al., 2022; Garwood, 2022; Gray, 2022; Morrow, 2022; Penaluna & Ross, 2022; Sopcak & Hood, 2022; Rossi, 2022; and Thacker & McKenzie, 2022).

We know that the voices of higher education professionals and practitioners deserve to be further elevated and amplified and we encourage more knowledge sharing from those who work in non-academic units.

Although the contributors to this volume represent many provinces of Canada, we recognize that not all regions are represented, such as those from the northern territories or the Atlantic provinces. This is both a limitation and an opportunity. As work on ethics and integrity in Canadian educational contexts continues to develop, it is essential to extend the dialogue to all regions of the country.

We acknowledge topics that we have not fully addressed in this volume that merit further inquiry such as engaging students as partners in academic integrity, as well as the ways machine learning and artificial intelligence are rapidly changing how we learn and teach. These omissions are also opportunities and there is no doubt in our minds that Canadians will continue to contribute to the knowledge base of ethics and integrity in educational contexts over time.

Concluding Remarks

Canadians are no longer obliged to rely on research from other countries to try and understand academic ethics and integrity in our own country. This volume provides a robust compendium of evidence of research, scholarship, and professional practice about academic integrity in Canada that not only showcases new and original thinking, but provides a base for future research, as well as policy and practice development. The chapters also contribute to the growing body of global scholarship on educational integrity, and provide substantive content that may be relevant to readers in other countries.

References

Alberta Council on Academic Integrity (ACAI). (2020). Statement Against Racism in Matters Relating to Academic Integrity. https://albertaacademicintegrity.files.wordpress.com/2020/06/alberta-council-on-academic-integrity-statement-against-racism-2020-06-04.pdf

Bens, S. (2022). Helping students resolve the ambiguous expectations of academic integrity. In: *Academic integrity in Canada: An enduring and essential challenge*. Springer.

Boisvert, S., Teymouri, N., Medicine Crane, J. A., & Eaton, S. E. (2020). Exploring Racism and Academic Integrity through a Circle Process. Paper presented at the Alberta Teachers' of English as a Second Language (ATESL) Annual Conference, Online. http://hdl.handle.net/1880/112689

Christensen Hughes, J. (2022). Academic integrity across time and place: Higher education's questionable moral calling. In S. E. Eaton & J. Christensen Hughes. (Eds.), *Academic integrity in Canada: An enduring and essential challenge*. Springer.

Christensen Hughes, J., & Bertram Gallant, T. (2016). Infusing ethics and ethical decision making into the curriculum. In T. Bretag (Ed.), *Handbook of academic integrity* (pp. 1055–1073). Singapore: Springer Singapore.

Christensen Hughes, J., & Eaton, S. E. (2022a). Academic misconduct in Canadian higher education: Beyond student cheating. In S. E. Eaton & J. Christensen Hughes (Eds.), *Academic integrity in Canada: An enduring and essential challenge*. Springer.

Christensen Hughes, J., & Eaton, S. E. (2022b). Student integrity violations in the academy: More than a decade of growing complexity and concern In S. E. Eaton & J. Christensen Hughes (Eds.), *Academic integrity in Canada: An enduring and essential challenge*. Springer.

Christensen Hughes, J. M., & McCabe, D. L. (2006a). Academic misconduct within higher education in Canada. *The Canadian Journal of Higher Education*, 36(2), 1–21. http://journals.sfu.ca/cjhe/index.php/cjhe/article/view/183537/183482

Christensen Hughes, J. M., & McCabe, D. L. (2006b). Understanding academic misconduct. *Canadian Journal of Higher Education*, 36(1), 49-63. Retrieved from https://journals.sfu.ca/cjhe/index.php/cjhe/article/view/183525

Crossman, K. (2022). Education as a financial transaction: Contract employment and contract cheating. In S. E. Eaton & J. Christensen Hughes (Eds.), *Academic integrity in Canada: An enduring and essential challenge*. Springer.

deMontigny, D. (2022). Managing academic integrity in Canadian engineering schools. In S. E. Eaton & J. Christensen Hughes (Eds.), *Academic integrity in Canada: An enduring and essential challenge*. Springer.

Eaton, S. E. (2020). Race-based data in student conduct: A call to action. University of Calgary. http://hdl.handle.net/1880/112157.

Eaton, S. E. (2021). *Plagiarism in higher education: Tackling tough topics in academic integrity*. Santa Barbara, CA: Libraries Unlimited.

Eaton, S. E. (2022). Contract cheating in Canada: A comprehensive overview. In S. E. Eaton & J. Christensen Hughes (Eds.), *Academic integrity in Canada: An enduring and essential challenge*. Springer.

Eaton, S. E., & Christensen Hughes, J. (2022). Academic integrity in Canada: Historical perspectives and current trends. In S. E. Eaton & J. Christensen Hughes (Eds.), *Academic integrity in Canada: An enduring and essential challenge*. Springer.

Eaton, S. E., & Edino, R. I. (2018). Strengthening the research agenda of educational integrity in Canada: A review of the research literature and call to action. *International Journal of Educational Integrity*, *14*(1). https://doi.org/10.1007/s40979-018-0028-7

Foeger, N., & Zimmerman, S. (2016). Research Integrity: Perspectives from Austria and Canada. In T. Bretag (Ed.), *Handbook of academic integrity* (pp. 809–821). Singapore: Springer Singapore.

Foxe, J. P., Miller, A., Farrelly, G., Hui, V., Nubla, D., & Schindler-Lynch, C. (2022). Visual plagiarism: Seeing the forest and the trees. In S. E. Eaton & J. Christensen Hughes (Eds.), *Academic integrity in Canada: An enduring and essential challenge.*

Garwood, K. (2022). Supporting academic integrity in the writing centre: Perspectives of student consultants. In S. E. Eaton & J. Christensen Hughes (Eds.), *Academic integrity in Canada: An enduring and essential challenge*. Springer.

Gladue, K. (2021). Indigenous Academic Integrity. Calgary, Canada: University of Calgary. Retrieved from https://taylorinstitute.ucalgary.ca/resources/indigenous-academic-integrity

Gray, B. C. (2022). Ethics, ed tech, and the rise of contract cheating. In S. E. Eaton & J. Christensen Hughes (Eds.), *Academic integrity in Canada: An enduring and essential challenge*. Springer.

Hamilton, M. J., & Wolsky, K. L. (2022). The barriers to faculty reporting incidences of academic misconduct at community colleges. In S. E. Eaton & J. Christensen Hughes (Eds.), *Academic integrity in Canada: An enduring and essential challenge*: Springer.

Hill, E., Tiefenthäler, A., Triebert, C., Jordan, D., Willis, H., & Stein, R. (2020). How George Floyd Was Killed in Police Custody. *New York Times*. https://www.nytimes.com/2020/05/31/us/george-floyd-investigation.html

Hunter, J., & Kier, C. A. (2022). Canadian open digital distance education universities and academic integrity. In S. E. Eaton & J. Christensen Hughes (Eds.), *Academic integrity in Canada: An enduring and essential challenge*. Springer.

Kenny, N., & Eaton, S. E. (2022). Academic integrity through a SoTL lens and 4M framework: An institutional self-study. In S. E. Eaton & J. Christensen Hughes (Eds.), *Academic integrity in Canada: An enduring and essential challenge*. Springer.

Lindstrom, G. (2022). Accountability, relationality and Indigenous epistemology: Advancing an Indigenous perspective on academic integrity. In S. E. Eaton & J. Christensen Hughes (Eds.), *Academic integrity in Canada: An enduring and essential challenge*. Springer.

McNeill, L. (2022). Changing "hearts" and minds: Pedagogical and institutional practices to foster academic integrity. In S. E. Eaton & J. Christensen Hughes (Eds.), *Academic integrity in Canada: An enduring and essential challenge*. Springer.

Miron, J. B. (2022). Academic integrity in work-integrated learning (WIL) settings. In S. E. Eaton & J. Christensen Hughes (Eds.), *Academic integrity in Canada: An enduring and essential challenge*. Springer.

Morrison, M., & Zachariah, P. (2022). Student academic misconduct through a Canadian legal lens. In S. E. Eaton & J. Christensen Hughes (Eds.), *Academic integrity in Canada: An enduring and essential challenge*. Springer.

Morrow, L. (2022). Beyond the traditional: academic integrity in Canadian librarianship. In S. E. Eaton & J. Christensen Hughes (Eds.), *Academic integrity in Canada: An enduring and essential challenge*. Springer.

Newton, P. M., & Lang, C. (2016). Custom essay writers, freelancers, and other paid third parties. In T. Bretag (Ed.), *Handbook of academic integrity* (pp. 249–271). Springer.

Packalen, K., & Rowbotham, K. (2022). Student insight on academic integrity. In S. E. Eaton & J. Christensen Hughes (Eds.), *Academic integrity in Canada: An enduring and essential challenge*. Springer.

Parnther, C. (2020). Creating a Culture of Equity in Academic Integrity: Best Practices for Teaching and Learning. Webinar presented at the Taylor Institute for Teaching and Learning, University of Calgary. https://youtu.be/59mBo9neEgY

Penaluna, L.-A., & Ross, R. (2022). How to talk about academic integrity so students will listen. In S. E. Eaton & J. Christensen Hughes (Eds.), *Academic integrity in Canada: An enduring and essential challenge*. Springer.

Peters, M., Fontaine, S., & Frenette, E. (2022). Teaching the teachers: To what extent do preservice teachers cheat on exams and plagiarise in their written work? In S. E. Eaton & J. Christensen Hughes (Eds.), *Academic integrity in Canada: An enduring and essential challenge*. Springer.

Poitras Pratt, Y., & Gladue, K. (2022). Re-defining academic integrity: Embracing Indigenous truths. In S. E. Eaton & J. Christensen Hughes (Eds.), *Academic integrity in Canada: An enduring and essential challenge*. Springer.

Rogerson, A. M., & Basanta, G. (2016). Peer-to-peer file sharing and academic integrity in the Internet age. In T. Bretag (Ed.), *Handbook of Academic Integrity* (pp. 273–285). Springer.

Rossi, S. L. (2022). Revisioning paraphrasing instruction. In S. E. Eaton & J. Christensen Hughes (Eds.), *Academic integrity in Canada: An enduring and essential challenge*. Springer.

Sopcak, P., & Hood, K. (2022). Building a culture of restorative practice and restorative responses to academic misconduct In S. E. Eaton & J. Christensen Hughes (Eds.), *Academic integrity in Canada: An enduring and essential challenge*. Springer.

Stoesz, B. M. (2022). Understanding provincial and territorial academic integrity policies for elementary and secondary education in Canada. In S. E. Eaton & J. Christensen Hughes (Eds.), *Academic integrity in Canada: An enduring and essential challenge*. Springer.

Teymouri, N., Boisvert, S., & John-West, K. (2022). Promotion of academic integrity through a marketing lens for Canadian post-secondary institutions. In S. E. Eaton & J. Christensen Hughes (Eds.), *Academic integrity in Canada: An enduring and essential challenge*. Springer.

Thacker, E. J., & McKenzie, A. (2022). Using quality assurance frameworks to support an institutional culture of academic integrity at Canadian universities. In S. E. Eaton & J. Christensen Hughes (Eds.), *Academic integrity in Canada: An enduring and essential challenge*. Springer.

Watson Hamilton, J. (2022). The distinctive nature of academic integrity in graduate legal education. In S. E. Eaton & J. Christensen Hughes (Eds.), *Academic integrity in Canada: An enduring and essential challenge*. Springer.

Sarah Elaine Eaton Ph.D., is an Associate Professor in the Werklund School of Education and the inaugural Educational Leader in Residence, Academic Integrity, University of Calgary. She is also the Editor-in-Chief of the *International Journal for Educational Integrity* and the author of *Plagiarism in Higher Education: Tackling Tough Topics in Academic Integrity* (Eaton, 2021b). Her research focuses on ethics and integrity in higher education and she has led numerous research teams and the local and national levels. Eaton advocates for pro-active and multi-stakeholder approaches to upholding and enacting integrity throughout the academy.

Julia Christensen Hughes Ph.D., has long advocated for ensuring the highest standards of academic integrity in higher education—in teaching, research and administrative practice. Her article, Academic Misconduct within Higher Education in Canada, with the late Don McCabe (published in 2006, in the *Canadian Journal of Higher Education*), received the Sheffield Award for research excellence (2007), from the Canadian Society for Studies in Higher Education. As former and founding Dean of the Gordon S. Lang School of Business and Economics (2009-2019) at the University of Guelph, Julia was a champion of business ethics, corporate social responsibility and the need for business schools to be aligned with the UN's Sustainable Development Goals (SDG's). In her new role as President of Yorkville University, Julia is looking forward to supporting and strengthening the institution's long-standing commitment to integrity.

Correction to: Academic Integrity in Canada

Sarah Elaine Eaton and Julia Christensen Hughes

Correction to: S. E. Eaton and J. Christensen Hughes (eds.), *Academic Integrity in Canada*, Ethics and Integrity in Educational Contexts 1, https://doi.org/10.1007/978-3-030-83255-1

The original version of the book was inadvertently published with incorrect ISSNs for print and electronic versions in the copyright page, which have now been corrected. The erratum chapter has been updated with the changes.

The updated version of the book can be found at
https://doi.org/10.1007/978-3-030-83255-1

S. E. Eaton and J. Christensen Hughes (eds.), *Academic Integrity in Canada*,
Ethics and Integrity in Educational Contexts 1,
https://doi.org/10.1007/978-3-030-83255-1_32

CPSIA information can be obtained
at www.ICGtesting.com
Printed in the USA
LVHW080704280922
729462LV00004B/72